Grade 4

Addison-Wesley Mathematics

Robert E. Eicholz
Sharon L. Young
Phares G. O'Daffer
Carne S. Barnett
Randall I. Charles

Stanley R. Clemens
Freddie L. Renfro
Gloria F. Gilmer
Mary M. Thompson
Andy Reeves
Carol A. Thornton

Addison-Wesley Publishing Company

Menlo Park, California ■ Reading, Massachusetts ■ New York
Don Mills, Ontario ■ Wokingham, England ■ Amsterdam ■ Bonn
Sydney ■ Singapore ■ Tokyo ■ Madrid ■ San Juan ■ Paris
Seoul ■ Milan ■ Mexico City ■ Taipei

Program Advisors

John A. Dossey Professor of Mathematics
Illinois State University, Normal, Illinois

Bonnie Armbruster Associate Professor, Center for the Study of Reading
University of Illinois, Champaign, Illinois

Karen L. Ostlund Associate Professor of Science Education
Southwest Texas State University, San Marcos, Texas

Betty C. Lee Assistant Principal
Ferry Elementary School, Detroit, Michigan

William J. Driscoll Chairman, Department of Mathematical Sciences
Central Connecticut State University, New Britain, Connecticut

David C. Brummett Educational Consultant
Palo Alto, California

Multicultural Advisors

Ann Armand-Miller
Bill Bray
Valerna Carter
Moyra Contreras
Gloria Dobbins
Paula Duckett
Barbara Fong
Jeanette Haseyama
James Hopkins
Carol Artiga MacKenzie
Gloria Maldonado
Mattie McCloud
Dolores Mena
Irene Miura
Marsha Muhammad
A. Barretto Ogilvie
Margarita Perez
May-Blossom Wilkinson
Glenna Yee

Contributing Writers

Betsy Franco
Mary Heinrich
Penny Holland
Marilyn Jacobson
Ann Muench
Gini Shimabukuro
Marny Sorgen
Connie Thorpe
Sandra Ward
Judith K. Wells

Executive Editor

Diane H. Fernández

Cover Photo Credit: Digital Art/West Light

TI-12 Math Explorer™ is a trademark of Texas Instruments.

ISBN: 0-201-86504-1

2 3 4 5 6 7 8 9 10 11 12 -VH- 98 97 96 95 94

Contents

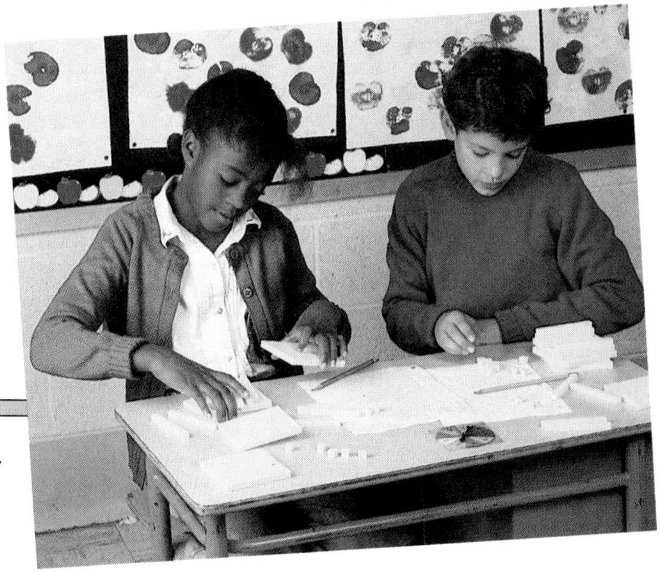

3

ADDITION AND SUBTRACTION OF WHOLE NUMBERS

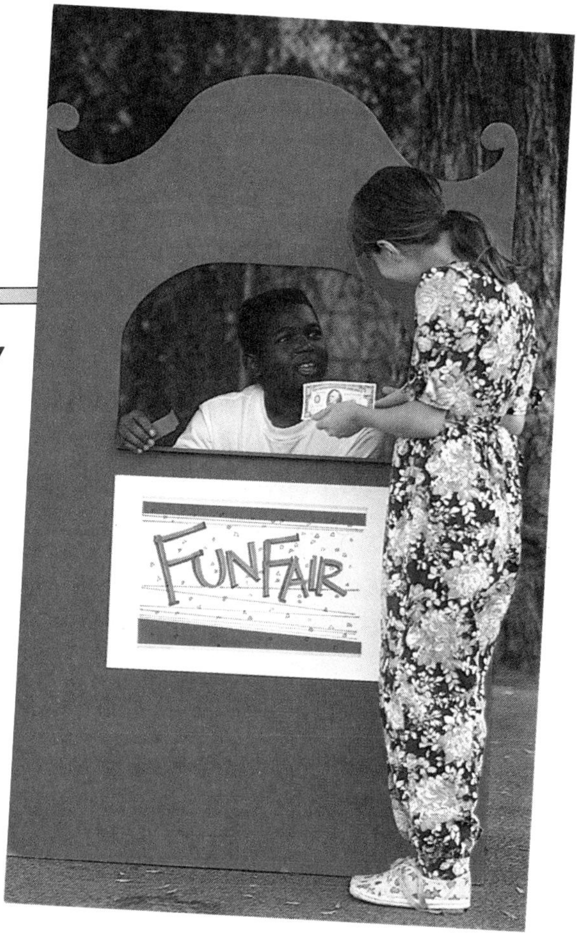

4

DATA, GRAPHS, AND PROBABILITY

5

MULTIPLICATION CONCEPTS AND BASIC FACTS

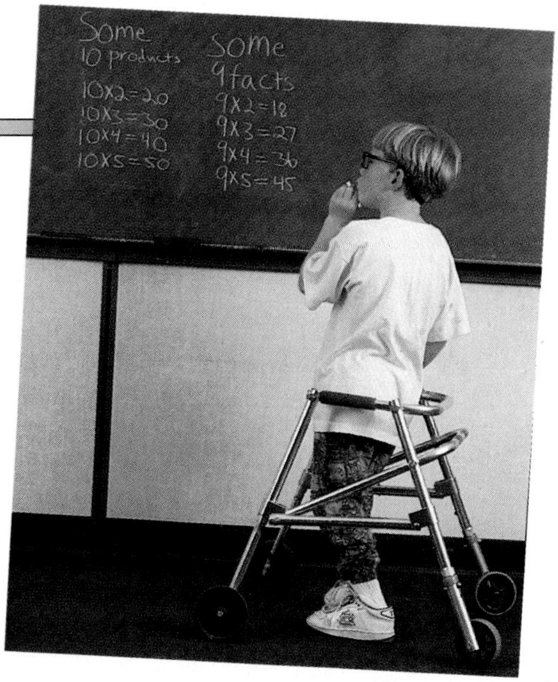

6

MULTIPLYING BY 1-DIGIT FACTORS

7

MULTIPLYING BY 2-DIGIT FACTORS

8

TIME AND CUSTOMARY MEASUREMENT

9

DIVISION: CONCEPTS AND BASIC FACTS

10

DIVISION: 1-DIGIT DIVISORS

11

GEOMETRY

12

FRACTION CONCEPTS

13

DECIMAL CONCEPTS

14

METRIC MEASUREMENT

15

ADDITION AND SUBTRACTION: FRACTIONS & DECIMALS

16

DIVISION: 2-DIGIT DIVISORS

RESOURCE BANK AND APPENDIX

Dear Student:

Welcome to an exciting world of mathematics. We have many activities for you to enjoy—activities that will increase your skill with numbers.

You are going to take the ideas you have already learned and apply them in interesting, new ways. You will do problem solving activities by drawing pictures. You will learn to estimate with money, a very useful skill. You will discover interesting things about circles, triangles and squares. You will explore numbers from fractions to millions.

You are going to become a whiz at multiplication this year! You will start on division. You will also work in groups to share your learning experience with others. That will make mathematics fun for everyone.

This is a very important year for you. We know you will enjoy all these new ways to use math.

From your friends at Addison-Wesley.

1

Addition and Subtraction Concepts and Basic Facts

THEME: NATURE

MATH AND SCIENCE

DATA BANK

Use the Science Data Bank on page 468 to answer the questions.

1 Which animal can live longer in the wild, a squirrel or a box turtle?

2 In captivity, how much longer can a raccoon live than a cottontail rabbit?

3 In the wild, the life span of a chipmunk can be 10 years more than that of a white-footed mouse. What is the life span of a wild chipmunk?

4 **Use Critical Thinking** Look at the graph and tell what part of the day the red-backed salamander is least active. Can you think of a reason why?

A nature museum is a good place to get a close look at animals and learn about their habits.

Problem Solving
Understanding Addition and Subtraction

UNDERSTAND
FIND DATA
PLAN
ESTIMATE
SOLVE
CHECK

LEARN ABOUT IT

When the action is **put together,** you **add.** When the action is **take away,** you **subtract.** Show the other subtraction actions below with counters. Complete the equations.

3	+	2	=	5
addend		**addend**		**sum**
5	−	**2**	=	**3**
sum		**addend**		**addend**

Problem	Action	Operation
	Compare	**Subtract**
On a nature walk, you count 5 red squirrels and 3 gray ones. How many fewer are gray?		$5 - 3 = \square$
	Find the Missing Part	
A tree squirrel has 6 young squirrels. 2 are male. How many are female?		$6 - 2 = \square$
	How Many More Are Needed?	
You want to find pictures of 6 kinds of squirrels. You have found 4 kinds. How many more must you find?	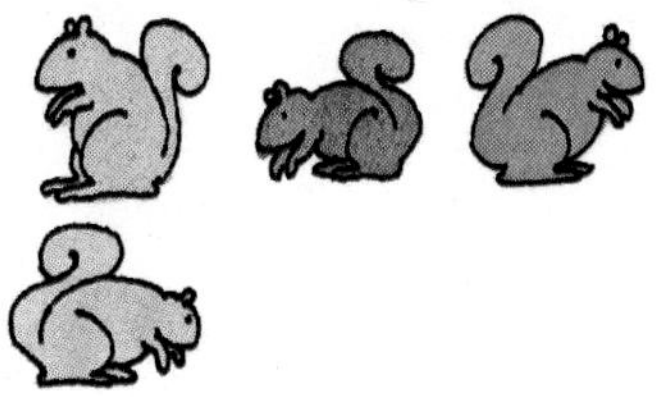	$6 - 4 = \square$

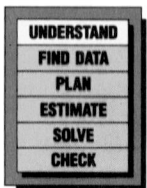

TRY IT OUT

Use counters to find the answer. Choose the correct equation.

1. The Wildlife Rescue Center is caring for 7 flying squirrels and 4 fox squirrels. How many more flying squirrels are there?
   a. $7 + 4 = 11$ **b.** $7 - 4 = 3$

2. You see 5 squirrels near your campsite. 3 are fox squirrels and the rest are gray squirrels. How many are gray?
   a. $5 - 3 = 2$ **b.** $5 + 3 = 8$

PRACTICE

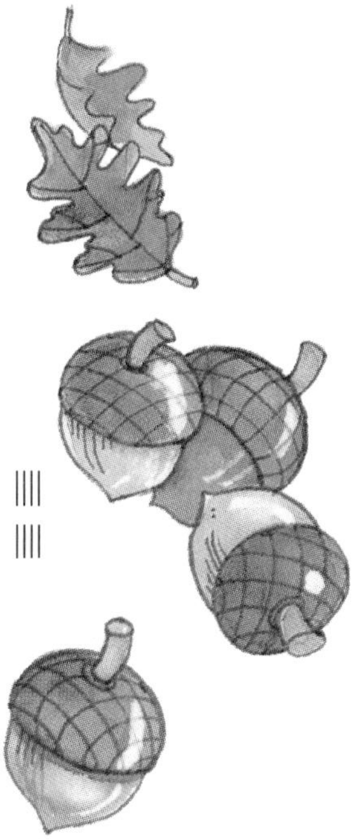

Use counters to find each answer. Then complete the equation that gives the same answer.

1. 5 squirrels are hiding nuts. 3 squirrels join them. How many squirrels are there?

$5 + 3 = \square$
$5 - 3 = \square$

2. 7 chipmunks are eating seeds. A noise scares 2 away. How many are still eating?

$7 + 2 = \square$
$7 - 2 = \square$

3. You count 8 red squirrels in the park. Then you count 3 gray squirrels. How many more red squirrels are there?

$8 - 3 = \square$
$8 + 3 = \square$

4. It takes 6 beavers to build a dam. 2 are working now. How many more are needed?

$6 + 2 = \square$
$6 - 2 = \square$

5. 7 ground squirrels are in a nest. 2 are parents. How many are young?

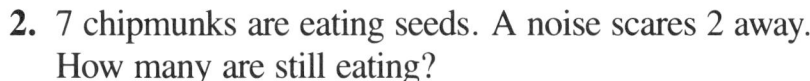

$7 - 2 = \square$
$7 + 2 = \square$

▶ WRITE YOUR OWN PROBLEM

6. Write a story problem that can be solved by adding.

7. Write a story problem that can be solved by subtracting.

More Practice, page 512, set C

Addition Properties

LEARN ABOUT IT

EXPLORE **Think About the Situation**

In Germany, some roads have underpasses so that frogs can cross safely. Hans and Will watched for an hour and saw 3 frogs, 4 toads, and 5 newts come through the underpass. To find the total number Hans thought:

> I'll add 3 and 4 to get 7. Then I'll add 5 to get 12.

$$(3 + 4) + 5 = 12$$

Will thought:

> I'll add 4 and 5 to get 9. Then I'll add 3 to get 12.

$$(4 + 5) + 3 = 12$$

The parentheses ( ) tell which numbers are added first.

TALK ABOUT IT

1. Which two numbers did Hans add first? Which did Will add first?

2. Does adding 3 and 5 first give a different sum?

The grouping property helps when you have 3 addends.

Grouping Property
Changing the grouping of addends does not change the sum.
$(2 + 3) + 4 = 9$, so $2 + (3 + 4) = 9$

You may remember other properties that help in finding addition facts.

Order Property	**Zero Property**
Changing the order of addends does not change the sum. $7 + 3 = 10$, so $3 + 7 = 10$	The sum of a number and zero is that number. $8 + 0 = 8$

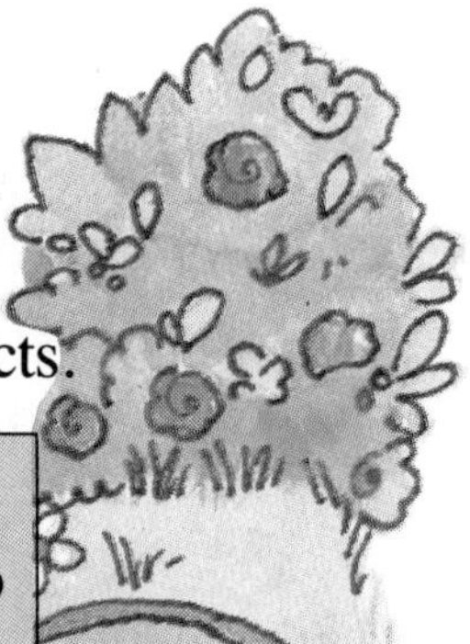

TRY IT OUT

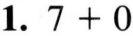

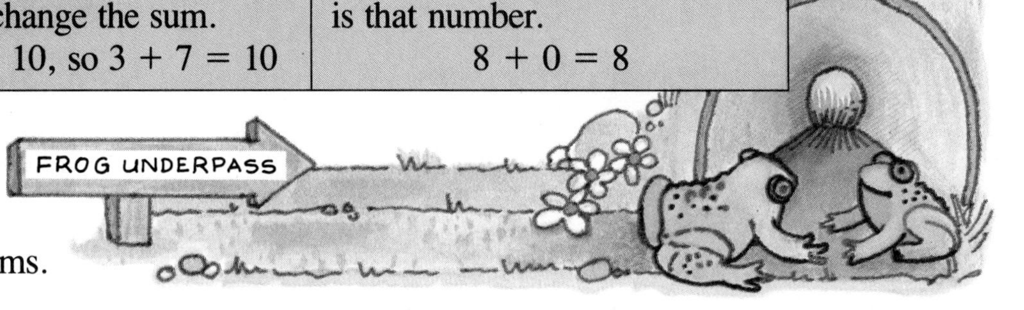

Find these sums.

1. $7 + 0$ **2.** $0 + 7$ **3.** $5 + (2 + 3)$ **4.** $(5 + 2) + 3$

PRACTICE

Add.

1. $8 + 3$
2. $3 + 8$
3. $7 + 9$
4. $9 + 7$
5. $6 + 5$
6. $5 + 6$
7. $9 + 0$
8. $0 + 9$
9. $8 + 8$
10. $0 + 6$
11. $6 + 0$
12. $7 + 7$
13. $4 + 5$
14. $5 + 4$
15. $8 + 9$
16. $9 + 8$
17. $9 + 2$
18. $2 + 9$
19. $(2 + 4) + 7$
20. $2 + (4 + 7)$
21. $(2 + 7) + 4$

APPLY

MATH REASONING Use the sums in the box to find these sums.

22. $249 + 368$
23. $537 + (368 + 249)$
24. $368 + 537$
25. $537 + 249 + 368$

$537 + 368 = 905$
$368 + 249 = 617$
$(537 + 368) + 249 = 1{,}154$

PROBLEM SOLVING

26. Amy's backyard frog, Slurpy, ate 3 more flies one night than it had eaten that morning. If Slurpy ate 6 flies in the morning, how many did it eat that day?

27. **Science Data Bank** How many minutes is a red-backed salamander active from 6 a.m. to 8 a.m.? See page 468.

MIXED REVIEW

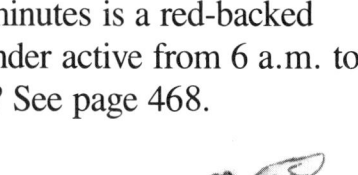

Add.

28. $8 + 5$
29. $5 + 8$
30. $2 + 7$
31. $7 + 2$
32. $3 + 0$
33. $8 + 0$
34. $(2 + 6) + 5$
35. $2 + (6 + 5)$
36. $(7 + 3) + 0$
37. $4 + 5 + 8$

Using Addition to Subtract

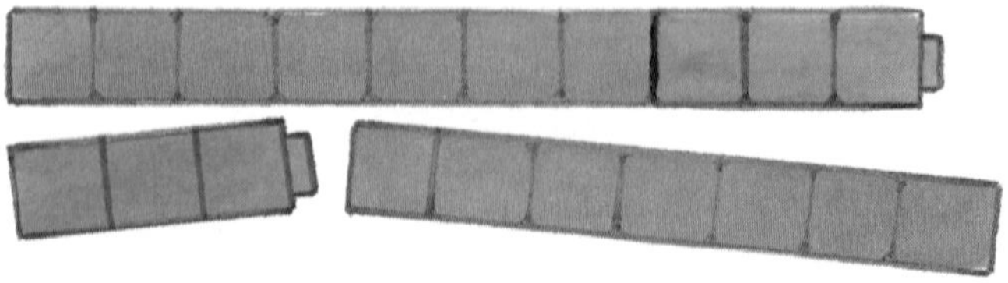

LEARN ABOUT IT

EXPLORE **Use Snap Cubes**

Since addition and subtraction are related, you can use addition to find differences. Work in groups. Use red and blue snap cubes to show the parts of this fact family.

Now use 10 cubes with another combination of red and blue to show a different fact family.

Fact Family

$7 + 3 = 10$
$10 - 3 = 7$
$3 + 7 = 10$
$10 - 7 = 3$

TALK ABOUT IT

1. Look at one of your fact families. What action did you use to show each fact?
2. Use the 10 cubes and a fact family to explain how addition and subtraction are related.

Math Point

When 0 is subtracted from a number, the difference is that number.

$6 - 0 = 6$

When a number is subtracted from itself, the difference is 0.

$6 - 6 = 0$

An addition fact shows two addends and their sum. The related subtraction fact shows the sum and one addend. You use the sum and this addend to find the other addend.

What number adds to 9 to give 12?

$12 - 9 =$ ||||

The missing addend is 3.

$$\begin{array}{r} 14 \\ -\ 7 \\ \hline \text{||||} \end{array}$$

What number adds to 7 to give 14?

The missing addend is 7.

TRY IT OUT

Subtract. Think about finding the missing addend.

1. $11 - 3 =$ |||| **2.** $12 - 6 =$ |||| **3.** $10 - 4 =$ |||| **4.** $16 - 8 =$ ||||

PRACTICE

Give an addition fact for each subtraction fact.

1. $11 - 9 = 2$ **2.** $12 - 3 = 9$ **3.** $8 - 5 = 3$ **4.** $7 - 4 = 3$

Subtract. Think about finding the missing addend.

5. $18 - 9$ **6.** $12 - 7$ **7.** $10 - 8$ **8.** $16 - 7$ **9.** $9 - 6$ **10.** $11 - 8$

11. $15 - 6$ **12.** $13 - 8$ **13.** $14 - 6$ **14.** $17 - 8$ **15.** $11 - 6$ **16.** $14 - 8$

17. $6 - 4$ **18.** $18 - 9$ **19.** $16 - 7$ **20.** $15 - 7$ **21.** $12 - 3$

22. $14 - 9$ **23.** $16 - 5$ **24.** $13 - 6$ **25.** $7 - 5$ **26.** $10 - 6$

APPLY

MATH REASONING Give the fact family for each pair of addends.

27. 4, 9 **28.** 6, 8 **29.** 3, 6 **30.** 7, 7

PROBLEM SOLVING

31. Keri has 8 animal stickers. How many more will she need to put one on each month of a calendar she is making?

32. Tim's sister gave him 7 snail shells. He found 6 more. How many more than a dozen does he have?

CALCULATOR

Enter the number 18 into a calculator and push these keys. [−] [9] [=] [=]

If 0 appears, your calculator has a subtraction constant. Estimate how many times you will have to subtract to reach 0 in each problem. Check.

33. Enter 24. Subtract 6. **34.** Enter 144. Subtract 12.

35. Enter 48. Subtract 3. **36.** Enter 56. Subtract 4.

More Practice, page 512, set D

Problem Solving
Introduction

LEARN ABOUT IT

Problems you can solve using one addition or one subtraction equation are called one-step problems. For one-step problems, you can use the strategy **Choose the Operation.**

A North American opossum sleeps 19 hours a day. A gray wolf sleeps 13 hours a day. How many more hours does an opossum sleep than a gray wolf?

The checklist can help you solve problems.

Understand the Situation — I want to compare the number of hours each animal sleeps.

Find Data — North American opossum: 19 hours
Gray wolf: 13 hours

Plan the Solution — Since I want to compare the two numbers, I should subtract.

Estimate the Answer — 19 − 13 is about 20 − 15 or 5.

Solve the Problem — 19 − 13 = 6
An opossum sleeps 6 hours more than a gray wolf.

Check the Answer — 6 is close to the estimate of 5, so 6 hours is a reasonable answer.

TRY IT OUT

Pick the number sentence you could use to solve the problem. Do not solve.

1. A giant armadillo sleeps 18 out of 24 hours. How long is it awake?

a. 24 − 18 **b.** 24 + 18

2. A roe deer sleeps 730 hours in a year. A rhesus monkey sleeps 2,555 more hours than a roe deer. How long does a rhesus monkey sleep in a year?

a. 2,555 − 730 **b.** 2,555 + 730

MIXED PRACTICE

Animal	Hours of Sleep Per Day
Arctic ground squirrel	16
Giant armadillo	18
Giant sloth	20
Goat	3
Gray seal	6
Mountain beaver	11
North American opossum	19
Owl monkey	17
Rhesus monkey	9

Pick the number sentence you could use to solve these problems.

1. How much more sleep does a giant sloth get than a mountain beaver?
   a. 20 − 11 **b.** 20 + 11

2. The black bear weighed 346 pounds when it went into hibernation. It lost 112 pounds in hibernation. How much does it weigh now?
   a. 346 + 112 **b.** 346 − 112

3. During winter vacation, Melissa slept 70 hours the first week. She slept 72 hours the second week. How much sleep did she get during vacation?
   a. 70 + 72 **b.** 72 − 70

Solve these problems.

4. The owl monkey has already slept 9 hours. How many more hours will he sleep today?

5. Lincoln the cat slept 7 hours during the day. Then he slept 7 hours at night. How many hours did he sleep all together?

6. There were 12 newborn chincilla rabbits sleeping in a hutch. 5 woke up. How many were still asleep?

7. How many fewer hours a day does a goat sleep than a North American opossum?

8. **Write Your Own Problem** Write two questions that can be answered using the data given in the table and the equations below.
   a. 20 − 3 **b.** 6 + 6

More Practice, page 512, set E

Using Critical Thinking

LEARN ABOUT IT

Teri gave this secret number riddle to Jessica and Bill.
"Well," said Bill, after thinking a minute. "This riddle is easy. The answer is the same number as my brother's age, 14!"
"Not so fast, Bill," said Jessica. "I think you missed something. This riddle has two answers!"

> 1. I'm even.
> 2. I am not 10 or 20 but I am between them.
> 3. You don't say me when you count by fours.
>
> What number am I?

TALK ABOUT IT

1. What does Teri ask? How do her friends reply?
2. What numbers are possible after the first clue? the second? the third?
3. Do you agree with Jessica that the riddle has two answers? Explain.
4. Can you give one more clue that would make the riddle have only one answer?

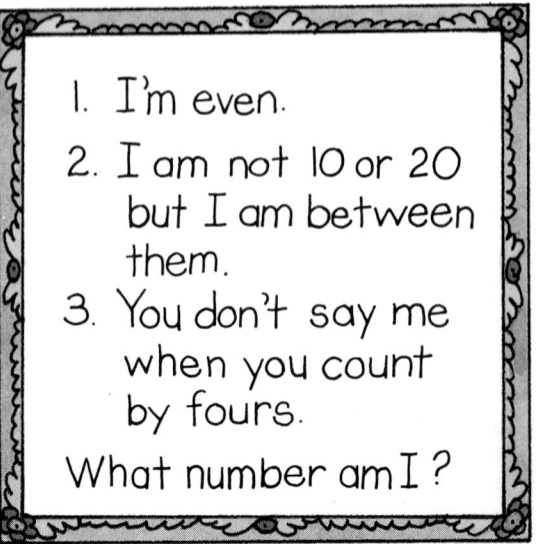

TRY IT OUT

Solve these secret number riddles.

1. a. I'm a double.
   b. I'm not a 2-digit number but I'm less than 100.
   c. My sum with 4 is more than 10.
   What number am I?

2. a. I'm a 3-digit number.
   b. I'm not odd.
   c. I couldn't be any greater.
   What number am I?

3. Make up a secret number riddle. Write 3 clues for your riddle. Give it to a classmate to solve.

Power Practice/Quiz

Find the sums.

1. $\begin{array}{r} 4 \\ +7 \\ \hline \end{array}$ **2.** $\begin{array}{r} 7 \\ +4 \\ \hline \end{array}$ **3.** $\begin{array}{r} 2 \\ 3 \\ +4 \\ \hline \end{array}$ **4.** $\begin{array}{r} 5 \\ 0 \\ +6 \\ \hline \end{array}$ **5.** $\begin{array}{r} 7 \\ 3 \\ +4 \\ \hline \end{array}$

6. $8 + 0$ **7.** $9 + 3$ **8.** $3 + 4$ **9.** $(2 + 3) + 5$

10. $8 + (2 + 3)$ **11.** $(8 + 2) + 3$ **12.** $8 + 0 + 5$ **13.** $5 + 3 + 3$

Write the addition fact you could use to answer each subtraction problem.

14. $12 - 7 = ?$ **15.** $8 - 8 = ?$ **16.** $5 - 4 = ?$ **17.** $16 - 9 = ?$

Find the differences.

18. $\begin{array}{r} 8 \\ -5 \\ \hline \end{array}$ **19.** $\begin{array}{r} 18 \\ -9 \\ \hline \end{array}$ **20.** $\begin{array}{r} 10 \\ -6 \\ \hline \end{array}$ **21.** $\begin{array}{r} 4 \\ -0 \\ \hline \end{array}$ **22.** $\begin{array}{r} 6 \\ -6 \\ \hline \end{array}$ **23.** $\begin{array}{r} 14 \\ -8 \\ \hline \end{array}$

Decide if you would add or subtract to answer each question.

24. 6 robins are in a tree. 4 cardinals join them.
  a. How many birds are in the tree?
  b. How many fewer cardinals are there than robins?

25. 7 baby foxes live in a den. 4 are playing inside the den. 1 leaves the den to be with the foxes outside.
  a. How many baby foxes are in the den?
  b. How many baby foxes are not in the den?

PROBLEM SOLVING

26. Today Jeno found 3 starfish. Yesterday he found 6. How many starfish has he found?

27. Liz needs 5 more shells to have as many as Tim has. If Liz has 8 shells, how many does Tim have?

28. Two numbers have a sum of 15. One number is 9. What is the other number?

29. Find two numbers whose sum is 12. What is the difference between the two numbers?

Mental Math
Breaking Apart Numbers

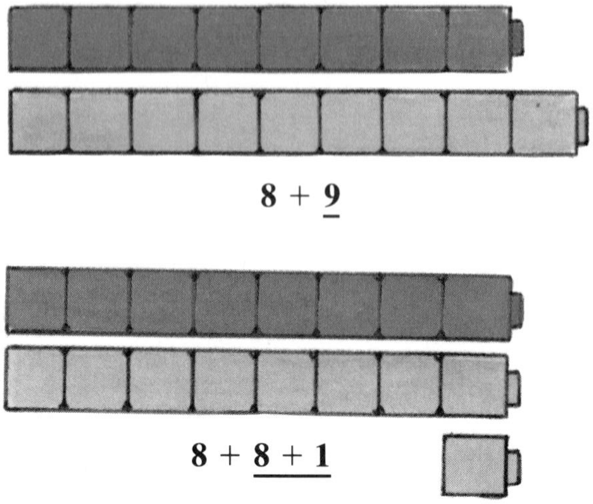

LEARN ABOUT IT

EXPLORE **Use Snap Cubes**

To help add numbers using mental math, you can break apart one of the addends. The snap cubes show one way to break apart the 9 in the sum 8 + 9.

Use snap cubes to show as many other ways as you can of breaking apart the 9.

TALK ABOUT IT

1. Describe the ways you found. How many were there?

2. Which way helped you most in finding 8 + 9? Explain.

Here are two addition strategies that are useful when you need to break apart an addend.

Make a double + 1.

7 + 8
↙ ↘
7 + 1

Break 8 into 7 + 1.
Find 7 + 7 plus 1.

Make 10 plus a number.

8 + 5
↙ ↘
2 + 3

Break 5 into 2 + 3.
Find 8 + 2 plus 3.

13 + 2
↙ ↘
10 + 3

Break 13 into 10 + 3.
Find 10 plus 3 + 2.

TRY IT OUT

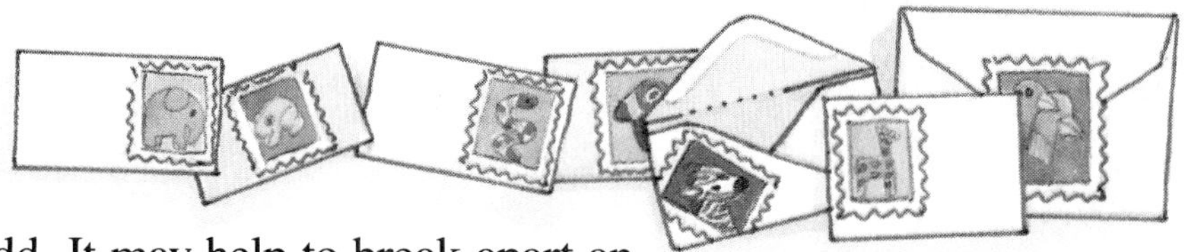

Use mental math to add. It may help to break apart an addend.

1. 6 + 7 **2.** 8 + 5 **3.** 13 + 2 **4.** 7 + 6 **5.** 15 + 3

6. 5 + 11 **7.** 9 + 12 **8.** 13 + 6 **9.** 4 + 9 **10.** 7 + 11

PRACTICE

Use mental math to add. If you need help, break apart an addend.

1. $9 + 5$
2. $7 + 6$
3. $14 + 5$
4. $6 + 5$
5. $12 + 7$
6. $11 + 6$
7. $8 + 6$
8. $12 + 4$
9. $8 + 9$
10. $11 + 8$
11. $16 + 3$
12. $7 + 8$
13. $14 + 5 = n$
14. $11 + 6 = n$
15. $7 + 9 = n$

APPLY

MATH REASONING Use mental math and the doubles in the table to find these sums.

36	+	36	=	72
57	+	57	=	114
79	+	79	=	158
126	+	126	=	252

16. $36 + 37$
17. $58 + 57$
18. $78 + 78$
19. $127 + 127$
20. $35 + 37$
21. $58 + 56$

PROBLEM SOLVING

22. **Data Hunt** Add the number of letters in your first and last names. Find a classmate whose name sum is larger than yours. Find one whose name sum is smaller.

23. Tim bought 6 animal stamps to put with the 9 he had already collected. How many did he then have?

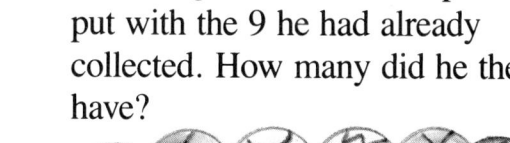

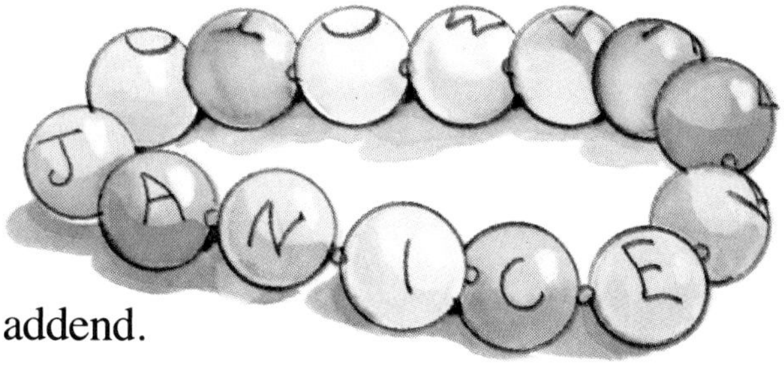

MIXED REVIEW

Subtract. Think about finding the missing addend.

24. $13 - 7$
25. $10 - 2$
26. $15 - 6$
27. $8 - 5$
28. $14 - 8$
29. $18 - 9$

Add. If it is useful, break apart an addend.

30. $13 + 0$
31. $6 + 9$
32. $12 + 7$
33. $9 + 8$
34. $2 + 16$
35. $15 + 4$

More Practice, page 500, set B

Mental Math
Using Compensation

LEARN ABOUT IT

EXPLORE **Discover a Relationship**
Follow these directions with 10 different pairs of addends. Use a calculator for larger numbers.

Choose any two addends.

$$\begin{array}{r} 5 \\ +\,9 \\ \hline \end{array}$$

Add a chosen amount to the first addend.
Subtract the same amount from the second addend.
Find and compare the sums.

$$\begin{array}{rl} 5 & \text{up } 2 \rightarrow 7 \\ +\,9 & \text{down } 2 \rightarrow \underline{7} \end{array}$$

TALK ABOUT IT

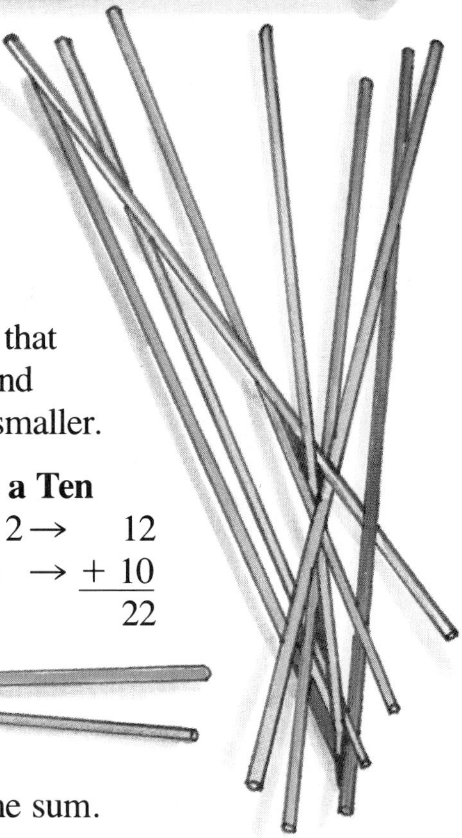

1. Tell what happened in the above example.
2. If you add 3 to one addend and subtract 3 from the other, will the sum change? Explain.
3. What did you discover when you tried this with other addends?

You can sometimes change a sum into an easier sum that has the same answer. To do this, you make one addend larger and **compensate** by making the other addend smaller.

Change to a Double

$$\begin{array}{rcr} 9 & \text{— down } 1 \rightarrow & 8 \\ +\,7 & \text{— up } 1 \rightarrow & +\,8 \\ \hline 16 & & 16 \end{array}$$

Change to a Ten

$$\begin{array}{rcr} 14 & \text{— down } 2 \rightarrow & 12 \\ +\,8 & \text{— up } 2 \rightarrow & +\,10 \\ \hline 22 & & 22 \end{array}$$

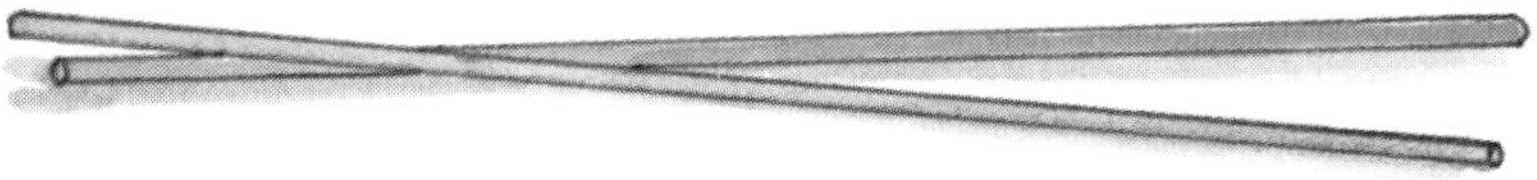

TRY IT OUT

Compensate as shown and use mental math to find the sum.

1. 8 down 2
+ 4 up 2

2. 8 up 2
+ 12 down 2

3. 14 down 3
+ 7 up 3

4. 9 up 1
+ 7 down 1

PRACTICE

Compensate and use mental math to find the sum.

1. 7 down 2 + 3 up 2	**2.** 9 up 1 + 11 down 1	**3.** 6 up 1 + 8 down 1	**4.** 11 down 2 + 7 up 2
5. 9 up 1 + 11 down 1	**6.** 11 down 1 + 9 up 1	**7.** 8 down 2 + 4 up 2	**8.** 12 down 2 + 8 up 2

Add. If it is helpful, use compensation.

9. 9 + 7	**10.** 8 + 15	**11.** 14 + 8	**12.** 12 + 9	**13.** 6 + 9	**14.** 11 + 7
15. 13 + 9	**16.** 9 + 4	**17.** 11 + 8	**18.** 7 + 12	**19.** 15 + 9	**20.** 6 + 12

APPLY

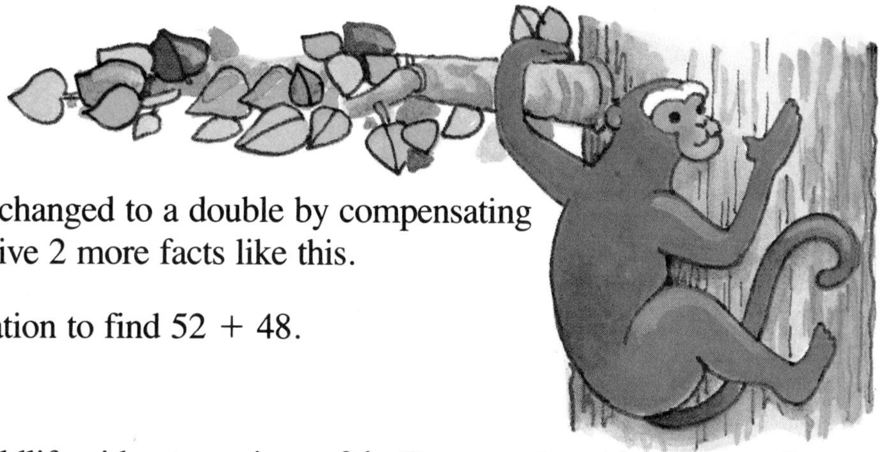

MATH REASONING

21. 9 + 7 can be changed to a double by compensating down-up 1. Give 2 more facts like this.

22. Use compensation to find 52 + 48.

PROBLEM SOLVING

23. Jill made 8 wildlife video tapes in the summer. She made 6 more in the fall. How many tapes did she make?

24. Tom ran the video camera for 9 minutes. Then he ran it for 15 more minutes. How long was the total video?

USING CRITICAL THINKING Logical Reasoning

Is the statement about addition with whole numbers always, sometimes, or never true?

25. The sum is less than either addend.

26. Different sums must have different addends.

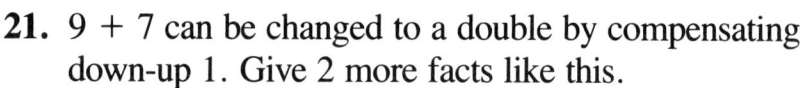

More Practice, page 500, set C

Group Decision Making

UNDERSTAND
FIND DATA
PLAN
ESTIMATE
SOLVE
CHECK

Group Skills
Listen to Others
Encourage and Respect Others
Explain and Summarize
Check for Understanding
Disagree in an Agreeable Way

You will work as part of a team for many lessons in this book. It is important for a team to listen to everyone's ideas before making decisions. The group skills in this chart are some of the ways your group can show that they appreciate everyone's ideas.

Work with your group. Think of at least 3 examples of how you know when a group member is not listening to others. When you do the cooperative activity, look for ways to show you are a good listener.

Cooperative Activity

Each person in your group will need 5 small paper squares and some graph paper. Your goal is to make patterns so that the edge of each square touches the edge of another square. Touching only by corners or by part of an edge is not allowed. All five squares must be used for each pattern.

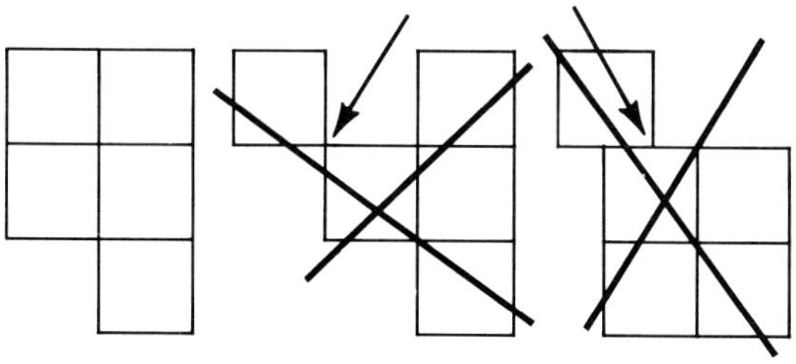

See if your group can find at least 10 different patterns. Cut each pattern out of graph paper. Patterns are different if they do not fit on top of each other no matter which way they are turned or flipped. Put the ones that are alike together.

Some Questions to Answer

1. How did you make sure everyone in your group understood what to do?
2. How many ways did your group find?
3. Did your group agree about which patterns were the same and which were different? What did you do if you did not agree?
4. Predict which of your patterns will fold to become the size of one of the squares. Try it to check your predictions.

Check Your Group Skills

5. What could your group do to improve how you listen to each other?

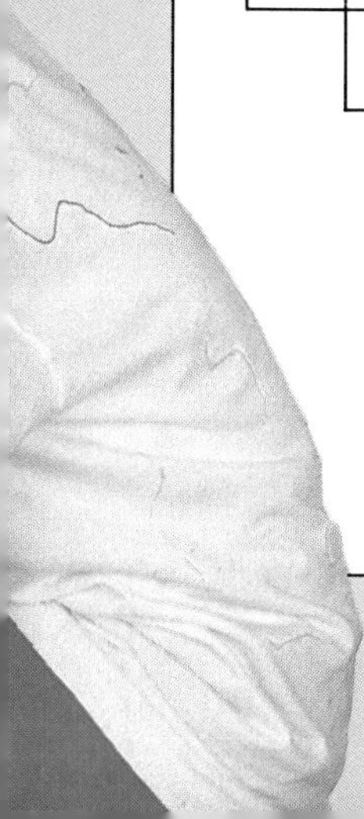

WRAP UP

Operation Sort

If you saw these sentences in story problems, would you need to add or subtract?

1. How many are there in all?
2. How many more are needed?
3. Who is older?
4. How much is it all together?
5. Compare the weights.
6. How many are still here?
7. Calculate the sum.
8. How many are left over?
9. What is the total?
10. Find the difference.

Sometimes, Always, Never

Which word should go in the blank, sometimes, always, or never?

11. You may __?__ add numbers in any order.
12. Fact families __?__ have two subtraction and two addition equations.
13. You __?__ use compensation to change sums.

Project

14. Use one of these facts to make up an addition problem and the other to make up a subtraction problem. Then find one more interesting animal fact and use it to make up another addition or subtraction problem.

- The tarantula spider can live 2 years without food and 7 months without water. The snail can go 5 years without food.
- If you have been sprayed by a skunk, you can get rid of the odor with tomato juice! It takes 3 large cans of juice each to make one boy and one dog smell all right again.

Power Practice/Test

Part 1 Understanding

Write a number sentence for each.

1. 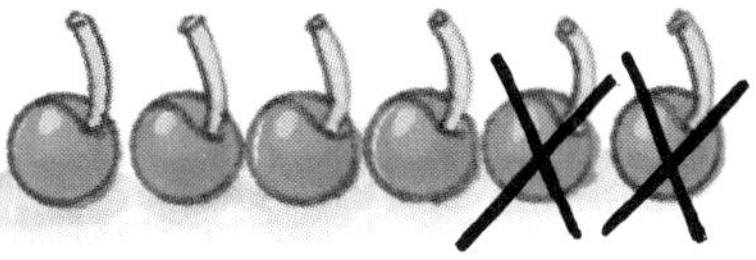

2. 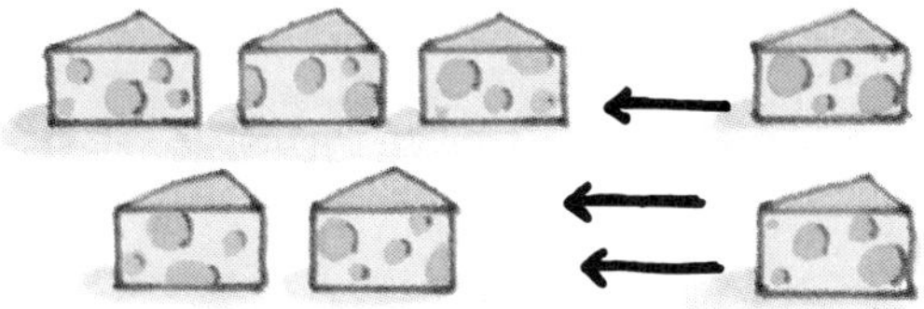

3. 6 + (4 + 3) = 13
   What does (6 + 4) + 3 equal?

4. If you add zero to a number, the sum will be the number. Why?

5. Write the rest of the fact family for:
   5 + 9 = 14

6. Use compensation to change 7 + 13 to a double. Write the new addends and sum.

Part 2 Skills

Add or subtract.

7. 6 + 8 **8.** 15 − 9 **9.** 11 − 0 **10.** $\begin{array}{r} 13 \\ -\ 5 \\ \hline \end{array}$ **11.** $\begin{array}{r} 14 \\ +\ 9 \\ \hline \end{array}$ **12.** $\begin{array}{r} 16 \\ -\ 8 \\ \hline \end{array}$

Give the fact family for each pair of addends.

13. 4, 7 **14.** 5, 9 **15.** 6, 6

Add, using mental math. Break apart an addend.

16. 7 + 4 **17.** 8 + 4 **18.** 11 + 7

Part 3 Applications

19. A rabbit ate 17 carrots and 9 turnips. What number sentence could you use to find how many more carrots than turnips it ate?

20. A snail crawled 9 inches in an hour. Then it crawled 6 more inches to a tidal pool. How far did the snail crawl?

21. Two numbers give a sum of 13 and a difference of 1. What are the numbers?

22. **Challenge** Use compensation and mental math to find the sum of 227 and 273. Compensate up-down 3, then break apart addends.

ENRICHMENT
Using and Making Flow Charts

Flow charts give directions for doing things. Special shapes signal different parts of the flow chart.

Here are two flow charts for you to copy and complete by giving the missing instructions or numbers.

Watch a TV Show

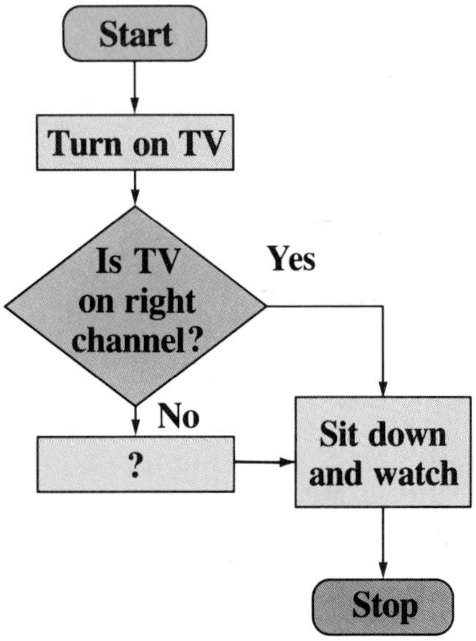

Try a Number Surprise

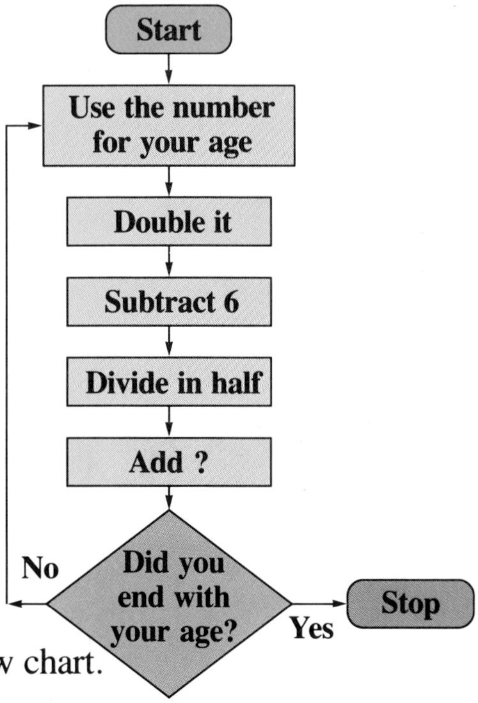

Put these instructions in order and make a flow chart.

1. Crossing the Street

Is anything coming?

Start. Stop.

Cross the street.

Wait at the corner.

Look both ways.

2. Calling on the Phone

Hang up. Start. Stop.

Does anyone answer?

Talk.

Pick up the receiver.

Dial the number.

CUMULATIVE REVIEW

Add or subtract.

1. $\begin{array}{r} 5 \\ +\ 9 \\ \hline \end{array}$

A 13 **B** 15

C 14 **D** 4

2. $\begin{array}{r} 15 \\ -\ 6 \\ \hline \end{array}$

A 9 **B** 10

C 11 **D** 21

3. $\begin{array}{r} 12 \\ -\ 8 \\ \hline \end{array}$

A 6 **B** 4

C 20 **D** 3

4. $\begin{array}{r} 5 \\ +\ 6 \\ \hline \end{array}$

A 7 **B** 11

C 10 **D** 12

Which property does each number sentence show?

5. $3 + (6 + 7) = 3 + (7 + 6)$

A grouping **B** order

C multiplication **D** zero

6. $6 + (4 + 5) = (6 + 4) + 5$

A grouping **B** order

C multiplication **D** zero

The mental math break apart method would be helpful in solving these problems. Choose the best way to break apart an addend.

7. $8 + 9$

A $3 + 6$ **B** $4 + 4$

C $8 + 1$ **D** $9 + 8$

8. $13 + 6$

A $3 + 3$ **B** $10 + 4$

C $10 + 3$ **D** $5 + 8$

9. Lia must mail 15 letters. She has 8 stamps. How many stamps should she buy?

A 23 **B** 6

C 8 **D** 7

10. Ron found $79 + 36 = 115$ with his calculator. Which sum can he now find using mental math?

A $76 + 39$ **B** $88 + 63$

C $97 + 67$ **D** $115 + 179$

2

PLACE VALUE AND MONEY

THEME: AMERICAN INDIANS

MATH AND SOCIAL STUDIES

DATA BANK

Use the Social Studies Data Bank on page 472 to answer the questions.

1 Which of the Indian dwellings had the greatest number of rooms?

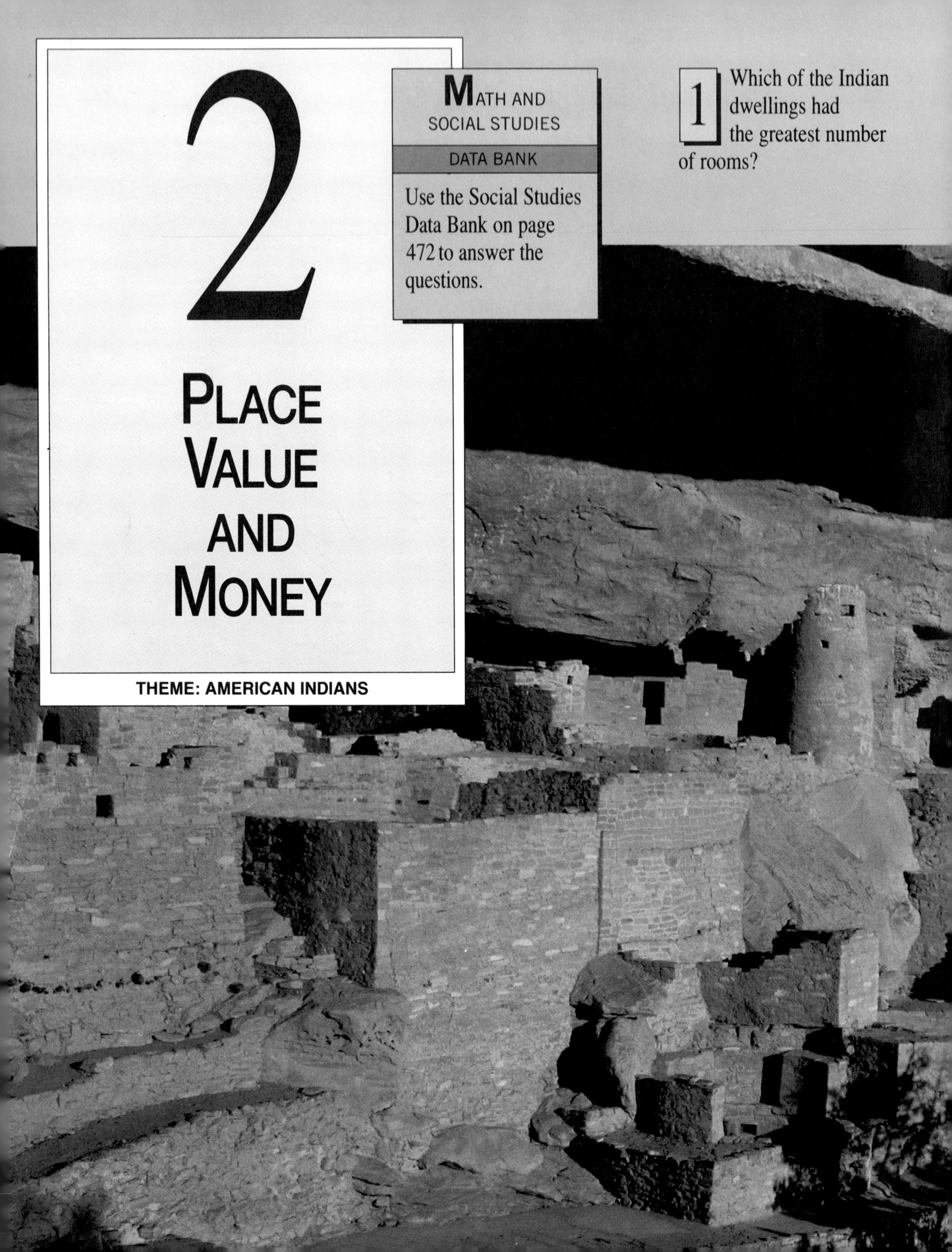

2 Name a building that had fewer than 90 rooms.

3 Name two buildings that had about the same number of rooms.

4 **Use Critical Thinking** What can you say about the sizes of Indian groups living in Canyon de Chelly, Chaco Canyon, and Mesa Verde? Explain.

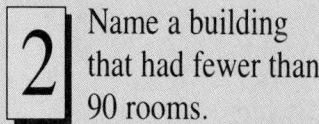

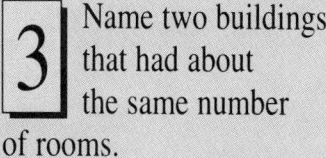

Centuries ago, ancestors of today's Pueblo Indians lived in protected villages built high in stone cliffs.

Understanding Place Value

LEARN ABOUT IT

EXPLORE **Use a Place Value Model**

You can write any whole number using the **digits** 1, 2, 3, 4, 5, 6, 7, 8, 9, 0, and place value.

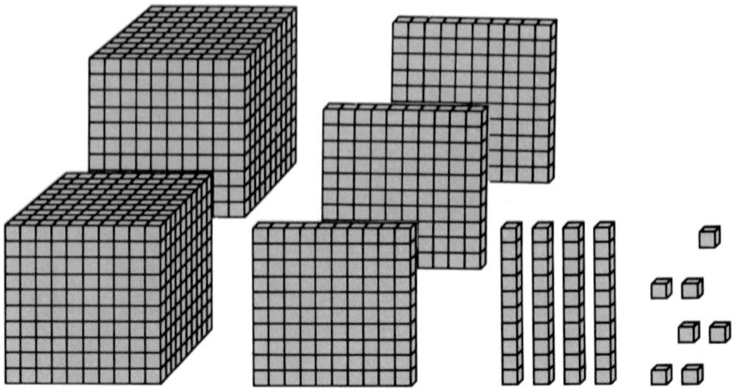

Work in groups. Use place value blocks to show a number with more thousands than are in the picture. Then show a number with fewer tens and a number with no hundreds. Write each number after you show it.

These blocks show a number.

You write, **2,347**.

You read, "**two thousand, three hundred forty-seven**."

TALK ABOUT IT

1. What did you do to show more thousands than are in 2,347?
2. How did your blocks show a number with no hundreds?
3. How do you write a number with no hundreds? with no tens?

You can find the **place value** of a digit by looking at its place in the number. The chart shows the place values for the digits in 5,698.

The expanded form helps you see the value of each place.

	Thousands		Hundreds		Tens		Ones
standard form →	5	,	6		9		8
expanded form →	5,000	+	600	+	90	+	8

TRY IT OUT

Use place value blocks. Show, read, and write each number.

1. 4 hundreds, 4 tens, and 3 ones
2. 2 thousands, 4 hundreds, and 2 ones
3. 2 thousands, 3 hundreds, and 6 tens
4. 1 thousand and 9 tens
5. Write 3 thousands, 9 hundreds, and 6 ones in expanded form.

PRACTICE

How many thousands, hundreds, tens, and ones are in each number? Write the number.

1.

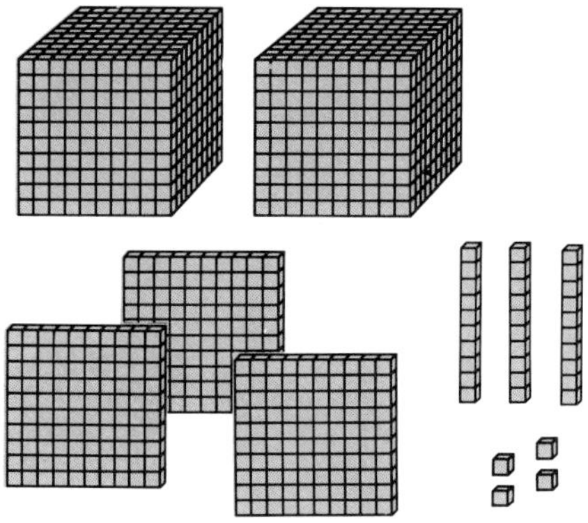

2.

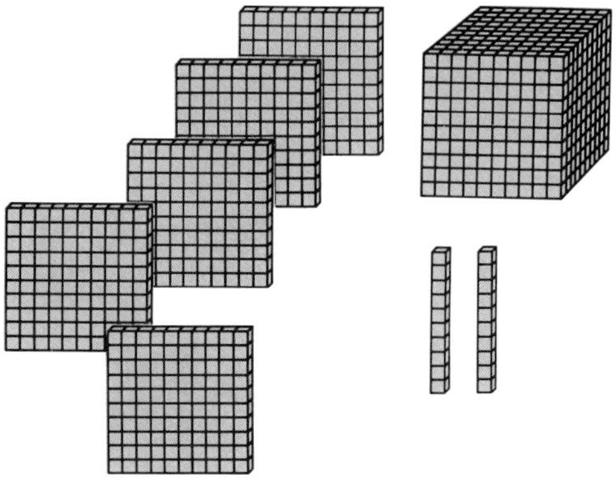

Write the number in standard form and in expanded form.

3. five thousand, eight hundred seventy-five

4. nine thousand, ninety-nine

5. two thousand, four hundred ten

APPLY

MATH REASONING Give the numbers from the box in which the digit 7 has the given value.

3,875	6,704	5,713
7,025	1,847	2,427
4,725	7,023	9,378

6. 700 **7.** 70 **8.** 7

PROBLEM SOLVING

9. What number would this picture show if it had 2 more hundreds? if it had 3 more tens?

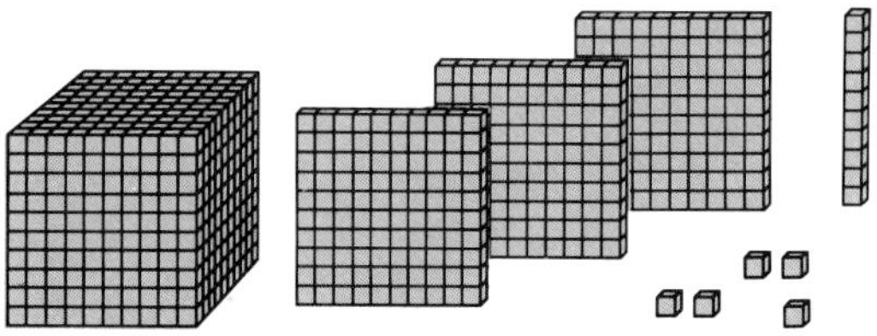

ALGEBRA

Use models to find the number you can put in the box to make the sentence true.

10. 3 thousands = ▢ hundreds

11. 3 thousands = ▢ tens

12. 3 thousands = ▢ ones

> Tens, hundreds, and thousands are related.
>
> 10 tens = 1 hundred
>
> 10 hundreds = 1 thousand

More Practice, page 512, set F

Using Larger Numbers

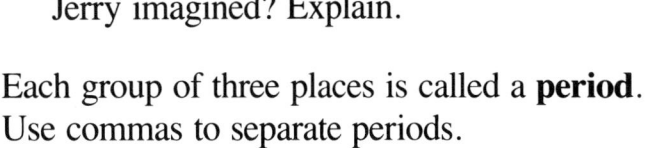

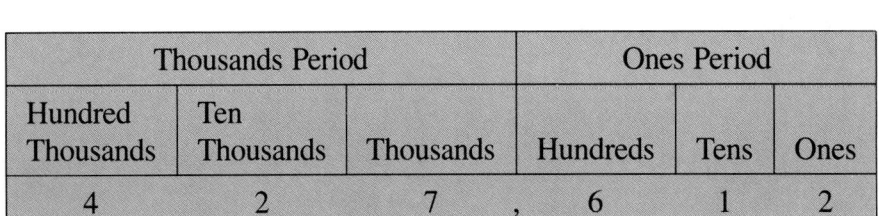

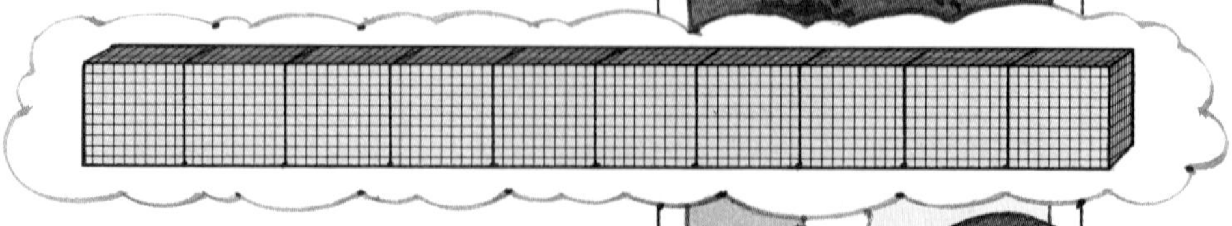

LEARN ABOUT IT

EXPLORE **Think About the Situation**

Jerry read that it took over 10,000 adobe blocks to build some ancient Indian homes. He thought about how he could show this large number with place value blocks.

TALK ABOUT IT

1. How could you convince someone that there are 1,000 ones cubes in the thousands cube Jerry is holding?
2. How many ones are there in the long row of cubes Jerry imagined? Explain.

Each group of three places is called a **period**. Use commas to separate periods.

Thousands Period			Ones Period		
Hundred Thousands	Ten Thousands	Thousands	Hundreds	Tens	Ones
4	2	7 ,	6	1	2

400,000 + 20,000 + 7,000 + 600 + 10 + 2

You write, **427,612**. You read, "**four hundred twenty-seven thousand, six hundred twelve**."

TRY IT OUT

1. Write and read a 5-digit number with 3 in the ten thousands place and 4 in the thousands place.

   3 4, ___ ___ ___

2. Write and read a 6-digit number with 7 in the hundred thousands place and 2 in the hundreds place.

   ___ ___ ___, ___ ___ ___

PRACTICE

Write and read each number.

1. A 5-digit number with 6 in the thousands place and 0 in the hundreds place
2. A 6-digit number with 9 in the ten thousands place and 5 in the tens place

Write the digit for the given place in the number 384,019.

3. hundreds
4. ten thousands
5. thousands
6. hundred thousands

Write the numbers from the box in which the digit 3 has the given value.

385,219	463,218
443,276	538,425
832,104	645,318
221,378	308,467

7. 300
8. 300,000
9. 3,000
10. 30,000

Write the number.

11. seventy thousand, three hundred four
12. two hundred sixty-three thousand, four hundred eighty-two

APPLY

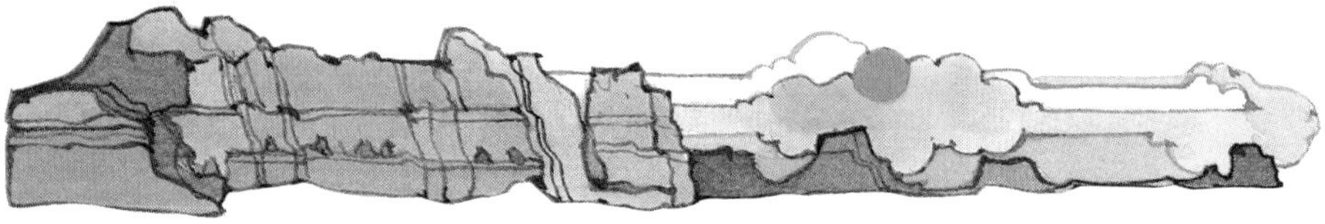

MATH REASONING

13. Give the next number in this pattern. 203 2,004 20,005

PROBLEM SOLVING

DATA BANK

14. One ancient Indian building used about 34,000 blocks. How many thousands cubes would Jerry need to show this?
15. **Social Studies Data Bank** How many tens are in the number of rooms in Long House? See page 472.

CALCULATOR

Change the digit by adding or subtracting just once. The other digits stay the same. Tell how you made each change.

16. Change the 8 in 586,204 to 0.
17. Change the 4 in 234,198 to 0.
18. Change the 3 in 765,382 to 4.

Comparing and Ordering Numbers

LEARN ABOUT IT

EXPLORE Study the Data

You can compare these numbers to find which is greater or less. Then you can put them in order by size.

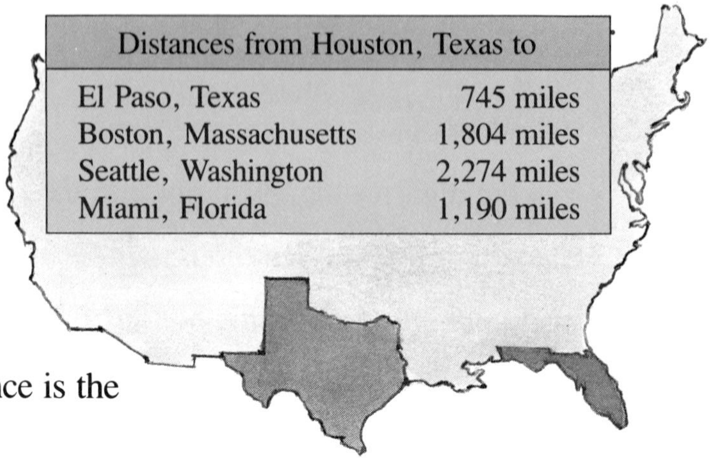

Distances from Houston, Texas to	
El Paso, Texas	745 miles
Boston, Massachusetts	1,804 miles
Seattle, Washington	2,274 miles
Miami, Florida	1,190 miles

TALK ABOUT IT

1. Can you tell quickly which distance is the shortest? How?
2. Which is the greatest distance from Houston—Boston or Miami? Explain how you know.

Use these symbols to compare numbers.

<	means *is less than*
>	means *is greater than*
=	means *is equal to*
≠	means *is not equal to*

You can use place value to compare numbers such as 7,289 and 7,294.

To compare, start at the left. Find the first place where the digits are not equal.

7,289
7,294

Compare the digits in that place.

8 **<** 9

The numbers compare the same way.

7,289 < 7,294

To order this list of numbers,
7,289 798 7,294 6,813,
compare the numbers two at a time.

798 < 6,813
6,813 < 7,289
7,289 < 7,294

Then list them from least to greatest or greatest to least.

798 6,813 7,289 7,294
7,294 7,289 6,813 798

TRY IT OUT

Compare. Write < or > for each ||||.

1. 578 |||| 579 **2.** 3,407 |||| 3,470 **3.** 72,885 |||| 72,588

4. Order these numbers. 5,817 587 5,871 5,819

PRACTICE

Compare. Write < or > for each ||||.

1. 197 |||| 179 **2.** 678 |||| 868 **3.** 98 |||| 111

4. 2,734 |||| 2,785 **5.** 769 |||| 2,032 **6.** 5,524 |||| 5,454

Order these numbers from least to greatest.

7. 1,501 369 1,522 1,487 **8.** 34,967 4,967 5,867 34,867

Use the numbers in the box.

9. List the numbers greater than 8,371.

10. List the numbers less than 5,419.

11. List the numbers between 4,500 and 9,050.

3,218	5,500
7,081	5,411
10,000	2,480
3,692	9,035

APPLY

MATH REASONING Think about the number 5,000. Then write the numbers.

12. Write 3 numbers that are a little more than 5,000.

13. Write 3 numbers that are much more than 5,000.

PROBLEM SOLVING

14. St. Louis is 779 miles from Houston. Atlanta is 789 miles from Houston. Which city is nearest to Houston?

15. Use these digits. What is the greatest 4-digit number you can write? What is the least 4-digit number you can write?

2	4
6	8

ESTIMATION

16. Without counting, list the pictures in order from most dots to fewest dots.

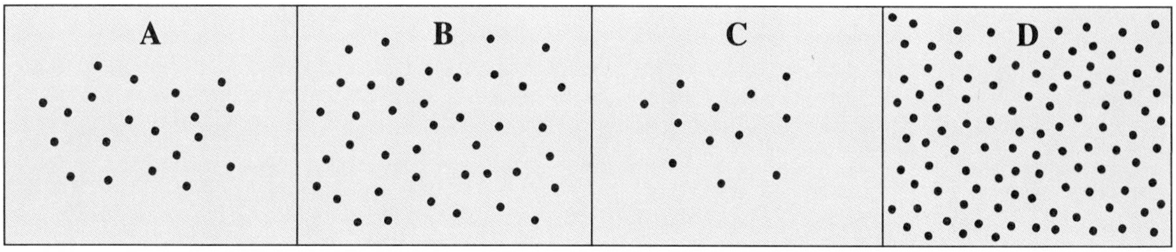

More Practice, page 500, set D

Exploring Algebra

LEARN ABOUT IT

The first two scales below are balanced. All the shapes are the same in all the pictures.

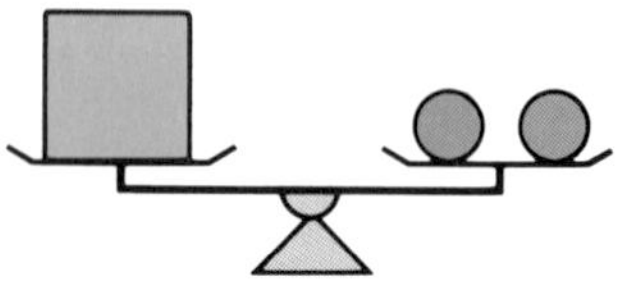

1 box balances 2 balls.

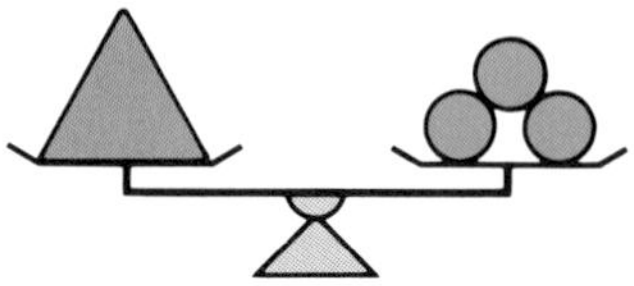

1 triangle balances 3 balls.

TALK ABOUT IT

1. Would a box balance a triangle? Explain.

2. How many balls would balance 2 boxes?

TRY IT OUT

Some of these scales will balance and some will not. Decide which ones are really balanced.

1.

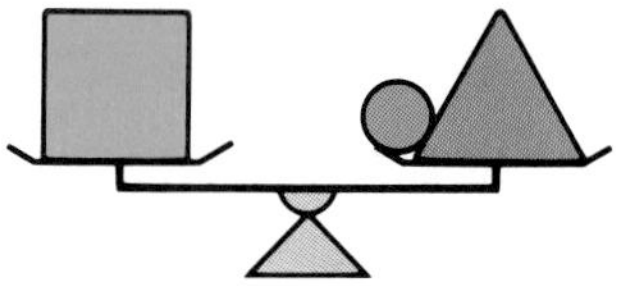

2.

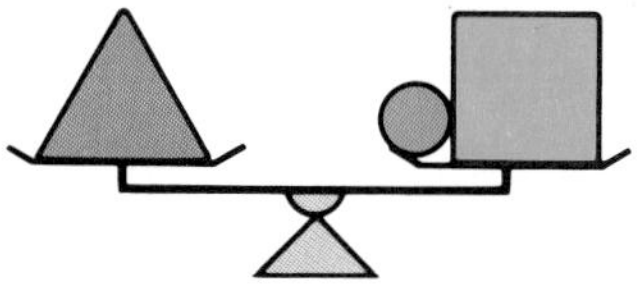

3.

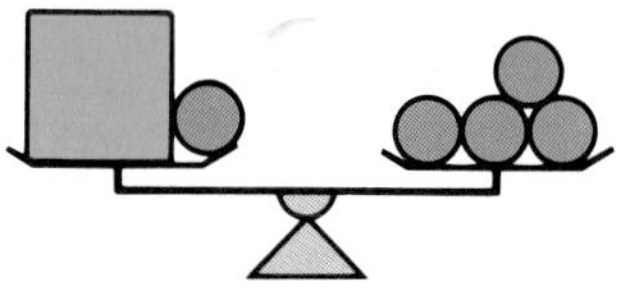

4.

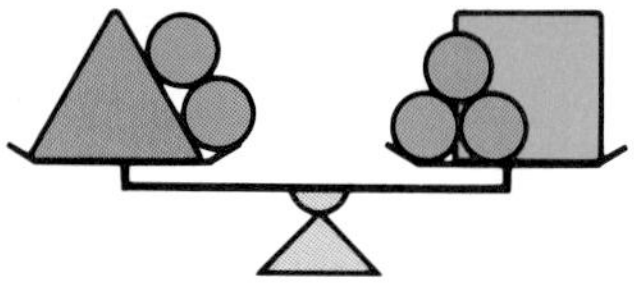

Find 3 ways to write one number in the ◯ and one number in the ☐ to make the left side equal the right side.

5. 5 + ◯ = 2 + ☐

6. ◯ − 3 = 6 − ☐

POWER PRACTICE/QUIZ

Write the number in standard form.

1. a 3-digit number with 4 in the tens place and 1 in the hundreds place
2. a 6-digit number with 2 in the ten-thousands place and 0 in the ones place
3. seven hundred twenty-one
4. five thousand, ninety
5. four hundred thousand, seventy-eight
6. six hundred thousand, forty-one

Write the numbers from the box in which the digit 4 has the given value.

425,708	5,452
139,645	243,100
34,231	38,467
42,689	372,040

7. 40,000
8. 40
9. 400
10. 400,000

11. Which of these numbers are less than 5,000?
    5,476   4,567   672   5,027

12. Which of these numbers are between 3,050 and 4,500?
    4,507   4,075   5,423   3,250

13. Order these numbers from least to greatest.
    26,341   26,355   2,989   13,289

Write $<$ or $>$ for each ▒.

14. 2,150 ▒ 2,015
15. 48,720 ▒ 4,872
16. 62,758 ▒ 62,785

PROBLEM SOLVING

Use the digits in the box. A digit may be used only once in a problem.

1	5	8	2

17. What is the greatest 3-digit number you can write?
18. What is the least 4-digit number you can write?
19. What 3-digit number can you write that is less than 251?
20. How many 4-digit numbers can you write that are greater than 5,812?

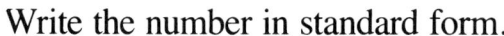

Problem Solving
Draw a Picture

- UNDERSTAND
- FIND DATA
- PLAN
- ESTIMATE
- SOLVE
- CHECK

LEARN ABOUT IT

To solve some problems, you may find it helpful to **Draw a Picture**.

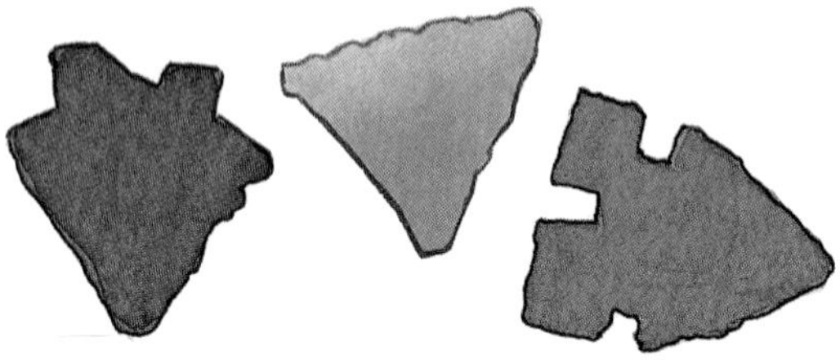

Four trees grow along a path. The birch tree is west of the pine. The oak is between the birch and the pine. The birch is east of the fig. The Indian arrowhead is buried under the tree that is farthest to the west. Where is the arrowhead buried?

First, I'll draw the trail.

The birch is west of the pine.

The oak is between the birch and the pine.

The birch is east of the fig.

The arrowhead is buried under the fig tree!

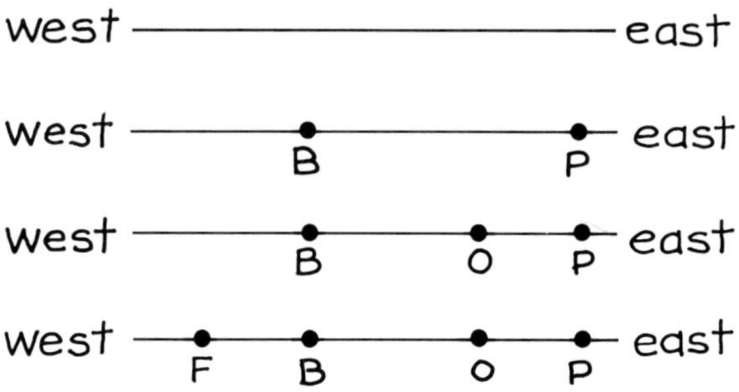

TRY IT OUT

Haida Indian totem poles made of cedar wood show pride in family ancestors.

Read this problem and finish the solution.

On the Indian totem pole, the bear is above the thunderbird. The beaver is under the thunderbird. The bear is under the eagle. Which animal is on top?

- Since the bear is above the thunderbird, could the thunderbird be on top?
- Which animal is just under the eagle?
- Copy the picture and finish drawing it to solve the problem.

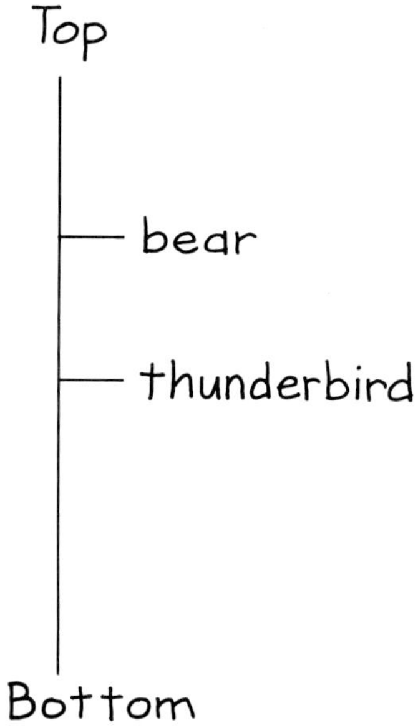

PRACTICE

Draw a picture to help you solve each problem.

1. At the Indian Festival, there were 4 booths in a row. Sand painting was east of jewelry. Drinks were west of jewelry. Belts were between jewelry and sand painting. Which booth was farthest east?

2. Dan was between Joe and Tae in the line for the Kachina doll booth. Dan was ahead of Tae. Tae was ahead of Luis. Who was third in line?

MIXED PRACTICE

Solve. Choose a strategy from the list or use other strategies that you know.

Some Strategies
Act It Out
Use Objects
Choose an Operation
Draw a Picture

3. On one totem pole, the beaver's head is 17 inches high. Its mouth is 8 inches high. How high is the rest of the head?

4. Michelle has 6 arrowheads in her collection. Her father has 15. How many more arrowheads does the father have than the daughter?

5. How many major Indian tribes are in Oklahoma and Alaska?

6. How many major Indian tribes in all are there in California, New Mexico, and Arizona?

7. On a leather bookmark, there are 4 symbols. The sun is above the rain. The mountain is above the sun. The rain is above the bird. Which picture is on the bottom?

8. Kara was sitting in the middle on a bench full of people watching the Indian dancing. She had 6 people to her left. How many people were on the bench?

State	Number of Major Indian Tribes
Alaska	6
Arizona	6
California	5
Florida	2
Montana	5
New Mexico	3
New York	4
Oklahoma	9
Oregon	6

More Practice, page 513, set B

Rounding

LEARN ABOUT IT

EXPLORE **Use a Number Line**

Draw this number line. Write in some numbers that are closer to 300 than to 200 or 400.

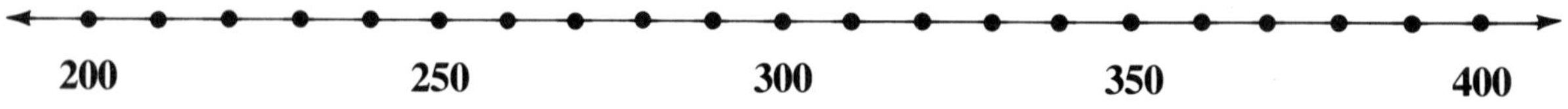

TALK ABOUT IT

1. Are any of your numbers less than 250? greater than 350? Explain.
2. Give some numbers that are about 290. They should be closer to 290 than to 280 or 300.

Use this method to round numbers to any place.

Find the place to which you are rounding.	→	Look at the digit to the right of that place. Compare it to 5.	→	**Round up** if it is 5 or greater. **Round down** if it is less than 5.

Round to the **nearest ten**.	43 365	43 365	43 round to 40. 365 rounds to 370.
Round to the **nearest hundred.**	343 4,789	343 4,789	343 rounds to 300. 4,789 rounds to 4,800.
Round to the **nearest dollar**.	\$3.26 \$8.61	\$3.26 \$8.61	\$3.26 rounds to \$3.00. \$8.61 rounds to \$9.00.

TRY IT OUT

Round the numbers to the nearest ten. Then round them to the nearest hundred.

1. 589 **2.** 831 **3.** 219 **4.** 450 **5.** 98 **6.** 6,720

Round to the nearest dollar. **7.** \$4.39 **8.** \$1.74 **9.** \$11.50

PRACTICE

First round the numbers to the nearest ten. Then round them to the nearest hundred.

1. 168	**2.** 345	**3.** 256	**4.** 793	**5.** 487
6. 862	**7.** 104	**8.** 151	**9.** 496	**10.** 634

Round to the nearest hundred.

11. 3,576	**12.** 4,083	**13.** 7,449	**14.** 8,888	**15.** 13,175
16. 2,083	**17.** 8,450	**18.** 1,080	**19.** 5,111	**20.** 47,289

Round to the nearest dollar.

21. \$5.50	**22.** \$43.04	**23.** \$8.46	**24.** \$93.75	**25.** \$49.49
26. \$180.50	**27.** \$346.17	**28.** \$498.15	**29.** \$150.63	**30.** \$799.85

APPLY

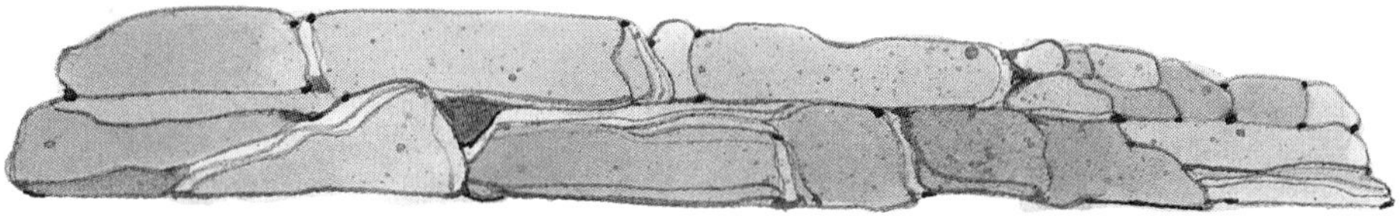

MATH REASONING

31. Give the smallest number that rounds to 170 when rounded to the nearest ten.

32. Give the largest amount of money that rounds to \$8.00 when rounded to the nearest dollar.

PROBLEM SOLVING

33. An explorer found 8 rooms in a cliff dwelling on a ledge and 9 more rooms in a cave. What is the total number of rooms rounded to the nearest ten?

34. **Data Hunt** Look in a newspaper. Find 3 numbers that have been rounded. Find 3 numbers that have not. If it makes sense, round these.

USING CRITICAL THINKING Draw Conclusions

35. I am a 3-digit number. Use these clues to find me.

- I am greater than 500.
- I am less than 557.
- My ones digit is a 2.
- I am 600 when rounded to the nearest hundred.

More Practice, page 500, set E

More About Rounding

LEARN ABOUT IT

EXPLORE **Think About the Situation**

Daryl gave a report on Richard Wetherill, a famous explorer of Southwest Indian ruins. In 1895 in Pueblo Bonito, Wetherill discovered a burial room with a basket containing 2,150 turquoise beads and 3,317 shell beads. Daryl decided to round these numbers to 2,000 turquoise beads and 3,000 shell beads.

TALK ABOUT IT

1. Why did it make sense for Daryl to round the numbers of beads?
2. Why did he round the number of shell beads to 3,000 instead of 4,000?
3. Would he have used the same number if there had been 3,525 shell beads? Why?

Remember! Find the digit to the right of the place to which you are rounding. **Round up** if the digit is 5 or more. **Round down** if the digit is less than 5.

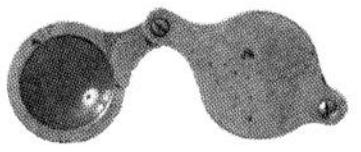

Round to the **nearest thousand**.

8,296 → 8,000   8,500 → 9,000   15,494 → 15,000

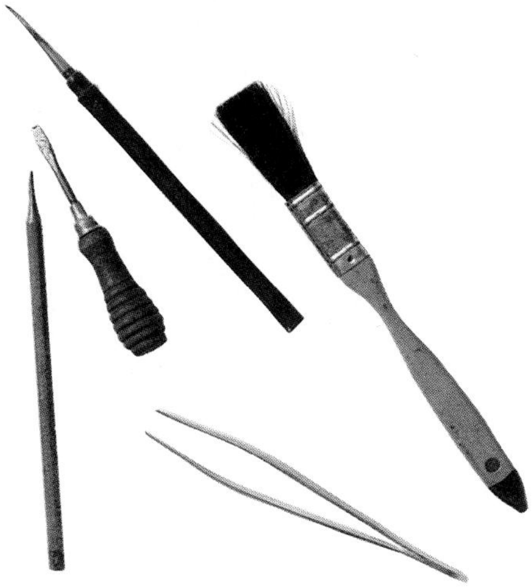

Be careful when you round up with the digit 9 in the place to which you are rounding.

Round to the nearest hundred. 975 → 1,000

Round to the nearest thousand. 9,858 → 10,000

TRY IT OUT

Round to the nearest thousand.

1. 3,586 **2.** 6,413 **3.** 9,620 **4.** 8,500 **5.** 19,613 **6.** 224,318

PRACTICE

Round to the nearest thousand.

1. 4,163	**2.** 3,200	**3.** 7,685	**4.** 6,500
5. 3,850	**6.** 4,075	**7.** 6,304	**8.** 8,987
9. 5,372	**10.** 9,634	**11.** 39,499	**12.** 39,500
13. 216,530	**14.** 499,821	**15.** 52,819	**16.** 39,499

APPLY

MATH REASONING

5	3
4	2

17. Use all the digits on these cards to make two numbers that each round to 2,500 as the nearest hundred, and round to 3,000 as the nearest thousand.

PROBLEM SOLVING

18. A room full of pottery the explorer Wetherill found in Chaco Canyon had 114 jars, 22 bowls, and 21 jar covers. If you wanted to report about how many of each he had found, what would your numbers be?

19. **Social Studies Data Bank** What are the numbers of rooms in each of the Mesa Verde dwellings rounded to the nearest ten? to the nearest hundred? See page 472.

DATA BANK

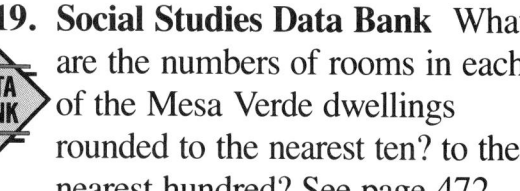

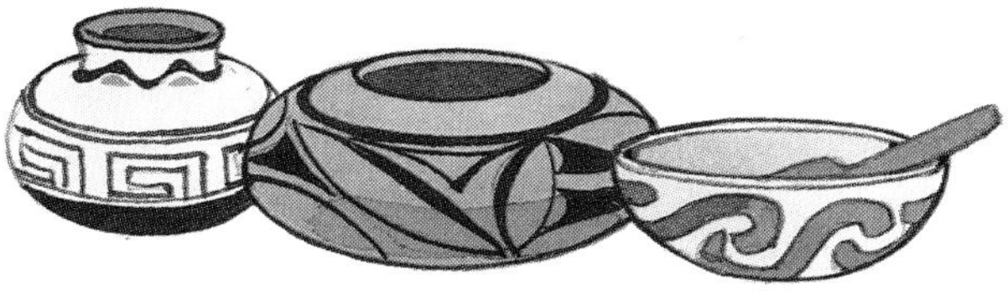

MIXED REVIEW

Add.

20. $9 + 4$ **21.** $4 + 9$ **22.** $8 + 6$ **23.** $6 + 8$ **24.** $7 + 0$ **25.** $2 + 0$

Subtract. Think about finding the missing addend.

26. $12 - 4$ **27.** $11 - 5$ **28.** $9 - 2$ **29.** $14 - 7$ **30.** $10 - 4$ **31.** $17 - 9$

More Practice, page 500, set F

Understanding Millions

LEARN ABOUT IT

EXPLORE **Think About the Situation**

Think how far a long line of students could reach.

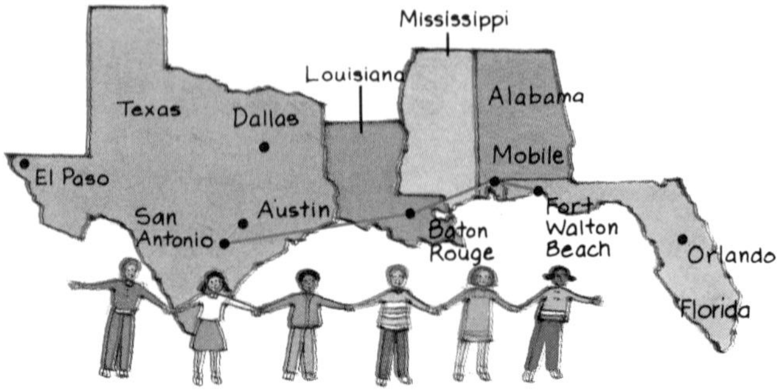

1,000 students → about 8 blocks
10,000 students → about 8 miles
100,000 students → from San Antonio to Austin (blue line)
1,000,000 students → from San Antonio to Fort Walton Beach (red line)

TALK ABOUT IT

1. How many thousands do you think are in one million? Explain your thinking.
2. Would a line of 10,000,000 students be 10 or 100 times as long as a line of 1,000,000 students? How do you know?

This table shows the place values for larger numbers.

Millions Period			Thousands Period			Ones Period		
Hundred Millions	Ten Millions	Millions	Hundred Thousands	Ten Thousands	Thousands	Hundreds	Tens	Ones
6	3	2 ,	5	8	7 ,	1	4	5

You write, **632,587,145**.

You read, "**six hundred thirty-two million, five hundred eighty-seven thousand, one hundred forty-five**."

TRY IT OUT

1. Write and read a 7-digit number with 5 in the millions place and 4 in the hundred thousands place.

   __, __ __ __, __ __ __

2. Write and read a 9-digit number with 3 in the hundred millions place and 0 in the millions place.

   __ __ __, __ __ __, __ __ __

PRACTICE

Write the number.

1. a 5-digit number with 2 in the ten thousands place and 4 in the tens place
2. fifty-three million, four hundred eighty-two thousand, one hundred six

Write the digit for the given place in 817,623,954.

3. millions
4. ten thousands
5. hundreds
6. hundred millions
7. ones
8. hundred thousands

Write two numbers from the box in which the digit 9 has the given value.

98,345,012	89,540,813
387,592,041	576,908,442
639,817,430	235,975,762
493,003,561	194,318

9. 900,000
10. 9,000,000
11. 90,000,000
12. 90,000

APPLY

MATH REASONING Give a number that is 1,000,000 more and another that is 1,000,000 less.

13. 23,418,000
14. 516,050,000
15. 9,300,000
16. 49,750,000

PROBLEM SOLVING

17. A calculator display shows 97,216,543. How can you add or subtract once to change the 7 to 8? Explain your method.
18. Use only the digits 1, 2, 3, 4, 5, 6, and 7. What are five 7-digit numbers between 4,000,000 and 5,000,000?

USING CRITICAL THINKING Discover a Pattern

Think about the pattern for the list of numbers. If you continued this pattern, which of these numbers would you use?

918,453,015
917,453,015
916,453,015
915,453,015

19. 902,453,015
20. 899,453,015
21. 899,000,000
22. 1,453,015

More Practice, page 513, set C

Counting Change

LEARN ABOUT IT

EXPLORE **Use Play Money**

Jeff and Tina each bought a T-shirt for $6.49. Jeff used exact change to pay. Tina used a ten-dollar bill. The clerk gave her some change.

Use play money to show how Jeff paid for the shirt. Then show how the clerk gave Tina her change.

TALK ABOUT IT

1. What coins and bills could Jeff use? How many ways did you find to show the amount?
2. What coins and bills might Tina have received in change? Explain how you decided.

Later Jeff used a ten-dollar bill to buy a game that cost $8.54. The clerk counted the change.

Start with the cost.	Count up, using coins of least value first.				End with the amount given.
$8.54	$8.55	$8.65	$8.75	$9.00	$10.00

Jeff received 1 penny, 2 dimes, 1 quarter, and a one-dollar bill in change.

TRY IT OUT

Count the change out loud. Write the numbers the clerk would say.

1. You give the clerk $1.00.

78¢

? ? ? ?

2. You give the clerk $5.00.

$3.69

? ? ? ?

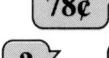

PRACTICE

Count the change out loud. Write the numbers the clerk would say.

1. You give the clerk $1.00.

63¢

? ? ? ?

2. You give the clerk $10.00.

$8.84

? ? ? ?

List the bills and coins you could use to pay the exact amount. List the bills and coins you could receive for a twenty-dollar bill.

3.

4.

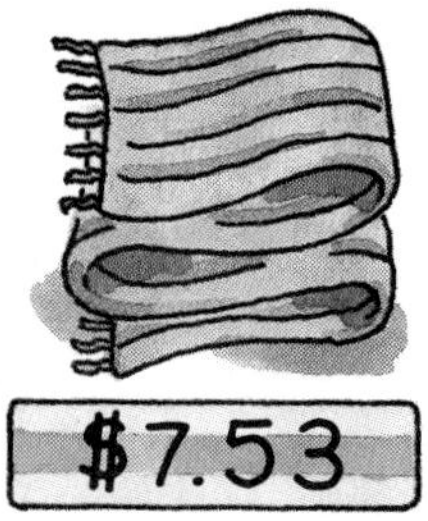

APPLY

MATH REASONING

5. Suppose you buy a belt for $6.89 and give the clerk a ten-dollar bill. Without counting, tell how much change you will get.

a. $1.11
b. $2.11
c. $3.11

PROBLEM SOLVING

6. A clerk counts your change as "$3.44, $3.45, $3.50, $3.75, $4, $5." How much did the item cost? What did you give the clerk? What bills and coins do you get back?

7. More Than One Answer How many ways can you show $1.00 using only quarters and dimes?

MENTAL MATH Counting On

Sometimes you can use mental math and count on by hundreds to add two numbers. To add 465 + 300, think: 465: 565, 665, 765.

Use mental math. Count on by hundreds to find these sums.

8. 294 + 200 **9.** 481 + 300 **10.** 318 + 100 **11.** 850 + 300

More Practice, page 513, set D

Estimating with Money
Using a Reference Point

4 quarters	=	$1.00
10 dimes	=	$1.00
5 dimes	=	50 cents
5 nickels	=	25 cents

You can use the table to help estimate.

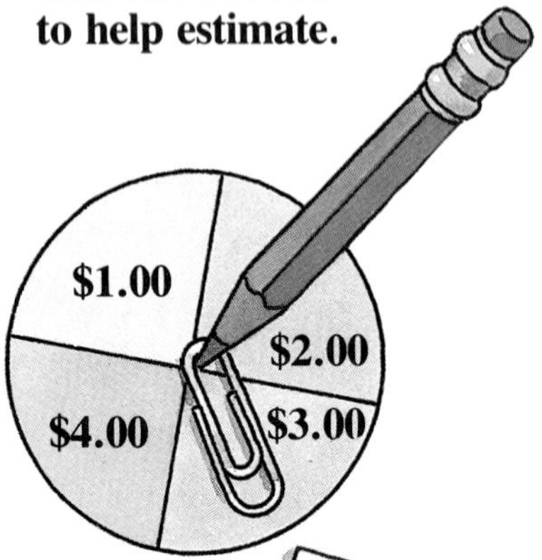

LEARN ABOUT IT

EXPLORE Use Play Money

Lay out a pile of play money coins. Spin a paper clip spinner marked in dollar amounts. Decide, without counting, if there is more or less than the spinner amount in the pile. Count to check. Try this several times.

TALK ABOUT IT

1. How did you decide if your pile of coins was more or less than $1.00 without counting the total?
2. Why would you want to know if you have more or less than a given amount of money?

You can estimate to decide if an amount is more or less than a given amount. The given amount is called a **reference point**.

Look at the coins. Since 4 quarters make $1.00 and 5 dimes make 50¢, it is easy to see at a glance that there is more than enough money to buy the sports cards.

$1.50

TRY IT OUT

Decide without counting if there is enough money to buy the item.

1.

PRACTICE

Decide without counting if there is enough money to buy the items.

1.

2.

APPLY

MATH REASONING Use play money to decide. Could the pile of coins be more than $4.00? Explain your thinking.

3. The pile has fewer than 9 quarters, fewer than 11 dimes, and fewer than 11 nickels.

4. The pile has fewer than 5 quarters, fewer than 31 dimes, and fewer than 6 nickels.

PROBLEM SOLVING

5. Ria had 6 quarters, 10 dimes, and fewer than 5 nickels in her pocket. Did she have enough to buy a $3.00 photo book of Indian cliff dwellings? Explain.

6. Lea had twice as many nickels as dimes. She had 30 coins, all dimes and nickels. Can she buy a map that costs $2.00?

MIXED REVIEW

Use mental math to add.

7. (3 + 5) + 7 **8.** (5 + 3) + 7 **9.** 2 + (6 + 4) **10.** (2 + 6) + 4

Use mental math. Break apart an addend if needed.

11. 7 + 5 **12.** 8 + 7 **13.** 12 + 6 **14.** 13 + 5

Add. Use compensation if needed.

15. 8 + 5 **16.** 9 + 6 **17.** 6 + 4 **18.** 7 + 9

More Practice, page 513, set E

Data Collection and Analysis
Group Decision Making

UNDERSTAND
FIND DATA
PLAN
ESTIMATE
SOLVE
CHECK

Doing a Survey
Group Skill:
Encourage and Respect Others

Your school newspaper has a section called "All Around the World." This month the paper will feature foods of many peoples. Your group is in charge of that section and you are going to conduct a survey to find what ethnic foods students prefer and why.

Collecting Data

1. Work with your group to make a list of 5 foods from around the world that you think students like to eat.
2. What are some reasons people like certain foods? Make a list of about 5 reasons.
3. Ask at least 25 students in your school which of the five foods on your list is their favorite. Then ask them to choose the one reason on your list which most describes why they like that particular food. Record the answers of each person you ask.

Organizing Data

4. Count how many people liked each food. Then mark the most popular food number 1, the next most popular number 2, and so on.
5. Make a table. On the left hand side of the table, write the names of the 5 foods, in order, from the most popular food to the least popular.

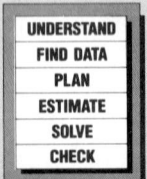

6. Beside the names of the foods, label columns with the reasons for choosing foods. Make tally marks in the table to show the reasons why people chose each food.

Presenting Your Analysis

7. What can you conclude from your table? What seems to be the most important reason for choosing a food? Did most people agree on their favorite ethnic food or were there many different responses?

Write a short paragraph for the school newspaper to summarize your results.

Use the data to write 5 true statements.

WRAP UP

Estimation Language Match

Match each phrase on the left with the correct amount of money or time on the right. Justify your choices.

1. just less than an hour	a. $18.70
2. a little less than fifty minutes	b. $20.56
3. a little over twenty dollars	c. $79.05
4. a little under eighty dollars	d. 59 minutes
5. almost twenty dollars	e. 48 minutes

Sometimes, Always, Never

Which word should go in the blank, sometimes, always, or never? Explain your choices.

6. 387 __?__ rounds to 400.

7. The millions period __?__ has more places than the ones period.

8. 6 hundred thousands is __?__ greater than 6 ten thousands.

Project

How far do you walk every day?

- Use string to show how far 10 steps is. How could you show 100 steps with string? How could you show 1,000 steps?
- Now estimate how many steps you take on the way to the school restroom. If you walked 100 steps from where you are now, where do you think you would be? What if you walked 1,000 steps?
- A million steps is about 400 miles. Look at a map. How far would you go if you walked 1,000,000 steps?

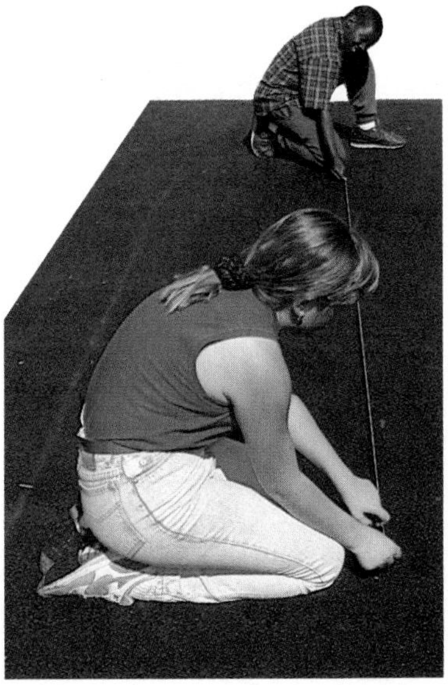

Power Practice/Test

Part 1 Understanding

1. Order these numbers from least to greatest.

4,628 43,628 43,816 4,682

Write the digit for the given place in 691,073,582.

2. millions **3.** ten millions **4.** hundred thousands

Part 2 Skills

Write each number in standard form.

5. seven thousand, nine hundred fourteen

6. seventy-eight thousand, one hundred sixteen

7. forty-two million, eight hundred thousand

Write $<$ or $>$ for each ||||.

8. 9,584 |||| 9,484 **9.** 31,772 |||| 31,780 **10.** 567,890 |||| 586,998

Write true or false.

11. To the nearest hundred, 182 rounds to 180.

12. To the nearest thousand, 74,495 rounds to 70,000.

13. To the nearest dollar, \$7.82 rounds to \$7

Part 3 Applications

14. Ed piled up 4 cubes. A red cube is above a blue cube. A green cube is on a pink cube. The blue cube is above the pink cube. Draw the pile.

15. Kay first gives you a penny as she says, "\$8.99." She continues to give you change and counts, "\$9, \$10." What did your purchase cost? How much did you give Kay? What is your change?

ENRICHMENT
Roman Numerals

I = 1
V = 5
X = 10

The Romans wrote numbers with letter symbols instead of digits. We still use Roman numerals, mostly for clocks and dates.

To read and write Roman numerals, add and subtract symbols.

III = 3	IV = 4	XV = 15
1 + 1 + 1 Add to get 3.	5 − 1 Subtract to get 4.	10 + 5 Add to get 15.

Think how many tens and ones you need. Put them together.

I	II	III	IV	V	VI	VII	VIII	IX	
1	2	3	4	5	6	7	8	9	
X	XX	XXX	XL	L	LX	LXX	LXXX	XC	C
10	20	30	40	50	60	70	80	90	100

Here's how to write the Roman numeral for the standard number.

38 You need 30 and 8.
XXXVIII

54 You need 50 and 4.
LIV

99 You need 90 and 9.
XCIX

1. What patterns do you see that tell when to add and when to subtract?

2. Find two Roman numerals that use addition.

3. Find two Roman numerals that use subtraction.

Write the Roman numeral for the standard number.

4. 27 **5.** 34 **6.** 76 **7.** 149

Write the standard number for the Roman numeral.

8. XXXV **9.** XVI **10.** CCI

CUMULATIVE REVIEW

1. $\begin{array}{r} 8 \\ +\ 7 \\ \hline \end{array}$

   A 1 **B** 6
   C 15 **D** 16

2. $\begin{array}{r} 16 \\ -\ 9 \\ \hline \end{array}$

   A 7 **B** 8
   C 10 **D** 25

3. 7 + 4

   A 3 **B** 11
   C 12 **D** 10

4. 13 − 5

   A 18 **B** 7
   C 9 **D** 8

5. Which number sentence belongs with the fact family for 5 + 6 = 11?

   A 11 − 5 = 6 **B** 6 − 5 = 11
   C 8 + 3 = 11 **D** 16 − 5 = 11

6. Which number fact could help you solve 6 + 7?

   A 5 + 3 = 8 **B** 6 + 6 = 12
   C 11 − 8 = 3 **D** 7 + 3 = 10

7. What sum helps you find 8 + 4 if you use down-up 2?

   A 6 + 6 **B** 7 + 3
   C 4 + 8 **D** 10 + 2

8. Find the missing number.
   12 − ▯ = 5

   A 17 **B** 8
   C 7 **D** 6

9. Add. Use the grouping strategy.
   7 + 4 + 3

   A 11 **B** 743
   C 14 **D** 21

10. Use the zero property to find 7 − 0.

    A 0 **B** 7
    C 70 **D** 6

11. Tanya counted the money in her purse and rounded it to $10. What is the largest amount she could have?

    A $9.49 **B** $9.99
    C $10.49 **D** $10.43

12. Which number has a 4 in the thousands place, a 9 in the hundreds place, and no tens?

    A 490 **B** 4,950
    C 34,901 **D** 94,004

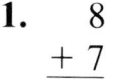

3

ADDITION AND SUBTRACTION OF WHOLE NUMBERS

THEME: ASTRONOMY

MATH AND SCIENCE

DATA BANK

Use the Science Data Bank on page 470 to answer the questions.

1 Name two planets that take less time than Earth to go around the sun. Name two planets that take more time.

2 In 1610, Galileo discovered 4 satellites of Jupiter with a simple telescope. How many more of Jupiter's satellites can now be seen?

3 List the names and diameters of the planets in order from smallest to largest.

4 **Use Critical Thinking** Which numbers in the chart about planets have probably been rounded? Which have not? Explain your thinking.

These families are looking at planets and the moon on a clear night. Have you ever looked through a telescope?

Mental Math
Special Sums and Differences

LEARN ABOUT IT

EXPLORE **Think About the Situation**
To help you make good estimates, you need to be able to use mental math to find sums like 600 + 300. You can think about hundred-dollar bills to help you find such sums.

6 hundred **3 hundred** **9 hundreds in all**

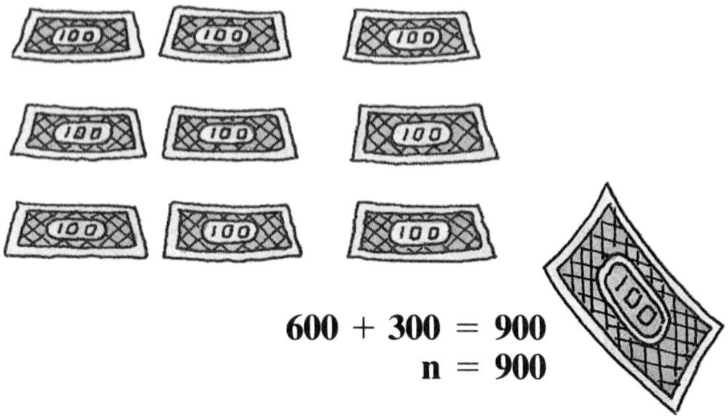

600 + 300 = 900
n = 900

TALK ABOUT IT

1. Explain how the sum of 6 and 3 helps you figure out the sum of 600 and 300 without using pencil and paper.
2. How would you use hundred-dollar bills to explain how to find 700–400?

You can use mental math to find special sums and differences by thinking about basic addition and subtraction facts.

To Find	Think	Say
90 + 70	9 + 7 tens	160
4,000 + 8,000	4 + 8 thousands	12,000
1,300 − 700	13 − 7 hundreds	600
16,000 − 9,000	16 − 9 thousands	7,000

To find the sum of 3 or more numbers, it sometimes helps to look for pairs of **compatible numbers** like 60 and 40 that can be easily found using mental math.

158
60 + 58 + 40

TRY IT OUT

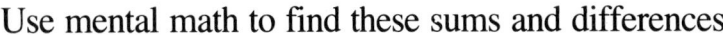

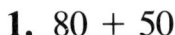

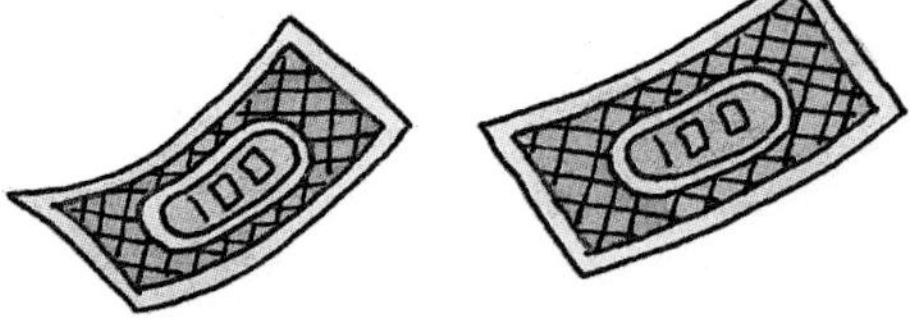

Use mental math to find these sums and differences.

1. 80 + 50 **2.** 160 − 90 **3.** 400 + 800 **4.** 900 − 500

5. 1,600 − 700 **6.** 14,000 − 9,000 **7.** 50 + 96 + 50 **8.** 80 + 69 + 20

PRACTICE

Use mental math to find these sums and differences.

1. 80 + 50 **2.** 7,000 + 8,000 **3.** 900 − 400 **4.** 7,000 + 3,000 **5.** 15,000 − 9,000

6. 90 − 50 **7.** 1,600 − 700 **8.** 12,000 − 3,000 **9.** 3,000 + 5,000 **10.** 400 + 900

11. 50 + 40 **12.** 4,500 − 300 **13.** 800 − 200 **14.** 2,300 + 400 **15.** 600 − 200

16. 50 + 78 + 50 **17.** 80 + 256 + 20 **18.** 96 + 60 + 40

APPLY

MATH REASONING Use mental math to find these sums and differences. Explain how you found each answer.

19. 21 + 30 **20.** 31 + 41 **21.** 62 − 31 **22.** 51 − 20

23. Give the next number in this pattern. 100 200 400 700

PROBLEM SOLVING

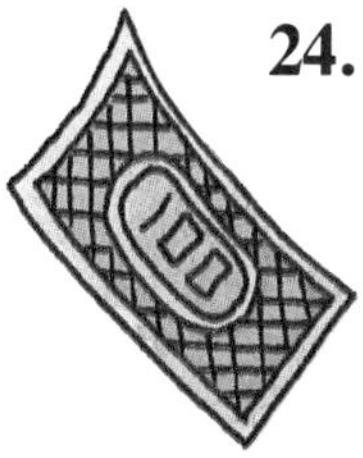

24. Juan doubled his starting score and then scored 100 more points to get a total of 900 points. What was his starting score?

25. Write Your Own Problem Use the following data to write a problem. Nan scored 800 points in the first game. She scored 500 points in the second game.

▶ **ALGEBRA**

26. A pair of numbers from this list has been written in the □ and △ to make a true number sentence. Show as many other ways as you can to do this.

10 20 30 40 50 60 70 80 90

Estimating Sums and Differences

LEARN ABOUT IT

EXPLORE **Read the Information**

Sometimes you only need to **estimate** an answer that is close to the exact answer. One way to estimate is to round the numbers before you add or subtract.

Pat played a computer game. The computer showed the points for each game. Pat wanted to score over 500 points in two games.

TALK ABOUT IT

1. To the nearest hundred, how many points did Pat score in the first game? in the second game?
2. Do you think the total number of points is more or less than 500? Explain.

You can estimate a sum or difference by rounding the numbers to the highest place of the smaller number and then adding or subtracting.

Nearest Ten

161	→	160
− 74	→	− 70
		Estimate: 90

Nearest Hundred

789	→	800
+ 518	→	+ 500
		Estimate: 1,300

Nearest Thousand

8,798	→	9,000
− 4,559	→	− 5,000
		Estimate: 4,000

You can also estimate dollar amounts by rounding to the nearest dollar.

$6.57	→	$7
+ $5.43	→	+ $5
		Estimate: $12

TRY IT OUT

Estimate. Round to the highest place of the smaller number.

1. 143 − 56

2. 697 + 436

3. 4,246 + 3,879

4. $9.56 − 4.98

5. 9,178 − 2,687

PRACTICE

Estimate the sum or difference.

1. $78 + 53$ **2.** $43 - 29$ **3.** $52 + 169$ **4.** $472 - 309$ **5.** $17 + 82$ **6.** $614 - 264$

7. $823 - 396$ **8.** $914 - 573$ **9.** $789 + 127$ **10.** $\$2.41 - 1.07$ **11.** $421 - 333$ **12.** $2{,}473 + 536$

13. $\$8.65 + 5.29$ **14.** $4{,}741 - 2{,}098$ **15.** $7{,}343 - 2{,}196$ **16.** $3{,}731 - 1{,}602$ **17.** $5{,}264 + 7{,}913$ **18.** $\$9.29 - 4.75$

APPLY

MATH REASONING Without finding the sums, decide which is greater.

19. 29 + 19 or 31 + 21 **20.** 59 + 34 or 56 + 26 **21.** 72 + 46 or 82 + 44

PROBLEM SOLVING

22. **Data Hunt** Find your weight in pounds. Choose a partner. Estimate the sum of your weights and the difference of your weights.

23. Tim weighed 127 pounds and Tami weighed 89 pounds. About what was the difference of their weights?

24. Jeff weighs more than Ann. Tina weighs less than Ann. Meg weighs more than Jeff. Who weighs most?

CALCULATOR

Draw squares like this and write the digits 4, 5, 6, 7, 8, and 9 in them to make these sums. Use each digit only once. Use your calculator to check.

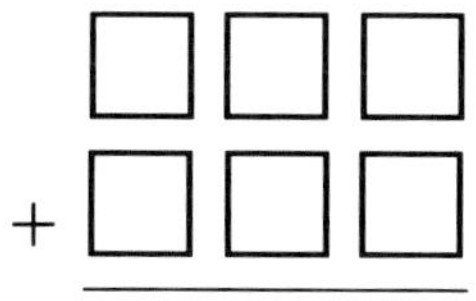

25. the largest sum possible

26. the smallest sum possible

27. the sum as close to 1,500 as possible

28. the sum as close to 2,000 as possible

More Practice, page 501, set B

Adding Whole Numbers
Making the Connection

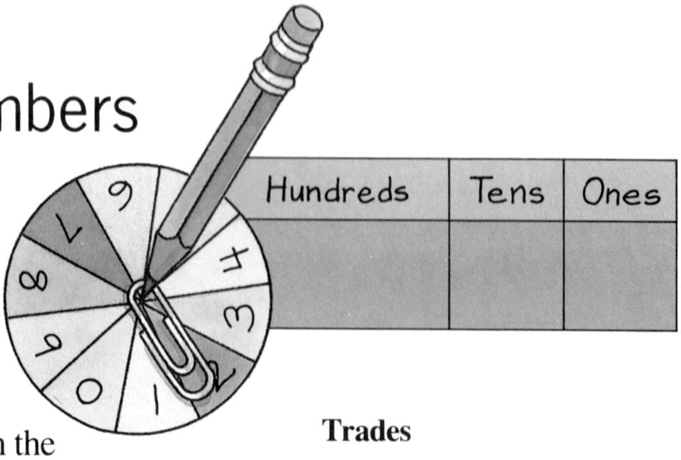

LEARN ABOUT IT

EXPLORE **Use a Place Value Model**

Work in groups. Use a spinner with the digits 0–9 and make piles of blocks.

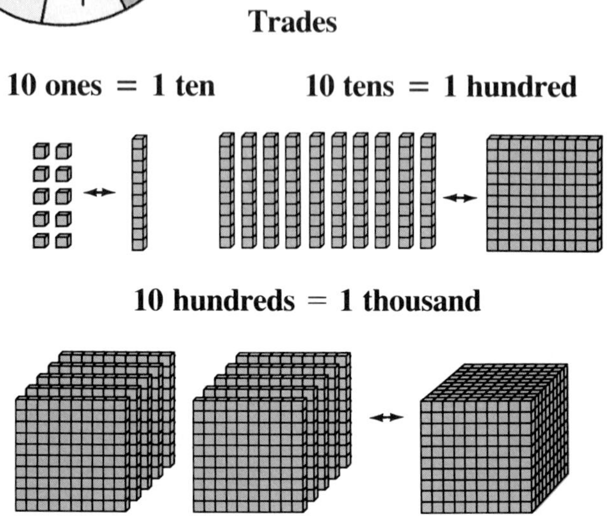

- Spin 3 times. The first spin gives the number of hundreds blocks for a pile. The second gives the number of tens and the third gives the number of ones. Make the pile and write the number for it in a table like the one given. Then repeat the steps.
- Push the two piles together and make all possible trades. When you get 10 or more of one type, trade for a larger block. Write the number for the resulting pile.
- Do this several times with different numbers.

TALK ABOUT IT

1. Use blocks and describe the trades that can be made.
2. Suppose you spin to make two piles of blocks and push them together. What are the smallest number of trades possible? the largest number? Explain using the blocks.
3. How does the number for the combined pile compare with the numbers for the original piles? Explain.

You have pushed blocks together, traded, and figured out how many in all. Now you will see a way to record what you have done. This process can help you find sums such as 382 + 256. Lay out blocks to start.

What You Do **What You Record**

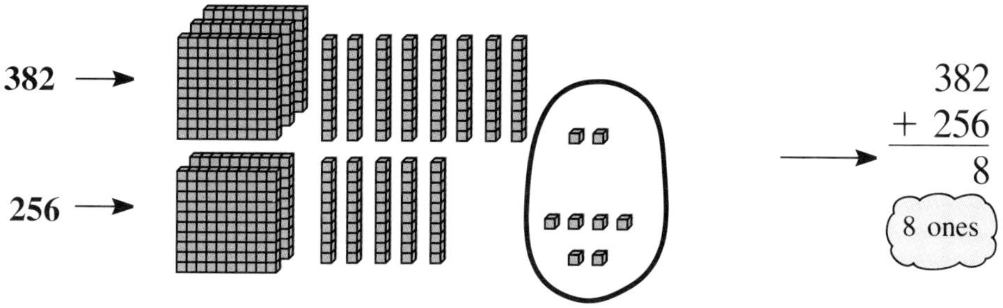

1. Are there enough ones to make a trade?

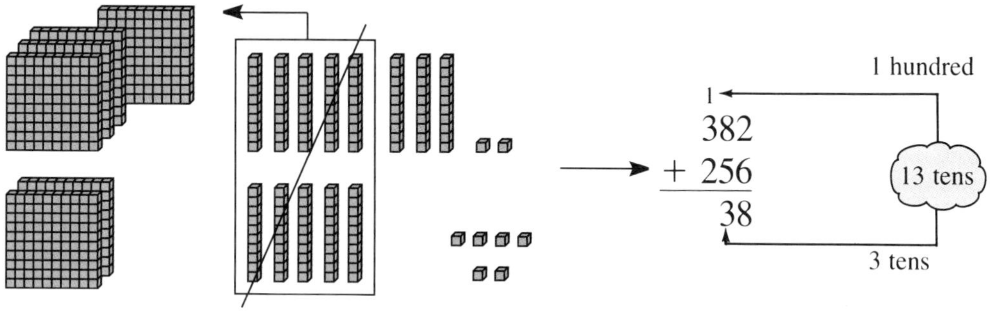

2. Are there enough tens to make a trade?

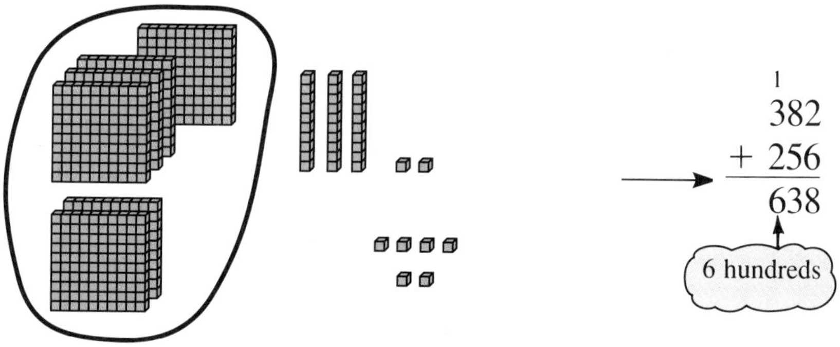

3. How many hundreds are there after the trade?

4. What is the sum of 382 and 256?

TRY IT OUT

Use blocks to find these sums. Record what you did.

1. 53 + 29 **2.** 173 + 48 **3.** 358 + 276 **4.** 367 + 475

5. Use blocks to find the sum of two 3-digit numbers of your choice.

Adding Whole Numbers

LEARN ABOUT IT

EXPLORE **Think About the Process**

Suppose you ride your bicycle for an hour and then stop at your friend's house to play tennis for an hour. How many calories do you use?

You add because you need to put together amounts to find the total.

Activity	Calories/hour
Bicycling	475
Rollerskating	370
Running	620
Swimming	425
Tennis	450

Add the ones. Trade if necessary.	Add the tens. Trade if necessary.	Add the hundreds.
$\begin{array}{r} 475 \\ +\ 450 \\ \hline 5 \end{array}$	$\begin{array}{r} {}^{1}\ \ \\ 475 \\ +\ 450 \\ \hline 25 \end{array}$	$\begin{array}{r} {}^{1}\ \ \\ 475 \\ +\ 450 \\ \hline 925 \end{array}$

TALK ABOUT IT

1. Why do you need to line up the digits?
2. How would you have estimated the sum?
3. Use a complete sentence to give a reasonable answer to the story problem.

Other Examples

14 hundreds equal 1 thousand and 4 hundreds → 1,469

A	B	C	D
$\begin{array}{r} 624 \\ +\ 845 \\ \hline 1{,}469 \end{array}$	$\begin{array}{r} {}^{1\,1}\ \ \\ 987 \\ +\ \ 38 \\ \hline 1{,}025 \end{array}$	$\begin{array}{r} {}^{1\ \ 1\,1}\ \ \\ 3{,}754 \\ +\ 5{,}489 \\ \hline 9{,}243 \end{array}$	$\begin{array}{r} {}^{1\ \ 1}\ \ \ \ \\ \$76.87 \\ 81.16 \\ \hline \$158.03 \end{array}$

TRY IT OUT

Add.

1. $\begin{array}{r} 39 \\ +\ 26 \\ \hline \end{array}$
2. $\begin{array}{r} 364 \\ +\ \ 72 \\ \hline \end{array}$
3. $\begin{array}{r} 576 \\ +\ 385 \\ \hline \end{array}$
4. $\begin{array}{r} 4{,}586 \\ +\ \ \ \ 635 \\ \hline \end{array}$
5. $\begin{array}{r} 7{,}674 \\ +\ 1{,}768 \\ \hline \end{array}$
6. $\begin{array}{r} \$25.89 \\ +\ 52.34 \\ \hline \end{array}$

PRACTICE

Find the sums.

1. 59 + 36	**2.** 493 + 21	**3.** 812 + 560	**4.** \$5.45 + 3.76	**5.** 9,052 + 876
6. 316 + 287	**7.** 1,486 + 3,039	**8.** 275 + 91	**9.** \$63.45 + 7.36	**10.** 6,525 + 7,680
11. 213 + 99	**12.** \$3.02 + 6.78	**13.** 9,163 + 708	**14.** 547 + 145	**15.** 2,568 + 3,846

16. 78 + 95 **17.** 467 + 295 **18.** \$83.00 + \$61.75 **19.** 9,154 + 258

20. 843 + 89 **21.** 3,556 + 82 **22.** 749 + 541 **23.** \$32.09 + \$4.78

24. 85 + 46 **25.** 425 + 81 **26.** 2,518 + 605 **27.** \$16.48 + \$5.02

APPLY

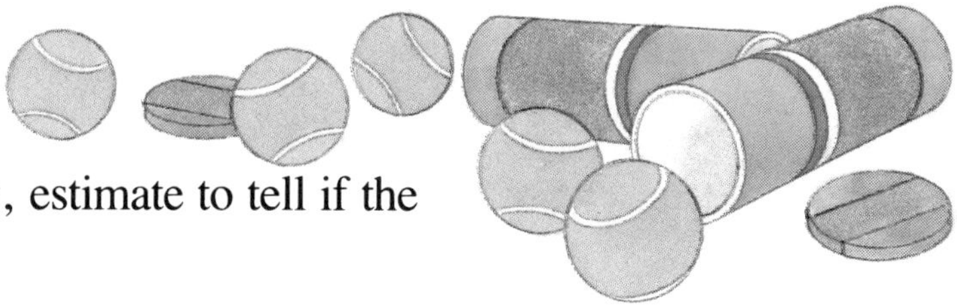

MATH REASONING Without adding, estimate to tell if the sum could be correct.

28. 57 + 39 = 67 **29.** 525 + 236 = 651 **30.** 354 + 128 = 482

PROBLEM SOLVING

31. A ham sandwich is 365 calories and a serving of hash brown potatoes is 197 calories. Would these foods together have more or less than 500 calories?

32. Use a calculator to find the next 3 numbers in this pattern. The same number is always added to get the next number. 28, 157, 286, __?__, __?__, __?__

COMMUNICATION Write to Learn

33. Write a paragraph that tells how you would use these place value blocks to show 346 + 182 = 528.

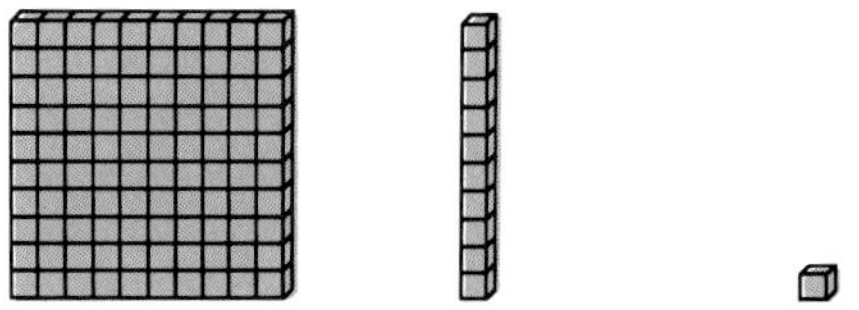

More Practice, page 501, set C

Column Addition

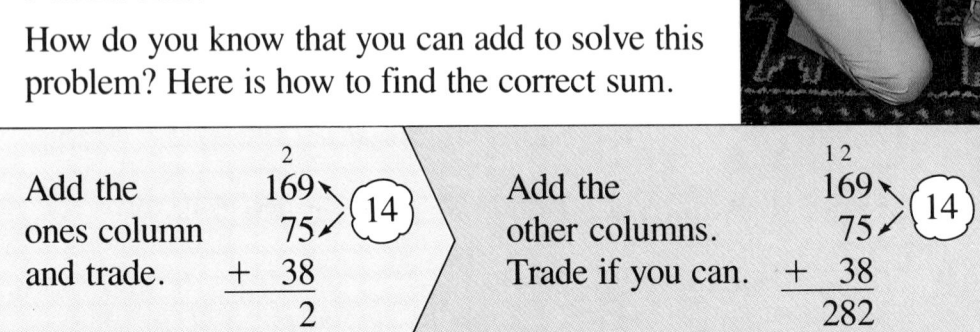

LEARN ABOUT IT

EXPLORE **Think About the Process**

Tyrone's father bought a telescope for $169, a tripod for $75, and a special color picture book about astronomy for $38. How much did these 3 items cost?

How do you know that you can add to solve this problem? Here is how to find the correct sum.

Add the ones column and trade.	Add the other columns. Trade if you can.
$\begin{array}{r} {}^{2} \\ 169 \\ 75 \\ +\ 38 \\ \hline 2 \end{array}$ (14)	$\begin{array}{r} {}^{1\,2} \\ 169 \\ 75 \\ +\ 38 \\ \hline 282 \end{array}$ (14)

TALK ABOUT IT

1. Why is it important to line up ones, tens, and hundreds when writing the numbers to be added?
2. Do you get the same sum if you begin at the bottom of a column and add up? Use this idea to check the addition.
3. How would you have estimated the sum?
4. Use a complete sentence to give a reasonable answer to the story problem.

TRY IT OUT

Add.

1.	2.	3.	4.	5.
42	27	346	725	$1.49
69	9	78	6,348	2.98
+ 38	+ 37	265	1,642	3.56
		+ 39	+ 76	+ 4.75

PRACTICE

1. $\begin{array}{r} 59 \\ 78 \\ +\ 36 \\ \hline \end{array}$ **2.** $\begin{array}{r} 35 \\ 47 \\ +\ 22 \\ \hline \end{array}$ **3.** $\begin{array}{r} 635 \\ 786 \\ +\ 429 \\ \hline \end{array}$ **4.** $\begin{array}{r} 349 \\ 8 \\ 67 \\ +\ 123 \\ \hline \end{array}$ **5.** $\begin{array}{r} 283 \\ 4{,}475 \\ 3{,}864 \\ +\quad 88 \\ \hline \end{array}$

6. $\begin{array}{r} 346 \\ 69 \\ +\ 287 \\ \hline \end{array}$ **7.** $\begin{array}{r} \$1.75 \\ 2.68 \\ 3.19 \\ +\ 0.79 \\ \hline \end{array}$ **8.** $\begin{array}{r} \$5.45 \\ 2.98 \\ +\ 3.76 \\ \hline \end{array}$ **9.** $\begin{array}{r} 36 \\ 948 \\ +\ 213 \\ \hline \end{array}$ **10.** $\begin{array}{r} 2{,}946 \\ 79 \\ 483 \\ +\quad 605 \\ \hline \end{array}$

11. 78 + 95 + 37 **12.** 4,627 + 5,748 + 1,236

APPLY

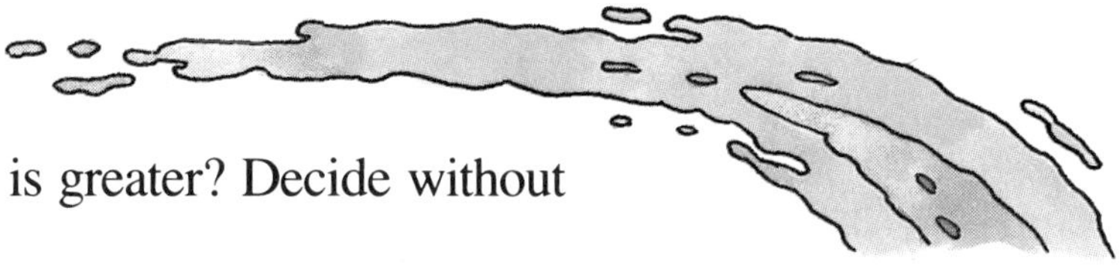

MATH REASONING Which sum is greater? Decide without finding the sum.

13. 89 + 75 + 42   79 + 65 + 32 **14.** 518 + 649 + 298   524 + 651 + 305

PROBLEM SOLVING

Astronomy Books	
Windows to the Universe	$6.45
A Look at the Stars	$11.98
All About Telescopes	$8.75
How Big Is Space?	$3.59

15. Tad bought 3 books about astronomy. He paid for them with a twenty-dollar bill and got some change back. Which 3 books did he buy?

16. Write a problem that you can solve using the data from this chart.

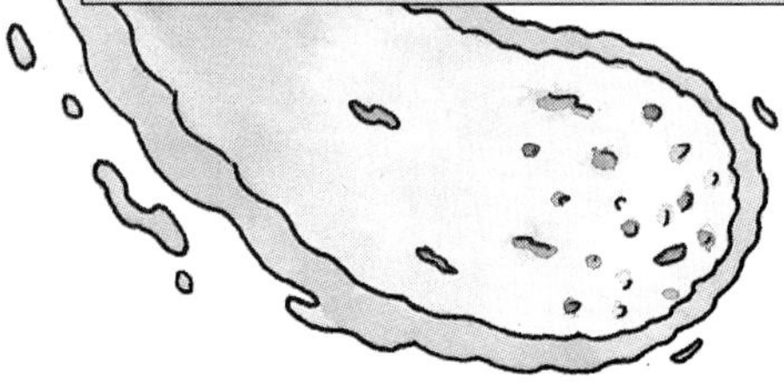

MIXED REVIEW

Give a subtraction fact for each addition fact.

17. 8 + 3 = 11 **18.** 7 + 8 = 15 **19.** 6 + 9 = 15 **20.** 9 + 9 = 18

Say and write this number.

21. 3 thousands, 6 hundreds, 4 tens, and 9 ones

Problem Solving
Make an Organized List

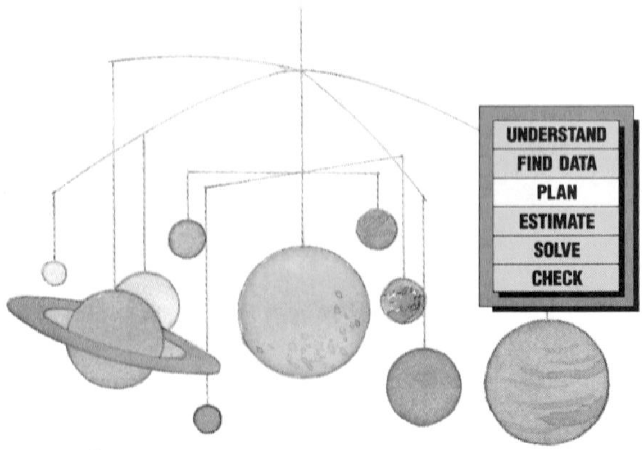

LEARN ABOUT IT

To solve some problems, you might need to make a list using the data in the problem. This strategy is called **Make an Organized List**.

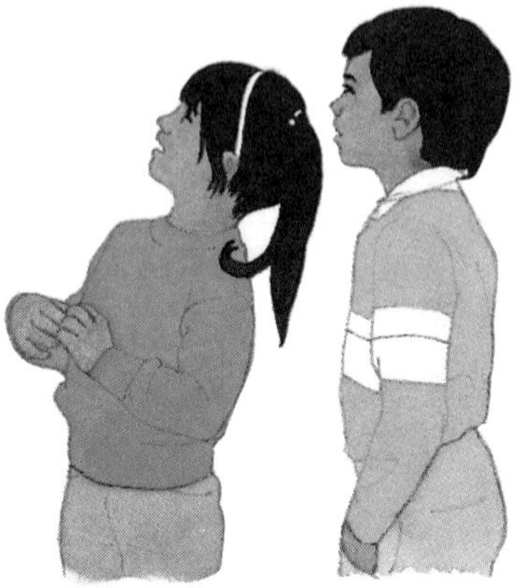

The morning events at the Adler Planetarium begin at 9:30, 10:30, and 11:30. At each time Joey and his sister can either see the star show or the demonstration on making navigation tools. How many different choices do they have?

If they choose the Star Show they can go at 3 different times.

If they choose the demonstration they can go at 3 different times.

Star Show	9:30 a.m.
Star Show	10:30 a.m.
Star Show	11:30 a.m.
Demonstration	9:30 a.m.
Demonstration	10:30 a.m.
Demonstration	11:30 a.m.

They have 6 different choices.

TRY IT OUT

Joey visited the planetarium with his sister Teresa, his mother, and his father. They went to the events in pairs, with one adult and one child going together. How many different ways could they pair up?

- How many different adults can Joey choose?
- Can Joey and Teresa go together?
- Copy and complete the list below to solve the problem.

Joey - mother
Joey - father

PRACTICE

Make an organized list to help you solve each problem.

1. The 3 kinds of sandwiches served at the planetarium lunch stand were chicken, ham, and cheese. The 2 choices of drinks were fruit juice and milk. How many different lunches could you choose?

2. Leroy could buy one book and one postcard in the planetarium shop. The books he liked were *The Life of a Star* and *Find That Constellation*. The postcards he liked were a photo of the earth and a drawing of Saturn. How many choices did he have?

MIXED PRACTICE

Solve. Choose a strategy from the list or use other strategies that you know.

3. Joe gave the clerk a \$5 bill. He bought juice and a sandwich for \$3.28. How much change did he get back?

4. Shirley wanted to write 50 facts in her star journal by New Year's Day. In October she had 21 facts. In November she had 15. How many facts did she need to write in her journal in December?

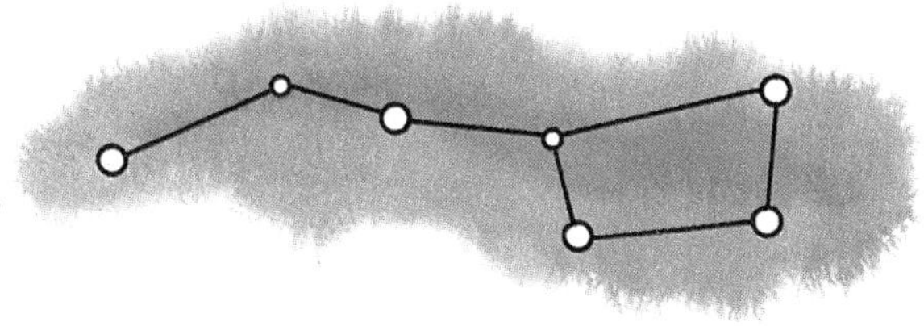

5. The Big Dipper is the easiest star group to find. There are 4 stars in its handle. The star Alioth is closer to the cup than Alkaid. Mizar is between Alioth and Alkaid. Alioth is farther from the cup than Megrez. Which star is at the end of the handle?

6. Yuri Gagarin was the first person to travel in space. His flight in April, 1961, lasted 108 minutes. Alan Shepard was the second. His flight in May, 1961, lasted 19 minutes. How many minutes did these 2 men fly in space?

Some Strategies

Act It Out
Use Objects
Choose an Operation
Draw a Picture
Make an Organized List

John Young Planetarium
(Orlando, Florida)

	Attendance in June	Attendance in January
laser show	3,000	3,526
star show	11,483	11,000

7. How many more people saw the laser show in January than in June?

8. What was the January attendance at the laser show and the star show?

More Practice, page 513, set F

Front-End Estimation

LEARN ABOUT IT

EXPLORE Examine the Data

To estimate the total cost of a shrimp dinner and a chicken dinner, Cindy added \$4 and \$5.

Think about her method. Try it with other pairs of dinners and decide if it is a good way to estimate the total.

TALK ABOUT IT

1. Is Cindy's estimate for the shrimp and chicken dinners more or less than the actual total? How do you know?
2. Does Cindy's method always give a low estimate? Explain.
3. Can you think of a way to improve Cindy's estimate?

Here is how you can use **front-end estimation** and adjust to find a closer estimate.

Estimate	**Adjust**
\$ 8.57	\$ 8.57
+ 7.39	+ 7.39 (about \$1)
15	

Estimate: \$16

Estimate	**Adjust**
867	867
352	352
+ 595	595 (about 200)
16	

Estimate: 1,800

PRACTICE

Use front-end estimation to estimate each sum.

1. \$9.45 + 5.69
2. 856 + 438
3. 232 + 985 + 361
4. 6,511 + 7,295
5. 3,128 + 8,693
6. Is \$7 enough for a \$5.49 dinner and a \$1.98 dessert?

More Practice, page 501, set E

POWER PRACTICE/QUIZ

Find the sums and differences using mental math.

1. $\begin{array}{r} 60 \\ +\ 30 \\ \hline \end{array}$ **2.** $\begin{array}{r} 400 \\ +\ 900 \\ \hline \end{array}$ **3.** $\begin{array}{r} 80 \\ -\ 50 \\ \hline \end{array}$ **4.** $\begin{array}{r} 600 \\ -\ 200 \\ \hline \end{array}$ **5.** $\begin{array}{r} 7{,}000 \\ +\ 4{,}000 \\ \hline \end{array}$ **6.** $\begin{array}{r} 500 \\ -\ 500 \\ \hline \end{array}$

Estimate the sum or difference.

7. $\begin{array}{r} 232 \\ +\ 741 \\ \hline \end{array}$ **8.** $\begin{array}{r} 837 \\ -\ 256 \\ \hline \end{array}$ **9.** $\begin{array}{r} 728 \\ -\ \ 64 \\ \hline \end{array}$ **10.** $\begin{array}{r} 583 \\ +\ \ 77 \\ \hline \end{array}$ **11.** $\begin{array}{r} \$7.23 \\ -\ 4.75 \\ \hline \end{array}$ **12.** $\begin{array}{r} 644 \\ +\ 365 \\ \hline \end{array}$

Find the sums.

13. $\begin{array}{r} 84 \\ +\ 19 \\ \hline \end{array}$ **14.** $\begin{array}{r} 367 \\ +\ 221 \\ \hline \end{array}$ **15.** $\begin{array}{r} 402 \\ +\ 689 \\ \hline \end{array}$ **16.** $\begin{array}{r} \$3.57 \\ +\ 4.99 \\ \hline \end{array}$ **17.** $\begin{array}{r} 843 \\ +\ \ 79 \\ \hline \end{array}$ **18.** $\begin{array}{r} 975 \\ +\ 268 \\ \hline \end{array}$

19. $\begin{array}{r} 27 \\ 45 \\ +\ 63 \\ \hline \end{array}$ **20.** $\begin{array}{r} 68 \\ 13 \\ +\ \ 9 \\ \hline \end{array}$ **21.** $\begin{array}{r} 452 \\ 68 \\ +\ 541 \\ \hline \end{array}$ **22.** $\begin{array}{r} \$8.95 \\ 4.21 \\ +\ 2.58 \\ \hline \end{array}$ **23.** $\begin{array}{r} 9{,}632 \\ 906 \\ +\ 1{,}843 \\ \hline \end{array}$ **24.** $\begin{array}{r} 846 \\ 3{,}257 \\ +\ 2{,}182 \\ \hline \end{array}$

25. 50 + 16 + 50 **26.** 80 + 45 + 20 **27.** 16 + 20 + 10

28. 89 + 458 + 35 **29.** 961 + 422 + 5 **30.** 1,356 + 15 + 408

PROBLEM SOLVING

31. Becky used place value blocks to show the addends 32 + 168. How many hundreds, tens, and ones pieces did she use? Which pieces did she need for the sum?

32. George has six place value blocks. He has two each of the hundreds, tens, and ones pieces. How many 3-digit numbers can he show if he does not use zero?

33. Dana's mom bought her 3 shirts, a white one, a blue one, and a red one. She also bought her a pair of blue jeans and a pair of white jeans. How many different outfits can Dana make?

34. Bob estimated that he would use 555 calories by rollerskating for one and a half hours and use 425 calories by swimming for one hour. Is this more or less than 1,000 calories?

Subtracting Whole Numbers
Making the Connection

LEARN ABOUT IT

EXPLORE Use a Place Value Model
Work in groups. Use a spinner with the digits 0–9 and make piles of blocks.

- Each partner spins 3 times. The first spin gives the number of hundreds blocks for your pile. The second gives the numbers of tens and the third gives the number of ones. Make your pile and write the number for it in the top row of a table like the one given.
- Each partner now spins 3 times to give the number of hundreds, tens, and ones to take away from your pile.
- Spin again as needed until the take away number is less than the number in your pile. Write the take away number in the table.
- Take from your pile the number of blocks shown. Trade if you need to. In the table write the number of blocks left.
- Do this several times.

	Hundreds	Tens	Ones
	6	2	5
Take Away	4	7	3
Number Left			

Take away.
Trade if needed.

TALK ABOUT IT

1. Describe a trade you might make when taking blocks from the pile
2. Is it better to start taking away th ones or should you start with the hundreds? Explain.

You have laid out blocks, taken some away, and found how many were left. Now you will see a way to record what you have done. This procedure can help you find differences such as 428 − 153. Lay out blocks to start.

What You Do	What You Record
428 → 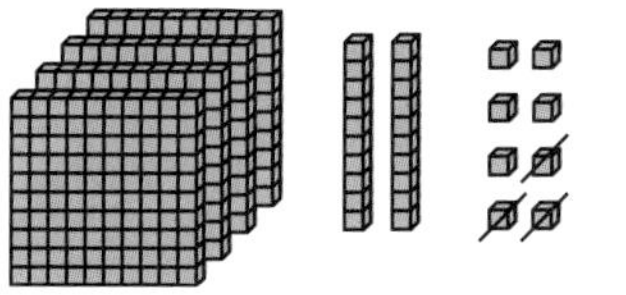	$\begin{array}{r} 428 \\ -\ 153 \\ \hline 5 \end{array}$
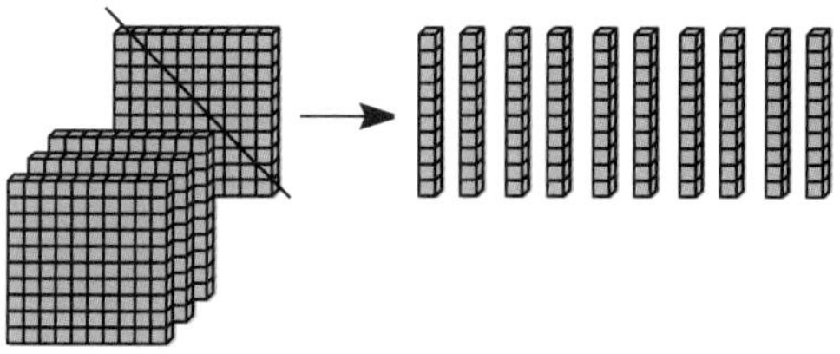	$\begin{array}{r} {\scriptstyle 3\ 12} \\ \not{4}\not{2}8 \\ -\ 153 \\ \hline 75 \end{array}$
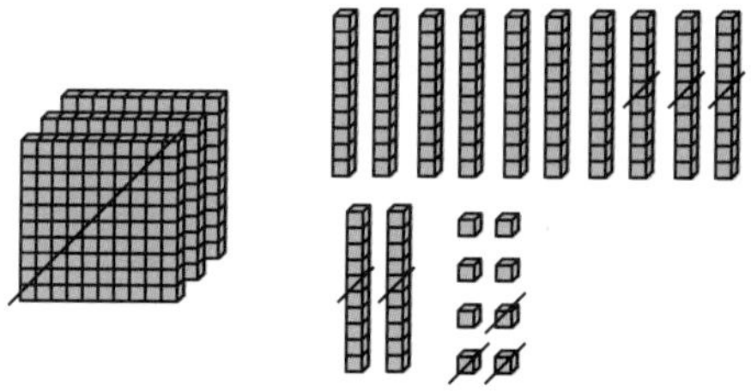	$\begin{array}{r} {\scriptstyle 3\ 12} \\ \not{4}\not{2}8 \\ -\ 153 \\ \hline 275 \end{array}$

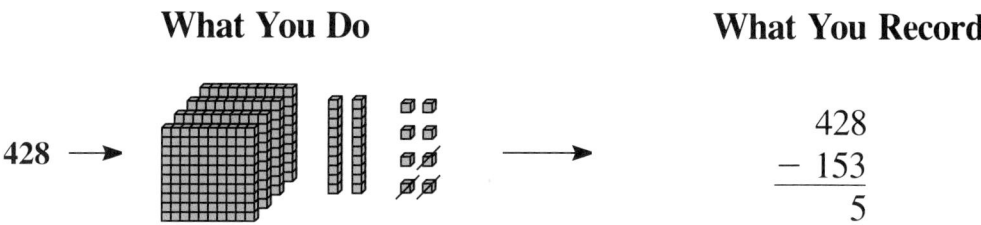

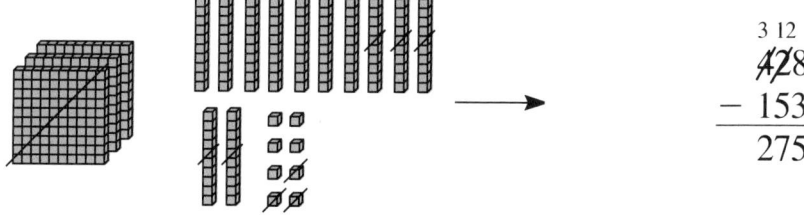

1. Can you take away 3 ones without trading?

2. Can you take away 5 tens without trading? Why?

3. How many hundreds and tens are left after the trade?

4. How many tens did you take away? How many hundreds?

5. What is 428 minus 153?

TRY IT OUT

Use blocks to find these differences. Record what you did.

1. 82 − 37 **2.** 175 − 58 **3.** 362 − 137 **4.** 436 − 271

5. Use blocks to find the difference of two 3-digit numbers of your choice.

Subtracting Whole Numbers

LEARN ABOUT IT

EXPLORE Analyze the Process

How many days longer than a year would a space flight to Mars take? A year is 365 days.

You subtract because you need to take away one amount from another to find the difference.

Space Flight from Earth	
to Mercury	206 days
to Venus	288 days
to Mars	514 days

Subtract the ones. Trade if necessary.

$$\begin{array}{r} {}^{0\ 14} \\ 5\,\cancel{1}\,4 \\ -\ 3\ 6\ 5 \\ \hline 9 \end{array}$$

Subtract the tens. Trade if necessary.

$$\begin{array}{r} {}^{4\ 10\ 14} \\ \cancel{5}\,\cancel{1}\,4 \\ -\ 3\ 6\ 5 \\ \hline 4\ 9 \end{array}$$

Subtract the hundreds.

$$\begin{array}{r} {}^{4\ 10\ 14} \\ \cancel{5}\,\cancel{1}\,4 \\ -\ 3\ 6\ 5 \\ \hline 1\ 4\ 9 \end{array}$$

TALK ABOUT IT

1. Why is it necessary to trade in the first step?
2. Explain the other trades.
3. How would you have estimated the difference?
4. Use a complete sentence to give a reasonable answer to the story problem.

Other Examples

A
$$\begin{array}{r} {}^{5\ 13\ 12} \\ \cancel{6}\,\cancel{4}\,\cancel{2} \\ -\ 1\ 7\ 9 \\ \hline 4\ 6\ 3 \end{array}$$

Check
$$\begin{array}{r} 463 \\ +\ 179 \\ \hline 642 \end{array}$$

B
$$\begin{array}{r} {}^{0\ 11\ 14} \\ \cancel{1}\,\cancel{2}\,4 \\ -\quad 7\ 8 \\ \hline 4\ 6 \end{array}$$

C
$$\begin{array}{r} {}^{4\ 15\ 12\ 14} \\ \cancel{5},\cancel{6}\,\cancel{3}\,\cancel{4} \\ -\ 2,9\ 5\ 6 \\ \hline 2,6\ 7\ 8 \end{array}$$

D
$$\begin{array}{r} {}^{3\ 15\ 10} \\ \$5\,\cancel{4}.\,\cancel{6}\,\cancel{0} \\ -\ 2\ 1.\ 8\ 5 \\ \hline \$3\ 2.\ 7\ 5 \end{array}$$

TRY IT OUT

1.	2.	3.	4.	5.	6.
64 − 48	548 − 73	462 − 235	6,825 − 409	7,256 − 6,184	$25.42 − 18.65

PRACTICE

Find the differences.

1. 59 − 45	**2.** 238 − 69	**3.** 593 − 465	**4.** \$8.26 − 3.81	**5.** 4,529 − 635

6. 78 − 45 **7.** 230 − 149 **8.** \$62.08 − \$38.52 **9.** 9,126 − 7,241

10. 6,843 − 2,589 **11.** \$3.59 − \$1.29 **12.** 8,942 − 1,385

13. 456 − 94 **14.** 1,549 − 425 **15.** 6,961 − 4,682

APPLY

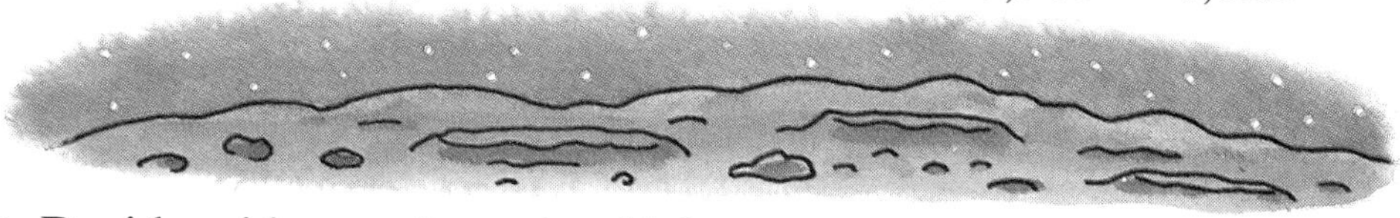

MATH REASONING Decide without subtracting if the difference is correct. Tell how you know.

16. 142 − 59 = 107 **17.** 356 − 28 = 298 **18.** 532 − 216 = 316

PROBLEM SOLVING

19. **Science Data Bank** Compare the number of days it takes Mars and Earth to go around the sun. Which takes longer? How many more days? See page 470.

DATA BANK

20. Temperatures on Venus can reach 850 degrees Fahrenheit. How much hotter is that than Earth's high temperature of 136 degrees?

CALCULATOR

When Jerry bought booklets about the planets, the price of the Mars booklet had been marked out. He discovered an easy way to use his calculator to find it. Here is what he did.

Booklets

Venus	\$2.49
Mercury	\$1.98
Mars	[redacted]
Total	\$5.64

Push	Enter	Push	Enter	Push	Enter	Push
ON/AC	**5.64**	−	**1.98**	−	**2.49**	=

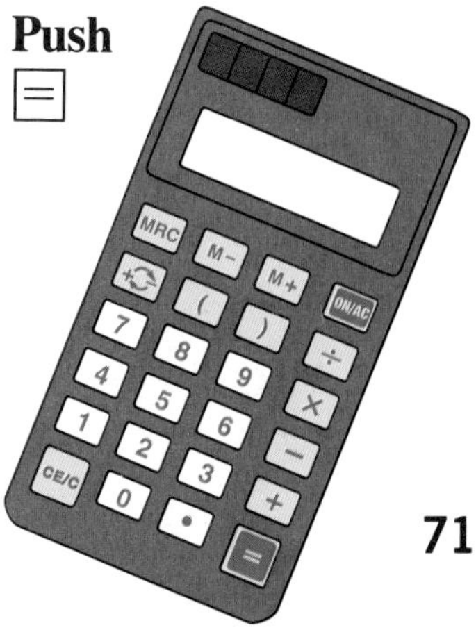

Use Jerry's method to find the missing numbers.

21. Find the Mars book price.

22. 57 + 86 + |||| = 237

Subtracting with Middle Zeros

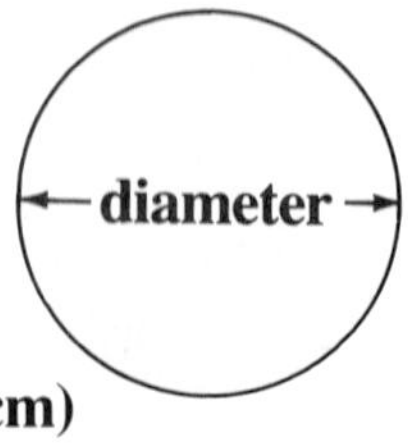

LEARN ABOUT IT

Observatory	Diameter of mirror (cm)
Hale (California)	508
Kitt Peak (Arizona)	401
Lick (California)	305
McDonald (Texas)	272
Hooker (California)	254
Mauna Kea (Hawaii)	223

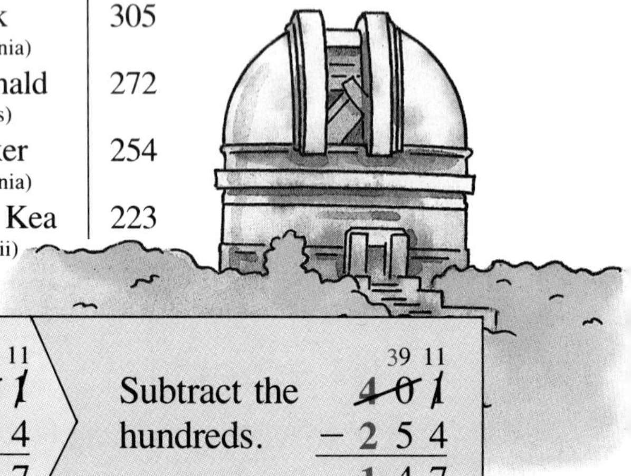

EXPLORE Analyze the Process

Some of the most powerful telescopes use circular mirrors to collect light from planets. How much greater is the diameter of the mirror at Kitt Peak Observatory than that of the mirror at Hooker Observatory?

How do you know that you can subtract to solve this problem?

Subtract the ones. Trade if necessary.	39 11 ~~4 0~~ ~~1~~ − 2 5 4 7	Subtract the tens. Trade if necessary.	39 11 ~~4 0~~ ~~1~~ − 2 5 4 4 7	Subtract the hundreds.	39 11 ~~4 0~~ ~~1~~ − 2 5 4 1 4 7

TALK ABOUT IT

1. How do you know that 4 hundreds and 0 tens are 40 tens?
2. How would you have estimated the difference?
3. Use a complete sentence to give a reasonable answer to the story problem.

Other Examples

A	B	C	D
49 13 ~~5 0~~ ~~3~~ − 6 8 4 3 5	9 14 1 ~~0~~ ~~4~~ − 6 7 3 7	79 10 ~~8 0~~ ~~0~~ − 7 6 4 3 6	699 13 ~~7, 0 0~~ ~~3~~ − 2, 5 6 8 4, 4 3 5

Think 700 tens

TRY IT OUT

1.	2.	3.	4.	5.
604 − 37	408 − 246	6,005 − 246	402 − 164	\$6.04 − 2.59

PRACTICE

Find the differences.

1. $\begin{array}{r} 703 \\ -\ 58 \\ \hline \end{array}$ **2.** $\begin{array}{r} 809 \\ -\ 528 \\ \hline \end{array}$ **3.** $\begin{array}{r} 501 \\ -\ 316 \\ \hline \end{array}$ **4.** $\begin{array}{r} 1{,}006 \\ -\ 981 \\ \hline \end{array}$ **5.** $\begin{array}{r} 2{,}308 \\ -\ 924 \\ \hline \end{array}$

6. $\begin{array}{r} 8{,}003 \\ -\ 2{,}416 \\ \hline \end{array}$ **7.** $\begin{array}{r} 4{,}602 \\ -\ 2{,}537 \\ \hline \end{array}$ **8.** $\begin{array}{r} 2{,}037 \\ -\ 428 \\ \hline \end{array}$ **9.** $\begin{array}{r} \$67.08 \\ -\ 4.63 \\ \hline \end{array}$ **10.** $\begin{array}{r} \$6.00 \\ -\ 5.25 \\ \hline \end{array}$

11. 6,403 − 378 **12.** 2,004 − 621 **13.** 502 − 81 **14.** $20.35 − $16.48

APPLY

MATH REASONING Show that these differences are all the same. Give the next 3 differences.

15. 104 − 67 **16.** 204 − 167 **17.** 304 − 267 **18.** 404 − 367

PROBLEM SOLVING

19. Unfinished problem Choose the question or questions that can be answered using the following data. The diameter of the largest mirror in a Russian telescope is 600 cm, in an Australian telescope, 389 cm, and in a Chilean telescope, 401 cm.

a. How much larger is the Russian telescope mirror than the Australian?

b. Which telescope mirror is the largest in the world?

ESTIMATION

20. Draw squares like this. Write the digits 4, 5, 6, 7, 8, and 9 in them to make the smallest difference, the largest difference, and the difference closest to 100. Check with your calculator.

More Practice, page 502, set B

Mental Math
Using Compensation

LEARN ABOUT IT

You have learned how to use compensation to find smaller sums. The same idea can be used to find larger sums and differences.

EXPLORE **Examine the Data**
Tom counted the number of vacationers who watched rocket launchings from a large park near Cape Canaveral. He made this table to show the data.

Rocket Launch	Number of People Watching
1	298
2	176
3	243
4	197
5	356

TALK ABOUT IT

1. Tom used mental math to find how many watched the first two launches. He increased 298 to 300. How should he change 176 before he adds?

2. Ben used mental math to find how many more people watched launch 3 than watched launch 4. He increased 197 to 200. How should he change 243 before he subtracts?

To use **compensation** to add, you increase one addend and decrease the other addend the same amount. To subtract, you increase or decrease each number the same amount.

■ Use compensation to find 198 + 256.

(200) (254)

198 + **256** = 454

Increase 198 by 2.
Decrease 256 by 2.

■ Use compensation to find 243 − 197.

(246) (200)

243 − **197** = 46

Increase 243 by 3.
Increase 197 by 3.

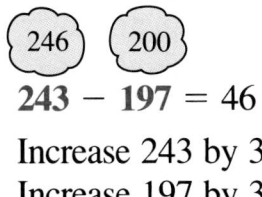

TRY IT OUT

Use compensation to find these sums or differences.

1. 97 + 538 **2.** 253 − 99 **3.** 38 + 56 **4.** 63 − 29

PRACTICE

Use compensation to find these sums or differences.

1. 19 + 63 **2.** 52 + 133 **3.** 147 + 31 **4.** 97 + 568

5. 125 + 198 **6.** 356 + 99 **7.** 439 + 296 **8.** 496 + 132

9. 96 − 52 **10.** 75 − 21 **11.** 135 − 97 **12.** 243 − 39

Estimate these sums or differences. Choose any method you wish.

13. 148 + 52 **14.** 496 + 45 **15.** 16 + 42 + 129 **16.** 876 + 114

APPLY

MATH REASONING

17. To find 76 + 98, Ted first found 76 + 100 = 176. How must he change 176 to get the correct sum for 76 + 98?

18. To find 72 − 37, Jan first found 72 − 40 = 32. How must she change 32 to get the correct difference for 72 − 37?

PROBLEM SOLVING

19. In the morning, 196 cars entered Cape Canaveral. In the afternoon, 348 cars entered. How many cars entered that day?

20. Jenny put 26 rocket buttons in one pile and 34 buttons in another pile. How many must she move from the large pile to the small pile to have the same number in each pile?

▶ USING CRITICAL THINKING Draw Conclusions

Find the missing digits. Complete the calculation.

21.
```
  □ 2 □
+ 5 □ 7
  8 7 5
```

22.
```
  3 □ 9
− 1 8 □
  □ 4 7
```

23.
```
  3 □ □
+ □ 4 8
  7 5 3
```

24.
```
    □ 6 2
+   4 □ □
1,  0 7 1
```

25.
```
  4 □ 5
− □ 1 6
  1 8 □
```

26.
```
  □ 5 □
+ 4 2 7
1,2 □ 2
```

27.
```
  5 8 □
− □ 3 2
  1 □ 4
```

28.
```
  1 7 4
+ 6 □ □
  □ 0 9
```

Problem Solving
Multiple-Step Problems

UNDERSTAND
FIND DATA
PLAN
ESTIMATE
SOLVE
CHECK

LEARN ABOUT IT

You may need to use more than one operation to solve some problems. These problems are called **Multiple-Step Problems.**

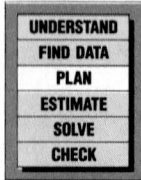

Ramona's lunch break at school is 55 minutes long. She spent 17 minutes in line and 19 minutes eating lunch. How much time did she have left?

First I'll add to find out how many minutes it took to go through the line and eat.

$17 + 19 = 36$

Then I'll subtract to find out how many minutes were left.

$55 - 36 = 19$

Ramona had 19 minutes left in her lunch break.

TRY IT OUT

1. Roman's lunch break at school is 55 minutes long. He spent 17 minutes in the hot lunch line and 19 minutes eating lunch. How much time did he have left?

2. Guido had \$1.05 for lunch. He bought a taco for \$0.89. Then he borrowed \$0.65 from John. How much more money does he need to buy another taco?

3. There are 47 students standing in the hot lunch line. 29 students are served and leave the line. 18 new students get in line. How many students are in the line now?

4. Joann brought \$2.60 for lunch. She spent \$1.37 on a hamburger and \$0.68 on a lemonade. How much money did she have left?

MIXED PRACTICE

Solve. Use any problem solving strategy. Use the survey for problems 1 and 2.

Survey questions: What is your favorite hot lunch?
What is your least favorite hot lunch?

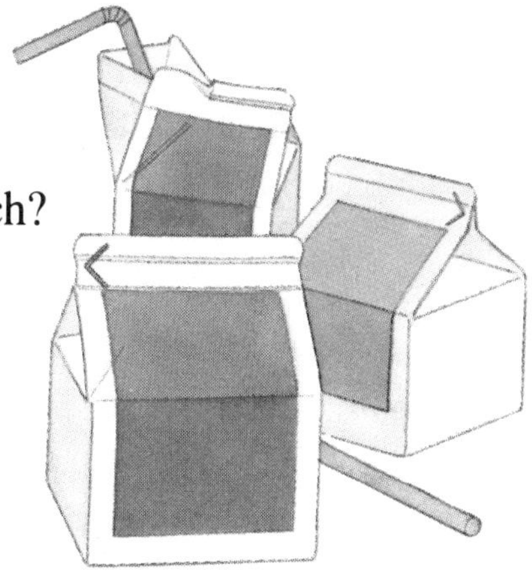

Favorite	Votes	Least Favorite	Votes
Pizza	98	Hot Dogs	123
Hamburgers	83	Sloppy Joes	63
Tacos	||||	Bean Tortillas	52

1. A total of 248 students voted for either tacos, hamburgers, or pizza as their favorite food. How many voted for tacos?

2. How many votes did hot dogs and sloppy joes get for least favorite lunch?

3. A book of lunch tickets for one week cost Jorge $6.85. Without the tickets, a week of lunches would cost $8.30. How much does Jorge save by buying tickets?

4. Ralph finished lunch before Josie. Matt finished after Josie. Vince finished between Josie and Matt. Who finished last?

5. On Tuesday, 224 students bought pizza, 140 students bought hamburgers, and 187 students brought their own bag lunches. How many more students bought pizza than ate a bag lunch?

Milk Cartons Sold in a Week

Day	Cartons
Monday	132
Tuesday	173
Wednesday	148
Thursday	131
Friday	138

6. How many more milk cartons were sold on Tuesday and Wednesday than on Thursday and Friday?

7. Students bought 689 milks in January and 726 in February. How many did they buy in those two months?

8. **Talk About Your Solution** Solve. Then explain your solution to a classmate. One rectangular cafeteria table seats 8 people. Two tables are pushed together to make one long table. How many people can be seated?

More Practice, page 514, set A

Adding and Subtracting Larger Numbers
Using a Calculator

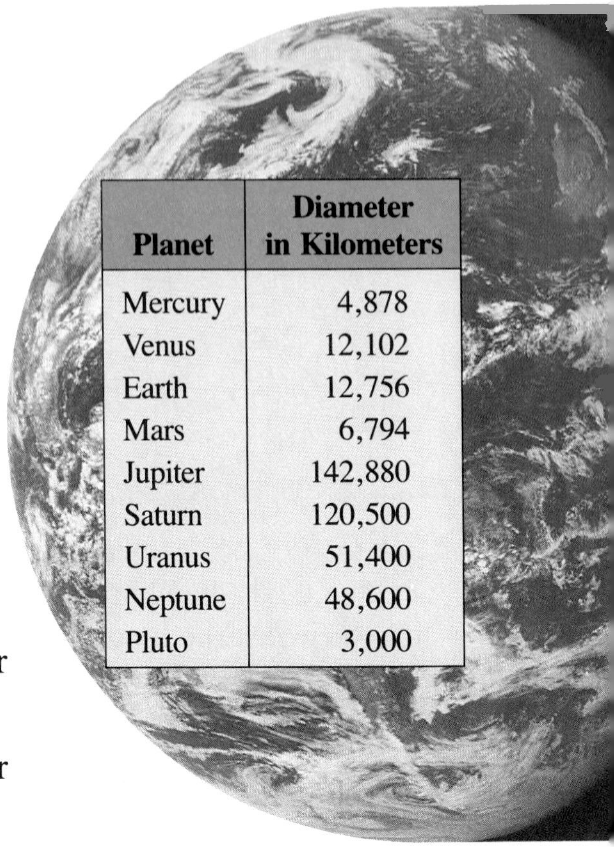

LEARN ABOUT IT

EXPLORE Read the Information

The diameter of a ball is the distance from one side to the other at the widest part. Even though the planets are far away, astronomers have invented ways to measure their diameters.

Planet	Diameter in Kilometers
Mercury	4,878
Venus	12,102
Earth	12,756
Mars	6,794
Jupiter	142,880
Saturn	120,500
Uranus	51,400
Neptune	48,600
Pluto	3,000

TALK ABOUT IT

1. Which planet is the largest? the smallest?
2. Pick 2 planets. How can you find how much larger the diameter of one is than the diameter of the other?
3. Estimate to pick 2 planets so that the diameter of one is double the diameter of the other. How can you check this?

Here is a way to calculate answers to the questions above.

Use a Calculator

To Add

Enter	Push	Enter	Push
6,794	+	6,794	=

To Subtract

Enter	Push	Enter	Push
51,400	−	12,102	=

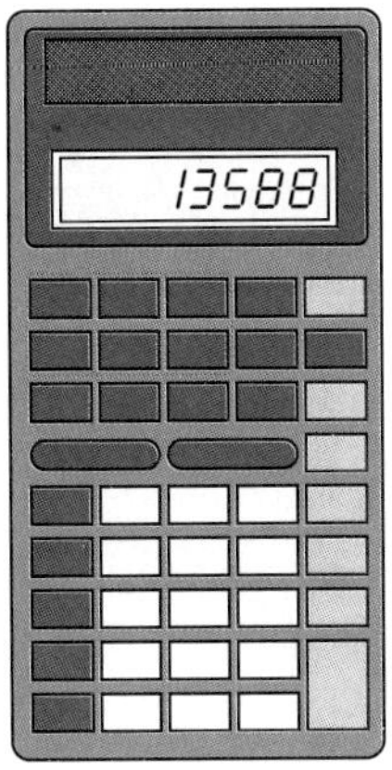

or

Use Pencil and Paper

Add or subtract in each place. Trade when necessary.

```
   1  1          4 11   3 9 10
   6, 7 9 4      5  1,  4 0  0
 + 6, 7 9 4    − 1  2,  1 0  2
  13, 5 8 8      3  9,  2 9  8
```

TRY IT OUT

How much greater is the diameter? Choose pencil and paper or a calculator.

1. Jupiter than Saturn
2. Mars than Mercury
3. Earth than Mars

PRACTICE

How much greater is the diameter? Use the chart on page 78. Decide whether to use pencil and paper or a calculator.

1. Uranus than Neptune
2. Saturn than Earth
3. Mercury than Pluto
4. Jupiter than Uranus
5. Venus than Mercury
6. Earth than Pluto
7. Is the diameter of Jupiter more or less than 3 times the diameter of Neptune?
8. Is the diameter of Earth more or less than 2 times the diameter of Mercury?

APPLY

MATH REASONING Use a calculator. Find the number for the ||||.

9. |||| − 6,276 = 57,698
10. |||| + 5,897 = 87,629

PROBLEM SOLVING

11. **Science Data Bank** How does the number of satellites circling Jupiter compare to the number circling Saturn? See page 470.

12. Mercury travels 170,500 kilometers per hour around the sun. The earth travels 107,220 kilometers per hour around the sun. How much faster does Mercury travel?

MIXED REVIEW

Give an addition fact for each subtraction fact.

13. 15 − 7 = 8
14. 11 − 6 = 5
15. 17 − 9 = 8
16. 14 − 8 = 6

Write the number in standard form.

17. eight hundred thirty-nine thousand, three hundred one
18. 600,000 + 80,000 + 2,000 + 40 + 9

More Practice, page 502, set D

Problem Solving
Deciding When to Estimate

UNDERSTAND
FIND DATA
PLAN
ESTIMATE
SOLVE
CHECK

LEARN ABOUT IT

When you solve problems, you sometimes need an exact answer. Other times you only need to know about how much or how many and you can make an estimate.

Fun Fair Tickets

Adults	$2.45
Children	$1.75
Senior Citizens	$1.25

Special Tickets

Cake Walk	$0.75
Lunch	$3.25

You have a ten-dollar bill. Is that enough to buy 5 adult tickets?

> All I need to know is whether I have enough money. I can estimate the total cost.

What will you have to pay the ticket seller for 1 adult ticket and 1 child ticket?

> The ticket seller must receive the exact amount. I need to find the exact answer.

When you need to decide about how many, or to compare an amount with a reference point, you can estimate. In other situations, you should find the exact answer.

TRY IT OUT

Decide whether you need an exact answer or an estimate. Tell why.

1. Is $5 enough to pay for 5 cakewalk tickets?
2. What should you pay the ticket taker for 3 student tickets?

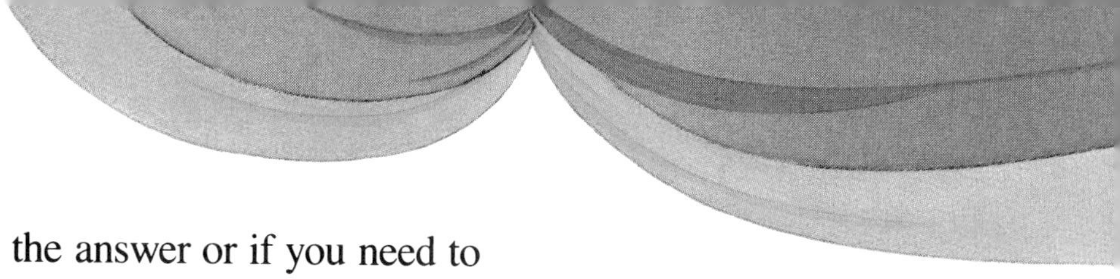

MIXED PRACTICE

Tell if you can estimate the answer or if you need to find an exact answer. Explain why.

1. On Friday, 148 people came to the Fun Fair. On Saturday, 156 people came. To tell her mother how successful the fair was, how many tickets should Janell say were sold?
2. The first night ticket sales were \$144.55 for adult tickets and \$155.75 for child tickets. What should the school newspaper report about the total ticket sales?
3. Mr. Thornquist wanted to buy lunch at the Fun Fair for 4 people in his family. He had \$20. Was that enough?
4. Megan ordered balloons for the Fun Fair. Last year, 78 balloons were used. She wanted to order twice as many this year. How many should Megan order?
5. William bought a child's ticket and a lunch ticket. How much should he pay the ticket seller?
6. There were 26 fourth grade and 27 fifth grade Fun Fair workers who received free tickets. How many free tickets should Erica report to the ticket takers? Would she give the same number to the person figuring the profits?
7. Sue bought 2 Fun Fair T-shirts for \$4.98 each. What amount should she use to tell a friend about the total cost?
8. Jake's father gave him money to spend at the fair. Jake bought a student ticket, walked for a cake, and ate lunch. What amount should he use to tell how much change he needed to return to his father?
9. Bo recorded the amount of time he spent at the Fun Fair. He was there 29 minutes on Friday and 116 minutes on Saturday. What amount should he use to tell a friend how much longer he was at the fair on Saturday than on Friday?
10. **Determining Reasonable Answers** Tell if the calculator answer for this problem is reasonable. If it is not reasonable, tell why. Jerod bought one ticket of each type at the Fun Fair. What was his total cost?

More Practice, page 514, set B

Applied Problem Solving
Group Decision Making

UNDERSTAND
FIND DATA
PLAN
ESTIMATE
SOLVE
CHECK

Group Skill:
Check for Understanding

You want to get a kitten from the animal pound. Your parents are concerned about the costs and problems of having a cat in the house. How can you convince them to let you have the kitten?

Facts to Consider

1. Before you can take the kitten home, it must have its shots. The pound charges $17 for the shots plus $10 for the office visit.
2. The kitten will need to eat 2 times a day. It will eat about 1 small can of cat food a day. Cat food costs about $0.35 a can.
3. A flea collar for the cat costs $3.29. A name tag for the collar costs $3.79.
4. A cat door costs $9.98.
5. A simple litter box costs $8.69. A fancy one that keeps the cat from kicking litter out costs $13.99.
6. A medium-sized bag of litter costs $2.89. It lasts about 1 week.

Some Questions to Answer

1. If you got the kitten, what things would you need to buy right away?
2. How would the cost change if you decided to buy only the necessary items? if you choose the cheaper litter box? What effects could these decisions have once the kitten had lived with you for a while?
3. How much would it cost to get the kitten's shots and buy all the things you would need to get started? Estimate the amount.
4. How much would it cost for food and litter each week? Estimate.

What Is Your Decision?

Write out a plan to give your parents. List the things you will need that will cost money. Show how much you estimate the kitten will cost in the beginning. Show the weekly cost. Tell how you plan to take care of the kitten.

WRAP UP

Strategy Search

Match each situation with one of the techniques or strategies that it suggests. Justify your choices.

1. To subtract 562 − 304, first subtract 4 from each number to make 558 − 300.
2. To estimate the difference of 628 and 312, subtract 300 from 600.
3. To decide if $4 is enough money to buy tape for $1.69 and glue for $2.77, add $1 + $2. Then add an estimate of $0.69 + 77.

a. using basic facts to find special sums

b. front-end estimation

c. estimating by rounding

d. using compensation

Sometimes, Always, Never

Which word should go in the blank, sometimes, always, or never? Explain your choices.

4. When adding whole numbers, if you have 10 or more ones blocks, tens blocks, or hundreds blocks, you should __?__ trade for a larger block.
5. A calculator __?__ gives the correct answer.

Project

Even numbers end in 2, 4, 6, 8, or 0.
Odd numbers end in 1, 3, 5, 7, or 9.

6. Use counters to show and then answer these addition and subtraction problems.

5 + 3 4 + 2 6 + 3 5 − 3 4 − 2 6 − 3

7. If you add two odd numbers is your answer odd or even? If you subtract two odd numbers is your answer odd or even?
8. Check your answers to problem 7 by showing several examples with your counters. What other patterns can you find for adding and subtracting odd and even numbers?

Power Practice/Test

Part 1 Understanding

Use mental math to find the sum or difference.
Explain how you found each answer.

1. 399 + 464 **2.** 1,500 − 700 **3.** 400 + 335 + 600

Part 2 Skills

Estimate the sum or difference.

4. 86 + 43 **5.** 730 − 285 **6.** 668 − 45

Use front-end estimation to find the sum or difference.

7. $7.88 + 5.25

8. 5,709 − 1,383

9. 386 + 977 + 591

10. 425 − 210

Add or subtract.

11. 427 + 368

12. 548 − 399

13. 603 − 357

14. 12,536 + 40,805

15. 54 + 793 **16.** 762 − 465 **17.** 8,006 − 541 **18.** 1,608 + 523

19. 872 + 333 + 164 + 21 **20.** 3,608 + 753 + 6,551

Part 3 Applications

21. Ed writes on a computer. He writes 234 words on page 1 and 188 words on page 2. How many more words does he need for a 500-word story?

22. Last year Rita used 27 cups at her party. This year she needs to double the number of cups. Should she find an estimate or an exact answer? How many cups should she buy?

ENRICHMENT
Palindromes

The words and numbers below are called palindromes. Palindromes have a special pattern.

1. What is the pattern?

dad	toot	level	deed	madam
66	747	3,883	52,125	753,357

2. Tell which of the following are not palindromes. Why not?

505 12,345 yoyo mom moon

3. Make up a word palindrome with 2 vowels.

The flow chart steps tell how to create a number palindrome.

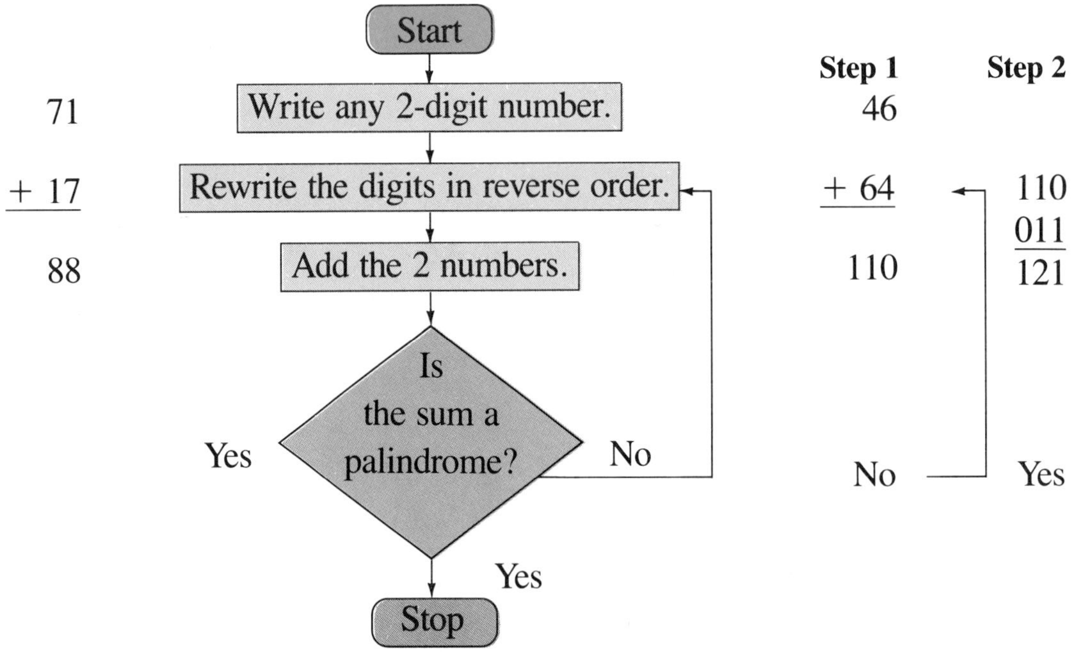

4. Follow the flow chart. Use 5 different starting numbers. Does it always work? Do you always use the same number of steps to make a palindrome? Explain.

CUMULATIVE REVIEW

1. 47 − 28

A 21 **B** 19
C 29 **D** 55

2. 37 + 56

A 81 **B** 19
C 83 **D** 93

3.
$$\begin{array}{r} 134 \\ -\ 39 \\ \hline \end{array}$$

A 95 **B** 115
C 105 **D** 173

4. To find 698 + 965, how many trades must you make?

A 0 **B** 2
C 1 **D** 3

5. What odd number is greater than 10, rounds to 20, and is said when you count by 5?

A 11 **B** 15
C 13 **D** 20

6. In 300 + 177 + 700, which are compatible numbers?

A 300 + 700 **B** 100 + 77
C 177 + 700 **D** 177 + 300

7. Estimate the difference between 783 and 231.

A 500 **B** 900
C 600 **D** 1,000

8. Which number is two hundred thousand, seventy-five?

A 275 **B** 275,000
C 20,750 **D** 200,075

9. What is 45,682 rounded to the nearest hundred?

A 45,700 **B** 46,000
C 45,600 **D** 45,000

10. In the city election, Ms. Ryan got 36,348 votes and the only other candidate, Mr. Sanchez, got 40,659 votes. How many people voted?

A 76,007 **B** 4,311
C 76,907 **D** 77,007

11. Rico made posters that were either blue, white, or red. Each poster had a single large star, eagle, or banner. How many poster combinations were there?

A 3 **B** 9
C 6 **D** 12

4

DATA, GRAPHS, AND PROBABILITY

THEME: MOUNTAINS AND RIVERS

MATH AND SOCIAL STUDIES

DATA BANK

Use the Social Studies Data Bank on page 473 to answer the questions.

1 How many mountains in the United States are more than 14,000 feet above sea level?

2 What is the longest river formed in the Rocky Mountains? Does it flow east or west?

3 The Rio Grande River goes about 800 miles before it becomes the US/Mexico border. For about how many miles is the river a border?

4 **Use Critical Thinking** Which two rivers put end-to-end would come closest to equaling the longest river in the table?

Place names in the Rocky Mountains remind us of the languages of many different groups of people.

Getting Information From a Graph

LEARN ABOUT IT

EXPLORE **Think About Graphs**

Graphs give us information by showing data. They use bars, lines, or pictures. Study these two graphs.

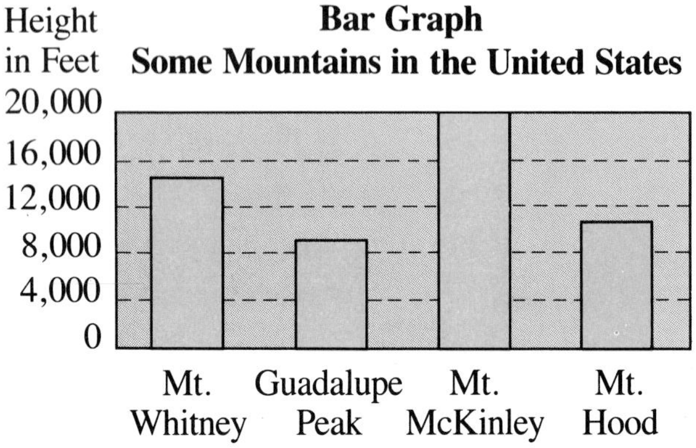

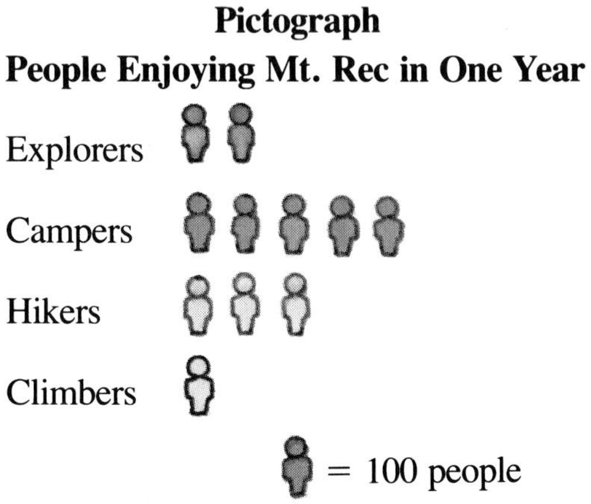

TALK ABOUT IT

1. What is the title of the bar graph? the pictograph? Why do you think the title is important?
2. Which mountain in the bar graph is the highest? the lowest?
3. Who used Mt. Rec the most? the least?
4. What else do the graphs tell us?

Every graph has a title that tells what it is about. It also has labels to tell what it shows. A number scale shows the units used on the graph.

TRY IT OUT

1. In the bar graph, what numbers are used to show heights of the mountains?
2. In the pictograph, what does the  stand for?
3. How many hikers enjoy Mt. Rec in one year?

PRACTICE

Answer these questions about this bar graph.

1. What is the title of the graph?
2. Name one of the trails on the bar graph.
3. Why do you think one of the trails is called Short Stretch?
4. Which trail is longer than 2 miles, but less than 4 miles?

Length of Some Mountain Hiking Trails

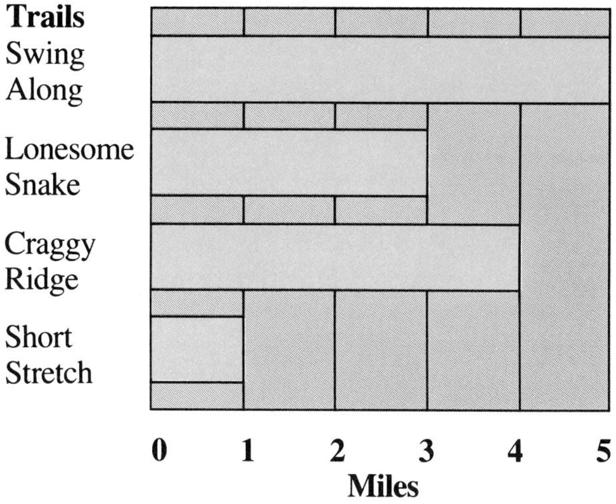

Answer these questions about this pictograph.

5. What kinds of birds does the pictograph show?
6. How many birds does each  represent?

Large Birds Spotted on a Mountain Trail

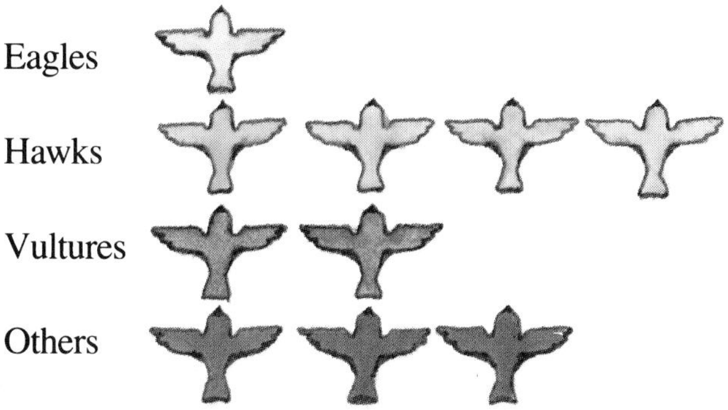

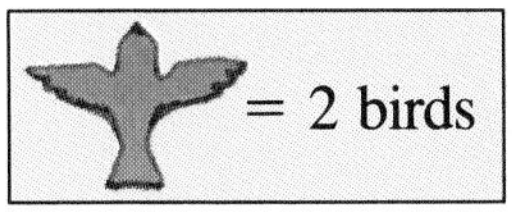

APPLY

MATH REASONING

7. What if each  represented 5 birds? How many hawks would the graph then show?

DATA BANK

PROBLEM SOLVING

8. **Social Studies Data Bank** What state would you visit to see the greatest number of high peaks? See page 473.

COMMUNICATION Write About It

9. Write a short paragraph about a mountain hike. In your story, use data from the graphs shown in this lesson.

Reading and Making Bar Graphs

LEARN ABOUT IT

EXPLORE **Use a Spinner**

Work in groups. The bar graph shows the results of spinning the first two spinners 30 times each.

Use a spinner like Spinner 3 and spin it 30 times. Decide how you could use the results to complete the bar graph.

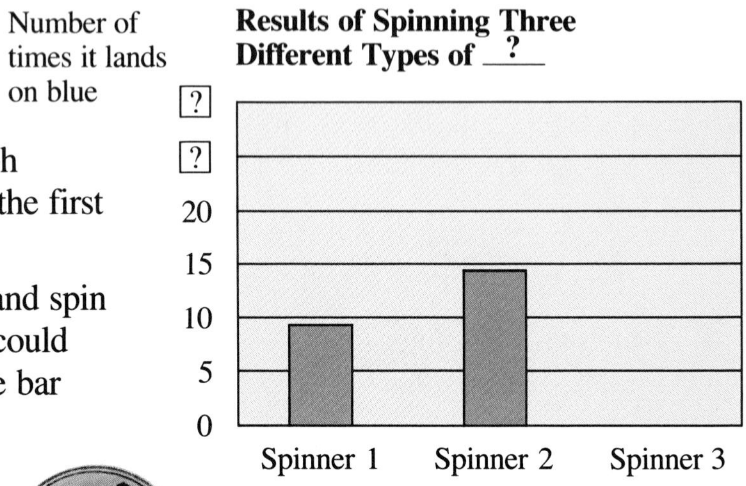

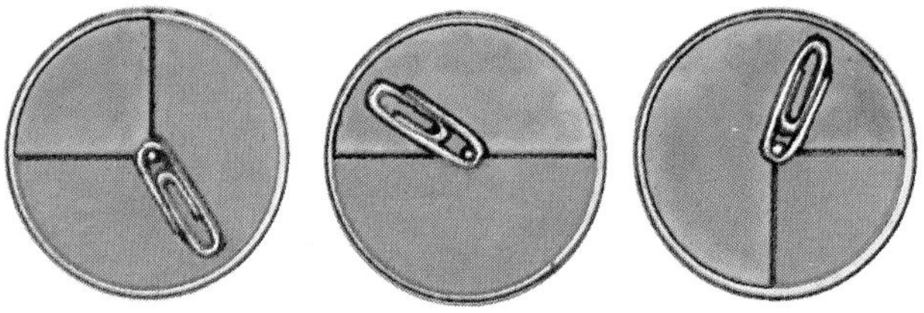

Spinner 1 Spinner 2 Spinner 3

TALK ABOUT IT

1. What do the red bars show?
2. How would you complete the title of the graph?
3. How would you complete the number scale?
4. What can you tell about the outcomes of spinning these spinners? Are the results equally likely or not equally likely?

Here is how to make a bar graph.

- Create a scale. Label the side and bottom of the graph.
- Draw the bars to show the data.
- Title the graph.

TRY IT OUT

1. Copy and complete the graph above.
2. Make a bar graph using the data in this table.

	Spinner 1	Spinner 2	Spinner 3
Red Spins in 30 Tries	20	16	6

PRACTICE

Record of 50 Coin Tosses

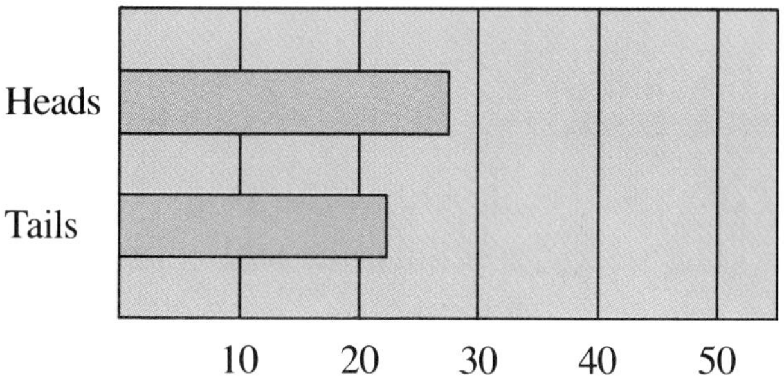

1. What is the title of the graph?
2. How many times was the coin tossed?
3. Which came up more, heads or tails? Is this what you would expect?
4. About how many times did each side come up?
5. Jason tossed a paper cup on the table 50 times. He recorded the results. Use his data to make a bar graph.

	Down	Up	Sideways

Number of Outcomes	18	5	27

APPLY

MATH REASONING

6. Suppose you spin this spinner 30 times. Do you think you would spin blue more than half the time? Why or why not?

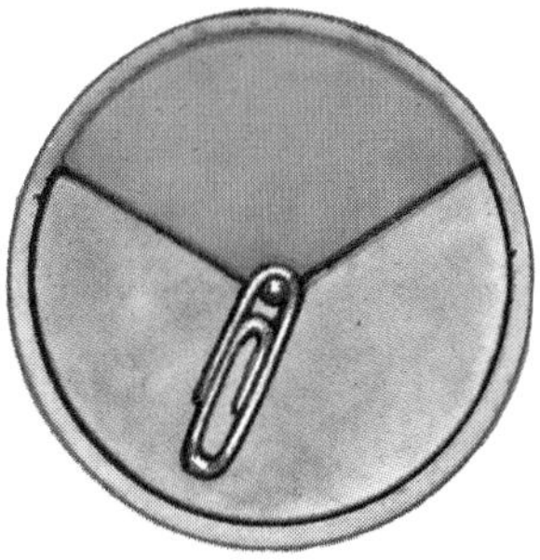

PROBLEM SOLVING

7. One bar on a graph was a little bit above 50. Another bar was a little below 20. Is the difference of the numbers the bars show more or less than 30? Tell why.

ALGEBRA

Copy this number scale.

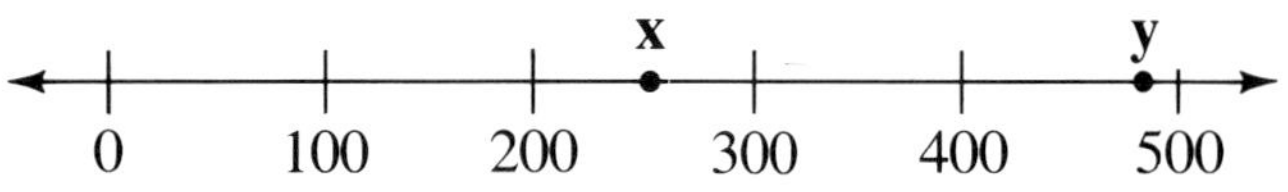

8. Show about where X + 100 would be.
9. Show about where Y − 100 would be.
10. Show about where X − 150 would be.

More Practice, page 514, set D

Reading and Making Pictographs

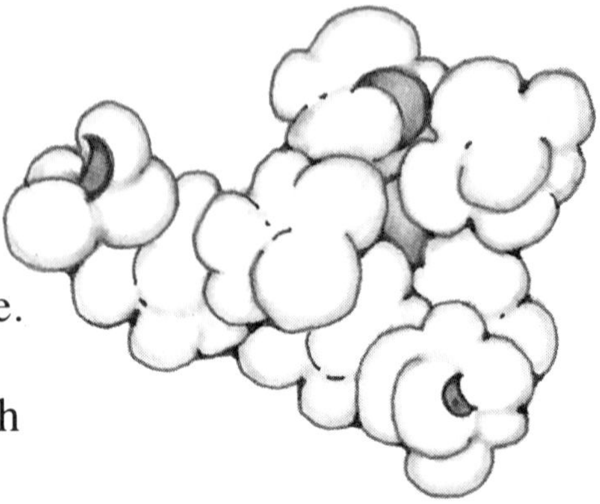

LEARN ABOUT IT

EXPLORE **Think About the Data**

The pictograph illustrates the information in the table. When the pictograph is complete, it will tell how much popcorn a small popcorn company sold in each season of one year.

Table

Popcorn Sold	
Season	Pounds
Spring	4,500
Summer	2,000
Fall	6,000
Winter	8,500

Pictograph

Pounds of Popcorn Sold in Each Season

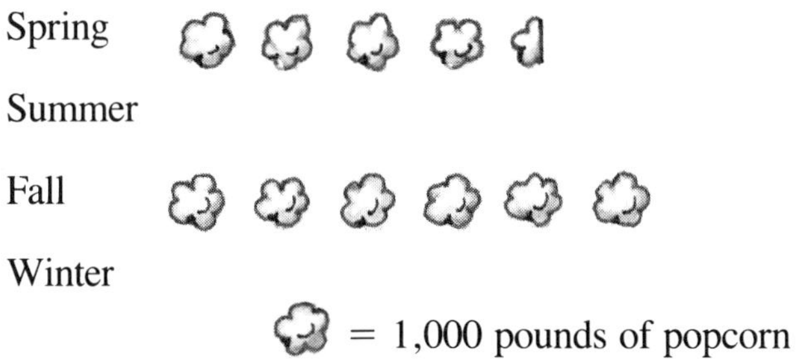

TALK ABOUT IT

1. In the pictograph, what does one kernel of popcorn represent?
2. Would it be a good idea for one kernel to equal 10 pounds? Why or why not?
3. What is the difference between seeing the information in a table and seeing it in a pictograph?

Here is how to make a pictograph.

- Choose a picture symbol. Tell what it represents.
- Decide how many pictures you need for each number.
- Label the graph. Draw the correct number of pictures.
- Give the graph a title.

TRY IT OUT

1. Copy and complete the pictograph above.
2. Make a pictograph to show this data.

Popcorn Jars Made in a Week

Monday	500
Tuesday	650
Wednesday	800
Thursday	350
Friday	200

PRACTICE

Ways We Pop Popcorn

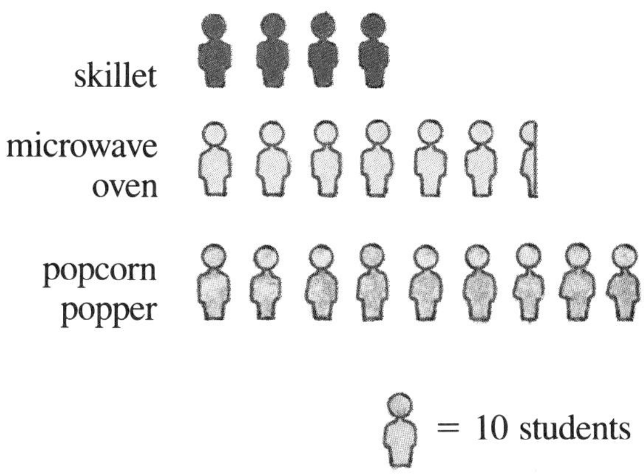

A class made this pictograph about a school survey. Answer these questions.

1. What does one picture symbol stand for on the graph?
2. How many students make popcorn in a skillet?
3. How many more students make their popcorn in popcorn poppers than in microwave ovens?
4. The fourth grade sent a questionnaire asking what students most like to do while they eat popcorn. 50 students answered. These are the results. Make a pictograph to show this data.

Watch TV	25
Play a game	10
Read a book	15

APPLY

MATH REASONING Suppose 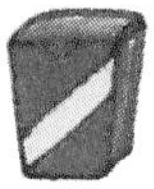 stands for 100 boxes of popcorn. Draw what would stand for these amounts.

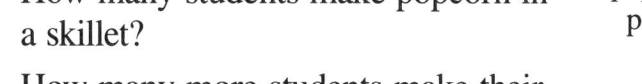

5. 50 boxes **6.** 200 boxes **7.** 150 boxes

PROBLEM SOLVING

8. People like to eat popcorn in different ways. In a survey, 9 people said they liked it plain, 5 liked salt only, 3 liked butter only, and 8 liked both butter and salt. How many took part in the survey?

MIXED REVIEW

First round each number to the nearest ten. Then round the number to the nearest hundred.

9. 273 **10.** 99 **11.** 833 **12.** 611 **13.** 441

Find the sums and differences using mental math.

14. $60 + 70 = n$ **15.** $36{,}000 - 15{,}000 = n$ **16.** $400 + 500$

Reading and Making Line Graphs

LEARN ABOUT IT

EXPLORE **Study the Graph**

Stacy hiked up a mountain on her vacation. She made this line graph to show how the temperature changed. The graph uses data she recorded in the table below.

Mountain Temperatures (°F)

At the base	59°	3,000 ft. up	48°
1,000 ft. up	57°	4,000 ft. up	47°
2,000 ft. up	52°	5,000 ft. up	41°

Temperature Changes as You Climb a Mountain

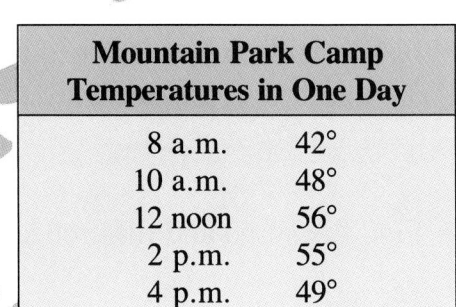

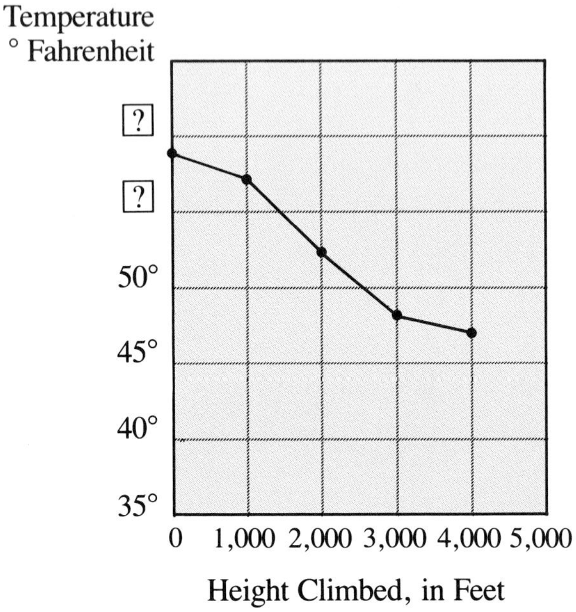

TALK ABOUT IT

1. Do the points on the graph show the data in the table? Explain.

2. Does the line on the graph go up or down? What does this tell you about the temperature?

This is how to make a line graph.

- Create scales. Label the side and bottom of the graph.
- Mark points that match the data on the bottom scale with the data on the side scale.
- Draw lines to connect the points.
- Give the graph a title.

TRY IT OUT

1. Copy and complete the line graph above.

2. Use this data to make a line graph.

Mountain Park Camp Temperatures in One Day	
8 a.m.	42°
10 a.m.	48°
12 noon	56°
2 p.m.	55°
4 p.m.	49°

PRACTICE

Answer questions 1–4 about the line graph.

Attendance at Mountain Park Camp

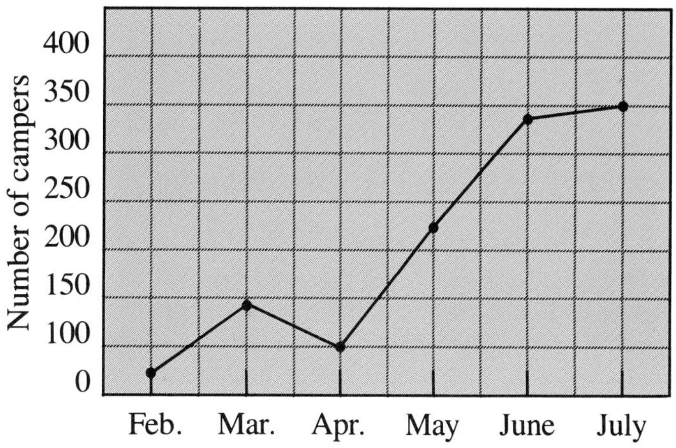

1. About how many attended the camp in March?
2. Which month had the lowest attendance?
3. In which months was the attendance greater than 200?
4. In what two months did the attendance stay about the same?
5. Make a line graph for this data.

Cost of Attending Camp	
1986, $200	1987, $245
1988, $255	1989, $240

APPLY

MATH REASONING

6. Match the words <u>decrease</u>, <u>no change</u>, and <u>increase</u> with graphs A, B, and C.

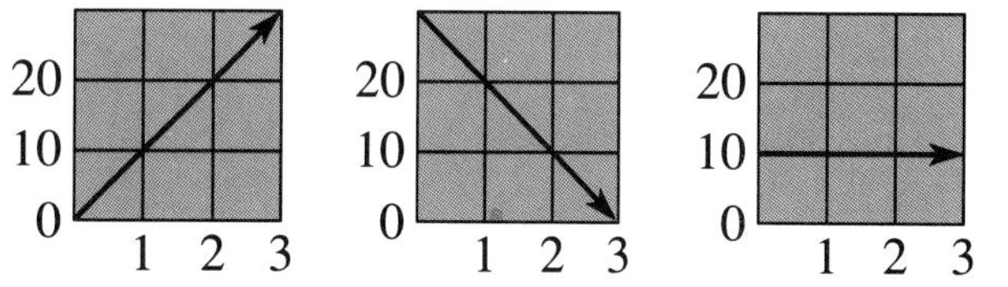

A | **B** | **C**

increase | **decrease** | **no change**

PROBLEM SOLVING

7. **Social Studies Data Bank** DATA BANK Two rivers formed in the Rocky Mountains flow east and become part of another river. What river do they join? Which of the two flows the greater distance? See page 473.

COMMUNICATION Write About It

8. Jane recorded the temperatures as she hiked on a mountain. Write two or three sentences to describe what this graph tells about her hike.

Temperature Changes on My Hike

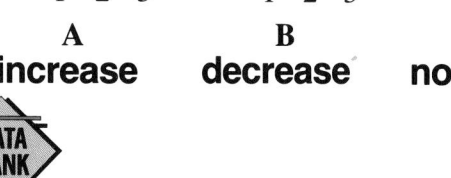

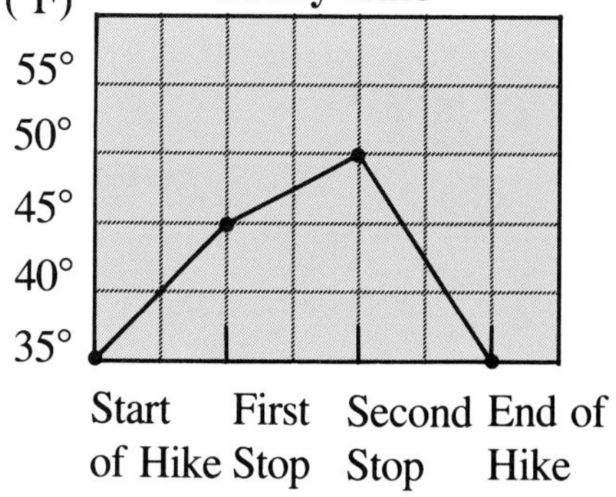

Using Critical Thinking

LEARN ABOUT IT

"Wow! What's that?" asked Meri, as she looked at Tim's paper.

"I call it an arrow graph," said Tim. "It tells about my grandfather, my grandmother, their children, and their grandchildren."

"It doesn't make sense to me," exclaimed Meri. "How does it work?"

"Simple," said Tim. "A red arrow points to a person's mother. A blue arrow points to a person's father."

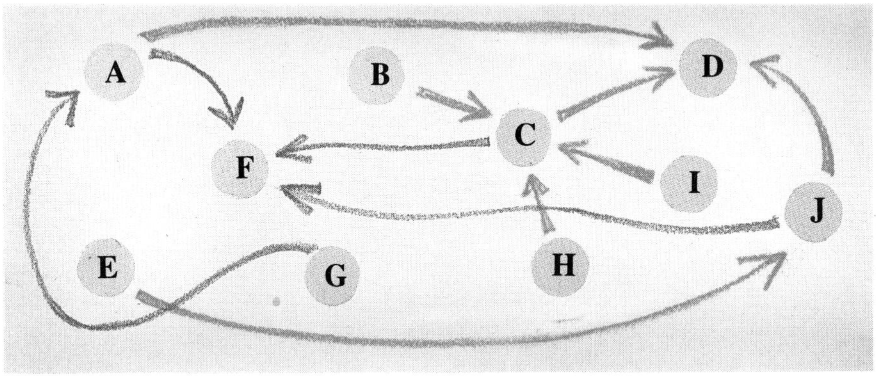

TALK ABOUT IT

1. What does the red arrow from I to C show? What does the blue arrow from C to F show?
2. Is person D male or female? Explain.
3. What letter represents the grandmother? the grandfather? Explain.

TRY IT OUT

1. How many children did the grandparents have? Which letters represent these children?
2. How many grandchildren did the grandparents have? Which letters represent these grandchildren?

POWER PRACTICE/QUIZ

In an experiment, a table tennis ball was hidden under one of four cups. The tally chart shows which cup each person guessed.

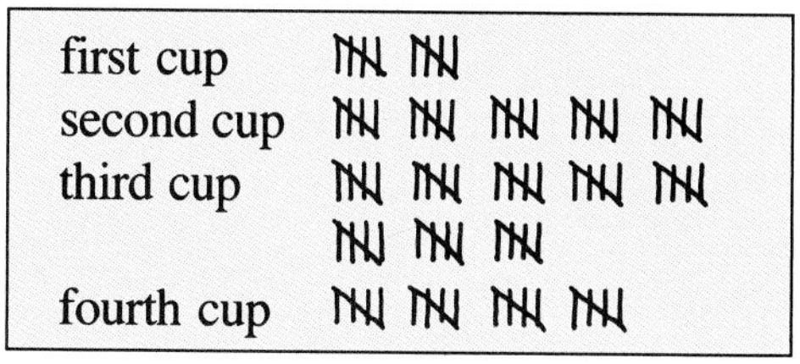

1. How many people chose each cup? How many people were guessing?

Make a pictograph of the data. Use  = 10 people.

2. What picture did you use for 5 people?

3. What would  mean?

4. What title did you give your pictograph?

5. Use the information in the tally chart to make a bar graph.

6. What scale did you use? How did you label the side of the graph? How did you label the bottom?

PROBLEM SOLVING

7. The line graph will show temperatures from 6:00 a.m. until noon. Copy and complete the graph, using the temperatures in the table.

Time	Temperature °F
2 a.m.	13°
4 a.m.	14°
6 a.m.	15°
8 a.m.	15°
10 a.m.	26°
noon	32°

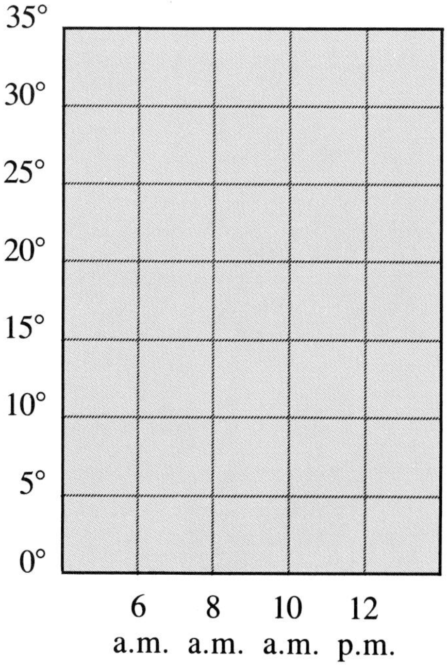

8. What was the temperature at 8 a.m.?

9. During which period of time was the temperature rising? Explain.

Problem Solving
Extra Data

UNDERSTAND
FIND DATA
PLAN
ESTIMATE
SOLVE
CHECK

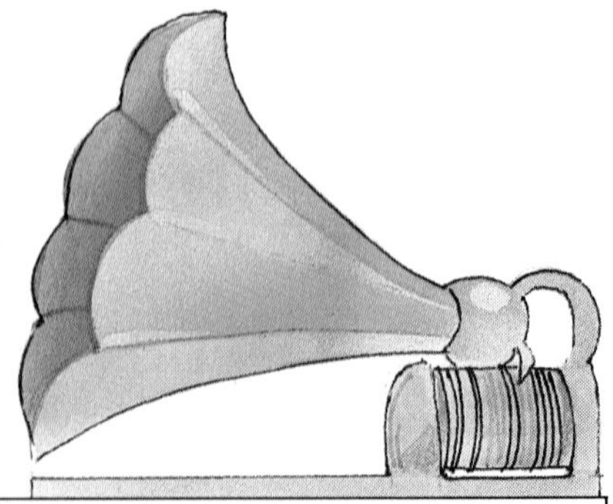

LEARN ABOUT IT

Sometimes a problem has extra data that you do not need to solve the problem.

Decibels measure the loudness of a sound. Without his hearing aid, Tony can hear only sounds louder than 110 decibels. Normal talking is about 65 decibels. A rock band is about 120 decibels. How many decibels louder than normal talking is a rock band?

I'll find the data I need to solve the problem.

Normal talking is about 65 decibels.
A rock band is about 120 decibels.

Some data is extra.

Tony hears only sounds louder than 110 decibels.

I'll solve the problem using only the data I need.

$$\begin{array}{r} 120 \\ -\ 65 \\ \hline 55 \end{array}$$

A rock band is 55 decibels louder than normal talking.

TRY IT OUT

Tell what data is extra. Then solve the problem.

1. The noise in the train station 2 miles from Ted's house is about 110 decibels. Music on Ted's headphones is about 75 decibels. How much louder is the noise in the train station?

2. Look at the graph. How many decibels louder is loud talking than soft talking?

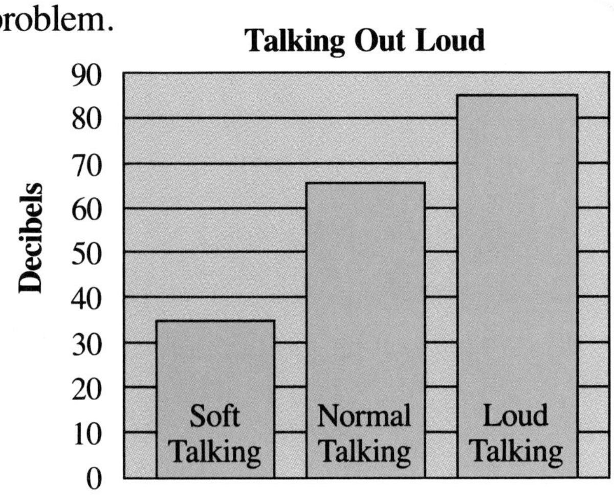

MIXED PRACTICE

1. Jim, David, Rod, and Li worked in pairs to practice sign language. What are the different pairs they could form?

2. John's friend Ben is deaf. John and his dad decided to learn sign language. The first 2 months, they learned 128 signs. The next 2 months, they learned 168 more signs. How many did they learn in all?

3. Use the pictograph. How many decibels louder is the sound of talking nearby than the sound of a pencil writing?

4. On the pictograph, how many decibels louder is a car horn than the sound of people talking far away?

5. Without her hearing aid, Carmina can hear only sounds starting at 82 decibels. According to the pictograph, can she hear the sound of people talking nearby?

6. Ferman learned how to finger sign the first 12 letters of the alphabet. Then he learned 11 more letters. How many letters did he know all together?

7. **Understanding the Operations** Tell the operation you would use to solve the problem. Use objects to solve. Janet learned 7 signs. There are 16 signs in her first lesson. How many more does she have to learn to know all the signs in the first lesson?

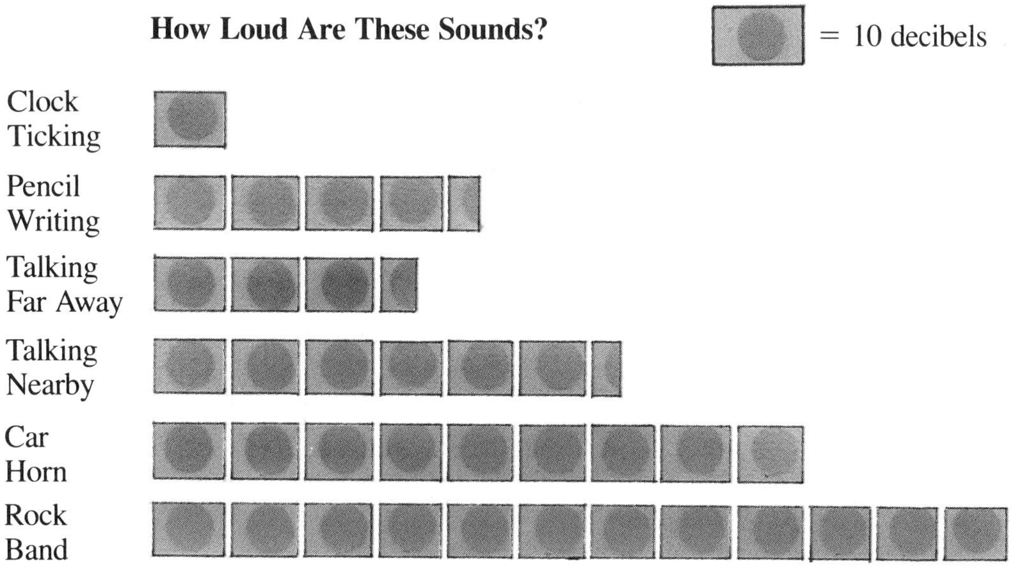

More Practice, page 515, set B

Fair and Unfair Games

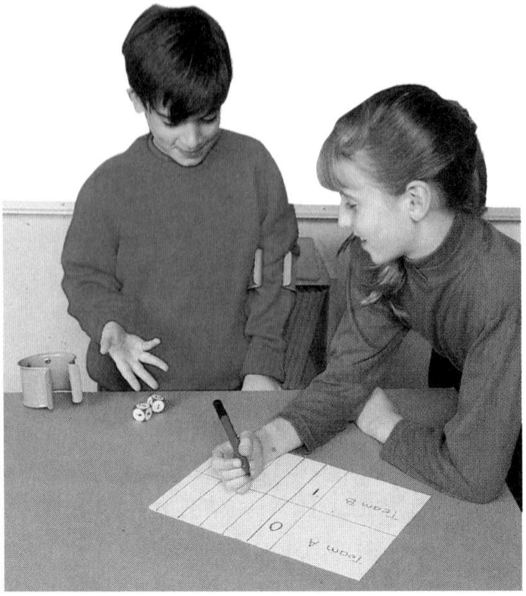

LEARN ABOUT IT

EXPLORE **Use Number Cubes**

Work in groups. Form two teams to play a game in your group.

Use two number cubes, each marked with two 1s, two 2s, and two 3s.

Here are the rules:

Roll.

Compare.

The numbers match.

Score.

Team A gets a point when the numbers match.

Team A	1			
Team B	0			

Team B gets a point when the numbers do not match.

The first team to score 10 wins!

TALK ABOUT IT

1. Were the games close?
2. Do you think the game is fair to both teams?
3. How could you change the game to make it fair?
4. Think about some games you and your friends play. Are they fair?

A game is fair if all players have an equal chance or **probability** of winning.

TRY IT OUT

Play the game above with cubes that have three 1s and three 2s on each of them. Do you think it is a fair game? Tell why or why not.

PRACTICE

Play these games with your group. Use two spinners marked 1, 2, 3, and 4 in even spaces. Are the games fair? Why?

1. Odds and Evens Match Game

Rules: Spin both spinners. If both numbers are odd or both are even, one team scores. The other team scores if one number is odd and the other is even. The first team to get 10 points wins.

2. Odd and Even Differences Game

Rules: Spin both spinners. If the difference between the two numbers is odd, one team scores. The other team scores if the difference is even. The first team to get 10 points wins.

APPLY

MATH REASONING

3. Suppose you use two spinners marked 1, 2, and 3 in even spaces. Would the game in exercise 1 be a fair game? Why or why not?

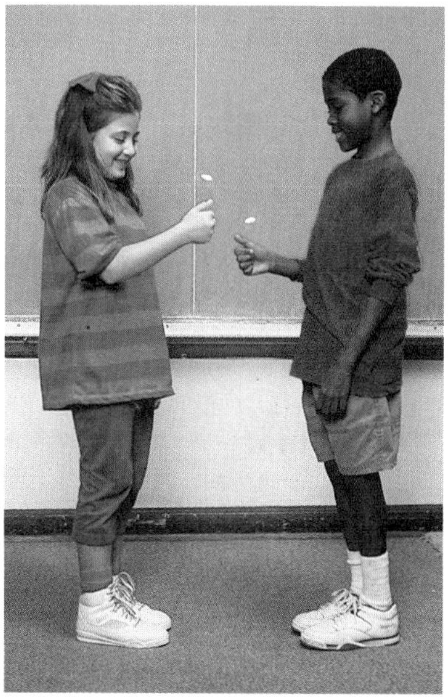

PROBLEM SOLVING

4. Joe and Victoria each flip a coin. If both coins come up heads or both come up tails, Joe wins. If one coin comes up heads and one comes up tails, Victoria wins. Is this a fair game? Why or why not?

MIXED REVIEW

Find the sums.

5. $12 + (25 + 41) = n$ **6.** $36 + (0 + 14) = n$ **7.** $(41 + 12) + 25 = n$

Use mental math and break apart an addend to find the sums.

8. $18 + 6$ **9.** $36 + 9$ **10.** $78 + 7$ **11.** $56 + 8$

Use mental math and compatible numbers to find the sums.

12. $25 + 16 + 15$ **13.** $37 + 43 + 7$ **14.** $38 + 12 + 21$

More Practice, page 515, set C

Probability and Prediction

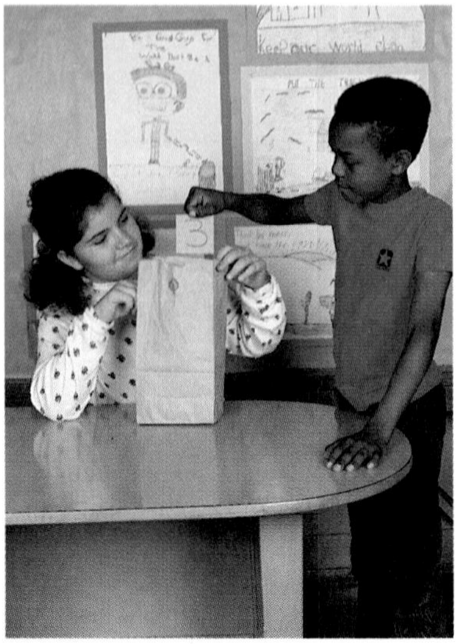

LEARN ABOUT IT

EXPLORE **Play a Game**

Work in groups.

- Cut out five small squares of paper. Write the numbers from 1 to 5 on the squares.
- Think of a lucky number from 1 to 5. Put the squares in a paper bag and shake the bag. How many draws does it take to get your lucky number?

TALK ABOUT IT

1. Suppose you draw one square from the bag without looking. Are you more likely to draw a 3 or a 5? Are the chances the same? Why or why not?
2. Suppose one team gets a point every time someone draws an even number. The other team gets a point every time someone draws an odd number. Do you think this is a fair game? Why or why not?

Probability is the chance that something will or will not happen. If there are more chances of something happening, there is a higher probability.

Suppose the game is played with these pieces of paper. There are more 5s than 3s, so there is a higher probability of drawing a 5 than a 3.

TRY IT OUT

Use paper squares for this experiment.

Predict whether you will get more even numbers or more odd numbers.

Draw a number from a bag 30 times. Return the number after each draw.

What actually happened? Compare this to your prediction.

PRACTICE

1. Predict about how many Bs you will get.

Draw a letter from a bag 50 times. Return the letter after each draw. How did what actually happened compare to your prediction?

2. Predict whether you will get more R's or E's or about the same number of R's and E's.

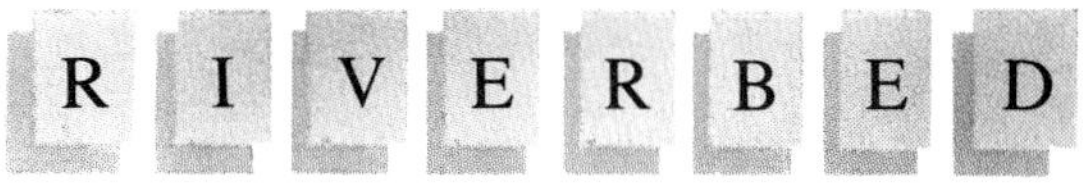

Draw a letter from a bag 30 times. Return the letter after each draw. How did what actually happened compare to your prediction?

3. Do you think there is a high or low probability that it will snow in the Sahara Desert during June?

4. Do you think there is a high or low probability that you will sleep sometime during the next 24 hours?

APPLY

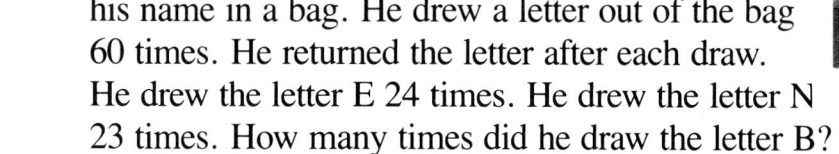

MATH REASONING

5. You flip a penny. Is there a high probability of getting heads or of getting tails? Or are the probabilities the same?

PROBLEM SOLVING

6. **Understand the Question** Ben put the letters of his name in a bag. He drew a letter out of the bag 60 times. He returned the letter after each draw. He drew the letter E 24 times. He drew the letter N 23 times. How many times did he draw the letter B?

▶ MENTAL MATH

You can halve a number by halving its parts. For example, 118 halved = half of 100 + half of 18. So half of 118 is 50 plus 9, or 59. Find half of these numbers.

7. 56 **8.** 84 **9.** 124 **10.** 250 **11.** 450 **12.** 616

More Practice, page 515, set D

Problem Solving
Guess and Check

UNDERSTAND
FIND DATA
PLAN
ESTIMATE
SOLVE
CHECK

LEARN ABOUT IT

For some problems, you cannot just add or subtract to find the answer. You can sometimes use a strategy called **Guess and Check**.

Joe divided 12 computer games into two piles: games he owns and games he has borrowed. He owns 2 more games than he has borrowed. How many are in the pile of borrowed games?

I'll guess he borrowed 4.
That means he owns 6.
My guess is too small.

Guess: Borrowed 4
Check: Owned $4 + 2 = 6$
Total $4 + 6 = 10$

I'll guess again. This time I'll guess a higher number.
It checks! My guess is right.

Guess: Borrowed 5
Check: Owned $5 + 2 = 7$
Total $5 + 7 = 12$

There were 5 games in the pile of borrowed games.

TRY IT OUT

Read the problem and finish the solution.

Jill bought 2 used computer games from Terry. Together the games cost \$24. *Ghost Hunt* cost \$4 more than *Home Run*. How much did *Home Run* cost?

- Which game cost more?
- How much did the games cost all together?

Copy and use this table to help.

	Home Run	Ghost Hunt
Guess Check	\$8 \$8 + \$12 = \$20	\$8 + \$4 = \$12
Guess Check		

PRACTICE

Guess and check to help you solve each problem.

1. Tena and Joan played on the computer for 20 minutes. Tena played 5 minutes longer than Joan. How long did Tena play?

2. Itaro invited his friends to play computer games for his birthday. He invited 10 friends in all. There were 2 more boys than girls. How many girls were there?

MIXED PRACTICE

Solve. Choose a strategy from the list or use other strategies that you know.

Some Strategies
Act It Out
Use Objects
Choose an Operation
Draw a Picture
Make an Organized List
Guess and Check

3. Lisa played the computer game *Adventures of Bo* for 30 minutes. She had 300 seconds to find the way out of the haunted castle. She used up 158 seconds. How many seconds did she have left?

4. It took Jeff 14 weeks to win *Crystal Search* and *Triple Dragon*. It took him 4 weeks longer to win *Triple Dragon* than *Crystal Search*. How long did he take to win *Crystal Search*?

5. Mike has 3 computer games: *Racer*, *Triple Dragon*, and *Baseball Player*. Yesterday he had time to play 2 games. List the choices. How many different choices of 2 games did he have?

6. Use the survey from Super Games Magazine. How many more votes did *Land of Zando* get than *Triple Dragon*?

7. Use the survey from Super Games Magazine below. Estimate the total number of votes for the two most popular games.

Super Games Magazine Survey
"What is your favorite game?"

Game	Votes
Baseball Player	359
Land of Zando	328
Triple Dragon	283
Safari Sisters	228
Crystal Search	192

Data Collection and Analysis
Group Decision Making

UNDERSTAND
FIND DATA
PLAN
ESTIMATE
SOLVE
CHECK

Doing a Survey
Group Skill:
Listen to Others

Look at the finger pads of the members of your group. Most fingerprints are composed of one or more of the three main types.

Look at the thumb pads of your group. Predict whether the thumb prints of both hands are the same type or different types for most people. Conduct an investigation to find out if your prediction was correct.

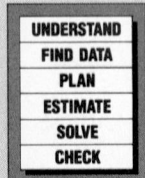

Collecting Data

1. Look at both thumb pads of at least 20 people. Record whether or not the thumb prints are the same type or different. Make a table.

Thumb Prints	
Same	Different
Angelita Gabriel Tony Penny Gina	Jerry Patrick

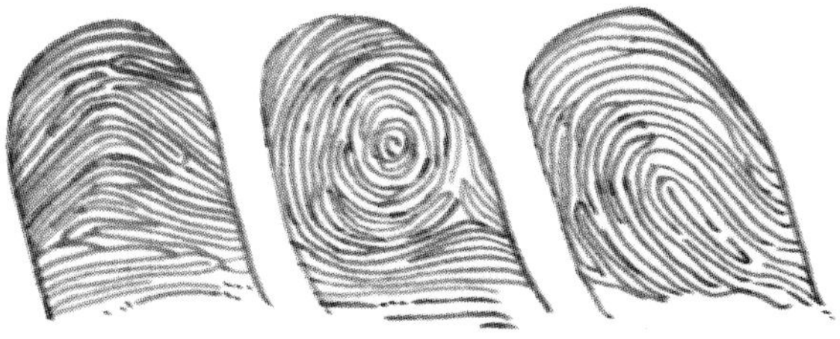

Organizing Data

2. Make a bar graph using the data in your table.

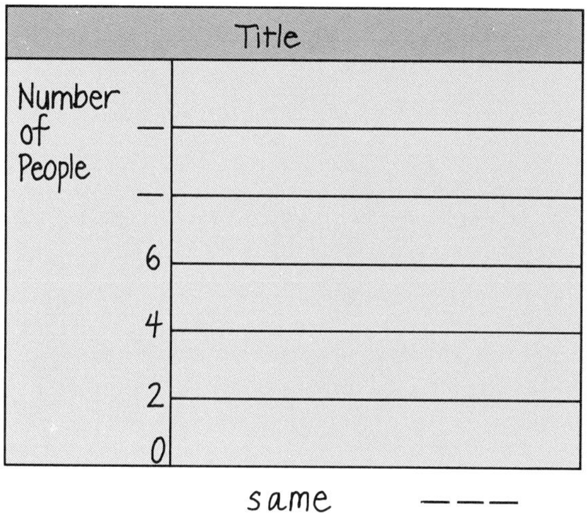

3. Did you label and give a title to your graph?

Presenting Your Analysis

4. Write a summary of your findings. Compare your findings with those of other groups.
5. Write at least two other questions you could ask about fingerprints.
6. Predict what you would discover if you looked at the thumb pads of 20 more people.

WRAP UP

What Are Your Chances?

Each sentence contains an expression associated with probability. Decide whether the expression means that the situation has a high, low, or even chance of happening.

1. There is little chance of snow tonight.

2. Eve and Ruth are likely to tie.

3. All experts favor the Central Division team.

4. There is only a slim chance that she will come.

5. Chances are great that he will get lost.

6. I have a 50-50 chance of being picked.

7. Mia has a clear advantage over Paco.

8. Which racer is better? It's a toss-up!

Sometimes, Always, Never

Which word should go in the blank, sometimes, always, or never? Explain your choices.

9. Pictograph symbols __?__ stand for even numbers.

10. Bar graphs __?__ help you compare data.

11. A bar graph should __?__ use a scale that helps show information clearly.

12. A fair game __?__ gives you a better chance than your opponent to win.

Project

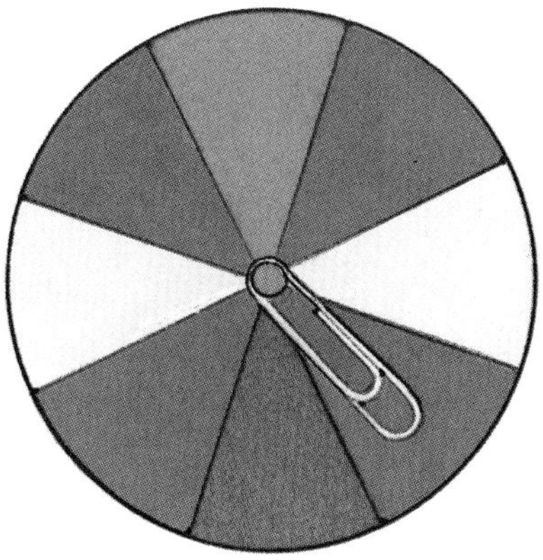

Use a spinner like this one to figure out a probability experiment. Predict what might happen and then do the experiment at least 30 times. Record your results and present them in a graph.

POWER PRACTICE/TEST

Part 1 Understanding

1. Pictographs present data by using __?__.

2. Explain what it means when a game is fair.

3. 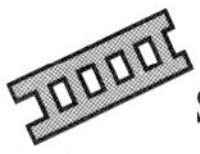 stands for 300 ladders. Draw what a pictograph might show for 150 ladders.

4. Describe a reasonable scale to use on a bar graph of the ages of people in your family.

Part 2 Skills

Use the line graph to answer these questions.

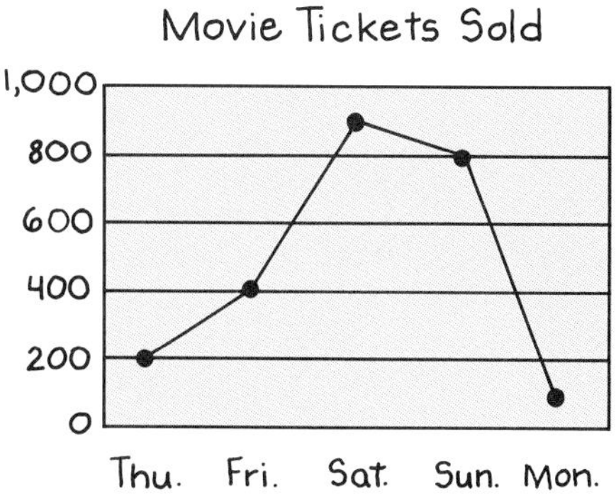

5. About how many tickets were sold on Friday?

6. On what day were over 800 movie tickets sold?

7. Estimate the total number of tickets sold.

Use the bar graph to answer these questions.

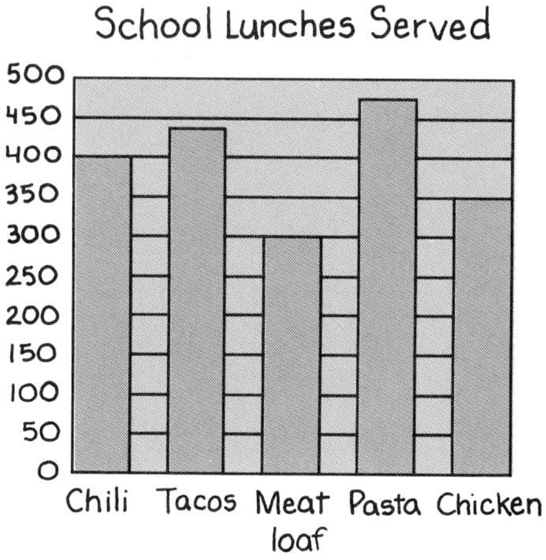

8. What does the scale tell?

9. Which lunch was the most popular?

10. Which food was served in about 350 lunches?

11. How many more taco lunches were served than chili lunches?

12. Which lunch was the least popular?

Part 3 Applications

13. Amy's and Beth's ages total 18 years. Beth is 4 years older than Amy. How old is each girl?

14. **Challenge** Li flips two dimes at once. Is the probability of getting two heads the same as that of getting one head and one tail? Explain.

ENRICHMENT
Listing Possible Outcomes

RATS! is a probability experiment. To do the experiment, you will need two number cubes labeled with the numbers 0 through 5. The letters in RATS stand for <u>R</u>oll, <u>A</u>dd, and <u>T</u>ally the <u>S</u>ums.

<u>R</u>oll

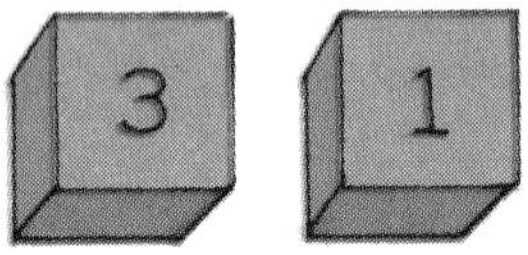

<u>A</u>dd

3 + 1 = 4

<u>T</u>ally the <u>S</u>um

Sum	Tally	Total
0		
1		
2		
3		
4		

Before you do RATS!, answer these questions to learn more about the possible sums you could roll.

1. What is the smallest sum you could roll? the largest?

2. Can you roll a sum in more than one way? Give an example.

3. Copy and complete a table to list all the possible ways to roll the sums. Consider the roll [1] [3] the same roll as the roll [3] [1].

Sum	Ways to Roll the Sum	Total Number of Ways to Roll the Sum
0	[0] [0]	1
1	[1] [0]	1
2	[1] [1] [2] [0]	2

4. When you do RATS!, which three sums do you predict will appear most often? least often? Explain your thinking.

5. Now do RATS! 50 times. Tally your results in a table like the one on this page. Tell how the outcome compares with your predictions.

Cumulative Review

1. Which equation is in a fact family with 7 + 2 = 9?

   A 6 + 3 = 9 B 7 + 3 = 10
   C 9 − 7 = 2 D 9 − 9 = 0

2. Compensate to find the sum of 11 + 8.

   A 19 B 20
   C 18 D 3

3. Which property tells you that 5 + 4 equals 4 + 5?

   A order B grouping
   C zero D compensation

4. In the number 4,307, which digit is in the thousands place?

   A 0 B 4
   C 3 D 7

5. Which number is greater than 802,573?

   A 802,537 B 801,999
   C 802,568 D 802,576

6. Which number is between 6,850 and 7,200?

   A 6,720 B 6,820
   C 7,159 D 7,210

7. What is $45.45 rounded to the nearest dollar?

   A $40.00 B $45.00
   C $50.00 D $46.00

8. What is 58,620 rounded to the nearest thousand?

   A 59,000 B 58,600
   C 58,000 D 60,000

9. Which number has a 5 in the ten millions place?

   A 531,726,894 B 405,394,662
   C 123,456,789 D 952,736,104

10. You pay for a $7.75 tie with $10.00. What is your change?

    A $2.75 B $3.75
    C $3.25 D $2.25

11. 537 − 288

    A 825 B 351
    C 249 D 251

12. 786 + 409

    A 1,185 B 1,195
    C 1,095 D 377

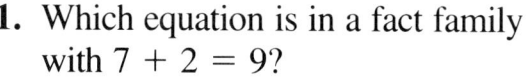

5

MULTIPLICATION CONCEPTS AND BASIC FACTS

THEME: STORYTELLING

MATH AND LANGUAGE ARTS

DATA BANK

Use the Language Arts Data Bank on page 476 to answer the questions.

1 During a drought, Pecos Bill watered his cattle by lassoing the Rio Grande River. In 3 days, how many miles of river did he lasso?

2 Paul Bunyan made rubber boots from the legs of a Gumbaroo. How many rubber legs does a Gumbaroo have? Count by twos to find the answer.

3 How many steel rails did Joe Magarac make when he squeezed with both hands at once?

4 **Use Critical Thinking** Explain how you would find the number of days it took Alfred's Octopus to get untied.

This Cochiti Indian girl listens as her grandfather tells her stories about the drums he makes.

Problem Solving
Understanding Multiplication

UNDERSTAND
FIND DATA
PLAN
ESTIMATE
SOLVE
CHECK

LEARN ABOUT IT Tall tales tell of Paul Bunyan, the greatest logger of them all.

Multiplication is like addition because you put together groups to find the total. When the groups are the same size, you can multiply.

The actions below help you decide when to use multiplication. Show the actions with counters. Complete the equations.

Problem	Action	Operation
Paul Bunyan ate 6 pancakes in one bite. How many pancakes did he eat in 3 bites?	**Put Together Same-Size Groups** 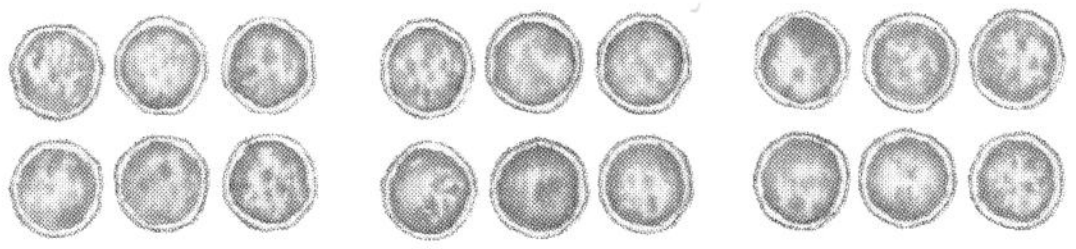	**Multiply** **3 × 6 = ?**
Paul's friend could flip 3 bike tire-size pancakes in the air at one time. Paul could flip 4 times that many. How many could Paul flip?	**Find a Number of Times as Many** 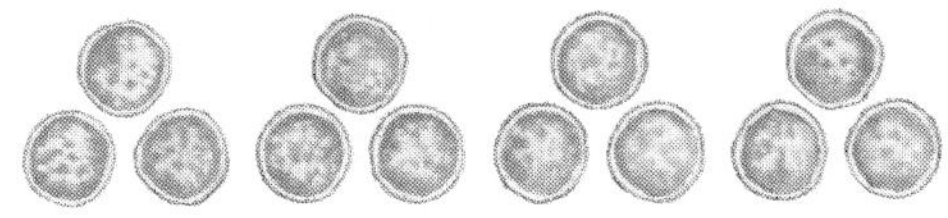	**Multiply** **4 × 3 = ?**

 **= 1 pancake**

TRY IT OUT

Use counters to find the answer. Write an equation.

1. The lumberjacks used a griddle that could cook 9 large pancakes at once. Paul built a griddle that could cook 3 times as many tractor tire-size pancakes at once. How many pancakes could Paul cook at once?

2. Paul had a plate so big that he could pile 6 of his giant pancakes on it. He used 3 plates piled full to start his breakfast. How many pancakes was that?

PRACTICE

Use counters to find the answer. Then write a multiplication equation that gives the same answer.

1. Pecos Bill roped four cattle in each throw. He threw 3 times. How many cattle did he rope?

2. Pecos Bill could herd 6 cows at a time, just by looking hard at them. His dog, Norther, could herd 4 times as many. How many cows could Norther herd?

3. Pecos Bill's friend, Bean Hole, could make 5 pancakes fly into the air, turn over, and return to their exact places. Bill could do this with 3 times as many pancakes. How many pancakes could Bill make flip and return?

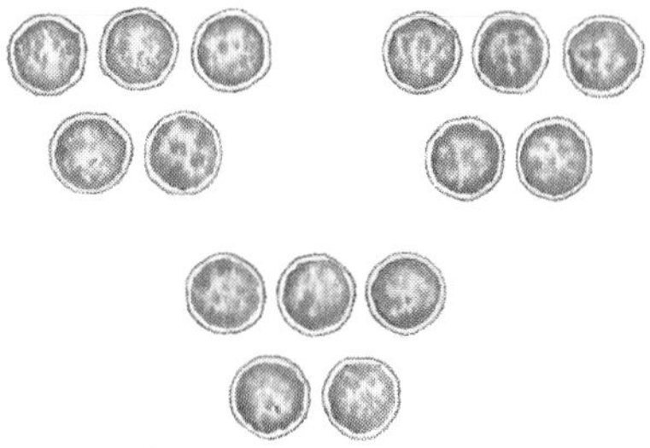

4. To build a fence from El Paso, Texas, to the Pacific Ocean, Bill bit off 4 fence posts at a time with his teeth. To begin, he took 5 bites and went to work. How many posts did he have to work with?

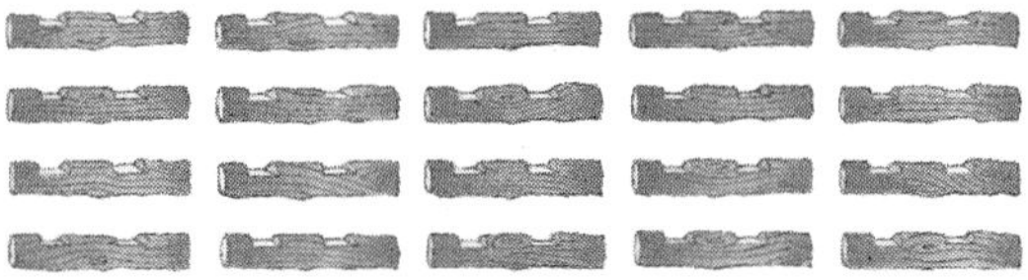

WRITE YOUR OWN PROBLEM

5. Write two story problems that can be solved by multiplying. Use a different action in each.

Multiplication Properties

LEARN ABOUT IT

EXPLORE **Use Counters**

Work in groups. Paul Bunyan could chop down many trees with one stroke of his ax. Here is one way to show how many trees he chopped down. Use counters to show other ways the trees could be laid in equal rows.

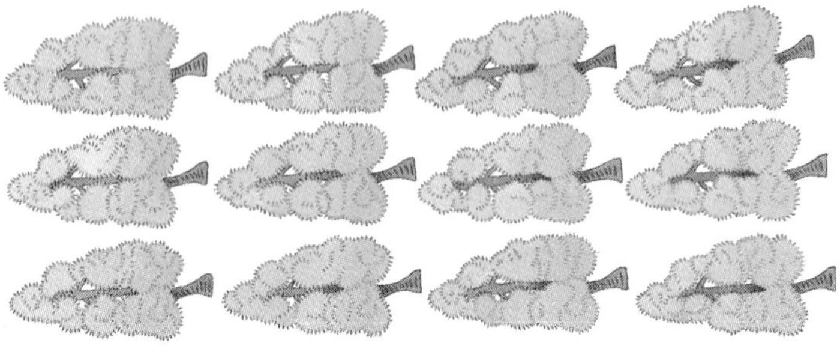

TALK ABOUT IT

1. How many ways did you find? Write a multiplication fact for each way of making equal rows.
2. Do 3×4 and 4×3 give the same product? Tell how you know.

Multiplication Fact

$$\underset{\text{factor}}{3} \times \underset{\text{factor}}{4} = \underset{\text{product}}{12}$$

$$\begin{array}{r} 3 \leftarrow \text{factor} \\ \underline{\times\ 4} \leftarrow \text{factor} \\ 12 \leftarrow \text{product} \end{array}$$

These multiplication properties will help you find certain multiplication facts.

Order Property	One Property	Zero Property
Changing the order of factors does not change the product. **5 × 3 = 3 × 5**	The product of a number and 1 is that number. **8 × 1 = 8**	The product of a number and 0 is 0. **4 × 0 = 0**

TRY IT OUT

Find each missing number.

1. $2 \times 4 = 8$ **2.** $3 \times 2 = 6$ **3.** $5 \times 4 = 20$ **4.** $6 \times 1 =$ |||| **5.** $3 \times 0 =$ ||||

$4 \times 2 =$ |||| $2 \times 3 =$ |||| $4 \times 5 =$ |||| $1 \times 6 =$ |||| $3 \times$ |||| $= 0$

PRACTICE

Find each answer.

1. $2 \times 9 = 18$
$9 \times 2 = n$

2. $6 \times 8 = 48$
$8 \times 6 = n$

3. $7 \times 3 = 21$
$3 \times 7 = n$

4. $4 \times 5 = 20$
$5 \times 4 = n$

5. 0×3 **6.** 6×1 **7.** 1×3 **8.** 0×4 **9.** 1×7 **10.** 8×1 **11.** 0×9

APPLY

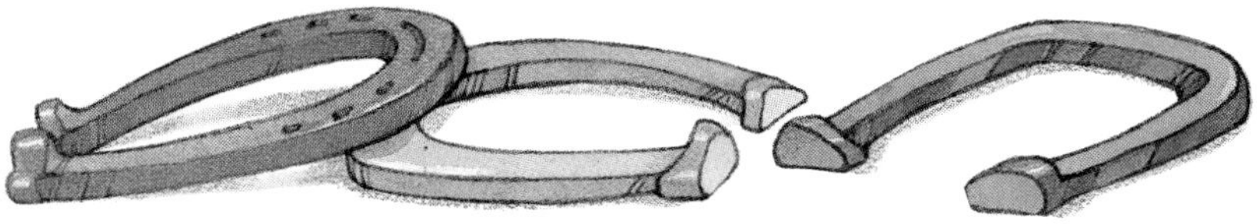

MATH REASONING

12. Write a multiplication fact for the sentence, "Two fives are ten."

Write a multiplication fact for the sentence, "Five twos are ten."

13. Write a multiplication fact for $2 + 2 + 2 = 6$.

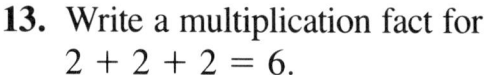

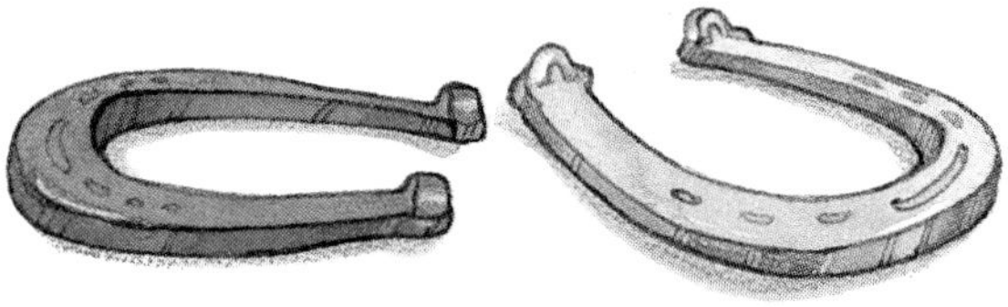

PROBLEM SOLVING

14. Ole could shoe 6 horses at a time. To shoe the hooves of 3 horses, how many horseshoes did he need?

15. DATA BANK **Language Arts Data Bank** How many slabs of bacon did his men use to grease Paul Bunyan's hotcake griddle? See page 476.

MIXED REVIEW

Compare. Write $<$ or $>$ in each ▥.

16. 897,234 ▥ 879,234

17. 33,410 ▥ 33,401

Find each sum.

18. $476 + 378$ **19.** $\$2.95 + 6.50$ **20.** $809 + 793$ **21.** $\$3.89 + 5.67$ **22.** $812 + 702$

Find each difference.

23. $769 - 727$ **24.** $109 - 87$ **25.** $\$9.50 - 7.75$ **26.** $412 - 398$ **27.** $981 - 195$

2 and 5 As Factors

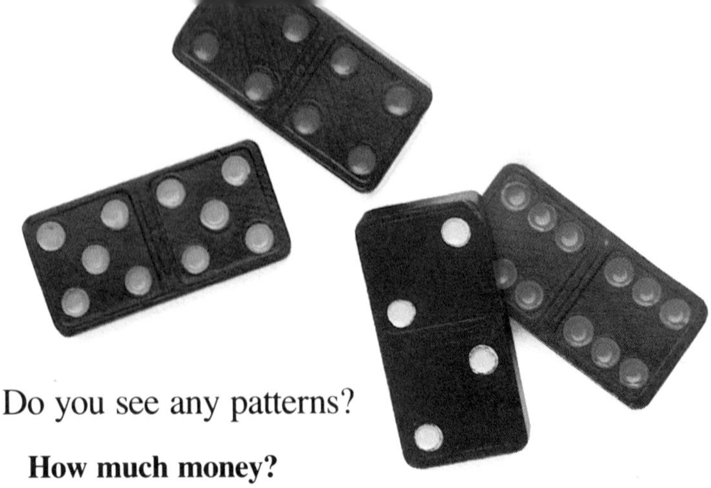

LEARN ABOUT IT

EXPLORE **Discover a Pattern**

Think about the pictures and equations. Do you see any patterns?

How many?

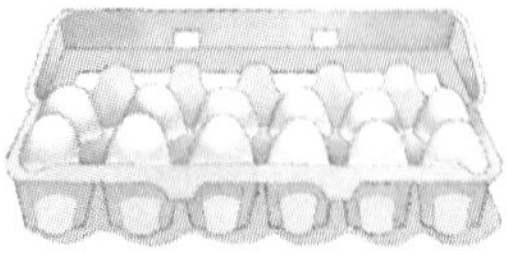

2 sixes
$2 \times 6 = n$

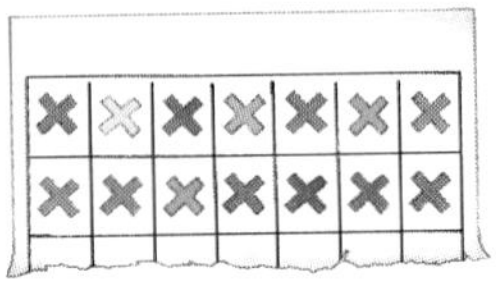

2 sevens
$2 \times 7 = n$

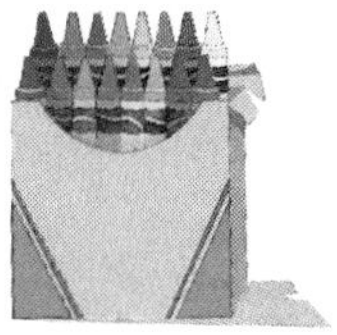

2 eights
$2 \times 8 = n$

2 nines
$2 \times 9 = n$

How much money?

$2 \times 5 = n$

$3 \times 5 = n$

$4 \times 5 = n$

TALK ABOUT IT

1. Make an ordered list for the facts of 2. What patterns do you see?
2. Explain how using addition doubles can help you multiply when 2 is a factor.
3. Make an ordered list for the facts of 5. What patterns do you see?
4. Explain how using nickel counting patterns can help you multiply when 5 is a factor.

- To find a 2 fact, you can think about addition doubles.
- To find a 5 fact, you can think about counting nickels.

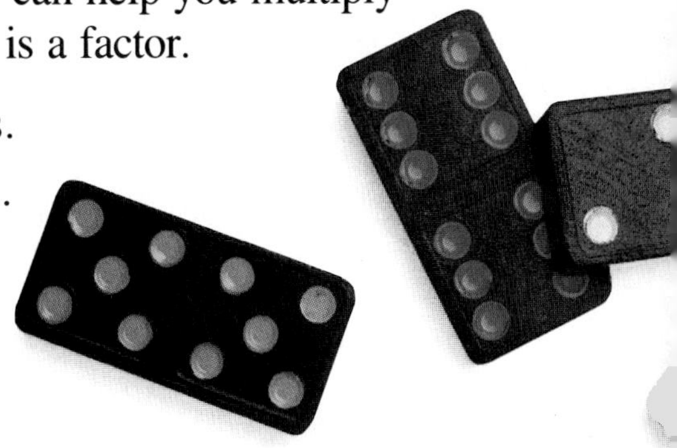

TRY IT OUT

Find each product.

1. $2 \times 5 = n$ **2.** $8 \times 5 = n$ **3.** $2 \times 8 = n$ **4.** $7 \times 5 = n$

5. 5×4 **6.** 5×6 **7.** 2×7 **8.** 3×2 **9.** 6×5

PRACTICE

Find each product.

1. $\begin{array}{r} 2 \\ \times 5 \\ \hline \end{array}$	**2.** $\begin{array}{r} 5 \\ \times 8 \\ \hline \end{array}$	**3.** $\begin{array}{r} 2 \\ \times 3 \\ \hline \end{array}$	**4.** $\begin{array}{r} 9 \\ \times 5 \\ \hline \end{array}$	**5.** $\begin{array}{r} 7 \\ \times 2 \\ \hline \end{array}$	**6.** $\begin{array}{r} 5 \\ \times 5 \\ \hline \end{array}$
7. $\begin{array}{r} 8 \\ \times 2 \\ \hline \end{array}$	**8.** $\begin{array}{r} 5 \\ \times 3 \\ \hline \end{array}$	**9.** $\begin{array}{r} 2 \\ \times 2 \\ \hline \end{array}$	**10.** $\begin{array}{r} 7 \\ \times 5 \\ \hline \end{array}$	**11.** $\begin{array}{r} 2 \\ \times 4 \\ \hline \end{array}$	**12.** $\begin{array}{r} 6 \\ \times 5 \\ \hline \end{array}$

13. $4 \times 5 = n$ **14.** $6 \times 2 = n$ **15.** $5 \times 8 = n$ **16.** $2 \times 7 = n$

17. $5 \times 2 = n$ **18.** $5 \times 9 = n$ **19.** $2 \times 9 = n$ **20.** $6 \times 5 = n$

Find the missing numbers.

21. $\square \times 5 = 45$ **22.** $2 \times \square = 18$ **23.** $8 \times \square = 40$

APPLY

MATH REASONING

24. If $2 + 2 + 2 = 6$ goes with $3 \times 2 = 6$, what goes with $4 \times 5 = 20$?

25. When you multiply an even number by 5, what is always true about the last digit in the product?

PROBLEM SOLVING

26. Unfinished Problem Tickets for the magic show cost $5. Juan bought 3 tickets and Emilia bought 6. Write a question to finish the problem.

27. Janey put fortune cookies in packages of 5. How many cookies did she need to fill 8 packages?

CALCULATOR

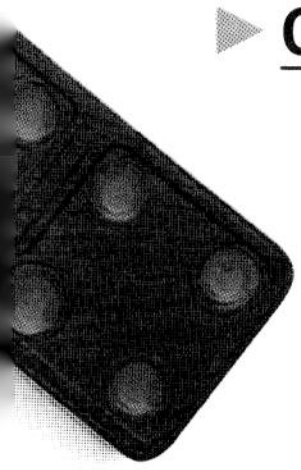

28. Give the numbers that go in the $\square$ and $\triangle$. Use your calculator and make 5 more cards like these with larger factors. What do you discover?

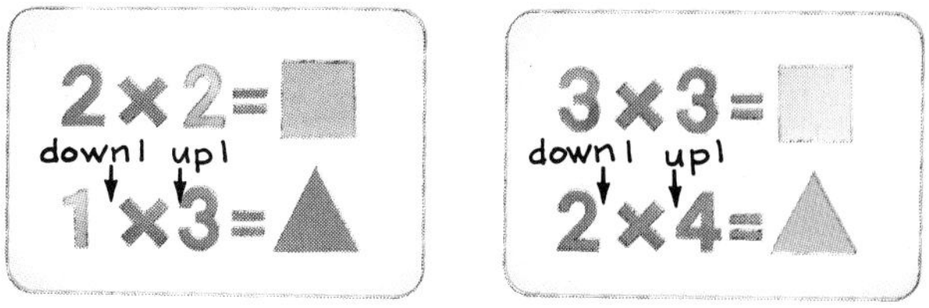

More Practice, page 502, set F

9 As a Factor

LEARN ABOUT IT

EXPLORE **Discover a Pattern**

Tim wrote some 9 facts and 10 products on his paper. He said he used patterns to find the 9 facts. See what patterns you can find.

Some 10 products	Some 9 facts
$10 \times 2 = 20$	$9 \times 2 = 18$
$10 \times 3 = 30$	$9 \times 3 = 27$
$10 \times 4 = 40$	$9 \times 4 = 36$
$10 \times 5 = 50$	$9 \times 5 = 45$

TALK ABOUT IT

1. Look at the products for the 9 facts. What do you discover about the sum of the digits?
2. For 9×2, the product starts with a 1. For 9×3, the product starts with a 2. Tell about this pattern.
3. Look at a 10 product. Then look at a matching 9 fact. How can you use the 10 products to find the 9 facts?

Here are some ways to find a product when 9 is a factor.

Use a Pattern

$9 \times 5 = 45$ (−1 from 5 gives 4; Sum = 9)

$9 \times 7 = 63$ (−1 from 7 gives 6; Sum = 9)

Use 10 Products

$\underline{10} \times 5 = 50$ **10 fives - 5** → $\underline{9} \times 5$ **is** 45

$\underline{10} \times 7 = 70$ **10 sevens - 7** → $\underline{9} \times 7$ **is** 63

TRY IT OUT

1. $2 \times 9 = n$ **2.** $4 \times 9 = n$ **3.** $7 \times 9 = n$ **4.** $9 \times 8 = n$

5. $9 \times 0 = n$ **6.** $9 \times 1 = n$ **7.** $9 \times 3 = n$ **8.** $0 \times 9 = n$

9. $\begin{array}{r} 3 \\ \times 9 \\ \hline \end{array}$ **10.** $\begin{array}{r} 6 \\ \times 9 \\ \hline \end{array}$ **11.** $\begin{array}{r} 9 \\ \times 5 \\ \hline \end{array}$ **12.** $\begin{array}{r} 9 \\ \times 9 \\ \hline \end{array}$ **13.** $\begin{array}{r} 5 \\ \times 9 \\ \hline \end{array}$

PRACTICE

Multiply.

1. 9×5 2. 3×9 3. 9×6 4. 2×5 5. 0×9 6. 4×9 7. 0×5

8. 9×9 9. 9×7 10. 1×9 11. 5×2 12. 5×5 13. 1×9 14. 9×8

15. $4 \times 9 = a$ 16. $9 \times 7 = a$ 17. $5 \times 9 = a$ 18. $1 \times 9 = a$

Find the missing numbers.

19. $9 \times \square = 36$ 20. $9 \times \square = 72$ 21. $\square \times 9 = 27$ 22. $\square \times 9 = 9$

23. Find the product of 9 times 3. 24. Multiply 10 by 9.

APPLY

MATH REASONING Give the number just before and just after each product.

25. 7×9 26. 6×5 27. 2×9 28. 8×9 29. 9×9

30. Give the next six numbers in this pattern. 0 9 18 27,

PROBLEM SOLVING

31. **Missing Data** What data is needed? Tina earned $9 each week helping her father. How much did she earn?

32. Cindy sold 9 boxes of flower seeds that had 6 packs of seeds in each. How many packs did she sell?

USING CRITICAL THINKING Logical Reasoning

33. Can you find the secret number? Here are some clues.

- It is odd and it is a 5 fact.
- It is not more than 30.
- If you had half that many eggs, then you would still have more than a dozen.

3 and 4 As Factors

LEARN ABOUT IT

EXPLORE Study the Pictures

You can break apart a factor and use the 2 facts to multiply by 3 or 4.

3 × 8

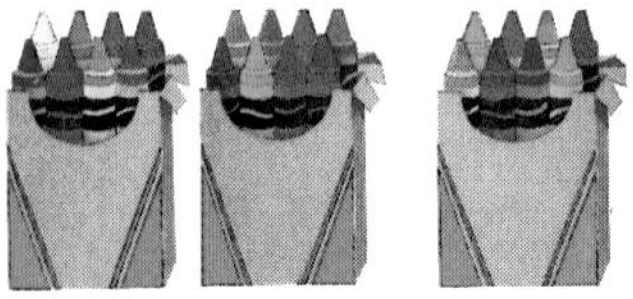

2 × 8 and 8 more

4 × 8

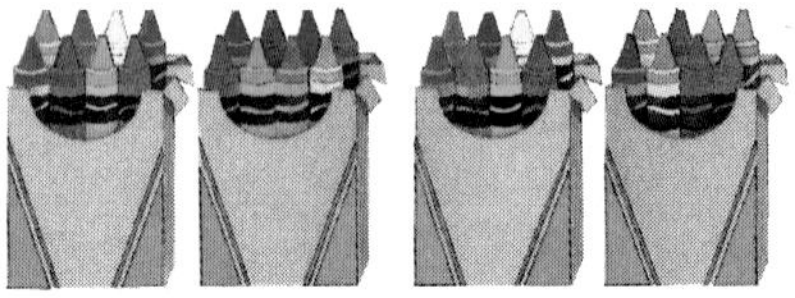

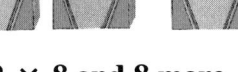

2 × 8 plus 2 × 8

TALK ABOUT IT

1. How do the pictures show that 3 × 8 is 2 × 8 and 8 more?
2. How do the pictures show that 4 × 8 is 2 × 8 and 2 × 8?
3. How would you use the same ideas to find 3 × 6 and 4 × 6?
4. Lenny said, "To multiply by 4, I just double a double!" What did he mean?

To multiply a number by 3, add the number to its double.
To multiply a number by 4, double it, then double again.

(2 × 7 plus 7 more)

3 × 7 = 21

Double the 7 to get 14.
Add 7 more to get 21.

(2 × 5 plus **2** × 5)

4 × 5 = 20

Double the 5 to get 10.
Double the 10 to get 20.

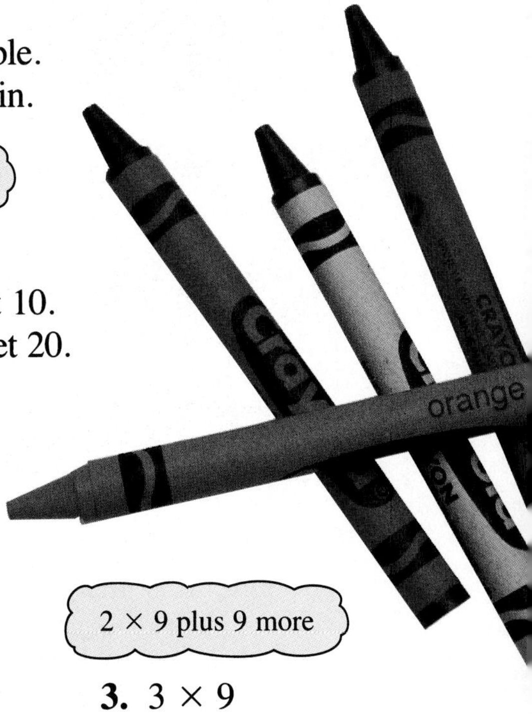

TRY IT OUT

Find the products mentally.

(2 × 5 plus 5 more)

1. 3 × 5

(2 × 7 plus 2 × 7)

2. 4 × 7

(2 × 9 plus 9 more)

3. 3 × 9

4. 3 × 7 = |||| **5.** 4 × 3 = |||| **6.** 4 × 8 = |||| **7.** 3 × 9 = ||||

PRACTICE

Multiply.

1. 3×6 2. 4×7 3. 9×3 4. 5×4 5. 4×8 6. 3×7 7. 8×3

8. 6×5 9. 9×8 10. 6×7 11. 9×9 12. 7×8 13. 6×6 14. 6×8

15. 3×7 **16.** 4×6 **17.** 2×0 **18.** 3×1 **19.** 5×8 **20.** 7×3

21. 4×5 **22.** 4×3 **23.** 3×8 **24.** 1×4 **25.** 9×3 **26.** 7×9

APPLY

MATH REASONING What number goes in the box to show a multiplication fact?

27. $\square \times 3 = 24$ **28.** $\square \times 4 = 32$ **29.** $3 \times \square = 21$

30. 3×8 is a name for the number 24. Write three other names for 24.

PROBLEM SOLVING

31. Data Hunt Make a table of items that come in packages, showing how many are in each package. For each item, how many are in 3 packages? in 4 packages?

MENTAL MATH

To do mental math, it helps if you can remember one number while computing with other numbers. To practice this, do these without pencil and paper. Which fact is greater?

32. 4×3 or 2×7 **33.** 3×5 or 4×4 **34.** 2×9 or 4×6

35. 4×7 or 9×3 **36.** 6×5 or 4×8 **37.** 7×3 or 5×4

Exploring Algebra

LEARN ABOUT IT

In these equations, each shape holds a place for just one number. Find the number that goes in each shape.

$$\square \times \square = 9$$

$$\triangle + \square = 10$$

TALK ABOUT IT

1. Look at the first equation. How many basic facts have a product of 9?
2. In the first equation, will the factors be the same or will they be different? Why is this important?
3. If you know what goes in $\square$, how can you find what goes in $\triangle$? Tell why.

TRY IT OUT

Find the number that goes in each shape.

1. $\square + \triangle = 7$

$\triangle \times \triangle = 4$

2. $\triangle + 8 = 8$

$\square - \triangle = 6$

3. $\square \times \triangle = 27$

$\square - \triangle = 6$

4. $\square \times \triangle = 30$

$\square \times \square = 36$

5. $\triangle + \triangle = \bigcirc + 3$

$\bigcirc + \square = 8$

$\square \times \triangle = \triangle$

6. $\square + \triangle = \bigcirc$

$5 \times \triangle = 5$

$\square + \square = 6$

7. Make up a problem like the one on this page. Exchange with a classmate and find the missing numbers.

Power Practice/Quiz

Draw a picture to show that the key action is **put together same-size groups**.

1. May planted 3 rows of tulips. She put 5 tulips in each row. How many tulips did she plant?

2. The pet store has 2 bowls of goldfish. There are 6 goldfish in each bowl. How many goldfish are in the bowls?

3. Liz has 9 nickels. How much money does she have?

Find the products.

4. 4×1 **5.** 2×5 **6.** 5×9 **7.** 0×2 **8.** 3×5 **9.** 1×3 **10.** 9×2

11. 9×1 **12.** 3×2 **13.** 4×9 **14.** 2×8 **15.** 1×5 **16.** 5×0 **17.** 8×9

18. 2×3 **19.** 4×5 **20.** 0×9 **21.** 2×2 **22.** 7×9 **23.** 4×2 **24.** 0×3

25. 5×6 **26.** 7×5 **27.** 1×0 **28.** 9×6 **29.** 6×2

30. 9×9 **31.** 8×5 **32.** 9×3 **33.** 2×7 **34.** 5×5

PROBLEM SOLVING

35. The art room has 9 tables. 4 students sit at each table. How many students can sit at the tables?

36. A quarter is worth 5 nickels. Ray has 7 quarters. How many nickels can Ray get for his 7 quarters?

37. June has 3 nickels, 2 dimes, and 2 quarters. How much money does she have?

38. Ben has 3 pairs of tennis shoes and 1 pair of dress shoes. How many pairs of shoes does he have? How many shoes is that?

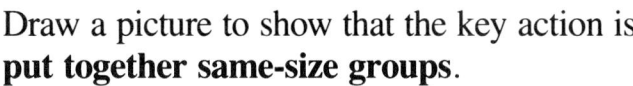

Problem Solving
Understanding the Question

UNDERSTAND
FIND DATA
PLAN
ESTIMATE
SOLVE
CHECK

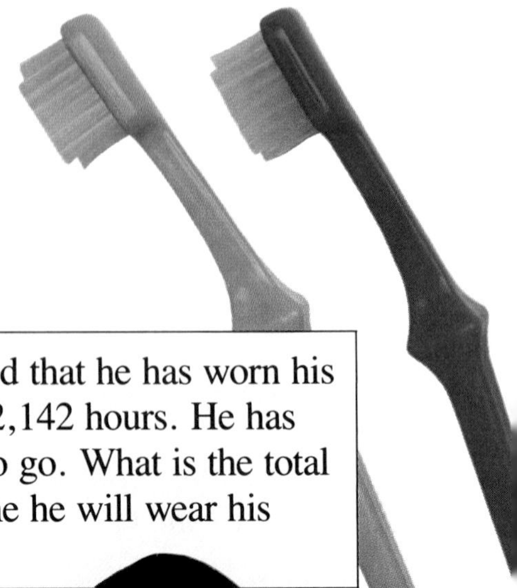

LEARN ABOUT IT

One of the first things you must do when you solve a problem is to understand the question. Sometimes it helps to put the question in your own words or to ask it in a different way.

Matt calculated that he has worn his headgear for 2,142 hours. He has 5,523 hours to go. What is the total amount of time he will wear his headgear?

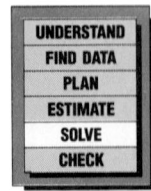

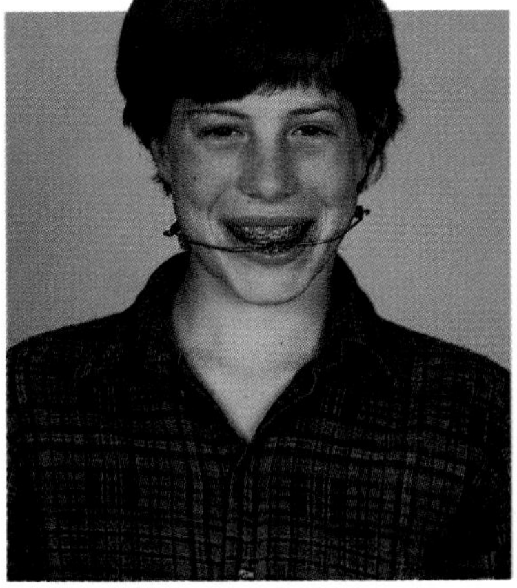

First I'll read the question.

What is the total amount of time he will wear his headgear?

Then I'll ask the question in a different way.

How many hours must Matt wear his headgear in all?

TRY IT OUT

Read each problem. Then decide which question asks the same thing.

1. An adult human has 32 teeth. A whale shark can have 4,000 teeth. What is the difference in the number of teeth?
a. How many more teeth does a whale shark have?
b. How many teeth do humans and whale sharks have all together?

2. Dr. Li is a children's dentist. She takes care of 15 patients a day. What is the total number of patients she sees in 5 days?
a. How many patients does she see each day?
b. In 5 days, how many patients does she see all together?

Write each question in a different way. Then solve.

3. Dr. Verne, the orthodontist, saw 365 patients in August. He saw 287 patients in September. How many fewer patients did he see in September?

4. Dr. Mudd displays pictures of some of his patients. There are 9 rows of pictures with 9 pictures in each row. What is the total number of pictures?

MIXED PRACTICE

Write each question in a different way. Then solve.

Dr. Fisher's Dental Office Number of Patients		
	Adults	Children
1989	2,177	1,334
1990	2,189	1,399
1991	2,161	1,442

1. How many more adults than children did Dr. Fisher see in 1990?
2. How many children did Dr. Fisher see all together from 1989 to 1991?
3. Did Dr. Fisher see fewer than 6,000 adults from 1989 to 1991? Tell how you know.
4. For the first 3 nights, Charlie wore his headgear for 6 hours each night. For the next 4 nights, he wore it for 8 hours each night. How long did he wear it in all?
5. For her prize box, Dr. Rose bought 5 packages of rings with 8 rings in each package. She also bought 36 stickers. How many rings did she buy?
6. José waited in the dentist's waiting room 20 minutes. His checkup took 45 minutes. What is the total amount of time José was at the dentist's office?

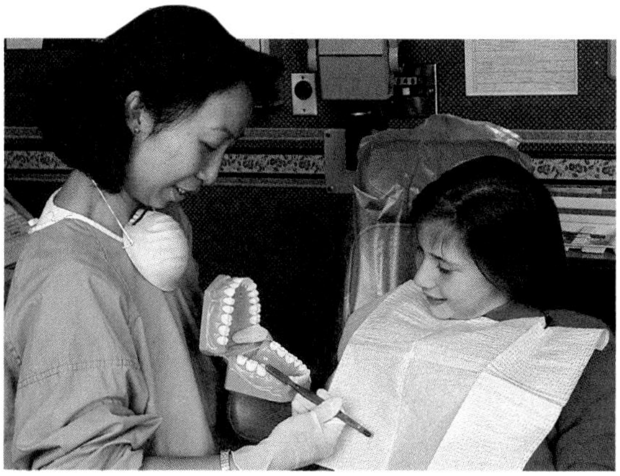

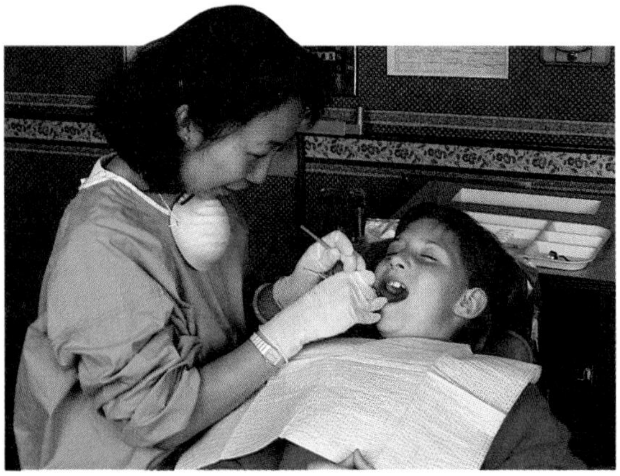

7. Mrs. Osawa has 8 times as many teeth as baby Keisi. Keisi has 4 teeth. How many teeth does Mrs. Osawa have?
8. **Think About Your Solution**
   A wire on Judy's braces came loose. She could see Dr. Brown, Dr. Pan, or Dr. Bernstein. She could get an appointment during school or after school. How many choices does she have?

   a. Show the steps you took to solve the problem.

   b. Write your answer in a complete sentence.

   c. Tell the strategy or strategies you used to solve the problem.

More Practice, page 516, set B

Mental Math
More Breaking Apart Numbers

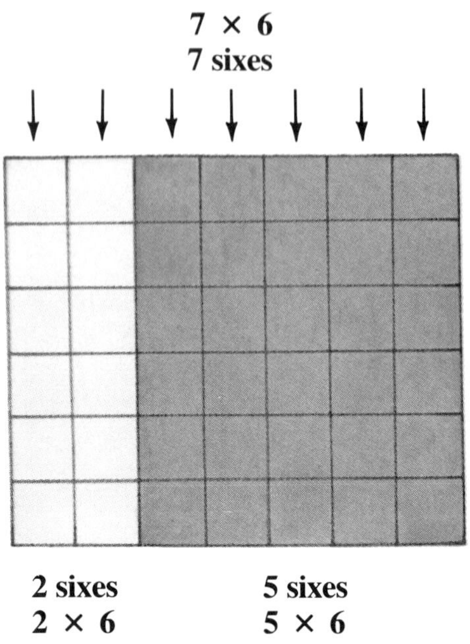

LEARN ABOUT IT

EXPLORE **Use Graph Paper**

Here is one way to break apart the factor 7 in 7 × 6. Color graph paper to show as many other ways to do this as you can.

TALK ABOUT IT

1. How can you use this idea to find 7 × 6?
2. Complete the following in 3 different ways.
   7 sixes = __?__ sixes and __?__ sixes.
3. Show how each way can be used to find 7 × 6.

Multiplication-Addition Property
When you multiply, you can break apart a factor.

You can find a product by breaking apart a factor, multiplying twice and then adding.

Break apart the factor.	**Multiply twice, then add.**
	5 × 6 plus 2 × 6
Break 7 into 5 and 2.	7 × 6 is 30 plus 12, or 42.

TRY IT OUT

Find each product.

3 × 6 plus 3 × 6	5 × 8 plus 2 × 8	5 × 6 plus 3 × 6
1. 6 × 6 = *n*	**2.** 7 × 8 = *n*	**3.** 8 × 6 = *n*

Find each product. Break apart the red factor.

4. 8 × 4 **5.** 9 × 2 **6.** 4 × 9 **7.** 7 × 7 **8.** 6 × 4

PRACTICE

Find each product.

3×6 plus 2×6	6×5 plus 1×5	5×6 plus 4×6
1. $5 \times 6 = n$	**2.** $7 \times 5 = n$	**3.** $9 \times 6 = n$

Find the products. Break apart the red factor.

4. 5×7 **5.** 6×3 **6.** 4×5 **7.** 6×8 **8.** 8×8 **9.** 7×4

10. 5×8 **11.** 4×7 **12.** 8×9 **13.** 3×9 **14.** 5×9 **15.** 6×4

APPLY

MATH REASONING Give the missing number. Then give the underlined product.

16. 5×6 is 30, so $\underline{6 \times 6}$ is 30 + ___?___

17. 5×7 is 35, so $\underline{6 \times 7}$ is 35 + ___?___

PROBLEM SOLVING

18. Each member of a group made up 8 short tall tales. There were 4 members in the group. How many tall tales were there?

19. A class Tall Tales Booklet had 9 pages. Each page except the first had 6 tall tales on it. The first page had 3 tall tales. How many tall tales were in the booklet?

MENTAL MATH

Use mental math. First find the larger doubles in Exercises 21–24. Then use your skill in finding larger doubles to find the products in Exercises 25 and 26.

20. 12 + 12 **21.** 14 + 14 **22.** 15 + 15 **23.** 16 + 16 **24.** 18 + 18

25. $\mathbf{14} \times 3 = (\mathbf{7} \times 3)$ plus $(\mathbf{7} \times 3) =$ ___?___

26. $\mathbf{16} \times 5 = (\mathbf{8} \times 5)$ plus $(\mathbf{8} \times 5) =$ ___?___

More Practice, page 503, set C

The Last Six Facts

LEARN ABOUT IT

EXPLORE **Use Graph Paper**

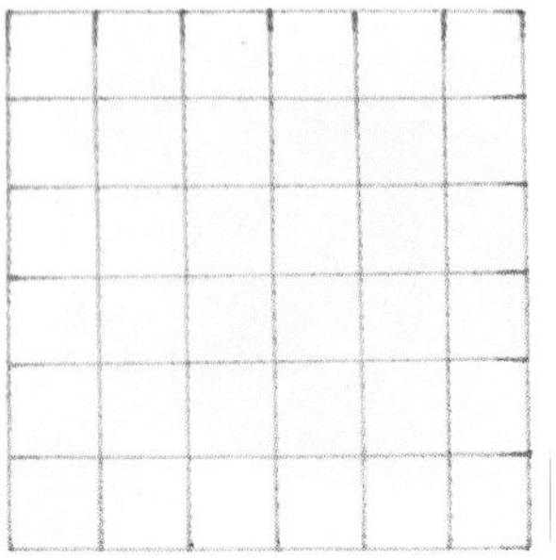

This square piece of graph paper shows a square fact. It has 6 rows of 6 small squares, or 36 squares in all.

Draw squares on graph paper to show as many other square facts as you can. Write a number sentence for each fact. Circle those facts not presented in earlier lessons.

TALK ABOUT IT

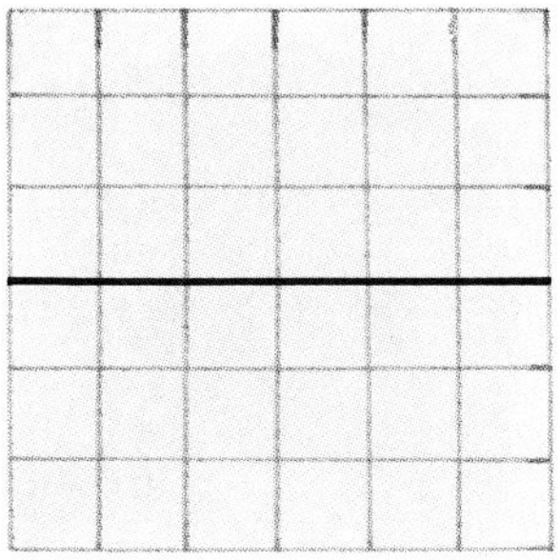

1. How many square facts did you find? How many of these are new facts?
2. How could you use the graph paper square to help find 6 × 6?
3. Explain how this square shows that 6 × 6 is 3 × 6 plus 3 × 6.

Here is one way to break apart factors to find the last six facts. Use mental math and the facts you already know.

6 facts

6 × 6 3 × 6 plus 3 × 6
6 × 6 is a square fact.

6 × 7 3 × 7 plus 3 × 7

6 × 8 3 × 8 plus 3 × 8

7 fact

7 × 7 5 × 7 plus 2 × 7
7 × 7 is a square fact.

8 facts

8 × 7 4 × 7 plus 4 × 7

8 × 8 4 × 8 plus 4 × 8
8 × 8 is a square fact.

TRY IT OUT

Find each product.

1. 8 × 7 **2.** 7 × 7 **3.** 6 × 6 **4.** 8 × 8 **5.** 7 × 8 **6.** 6 × 8

PRACTICE

Find each product.

1. $\begin{array}{r} 8 \\ \times 6 \\ \hline \end{array}$ 2. $\begin{array}{r} 6 \\ \times 7 \\ \hline \end{array}$ 3. $\begin{array}{r} 7 \\ \times 7 \\ \hline \end{array}$ 4. $\begin{array}{r} 8 \\ \times 7 \\ \hline \end{array}$ 5. $\begin{array}{r} 9 \\ \times 7 \\ \hline \end{array}$ 6. $\begin{array}{r} 6 \\ \times 6 \\ \hline \end{array}$ 7. $\begin{array}{r} 8 \\ \times 8 \\ \hline \end{array}$

8. $\begin{array}{r} 6 \\ \times 9 \\ \hline \end{array}$ 9. $\begin{array}{r} 8 \\ \times 9 \\ \hline \end{array}$ 10. $\begin{array}{r} 4 \\ \times 8 \\ \hline \end{array}$ 11. $\begin{array}{r} 7 \\ \times 6 \\ \hline \end{array}$ 12. $\begin{array}{r} 9 \\ \times 9 \\ \hline \end{array}$ 13. $\begin{array}{r} 7 \\ \times 8 \\ \hline \end{array}$ 14. $\begin{array}{r} 3 \\ \times 7 \\ \hline \end{array}$

15. 6×7 **16.** 8×9 **17.** 7×8 **18.** 6×9 **19.** 9×7 **20.** 4×4

21. Find the product of 6 and 8.

22. What times 6 is equal to 54?

APPLY

MATH REASONING Find each product.

23. I am a square fact. One of my factors is 8. What is my product?

24. One of my factors is 6. My other factor is 2 more than the first. What is my product?

PROBLEM SOLVING

25. Stormalong was 4 fathoms tall. He fought the sea monster Guznod who was 10 fathoms long. A fathom is 6 feet. How many feet longer than Stormalong's height was Guznod's length?

26. **Language Arts Data Bank** If Joe Magarac squeezed 7 times, how many steel rails did he make? See page 476.

DATA BANK

MIXED REVIEW

Give the missing number.

27. $(15 + 25) + 36 = (36 + ▒) + 15$

28. $9 + (43 + 37) = (37 + 43) + ▒$

Use mental math.

29. $40 + 63 + 60$ **30.** $50 + 89 + 50$ **31.** $80 + 58 + 20$

Multiples

LEARN ABOUT IT

EXPLORE Use Graph Paper

You can cut graph paper strips to help you learn about some special sets of numbers.

These graph paper strips show the results when you multiply 0, 1, 2, 3, and 4 by 2. The table shows the products when you multiply by 2.

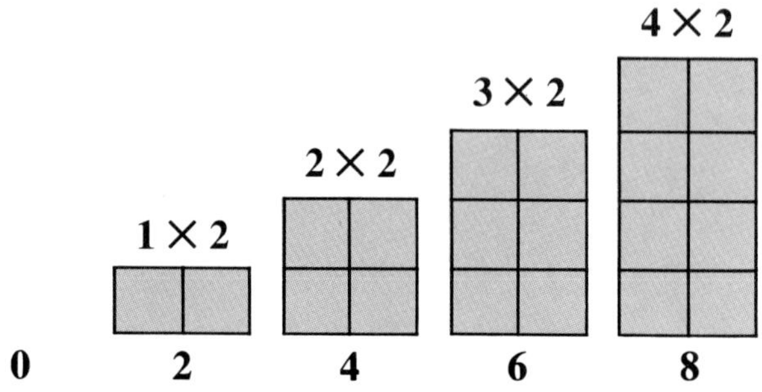

The **multiples** of a number are the products when that number is one of the factors.

Multiples of 2	×	0	1	2	3	4
	2	0	2	4	6	8

Multiples of 2 are called **even numbers.** All other whole numbers are called **odd numbers.**

TALK ABOUT IT

1. Name 5 odd numbers.
2. You can skip count by twos to get multiples of 2. How would you count to get multiples of 3?
3. What would graph paper strips that showed multiples of 5 look like?

TRY IT OUT

1. Cut graph paper strips to show multiples of 4.
2. Make a table to show multiples of 3.

PRACTICE

Copy and complete these multiple tables. Look at your tables. What patterns do you see?

1.

Multiples of 4	×	0	1	2	3	4	5	6	7	8	9	10
	4	0	4	8								

2.

Multiples of 6	×	0	1	2	3	4	5	6	7	8	9	10
	6	0	6	12								

3.

Multiples of 9	×	0	1	2	3	4	5	6	7	8	9	10
	9											

4. Write the first 10 even numbers.

5. Write the first 10 odd numbers.

APPLY

MATH REASONING

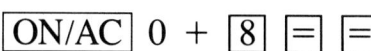

6. Solve this riddle. "Of the numbers with two digits, I'm the smallest with this fate. I'm a multiple of 6 and a multiple of 8. Who am I?"

PROBLEM SOLVING

7. Paul Bunyon's blacksmith made shoes for Babe the Blue Ox only in groups of 4. Paul thought between 40 and 50 shoes would last Babe for about a week, so he asked a friend to buy a week's supply. How many do you think he bought?

▶ USE A CALCULATOR

These keystrokes will give some multiples of 8:

Use the constant function on your calculator to find multiples of the numbers given below. Record the first 10 multiples of each.

[ON/AC] 0 + [8] [=] [=]

8. 8 **9.** 9 **10.** 12 **11.** 13 **12.** 15

More Practice, page 503, set E

Problem Solving
Make a Table

UNDERSTAND
FIND DATA
PLAN
ESTIMATE
SOLVE
CHECK

LEARN ABOUT IT

To solve some problems, you may need to make a table using the data in the problem. This strategy is called **Make a Table**.

Jim is making a batch of bubble mixture for making giant bubbles. He uses water, 2 cups of dishwashing soap, and 6 tablespoons of glycerine. How many cups of soap does he need if he uses 24 tablespoons of glycerine?

First I'll make a table and write what I know.

cups of soap	2
tablespoons of glycerine	6

Now I'll fill in the table to find the solution to the problem.

Add 2 more cups. +2 +2 +2

cups of soap	2	4	6	8
tablespoons of glycerine	6	12	18	24

Add 6 more tablespoons. +6 +6 +6

Jim will need 8 cups of soap.

TRY IT OUT

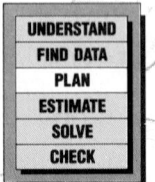

Read this problem and finish the solution.

At the Pinewood Bubble Festival, there were 2 bubble demonstrations every 10 minutes. How many shows were there in 60 minutes?

- How many demonstrations are given at a time?
- How long does it take to give 2 demonstrations?
- Copy and complete the table to solve the problem.

demonstrations	2	4	6			
minutes	10	20	30			

PRACTICE

Copy and complete each table to help you solve these problems.

1. On a dry day, the bubble recipe calls for 10 cups of water and 3 tablespoons of glycerine. How many tablespoons of glycerine will Janelle need if she uses 50 cups of water?

water	10	20			
glycerine	3	6			

2. Five tickets to the Bubble Festival cost $4. How much would it cost to buy tickets for a class of 25 students?

tickets	5	10	15		
price	$4	8	12		

MIXED PRACTICE

Choose a strategy from the list or use other strategies you know to solve these problems.

Some Strategies
Act It Out
Use Objects
Choose an Operation
Draw a Picture
Make an Organized List
Guess and Check
Make a Table

3. Jimbo made 3 bubble chains with 7 bubbles in each chain. Then he made 5 bubble chains with 9 bubbles each. How many bubbles in all were in both chains?

4. To make bubbles with her bubble wand, Juanita needs dishwashing soap. The 3 different brands it comes in are Glow, Sparkle, and Lemon Clear. The 2 sizes are large and small. How many different choices does Juanita have?

5. About how many people attended these three demonstrations?

Demonstration	Number of Spectators
Walking Through Bubbles	682
Barehanded Bubble Making	478
Building Bubble Castles	394

6. A Bubble Pack contains 2 bubble blowers and 8 ounces of bubbles. Janell bought enough packs to get 32 ounces of bubbles. How many blowers did she get?

blowers	2	4
bubbles	8	16

More Practice, page 516, set C

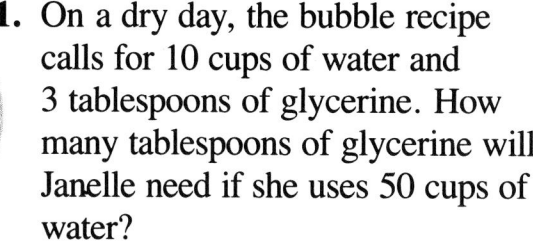

Applied Problem Solving
Group Decision Making

UNDERSTAND
FIND DATA
PLAN
ESTIMATE
SOLVE
CHECK

Group Skill:
Encourage and Respect Others

At the school Round-Up, your class is going to run the ball-tossing booth. First decide how many prizes you will need all together. Then decide how many of each type of prize you want to buy.

Facts to Consider

1. You can expect to award from 15 to 25 prizes each hour.
2. The Round-Up will last about 6 hours.
3. You have only $140 to spend.
4. There are only 9 packages of each type of prize at Max's Variety Store.

Max's Variety Store		
Prize	**Number in a Package**	**Cost per Package**
Skeletons	8 per package	$7
Rings	6 per package	$4
Whistles	5 per package	$2
Small spiders	5 per package	$4
Small dinosaurs	6 per package	$4
Finger monsters	7 per package	$4
Tiny race cars	4 per package	$2
Bouncy balls	3 per package	$4
Silly glasses	3 per package	$2

Some Questions to Answer

1. How many prizes will you need to buy if you award 15 prizes each hour?
   Hint:
   $15 + 15 + 15 + 15 + 15 + 15 = n$
2. How many prizes will you need to buy if you award 25 prizes each hour?
3. Suppose you bought 5 packages of rings at Max's Variety Store. How many prizes would you have? How much would they cost?
4. Suppose you bought 8 packages of silly glasses at Max's Variety Store. How many prizes would you have? How much would they cost?
5. How would a table or list help you to keep track of the number of prizes you will buy and the amount they will cost?

What Is Your Decision?

Show the prizes you have decided to buy.
Show how much money you will spend on each type of prize.
Show how much the prizes will cost all together.

Wrap Up

Operation Classification

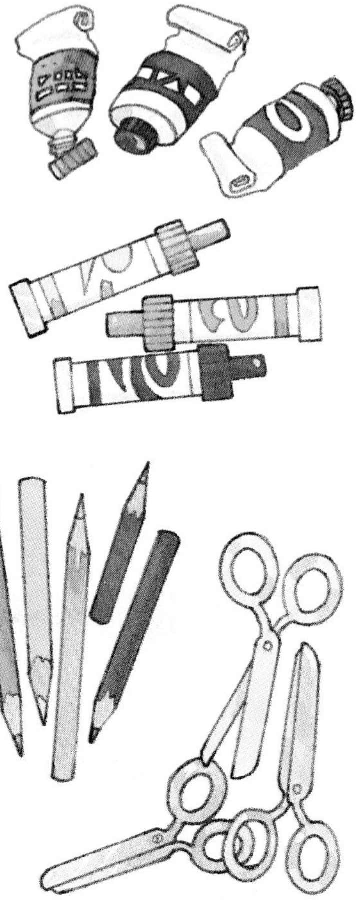

Decide whether you might add, subtract, or multiply to solve a problem about each situation. Some situations may suggest more than one operation. Justify your choices.

1. The class has 5 sets of markers with 8 in a set.
2. Gene took 28 photos. An album holds 50.
3. The art room has 452 tubes of paint, but 26 have dried out.
4. Tina counted 9 spiders, each with 8 legs.
5. Ky is 13. His sister is 6 years younger.

Sometimes, Always, Never

Which word should go in the blank, sometimes, always, or never? Explain your choices.

6. Multiples of 3 are __?__ odd numbers.
7. The product of two odd factors is __?__ odd.
8. The product of two even factors is __?__ odd.

Project

9. Look at the pattern in row A and in row B and complete this number chart.

Row A	2	3	4	5					
Row B	4	6	8	10					

10. What is the relationship between each pair of numbers in a column?
11. Using the rule you found, add 5 more columns to your chart.

POWER PRACTICE/TEST

Part 1 Understanding

Write a multiplication equation that is an example of each property.

1. order property **2.** one property **3.** zero property

Match each word with an example.

4. factors a. 3, 6, 9, 12

5. multiplication equation b. 6×5

6. multiples c. $5 \times 5 = 25$

7. Complete the sentence.

To break apart 7×6, you might use the sets of factors |||| and ||||.

Part 2 Skills

Find the products.

8. $\begin{array}{r} 2 \\ \times 8 \\ \hline \end{array}$ **9.** $\begin{array}{r} 4 \\ \times 9 \\ \hline \end{array}$ **10.** $\begin{array}{r} 6 \\ \times 8 \\ \hline \end{array}$ **11.** $\begin{array}{r} 7 \\ \times 3 \\ \hline \end{array}$ **12.** $\begin{array}{r} 9 \\ \times 4 \\ \hline \end{array}$

13. 6×0 **14.** 4×8 **15.** 7×7 **16.** 5×8 **17.** 8×1

Find a number to fill the squares and another number to fill the triangles.

18. $\square \times \triangle = 18$ **19.** $\triangle - \square = 7$

Part 3 Applications

20. A fruit salad recipe calls for 5 apples and 2 oranges. If Ray wants to use 35 apples, how many oranges does he need?

21. Write the question another way, then solve. On Monday, Amir's Restaurant served 357 lunches and 464 dinners. What is the total number of meals served?

ENRICHMENT
Multiplication Table Patterns

You know that a multiplication table helps you find the product of a pair of factors. You can also explore the rows, columns, and diagonals of the table to discover some interesting number patterns and relationships.

x	0	1	2	3	4	5	6	7	8	9
0	0	0	0	0	0	0	0	0	0	0
1	0	1	2	3	4	5	6	7	8	9
2	0	2	4	6	8	10	12	14	16	18
3	0	3	6	9	12	15	18	21	24	27
4	0	4	8	12	16	20	24	28	32	36
5	0	5	10	15	20	25	30	35	40	45
6	0	6	12	18	24	30	36	42	48	54
7	0	7	14	21	28	35	42	49	56	63
8	0	8	16	24	32	40	48	56	64	72
9	0	9	18	27	36	45	54	63	72	81

1. How could the table help you count by 2s? by 3s? by 5s?

2. Which rows of the table have all numbers even? Does any row have all numbers odd?

3. Use the table to help you complete these "equations."
   a. even × even = ||||
   b. even × odd = ||||
   c. odd × odd = ||||

4. Compare the 3 row with the 3 column. What do you discover? Is this true for other rows and columns?

5. The blue line connects two identical products. How many other pairs of identical non-zero products like this can you find? Explain why this happens.

6. Look at the non-zero products, such as 36, in row 9. Add the digits in each product, in this case 3 + 6. What do you discover?

7. Is what you discovered in exercise 6 true for other rows? What patterns, if any, do you see in other rows?

8. Add any product in the 1 row to the product below it in the 2 row. What do you discover about the sum? Try this with other rows. Does it always work this way?

Cumulative Review

1. Which numbers can fill the box and the circle to make the equation true?
   6 + □ = 3 + ○

   A $\boxed{6}$, ③ **B** $\boxed{4}$, ④
   C $\boxed{5}$, ⑧ **D** $\boxed{2}$, ③

2. A, E, M, and T spell a word. T comes before E. M comes after A. The vowels are together. What is the word?

   A mate **B** team
   C meat **D** tame

3. Use front-end estimation and adjust to estimate \$4.49 + \$8.44.

   A \$13 **B** \$12
   C \$14 **D** \$11

4. Use compensation to find the difference of 497 and 98.

   A 400 **B** 398
   C 399 **D** 401

5. 593 + 688

   A 1,281 **B** 1,271
   C 1,181 **D** 1,211

6. 442 + 1,296 + 375 + 803

   A 2,816 **B** 2,916
   C 3,016 **D** 17,496

7. About 10,000 fans liked which sport?

   A tennis **B** basketball
   C hockey **D** wrestling

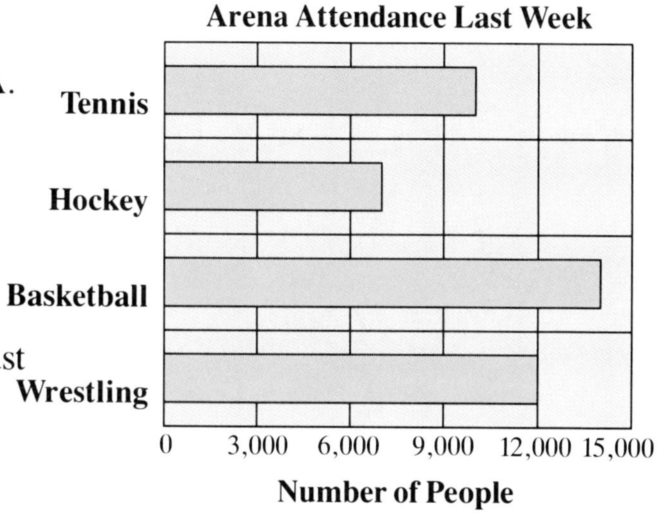

8.  stands for 25 trees. If 250 trees are planted, how many tree symbols would a pictograph show?

   A 5 **B** 10
   C 50 **D** 25

9. A grab bag has 7 books, 2 puzzles, 2 tapes, and 1 art set. Which has the highest probability of being picked?

   A book **B** puzzle
   C tape **D** art set

6

MULTIPLYING BY 1-DIGIT FACTORS

THEME: NATURE

MATH AND SCIENCE

DATA BANK

Use the Science Data Bank on page 469 to answer the questions.

1 Which bird on the list lays the same number of eggs in 1 year as the lark does?

2 A turkey's heart beats 28 more times per minute than an ostrich's heart does. How many times per minute does a turkey's heart beat?

3 Which of the birds lays the greatest number of eggs in 1 year? Which bird lays the least number of eggs in 1 year?

4 **Use Critical Thinking** What do you notice about the number of wingbeats per second when you compare the sizes of the hummingbirds?

A hummingbird's special wings make it able to hang still in the air and also to fly backward.

Mental Math
Special Products

LEARN ABOUT IT

EXPLORE Think About the Situation

Dana bought a package of 300 stickers for each of 4 friends. The packages had sheets with 100 stickers on a sheet.

4 × 3 hundred stickers are |||| hundred stickers?
4 × 300 = ||||

TALK ABOUT IT

1. How many sticker sheets did Dana buy for each friend?
2. How many sticker sheets did Dana buy in all? How many stickers is this? Explain how you decided.

You can break apart numbers and use basic multiplication facts to find products like 4 × 80, 6 × 500, and 8 × 3,000.

To Find	Think	
4 × 80	4 × 8 tens	320
6 × 500	6 × 5 hundreds	3,000
8 × 3,000	8 × 3 thousands	24,000

You can use this mental math skill and a method called **clustering** to help you estimate sums of certain addends.

The addends cluster around 500. The sum is about 3 × 500, or 1,500.

496 + 508 + 487

TRY IT OUT

Use mental math to find the products.

1. 6 × 100 **2.** 7 × 30 **3.** 8 × 4,000 **4.** 4 × 500

5. Use clustering to estimate the sum 687 + 699 + 716 + 708.

PRACTICE

Copy each equation and give the numbers for the □ and the △.

1. Since 8 × 7 = □, then 8 × 70 = △.
2. Since 3 × 8 = □, then 3 × 80 = △.
3. Since 6 × 9 = □, then 6 × 900 = △.

Estimate the sums.

4. 397 + 411 + 385 + 403
5. 191 + 175 + 230 + 213
6. 921 + 897 + 884

Find the products. Write only the answers.

7. 4 × 600
8. 7 × 700
9. 9 × 6,000
10. 800 × 3
11. Multiply 6 and 400.
12. Find the product of 9 and 2,000.

APPLY

MATH REASONING

13. The equation 3 × 40 has the same product as 4 × 30, 2 × 60, and 6 × 20. Give 3 equations that have the same product as 9 × 20.

PROBLEM SOLVING

14. **Extra Data** Solve the problem, then tell what data was not needed. Eve bought 4 sheets with 50 stickers on a sheet for 60¢. Fran bought 3 sheets of 80 stickers for 70¢. How many more stickers did Fran get?

15. Stan wanted to buy enough packages containing 4 sheets with 50 stickers each to have 1,000 stickers. How many packages must he buy?

USING CRITICAL THINKING Support Your Conclusion

16. Without using pencil and paper or a calculator, convince someone that a goose flying at a top speed of 63 miles per hour cannot fly 190 miles in 3 hours.

More Practice, page 503, set F

Estimating Products

LEARN ABOUT IT

EXPLORE **Make a Decision** Julie's nature club wanted to buy bird feeders to put at the windows in a senior citizens' home. Each feeder costs \$19. The children had earned \$150. Did they have enough money to buy 7 feeders?

TALK ABOUT IT

1. Should the children use \$10 or \$20 when estimating the cost of each bird feeder? Why?
2. Will their estimate be more or less than the actual cost?

You can round numbers when you want to estimate a product to decide if it is close to a reference point.

Is \$150 enough to buy 7 bird feeders that cost \$19?

Round to the nearest 10.	\$19 × 7	⟶	\$20 × 7
Estimate.			\$140

The reference point is \$150. The estimate, \$140, is over the actual cost. So \$150 is more than enough to buy the 7 bird feeders.

Other Examples

A Nearest Ten

3 × 45 (3 × 50 = 150)

About 150

B Nearest Hundred

4 × 678 (4 × 700 = 2,800)

About 2,800

C Nearest Dollar

7 × \$5.89 (7 × \$6)

About \$42

TRY IT OUT

Round to the nearest ten, hundred, or dollar. Then estimate the product.

1. 8 × 23 **2.** 9 × 855 **3.** 5 × \$6.98 **4.** 7 × \$3.19

PRACTICE

Round to the highest place or the nearest dollar. Then estimate the product.

1. 5×68 **2.** 9×74 **3.** $\$57 \times 4$ **4.** 266×7

5. 4×824 **6.** 341×3 **7.** $\$4.70 \times 2$ **8.** 6×36

Use rounding to estimate each product. Then decide whether the actual product is over or under the reference point 800.

9. 199×4 **10.** 8×87 **11.** 390×2 **12.** 186×5

APPLY

MATH REASONING

13. The product of 8 and one of these numbers is 2,456. Use estimation to find the number. Explain how you chose your answer.

PROBLEM SOLVING

14. One day in late March, Mr. Abbott counted 27 Rocky Mountain blue birds on a fence in his pasture. At this rate, how many would he see in 4 days?

15. A kids' nature club in Florida earned $2,200 for a bald eagle exhibit by recycling aluminum cans. If they collected 3,789 cans in April, how many fewer was this than the 5,068 cans they collected in May?

MIXED REVIEW

Estimate the sum or difference.

16. $89 + 41$ **17.** $686 - 475$ **18.** $\$23.19 + 11.87$ **19.** $\$49.89 - 37.50$ **20.** $6{,}791 + 3{,}211$

Add.

21. $527 + 8{,}436 + 59$ **22.** $\$20.32 + 1.68 + .19$ **23.** $678 + 45 + 123$ **24.** $12{,}765 + 476 + 6{,}928$ **25.** $32{,}123 + 87 + 51$

Mental Math
Multiply and Then Add

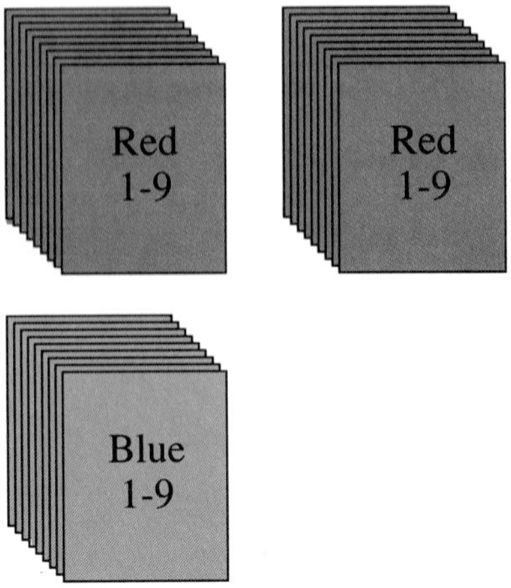

LEARN ABOUT IT

EXPLORE Use Number Cards
Work in groups. Play this game with 3 decks of cards, 2 red and 1 blue. Each deck is numbered 1 to 9. Pick a card from each deck. Play by the rules shown. Take turns and use mental math.

Rules
- **Multiply red × red.**
- **Add the blue.**

TALK ABOUT IT

1. Kathy picked these cards. What was her score?
2. What is the largest possible score for this game? the smallest possible score?

Here is how you can find a score.

Find 9 × 7.
Then add 3.
9 × 7 = 63
63 + 3 = 66

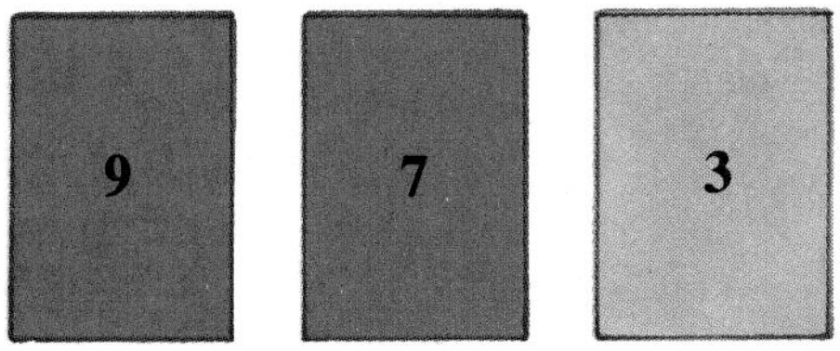

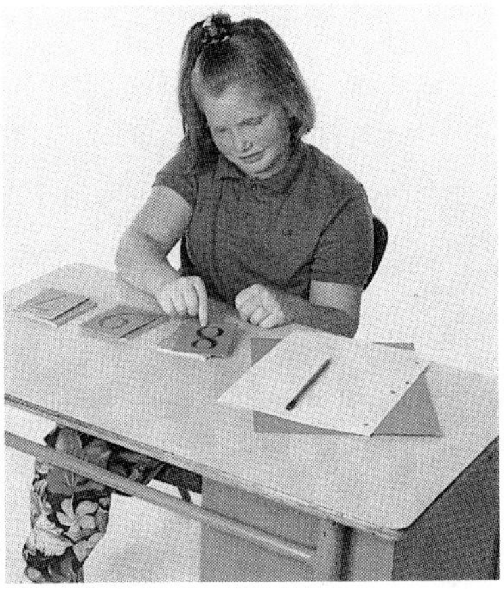

TRY IT OUT

Give the score for each turn below.

1.

2.
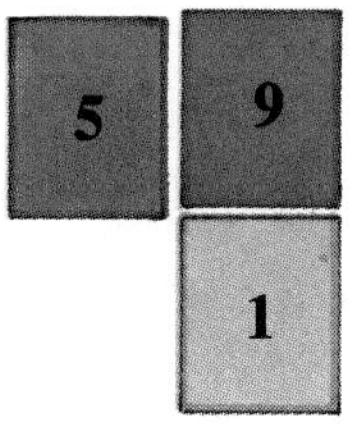

3.
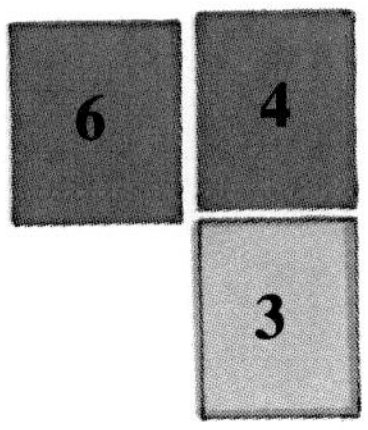

4.
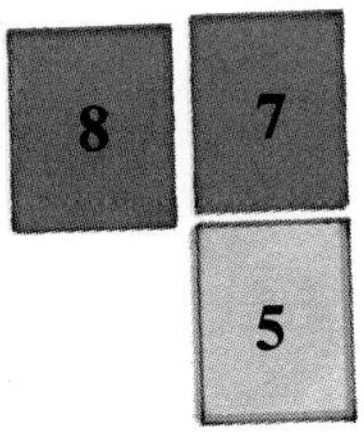

PRACTICE

Multiply the first 2 numbers. Then add the third. Write only the answers.

1. 7 × 3 4 **2.** 5 × 6 5 **3.** 4 × 8 7 **4.** 7 × 6 3

5. 8 × 6 3 **6.** 3 × 9 8 **7.** 8 × 8 6 **8.** 4 × 5 5

Multiply the red number by each of the first 2 numbers. Then add the products.

9. 20 3 2 **10.** 12 6 2 **11.** 9 1 8 **12.** 10 4 3

13. 60 2 4 **14.** 40 2 3 **15.** 30 4 5 **16.** 50 3 3

APPLY

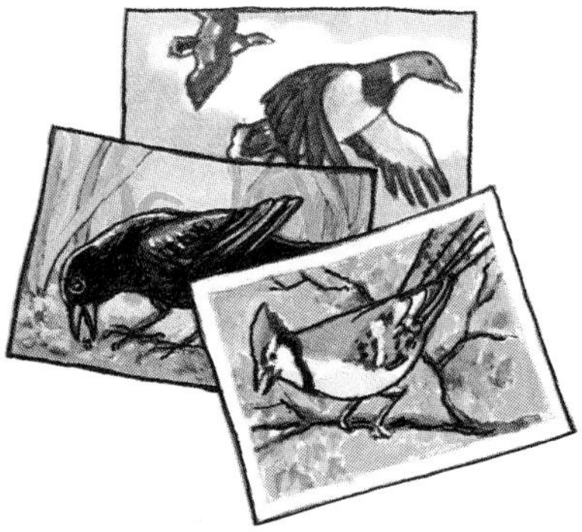

MATH REASONING Give the number for each ||||.

17. 3 × 4 + |||| = 13 **18.** 5 × 6 + |||| = 34

19. 8 × 5 + |||| = 45 **20.** 7 × 9 + |||| = 65

PROBLEM SOLVING

21. Beth collects bird photos. Every time she gets a new photo she writes 3 facts to describe the bird. When she has 9 photos, how many facts will she have written?

22. Manuel bought six 30¢ stamps and three 5¢ stamps. How much did he pay?

CALCULATOR

Think about the 2 numbers on the top cards. Use mental math to multiply each by the blue number card. Then use the calculator to find the sum of the products.

23.

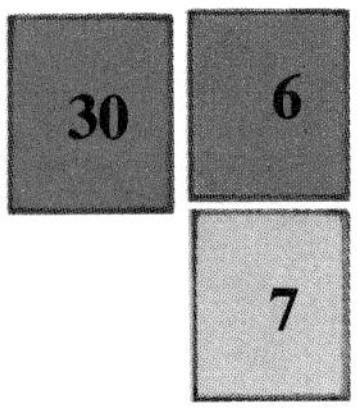

24.

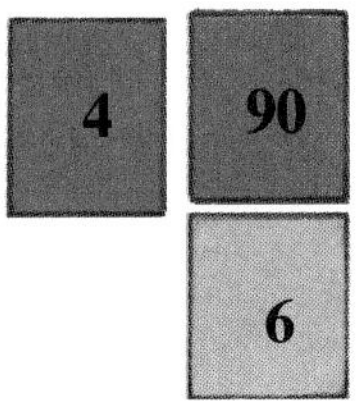

25.

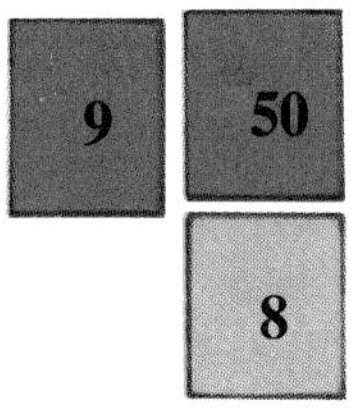

26.

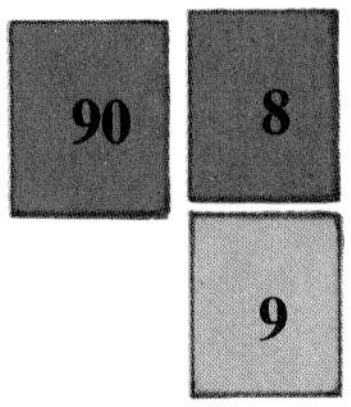

Multiplying Whole Numbers
Making the Connection

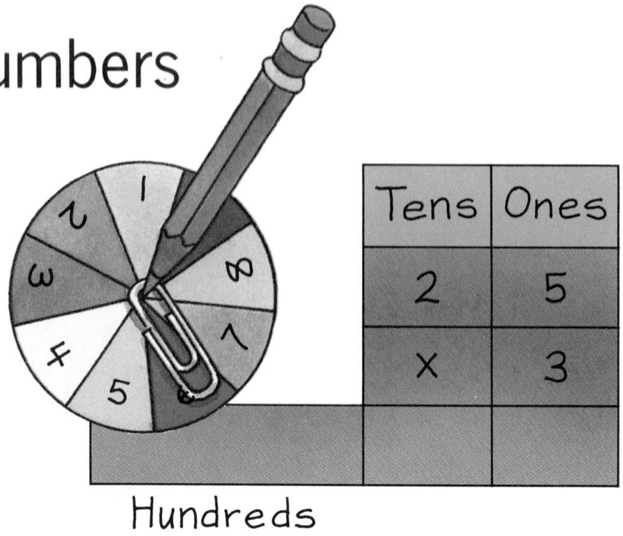

LEARN ABOUT IT

EXPLORE Use a Place Value Model
Work in groups. Use a spinner with the digits 1–9.

- Spin 2 times. The first spin gives the number of tens. The second gives the number of ones. Make a table like the one shown and record this number in the top row.
- Spin again. If you land on an even number, write 2 beside the × sign in the table. Then lay out 2 piles of blocks, each with the number of tens and ones in the top number. If you land on an odd number, write 3 and lay out 3 piles of blocks.
- Push the piles together and make all possible trades. When you get 10 or more of one type, trade for a larger block. Write the number for the resulting pile in the bottom row of the table.
- Do this several times. Make a separate table each time.

TALK ABOUT IT

1. Look at one of your tables and tell what trades, if any, you made when you pushed the piles together.
2. Can you show a situation in which you must make two trades to find the total? one trade? no trades?

You have pushed same-size piles of blocks together, traded, and figured out how many in all. Now you will see a way to record what you have done. This process can help you find products such as 47 × 3.

What You Do | **What You Record**

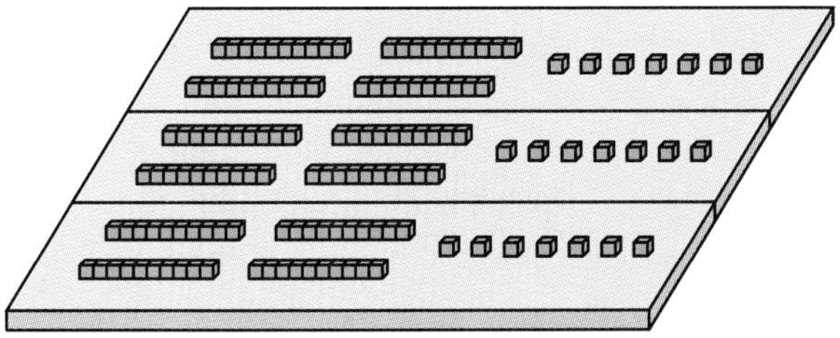

$$\begin{array}{r} 47 \\ \times\ 3 \\ \hline \end{array}$$

1. Are there enough ones on the table to trade?

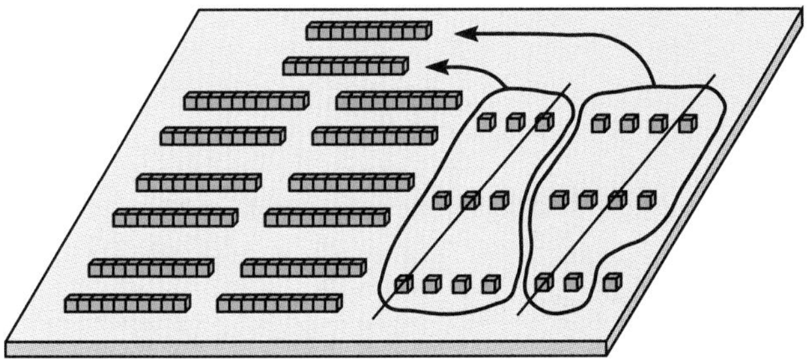

$$\begin{array}{r} {\scriptstyle 2} \\ 47 \\ \times\ \ 3 \\ \hline 1 \end{array}$$

2. How many ones are left after the trades? How many tens?

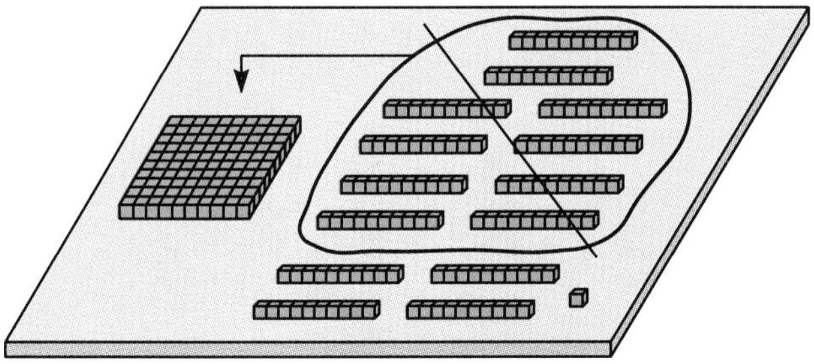

$$\begin{array}{r} {\scriptstyle 2} \\ 47 \\ \times\ \ 3 \\ \hline 141 \end{array}$$

3. Are there enough tens for a trade?

4. What is the product 3 × 47?

TRY IT OUT

Use blocks to find these products. Trade when you can. Record what you did.

1. 42 × 3 **2.** 17 × 4 **3.** 16 × 5 **4.** 72 × 8 **5.** 58 × 6

6. Use blocks to solve a multiplication problem of your choice.

Multiplying 2-Digit Numbers

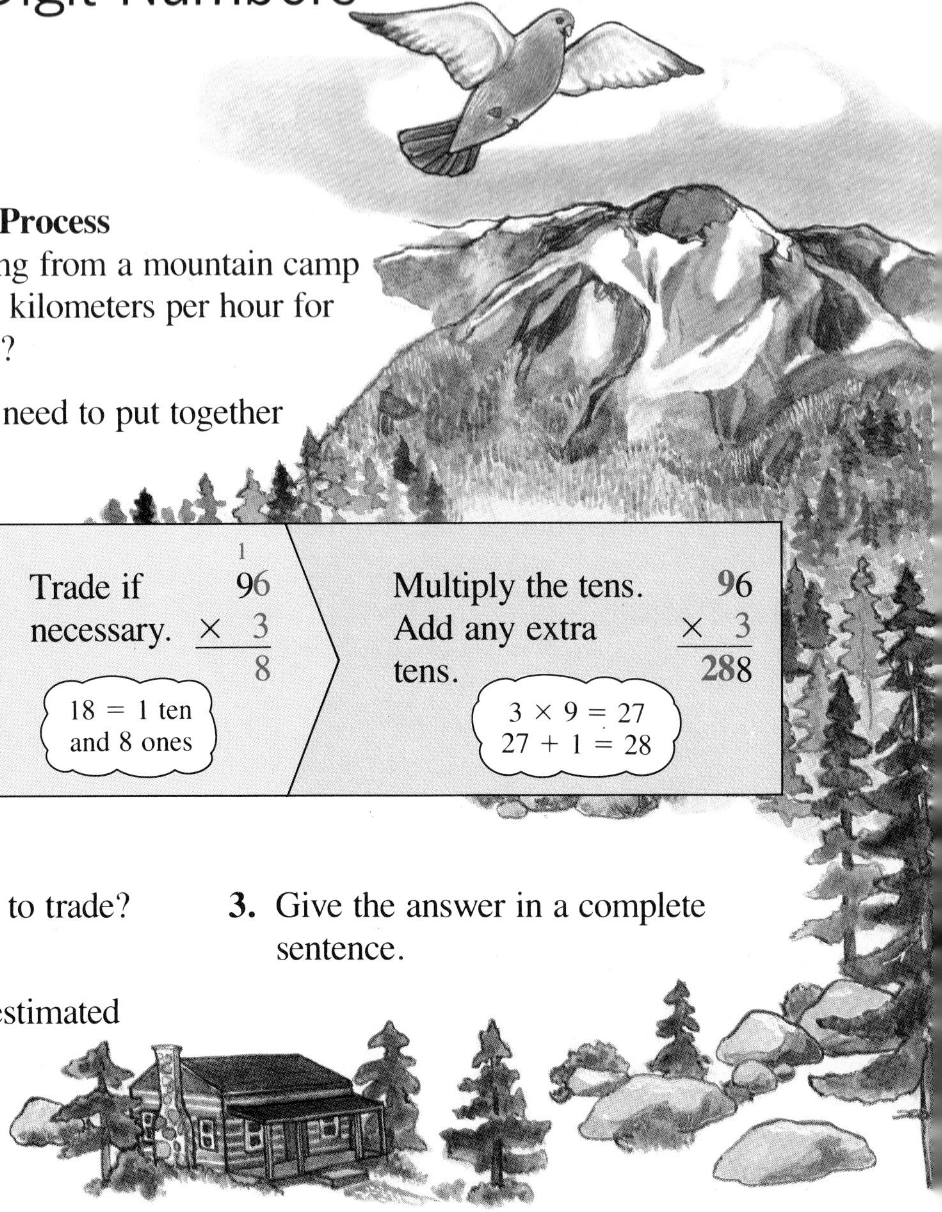

LEARN ABOUT IT

EXPLORE **Think About the Process**

A homing pigeon was flying from a mountain camp to headquarters. It flew 96 kilometers per hour for 3 hours. How far did it fly?

You multiply because you need to put together same-size groups.

Multiply the ones.	Trade if necessary.	Multiply the tens. Add any extra tens.
$\begin{array}{r} 96 \\ \times\ 3 \\ \hline \end{array}$	$\begin{array}{r} ^{1}\ \\ 96 \\ \times\ 3 \\ \hline 8 \end{array}$	$\begin{array}{r} 96 \\ \times\ 3 \\ \hline 288 \end{array}$
$3 \times 6 = 18$	18 = 1 ten and 8 ones	$3 \times 9 = 27$ $27 + 1 = 28$

TALK ABOUT IT

1. When was it necessary to trade? Why?
2. How would you have estimated the distance?
3. Give the answer in a complete sentence.

Other Examples

A	B	C	D	E
$\begin{array}{r} 23 \\ \times\ 3 \\ \hline 69 \end{array}$	$\begin{array}{r} 52 \\ \times\ 3 \\ \hline 156 \end{array}$	$\begin{array}{r} ^{1}\ \\ 43 \\ \times\ 6 \\ \hline 258 \end{array}$	$\begin{array}{r} ^{2}\ \\ 35 \\ \times\ 5 \\ \hline 175 \end{array}$	$\begin{array}{r} ^{2}\ \\ 75 \\ \times\ 4 \\ \hline 300 \end{array}$

TRY IT OUT

1.	2.	3.	4.	5.
$\begin{array}{r} 36 \\ \times\ 4 \\ \hline \end{array}$	$\begin{array}{r} 64 \\ \times\ 5 \\ \hline \end{array}$	$\begin{array}{r} 25 \\ \times\ 7 \\ \hline \end{array}$	$\begin{array}{r} 86 \\ \times\ 3 \\ \hline \end{array}$	$\begin{array}{r} 18 \\ \times\ 6 \\ \hline \end{array}$

PRACTICE

Find the products.

1. 43×6
2. 58×4
3. 72×8
4. 94×7
5. 31×6
6. 62×5
7. 29×4
8. 47×3
9. 68×1
10. 89×9

11. 78×5 **12.** 4×67 **13.** 28×7 **14.** 0×35

15. 43×9 **16.** 3×83 **17.** 53×8 **18.** 84×6

19. Multiply 6×27.

20. Find the product of 43 and 8.

APPLY

MATH REASONING Find only the products that are over 500. Write under for the others.

21. 49×3 **22.** 78×7 **23.** 51×9 **24.** 73×6 **25.** 86×7

PROBLEM SOLVING

26. A sparrow flew south at a speed of 40 kilometers per hour for 6 hours. A Canada goose flew in the same direction at a speed of 87 kilometers per hour for 3 hours. Which bird flew farther? How much farther did it fly?

27. DATA BANK **Science Data Bank** How many more times would a hummingbird weighing 2 grams beat its wings than a hummingbird weighing 6 grams if both birds hovered for 5 seconds? See page 469.

COMMUNICATION Write to Learn

28. Write a paragraph that tells how you would solve the equation 24×3 using blocks. Use these words: lay out, put together, trade, ones, tens, count.

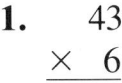

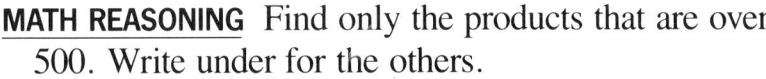

Multiplying Larger Numbers
1 Trade

LEARN ABOUT IT

EXPLORE Think About the Process

The school auditorium could seat 293 people. If the seats were full for each of 3 puppet shows, how many people saw the shows?

You multiply because you need to find the total for equal numbers of people.

Multiply the ones. Trade if necessary.	Multiply the tens. Add any extra tens. Trade if necessary.	Multiply the hundreds. Add any extra hundreds.
$\begin{array}{r} 293 \\ \times\ \ 3 \\ \hline 9 \end{array}$	$\begin{array}{r} {}^{2} \\ 293 \\ \times\ \ 3 \\ \hline 79 \end{array}$	$\begin{array}{r} {}^{2} \\ 293 \\ \times\ \ 3 \\ \hline 879 \end{array}$

TALK ABOUT IT

1. How would you estimate the number of people who saw the shows?
2. Use a complete sentence that gives a reasonable answer to the story problem.

Other Examples

Trading Ones	Trading Tens	Trading Hundreds
A $\begin{array}{r} {}^{2} \\ 216 \\ \times\ \ 4 \\ \hline 864 \end{array}$	**B** $\begin{array}{r} {}^{1} \\ 380 \\ \times\ \ 2 \\ \hline 760 \end{array}$	**C** $\begin{array}{r} 301 \\ \times\ \ 5 \\ \hline 1{,}505 \end{array}$

TRY IT OUT

1. $\begin{array}{r} 213 \\ \times\ \ 7 \\ \hline \end{array}$ **2.** $\begin{array}{r} 652 \\ \times\ \ 3 \\ \hline \end{array}$ **3.** $\begin{array}{r} 741 \\ \times\ \ 6 \\ \hline \end{array}$ **4.** $\begin{array}{r} 109 \\ \times\ \ 5 \\ \hline \end{array}$ **5.** $\begin{array}{r} 317 \\ \times\ \ 2 \\ \hline \end{array}$

PRACTICE

Find the products.

1. 315×4 **2.** 206×9 **3.** 941×5 **4.** 174×2 **5.** 503×7

6. 642×3 **7.** 741×7 **8.** 539×2 **9.** 416×6 **10.** 880×8

11. 708 × 5 **12.** 121 × 8 **13.** 3 × 318 **14.** 861 × 4

15. 473 × 2 **16.** 6 × 712 **17.** 510 × 9 **18.** 7 × 271

19. Multiply 6 × 207. **20.** Find the product of 413 and 5.

APPLY

MATH REASONING For each problem decide whether to use pencil and paper, mental math, or a calculator. Then solve the problems.

21. 300 × 6 **22.** 2 × 34 **23.** 6,478 × 298 **24.** 314 × 6

PROBLEM SOLVING

25. Jeff sold some $2 and some $5 tickets to a puppet show. He sold $35 worth of tickets all together. How many of each type ticket could he have sold? Give 3 possible combinations.

26. The puppet show project made $204 for a charity. A can collection project made $159. How much more did the puppet show make?

▶ ALGEBRA

Estimate to find the number for the ||||. Check your estimate with a calculator.

27. 316 × |||| = 1,580 **28.** 832 × |||| = 3,328 **29.** 271 × |||| = 2,168

30. 490 × |||| = 3,430 **31.** 909 × |||| = 3,636 **32.** 826 × |||| = 2,478

More Practice, page 504, set C

Multiplying Larger Numbers
2 or More Trades

LEARN ABOUT IT

EXPLORE Think About the Process

The heartbeat rate of a robin is about 4 times the heartbeat rate of a dove. The heartbeat rate of a dove is 135 beats a minute. About what is the heartbeat rate of a robin?

You multiply because you need a total for equal numbers of heartbeats.

Multiply the ones. Trade if necessary.	$\begin{array}{r} {\scriptstyle 2} \\ 135 \\ \times\ \ 4 \\ \hline 0 \end{array}$
Multiply the tens. Add any extra tens. Trade if necessary.	$\begin{array}{r} {\scriptstyle 1\,2} \\ 135 \\ \times\ \ 4 \\ \hline 40 \end{array}$
Multiply the hundreds. Add any extra hundreds.	$\begin{array}{r} {\scriptstyle 1\,2} \\ 135 \\ \times\ \ 4 \\ \hline 540 \end{array}$

TALK ABOUT IT

1. How would you have estimated the heartbeat rate of the robin?
2. Give the answer in a complete sentence.

Other Examples

A $\begin{array}{r} {\scriptstyle 3} \\ 318 \\ \times\ \ 4 \\ \hline 1,272 \end{array}$ **B** $\begin{array}{r} {\scriptstyle 1\,2} \\ 237 \\ \times\ \ 3 \\ \hline 711 \end{array}$ **C** $\begin{array}{r} {\scriptstyle 1} \\ 706 \\ \times\ \ 2 \\ \hline 1,412 \end{array}$

TRY IT OUT

Find the products.

1. $\begin{array}{r} 354 \\ \times\ \ 3 \\ \hline \end{array}$ **2.** $\begin{array}{r} 572 \\ \times\ \ 4 \\ \hline \end{array}$ **3.** $\begin{array}{r} 879 \\ \times\ \ 6 \\ \hline \end{array}$ **4.** $\begin{array}{r} 727 \\ \times\ \ 3 \\ \hline \end{array}$ **5.** $\begin{array}{r} 515 \\ \times\ \ 4 \\ \hline \end{array}$

PRACTICE

Find the products.

1. $\begin{array}{r} 456 \\ \times \quad 3 \\ \hline \end{array}$
2. $\begin{array}{r} 343 \\ \times \quad 6 \\ \hline \end{array}$
3. $\begin{array}{r} 169 \\ \times \quad 9 \\ \hline \end{array}$
4. $\begin{array}{r} 826 \\ \times \quad 4 \\ \hline \end{array}$
5. $\begin{array}{r} 369 \\ \times \quad 7 \\ \hline \end{array}$

6. 728 × 6 **7.** 571 × 4 **8.** 8 × 733 **9.** 879 × 3

10. 428 × 8 **11.** 2 × 683 **12.** 256 × 5 **13.** 9 × 354

14. Multiply 7 × 409. **15.** Find the product of 537 and 9.

APPLY

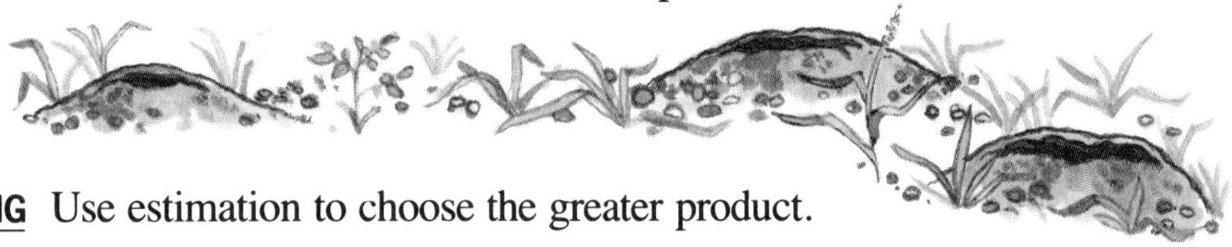

MATH REASONING Use estimation to choose the greater product.

16. 398 × 4 or 498 × 3 **17.** 508 × 8 or 608 × 7 **18.** 999 × 4 or 499 × 9

PROBLEM SOLVING

19. Science Data Bank The heartbeat rate of a hummingbird is about 3 times the heartbeat rate of a starling. About what is the heartbeat rate of a hummingbird? See page 469.

DATA BANK

20. An ostrich takes 45 breaths per minute when the weather is warm. In cool weather, an ostrich takes 5 breaths per minute. How many more breaths per minute does an ostrich take in warm weather?

MIXED REVIEW

The 2 scales are balanced. Each shape has the same value in all the pictures.

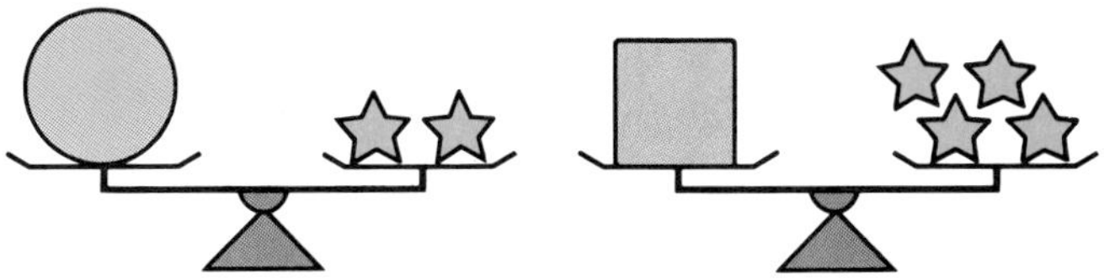

Write yes if each scale below is balanced. Write no if it is not.

21.

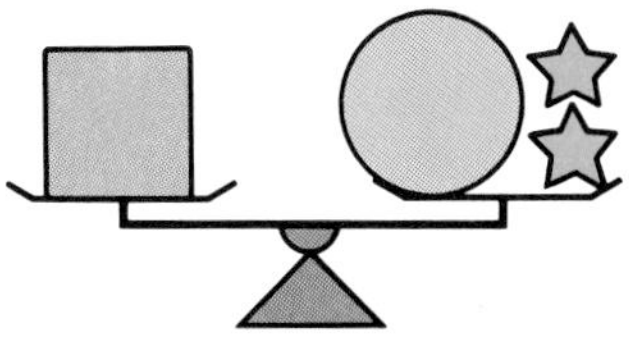

22.

More Practice, page 504, set D

Using Critical Thinking

LEARN ABOUT IT

Rudy and Sara sometimes work at the class store.
"How much will 3 notepads be?" asked Derrick.
"I forgot my calculator!" exclaimed Sara. "I guess we'll have to use pencil and paper."
"Wait," said Rudy. "I thought about dimes and pennies and invented a way to do it in my head!"

TALK ABOUT IT

1. What method might Rudy have invented?
2. Invent a method of your own for finding the product.
3. How much did the 3 notepads cost? How could you prove that your answer is correct?

TRY IT OUT

Use a mental math method to find the cost of each of these items.

1. 3 pencils **2.** 4 pencils **3.** 2 notepads

4. 2 pens **5.** 4 notepads **6.** 2 tablets

POWER PRACTICE/QUIZ

Find the products. Write answers only.

1. 7 × 10 **2.** 8 × 40 **3.** 500 × 6 **4.** 3 × 9,000

Round to the highest place and then multiply to estimate the product.

5. 4 × 909 **6.** 5 × \$7.89 **7.** 8 × 674 **8.** 398 × 2

Estimate the product. Is it less than \$10?

9. 3 × \$2.77 **10.** 6 × \$0.98 **11.** \$4.25 × 2 **12.** 5 × \$2.37

Multiply the two numbers. Then add 3. Write answers only.

13. 4 and 3 **14.** 9 and 7 **15.** 7 and 7 **16.** 6 and 8

Multiply each number by 4. Then add the products.

17. 30 and 2 **18.** 10 and 4 **19.** 70 and 6 **20.** 80 and 5

Find the products.

21. 32 × 3 **22.** 16 × 7 **23.** 783 × 2 **24.** 126 × 9 **25.** \$3.75 × 8

26. 821 × 5 **27.** 84 × 5 **28.** 308 × 9 **29.** 496 × 6 **30.** 515 × 4

31. 632 × 7 **32.** 72 × 9 **33.** 36 × 8 **34.** 224 × 3 **35.** \$7.77 × 4

PROBLEM SOLVING

36. Peter used place value blocks to show these four problems. For which problems did he trade ones for tens? For which did he trade tens for hundreds?

A 61 × 7
B 27 × 3
C 32 × 3
D 42 × 5

37. Chris has 8 coins in his pocket that total 75¢. Which coins are they? Can you find another possibility?

Mental Math
Multiplying 3 Factors

1 carton of
2 boxes

LEARN ABOUT IT

EXPLORE **Think About the Situation**

Liz and John sold 4 cartons of holiday candles. Each carton contained 2 boxes of 3 candles each. One box had red candles and the other had green. How many candles did Liz and John sell?

TALK ABOUT IT

1. What numbers do you multiply first to find out how many candles were in each carton? What second step do you need to take?
2. If you find the total number of red candles first and then multiply by 2, will the answer change?

Grouping Property for Multiplication
Changing the grouping of factors does not change the product.

The parentheses tell which digits to multiply first. When no parentheses are shown, you can pick any 2 factors to multiply first.

1. **Multiply these.** ↙ ↘

$(3 \times 2) \times 4$

$6 \times 4 = 24$

2. **Multiply these.** ↙ ↘

$3 \times (2 \times 4)$

$3 \times 8 = 24$

3. **Pick any two. Try these.** ↙ ↘

$3 \times 2 \times 4$

$12 \times 2 = 24$

TRY IT OUT

Decide whether to use mental math, pencil and paper, or a calculator. Then find the products.

1. $(3 \times 2) \times 5$ **2.** $3 \times (5 \times 4)$ **3.** $(2 \times 5) \times 8$ **4.** $4 \times (9 \times 7)$

5. $2 \times 94 \times 5$ **6.** $48 \times 25 \times 4$ **7.** $50 \times 78 \times 2$ **8.** $8 \times 67 \times 9$

More Practice, page 504, set E

Problem Solving Using a Calculator

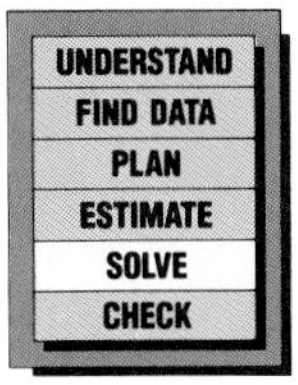

LEARN ABOUT IT

This square with numbers is a magic square because the sum of the numbers in each row, column, and diagonal is the same. The sum is called the magic number. In this square the magic number is 15. You can use a calculator to solve magic square problems.

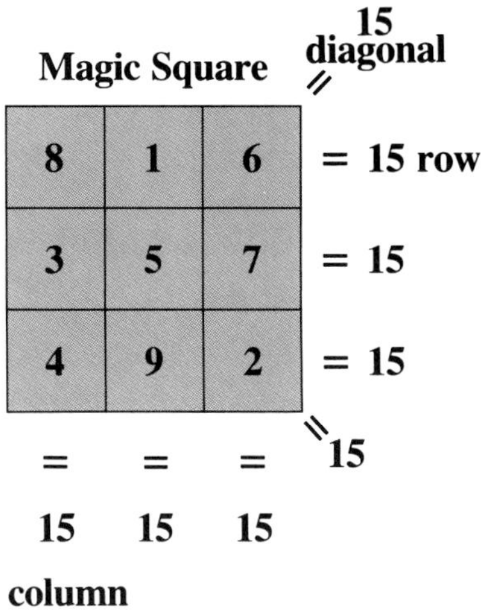

Find the missing number to make this a magic square.

297	45	225
117	189	261
153	333	?

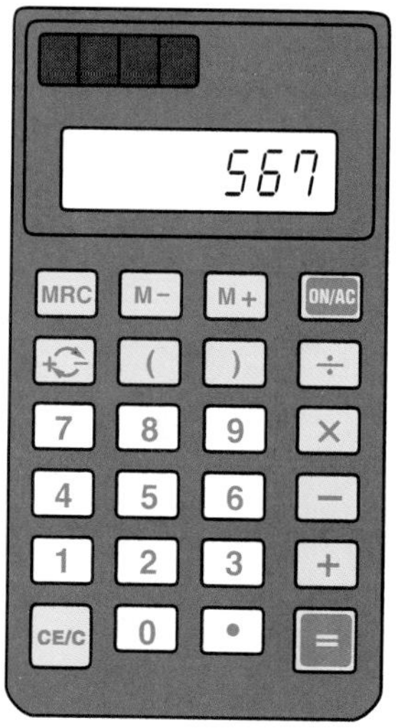

Here's how. Use your calculator to add any row or column to find the magic number. Then look at a row or column with the missing number. With the magic number still on your calculator, use these key strokes.

[ON/AC] [−] 225 [=] _?_ [−] 261 [=] _?_

This missing number is 81.
Check by adding all 3 numbers.

TRY IT OUT

1. What missing numbers will make this a magic square?
2. Multiply each number in the square by 99. Is this still a magic square?
3. Add 99 to each number in the square. Is this still a magic square?

414	?	360
?	270	?
180	?	126

More Practice, page 504, set F

Multiplying Larger Numbers
All Trades

LEARN ABOUT IT

EXPLORE Think About the Process

The length of the Chesapeake Bay Bridge is 5 times the length of the Golden Gate Bridge. How long is the Chesapeake Bay Bridge?

Lengths of World's Longest Suspension Bridges

Place	meters
Akashi-Kaykyo, Japan	1,780
Humber, England	1,410
Golden Gate, California	1,280

Multiply the ones. Trade if necessary.	Multiply the tens. Add any extra tens. Trade if necessary.	Multiply the hundreds. Add any extra hundreds. Trade if necessary.	Multiply the thousands. Add any extra thousands.
1,280 × 5 0	4 1,280 × 5 00	1 4 1,280 × 5 400	1 4 1,280 × 5 6,400

TALK ABOUT IT

1. How would you estimate the product?
2. Give the answer in a complete sentence.

Other Examples

A	B	C
1 1 3 3,428 × 4 13,712	3 3 2,505 × 6 15,030	4 8 1,049 × 9 9,441

TRY IT OUT

Find the product.

1.	2.	3.	4.
3,154 × 3	1,578 × 4	3,879 × 6	9,221 × 7

PRACTICE

Find the products.

1. $1{,}473 \times 4$
2. $6{,}201 \times 6$
3. $3{,}472 \times 2$
4. $8{,}307 \times 7$
5. $9{,}195 \times 6$
6. $3{,}276 \times 5$
7. $4{,}009 \times 8$
8. $6{,}428 \times 3$
9. $5{,}066 \times 9$
10. $7{,}183 \times 8$
11. $7{,}206 \times 6$
12. $2 \times 7{,}956$
13. $1{,}840 \times 5$
14. $9 \times 9{,}074$
15. Multiply $7 \times 4{,}098$.
16. Find the product of 9,537 and 9.

APPLY

MATH REASONING

17. Use estimation to pick the two numbers below with the product 28,476.

2   4   6   8   1,258   3,964   5,568   7,119   9,985

PROBLEM SOLVING

18. A mile is 5,280 feet. The Golden Gate Bridge is 4,199 feet long. How much more or less than a mile is the length of the Golden Gate Bridge?

19. A meter is a little more than 3 feet. Look at the table on page 164 and tell if the Akashi-Kaykyo Bridge in Japan is more or less than a mile long.

MENTAL MATH

Choose a method or methods from this chart to answer these problems. Tell what method you used.

20. $2{,}010 \times 3$
21. $78 \times 25 \times 4$
22. $2{,}198 + 3$
23. $3{,}333 + 198$
24. $2{,}100 \times 4$
25. $4{,}500 - 2$

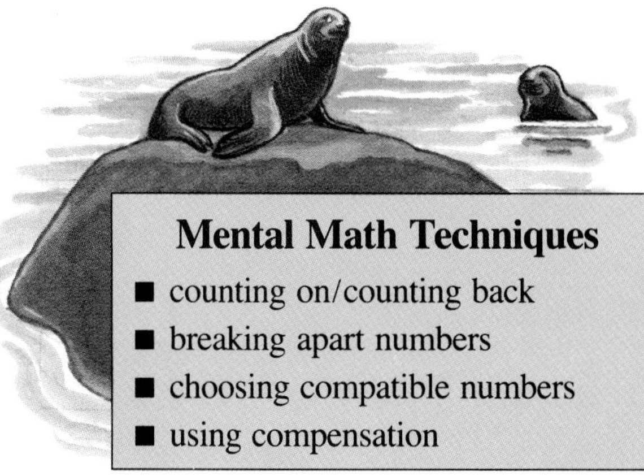

Mental Math Techniques

- counting on/counting back
- breaking apart numbers
- choosing compatible numbers
- using compensation

Multiplying with Money

LEARN ABOUT IT

EXPLORE **Think About the Situation**

A pet store owner checked to see what it would cost to stock items to sell to owners of parrots. Use a calculator and the information in the ad to find how much 6 of an item of your choice would cost. Do this for several items. Make a table to show the results.

TALK ABOUT IT

1. What process did you use to find your answers?
2. If you changed the cost of a box of birdseed to all cents, how many cents would you have? Explain.
3. How would you write 856¢ using the $ symbol?

You can multiply money just like you multiply whole numbers. Here is an example.

How much would 6 boxes of birdseed at $4.79 each cost?

$$\begin{array}{r} \$4.79 \\ \times\quad 6 \\ \hline \$28.74 \end{array}$$

Multiply as with whole numbers.

Show dollars and cents.

TRY IT OUT

1. $\begin{array}{r} \$9.43 \\ \times\quad 2 \\ \hline \end{array}$ **2.** $\begin{array}{r} \$13.59 \\ \times\quad 5 \\ \hline \end{array}$ **3.** $\begin{array}{r} \$10.72 \\ \times\quad 9 \\ \hline \end{array}$ **4.** $\begin{array}{r} \$0.87 \\ \times\quad 4 \\ \hline \end{array}$ **5.** $\begin{array}{r} \$6.82 \\ \times\quad 5 \\ \hline \end{array}$

6. 9 × $2.98 **7.** 8 × $1.25 **8.** 7 × $6.08 **9.** 4 × $5.16

10. 6 × $3.05 **11.** 2 × $4.36 **12.** 5 × $1.32 **13.** 3 × $8.54

PRACTICE

Multiply to decode the message.

1. $4.19 × 7 R	**2.** $6.05 × 8 U	**3.** $3.18 × 6 Y	**4.** $5.46 × 4 W
5. $10.32 × 8 T	**6.** $3.68 × 4 A	**7.** $19.78 × 3 E	**8.** $18.27 × 5 O
9. $8.57 × 7 Z	**10.** $38.79 × 2 H	**11.** $60.94 × 6 M	**12.** $14.56 × 3 I

Message

Y	**O**	**U**	*	___	___	___	*	___
$19.08	$91.35	$48.40		$14.72	$29.33	$59.34		$14.72

___	___	___	___	*	___	___	___	___
$365.64	$14.72	$82.56	$77.58		$21.84	$77.58	$43.68	$59.99

APPLY

MATH REASONING Estimate which product is greater. Use < or >.

13. $2.92 × 7 ▯ $1.99 × 8

14. $42.09 × 6 ▯ $59.67 × 5

PROBLEM SOLVING

15. Tammy bought 6 tropical fish that cost $4.65 each. The store reduced the total cost by $2. What did Tammy pay?

CALCULATOR

Here are some items ordered by the manager of a pet store. Find the missing numbers.

Item	Aquarium	Book	Fish
Cost of Item	$54.98	$16.79	?
Number of Items	25	?	12
Total Cost	?	$117.53	$69

Problem Solving
Look for a Pattern

UNDERSTAND
FIND DATA
PLAN
ESTIMATE
SOLVE
CHECK

LEARN ABOUT IT

You can solve some problems by using a strategy called **Look for a Pattern.** To help you discover the pattern, try making a table.

Fred arranged comic books on 6 shelves in the Comics Store. The picture shows the first three shelves. If he continued the pattern, how many books did Fred put on the 6th shelf?

Row 1

Row 2

Row 3

I'll make a table and look for a pattern.

I see the pattern. There are 3 more comic books on each shelf. I'll complete the table to shelf 6.

Shelf Number	1	2	3	4	5	6
Comic Books	1	4	7	10	13	16

Fred put 16 comic books on shelf 6.

TRY IT OUT

Read this problem and finish the solution.

Jessie draws for the school paper. She drew 5 comic strips the first month, 10 the second month, 15 the third, and so on. In this pattern, how many did she draw the sixth month?

- How many comic strips did Jessie draw the first month? the second month? the third month?
- Copy and complete the table to solve the problem.

month	1	2	3	4	5	6
comic strips	5	10	15			

PRACTICE

Make a table to help solve each problem.

1. When The Comics Store first opened, Ben had to sort all the comics into bins. The first day he sorted 1 box, the second day 2, the third day 4, the fourth day 8, and so on. How many boxes did he sort the sixth day?

2. Comics sell for $1.50 in bin 1, $1.75 in bin 2, $2.00 in bin 3, and so on. How much would a comic book in bin 7 cost?

MIXED PRACTICE

Choose a strategy from the strategies list or use other strategies you know to solve these problems.

Some Strategies
Act It Out
Use Objects
Choose an Operation
Draw a Picture
Make an Organized List
Guess and Check
Make a Table
Look for a Pattern

3. Posters at The Comics Store cost $7.99 each. Buttons are $1.99 each. How much did Maria pay for 6 posters?

4. George displayed the most expensive comics on the wall behind the counter. He put 3 comics in the top row, 7 in row 2, 11 in row 3, 15 in row 4, and so on. How many comics did he put in row 9?

5. Joe writes a comic strip every day in the newspaper. Each strip has 4 frames in it. How many frames does he draw in a year?

6. The 4 most expensive comic books in the store cost $132.98, $115.98, $95.98, and $87.98. How much are they worth all together?

7. A box of 5 Rocket Ron comic books costs $6. How much would 30 Rocket Ron comic books cost?

8. Mark bought 3 comics at $1.59 each. He also bought an old comic book for $6.95. How much did he pay in all?

More Practice, page 516, set D

Data Collection and Analysis
Group Decision Making

UNDERSTAND
FIND DATA
PLAN
ESTIMATE
SOLVE
CHECK

Doing a Questionnaire
Group Skill:
Check for Understanding

How do students your age like to study? Your group is in charge of making a **questionnaire** to gather information about study habits. A questionnaire is a written list of questions used to gather information.

Collecting Data

1. A **multiple choice question** is one type of question that can be used on a questionnaire. A multiple choice question usually gives 3 or 4 choices for answers. The sample questionnaire has 2 multiple choice questions. Why is it useful on question 2 to include "other" as one of the choices?

2. Work with your group to make a questionnaire with at least 4 multiple choice questions about study habits.

3. Test your questionnaire with 2 or 3 people. Revise the questions that are unclear.

4. Make at least 20 copies of your questionnaire. Give the questionnaire to 20 students.

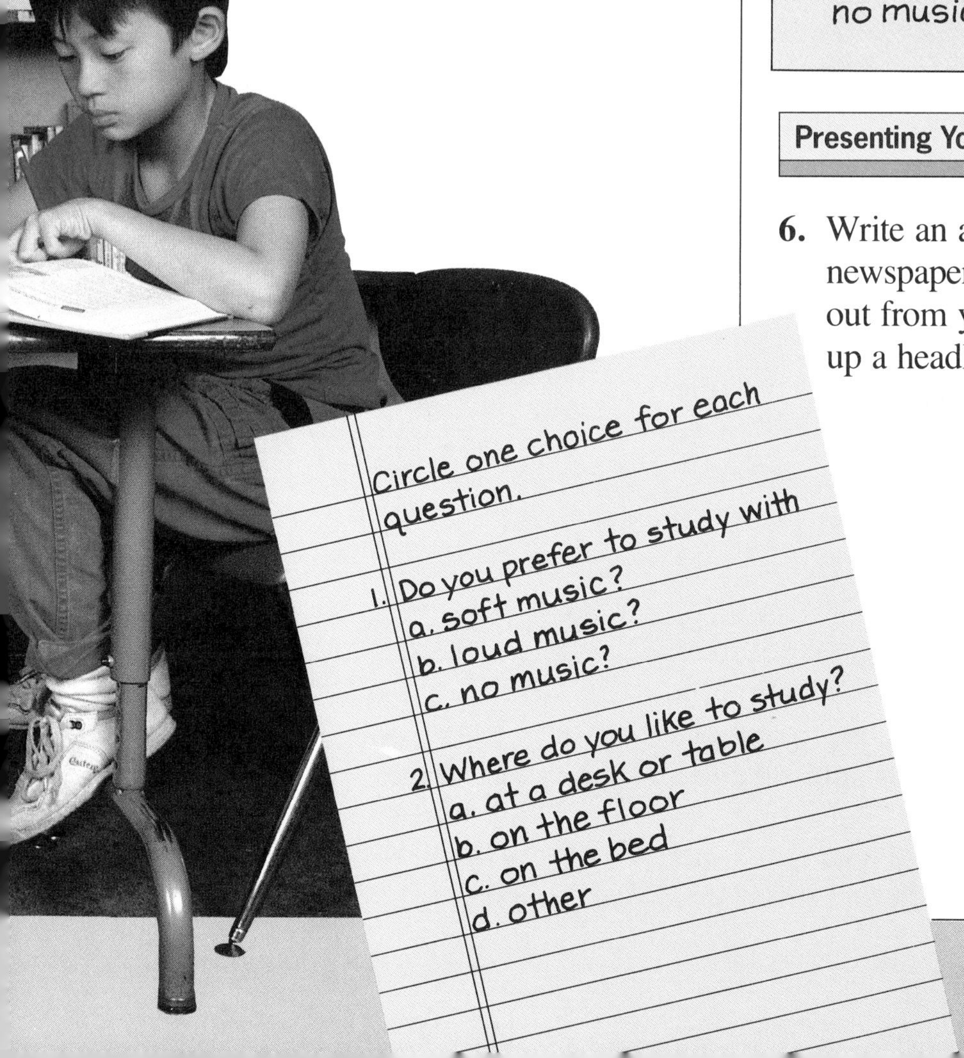

5. Make a table to show the results of each question on your questionnaire. Mark a tally for each response on your table. Count and record the total number of responses. This is an example.

1. Do you prefer to study with		Total
soft music	‖‖‖‖ ‖‖‖‖	10
loud music	‖‖‖	3
no music	‖‖‖‖ ‖‖	7

6. Write an article for a school newspaper about what you found out from your questionnaire. Make up a headline for your article.

Circle one choice for each question.

1. Do you prefer to study with
 a. soft music?
 b. loud music?
 c. no music?

2. Where do you like to study?
 a. at a desk or table
 b. on the floor
 c. on the bed
 d. other

WRAP UP

Number Phrase Match

Match each phrase with a number expression. Explain your choices.

1. six hundreds	a.	6×12
2. the product of six and twelve	b.	12×4
3. double six	c.	4×6
4. twelve groups of four each	d.	9×3
5. twelve times two	e.	6×100
6. six multiplied by four	f.	$(9 \times 3) + 2$
7. a pair of odd factors	g.	\$6.12
8. six dollars twelve cents	h.	2×6
9. two more than the product of nine and three	i.	12×2

Sometimes, Always, Never

Which word should go in the blank, sometimes, always, or never? Explain your choices.

10. The product of a number and 1 is __?__ that number.

11. Factors __?__ may be multiplied in any order.

12. Multiplying a number by a 2-digit or 3-digit factor __?__ requires trading.

Project

13. Has anyone ever told you that you eat like a bird? If you really ate like some songbirds, you would eat your weight in food every day. Find out how many of each of these foods you would have to eat if you had a songbird's appetite! To begin, you will need to know how much you weigh.

Food	Number in one pound
hamburger	4
orange	3
egg	5
piece of bread	8

POWER PRACTICE/TEST

Part 1 Understanding

Copy each equation and give the numbers for the $\square$ and the $\triangle$.

1. Since $6 \times 4 = \square$, then $600 \times 4 = \triangle$.

2. Since $\square \times 5 = 40$, then $\triangle \times 5 = 400$.

3. Which factors would you multiply first in $4 \times 7 \times 5$? Why? Find the product.

Which method would you suggest using to solve each of these problems? Explain your reasoning.

4. 400×7 a. calculator

5. $3{,}984 \times 687$ b. mental math

6. 216×6 c. paper and pencil

Part 2 Skills

Round, then estimate the product.

7. $7 \times \$5.22$

8. 6×88

Multiply and add. Use mental math.

9. $(4 \times 7) + 3$

10. $(3 \times 6) + 5$

Multiply.

11. $\begin{array}{r} 26 \\ \times \ 4 \\ \hline \end{array}$

12. $\begin{array}{r} 373 \\ \times \ 3 \\ \hline \end{array}$

13. $\begin{array}{r} 4{,}971 \\ \times \ 6 \\ \hline \end{array}$

14. $\begin{array}{r} \$20.77 \\ \times \ 3 \\ \hline \end{array}$

Part 3 Applications

15. Roy delivers 77 papers a day. Estimate his weekly total by rounding. Is the weekly total more or less than 500?

16. Sue is making a design. She puts 5 tiles in row 1, 11 tiles in row 2, 17 tiles in row 3, and 23 tiles in row 4. How many tiles will be in row 7?

ENRICHMENT
What Else Do You Need to Know?

- In 1986, people in Florida built the world's tallest sand castle. It was 5 stories tall and weighed 48,400 tons.
- In 1986, a California man rocked in a rocking chair for 453 hours and 40 minutes.
- In 1986, a man in Japan set a distance record. He spent 8 hours 21 minutes climbing up and down the foothills of Mount Fuji on a pogo stick.

Rita found these facts in a book of world records. As she thought about each fact, she realized she wanted to know more. So Rita made up these questions about the sand castle.

1. How tall is a story?
2. Is the given weight exact or estimated?
3. How could someone weigh a sand castle?

Think about the three records. For each record write three questions to explore information that is missing. You do not have to answer the questions.

Then use a book of world records to find another interesting record. Write three questions you would like to ask the record holder.

CUMULATIVE REVIEW

1. Lynette needs to trade 1 ten for 10 ones. Which number is she subtracting from 234?

   A 234 B 181

   C 78 D 34

2. Estimate the sum of 673 and 821.

   A 1,494 B 1,500

   C 1,400 D 1,600

3. To find the number of apples you need to give 2 each to 15 children, what kind of answer would be best?

   A estimate B rounded

   C difference D exact

4. Which equation fits the picture?

   A $2 + 7 = 9$ B $7 \times 3 = 21$

   C $2 \times 7 = 14$ D $14 - 7 = 7$

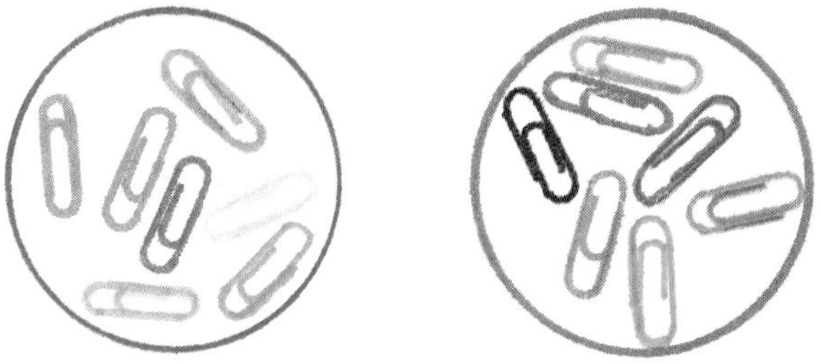

5. 9×4

   A 36 B 45

   C 32 D 40

6. 6×1

   A 6 B 5

   C 7 D 1

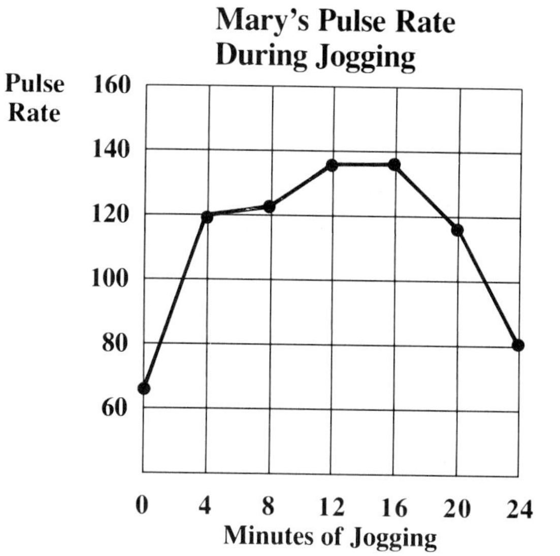

7. How is the data given in the graph?

   A bars B lines

   C pictures D words

8. Look at the graph and tell what Mary's pulse rate was after she ran 12 minutes.

   A 120 B 130

   C 135 D 140

9. During which part of her run did Mary's pulse rate change the least?

   A 0–4 min B 4–8 min

   C 8–12 min D 12–16 min

10. At what time do you think Mary began to slow down?

    A 16 min B 24 min

    C 12 min D 20 min

7

MULTIPLYING BY 2-DIGIT FACTORS

THEME: ACTIVE GAMES

MATH AND HEALTH AND FITNESS

DATA BANK

Use the Health and Fitness Data Bank on page 481 to answer the questions.

1 Which is greater, the number of aerobic points for 3 hours of playing baseball or for 1 hour of skipping rope?

2 In double unders, the rope turns 2 times per jump. Find the world record for fourth graders in this event.

3 In triple unders, the rope turns 3 times per jump. Find the world record for fourth graders in this event.

4 **Use Critical Thinking** One hour of bicycling uses 16 aerobic points. Name another activity that uses about this number of aerobic points.

These children in China are doing exercises in their school yard. Does your class exercise together?

Mental Math
Special Products

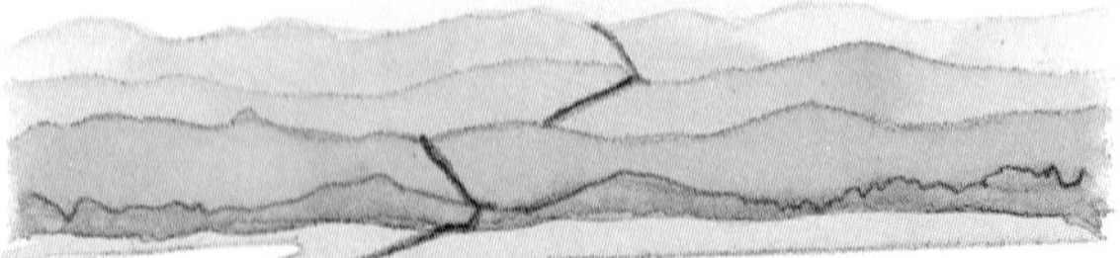

LEARN ABOUT IT

EXPLORE **Solve to Understand**

Daniela made up these Far Out Facts problems that can be solved using mental math.

Far Out Facts Problems
1. There is enough lead in one pencil to draw a line 40 miles long. How long a line could you draw with a pack of 20 pencils?
2. The average dollar bill wears out in 20 months. How many days is this? Use 30 days in a month.

TALK ABOUT IT

1. How many times as large as 40×2 is the answer to problem 1? Explain.
2. How many times as large as 20×3 is the answer to problem 2? Explain.
3. How many times as large as 2×3 is the answer to problem 2? Explain.

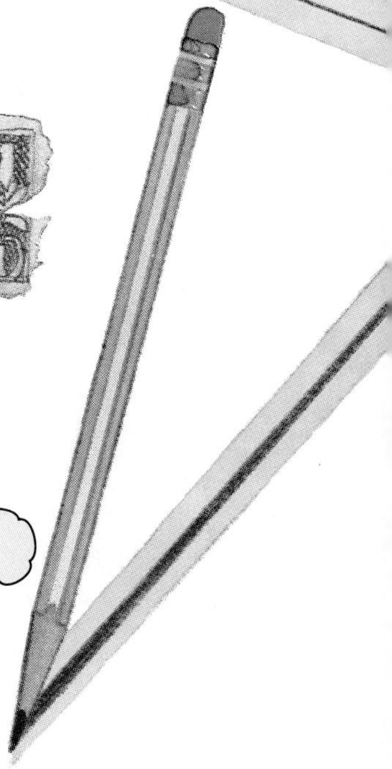

This mental math method gives you a quick way to find products like 40×20.

- To find $4\underline{0} \times 2\underline{0}$, find 4×2 and then multiply by $1\underline{00}$.

4 tens × 2 tens = 8 hundreds

$$\mathbf{4\underline{0} \times 2\underline{0} = 8\underline{00}}$$

Here are more examples.

$60 \times 10 = 600$ 6 tens × 1 ten = 6 hundreds

$50 \times 60 = 3{,}000$ 5 tens × 6 tens = 30 hundreds or 3 thousands

TRY IT OUT

1. 70×10 **2.** 30×70 **3.** 80×40 **4.** 40×50

5. 50×20 **6.** 60×70 **7.** 40×90 **8.** 50×80

PRACTICE

Copy each equation and give the numbers for the □ and △.

1. Since $9 \times 4 = \square$, then $90 \times 40 = \triangle$.

2. Since $2 \times 7 = \square$, then $20 \times 70 = \triangle$.

Find the products. Use pencil and paper for answers only.

3. 90×10
4. 20×30
5. 50×10
6. 40×40
7. 40×60
8. 90×50
9. 20×30
10. 80×50
11. Multiply 60 and 70.
12. Find the product of 90 and 20.

APPLY

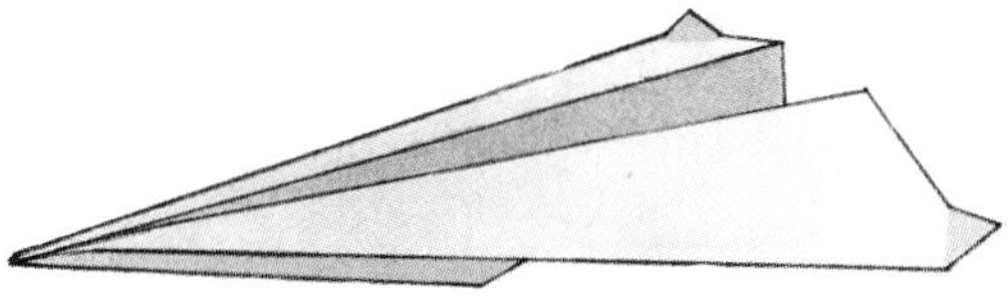

MATH REASONING

13. What product would give the best estimate for 55×55? Why?
    a. 60×60 b. 60×50 c. 50×50 d. 50×40

PROBLEM SOLVING

14. A hen's egg was once thrown 90 meters without being broken. The record for throwing a paper airplane is 10 times that far. How many meters did the paper airplane fly?

15. A cat was taken away in a moving van by mistake. To get home it had to travel 640 kilometers. If it went 10 kilometers a day for 60 days, how much further would it still have to go?

USING CRITICAL THINKING Discover a Sequence

16. These cards give a shortcut for finding products such as 60×40. What is their correct sequence?

Add on the number of zeros in the factors.	Look at the factors.	Multiply the front-end digits.	Count the number of zeros in the factors.

Estimating Larger Products

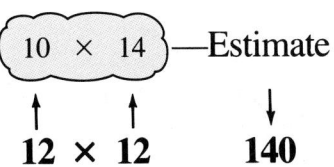

LEARN ABOUT IT

EXPLORE Think About the Situation

Phil was making his sister Patti a funny card for her 12th birthday. He wanted to write on it her estimated age in weeks and months.

TALK ABOUT IT

1. Phil first estimated Patti's age in weeks. He rounded 12×52 to 10×50 and got 500. Is this an overestimate or an underestimate? Explain.
2. His older brother suggested he use 10×60 instead. Would this give a closer estimate? Explain.

1 year = 52 weeks
1 year = 12 months

Here is how to estimate the age in months.

If you round 12×12 to the nearest 10, you get an underestimate.

$10 \times 10 = 100$

To get a closer estimate, round one factor up and the other down.

10×14 —Estimate

↑ ↑ ↓

12 × 12 **140**

Look at these additional examples.

43 × 589	**32 × \$5.75**
40 × 600	30 × \$6
About 24,000	**About \$180**

TRY IT OUT

Round to the highest place to make an estimate. Decide if the estimate is an underestimate, an overestimate, or if you can't tell. Give a closer estimate if possible.

1. 53×84 **2.** 39×21 **3.** 264×35 **4.** 623×46 **5.** $54 \times \$3.79$

PRACTICE

Round to the highest place to estimate the product. Write underestimate, overestimate, or can't tell. Then give a closer estimate if possible.

1. 25 × 68 **2.** 37 × 52 **3.** \$5.52 × 28 **4.** 237 × 46

5. 24 × 834 **6.** 61 × 78 **7.** 88 × 717 **8.** \$3.54 × 62

9. 769 × 63 **10.** 82 × \$3.06 **11.** 54 × 51 **12.** 97 × 536

Your reference point is 24,000. Estimate to tell if these products will be over or under the reference point.

13. 399 × 57 **14.** 49 × 547 **15.** 38 × 789 **16.** 368 × 51

APPLY

MATH REASONING Use estimation to choose the best number for each box.

17. 49 × □ = 1,421 **a.** 19 **b.** 29 **c.** 39

18. □ × 25 = 1,100 **a.** 24 **b.** 34 **c.** 44

PROBLEM SOLVING

19. Katrina is 9 years and 15 weeks old. What is her age in weeks?

20. Steve is 52 months old. How many months less than 8 years is this?

MIXED REVIEW

Find the products.

21. 3 × 2 **22.** 9 × 1 **23.** 0 × 5 **24.** 1 × 7 **25.** 4 × 0

26. 5 × 4 **27.** 2 × 9 **28.** 8 × 5 **29.** 7 × 2 **30.** 5 × 7

Multiply and then add the number given.

31. 6 × 5 8 **32.** 7 × 4 3 **33.** 3 × 9 7 **34.** 7 × 8 4

More Practice, page 505, set D

Multiplying by Multiples of 10

LEARN ABOUT IT

EXPLORE **Think About the Process**

How many times would your heart beat in one hour on a slow walk, if it beats 84 times a minute? An hour is 60 minutes.

You multiply to find the total number of heartbeats when you have an equal number per minute for 1 hour.

Multiply by the digit in the ones place.	84 × 60 0	Multiply by the digit in the tens place.	2 84 × 60 **5,040**	6 tens × 84 = 504 tens

TALK ABOUT IT

1. What product does the first 0 in the answer represent?
2. Why is 504 written to the left of the 0 in the second step?
3. How would you have estimated the total?
4. Give the answer in a complete sentence.

Other Examples

	A	B	C	D
	64 × 10 640	3 46 × 50 2,300	4 75 × 80 6,000	40 × 30 1,200

TRY IT OUT

Multiply.

1. 36 × 20 **2.** 76 × 50 **3.** 53 × 30 **4.** 89 × 40 **5.** 16 × 90

PRACTICE

Find the products.

1. 52×20
2. 67×40
3. 35×80
4. 95×60
5. 76×40
6. 41×90
7. 26×10
8. 83×50
9. 66×50
10. 39×30
11. 46×60
12. Find the product when the factors are 83 and 60.

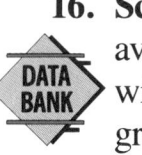

APPLY

MATH REASONING Use mental math to find the products. The first fact can help you find the second.

13. a. 25×10 **b.** 25×20

14. a. 25×4 **b.** 25×40

PROBLEM SOLVING

15. While Rosella was running, her heart beat 96 times a minute. At this rate, how many times would it beat during a 30-minute run?

16. DATA BANK **Science Data Bank** Compare the average resting heartbeat for girls with that of women. How much greater is the average number of heartbeats for girls than for women? See page 481.

ESTIMATION

Use one or more of these methods to estimate the answers. Tell which method you used.

Choose an Estimation Method
■ Front-end ■ Rounding ■ Clustering

17. 98×60
18. 48×22
19. $579 + 617 + 589 + 624$
20. $456 + 848$

Multiplying with 2-digit Factors

LEARN ABOUT IT

Mary lived in England many years ago. She discovered a secret garden and a new friend.

EXPLORE **Think About the Process**

Mary, in the book *The Secret Garden*, could only skip up to 20 when she first got her jump rope. By practicing each day she could soon jump more than 100 times. If it took her 28 jumps to go around a flower bed in the garden, how many jumps would she make after going around 2 dozen times?

You multiply because you need to find the total number of jumps in 24 trips around the flower bed.

Multiply by the digit in the ones place.	Multiply by the digit in the tens place.	Add the two products.
$\begin{array}{r} ^{3} \\ 28 \\ \times\ 24 \\ \hline \mathbf{112} \end{array}$	$\begin{array}{r} ^{1} \\ 28 \\ \times\ 24 \\ \hline 112 \\ \mathbf{560} \end{array}$	$\begin{array}{r} 28 \\ \times\ 24 \\ \hline 112 \\ 560 \\ \hline \mathbf{672} \end{array}$

TALK ABOUT IT

1. How would you have estimated the answer?

2. Give the answer in a complete sentence.

Other Examples

A $\begin{array}{r} 32 \\ \times\ 23 \\ \hline 96 \\ 640 \\ \hline 736 \end{array}$

B $\begin{array}{r} ^{1} \\ 34 \\ \times\ 24 \\ \hline 136 \\ 680 \\ \hline 816 \end{array}$

C $\begin{array}{r} ^{2} \\ 54 \\ \times\ 65 \\ \hline 270 \\ 3{,}240 \\ \hline 3{,}510 \end{array}$

TRY IT OUT

Multiply.

1. $\begin{array}{r} 26 \\ \times\ 34 \\ \hline \end{array}$ **2.** $\begin{array}{r} 74 \\ \times\ 25 \\ \hline \end{array}$ **3.** $\begin{array}{r} 46 \\ \times\ 28 \\ \hline \end{array}$ **4.** $\begin{array}{r} 67 \\ \times\ 42 \\ \hline \end{array}$ **5.** $\begin{array}{r} 82 \\ \times\ 76 \\ \hline \end{array}$

PRACTICE

Find the products.

1. $\begin{array}{r} 53 \\ \times\ 26 \\ \hline \end{array}$ 2. $\begin{array}{r} 36 \\ \times\ 17 \\ \hline \end{array}$ 3. $\begin{array}{r} 93 \\ \times\ 84 \\ \hline \end{array}$ 4. $\begin{array}{r} 85 \\ \times\ 62 \\ \hline \end{array}$ 5. $\begin{array}{r} 74 \\ \times\ 53 \\ \hline \end{array}$

6. 66×58 7. 56×78 8. 68×16 9. 75×85

10. Multiply 36×47.

11. Find the product of 73 and 28.

APPLY

MATH REASONING Use mental math to make up multiplication problems of 2-digits times 2-digits with these products.

12. 2,000 13. 4,800 14. 7,200 15. 3,000

PROBLEM SOLVING

16. In "Rock the Boat" you skip rope and bounce a ball at the same time. Arlene tried twice. The first time she went 58 skips without missing. The second time she skipped to 116. How much better did she do the second time?

17. 13 of the fourth grade girls played "Chase the Fox." They ran through the rope 3 times before anyone missed. If they each jumped once the first time through, twice the second time, and 3 times the third time, how many jumps did they make all together?

MIXED REVIEW

18. $\begin{array}{r} 3 \\ \times\ 6 \\ \hline \end{array}$ 19. $\begin{array}{r} 7 \\ \times\ 4 \\ \hline \end{array}$ 20. $\begin{array}{r} 4 \\ \times\ 9 \\ \hline \end{array}$ 21. $\begin{array}{r} 3 \\ \times\ 3 \\ \hline \end{array}$ 22. $\begin{array}{r} 3 \\ \times\ 4 \\ \hline \end{array}$ 23. $\begin{array}{r} 4 \\ \times\ 8 \\ \hline \end{array}$

24. $\begin{array}{r} 7 \\ \times\ 8 \\ \hline \end{array}$ 25. $\begin{array}{r} 8 \\ \times\ 7 \\ \hline \end{array}$ 26. $\begin{array}{r} 6 \\ \times\ 6 \\ \hline \end{array}$ 27. $\begin{array}{r} 7 \\ \times\ 6 \\ \hline \end{array}$ 28. $\begin{array}{r} 8 \\ \times\ 8 \\ \hline \end{array}$ 29. $\begin{array}{r} 7 \\ \times\ 7 \\ \hline \end{array}$

30. 36×6 31. 72×7 32. 69×5 33. 82×3

More Practice, page 505, set F

Multiplying with 2- and 3-Digit Factors

1 regular year = 365 days
1 leap year = 366 days Every 4th year is a leap year.

LEARN ABOUT IT

EXPLORE Think About the Process

Katsumi Suzuki holds world records in 3 jump rope events. Usually, Mr. Suzuki skips rope for 2 hours each day. This has an aerobic value of 48 points. How many aerobic points would he have for skipping rope every day in a year that is not a leap year?

You multiply to find the total aerobic points when the same number is earned each day for a year.

Multiply by ones.	Multiply by tens.	Add the products.
$\begin{array}{r} {\scriptstyle 5\,4} \\ 365 \\ \times\ 48 \\ \hline \mathbf{2{,}920} \end{array}$	$\begin{array}{r} {\scriptstyle 2\,2} \\ 365 \\ \times\ 48 \\ \hline 2{,}920 \\ \mathbf{14{,}600} \end{array}$	$\begin{array}{r} 365 \\ \times\ 48 \\ \hline \mathbf{2{,}920} \\ \mathbf{14{,}600} \\ \hline \mathbf{17{,}520} \end{array}$

TALK ABOUT IT

1. How would you have estimated the answer?

2. Give the answer in a complete sentence.

Other Examples

A $\begin{array}{r} 286 \\ \times\ \ 23 \\ \hline 858 \\ 5{,}720 \\ \hline 6{,}578 \end{array}$

B $\begin{array}{r} 305 \\ \times\ \ 82 \\ \hline 610 \\ 24{,}400 \\ \hline 25{,}010 \end{array}$

C $\begin{array}{r} 840 \\ \times\ \ 37 \\ \hline 5{,}880 \\ 25{,}200 \\ \hline 31{,}080 \end{array}$

TRY IT OUT

Multiply.

1. $\begin{array}{r} 542 \\ \times\ 23 \\ \hline \end{array}$

2. $\begin{array}{r} 704 \\ \times\ 57 \\ \hline \end{array}$

3. $\begin{array}{r} 680 \\ \times\ 39 \\ \hline \end{array}$

4. $\begin{array}{r} 500 \\ \times\ 24 \\ \hline \end{array}$

PRACTICE

Find the products.

1. $\begin{array}{r} 572 \\ \times\ 26 \\ \hline \end{array}$

2. $\begin{array}{r} 813 \\ \times\ 94 \\ \hline \end{array}$

3. $\begin{array}{r} 546 \\ \times\ 67 \\ \hline \end{array}$

4. $\begin{array}{r} 725 \\ \times\ 13 \\ \hline \end{array}$

5. $\begin{array}{r} 489 \\ \times\ 76 \\ \hline \end{array}$

6. $\begin{array}{r} 360 \\ \times\ 47 \\ \hline \end{array}$

7. $\begin{array}{r} 273 \\ \times\ 65 \\ \hline \end{array}$

8. $\begin{array}{r} 361 \\ \times\ 88 \\ \hline \end{array}$

Estimate the products.

9. 397×48 **10.** 617×89 **11.** 84×791

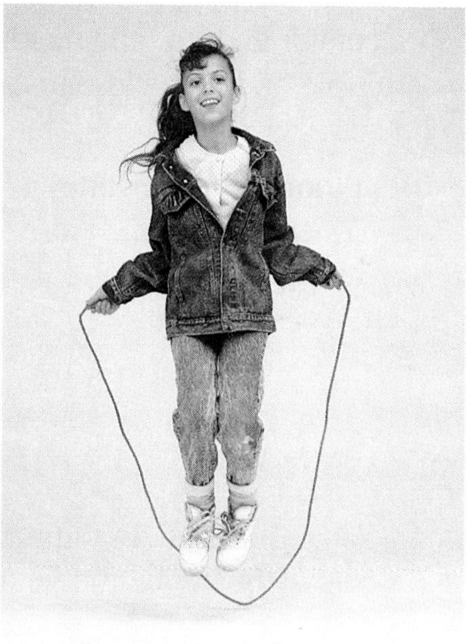

APPLY

MATH REASONING Without using pencil and paper, tell which equation has the larger product.

12. 36×487 or 46×487

13. 58×649 or 58×639

PROBLEM SOLVING

14. Manuel's fastest jump rope time was 105 times in a minute. At that rate, how many jumps would he make in 12 tries?

15. How many more hours are in a leap year than in an ordinary year? A day has 24 hours.

CALCULATOR

16. Use a calculator. Multiply any number by 9 and add together the digits in your answer. If the result is more than 1 digit, add those together until you get a 1-digit answer. Do this with several other numbers, always using 9 as a factor. Do you think it is always, sometimes, or never true that the digits in the answer will add up to 9? Would you give the same answer for multiplying by 90?

Multiply	Add the Digits
$9 \times 6 = 54$	$5 + 4 = 9$
$9 \times 62 = 558$	$5 + 5 + 8 = 18$ $1 + 8 = 9$

Using Critical Thinking

LEARN ABOUT IT

Brad showed Beth his calculator. "I've used the x^2 key on my calculator to multiply a number by itself. The product is 1,024," said Brad. "Can you use my calculator and find the number? I'll tell you what multiple of 10 it's close to, so you'll know where to start!"

Beth thought for a while. "No thanks," she said. "I won't need your hint. I already know where to start!"

Beth was thinking:

30 × 30 is 900
40 × 40 is 1,600
3? × 3? = 1,024

TALK ABOUT IT

1. What did Brad do to produce 1,024 on his calculator? What did he ask Beth to do?
2. What did Beth learn about Brad's number from the products she thought about?
3. What multiple of 10 is Brad's number closest to? How do you know?
4. How would you use a calculator to find Brad's number?

TRY IT OUT

Each number below is the product of a number multiplied by itself. First decide what multiples of 10 it is between. Then use a calculator to find the number.

1. 1,849 **2.** 5,476 **3.** 729
4. 3,136 **5.** 6,561 **6.** 625

POWER PRACTICE/QUIZ

Estimate each product.

1. 44 × 53 **2.** 29 × \$7.67 **3.** 72 × 429 **4.** 655 × 19

Decide if each estimate in red is an overestimate or an underestimate. Then give a closer estimate.

5. 37 × 28 1,200

6. 32 × \$5.42 \$150.00

7. 88 × 366 36,000

8. 243 × 97 20,000

Find the products. Use estimation and mental math to decide if your answer is reasonable.

9. 20 × 30 **10.** 24 × 50 **11.** 78 × 90 **12.** 90 × 30

13. 70 × 60 **14.** 63 × 80 **15.** 50 × 20 **16.** 80 × 70

17. 72 × 30 **18.** 64 × 16 **19.** 88 × 55 **20.** 32 × 75 **21.** 105 × 39

22. 681 × 26 **23.** 95 × 48 **24.** 37 × 18 **25.** 607 × 87 **26.** \$7.25 × 84

27. 28 × 35 **28.** \$4.95 × 26 **29.** 479 × 60 **30.** 700 × 41 **31.** \$1.98 × 14

PROBLEM SOLVING

32. If an elephant's heart beats 33 times in 1 minute, how many times does it beat in 1 hour? An hour is 60 minutes.

33. In one minute, a canary's heart beats about 22 times faster than an elephant's heart. Which of these 3 products give the closest estimate?

a. 20 × 30
b. 25 × 30
c. 22 × 30

34. When Billy runs, his heart beats about twice as fast as normal. After a short rest, Billy's heart rate drops 30 beats per minute to reach 110. What is his normal heart rate?

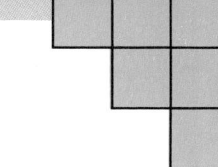

Problem Solving
Use Logical Reasoning

UNDERSTAND
FIND DATA
PLAN
ESTIMATE
SOLVE
CHECK

The students are doing an Ibo dance from Nigeria in western Africa.

LEARN ABOUT IT

To solve some problems, a helpful strategy is **Use Logical Reasoning.**

The Folk Dance Festival presented dances from many different countries. 25 children joined in the African dances. 16 danced the Umoya Spirit Dance and 14 danced the Aredze Game Dance. How many children danced in both dances?

I'll draw a Venn diagram.

I'll put 16 counters inside the Spirit Dancers circle.
I'll put 14 counters inside the Game Dancers circle.

To do this with only 25 counters, I must place 5 counters so that they are inside *both* circles.

5 children danced both dances.

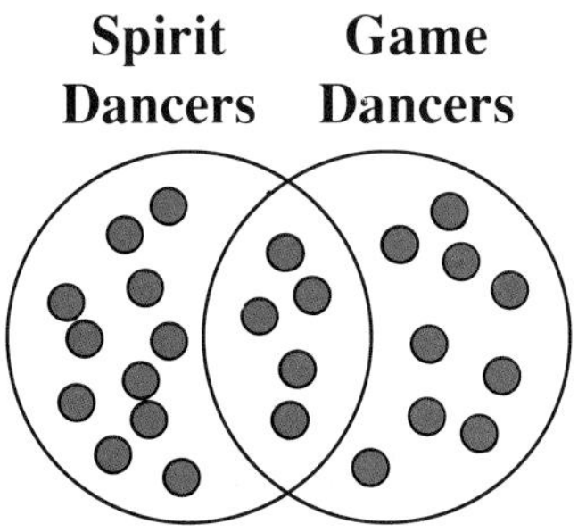

Venn Diagram

TRY IT OUT

Tell if the statement about the dance problem is true or false.

1. **All** of the 25 dancers joined two different dances.

2. **Every** child danced at least once, and **some** children danced twice.

3. **Many** of the children danced at least one dance.

4. Copy this Venn diagram and solve using counters.

   There were 16 dances in the Festival. 9 dances were performed in the morning and 12 in the afternoon. How many dances were performed both times?

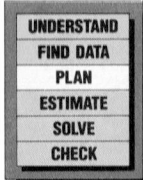

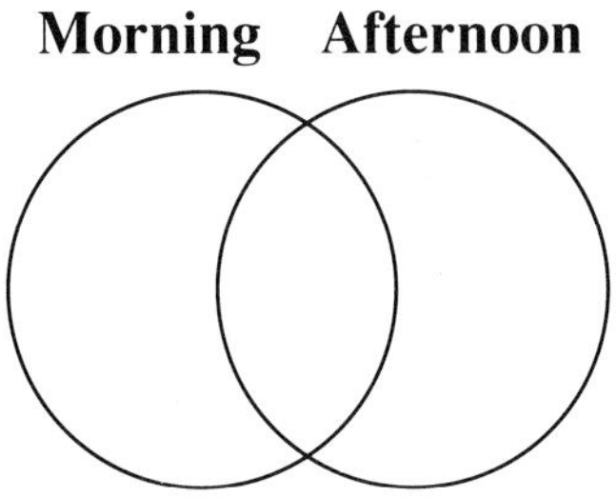

PRACTICE

Use logical reasoning to solve each problem.

1. The 27 students in Edwa's class learned some American Indian dances. 18 learned the Buffalo dance and 13 learned the Snake dance. How many students learned both dances?

2. A total of 57 people bought tee shirts at the festival. 36 bought shirts with dance pictures and 37 bought festival name shirts. How many people bought both types of shirts?

MIXED PRACTICE

Choose a strategy from the strategies list or use other strategies you know to solve these problems.

Folk Dances

Name of Dance	Number of Dancers	Time for Dance
African Ibo	16	12 min
Greek Syrto	9	6 min
Russian Karapyet	12	5 min
Texas Square	8	8 min

Some Strategies

Act It Out
Use Objects
Choose an Operation
Draw a Picture
Make an Organized List
Guess and Check
Make a Table
Look for a Pattern
Use Logical Reasoning

3. How many people are needed to dance the four dances in the chart if no one dances more than one dance?

4. Use mental math to find how long the program of dances in the chart would last.

5. Jeremy watched the festival dances from 11:30 a.m. to 2:45 p.m. For how long did he watch dancing?

6. A festival tee shirt costs $8.75. How much would 5 tee shirts cost?

7. Mrs. Ramirez bought some African pottery costing $42.35. She used a $50 bill to pay. How much change did she get?

8. On Friday and Saturday a total of 15 visitors from different countries came to the festival. 9 came on Friday and 12 on Saturday. How many visitors came to the festival both days?

Multiplying with Money

LEARN ABOUT IT

EXPLORE **Make a Decision**

Mrs. Wingate wants to order special award trophies for each of the 23 students who won sports honors during the year. She saw this ad in the school catalog. She needs to decide whether to buy 23 trophies at the regular price or to buy 25 at the reduced price.

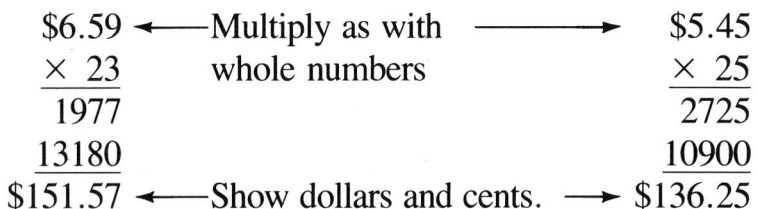

TALK ABOUT IT

1. What process would you use to make the choice?
2. If you changed the single sports trophy price to all cents, how many cents would you have?

You can multiply money just like you multiply whole numbers.

\$6.59	← Multiply as with whole numbers →	\$5.45
× 23		× 25
1977		2725
13180		10900
\$151.57	← Show dollars and cents. →	\$136.25

Sports Trophies
\$6.59 each
Only \$5.45 each with the purchase of 25 or more

Mrs. Wingate should buy 25 sports trophies at the cheaper price.

TRY IT OUT

Multiply.

1. \$3.24 × 18 **2.** \$9.38 × 38 **3.** \$3.75 × 22 **4.** \$0.75 × 44 **5.** \$6.09 × 11

6. \$2.78 × 12 **7.** \$6.05 × 49 **8.** \$1.99 × 20 **9.** \$7.10 × 29 **10.** \$4.31 × 15

11. 11 × \$3.80 **12.** 17 × \$2.35 **13.** 20 × \$0.85

PRACTICE

Find the products.

1. $\$3.86 \times 12$
2. $\$2.81 \times 21$
3. $\$5.79 \times 32$
4. $\$3.68 \times 45$
5. $\$8.20 \times 29$
6. $\$0.98 \times 60$
7. $\$9.00 \times 71$
8. $\$0.56 \times 28$
9. $\$7.14 \times 86$
10. $\$9.49 \times 45$

11. 15 × $0.89 **12.** $7.09 × 78 **13.** $4.30 × 68 **14.** 59 × $7.40

15. $4.28 × 23 **16.** $8.27 × 47 **17.** 17 × $0.75 **18.** $3.05 × 18

Estimate these products.

19. $1.98 × 49 **20.** $4.89 × 52 **21.** $6.07 × 19 **22.** $9.98 × 25

APPLY

MATH REASONING Solve. Look for a pattern and give the next 3 products.

23. $\$0.50 \times 50$
24. $\$0.51 \times 49$
25. $\$0.52 \times 48$
26. $\$0.53 \times 47$
27. $\$0.54 \times 46$

PROBLEM SOLVING

28. Award certificates for a team cost $9.75. Mrs. Wingate bought certificates for 3 teams. How much did she pay?

29. Jeff's soccer coach bought 3 trophies for $4 each. He bought some more trophies for $5 each. The total cost was $22. How many $5 trophies did he buy?

MENTAL MATH

Use mental math to multiply by 4. To do this, double and then double again.

30. $32 **31.** $2.50 **32.** $5.25 **33.** $4.15 **34.** $12.20

35. $16 **36.** $6.08 **37.** $7.10 **38.** $8.22 **39.** $92.00

More Practice, page 506, set A

Problem Solving
Choosing a Calculation Method

UNDERSTAND
FIND DATA
PLAN
ESTIMATE
SOLVE
CHECK

LEARN ABOUT IT

Calculation Methods

- Mental Math
- Paper and Pencil
- Calculator

When you solve a problem, you must choose which of these calculation methods is best to use.

Wacky Records adapted from the *Guinness Book of World Records*	
■ Balancing on 1 foot — 34 hours —5-minute rest breaks after each hour	■ Crawling — 27 miles —always moving, with one or the other knee always touching the ground
■ Standing Up — 17 years —leaning against a board while sleeping	■ Walking on Hands — 871 miles —in 55 daily 10-hour periods

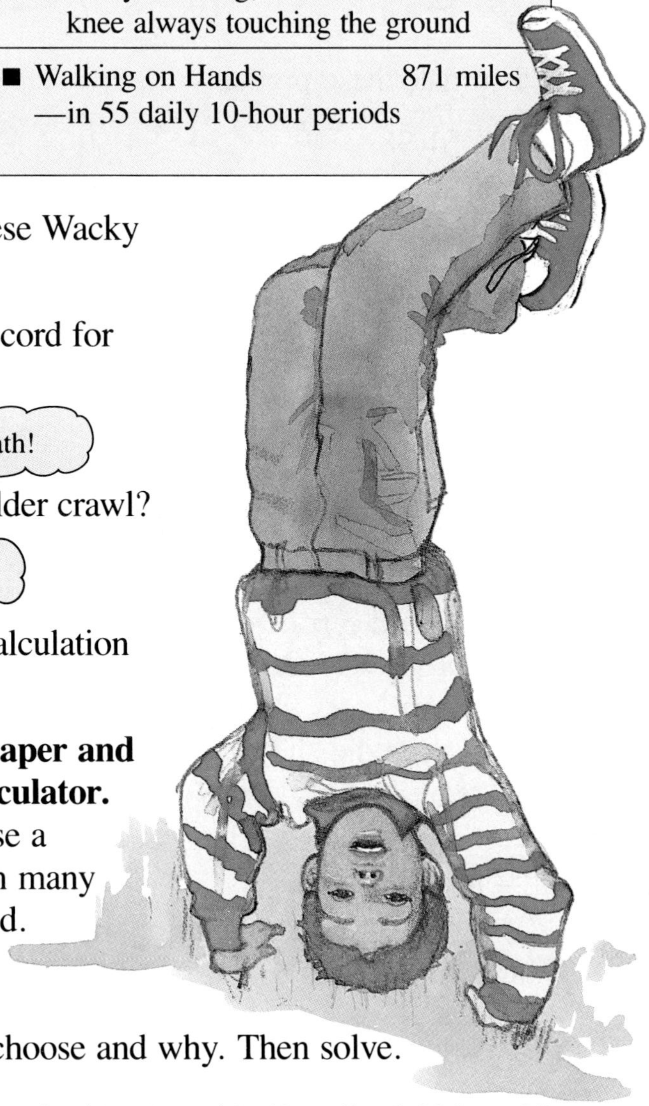

Which methods would you use to solve these Wacky Records problems?

How many hours did it take to reach the record for walking on hands?

55×10 — I can do this using mental math!

How many feet did the crawling record holder crawl?

$5{,}280 \times 27$ — I think I'll use a calculator.

Use these hints when you are choosing a calculation method.

- **First try mental math.** Look for easy computations.
- **Then choose paper and pencil or a calculator.** It is better to use a calculator when many steps are needed.

TRY IT OUT

Tell which calculation method you would choose and why. Then solve.

1. 7×100 **2.** $362 - 99$ **3.** 3×13 **4.** \$9.58 + \$0.42 **5.** $5{,}280 \times 39$

MIXED PRACTICE

Tell which calculation method you choose and why. Then solve.

1. $25 \times 68 \times 4$

2. $300 - 199$

3. 967×346

4. 60×40

5. 123×3

6. $101 + 100 + 99$

7. 155×5

8. $\$967 - \$38.69$

9. $86 + 5$

10. 3×21

11. 31×20

12. 45×26

Solve. Give the calculation method you chose.
Use the Wacky Records on page 194.

13. Joe balanced on one foot for 3 hrs. How many hours longer than this is the official record?

14. Between the start and the finish, how many minutes of rest did the person who set the balancing on one foot record get?

15. How many days did the person who set the standing record stand? Use 365 days in a year.

16. How many more miles is the walking on hands record distance than the crawling record distance?

17. Jonathan crawled 1 mile in 30 minutes. How many minutes would it take for him to crawl as far as the world record holder did?

18. Lila is 9 years old. How many more years did the standing record holder stand than Lila has been alive?

19. How many more miles would the record holder have had to walk on his or her hands to have walked 1,000 miles?

20. **Write Your Own Problems** Write a problem that you would solve **a.** using mental math, **b.** using paper and pencil, and **c.** using a calculator.

Problem Solving
Multiple-Step Problems

UNDERSTAND
FIND DATA
PLAN
ESTIMATE
SOLVE
CHECK

LEARN ABOUT IT

To solve some problems, you will need to use more than one of the operations of addition, subtraction, and multiplication. These problems are called multiple-step problems.

Mario's goal in the Reading Marathon was to read 1,550 pages. He read 35 pages a day for 59 days. How many pages over his goal did he go?

First I'll multiply to find how many pages he read in all.

$$35 \times 59 = 2{,}065$$

Then I'll subtract to find how many pages he read over his goal.

$$2{,}065 - 1{,}550 = 515$$

He read 515 pages over his goal.

TRY IT OUT

1. Mrs. Finch made a mistake when she wrote a check for $9.02. Her daughter had ordered 2 books at $1.69 each and 3 books at $1.49 each. How much money should Mrs. Finch get back?

2. Marta's goal was to make $20.00 from her sponsors in the Reading Marathon. She read 23 books and collected a total of $0.75 for each book. How much under her goal was she?

Use the order form on page 197 to solve these problems.

3. How much more did the fourth grade classes spend on *The Phantom Tollbooth* by Norton Juster than on *Voyage to the Misty Isles*?

4. Last month, the fourth graders spent $35.32 on software. How much less did they spend this month?

MIXED PRACTICE

You may need to use the book club order form below to solve these problems.

1. The longest book Stacey had ever read was 304 pages. She just finished *The Wind in the Willows* by Kenneth Grahame with 258 pages. How much shorter was this than the longest book she had read?

2. Last month, the fourth graders bought a total of 71 items and spent a total of $136.98 on their book club orders. How much less was spent on this book order?

3. There are 30 shelves in the children's section of the library. There are about 20 books on each shelf. About how many books are in the children's section?

4. Stacey bought one each of items 3 through 6 on the book order form. How much did she spend?

5. A total of 16 students bought old time favorites. How many students bought both old time favorites?

6. **Understanding the Operations** Tell what operation you would use. Use objects to solve the problem. Lita had a box of detective mysteries. She gave 9 books away. She has 8 books left. How many books did she have in the beginning?

Triangle Book Club
Order Form Rooms 6, 7, and 8

Item	Qty	Title	Cost each
Paperbacks			
1	14	James and the Giant Peach	$1.49
2	7	Little House on the Prairie	$1.69
3	11	Little Women **Old Time Favorite**	$1.95
4	3	Mystery of Slimey Gulch	$1.49
5	12	The Phantom Tollbooth	$1.49
6	6	Voyage to the Misty Isles	$1.69
7	9	Wind in the Willows **Old Time Favorite**	$1.95
Software			
8	2	Math Whiz	$8.85
9	1	Write Your Own Jokes	$7.95
Total Items	65	Total Cost	$129.83

More Practice, page 517, set B

Applied Problem Solving
Group Decision Making

UNDERSTAND
FIND DATA
PLAN
ESTIMATE
SOLVE
CHECK

Group Skill:
Explain and Summarize

Rick's family is thinking about becoming members of the large zoo near them. What do you think they should do?

Facts to Consider

1. A family membership costs $35.
2. These are the benefits of a family membership.
   - free admission to zoo grounds
   - subscription to zoo magazine
   - free admission to insect and petting zoo
   - one 50¢ coupon for a purchase of $5.00 or more at the zoo gift store

3. These are the regular admission fees.
   - adult $2.25
   - child $0.75
   - insect and petting zoo, per person $0.75
4. Rick's entire family usually goes to the zoo about 3 times a year. There are 3 children and 2 parents in the family.

5. The family always goes to the insect and petting zoo.
6. The family usually spends about $5.00 at the zoo store each visit.

Some Questions to Answer

1. How much does Rick's family pay for admission fees each time they go to the zoo?
2. How much does his family pay to go to the insect and petting zoo?
3. How much money does Rick's family spend in all for each zoo visit, not including the zoo store?
4. How much do they spend in 2 visits?
5. If they were members, how much would they get back from the zoo store each time?

What Is Your Decision?

Make a list or chart to show why you think Rick's family should or should not become members of the zoo.

WRAP UP

Multiplication Match

Use the term that best completes each sentence.

whole numbers	mental math
underestimates	multiple steps

1. When you multiply front-end digits of factors your products are usually __?__.
2. You can multiply with money just like you multiply with __?__.
3. When numbers are easy to work with you can use __?__.
4. If you must use more than one operation to solve a problem, the problem has __?__.

Sometimes, Always, Never

Which word should go in the blank, sometimes, always, or never? Explain your choices.

5. The product of two even numbers is __?__ an odd number.
6. It is __?__ wiser to overestimate than to underestimate.
7. In a multiple-step problem, you __?__ do the multiplication step first.

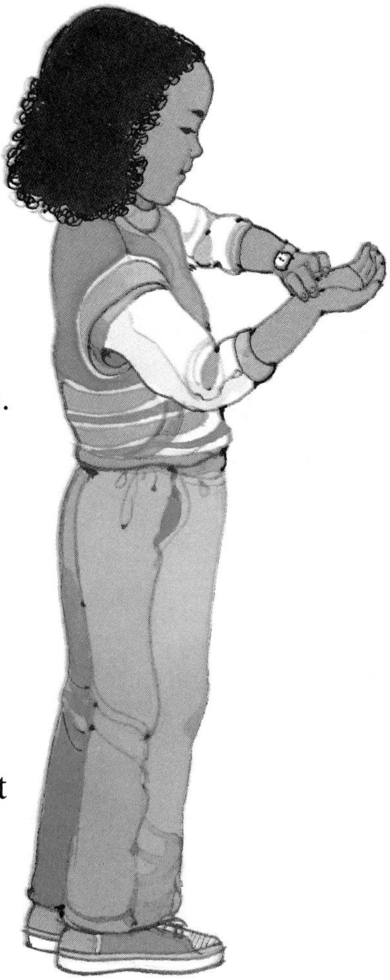

Project

For one minute, count how many times these things happen.

- your heart beats
- you swallow
- your eyes blink
- you breathe in and out

After you collect the exact data, estimate how many times you do each activity in one hour, then in one day. Explain how some of the estimates might vary over 24 hours.

Power Practice/Test

Part 1 Understanding

1. What fact helps you find the product for 40×60?
2. What fact helps you find the product for 70×80?
3. One way to estimate 27×78 is to use 30×80. Will your product be an overestimate or an underestimate? Why?
4. Make the best match you can.

■ to find 5,684 + 4,692 + 3,425	a. use mental math
■ to find 582 + 32 + 14	b. use pencil and paper
■ to find 3,000 × 40	c. use a calculator

Part 2 Skills

5. 50×70
6. 40×40
7. 83×30
8. 68×60
9. 48×75
10. 19×91
11. 34×84
12. 61×27
13. 804×39
14. 773×52
15. $\$6.15 \times 89$
16. $\$3.63 \times 40$

Part 3 Applications

17. A magician does 13 coin tricks using dimes and nickels. In 7 of the tricks she uses dimes. In 10 of the tricks she uses nickels. In how many tricks does she use both dimes and nickels?

18. The magician needs a dozen scarves that cost $2.75 each. She has a $20 bill. How much more money does she need?

19. A bowling ball weighs 17 times more than a 15-ounce football. How much does the bowling ball weigh?

20. **Challenge** Ky can do 33 sit-ups a minute. If he kept that pace for 24 hours, how many sit-ups would he do?

ENRICHMENT
The Unfinished Table

The multiplication table below is incomplete. There are some missing factors and products. Find your detective hat and your calculator. Complete the table. Hint: How are multiplication and division related?

1.

X			28	163
49	19,943	3,038		
				15,322
			1,680	
57				

Then find the missing digits in these examples.

2. □□□ × 28 = 11,116

3. 283 × □□ = 18,678

4. □78 × 25 = 11,950

Cumulative Review

1.

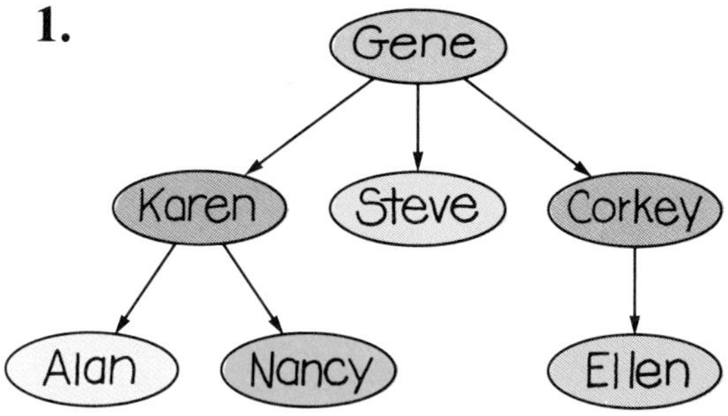

Gene made a family tree. Find the number of children Gene has.

A 5 **B** 4

C 3 **D** 6

2.

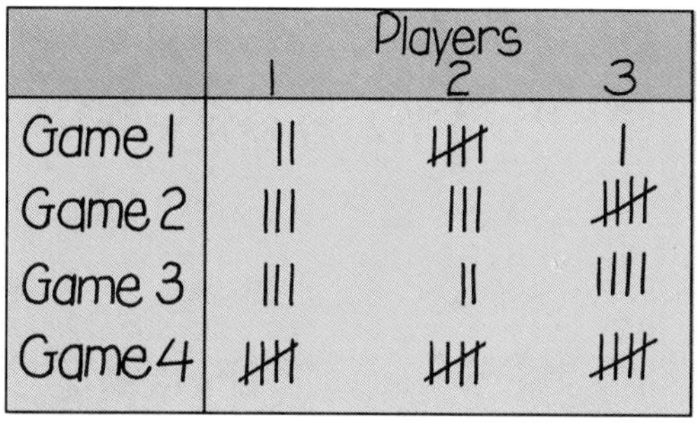

Look at the scores of the 3 players trying each game. Which game seems the least fair?

A Game 1 **B** Game 2

C Game 3 **D** Game 4

3. 10×0

A 10 **B** 100

C 0 **D** 1

4. 7×5

A 12 **B** 35

C 0 **D** 70

5. Which is a multiple of 8?

A 4 **B** 20

C 18 **D** 32

6. Find the product of 3 and 9.

A 27 **B** 6

C 28 **D** 12

7. 308×3

A 911 **B** 904

C 924 **D** 964

8. 314×6

A 1,864 **B** 2,064

C 1,884 **D** 1,984

9. Find the product of 5,073 and 8.

A 40,584 **B** 45,084

C 40,544 **D** 44,084

10. A rubber nose costs 85¢. Use mental math to find the cost of 4 rubber noses.

A $3.40 **B** $1.70

C $3.20 **D** $2.60

11. Clown makeup jars are on display in rows. Row 1 has 5 jars, row 2 has 8 jars, and row 3 has 11 jars. How many jars are in row 6?

A 30 **B** 17

C 23 **D** 20

8

TIME AND CUSTOMARY MEASUREMENT

THEME: TIME ZONES

MATH AND SOCIAL STUDIES

DATA BANK

Use the Social Studies Data Bank on page 474 to answer the questions.

1 What time is shown on each clock on the map of time zones?

2 In which time zone is the time one hour later than in the Pacific time zone? 2 hours later? 3 hours later?

3 Do you lose or gain time when you travel from New York to California?

4 **Use Critical Thinking** The time difference from Alaska to Hawaii is 1 hour. Hawaii is farther west, so is the time there earlier or later?

When this clock in London, England, shows 3 o'clock, would a clock at your school show the same time?

Telling Time
Minutes

LEARN ABOUT IT

Linda's clock

Russ's clock

EXPLORE **Compare the Methods**

Linda and Russ planned to meet at the science museum. Linda said, "I'll leave my house at 15 minutes to 4." Russ looked at his clock and said, "I thought I'd leave my house at 45 minutes past 3. Does that mean we'll leave at the same time?" "I think so," said Linda, "but let's count on our clocks to check."

TALK ABOUT IT

1. Who counted from the 12 on the clock to find the time? Who counted from the 9?
2. Linda said another way to think about the time was to say "quarter to four." Explain why that works.

Here are some ways to read and write times.

You read five-fifteen, 15 minutes past 5, or quarter past five.

You read ten-thirty, 30 minutes past 10, or half past ten.

You read seven-forty-two, 42 minutes past 7, or 18 minutes to 8.

TRY IT OUT

Give each time in three different ways.

1. 

2. 

3. 

4. 

PRACTICE

Write each time as it would look on a digital clock.

1. 

2. 

3. 

4. 

5. 

6. 

7. 

8. 

APPLY

MATH REASONING

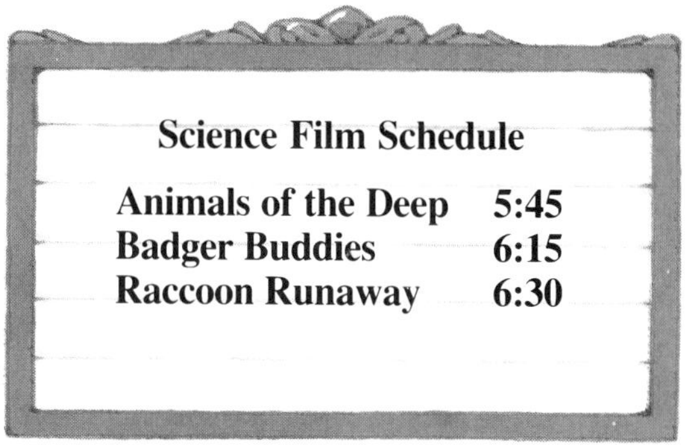

Science Film Schedule
Animals of the Deep 5:45
Badger Buddies 6:15
Raccoon Runaway 6:30

9. Which film starts at a quarter past six?

10. Which film starts at half past 6?

11. Which film starts at a quarter to 6?

PROBLEM SOLVING

12. Where is the hour hand at 14 minutes to 6? Where is the minute hand?

13. Social Studies Data Bank
When it is 5:00 in Arkansas (AR), what time is it in New York (NY)? See page 474.

DATA BANK

ESTIMATION

14. The minute hand is missing from this clock. Choose the best estimate for the time.

a. close to 8:00 **b.** close to 9:00

A.M. and P.M.

LEARN ABOUT IT

a.m.

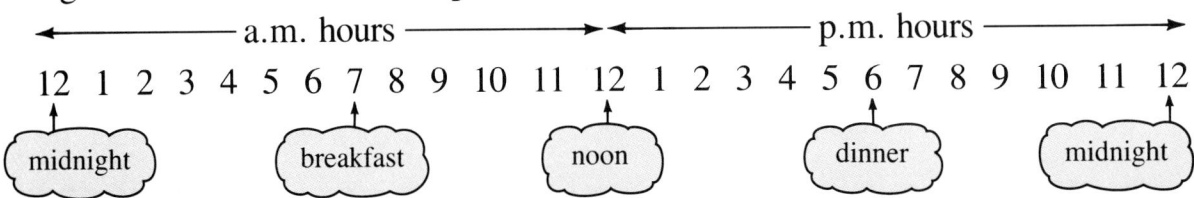

p.m.

EXPLORE **Study the Information**

The hour hand goes around the clock twice each day. It goes around once for the **a.m.** hours, which are before noon. It also goes around once for the **p.m.** hours, which are after noon.

TALK ABOUT IT

1. How many hours does it take for the hour hand to go around the clock once? twice?
2. Explain why it is important to know if a given time is in the a.m. hours or p.m. hours.

Thinking of a time line like this can help you decide if a given time is in the a.m. or p.m. hours.

← a.m. hours → ← p.m. hours →

12 1 2 3 4 5 6 7 8 9 10 11 12 1 2 3 4 5 6 7 8 9 10 11 12

midnight (12) breakfast (7) noon (12) dinner (6) midnight (12)

PRACTICE

Use the time line to help answer these questions.

1. What are three things you do in the a.m. hours?
2. What are three things you do in the p.m. hours?
3. Are you in school more a.m. hours or p.m. hours?
4. Do you sleep more a.m. hours or p.m. hours?

Write a.m. or p.m. to complete each sentence.

5. Pernell woke up at 1:00 _?_ in the middle of the night.
6. Tessa napped at 2:45 _?_ in the afternoon.
7. Carla got home from school at 3:20 _?_.
8. Ho cooked his breakfast at 7:30 _?_.

More Practice, page 517, set D

Reading the Calendar

LEARN ABOUT IT

EXPLORE **Study the Calendar**

It is important to know the order of the days and weeks so you can talk about dates on the calendar.

August 8 is on Tuesday. It is the second Tuesday in the month.

TALK ABOUT IT

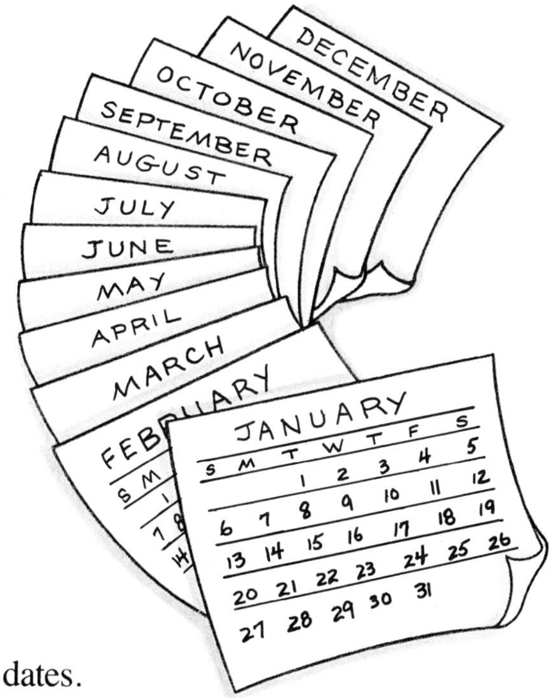

1. Tell which Thursday is the 24th of August.
2. What is the date of the fifth Wednesday in August?

There are 12 months in a year. You can use **ordinal numbers** to describe the months. August is the 8th month.

You can write dates two ways.

August 5, 1989   8/5/89

PRACTICE

Use the August calendar to name these dates.

1. The Camera Club meets on the third Monday of each month. When will it meet in August?
2. The Music Club meets on the second Friday of each month. When will it meet in August?

Name the month.

3. the 12th month
4. the 7th month
5. the 5th month

Write each date another way.

6. 9/11/88
7. June 29, 1985
8. 2/13/87
9. November 7, 1989

More Practice, page 518, set A

Mental Math
Elapsed Time

LEARN ABOUT IT

You can use mental math to find out how long an event lasts or when an event will end.

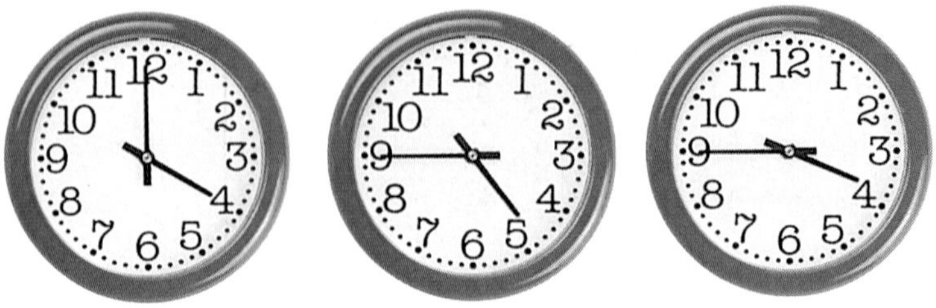

A B C

D E

EXPLORE **Study the Clocks**

- The Cinco de Mayo parade had bands, dancers, and horseback riders. It began at 1:15 and lasted for 3 hours. Which clock shows when it finished?
- Gloria's father was a parade monitor. Clock D shows his starting time. Clock E shows his ending time. How long did her father work at the parade?

TALK ABOUT IT

1. How did you choose the correct clock to show the time when the parade finished?
2. Look at Gloria's solution. How is it different from your solution?

Gloria's Solution

I'll begin at 12:30 and count on by hours, then by half hours and minutes.

12:30, 1:30, 2:30, 3:30, 4:00, 4:15
My father worked 3 hours, 45 minutes.

TRY IT OUT

Give the ending time.

1. The folkloric dancing started at 2:15. It lasted 4 hours.
2. Riders began to groom horses at 9:45. It took 2 hours, 15 minutes.

Give the amount of elapsed time.

3. Starting time 8:00 a.m.
   Ending time 11:00 p.m.
4. Starting time 6:15 p.m.
   Ending time 11:30 p.m.

PRACTICE

Use the list to tell how long each girl took to make her piñata.

> The Saturday before the holiday, Gloria and her friends made piñatas for Cinco de Mayo parties.
>
> Tina began at 9:30 a.m.
> Lina began at 10:30 a.m.
> Maya began at 11:15 a.m.
> Lara began at 3:15 p.m.
> Gloria began at 3:30 p.m.

1. Lara finished at 4:30 p.m.

2. Gloria finished at 5:35 p.m.

3. Lina finished at 1:30 p.m.

Use the list to give the ending time.

4. It took Tina 3 hours to make a piñata.

5. Maya worked for 55 minutes.

MATH REASONING

6. Which is a better estimate for the amount of time?

Starting time	2:15 p.m.	**a.** about 2 hours
Ending time	3:58 p.m.	**b.** about 3 hours

PROBLEM SOLVING

7. Gloria left the dancing at 6:05. She arrived home 1 hour and 35 minutes later. What time was it?

8. **Social Studies Data Bank** DATA BANK Gloria called from Iowa (IA) at 11:35 a.m. to tell her grandma in Ohio (OH) about the parade. What time was it in Florida? See page 474.

CALCULATOR

9. This list shows how long these children rode their horses in the riding contest. The contest began at 3:00. What time did it end?

Paco	23 minutes
Lisa	9 minutes
Reggie	19 minutes
Belva	24 minutes
Al	28 minutes
Yvonne	17 minutes

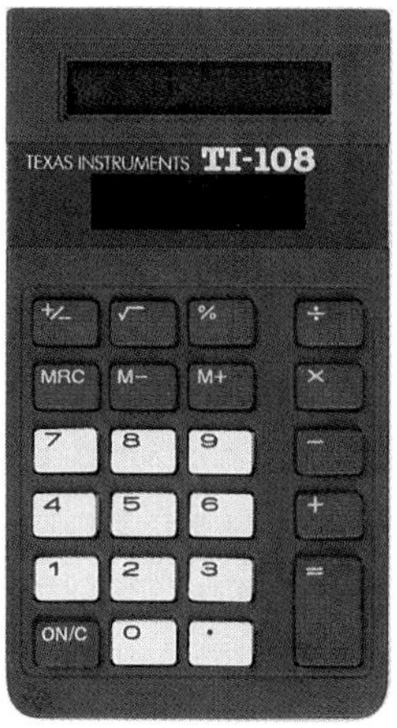

Problem Solving
Problems with More than One Answer

UNDERSTAND
FIND DATA
PLAN
ESTIMATE
SOLVE
CHECK

LEARN ABOUT IT

The parents at Hayes School were building two playground structures. While working under the slide, Mrs. Kuang could see only the legs of those walking by. She counted 10 legs in one group. What combination of dogs and children could have been in that group?

Some problems have more than one answer. When you find an answer to a problem, don't stop there. Ask yourself if there might be other answers.

Try 3 children and 2 dogs.
6 legs + 8 legs = 14 legs

I can use guess and check. That's too many legs.

Try 3 children and 1 dog.
6 legs + 4 legs = 10 legs.

Correct! Mrs. Kuang saw 10 legs.

I can check for other answers. I'll organize my work in a table.

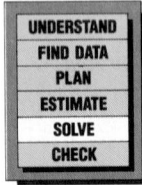

Children	Legs	Dogs	Legs	Total
1	2	2	8	10 That works.
2	4	2	8	12 That doesn't work.
3	6	1	4	10 That works.
4	8	1	4	12 That doesn't work.

There are two possible answers: 1 child and 2 dogs, or 3 children and 1 dog.

TRY IT OUT

Find as many answers as you can for each problem.

1. Brian counted 21 wheels on the bicycles and tricycles on the playground. How many tricycles and how many bicycles were there?

2. Bob's dad bought 100 pounds of sand to put under the structures. The sand came in 25-pound and 50-pound bags. How many bags of each size did he buy?

MIXED PRACTICE

Choose a strategy from the list or use other strategies you know to solve these problems.

Some Strategies
Act It Out
Use Objects
Choose an Operation
Draw a Picture
Make an Organized List
Guess and Check
Make a Table
Look for a Pattern
Use Logical Reasoning

1. Redwood posts for the structure cost $6.88 apiece. They are 8 feet long. How much did 9 posts cost?

2. Paolo's mother laid the 24 monkey bars into rows. There were the same number of bars in each row. How many were in each row? How many rows were there?

3. Mr. Chan arrived at 1:45 p.m. He worked until 4:20 p.m. How long did he work?

4. 25 parents volunteered to build the structure. 14 worked on the morning shift and 17 worked on the afternoon shift. How many worked both shifts?

5. Kara's father needs 17 feet of lumber for railings. He has some boards that are 5 feet long and some that are 6 feet long. How many 5-foot and 6-foot boards does he need?

6. How many more students will be using the large structure than the small structure?

Grade	Students	Structure
K	59	small
1–3	196	small
4–6	287	large

7. It took Mrs. Whitecloud 1 hour and 25 minutes to make the balance beams. She started at 2:45. When did she finish?

8. Jane's grandfather carried in 12 bags of sand. Each bag weighed 25 pounds. How heavy were the bags of sand all together?

More Practice, page 518, set C

Estimating and Measuring Length
Nonstandard Units

LEARN ABOUT IT

EXPLORE Use Body Units

Work in groups. Choose six items in your classroom. Estimate and measure the length of each item using one of your body units. Make a table like the one started below. Record your data in the table.

Item	Unit	Estimate	Measure

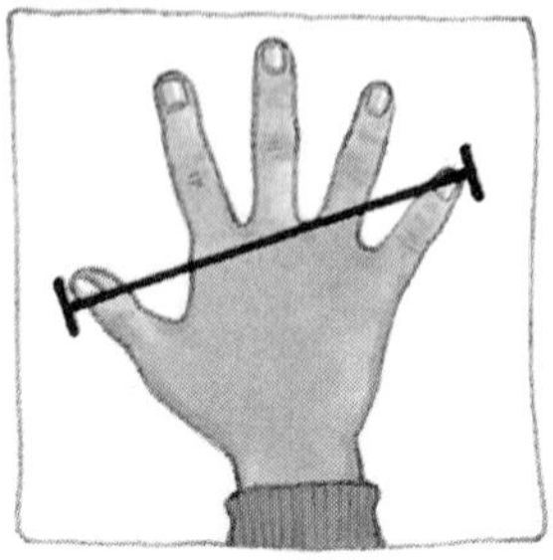

1 span

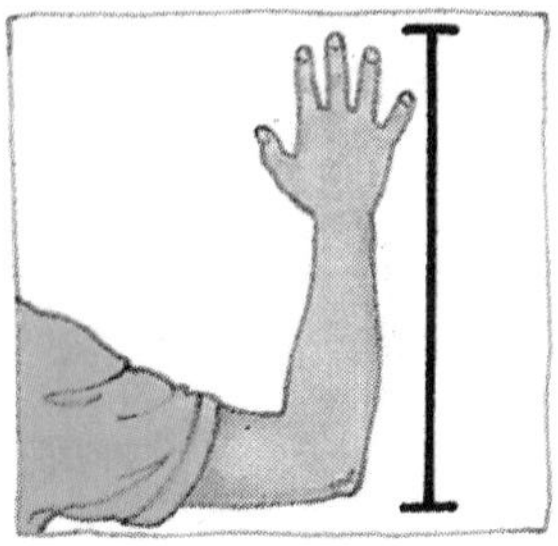

1 cubit

1 step

TALK ABOUT IT

1. How did you decide which unit to use with each item?
2. If everyone in your group used their hand span to measure a table, would the measures all be the same? Explain.

To measure the length of an object, choose a unit. Then count how many times you can lay that unit along the length of the object.

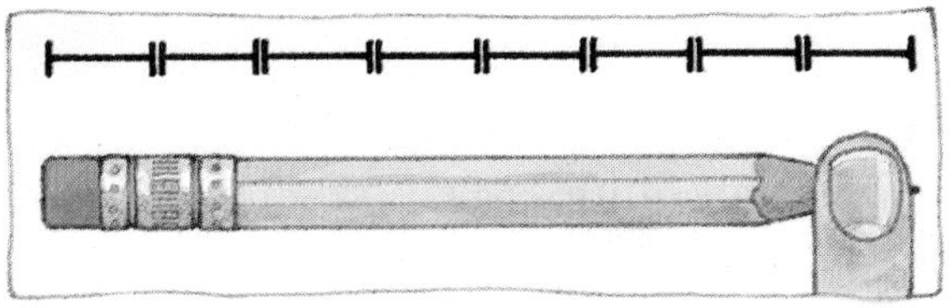

The length of the pencil is close to 7 thumb units.

TRY IT OUT

Estimate and measure the lengths of these pencils. Use your thumb as the unit of measurement.

1. 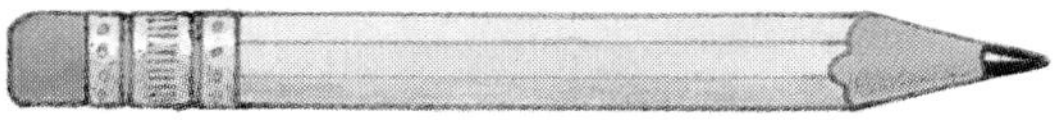

2. 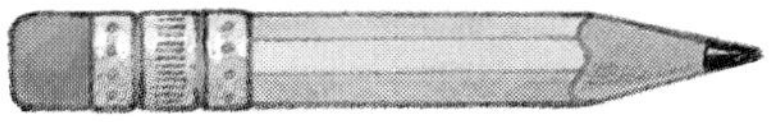

PRACTICE

Estimate and measure using your body units.

1. 

Item: chalkboard
Unit: step

2. 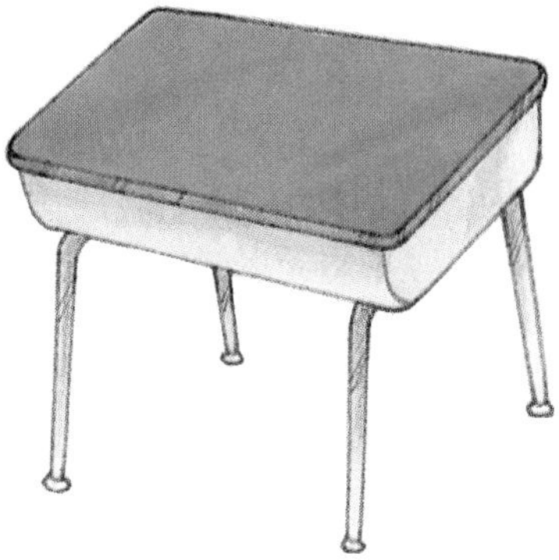

Item: your desk
Unit: hand span

3. Estimate the length of your hand span in thumb units. Check by measuring.

4. Estimate the length of your cubit in hand span units. Check by measuring.

APPLY

MATH REASONING

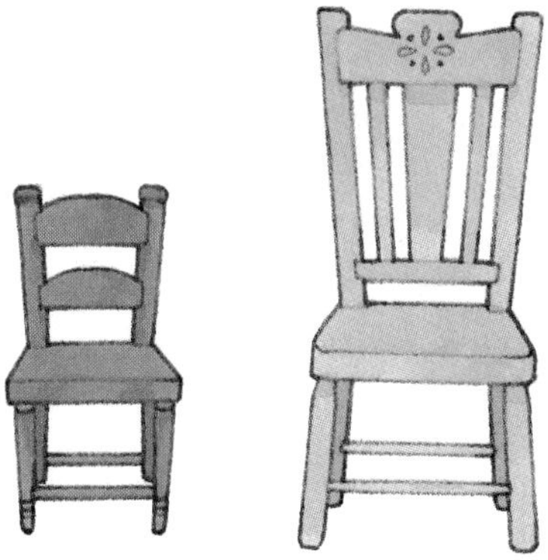

5. One chair is 10 cubits high. The other is 10 hand spans high. Which is higher? Explain how you know.

PROBLEM SOLVING

6. Which of the body units would give the largest measure for the width of your classroom? Why?

7. Bill's hand span is 9 thumbs long. Bill found that the length of his desk is 5 hand spans. How many thumbs long is the desk?

COMMUNICATION Write About It

8. Body units are not used to measure things in everyday life. Write a paragraph to explain why you think they are not used.

Inch, Foot, and Yard

LEARN ABOUT IT

The **inch**, the **foot**, and the **yard** are customary units of length that are often compared. To compare measurements made with different units, you may need to change those units.

inch (in.) ├──────────┤

1 foot (ft) = 12 inches

1 yard (yd) = 3 feet, or 36 inches

EXPLORE Create a Method

Do you think the distance around your open hand is closer to 6 inches, 12 inches, or 36 inches? Create a way to measure this distance to the nearest inch. Then decide if you can change your measurement into feet or yards.

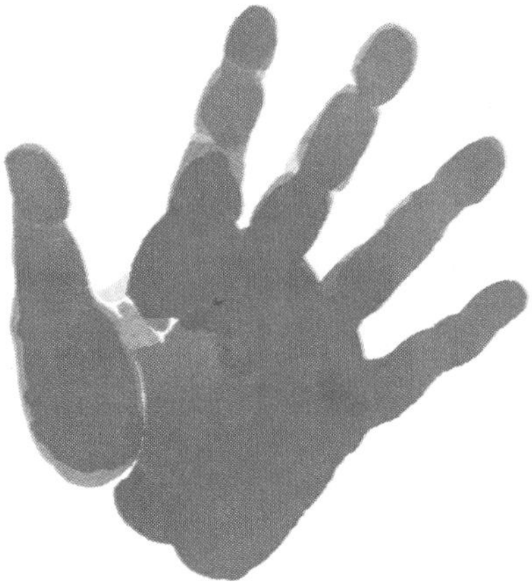

TALK ABOUT IT

1. How did you measure the distance?
2. How did you decide if your measurement could be changed into feet or yards?

Here is a way to compare measurements with different units. First decide which measurement has the larger unit. Then multiply that measurement to change it into the smaller unit.

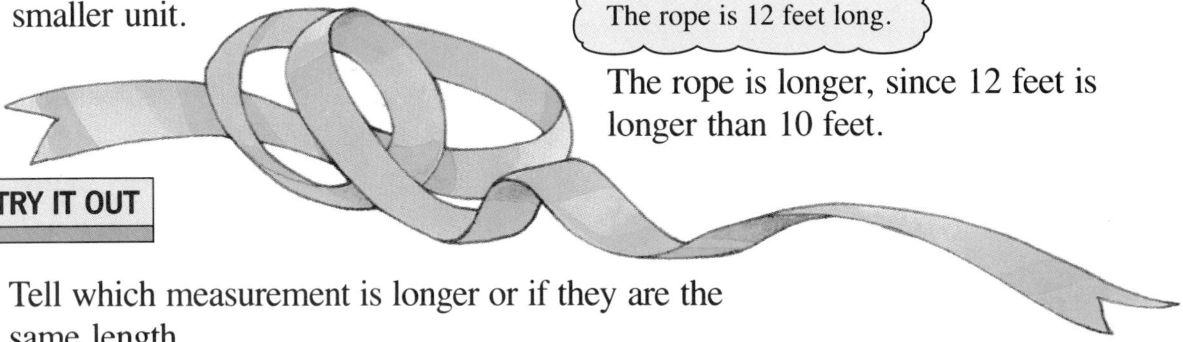

Which is longer—10 feet of ribbon or 4 yards of rope?

Yards is the larger unit, so I multiply 4×3 ft.

The rope is 12 feet long.

The rope is longer, since 12 feet is longer than 10 feet.

TRY IT OUT

Tell which measurement is longer or if they are the same length.

1. 5 yd 15 ft	**2.** 56 in. 2 ft	**3.** 2 yd 72 in.	**4.** 6 yd 12 ft
5. 3 yd 108 in.	**6.** 6 ft 3 yd	**7.** 4 ft 48 in.	**8.** 50 in. 4 ft

PRACTICE

Tell which is longer or if they are the same length.

1. Water ski
   Bow
2. Bow
   Arrow
3. Fishing pole
   Water ski
4. Arrow
   Fishing pole

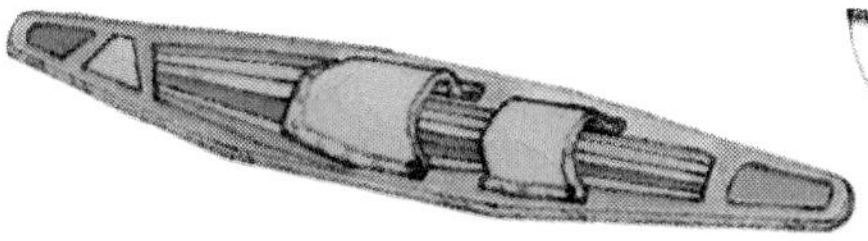

Water ski 72 in.

Fishing pole 2 yd

Bow 4 ft

Arrow 36 in.

APPLY

MATH REASONING Which is the better estimate for the length?

5. A garden hose is 25 ft long. **a.** about 8 yd **b.** about 9 yd

PROBLEM SOLVING

6. Margo is making a super-long balance beam. She laid 5 boards in a row, with the ends touching. Each board is 47 in. long. How long will her balance beam be?

7. **Developing a Plan** Spencer bought 4 rolls of twine. Each roll was 15 yd long. How many feet is that? Tell which steps you could use to solve this problem.

MIXED REVIEW

Find the products.

8. 475×7 **9.** 219×6 **10.** 937×2 **11.** 730×5 **12.** 555×5

13. 264×8 **14.** 827×3 **15.** 601×4 **16.** 967×6

17. 82×40 **18.** 57×90 **19.** 34×60 **20.** 69×50 **21.** 99×20 **22.** 21×70

More Practice, page 518, set E

Problem Solving
Deciding When to Estimate

LEARN ABOUT IT

When you solve a problem where a measurement is needed, you must decide whether to actually measure or just estimate. Knowing how the measurement will be used can help you decide.

Cora wants to grill hamburgers for 16 friends. Does she need to make a hamburger and weigh it to decide if she can buy the hamburger for $16?

Josh cooks in a restaurant that sells quarter-pound hamburgers. He has 20 pounds of meat to fill an order for 80 hamburgers. Is that enough meat? Does Josh need to weigh each hamburger patty?

The hamburgers Cora is making do not need to weigh exactly the same.

Cora can estimate that one pound will serve 4 people and so she will need 4 pounds. $4 \times \$2.98$ per pound is about $12.

The hamburgers Josh is making each need to weigh exactly a quarter pound, as they arc advertised.

Josh should weigh each amount of meat.

TRY IT OUT

Decide whether an estimate or an actual measurement is needed. Explain why.

1. Your dog is on a special diet. You were told to feed her only 1 pound of food each day. How much food should you give her today?

2. You are sick and your doctor wants to know how much your body temperature has risen in the last hour. What is your temperature?

MIXED PRACTICE

Decide whether you need to estimate or measure in each problem. Explain why. Then solve problems 1, 4, 8, and 9.

1. You are making a place mat that will cover the entire top of your desk. How long should the mat be? How wide should it be?

2. You want to hang a picture at your eye level. Where should you put the nail?

3. The Box It Up shop wraps packages for mailing. They charge $0.25 per pound to wrap a package. How much will it cost for them to wrap your package?

4. You are cutting gold yarn to fit exactly across the width of a bulletin board in your classroom. How many inches of yarn will you need?

5. You are cutting ribbon to wrap around a present. How long should the ribbon be?

6. You are making cupcakes for a goodbye party. The recipe says to bake the cupcakes for 12 minutes. How long have the cupcakes been baking in the oven?

7. You want to make enough punch for 6 friends. How much punch will you make?

8. Your teacher wants your class to make a height bar graph. The labels under the bars on the graph increase 1 inch at a time. Where will you record your height?

9. **Missing Data** Make up the missing data and solve the problem. You are making a ladder for your pet mouse, Cheesy. Cheesy's cage is 14 inches wide. How long and wide will you make the ladder?

Miles

LEARN ABOUT IT

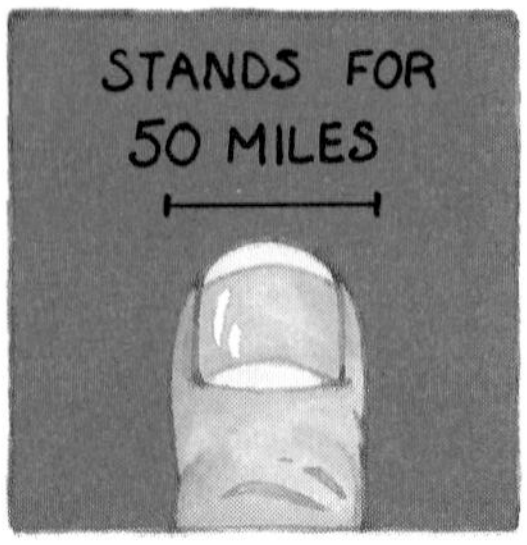

EXPLORE **Use the Map**
Find a place on the map where your thumb width is about the same as the distance between two towns. About how many miles is it between those towns?

TALK ABOUT IT

1. Explain how you can use your thumb width to estimate distances on the map.
2. About how many miles is it from White Eagle to Frogville?

The **mile** is another customary unit used to measure length. The relationships between miles, feet, and yards can help you understand how long a mile is.

1 mile (mi) = 5,280 ft = 1,760 yd
You can walk a mile in about 20 min.

PRACTICE

Estimate these distances in miles using your thumb width and the map above.

1. from Buffalo to White Eagle
2. from Frogville to Wild Horse
3. from Elk City to Buffalo
4. from Wild Horse to Beaver
5. from Beaver to Eagle City
6. from Elk City to Wild Horse

More Practice, page 519, set A

POWER PRACTICE/QUIZ

Write each time. Use a.m. and p.m.

1. Breakfast

2. Bedtime

3. Lunch

4. School ends

Answer these questions. You will need to use the calendar for some of them.

5. What is the fourth Saturday in April?

6. What day of the week is April 26?

7. What is another way to write April 3, 1990?

Estimate and measure the lengths of these things using body units. Then estimate their lengths in inches, and measure their lengths with a ruler.

8. Your leg **9.** Your shoe **10.** Your pencil

Tell if the distance is more than, less than, or the same as 1 mile.

11. 5,280 ft **12.** 1,000 yd **13.** 5,670 ft

PROBLEM SOLVING

14. The movie *Watchful Eyes* lasts 100 minutes. If the movie starts at 12:45, what time will it end?

15. The movie *Movin' On* begins at 6:30 and ends at 8:55. How long does this movie last?

16. Mr. Reed wants to buy fencing to put around his garden. Should he estimate or measure the distance around the garden?

17. Mrs. Reed is planting 28 tomato plants. She wants to put the same number in each row. How many plants can she put in each row? How many rows will she make?

Perimeter

LEARN ABOUT IT

The distance around a figure or an object is its **perimeter**.

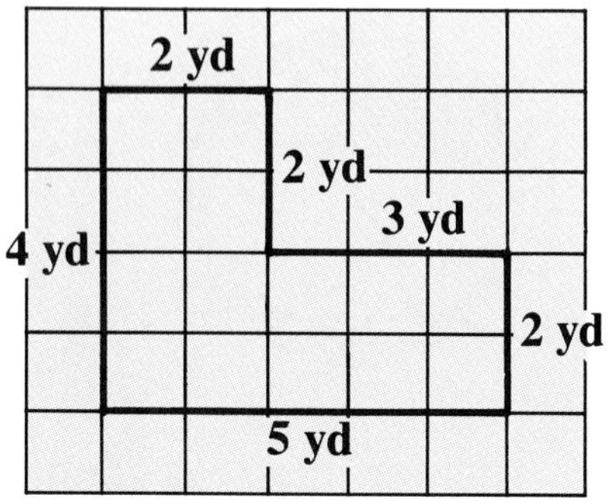

EXPLORE Use Graph Paper

Look at Rita's plan for a dog pen. The perimeter is 18 yd. Use graph paper to draw other plans for a dog pen with this perimeter. Use whole numbers for each side.

TALK ABOUT IT

1. Can you make a square dog pen with a perimeter of 18 yd? If so, tell the length of each side.
2. Do figures with the same perimeter have the same shape? Explain why or why not.

One way to find the perimeter of a figure or an object is to add the lengths of the sides.

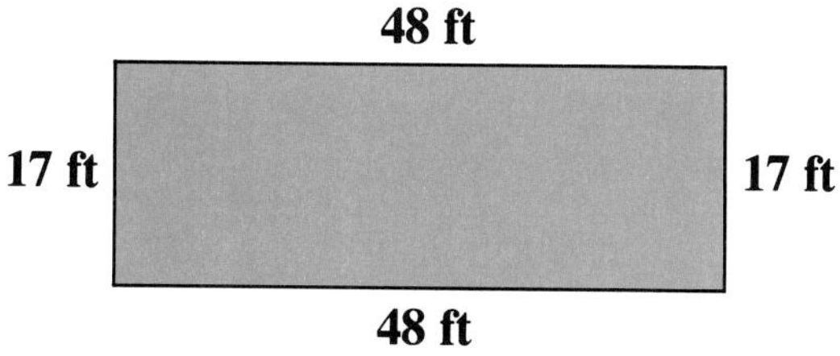

48 + 17 + 48 + 17 = 130 ft.
The perimeter is 130 ft.

To find the perimeter on the calculator, use this key code.
[ON/AC] side length [+] side length [+] side length [+] side length [=]

PRACTICE

1. Choose one of these nonstandard units and measure the perimeter of your classroom.
   a. your step   b. string as long as your armspan

Use a calculator to find the perimeters.

2. 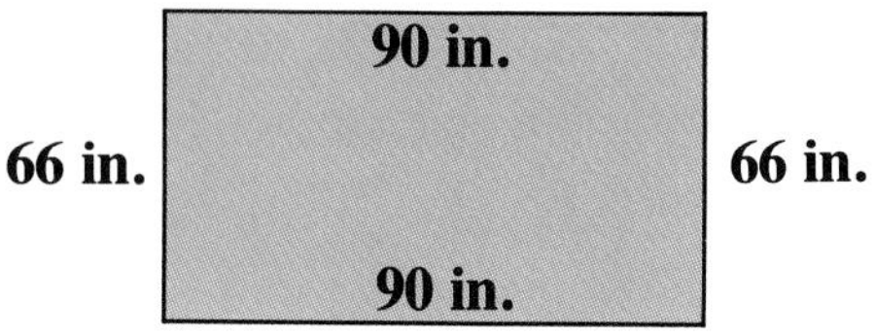

3. Rita walks her dog around a square park. Each side of the park is 155 ft long. What is the perimeter of the park?

More Practice, page 519, set B

Estimating Length, Width, and Perimeter
Using a Benchmark

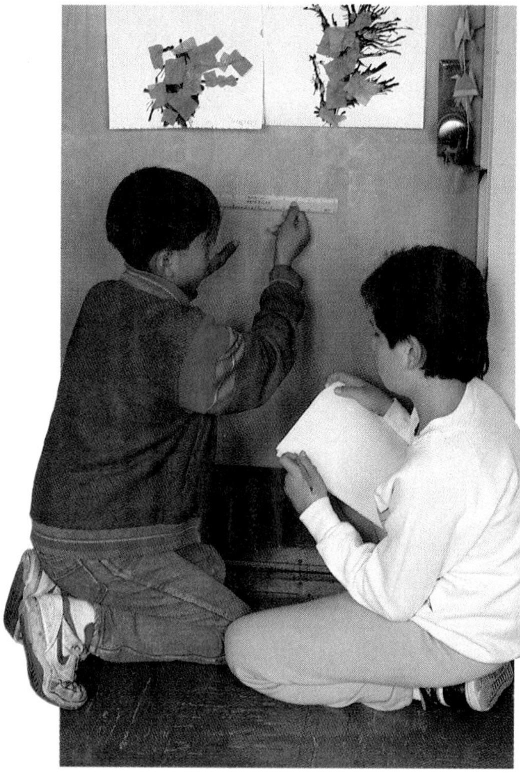

LEARN ABOUT IT

EXPLORE Use Classroom Objects
Work in groups. Without leaving your chairs, look for an object about 1 ft or 1 yd long. Thinking of that object, estimate the room's length and width. Check your estimates by measuring with a tape measure.

TALK ABOUT IT

1. How did you make your estimates? What object did you use?
2. How could you use your estimates to estimate the perimeter of the classroom?
3. What other objects could help you estimate lengths in feet and yards?
4. Would the length of a paperclip or a pencil be a good unit to use as a benchmark for estimating feet and yards? Explain your reasoning.

If you know that the length of an object is close to a given unit, you can use it as a **benchmark**. Then you imagine using that object as the unit and count about how many times it is used.

PRACTICE

Estimate the length, width, and perimeter of these objects in feet. Use a benchmark. Check your estimates by measuring with a tape measure.

1. Chalkboard **2.** Window **3.** Door

More Practice, page 519, set C

Problem Solving
Data from a Chart

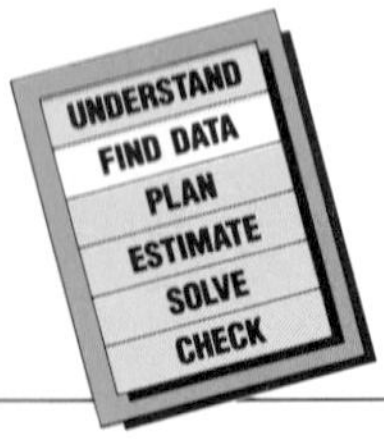

To solve some problems, you need to sort through numbers in a chart to find the data you need.

How much higher is the tallest building in Houston than the tallest building in Dallas?

Largest Cities in Texas

City	Population	Tallest Building	Rainfall per Year
Houston	1,595,138	Texas Commerce Tower, 1,002 ft	42 in.
Dallas	904,078	First Republic Bank Plaza, 939 ft	32 in.
San Antonio	786,023	Marriott River Center, 656 ft	28 in.
El Paso	425,259	—	8 in.
Fort Worth	385,141	City Center Tower II, 546 ft	32 in.
Austin	345,890	One American Center, 395 ft	42 in.

I'll find the data I need in the chart.

The Texas Commerce Tower is 1,002 ft high. The First Republic Bank Plaza is 939 ft high.

$1{,}002 - 939 = 63$

Now I'll solve the problem.

The tallest building in Houston is 63 feet taller than the tallest building in Dallas.

TRY IT OUT

Solve using data from the chart.

1. What is the total height of the Marriott River Center and the City Center Tower II?

2. Which cities get 4 times the amount of rainfall per year that El Paso gets?

MIXED PRACTICE

Solve these problems. Use the data from the chart.

1. Which building is 183 feet shorter than 3 times the height of One American Center in Austin?

2. What is the difference between the rainfall in the wettest and the driest cities in the chart?

3. The tallest building in the United States is the Sears Tower in Chicago at 1,454 feet. How much taller is this than the Texas Commerce Tower?

4. Houston and Dallas have a total of 64 universities and colleges. Dallas has 10 more than Houston. How many universities and colleges does Houston have?

5. How much higher is the tallest building in the table than the shortest?

6. Alonso Alvarez de Pineda of Spain mapped the Texas coast in 1519. The Texas Revolution against Mexico began 316 years later. In 1845 Texas became a state. What year did the Texas Revolution begin?

7. The highest point in Texas is 8,751 feet at Guadalupe Peak. The highest point in the United States is Mt. McKinley. Mt. McKinley is 11,569 feet higher than Guadalupe Peak. How high is Mt. McKinley?

8. What is the total amount of rainfall for Austin, Houston, and San Antonio?

9. **Using a Calculator** What is the total population of the three largest cities in Texas?

More Practice, page 519, set D

Estimating and Measuring Capacity

LEARN ABOUT IT

EXPLORE **Use Nonstandard Units**

Work in groups. Choose a container to use as a nonstandard unit. Estimate how many times you could pour that filled container into a milk carton. Then fill the milk carton to check your estimate. Do this again with the other nonstandard units.

TALK ABOUT IT

Which of the units gave the largest measure for the milk carton? Which gave the smallest? Explain.

These containers have the customary units of capacity.

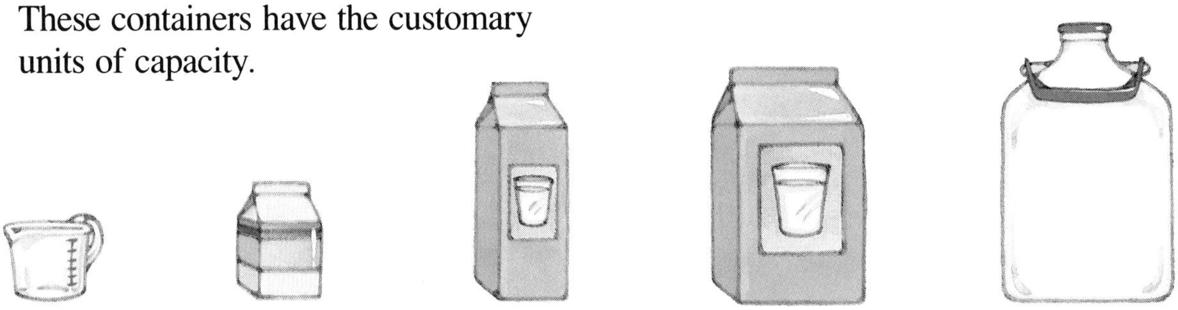

Cup **Pint** **Quart** **Half gallon** **Gallon**

Here are some relationships between these units.

8 fluid ounces (fl oz) = 1 cup (c)
2 c = 1 pint (pt)
2 pt = 1 quart (qt)
2 qt = 1 half gallon (half gal)
4 qt = 2 half gal = 1 gallon (gal)

You can find more relationships between the units. Multiply the larger unit to change it into the smaller unit.

3 gallons = |||| quarts

> Gallons is the larger unit, so I multiply 3 × 4 qt.

3 gallons = 12 quarts

TRY IT OUT

Multiply to find the relationships.

1. 3 gal = |||| qt **2.** 4 pt = |||| c **3.** 5 c = |||| fl oz

PRACTICE

Multiply to write these amounts another way.

1. Sour cream

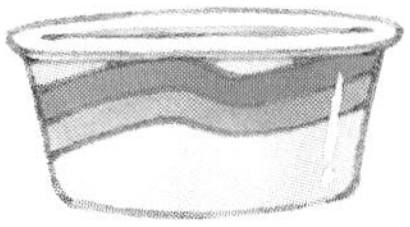

2 pt = |||| c

2. Milk

3 half gal = |||| qt

3. Juice

8 c = |||| fl oz

APPLY

MATH REASONING What is the better estimate for the amount?

4. Detergent
20 fl oz

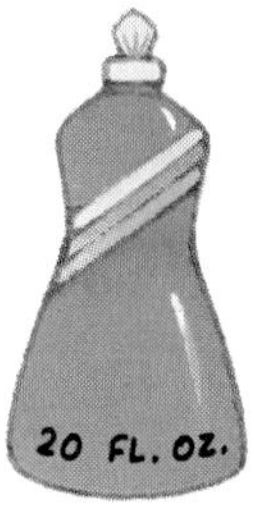

a about 2 cups
b about 1 cup

5. Cider
9 qts

a about 2 gallons
b about 3 gallons

6. Cottage cheese

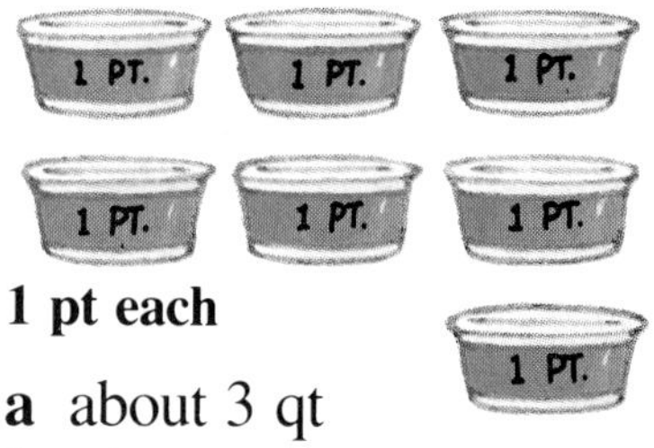

1 pt each

a about 3 qt
b about 5 qt

PROBLEM SOLVING

7. Ted needs 9 cups of yogurt. The container of yogurt has 5 pints in it. Does he have enough yogurt?

8. **Extra Data** Your recipe calls for 7 c of apple juice and 9 c of orange juice. How many fluid ounces of apple juice do you need?

MIXED REVIEW

Find the product.

9. 36 × 29
10. 47 × 81
11. 70 × 64
12. 598 × 27
13. 246 × 33
14. 805 × 69

Round to the highest place or nearest dollar.
Then estimate the product.

15. 5 × 47
16. 6 × $7.81
17. 9 × 412
18. 7 × 387

Estimating and Measuring Weight

LEARN ABOUT IT

The **pound** and the **ounce** are the customary units of weight.

1 pound (lb) = 16 ounces (oz)

EXPLORE Use a Scale
Work in groups. Find the pictured objects in your classroom. Estimate whether the weight of each object is closer to 1 ounce or closer to 1 pound. Check by weighing each object on a scale.

TALK ABOUT IT

1. How can you use the weight of these objects to estimate the weight of other objects?
2. Two erasers weigh 1 oz. About how many erasers would it take to weigh 1 lb?

To compare measurements of weight, you must often change the units. One way to do that is to multiply the larger unit to change it into the smaller unit.

Which is heavier—3 lb of spaghetti or 40 oz of noodles?

Pounds is the larger unit, so I multiply 3×16 oz.

The spaghetti weighs 48 oz.

The spaghetti is heavier, since 48 oz is more than 40 oz.

PRACTICE

Tell which weighs the most.

1. biscuits 2 lb
   rolls 30 oz
2. cookies 4 lb
   crackers 24 oz
3. plums 5 lb
   grapefruit 64 oz

Estimate the weight of these items in pounds.

4. 

5. 

6. 

More Practice, page 520, set A

Temperature
Degrees Fahrenheit

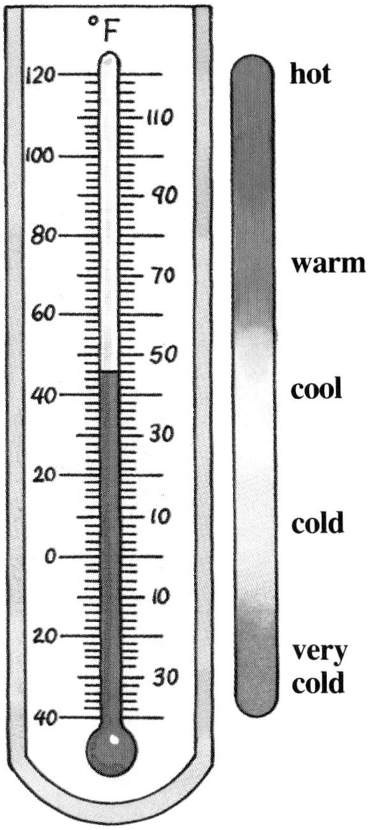

LEARN ABOUT IT

EXPLORE **Study the Thermometer**

A customary unit for measuring temperature is the **degree Fahrenheit** (°F). This thermometer reads 46°F. Every mark represents 2 degrees.

TALK ABOUT IT

1. How do you count to read the temperature on this thermometer?
2. Describe the weather at 68°F and at 42°F.
3. Give an example of a very cold temperature and an example of a hot temperature.

Examples

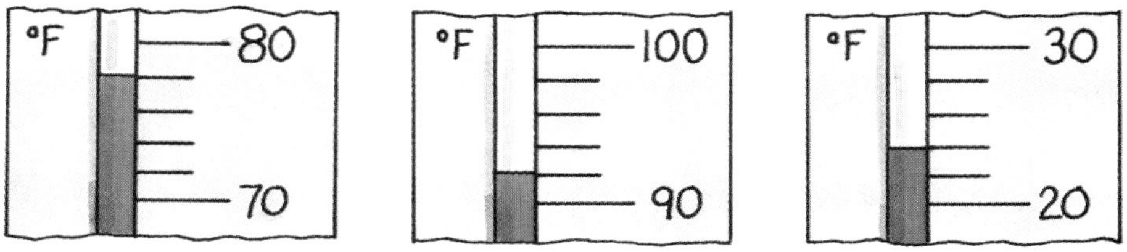

PRACTICE

Write each temperature.

1. 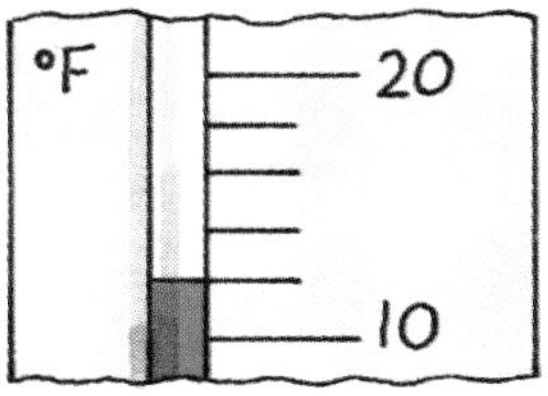

2. 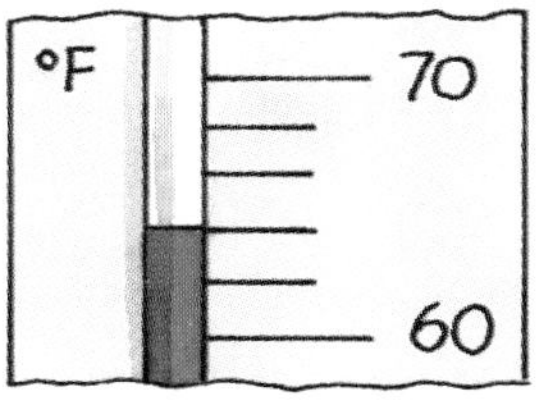

3. 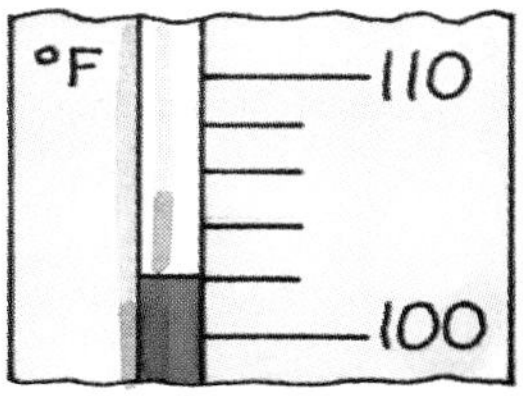

4. 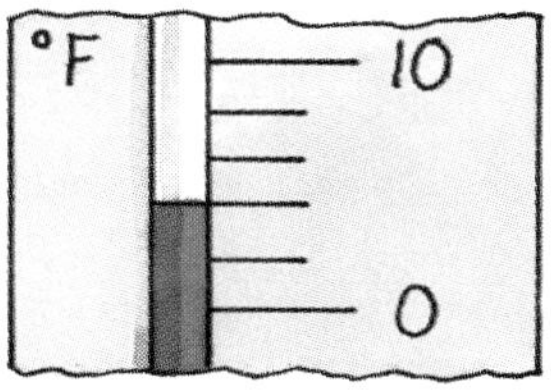

5. 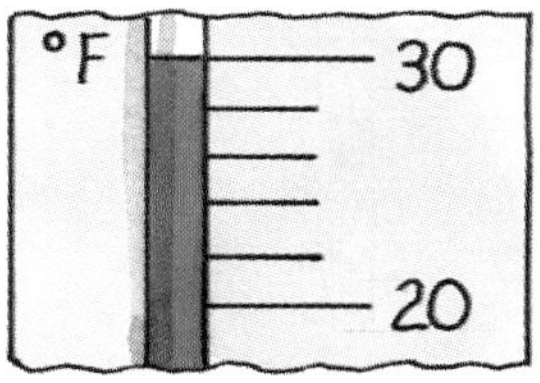

6. 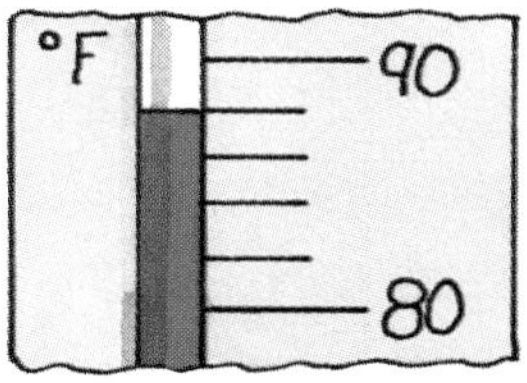

More Practice, page 520, set B

Data Collection and Analysis
Group Decision Making

UNDERSTAND
FIND DATA
PLAN
ESTIMATE
SOLVE
CHECK

Doing an Investigation
Group Skill:
Listen to Others

For this investigation your group will need two paper clips of any size. You can "flip" one of the paper clips by laying it on your desktop, then pushing down on the end of it with the end of the other clip. The bottom clip will jump like a tiddly wink. Try it! Do you think you can make the paper clip jump farther if you practice?

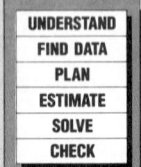

Collecting Data

1. Have each student in your group flip a paper clip and measure the distance it jumps in inches. Keep a record like the one below. There should be three trials for each student. Find the sum of your group's distances for each trial.

Trial 1	**Distance**
Dan	6 in.
Suzie	13 in.
Judy	9 in.
Jose	10 in.
Total	38 in.
Trial 2	
Dan	9 in.
Suzie	15 in.
Judy	12 in.
Jose	10 in.
Total	....
Trial 3	
Dan	....
Suzie	....
Judy	....
Jose	....
Total	....

Organizing Data

2. Make a bar graph to show your group's total distance for each trial. Adjust the scale so that the largest and smallest total distances will fit on the graph.

3. Check back. Did you title your graph? Did you label all of its parts?

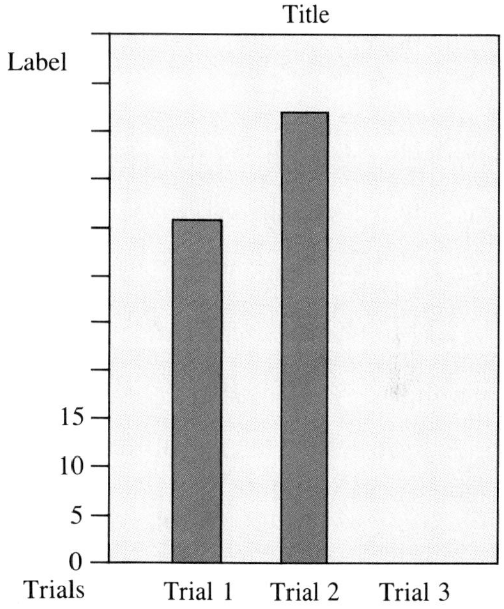

Presenting Your Analysis

4. Did your group get better with practice? Explain how your graph shows whether or not it did.

5. Prepare to share at least three things about your graph with your classmates.

Wrap Up

How Do You Measure Up?

Complete each sentence with a sensible unit of measure.

1. Many airplanes fly at an altitude of 30,000 __?__.
2. The new kitten weighed only 12 __?__.
3. Sally's curtain is two __?__ too long.
4. Mom's favorite bowl holds about a half __?__ of soup.
5. Since our family drinks lots of milk, we buy it by the __?__.
6. I need about 3 cups of juice, so I will buy a __?__.

Sometimes, Always, Never

Which word should go in the blank, sometimes, always, or never? Explain your choices.

7. Twelve-thirty is __?__ the same as half past noon.
8. A day __?__ has more a.m. hours than p.m. hours.
9. A Fahrenheit temperature of 89° would __?__ be good weather for making a snowman.
10. Figures with the same shape will __?__ have the same perimeter.

Project

Plant a seed in a small pot and care for it every day. Once it breaks through the soil, measure it once a week for a month. Record the measurements. Then make a bar graph to show the results. Can you find a pattern in the plant's growth? Explain what happened to make the pattern form as it did.

POWER PRACTICE/TEST

Part 1 Understanding

1. Tell two possible ways to find the perimeter of a triangle that has 3 equal sides, each 9 in. long.

2. List two activities you might do at 7:45 a.m. List two activities you might do at 7:45 p.m.

3. Find the date that came one month before 1/9/89. Write it in the other form for writing dates.

4. Draw a clock face that shows 5:49.

Part 2 Skills

5. Estimate and then measure the flute in thumb units.

6. Estimate and then measure the flute in inches.

In problems 7–13, tell which is the greater amount.

7. 7 yd or 20 ft

8. 5,000 ft or 1 mi

9. 50 fl oz or 5 c

10. 5 pt or 2 qt

11. 3 lb or 24 oz

12. 50 oz or 3 lb

13. the width of a chalkboard or its perimeter

14. Which room measurement is just under 4 feet?

15. To buy a window shade, would you estimate or measure its exact width?

Room Measurements	
window height	41 in.
window width	30 in.
door height	80 in.
door width	46 in.

Part 3 Applications

16. A soccer game began at 1:15 p.m. and ended after 1 hour and 55 minutes. At what time was the game over?

17. Pens come in packets of 3 or 5. Find 2 different combinations of packets that total 60 pens.

18. **Challenge** How would you measure 1 gallon of punch with a 1-pint measuring cup?

ENRICHMENT
Temperatures Below Zero

When the temperature is 32° Fahrenheit we say it is at freezing, because water will freeze at 32° F. When the temperature falls lower than 0° Fahrenheit, we say it is **below zero**. We write such very low temperatures as **negative numbers**.

Look at the thermometer as a vertical number line. On this thermometer the numbers below zero are blue. You write these numbers with a minus sign, for example, −2°F or −8°F. The red numbers are above zero. You write these without the minus sign, as 2° F and 8° F.

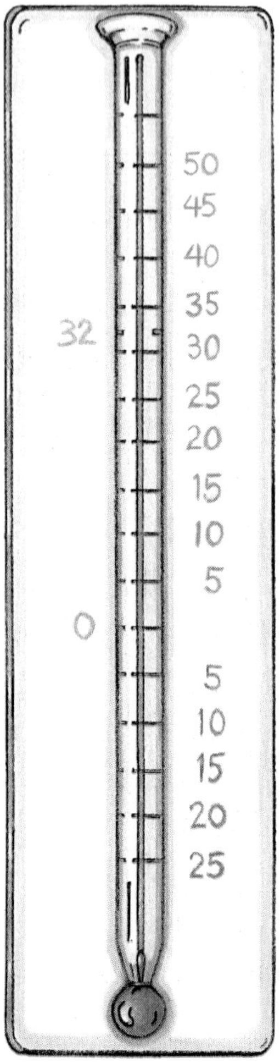

Look at the thermometer and answer these questions.

1. What number on a thermometer expresses a temperature 8 degrees colder than the point at which water freezes?
2. What temperature is 8 degrees above the freezing point?
3. How many degrees below the freezing point will the temperature fall before it reaches 0°F?
4. Write the Fahrenheit temperatures for 1 degree below zero and 5 degrees below zero. Explain which is colder.

Solve each weather problem.

5. At midnight it was −3°F in Billings, Montana. Three hours later the temperature was 10 degrees colder. How cold was it at 3 a.m.?

7. At dawn Ingrid's thermometer read −8°F. By noon the temperature had risen 12 degrees. What was the new temperature?

CUMULATIVE REVIEW

1. 6 × 7 is the same as 5 × 7 plus ▥.

A 1 × 7 B 7 × 7

C 7 × 5 D 1 × 6

2. 4, 8, 12, and 16 are some of the multiples of ▥.

A 32 B 5

C 12 D 4

3. □ + △ = 7 and △ × △ = 16
□ must be

A 5 B 4

C 3 D 2

4. Round in order to estimate the product of 6 × 314. The product is a little more than ▥.

A 6,300 B 1,500

C 1,800 D 2,400

5. 34 × 6

A 204 B 1,104

C 222 D 1,824

6. 6 × 5,000

A 3,000 B 11,000

C 5,600 D 30,000

7. 3 × 8 × 2

A 24 B 48

C 40 D 30

8. 70 × 80

A 560 B 56,000

C 5,600 D 70,800

9. 98 × 40

A 392 B 3,620

C 3,920 D 4,820

10. 43 × 79

A 688 B 3,387

C 5,600 D 3,397

11. Students sold 957 tickets to a play at $3 each. By how much did ticket sales go over the goal of $2,500?

A $371 B $1,540

C $5,371 D $2,871

12. 68 customers ate at a snack bar. 49 ate salad and 35 ate corn on the cob. How many ate both?

A 84 B 16

C 19 D 14

9

Division Concepts and Basic Facts

THEME: PUPPETS

MATH AND FINE ARTS

DATA BANK

Use the Fine Arts Data Bank on page 479 to answer the questions.

1 To cut all the wood strips for the controller for a 9-string marionette, how long a piece of wood do you need?

2 The Japanese art of Bunraku uses large, complex puppets. How many people would you see on stage operating 5 male Bunraku puppets?

3 How many people would you see on stage operating 3 female Japanese Bunraku puppets?

4 **Use Critical Thinking** How many feet of wood will you need to make the controller for one marionette?

Operators of the *Bunraku* puppets of Japan wear black and mask their faces on stage. Can you think why?

Problem Solving
Understanding Division

LEARN ABOUT IT

You can understand when to use division by trying the actions below. Show the actions with counters. Complete the equations.

Problem	**Action**	**Equation**
	Separate into Equal Groups Number in Each Group Given	
A puppeteer put 12 puppets in boxes, 3 in each box. How many boxes did he need?		**12 ÷ 3 = ?** **product factor factor**
	Share Equally among Groups Number of Groups Given	
It takes 12 people to operate 4 large puppets. How many people are needed for each puppet?	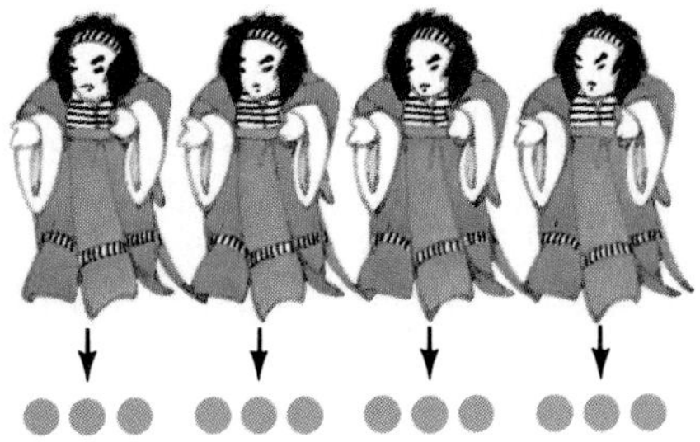	**12 ÷ 4 = ?**

TRY IT OUT

Use counters to find the answer. Write an equation.

1. Four wood strips are used to make the controllers for each marionette puppet. How many controllers can you make with 20 wood strips?
2. It takes 15 people to operate 5 large female puppets. How many people are needed for each puppet?

PRACTICE

Use counters to find the answer. Write an equation.

1. Each marionette puppet takes 9 strings. You have 18 strings.

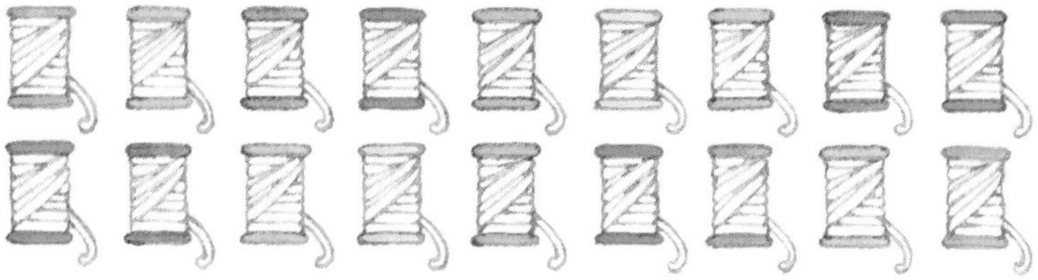

How many puppets can you make?

2. The 24 chairs at the puppet show were in rows of 6. How many rows were there?

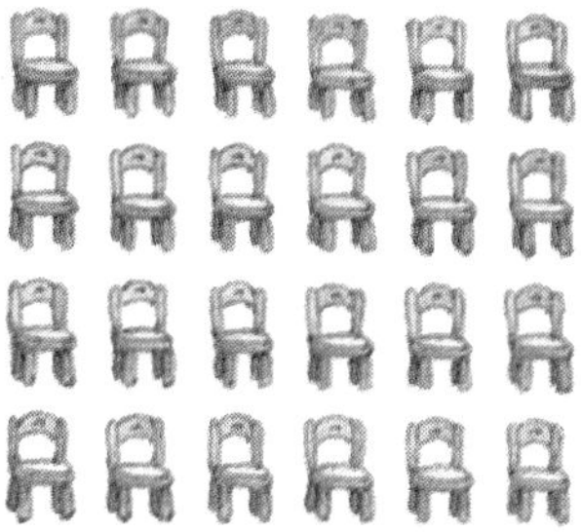

3. 15 puppets were stored in 3 boxes.

How many puppets were put in each box?

4. Bill had 20 strips of wood, just enough for 5 puppet controllers.

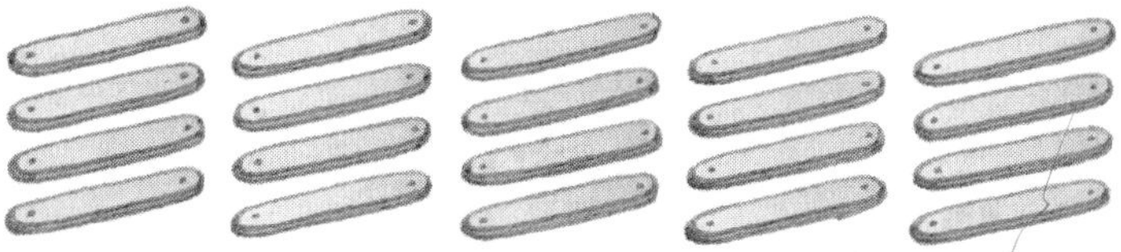

How many strips were needed for each controller?

WRITE YOUR OWN PROBLEM

5. Write two story problems that can be solved by dividing. Use a different action in each.

More Practice, page 506, set B

Relating Multiplication and Division

LEARN ABOUT IT

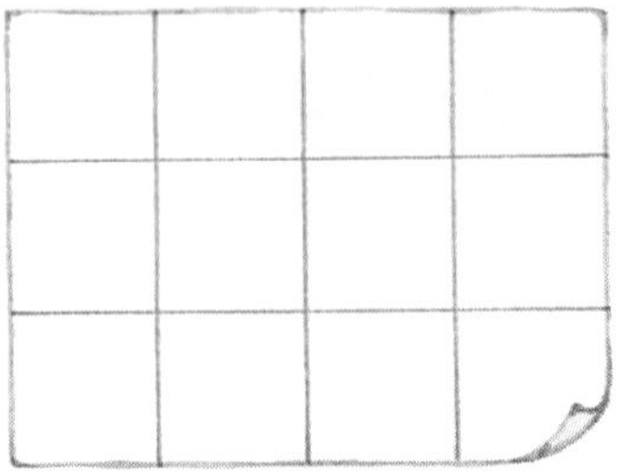

3 rows of 4 is 12

EXPLORE Use Graph Paper
Work in groups. Since multiplication and division are related, you can use multiplication to find quotients. Cut out graph paper rectangles to show that you have found the missing numbers in these examples.

Fact Family

$4 \times 3 = 12$	$3 \times 4 = 12$
$12 \div 4 = 3$	$12 \div 3 = 4$

A
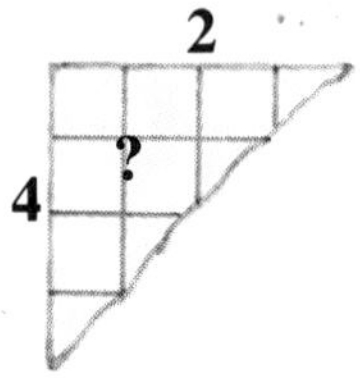

B
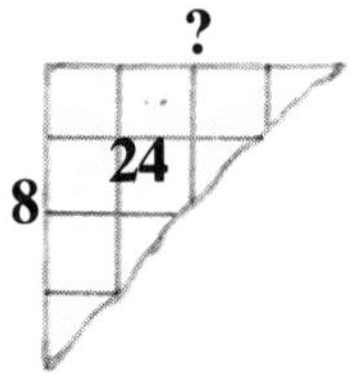

C
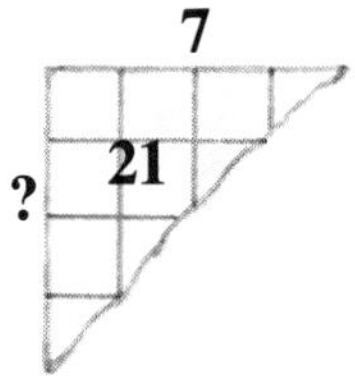

D
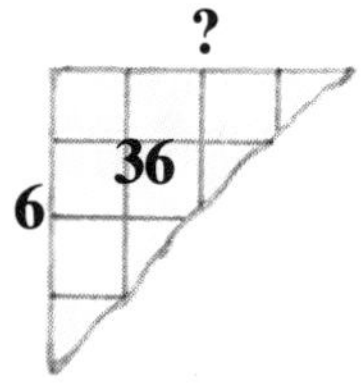

TALK ABOUT IT

1. In example A, how can you easily find the number that goes with 4 and 2?
2. Give a fact family for each example. Explain how multiplication and division are related.

In multiplication you know two factors and find the product. In division you know the product and one factor. You find the other factor.

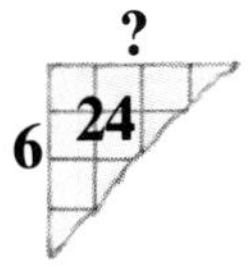

What number multiplied by 6 is 24?

$24 \div 6 = ?$ **The missing factor is 4.**

product factor factor

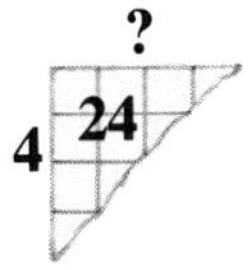

What number multiplied by 4 is 24?

$24 \div 4 = ?$ **The missing factor is 6.**

product factor factor

TRY IT OUT

Divide. Think about finding the missing factor.

1. $15 \div 3 =$ ▯ **2.** $28 \div 4 = $ ▯ **3.** $20 \div 5 = $ ▯ **4.** $14 \div 2 = $ ▯

PRACTICE

1. Write two multiplication and two division equations for this situation.

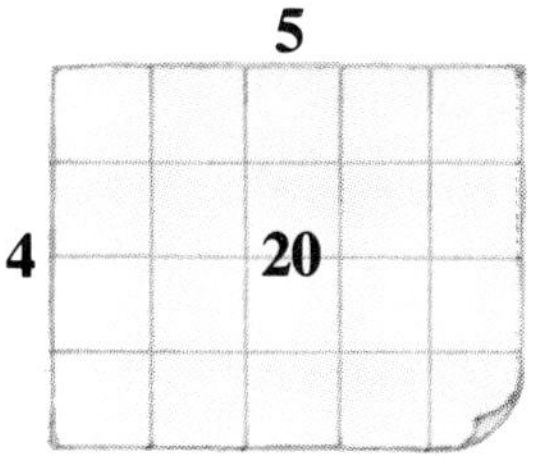

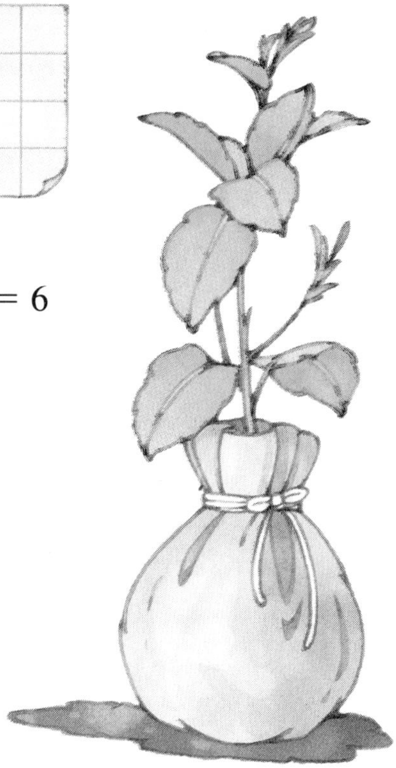

Give three or more equations in the same fact family.

2. $3 \times 2 = 6$ **3.** $2 \times 8 = 16$ **4.** $18 \div 3 = 6$

APPLY

MATH REASONING Give the fact family for each set of factors. Which is different from the others? Why?

5. 2, 5 **6.** 3, 6 **7.** 2, 9 **8.** 4, 3

9. 3, 3 **10.** 2, 6 **11.** 3, 7 **12.** 4, 8

PROBLEM SOLVING

13. Kristy pasted 8 stamps in each row in her stamp book. She filled 4 rows. How many stamps did she put in the book?

14. Rob planted 6 rows with 5 trees in each row. He had 3 extra trees. How many trees were there?

MIXED REVIEW

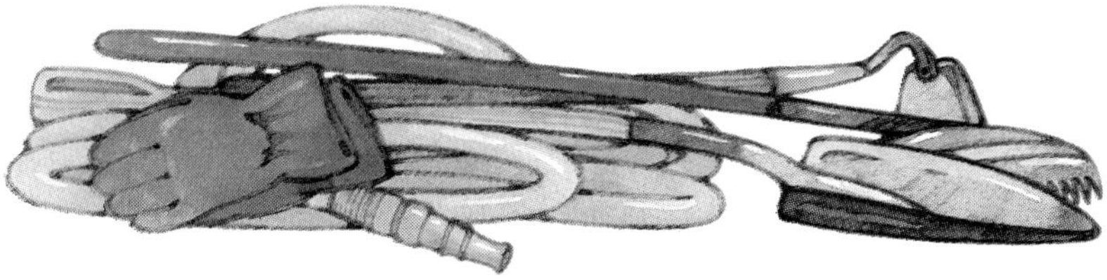

Find the product.

15. $3{,}798 \times 5$ **16.** $7{,}654 \times 9$ **17.** $2{,}639 \times 7$ **18.** $8{,}022 \times 6$

19. $9{,}606 \times 8$ **20.** $4{,}394 \times 4$ **21.** $\$22.99 \times 3$ **22.** $\$6.52 \times 2$

23. $4{,}526 \times 6$ **24.** $1{,}896 \times 5$ **25.** $2{,}004 \times 8$ **26.** $9{,}420 \times 7$

Write the correct time as you would see it on a digital clock.

27. quarter past five **28.** twelve minutes past eleven

29. seven-thirty **30.** half past two **31.** six-forty-five

More Practice, page 520, set C

Dividing by 2 and 3

LEARN ABOUT IT

EXPLORE **Discover a Relationship**

Knowing the multiplication facts for 2 and 3 can help you divide by 2 and 3.

Flower Bulbs

Kind	Number per Package	Number of Packages	Total Number of Bulbs Needed
Tulip	2	6	12
Daffodil	3	____	15
Iris	2	____	16
Crocus	3	____	24

TALK ABOUT IT

1. To find the number of packages of 3 daffodil bulbs it takes to have 15 bulbs, you find the missing factor when 15 is divided by 3. What multiplication fact would help you?

2. What missing factor would give the number of packages to buy to get 16 iris bulbs? 24 crocus bulbs? What multiplication facts would help you?

Here is how you can use multiplication to find a quotient. The division equation is shown in two ways.

2 times what number is 18?

$18 \div 2 = 9$

Check: $2 \times 9 = 18$

3 times what number is 27?

$$3\overline{)27}\ \text{quotient } 9$$

Check: $3 \times 9 = 27$

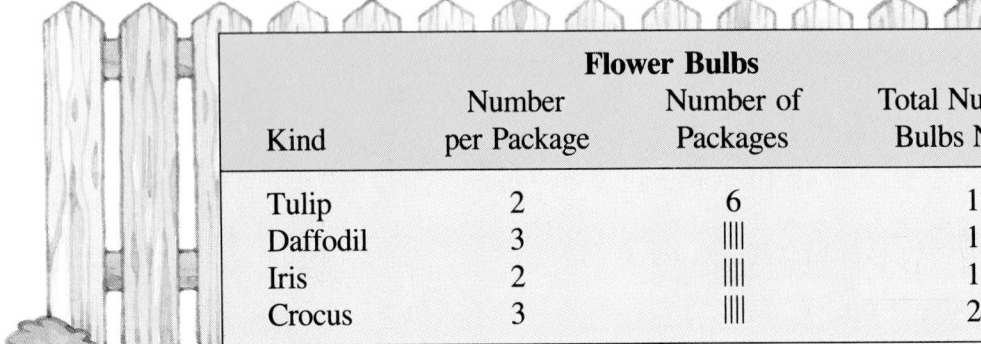

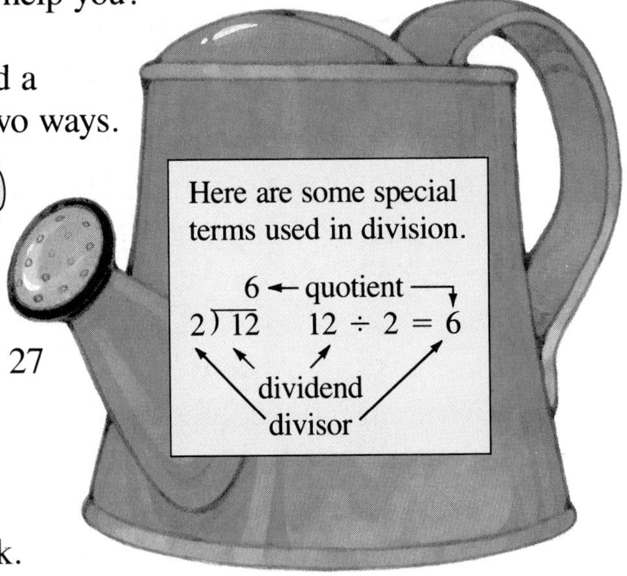

Here are some special terms used in division.
6 ← quotient
2)12
12 ÷ 2 = 6
dividend
divisor

TRY IT OUT

Divide. Use a multiplication equation to check.

1. $12 \div 3$ **2.** $16 \div 2$ **3.** $21 \div 3$ **4.** $18 \div 3$ **5.** $10 \div 2$

Find the quotients.

1. $12 \div 2$ **2.** $9 \div 3$ **3.** $14 \div 2$ **4.** $4 \div 2$

5. $15 \div 3$ **6.** $21 \div 3$ **7.** $8 \div 2$ **8.** $27 \div 3$

9. $10 \div 2$ **10.** $6 \div 3$ **11.** $24 \div 3$ **12.** $6 \div 2$

13. $16 \div 2$ **14.** $18 \div 3$ **15.** $18 \div 2$ **16.** $12 \div 3$

17. $3\overline{)15}$ **18.** $2\overline{)18}$ **19.** $3\overline{)27}$ **20.** $2\overline{)16}$ **21.** $3\overline{)24}$ **22.** $2\overline{)10}$

23. $3\overline{)12}$ **24.** $2\overline{)8}$ **25.** $2\overline{)12}$ **26.** $3\overline{)9}$ **27.** $2\overline{)4}$ **28.** $3\overline{)18}$

29. Find the quotient of 14 and 2. **30.** Divide 21 by 3.

APPLY

MATH REASONING Use the equations in the box to find these quotients.

31. $346 \div 2$ **32.** $327 \div 3$

33. $456 \div 3$ **34.** $486 \div 2$

$2 \times 243 = 486$
$3 \times 109 = 327$

$2 \times 173 = 346$
$3 \times 152 = 456$

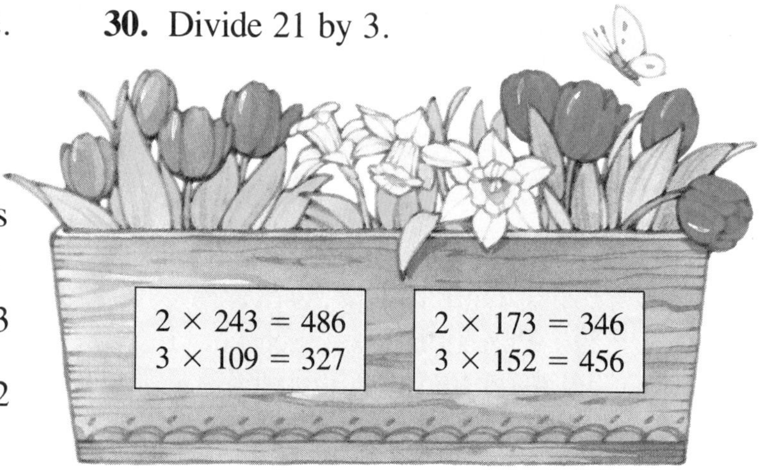

PROBLEM SOLVING

35. Tim bought 6 packages with 2 bulbs in each and 4 packages with 3 bulbs in each. How many bulbs did he buy?

36. Unfinished Problem Jessica needed 18 bulbs. There were 3 bulbs in each package. Write a question to finish the problem.

▶ **USING CRITICAL THINKING** Logical Reasoning

37. Can you find the secret number? Here are some clues.
- It is odd and has just one digit.
- It is not the number of days in a week.
- It can be divided by 3, but its quotient is not 3.

More Practice, page 506, set C

Dividing by 4 and 5

LEARN ABOUT IT

EXPLORE **Study the Chart**

Knowing the multiplication facts for 4 and 5 can help you divide by 4 and 5.

<table>
<tr><th colspan="4">Marionette Strings</th></tr>
<tr><th>Kind of Puppet</th><th>Strings per Puppet</th><th>Number of Puppets</th><th>Total Number of Strings</th></tr>
<tr><td>Horse Puppet</td><td>4</td><td>6</td><td>24</td></tr>
<tr><td>Girl Puppet</td><td>5</td><td>||||</td><td>30</td></tr>
<tr><td>Dragon Puppet</td><td>4</td><td>||||</td><td>32</td></tr>
<tr><td>Boy Puppet</td><td>5</td><td>||||</td><td>45</td></tr>
</table>

TALK ABOUT IT

1. How many girl puppets could be strung with 30 lengths of string? What multiplication fact would help you find this quotient?

2. What quotient would give the number of dragon puppets that can be strung with 32 lengths of string? the number of boy puppets that can be strung with 45 lengths of string?

When you divide, it helps to use multiplication.

4 times what number is 28?

$28 \div 4 = 7$

Check: $4 \times 7 = 28$

5 times what number is 40?

$$\begin{array}{r} 8 \\ 5\overline{)40} \end{array}$$

Check: $5 \times 8 = 40$

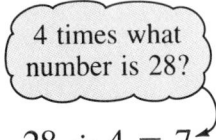

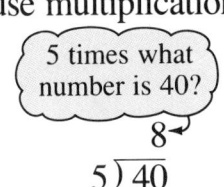

TRY IT OUT

Divide. Use a multiplication equation to check.

1. $25 \div 5$ **2.** $24 \div 4$ **3.** $30 \div 5$ **4.** $28 \div 4$ **5.** $36 \div 4$

6. $16 \div 4$ **7.** $10 \div 5$ **8.** $5 \div 5$ **9.** $20 \div 4$

PRACTICE

Find the quotients.

1. 12 ÷ 4
2. 25 ÷ 5
3. 32 ÷ 4
4. 20 ÷ 4
5. 10 ÷ 5
6. 18 ÷ 3
7. 35 ÷ 5
8. 24 ÷ 3
9. 16 ÷ 4
10. 15 ÷ 5
11. 18 ÷ 2
12. 12 ÷ 3
13. $5\overline{)20}$
14. $2\overline{)10}$
15. $3\overline{)15}$
16. $3\overline{)21}$
17. $5\overline{)30}$
18. $2\overline{)12}$
19. $2\overline{)16}$
20. $3\overline{)27}$
21. $4\overline{)8}$
22. $2\overline{)14}$
23. $4\overline{)28}$
24. $5\overline{)20}$
25. Find the quotient of 24 and 4.
26. Divide 35 by 5.

APPLY

MATH REASONING Use the equations in the table to find these quotients.

27. 325 ÷ 5
28. 248 ÷ 4
29. 456 ÷ 4
30. 490 ÷ 5

4 × 114	= 456
5 × 65	= 325
5 × 98	= 490
4 × 62	= 248

PROBLEM SOLVING

31. The art teacher cut 20 pieces of string for dragon puppets. How many dragon puppets will they make?

32. **Fine Arts Data Bank**
DATA BANK
How much string would you need to string a puppet with a 9-string double airplane controller? See page 479.

ALGEBRA

Choose a number from the basket that can be written in the □ to make a true sentence.

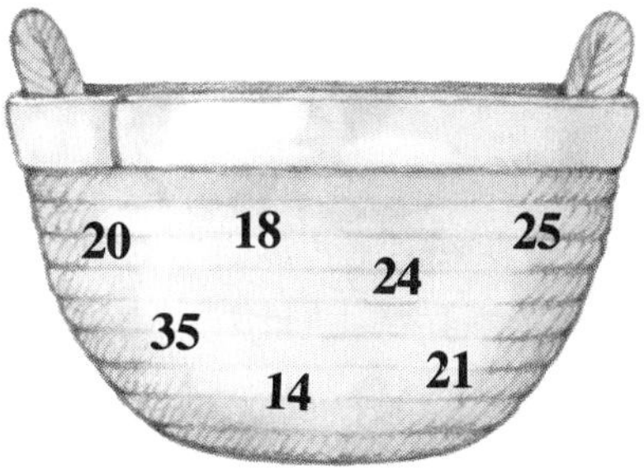

33. □ ÷ 2 = 7
34. □ ÷ 3 = 7
35. □ ÷ 4 = 5
36. □ ÷ 5 = 5
37. □ ÷ 5 = 7
38. □ ÷ 3 = 8

Problem Solving
Estimate the Answer

UNDERSTAND
FIND DATA
PLAN
ESTIMATE
SOLVE
CHECK

LEARN ABOUT IT

Before solving a problem, it is important to decide what would be a reasonable answer. To decide, you will need to **Estimate the Answer.**

At a music store sidewalk sale, Kizzie's mother was amazed by some of the instruments for sale. They had been invented thousands of years ago.

Kizzie's mother can spend $25. She wants to buy as many instruments as she can. Which ones can she buy?

East African Kettle Drum	$10.40
Nigerian Cow Bell	6.65
African Mbira Thumb Piano	15.60
Hopi Indian Gourd Rattle	7.85

I'll begin by rounding the data in the problem.

10.40 → 10   6.65 → 7
15.60 → 16   7.85 → 8

I'll use the rounded numbers to make an estimate.

10 + 7 + 16 + 8 = 41   Too much!
10 + 7 + 8 = 25   About right!

Now I'll solve the problem.

$10.40 + $6.65 + $7.85 = $24.90.

$24.90 is a reasonable answer because it is close to $25.

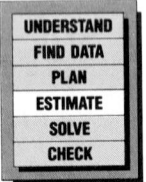

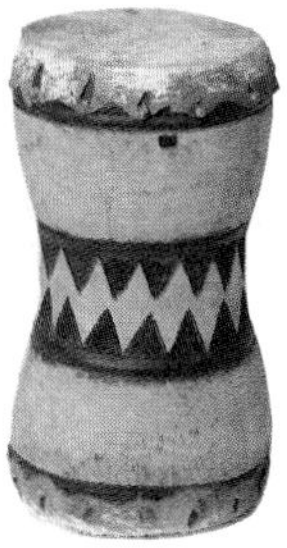

In African music several drummers may beat as many as six different rhythms together.

TRY IT OUT

Before solving each problem, estimate the answer. Then solve the problem and decide if your answer is reasonable.

1. Cliff had saved $142.50. He bought a guitar for $119.95. How much money does he have left?

2. It costs Betty $18 a month to rent a saxophone. How much is this per year?

3. Marlo practiced the piano 22 days this month. She practiced 35 minutes a day. How long did she practice in all?

4. It took Hyun 5 months to learn 25 piano pieces. He learned the same number each month. How many pieces did he learn a month?

MIXED PRACTICE

Estimate the answer. Then solve the problem and decide if your answer is reasonable.

1. Beethoven was born in 1770. When he was 49, he became totally deaf. What year was that?

2. The 37 band members sold greeting cards to raise money for 20 new uniforms. Each member needed to raise $24. How much money did they need to raise in all?

Use this chart to solve 3 and 4.

Drayer's Music Store	new	used
Saxophone	$750.00	$375.50
Clarinet	$450.00	$275.98
Electric Guitar	$169.99	$120.98

3. Bev has saved $87.75 for a brand new electric guitar. About how much more money does she need?

4. Joseph rented a saxophone at $16 a month for 12 months. How much more does it cost to buy a used saxophone than to rent one for a year?

The *mbira* or thumb piano is easy to make and play. It is used in many parts of Africa.

5. There are 27 students in Jerry's flute class at school. Mr. Note divided the students into 3 equal groups for testing. How many are in each group?

6. Betsy buys reeds for her clarinet in packages. Use the price list to find how much 45 reeds would cost.

Reeds	
Single reed	$1
Package of 9	$8

7. The 18 elementary school students in Newtown's Junior Orchestra come from 6 different schools. There are the same number of students from each school. How many students come from each school?

8. **Understanding the Question** Tell what operation you would use. Then solve the problem. At the age of 15, Bill came in first in a piano competition. Bill was 3 times as old as Mozart was when the composer wrote his first short pieces. At what age did Mozart write his first short pieces?

More Practice, page 520, set D

0 and 1 in Division

LEARN ABOUT IT

EXPLORE Use a Calculator

You can use a calculator to help you understand 0 and 1 in division.

A The art class spent several weeks making finger puppets. Lewis made 6 finger puppets to share among 6 friends. How many will each friend get?

key code: [ON/AC] 6 [÷] 6 [=]

B Julie made 6 finger puppets for 1 friend. How many puppets will the friend get?

key code: [ON/AC] 6 [÷] 1 [=]

C Terri planned to share her finger puppets with 3 friends, but her dog chewed them all up. How many puppets did each friend get?

key code: [ON/AC] 0 [÷] 3 [=]

D Miguel made 3 finger puppets, but he did not want to give any away. To how many friends could he give 0 puppets?

key code: [ON/AC] 3 [÷] 0 [=]

This does not make sense.

TALK ABOUT IT

1. What did the calculator display show when you pressed 3 [÷] 0 [=]?

2. Could Miguel give 0 puppets to 20 friends? 500 friends? Explain why it does not make sense to divide by zero.

3. Which of the examples above match each of these division rules?

- Zero divided by any number is 0.
- Never divide by 0.
- The quotient of a number divided by 1 is that number.
- The quotient of a number divided by itself is 1.

TRY IT OUT

Use your calculator to solve.

1. 6 ÷ 6 **2.** 0 ÷ 8 **3.** 5 ÷ 1 **4.** 0 ÷ 4

5. 37 ÷ 37 **6.** 0 ÷ 75 **7.** 86 ÷ 1 **8.** 78 ÷ 78

More Practice, page 506, set E

Power Practice/Quiz

Tell which division action is needed in each problem, share equally or separate same-size groups. Then draw a picture to solve the problem.

1. There are 24 students in Jack's gym class. The coach wants 8 teams for a tournament. He assigns one student to each team until all students are assigned. What is the size of each team?

2. In Jill's gym class there are also 24 students. Her coach needs teams with 4 members each. How many teams will there be?

Write four fact family equations for each set of numbers.

3. 3, 4, 12 **4.** 4, 7, 28 **5.** 6, 5, 30 **6.** 1, 2, 2

Give three more equations in the same family.

7. $8 \times 5 = 40$ **8.** $5 \times 2 = 10$ **9.** $27 \div 3 = 9$ **10.** $8 \div 4 = 2$

Divide. Use multiplication to check the division.

11. $18 \div 2$ **12.** $24 \div 3$ **13.** $20 \div 5$ **14.** $36 \div 4$

15. $5\overline{)15}$ **16.** $3\overline{)18}$ **17.** $2\overline{)12}$ **18.** $4\overline{)32}$ **19.** $3\overline{)9}$

20. $3\overline{)27}$ **21.** $2\overline{)10}$ **22.** $4\overline{)4}$ **23.** $5\overline{)45}$ **24.** $2\overline{)8}$

PROBLEM SOLVING

25. Lance has 24 photos to put in his scrapbook. Find 3 different ways he could put the same number of photos on each page. For each way, tell how many pages he would need.
26. Show two ways 21 students can split into teams so that each team has 3 or 4 players.
27. Find three ways Vera can throw 3 darts and score 20 points. Darts that miss the target score 0 points.

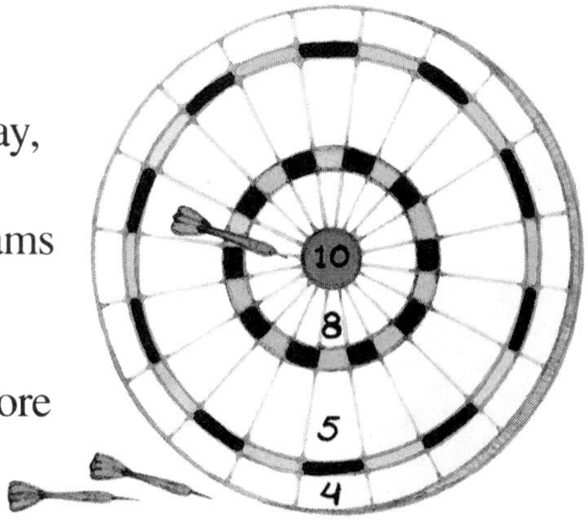

Dividing by 6 and 7

Bunraku Puppet Shows		
Number of Weeks	**Shows per Week**	**Total Number of Shows**
6	7	42
||||	7	56
||||	6	30
||||	6	54

LEARN ABOUT IT

EXPLORE Think About the Relationship
You can use the multiplication facts for 6 and 7 to help you divide by 6 and 7. A Bunraku puppet group did four tours in a year. Use the chart to figure out how many weeks were in each tour.

TALK ABOUT IT

1. What quotient would you find to decide how many weeks it took for 56 shows? What multiplication fact would help you find this quotient?
2. What quotient would give the number of weeks for 30 shows? for 54 shows? What multiplication facts would help you find these quotients?

You divide by finding a missing factor.

7 times what number is 28?

$28 \div 7 = 4$

Check: $7 \times 4 = 28$

6 times what number is 54?

$6\overline{)54}$ = 9

Check: $6 \times 9 = 54$

Bunraku puppets from Japan are about 4 feet tall. Some have movable faces.

TRY IT OUT

Divide. Multiply to check.

1. $35 \div 7$	**2.** $24 \div 6$	**3.** $36 \div 6$	**4.** $28 \div 7$	**5.** $63 \div 7$
6. $42 \div 7$	**7.** $18 \div 6$	**8.** $48 \div 6$	**9.** $12 \div 6$	**10.** $54 \div 6$
11. $7\overline{)49}$	**12.** $6\overline{)42}$	**13.** $7\overline{)56}$	**14.** $6\overline{)30}$	**15.** $7\overline{)21}$
16. $6\overline{)6}$	**17.** $7\overline{)14}$	**18.** $7\overline{)7}$	**19.** $7\overline{)63}$	**20.** $6\overline{)24}$

PRACTICE

Divide.

1. $12 \div 6$ **2.** $49 \div 7$ **3.** $48 \div 6$ **4.** $14 \div 7$

5. $36 \div 6$ **6.** $32 \div 4$ **7.** $63 \div 7$ **8.** $9 \div 3$

9. $18 \div 2$ **10.** $30 \div 6$ **11.** $25 \div 5$ **12.** $56 \div 7$

13. $7\overline{)49}$ **14.** $6\overline{)48}$ **15.** $4\overline{)28}$ **16.** $3\overline{)21}$ **17.** $7\overline{)7}$ **18.** $3\overline{)24}$

19. Find the quotient of 42 and 7.

20. Divide 56 by 7.

21. Write multiplication equations to check exercises 5, 10, 15, and 20.

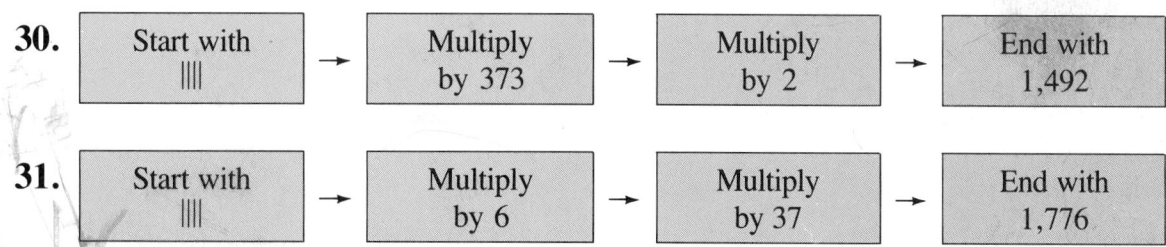

APPLY

MATH REASONING Sort these into even quotients and odd quotients. Is an even number divided by an even number always even? Explain.

22. $35 \div 7$ **23.** $54 \div 6$ **24.** $48 \div 6$ **25.** $21 \div 7$ **26.** $42 \div 7$ **27.** $30 \div 6$

PROBLEM SOLVING

28. The puppet group plans a 49-day tour next year. How many weeks will this tour be?

29. DATA BANK **Fine Arts Data Bank** How many people are needed to work 3 female and 4 male Bunraku puppets? See page 479.

CALCULATOR

Use a calculator and work backward to find the starting number.

30. Start with |||| → Multiply by 373 → Multiply by 2 → End with 1,492

31. Start with |||| → Multiply by 6 → Multiply by 37 → End with 1,776

Dividing by 8 and 9

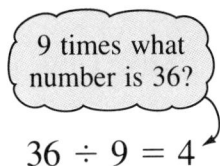

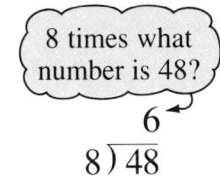

LEARN ABOUT IT

EXPLORE Study the Tables

The multiplication facts for 8 and 9 help you divide by 8 and 9. For several years groups of drama club members have performed in a city-wide puppet show contest. Use the chart to tell how many groups performed each year.

Puppet Show Contest		
Number of Groups	**Number in Each Group**	**Total Number of Students**
5	8	40
____	8	48
____	8	64
5	9	45
____	9	54

TALK ABOUT IT

1. What quotient would you find to decide how many groups performed if there were 48 students? What multiplication fact would help you find this quotient?
2. Give a quotient suggested by each row in the table. What multiplication facts would help you find these quotients?

Use multiplication to help you divide and check.

9 times what number is 36?

$36 \div 9 = 4$

Check: $9 \times 4 = 36$

8 times what number is 48?

$$\begin{array}{r} 6 \\ 8\overline{)48} \end{array}$$

Check: $8 \times 6 = 48$

TRY IT OUT

Divide. Multiply to check.

1. $45 \div 9$ **2.** $32 \div 8$ **3.** $81 \div 9$ **4.** $72 \div 8$ **5.** $63 \div 9$

6. $56 \div 8$ **7.** $54 \div 9$ **8.** $16 \div 8$ **9.** $27 \div 9$ **10.** $36 \div 9$

11. $8\overline{)64}$ **12.** $9\overline{)72}$ **13.** $9\overline{)18}$ **14.** $8\overline{)48}$ **15.** $9\overline{)63}$

PRACTICE

1. $18 \div 9$ **2.** $72 \div 8$ **3.** $40 \div 8$ **4.** $63 \div 9$

5. $0 \div 8$ **6.** $45 \div 9$ **7.** $72 \div 9$ **8.** $48 \div 8$

9. $9\overline{)0}$ **10.** $8\overline{)32}$ **11.** $6\overline{)48}$ **12.** $8\overline{)64}$ **13.** $8\overline{)24}$ **14.** $9\overline{)72}$

15. $9\overline{)63}$ **16.** $8\overline{)72}$ **17.** $9\overline{)9}$ **18.** $6\overline{)54}$ **19.** $8\overline{)48}$ **20.** $6\overline{)24}$

APPLY

MATH REASONING

21. Read this statement. Then write a sentence telling how to correct it.
When you multiply, you know two factors and you find the product. When you divide, you know the product and you find the two factors.

PROBLEM SOLVING

22. In the "Math Is Everywhere" puppet show, the queen, Delila Divide, gives each of her loyal subjects a bag of gold coins. She uses 36 coins. If she puts 9 in each bag, how many loyal subjects does she have?

23. Queen Delila gives each disloyal subject a bag of pebbles. She has 50 pebbles. How many more does she need to fill 7 bags with 9 pebbles in each?

MIXED REVIEW

Write the correct time as it would appear on a digital clock.

24. quarter past five **25.** six-forty-five **26.** seven-thirty

Are these measures the same amount? Write yes or no.

27. 128 ounces
8 pounds

28. 6 pints
4 quarts

29. 3 gallons
12 quarts

30. 4 cups
1 quart

More Practice, page 507, set A

Using Critical Thinking

LEARN ABOUT IT

"This is a great machine," said Carl. "You can put in a number and make it do any operation you want! It's easy to see that it is dividing by 4."

"It's not easy for me to see," said Lola. "I thought that the machine was subtracting!"

"You're both jumping to conclusions," said Ginger. "I just thought of a way that the machine could be subtracting *and* dividing!"

TALK ABOUT IT

IN	OUT
24	6

1. What does a function machine do?
2. Why did Carl think that the machine was dividing by 4?
3. What do you think Lola meant? How could the machine produce 6 by subtracting?
4. Could Ginger be correct? Work together to figure out a rule that the machine could use to begin with 24 and produce 6 by subtracting and dividing.
5. What additional information might help you decide what rule the machine is actually using? Give examples.
6. Make up a rule for a function machine. Give some "in" and "out" numbers and ask a partner to discover the rule.
7. Can you think of any real-world machines that could be made to work like a function machine? Explain.

TRY IT OUT

1. Matt pretended to be a function machine.

   When Jorie said 24, Matt said 4.

   When Jorie said 12, Matt said 2.

   When Jorie said 18, Matt said 3.

   What rule do you think Matt was using?

Give the output number for each of these input numbers.

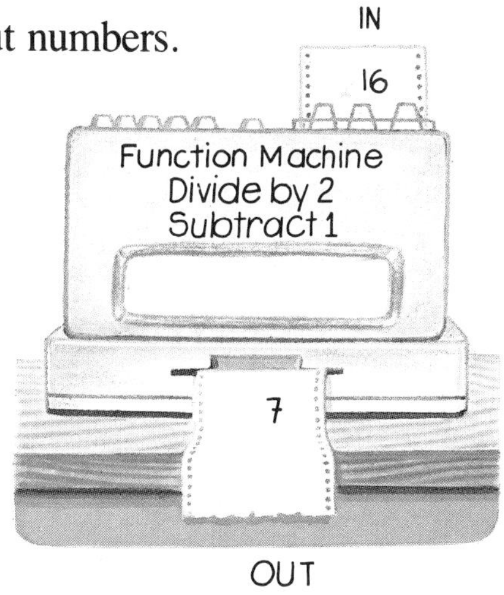

2. 8 **3.** 10

4. 14 **5.** 40

6. 20 **7.** 24

8. 16 **9.** 100

Think about what rule the function machine could be using. What do you think should go in each box?

	RULE	
	Multiply by 6.	
	IN	**OUT**
	3	18
10.	5	☐
11.	9	☐
12.	7	☐
13.	0	☐

	RULE	
14.	☐	
	IN	**OUT**
	6	2
	12	4
	3	1
	9	3
15.	24	☐

	RULE	
	Divide by 4. Add 3.	
	IN	**OUT**
	16	7
16.	12	☐
17.	8	☐
18.	24	☐
19.	36	☐

	RULE	
20.	☐	
	IN	**OUT**
	2	5
	3	7
	4	9
	5	11
21.	10	☐

Problem Solving
Work Backward

UNDERSTAND
FIND DATA
PLAN
ESTIMATE
SOLVE
CHECK

LEARN ABOUT IT

To solve some problems, you may need to undo the key actions in the problem. This strategy is called **Work Backward**.

The junior bowling teams came to Lucky Lanes. 14 bowlers had to wait for lanes to open up. The rest of the bowlers were assigned to the 6 open lanes. 4 bowlers were assigned to each lane. How many junior bowlers came to Lucky Lanes?

First, I'll multiply to find out how many bowlers were assigned to lanes.

$6 \times 4 = 24$

Now, I'll add back the number of bowlers waiting for lanes to see how many bowlers there were all together.

$24 + 14 = 38$

There were 38 bowlers all together.

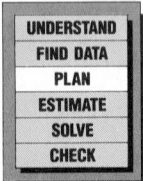

TRY IT OUT

Work backward to solve this problem. Copy and complete the steps.

Andy went bowling on 3 days. Each day he spent \$4. The last day, he also spent \$13 on bowling shoes. Andy had \$2 left. How much money did he have in the beginning?

- How much money does Andy have left?
  Start with the \$2 Andy has left.
- How much money did he spend on shoes?
  Add back the \$13.
  \$2 + \$13 = \$15
- How much money did he spend each day at the bowling alley?
  He spent 3 × \$4 bowling.
  3 × \$4 = ||||
- How much did he have in the beginning?
  |||| + |||| = \$||||

PRACTICE

Work backward to solve these problems.

1. Raul came in first in raising money for the Scout-A-Rama. He got a book of free bowling tickets as a prize. He gave away 5 tickets each to 4 friends. Then he gave 7 to his brother. Raul kept 13. How many bowling tickets did he win?

2. Alexa's grandmother gave her some birthday money. Alexa spent $5 on bowling. Then her sister gave her the $4 she owed her. Alexa now had $9. How much money did she get for her birthday?

MIXED PRACTICE

Choose a strategy from the list or use other strategies you know.

Some Strategies
Act It Out
Use Objects
Choose an Operation
Draw a Picture
Make an Organized List
Guess and Check
Make a Table
Look for a Pattern
Use Logical Reasoning
Work Backward

3. There are 9 junior bowling teams and 45 bowlers in all. Each team has the same number of bowlers. How large is each team?

4. Marco bowled his first frame. In the second frame he knocked down 4 pins. In the third frame he knocked down twice as many as in the second. His score so far is 21. How many pins did he knock down in the first frame?

5. In the girl's league, Lia had the top score for the season with 2,954 points. Her highest game was 234. Kim came in second with 2,527. Rhonda was third with 2,489. What was the difference between the first and the third place scores for the season?

6. The Brighton Bowling Alley has a package deal for birthday parties. It costs $3.50 for each person. Joe would like to invite 17 people. His mother says 7 is plenty. How much more would Joe's plan cost than his mother's?

More Practice, page 520, set E

Applied Problem Solving
Group Decision Making

UNDERSTAND
FIND DATA
PLAN
ESTIMATE
SOLVE
CHECK

Group Skill:
Encourage and Respect Others

To help clean up the neighborhood and save natural resources, your class is taking part in a neighborhood recycling program. Recycling is also a way to earn money for your class's outdoor education program.

A recycling company will buy items at the rates shown in the chart. Your class has decided to spend the money you earn to go and work for three days at a special farm school. The farm charges $30 for each student. Decide how long you will need to earn the necessary funds.

Facts to Consider

1. There are 25 students in the class.
2. The chart, when completed, will tell you how much the class collected and earned the first day of the program.

Some Questions to Answer

1. What was the total amount earned the first day?
2. Which item collected earned the most money?

Items for Recycling	Rate per Pound	Pounds Collected	Amount Earned
Aluminum cans	$.59	16	$9.44
Glass bottles/jars	.04	78	IIII
Plastic	.01	12	IIII
Newspapers	.01	IIII	.94
Cardboard	.02	IIII	.38

3. Which item seems easiest to collect?
4. Can the class expect to earn this amount each day?
5. How much will the farm trip cost all together?

What Is Your Decision?

How long do you think it will take to earn the money the class needs? Support your conclusions.

WRAP UP

Operations Match

Match each operation with its answer.

1. multiplication	**a.** quotient
2. division	**b.** sum
3. subtraction	**c.** difference
4. addition	**d.** product

Sometimes, Always, Never

Which word should go in the blank, sometimes, always, or never? Explain your choices.

5. You can __?__ check division with multiplication.

6. 15 ÷ 3 and 3 ÷ 15 __?__ give the same quotient.

7. Dividing by 2 __?__ tells you half of an amount.

8. Dividing by a smaller number __?__ gives a smaller quotient.

9. There are __?__ 4 equations in a fact family for multiplication or division.

Project

There are 28 students in art class. Small tables hold 3 students. Large tables hold 4 students.

a. If everybody wanted to sit at a full table, how many different ways could students be arranged? Explain each arrangement.

b. How many students would sit at large tables of 4 and how many at small tables of 3 to have the same number of each size table filled? Draw a picture of the arrangement.

POWER PRACTICE/TEST

Part 1 Understanding

Draw a picture, then write a division equation for the answer.

1. A store sells boxes of juice in packs of 3. How many packs can you make with 18 boxes?

2. 15 bananas will make 5 batches of banana bread. How many bananas go in each batch?

3. In multiplication, you have $\underline{\quad ? \quad}$ and you find the $\underline{\quad ? \quad}$. In division, you know the $\underline{\quad ? \quad}$ and one $\underline{\quad ? \quad}$. You use that information to find the other $\underline{\quad ? \quad}$.

4. Give the fact family for the factors 6 and 7.

Part 2 Skills

Find the quotients.

5. $14 \div 2$	**6.** $40 \div 5$	**7.** $49 \div 7$	**8.** $27 \div 3$
9. $4\overline{)16}$	**10.** $9\overline{)63}$	**11.** $5\overline{)0}$	**12.** $6\overline{)24}$

13. 32 divided by 8 **14.** 42 divided by 7 **15.** $\blacksquare \div 1 = 6$

Part 3 Applications

16. Jan traded 13 baseball cards to Dan for 4 new packs of 6 cards each. Jan lost 3 cards so now she has 75. How many did she have at the start?

Give an estimate and then find the exact solution.

17. Toy Town sells baseball cards at \$0.49 a pack. How much money will Elise, the clerk, collect if she sells 82 packs?

18. **Challenge** A display rack holds 21 sports cards in each of 9 rows. Figure out the total number of cards on two display racks.

ENRICHMENT
Factor Pair Fun

Here is one way you can cut a rectangle with 24 squares from a piece of graph paper. There are 4 rows of 6 squares, so 4 and 6 are a **factor pair** for 24.

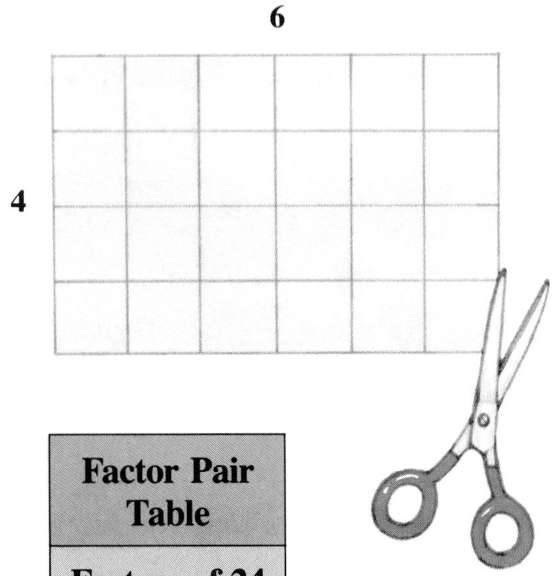

You can use graph paper in this way to find factor pairs and list all the factors of a number.

1. How many different ways can you find to cut a rectangle with 24 squares from graph paper? Show each way and list the factor pairs.
2. Copy and complete this factor pair table to show all of the factors of 24.
3. Cut graph paper squares and make a factor pair table to show all of the factors of 16. Make a list of the factors in numerical order.

Factor Pair Table		
Factors of 24		
1	×	
2	×	
3	×	
4	×	6

Just for fun, we could say that some numbers are *too full*, some are *hungry*, and some are *just right*! In these examples, add all the factors that are less than the number itself. Then tell why you think the numbers could have these names.

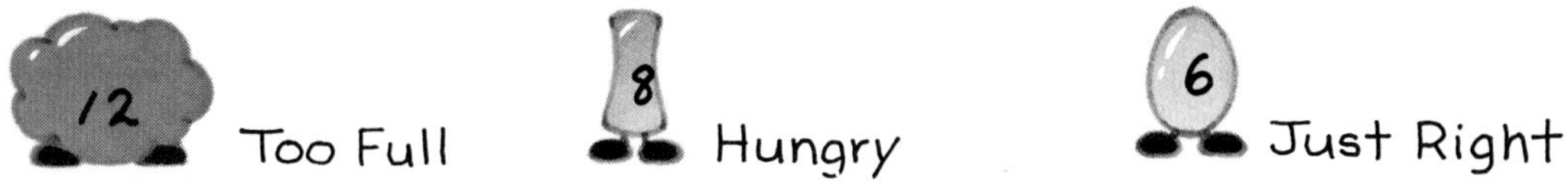

Factors: 1, 2, 3, 4, 6, 12 **Factors: 1, 2, 4, 8** **Factors: 1, 2, 3, 6**

4. Find all the factors of each number up to 20. Make a table that shows the factors and tells which numbers are *too full*, which are *hungry*, and which are *just right*.

CUMULATIVE REVIEW

1. 803×6

   A 4,808 B 4,868
   C 4,818 D 4,809

2. $(4 \times 40) + 4$

   A 444 B 164
   C 4,404 D 640

3. $\$62.48 \times 7$

   A \$437.36 B \$440.25
   C \$455.36 D \$476.36

4. 819×76

   A 10,647 B 62,234
   C 66,094 D 62,244

5. Which calculation method is probably best to find $(76 \times 68) + 47$?

   A pencil, paper B estimation
   C mental math D calculator

6. What is another way to write the date October 19, 1991?

   A 19/10/91 B 9/19/91
   C 10/19/91 D 10/91/19

7. The play started at 2:30 p.m. It lasted until 5:10 p.m. How long did it last?

   A 3 h 20 min B 2 h 10 min
   C 2 h 40 min D 7 h 40 min

8. Intermission began 1 hour and 23 minutes after the 2:30 p.m. start of the play. What time was that?

   A 4:03 p.m. B 3:53 p.m.
   C 3:48 p.m. D 3:57 p.m.

9. Which is less than 3 yards?

   A 90 in. B 12 ft
   C 9 ft D 300 in.

10. 4 gal = |||| qt

    A 64 B 1
    C 32 D 16

11. One side of a square patio measures 27 feet. Find the patio's perimeter.

    A 31 ft B 108 ft
    C 54 ft D 729 ft

12. Estimate the product of 49×80.

    A 3,920 B 4,000
    C 3,200 D 4,500

10

DIVISION 1-DIGIT DIVISORS

THEME: HISTORICAL SHIPS

MATH AND SOCIAL STUDIES

DATA BANK

Use the Social Studies Data Bank on page 475 to answer the questions.

1 How much shorter was a Viking cargo ship than a Viking longship?

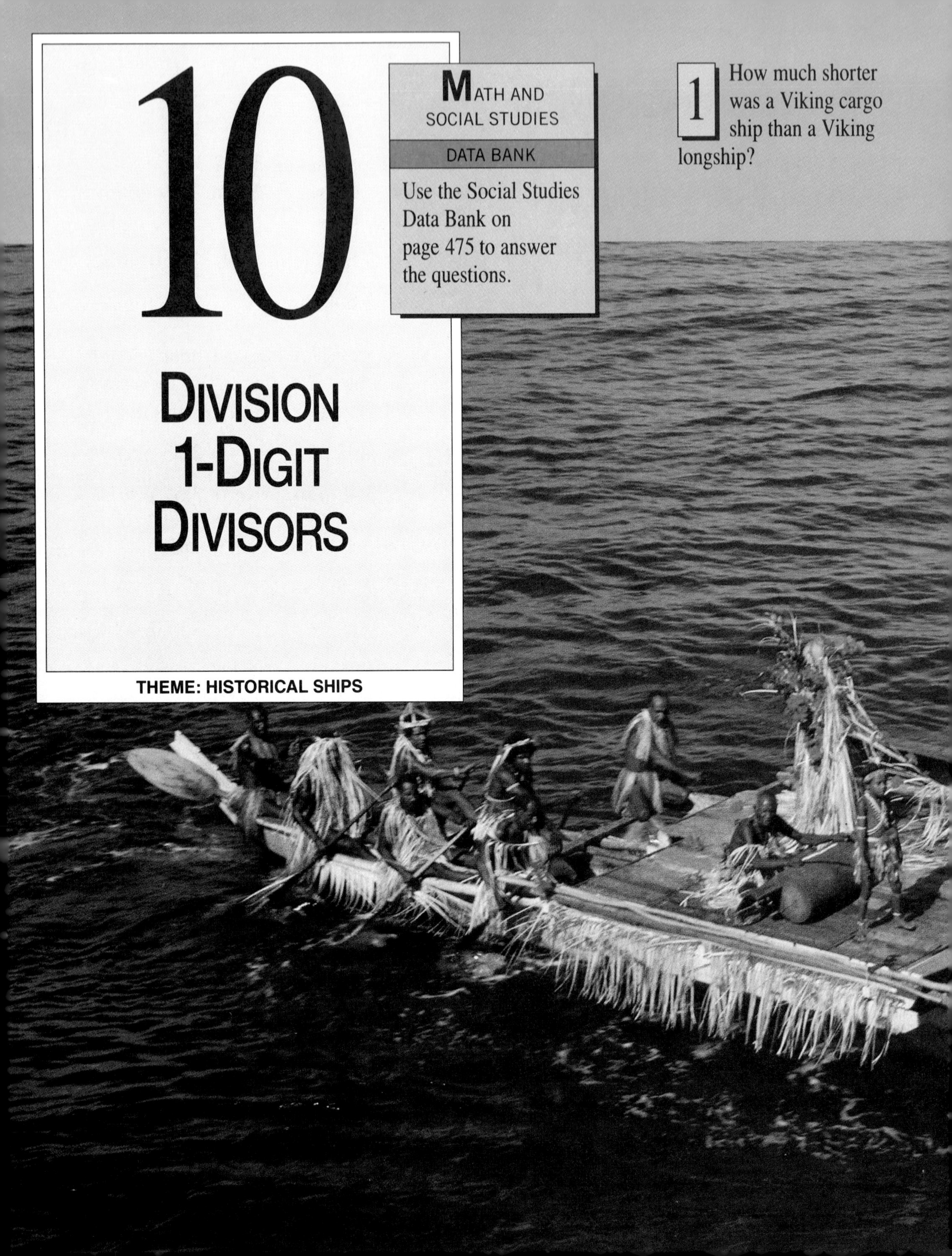

2 The crew of the *Niña*, Columbus' smallest ship, was 4 times the size of a small Viking ship crew. How many were in the *Niña's* crew?

3 If an equal number of rowers sat at the oars on each side of a small Viking ship, how many rowers would be on each side?

4 **Use Critical Thinking** Longer boats usually go faster than shorter boats. Would you predict that the *Pinta* or the long-ship would be faster?

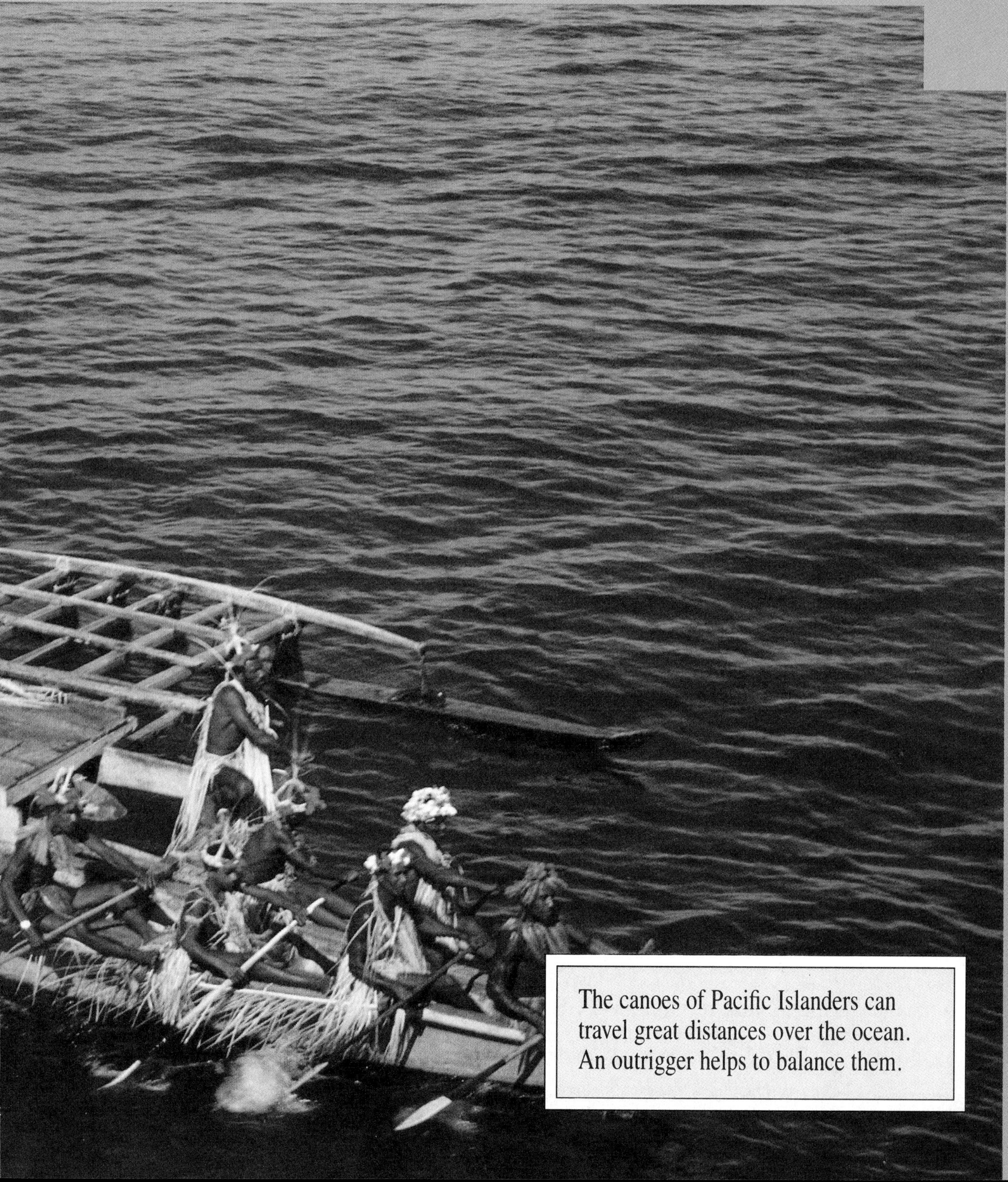

The canoes of Pacific Islanders can travel great distances over the ocean. An outrigger helps to balance them.

Finding and Checking Quotients and Remainders

LEARN ABOUT IT

EXPLORE **Think About the Process**

Pam made a picture book about different kinds of famous boats. She had 43 pictures and wanted to put 6 pictures on each page. How many pages would she need?

Since you must separate the pictures into equal groups, you divide to find the answer.

Here is how to find the correct quotient.

Estimate the quotient.	Multiply and subtract.	Compare. Write the remainder beside the quotient.	Check.
$6\overline{)42}$ $6\overline{)43}$ ↑ divisor	7 ← quotient $6\overline{)43}$ ← dividend (7 × 6) → − 42 1 ← remainder	7 R1 $6\overline{)43}$ − 42 (1 < 6) → 1	7 quotient × 6 divisor 42 + 1 remainder 43 dividend

TALK ABOUT IT

1. Which number in the third step shows the number of pictures? the number of pictures per page? the number of pages filled? the number of pictures left over?
2. Explain how to check the answer.
3. How would you have estimated the answer?
4. Use a complete sentence to give a reasonable answer to the story problem.

TRY IT OUT

Find the quotients and remainders. Check your answers.

1. $4\overline{)30}$ **2.** $6\overline{)38}$ **3.** $4\overline{)26}$ **4.** $2\overline{)13}$ **5.** $7\overline{)54}$ **6.** $9\overline{)57}$

PRACTICE

Check these division problems. Correct those with errors.

1.
```
   7 R1
4)29
  28
   1
```

2.
```
   9 R4
6)60
  56
   4
```

3.
```
   4 R5
8)37
  32
   5
```

4.
```
   6 R2
9)58
  56
   2
```

Find the quotients and remainders. Check.

5. 6)46 **6.** 4)39 **7.** $48 \div 5$ **8.** $16 \div 3$ **9.** $64 \div 8$

10. 7)51 **11.** 8)75 **12.** 9)80 **13.** 5)29 **14.** $15 \div 2$

15. $41 \div 6$ **16.** $24 \div 7$ **17.** $54 \div 4$ **18.** 3)27 **19.** $62 \div 9$

20. What is 66 divided by 9? **21.** What is 32 divided by 5?

APPLY

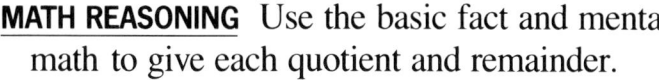

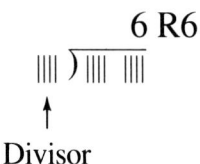

MATH REASONING Use the basic fact and mental math to give each quotient and remainder.

$56 \div 7 = 8$

22. 7)57 **23.** 7)58 **24.** 7)60 **25.** 7)62

PROBLEM SOLVING

26. Data Hunt What is the largest number of each of these size pictures you could paste, without overlapping, on a sheet of your tablet paper?

a. $2\frac{1}{2}$ in. by 3 in.
b. 3 in. × 6 in.
c. 7 in. × 8 in.

How many tablet sheets would you need for 81 of the $2\frac{1}{2}$ in. by 3 in. pictures? Can you find a pattern and decide, without dividing, how many sheets you will need for 81 of the other size pictures?

USING CRITICAL THINKING Analyze the Situation

27. All the digits are hidden except the answer. The divisor is a 1-digit number and the dividend is a 2-digit number. Write as many problems as you can for which this answer would be correct.

```
      6 R6
▒ )▒ ▒
↑
Divisor
```

More Practice, page 507, set B

Mental Math
Special Quotients

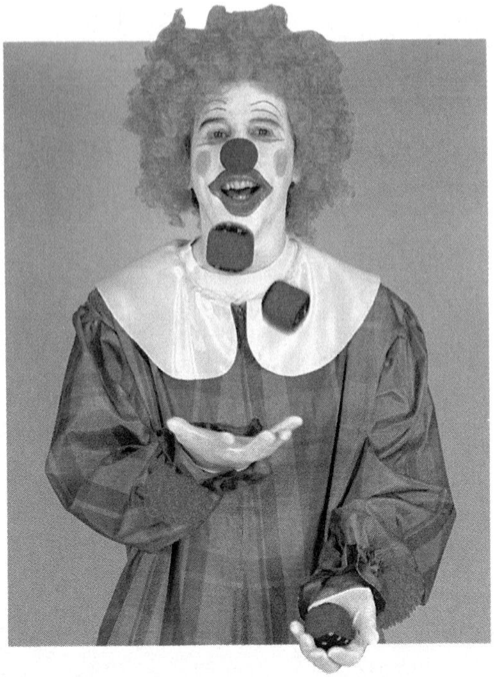

LEARN ABOUT IT

EXPLORE **Think About the Situation**

A circus runs a clown college. During one year 240 people attended the college. There was a new class every other month and each class was the same size.

TALK ABOUT IT

1. How many different classes were there in one year? Explain.
2. How many people were in each class? It may be helpful to use the guess and check strategy.
3. Suppose 24 people had attended the college and there were 6 classes. How many would be in each class? How does this number compare with the number you found in question 2?

The mental math method below gives a quick way to find quotients like 320 ÷ 4.

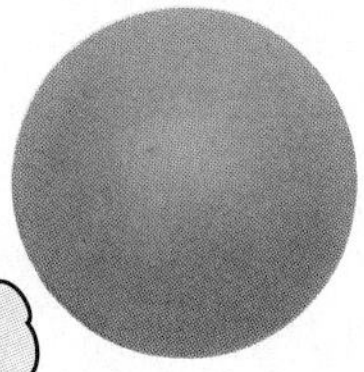

To find **320 ÷ 4**, find **32 ÷ 4** and then multiply by 10.

32 tens ÷ 4 = 8 tens

320 ÷ 4 = 80

Examples

60 ÷ 3 = 20 400 ÷ 5 = 80 360 ÷ 4 = 90

TRY IT OUT

Use mental math to find the quotients.

1. 80 ÷ 4 **2.** 320 ÷ 8 **3.** 280 ÷ 4 **4.** 640 ÷ 8

5. 250 ÷ 5 **6.** 420 ÷ 7 **7.** 360 ÷ 9 **8.** 300 ÷ 6

PRACTICE

Find the quotients. Check your answers by multiplying.

1. $80 \div 4$ **2.** $90 \div 9$ **3.** $180 \div 3$ **4.** $280 \div 7$

5. $180 \div 2$ **6.** $420 \div 7$ **7.** $250 \div 5$ **8.** $360 \div 6$

9. $640 \div 8$ **10.** $120 \div 4$ **11.** $320 \div 8$ **12.** $450 \div 9$

13. $490 \div 7$ **14.** $240 \div 3$ **15.** $810 \div 9$ **16.** $720 \div 8$

APPLY

MATH REASONING Tell which quotient is larger.

17. $342 \div 5$ or $322 \div 5$

18. $483 \div 9$ or $481 \div 8$

PROBLEM SOLVING

19. How many people were enrolled per month in the trapeze artist school?

20. Write Your Own Problem Use the data in the graph to write a division problem.

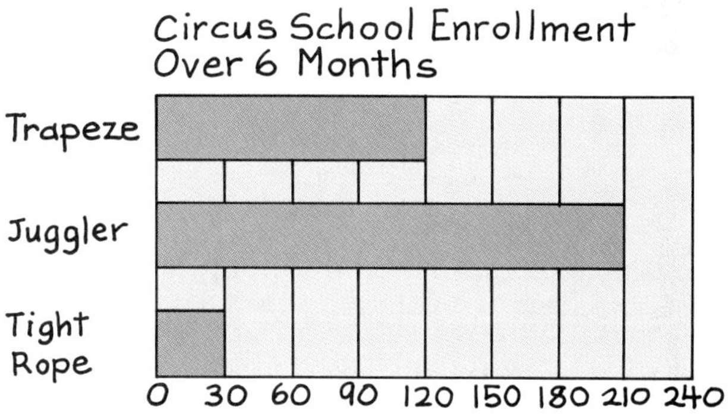

MIXED REVIEW

Tell which weighs the most.

21. corn chips 1 lb
onion dip 18 oz

22. laundry detergent 3 lb
bleach 32 oz.

23. potatoes 5 lb
asparagus 64 oz

24. flour 36 oz
corn meal 2 lb

Write four fact family equations for these factors and products. The order of the equations may vary.

25. 18 3 6

26. 7 28 4

27. 5 9 45

28. 7 56 8

Estimating Quotients

LEARN ABOUT IT

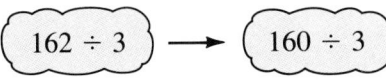

EXPLORE **Solve to Understand**

In the year 1010, a Viking named Thorfinn sailed for Vinland. His 3 ships carried 162 people. If each ship carried the same number of people, how many were on each?

TALK ABOUT IT

1. What numbers do you need to divide to get the answer?
2. If you round the number of people to the nearest ten, will you be able to estimate the answer easily? Explain.
3. How can you change the rounded number to make the problem into a basic fact?

When you estimate a quotient, sometimes rounding is not enough. You may need to substitute a compatible number that makes the computation easier.

To estimate $162 \div 3$, round the dividend to the nearest ten. $162 \div 3 \rightarrow 160 \div 3$

Then substitute a close number so you can estimate using a basic fact. $150 \div 3$

Each ship carried about 50 people. Since you reduced the dividend to find the estimate, the answer is an underestimate.

TRY IT OUT

Use rounding to estimate. Substitute if necessary. Tell if the estimate is over or under the exact answer.

1. $43 \div 4$ **2.** $67 \div 3$ **3.** $118 \div 6$ **4.** $157 \div 5$

PRACTICE

Use rounding to estimate the quotients. Substitute if necessary.

1. 66 ÷ 7	**2.** \$8.90 ÷ 5	**3.** 348 ÷ 4	**4.** 461 ÷ 9
5. 355 ÷ 6	**6.** 712 ÷ 8	**7.** $3\overline{)117}$	**8.** 164 ÷ 2
9. $5\overline{)242}$	**10.** \$48.66 ÷ 7	**11.** $9\overline{)269}$	**12.** 153 ÷ 4

Estimate each quotient. Tell whether the estimate is <u>over</u> or <u>under</u> the exact quotient.

13. 397 ÷ 5	**14.** 106 ÷ 6	**15.** 218 ÷ 3	**16.** 233 ÷ 8
17. $4\overline{)\$19.79}$	**18.** $7\overline{)294}$	**19.** 471 ÷ 5	**20.** 534 ÷ 9
21. 193 ÷ 2	**22.** 486 ÷ 8	**23.** $4\overline{)256}$	**24.** 542 ÷ 6

APPLY

MATH REASONING

25. The closer the divisor is to 1, the closer the dividend comes to equaling the __?__.

PROBLEM SOLVING

26. A copy of a Viking ship crossed the Atlantic Ocean in 28 days. The ship's length of 76 ft was about 4 times its width. About how wide was it?

27. Social Studies Data Bank DATA BANK
In 1970 a Norwegian explorer crossed the Atlantic Ocean in a reed boat he had made, called Ra II. 4 boats the length of Ra II would equal the length of a Viking longship. About how long was Ra II? See page 475.

CALCULATOR

28. Start with 510. Guess how many times you can subtract 34. Then try it with a calculator.

Begin your calculator steps like this.

[ON/AC] [−] 34 [Cons] 510 [Cons] 476 ⟶ 1 time [Cons] 442 ⟶ 2 times

More Practice, page 507, set D

Dividing Whole Numbers
Making the Connection

LEARN ABOUT IT

EXPLORE Use a Place Value Model
Work in groups. Use a spinner with digits 1–9 and make piles of blocks.

- Spin two times to give the number of tens and ones blocks for a pile. Record the numbers in a table like the first one shown.
- Spin the spinner again. If you land on an even number, write 2 on the blank line next to "equal sets." Then divide the pile into 2 equal piles. If you land on an odd number, write 3 and divide the pile into 3 equal piles. Trade a tens block for 10 ones blocks if necessary.
- Record any extras in the extra box.
- Do this several times. Make a separate table each time.

Divide.

Tens	Ones
7	4

Record results.

Tens (in each equal set)	Ones (in each equal set)
3	7

Extras
0

into 2 equal sets.

Separate into same-size piles to share the blocks equally.

TALK ABOUT IT

1. Look at one of your tables and tell what trades, if any, you made to divide up the pile.
2. Did you divide the tens or ones first? Which seems easier? Why?
3. When are there extras? Do you see a pattern?

You have used your blocks to divide numbers into 2 and 3 equal sets. Now you will see another way to record what you have done. This process can help you find quotients such as 74 ÷ 2.

What You Do | **What You Record**

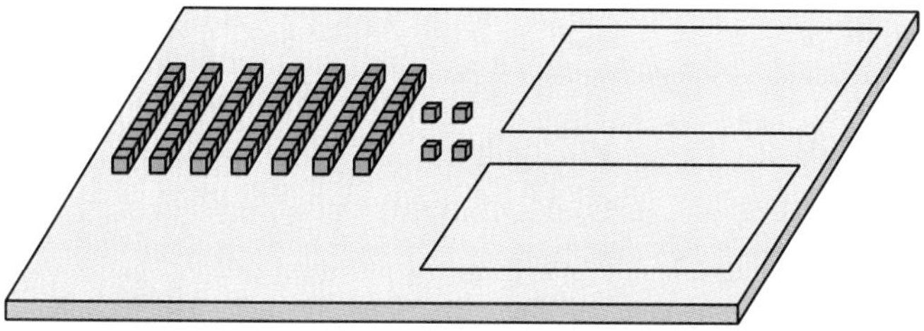

→ 2)74

1. How many tens can you put into each of the 2 sets?

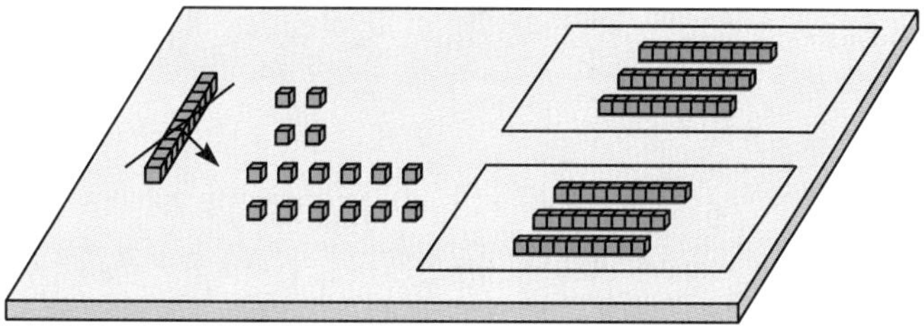

→

```
   3
2)74
  6
  14  ← 14 ones
```

2. How many ones do you have to divide after you trade the extra ten?

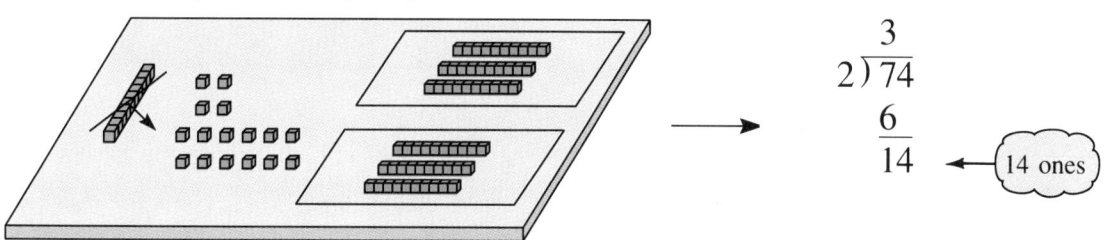

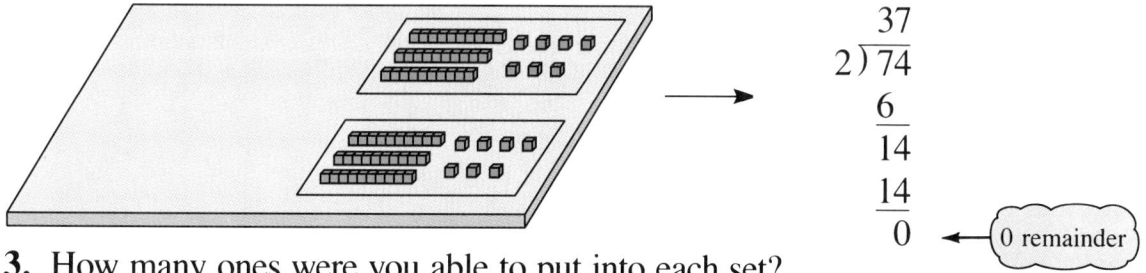

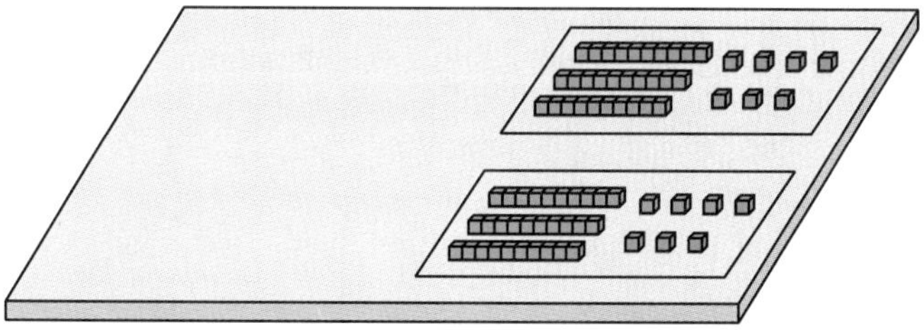

→

```
  37
2)74
  6
  14
  14
   0  ← 0 remainder
```

3. How many ones were you able to put into each set? How many extra ones were there?
4. How many are in each set? What is the quotient for 74 ÷ 2? What is the remainder?

TRY IT OUT

Use blocks to find answers to the following. Trade when necessary. Record what you do.

1. 46 ÷ 2 **2.** 52 ÷ 3 **3.** 27 ÷ 2 **4.** 35 ÷ 3

5. Use blocks to solve a division problem of your choice.

Dividing Whole Numbers
2-Digit Quotients

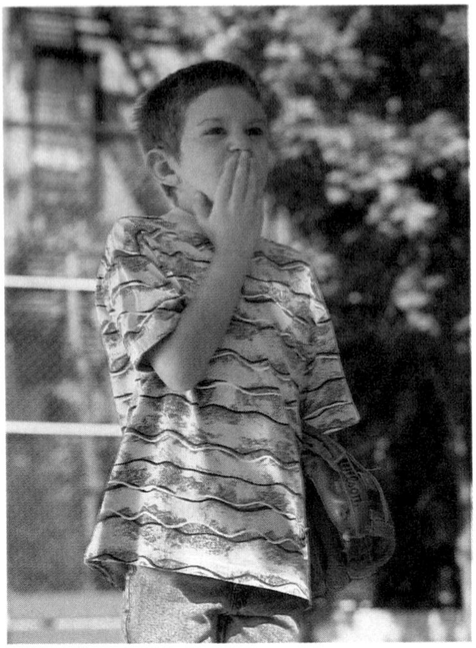

LEARN ABOUT IT

EXPLORE Think About the Process

Jonathan and his two friends were playing catch and by accident broke the neighbor's window. Repairing the window will cost $87. What is each child's fair share of the cost?

Since an amount of money is to be separated into equal groups, you divide to find the answer.

Divide the tens.		Divide the ones.		Write the remainder next to the quotient unless it is 0.
■ Estimate ■ Divide ■ Multiply ■ Subtract ■ Compare	$\begin{array}{r} 2 \\ 3\overline{)87} \\ -6 \\ \hline 2 \end{array}$	■ Bring down ■ Divide ■ Multiply ■ Subtract ■ Compare	$\begin{array}{r} 29 \\ 3\overline{)87} \\ -6 \\ \hline 27 \\ -27 \\ \hline 0 \end{array}$	$\begin{array}{r} 29 \\ 3\overline{)87} \\ -6 \\ \hline 27 \\ -27 \\ \hline 0 \end{array}$

TALK ABOUT IT

1. In step 1, 8 was divided into 3 groups. How many tens were in each group? How many tens were left over?
2. How would you have estimated the answer?
3. Give the answer in a complete sentence.

TRY IT OUT

1. $6\overline{)74}$ **2.** $8\overline{)93}$ **3.** $3\overline{)60}$ **4.** $4\overline{)94}$ **5.** $5\overline{)86}$

PRACTICE

Find the quotients and remainders.

1. $73 \div 4$ **2.** $98 \div 9$ **3.** $65 \div 3$ **4.** $70 \div 6$ **5.** $55 \div 4$

6. $7\overline{)86}$ **7.** $5\overline{)58}$ **8.** $2\overline{)69}$ **9.** $8\overline{)47}$ **10.** $9\overline{)46}$

11. Divide 84 by 6. **12.** Divide 93 by 4. **13.** Divide 78 by 7.

Estimate each quotient.

14. $85 \div 2$ **15.** $71 \div 3$ **16.** $89 \div 8$ **17.** $95 \div 5$ **18.** $23 \div 4$

APPLY

MATH REASONING For each exercise, make up and complete 3 division problems to help you give the number for the blank.

19. When an even number is divided by 2, the remainder is __?__.

20. When an odd number is divided by 2, the remainder is __?__.

PROBLEM SOLVING

21. **Developing a Plan** Choose the steps you could follow to solve this problem. Jack had 32 marbles. He found 4 more. Then he decided to give all of his marbles to 3 of his friends. How many marbles did each friend get?

a. Divide 32 by 3. Then add 4.
b. Add 32 and 4. Then divide by 3.
c. Add 32 and 4. Then multiply by 3.

22. Maria's mother bought tickets and lunch for Maria and 3 friends at the Oakland A's and Houston Astros game. The total cost was $52. How much was this per person?

ESTIMATION

23. Suppose there are 817 people in the whole picture. Estimate the number of people in one section.

More Practice, page 507, set E

Problem Solving
Interpreting Remainders

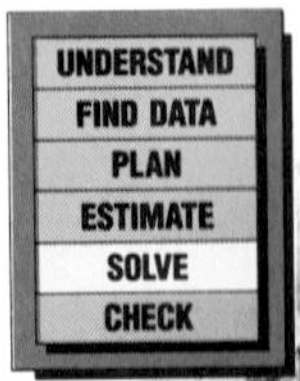

LEARN ABOUT IT

Sometimes division does not give you the complete answer to the problem. You need to understand the remainder.

At junior lifesaving camp at the beach, the counselors divided 88 campers into teams of 7 for the freestyle relay race. How many complete teams could they make?

$$\begin{array}{r} 12 \text{ R}4 \\ 7\overline{)88} \\ \underline{7} \\ 18 \\ \underline{14} \\ 4 \end{array}$$

They could make 12 teams.

> There aren't enough campers in the last group to make a team.

The camp counselors bought juice bars for the 86 campers who came on Tuesday. The bars come in boxes of 6. How many boxes should they buy?

$$\begin{array}{r} 14 \text{ R}2 \\ 6\overline{)86} \\ \underline{6} \\ 26 \\ \underline{24} \\ 2 \end{array}$$

They should buy 15 boxes.

> They need 14 full boxes. A 15th box is needed to have some for the 2 remaining campers.

TRY IT OUT

Read and then solve each problem.

1. One Saturday, 98 passengers rented paddleboats. A boat can hold 4 people. How many boat rides were needed for everyone to get a ride?
2. There were 53 people waiting to play in the White Sands Beach volleyball competition. They divided into teams of 5. How many complete teams could they form?

MIXED PRACTICE

Solve the problems. Use any problem solving strategy.

Some Strategies
Act It Out
Use Objects
Choose an Operation
Draw a Picture
Make an Organized List
Guess and Check
Make a Table
Look for a Pattern
Use Logical Reasoning
Work Backward

1. There were 95 campers on the beach. They formed teams of 7 for volleyball. How many campers were left over?

2. The Beach Store had a window display of 18 flying disks in different colors. Each disk was worth $6.99. How much were all the disks in the window worth?

The Outdoor Store		
Complete Windsurfing Boards	Regular	On Sale
Fantastic 304	$769	$599
Fantastic Seaviper	$1,499	$999
Fantastic Seaboa	$1,524	$1,199
Fantastic Cat	$1,894	$1,549

Use the table above to solve problems 3–6.

3. How much money would you save by buying a Fantastic Seaboa on sale?

4. A used windsurfing board is $399. Which new board on sale is almost 4 times as much as a used board?

5. Yang wants to start a windsurfing rental service at the beach. How much money would he save by buying 4 Fantastic 304s on sale rather than at the regular price?

6. How much would Yang pay for 3 Fantastic Seavipers on sale?

7. Mario spent $36 on a skin board. Then he bought 3 T-shirts at $11 each. He had $3 left. How much money did he start with?

8. Jon and his friends are renting wetsuits for surfing. They rent for $9 each. How many suits could they rent with $39?

More Practice, page 521, set A

3-Digit Quotients

LEARN ABOUT IT

EXPLORE Think About the Process

Columbus measured the distance he sailed in a unit called the Portuguese league, which is equal to 4 miles. A two-weeks' journey was about 944 miles. How many Portuguese leagues is 944 miles?

Since you want to separate a total number of miles into equal parts, you divide.

Divide the hundreds.		Divide the tens.		Divide the ones.	
	2		23		236
■ Estimate	4)944	■ Bring down	4)944	■ Bring down	4)944
■ Divide	8	■ Divide	8	■ Divide	8
■ Multiply	1	■ Multiply	14	■ Multiply	14
■ Subtract		■ Subtract	12	■ Subtract	12
■ Compare		■ Compare	2	■ Compare	24
					24
					0

TALK ABOUT IT

1. In each step, what did you compare?
2. How would you have estimated the answer?
3. Give the answer in a complete sentence.

TRY IT OUT

1. 3)646 **2.** 5)933 **3.** 2)974

4. 4)870 **5.** 8)962 **6.** 7)892

7. 4)575 **8.** 5)907 **9.** 2)685

PRACTICE

Find the quotients and remainders.

1. $6\overline{)692}$ **2.** $3\overline{)424}$ **3.** $8\overline{)985}$ **4.** $7\overline{)801}$

5. $2\overline{)783}$ **6.** $9\overline{)999}$ **7.** $4\overline{)569}$ **8.** $5\overline{)790}$

9. $815 \div 3$ **10.** $779 \div 7$ **11.** $838 \div 5$ **12.** $925 \div 2$

13. What is 642 divided by 5? **14.** What is 814 divided by 3?

Estimate these quotients.

15. $3\overline{)950}$ **16.** $8\overline{)843}$ **17.** $4\overline{)834}$ **18.** $2\overline{)550}$

APPLY

MATH REASONING

19. In these problems, what pattern do the remainders make?

$145 \div 9$, $146 \div 9$, $147 \div 9$, $148 \div 9$, $149 \div 9$, $150 \div 9$, $151 \div 9$, $152 \div 9$

PROBLEM SOLVING

20. A league in English-speaking countries is equal to 3 miles. How many more English leagues than Portuguese leagues is a distance of 600 miles? Remember a Portuguese league is equal to 4 miles.

DATA BANK

21. Social Studies Data Bank The length of a carrack was about 3 times the width. About how much wider was a man-of-war carrack than a merchant carrack? See page 475.

MIXED REVIEW

Tell if the object is closer to an ounce or a pound.

22. a feather **23.** a brick **24.** 2 pencils **25.** a watermelon

Find the quotients.

26. $18 \div 2$ **27.** $18 \div 3$ **28.** $27 \div 3$ **29.** $16 \div 2$ **30.** $12 \div 3$

31. $8 \div 2$ **32.** $20 \div 2$ **33.** $24 \div 3$ **34.** $21 \div 3$ **35.** $14 \div 2$

Finding Averages

LEARN ABOUT IT

EXPLORE Think About the Process

Jay read a mystery book in 6 days. He read 55 pages the first day, 62 the second, 109 the third, 78 the fourth, 123 the fifth, and 137 the last. Suppose you read the same book in 6 days by reading an equal number of pages every day. How many pages would you read per day?

TALK ABOUT IT

1. How many pages are in the book?
2. Do you think you would read more or less than 50 pages a day? more or less than 100 a day?

The number of pages you would be reading each day is called the average. To find the average of a set of numbers, add the numbers and divide by the number of addends.

Find the average of 243, 259, and 275.

Add:

$$\begin{array}{r} 243 \\ 259 \\ +\ 275 \\ \hline 777 \end{array}$$

Divide:

$$3\overline{)777} = 259$$

The average is 259.

You can use this key code to find the average on the calculator.

[ON/AC] 243 [+] 259 [+] 275 [=] |||| [÷] 3 [=] ||||

PRACTICE

Find the average of these numbers.

1. 36, 32, 43
2. 17, 24, 19, 16
3. 65, 59, 38, 47, 56
4. 138, 175, 143
5. 164, 196, 132, 128
6. 321, 339, 306

More Practice, page 521, set B

Power Practice/Quiz

Use rounding and substitution to estimate each quotient. Circle your estimate if it is over the actual quotient.

1. $86 \div 4$	**2.** $267 \div 3$	**3.** $95 \div 2$	**4.** $188 \div 6$
5. $335 \div 8$	**6.** $344 \div 5$	**7.** $410 \div 7$	**8.** $801 \div 9$

Check these division problems. Correct those with errors.

9.
$$\begin{array}{r} 7 \text{ R2} \\ 8\overline{)56} \\ \underline{54} \\ 2 \end{array}$$

10.
$$\begin{array}{r} 6 \text{ R2} \\ 7\overline{)40} \\ \underline{42} \\ 2 \end{array}$$

11.
$$\begin{array}{r} 31 \text{ R1} \\ 4\overline{)17} \\ \underline{12} \\ 5 \\ \underline{4} \\ 1 \end{array}$$

12.
$$\begin{array}{r} 9 \text{ R0} \\ 6\overline{)56} \\ \underline{56} \\ 0 \end{array}$$

Suppose you use blocks to show each problem. Write <u>T</u> if you would trade tens for ones. Write <u>R</u> if there will be ones remaining.

13. $4\overline{)89}$ **14.** $5\overline{)64}$ **15.** $3\overline{)27}$ **16.** $2\overline{)80}$ **17.** $7\overline{)90}$

Find the quotients and remainders.

18. $6\overline{)8}$	**19.** $2\overline{)11}$	**20.** $5\overline{)72}$	**21.** $3\overline{)87}$	**22.** $3\overline{)456}$
23. $8\overline{)96}$	**24.** $4\overline{)79}$	**25.** $7\overline{)783}$	**26.** $6\overline{)784}$	**27.** $6\overline{)62}$
28. $7\overline{)87}$	**29.** $2\overline{)42}$	**30.** $4\overline{)27}$	**31.** $8\overline{)907}$	**32.** $5\overline{)85}$
33. $5\overline{)903}$	**34.** $3\overline{)29}$	**35.** $9\overline{)999}$	**36.** $4\overline{)60}$	**37.** $7\overline{)40}$

38. Use multiplication to check. Explain what is wrong with this problem.

$$\begin{array}{r} 8 \text{ R7} \\ 6\overline{)55} \\ \underline{48} \\ 7 \end{array}$$

PROBLEM SOLVING

39. When Gretchen and some friends shared \$17, they had \$2 left over. How many friends might there have been? Can you find another way?

Deciding Where to Start

LEARN ABOUT IT

EXPLORE **Think About the Process**

A test driver in a compact car took 5 hours to drive 485 miles. At what speed was the car traveling?

Decide where to start. Divide the hundreds if possible.	Divide the tens.	Divide the ones.
$5\overline{)485}$ 5 > 4 Not enough hundreds. Divide the tens.	$\begin{array}{r} 9 \\ 5\overline{)485} \\ \underline{45} \\ 3 \end{array}$	$\begin{array}{r} 97 \\ 5\overline{)485} \\ \underline{45} \\ 35 \\ \underline{35} \\ 0 \end{array}$

TALK ABOUT IT

1. Why can't you divide the hundreds in step 1?
2. How many tens do you divide in step 2?
3. How would you have estimated the answer?
4. Give the answer in a complete sentence.

Other Examples

A $\begin{array}{r} 33\text{ R}3 \\ 4\overline{)135} \\ \underline{12} \\ 15 \\ \underline{12} \\ 3 \end{array}$

B $\begin{array}{r} 71\text{ R}1 \\ 8\overline{)569} \\ \underline{56} \\ 09 \\ \underline{8} \\ 1 \end{array}$

C $\begin{array}{r} 68 \\ 3\overline{)204} \\ \underline{18} \\ 24 \\ \underline{24} \\ 0 \end{array}$

TRY IT OUT

1. $5\overline{)637}$ **2.** $7\overline{)568}$ **3.** $4\overline{)239}$ **4.** $3\overline{)342}$

PRACTICE

Write whether you start by dividing tens or by dividing hundreds.

1. $6\overline{)432}$ **2.** $9\overline{)926}$ **3.** $2\overline{)634}$ **4.** $8\overline{)309}$

Divide and check.

5. $644 \div 4$ **6.** $826 \div 7$ **7.** $245 \div 5$ **8.** $773 \div 9$

9. Divide 381 by 6. **10.** Divide 925 by 8.

11. Divide 507 by 3. **12.** Divide 659 by 7.

Estimate these quotients.

13. $2\overline{)683}$ **14.** $7\overline{)146}$ **15.** $9\overline{)873}$ **16.** $6\overline{)452}$

APPLY

MATH REASONING

17. If a, b, and c represent numbers, how would you check the answer to this problem?

$$\begin{array}{r} c \\ a\overline{)b} \end{array}$$

PROBLEM SOLVING

18. **Missing Data** Tell what data is missing in this problem. In a famous auto race, a car finished in about 3 hours. The purse for the race was over $1,500,000. How fast did the car go?

19. Last year the speed record in an auto race was 147 miles per hour. This year the record was 162 miles per hour. How much faster is this year's record?

▶ MENTAL MATH

Use mental math and break apart the dividends to find the quotients.

20. $728 \div 7$ **21.** $812 \div 4$ **22.** $428 \div 4$ **23.** $614 \div 2$

24. $636 \div 6$ **25.** $921 \div 3$ **26.** $545 \div 5$ **27.** $832 \div 8$

28. $2\overline{)450}$ **29.** $3\overline{)618}$ **30.** $9\overline{)963}$ **31.** $3\overline{)627}$

More Practice, page 508, set B

Zero in the Quotient

LEARN ABOUT IT

EXPLORE Think About the Process

548 seats will be installed in a new Boeing 747 jet. How many rows of 9 can be put in? How many extra seats will there be for another row?

Decide where to start. Divide the hundreds if possible.	Divide the tens.	Divide the ones.
9 > 5 Not enough hundreds. $9\overline{)548}$	9 < 54 $\begin{array}{r} 6 \\ 9\overline{)548} \\ -\ 54 \\ \hline 0 \end{array}$	$\begin{array}{r} 60\text{ R}8 \\ 9\overline{)548} \\ -\ 54 \\ \hline 08 \\ -\ 0 \\ \hline 8 \end{array}$

TALK ABOUT IT

1. How would you have estimated the answer?
2. Give the answer in a complete sentence.

Other Examples

A $\begin{array}{r} 10\text{ R}5 \\ 6\overline{)65} \\ -\ 6 \\ \hline 05 \\ -\ 0 \\ \hline 5 \end{array}$

B $\begin{array}{r} 406\text{ R}1 \\ 2\overline{)813} \\ -\ 8 \\ \hline 01 \\ -\ 0 \\ \hline 13 \\ -\ 12 \\ \hline 1 \end{array}$

C $\begin{array}{r} 200\text{ R}2 \\ 3\overline{)602} \\ -\ 6 \\ \hline 00 \\ -\ 0 \\ \hline 02 \\ -\ 0 \\ \hline 2 \end{array}$

TRY IT OUT

1. $6\overline{)65}$ **2.** $6\overline{)638}$ **3.** $4\overline{)201}$ **4.** $5\overline{)904}$

5. $2\overline{)615}$ **6.** $8\overline{)165}$ **7.** $2\overline{)813}$ **8.** $3\overline{)602}$

PRACTICE

Divide.

1. $75 \div 7$	**2.** $640 \div 4$	**3.** $907 \div 9$	**4.** $252 \div 5$
5. $815 \div 2$	**6.** $803 \div 8$	**7.** $120 \div 6$	**8.** $928 \div 3$
9. $7\overline{)751}$	**10.** $5\overline{)508}$	**11.** $3\overline{)625}$	**12.** $8\overline{)483}$

Use mental math to find these quotients.

13. $3\overline{)363}$	**14.** $6\overline{)642}$	**15.** $4\overline{)164}$	**16.** $9\overline{)909}$

APPLY

MATH REASONING Use the first equation to find the missing numbers in the second.

17. $45 \times 7 + 3 = 318$ $318 \div 7 =$ ▯ R▯

PROBLEM SOLVING

18. A Boeing 727 holds 189 people. How many rows of 8 can there be? How many seats are left over?

19. The O'Neals paid $744 for three plane tickets to Disneyland. How much was each ticket if all fares were the same?

ALGEBRA

20. The output of function machine A is the input for function machine B. Study the example. Then figure out the two function rules and complete the table.

Input A	Output B
24	5
72	11
8	3
32	▯
40	▯
48	▯

Problem Solving
Choosing a Calculation Method

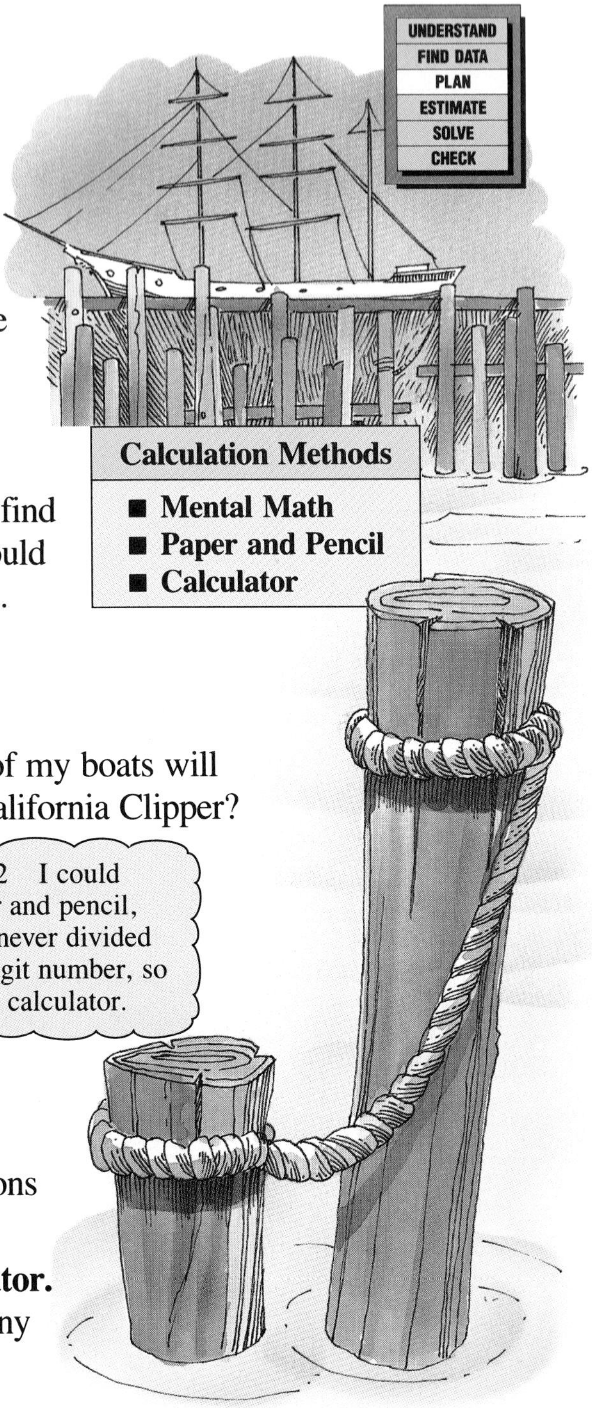

LEARN ABOUT IT

When you solve a problem, you must choose the calculation method that is best to use.

Which of the methods in the box would you use for this problem?

Calculation Methods

- **Mental Math**
- **Paper and Pencil**
- **Calculator**

Jack's sailboat was 12 ft long. He wanted to find how many boats like his, put end to end, would reach the length of these two historical ships.

Baltimore Clipper Ship	120 ft long
California Clipper Ship	216 ft long

How many of my boats will match the Baltimore Clipper?

120 ÷ 12 This is easy to do in my head. I'll use mental math.

How many of my boats will match the California Clipper?

216 ÷ 12 I could try paper and pencil, but I've never divided by a 2-digit number, so I'll use a calculator.

Use these hints when you are choosing a calculation method.

- **First try mental math.** Look for computations you can do easily in your head.
- **Then choose paper and pencil or a calculator.** It is often better to use a calculator when many steps or trades are needed.

TRY IT OUT

Tell which calculation method you choose and why. Then solve.

1. 54 − 40 **2.** 278 + 99 **3.** 56 × 28 **4.** \$69.58 + \$98.79 **5.** 576 ÷ 9

MIXED PRACTICE

Tell which calculation method you choose and why. Then solve.

1. $5 \times 18 \times 2$

2. $200 - 99$

3. 678×563

4. $160 \div 4$

5. $137 - 67$

6. $49 + 50 + 51$

7. 158×5

8. $\$72 - \$16.67$

9. $192 \div 8$

10. 8×21

11. $57 + 5$

12. $666 \div 2$

Solve. Choose the most useful calculation method.

13. How many 15 ft sailboats end to end would match a 150 ft Egyptian galley ship?

14. A whaling ship was 107 ft long. How much less was this length than the length of a 207 ft English warship?

15. A giant clipper ship was 8 times as long as it was wide. It was 432 feet long. How wide was it?

16. The largest clipper ship had 5 masts with 12 sails on each mast. It had another sail in front and in back. How many sails did it have?

17. A historical ship collection in a museum contained models of 29 sailing ships and 47 engine-driven ships. How many ships were in the collection?

18. A modern ocean liner might travel 38 miles per hour. A clipper ship could travel 22 miles per hour. How much faster is the ocean liner's speed?

19. The average amount of cloth per sail was 968 square feet. Use your answer to problem 16 to find how many square feet of cloth were needed to make all the sails on the ship.

WRITE YOUR OWN PROBLEM

Write a problem using each of these methods.

20. mental math
21. paper and pencil
22. a calculator

More Practice, page 521, set C

Dividing with Money

LEARN ABOUT IT

EXPLORE **Think About the Situation**

Tina and her best friend made silly photos of themselves in the mall photo booth. They paid \$3.92 for 8 photos. How much did each photo cost?

TALK ABOUT IT

1. How do you know to divide in this problem?
2. Will the photos cost more or less than \$0.50 each?

Think cents.

Divide as with whole numbers.

```
    49
8)$3.92    (392 cents)
 - 3 2
    72
  - 72
     0
```

Think dollars and cents.

Show dollars and cents in the quotient.

```
  $0.49
8)$3.92    (If there are no dollars, write a 0.)
 - 3 2
    72
  - 72
     0
```

Other Examples

```
  $0.91        $1.04        $0.05
5)4.55       8)$8.32      9)$0.45    (If there are no tens, write a 0.)
  0           - 8          -  0
  4 5           0 3            45
- 4 5             0          - 45
    05           32             0
     5         - 32
     0            0
```

TRY IT OUT

1. 4)\$8.20 **2.** 7)\$9.45 **3.** 6)\$1.38 **4.** 9)\$0.72

PRACTICE

1. 3)$4.38	**2.** 6)$9.72	**3.** 4)$1.36	**4.** 8)$0.96
5. 7)$0.63	**6.** 5)$8.80	**7.** 3)$6.09	**8.** 9)$8.46
9. 4)$9.00	**10.** 8)$5.52	**11.** 2)$7.06	**12.** 6)$8.28

Estimate these quotients.

13. 8)$2.50	**14.** 7)$7.65	**15.** 4)$9.28	**16.** 3)$10.00

APPLY

MATH REASONING Use number sense to complete the following.

17. If there are three 35s in 105, how many 35s will be in 210?

18. If there are four 52s in 208, how many 52s will be in 416?

PROBLEM SOLVING

19. Rita had a roll of film developed for $8.64. Her flash was not working so only 9 prints turned out. What did each print cost?

20. Rita had 5 reprints made of one photo and 3 reprints made of another photo. The total cost was $6.16. How much did the store charge per reprint?

21. At a photo shop it cost $0.50 per picture to develop a roll of 24 pictures. What was the total cost?

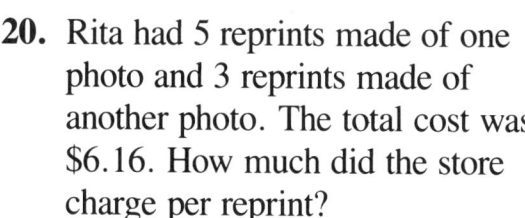

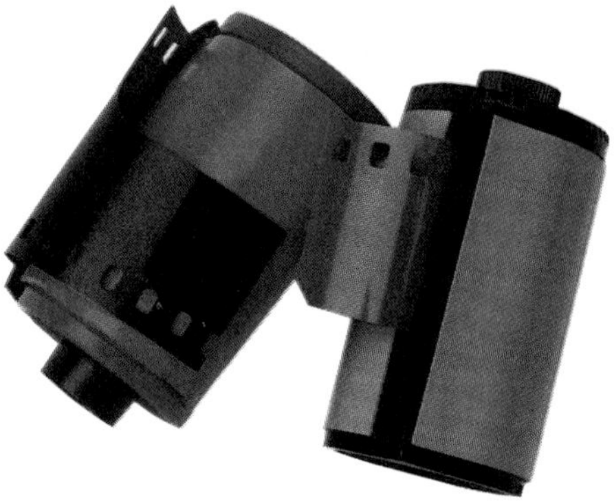

USING CRITICAL THINKING Careful Reasoning

22. You have savings accounts at 3 banks. You want to make 2 money transfers so that all accounts have the same amount. Tell what transfers you could make.

Last National Bank	Tight Wad Bank	Savers' National Bank
$35	$80	$35

More Practice, page 508, set D

Data Collection and Analysis
Group Decision Making

UNDERSTAND
FIND DATA
PLAN
ESTIMATE
SOLVE
CHECK

Doing a Questionnaire
Group Skill:
Check for Understanding

What do you like most to do after school? What do your friends like most to do? Make a prediction and then make a questionnaire to help you find out.

Collecting Data

1. Work with your group to make a list of things children often do after school. Try to include activities from many different groups of students at your school. Then choose three to five things that you think are the most common.

2. Use the activities you chose on a questionnaire and ask students to check their favorite. You may also want to ask them to tell other things they like to do and how long they spend doing their favorite activity.

Sample Questionnaire

Favorite After-School Activities

Check any of the activities that you sometimes like to do after school. *Circle* your favorite activity. Tell how long you usually spend doing your favorite activity.

__ **1.** Watch TV __ **2.** Listen to music

__ **3.** Play with a friend __ **4.** Play a sport

__ **5.** Other ______ Time: __ minutes

3. Give your questionnaire to one or two people. Ask if they understand what the questionnaire asks them to do. Change it if you need to.

4. Make enough copies of your questionnaire so that you can give one to each person in your class.

Organizing Data

5. For each activity, count the number of students who marked it as their favorite.

6. Have group members show different ways to display the data. Think about pictures, charts, and graphs. Discuss the advantages of each and decide which ones you want to use when you present the data to your class. Complete this bar graph as a sample.

Presenting Your Analysis

Share your analysis of the data from the questionnaires by discussing the answers to these questions with your classmates.

7. Which after-school activity was chosen most often as the favorite?

8. What is the next most favorite after-school activity?

9. About how much time do students generally spend on their favorite activity?

10. How did your prediction of the favorite activities compare with the results of the questionnaire?

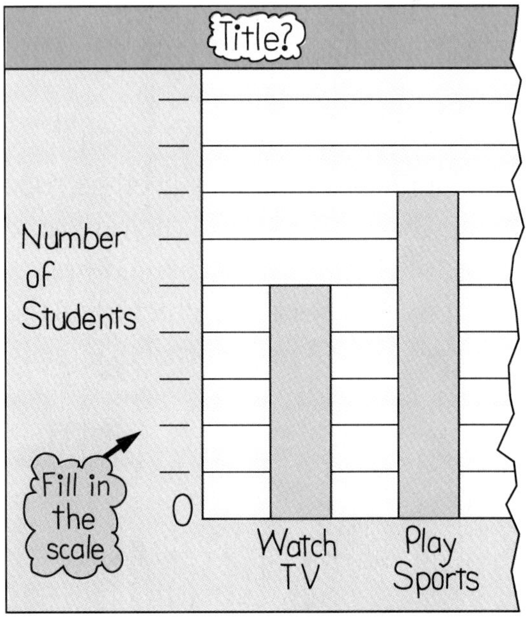

WRAP UP

Name That Number

Use this division example: $5\overline{)38}$ with quotient 7 R3

1. Which number is the divisor?
2. Which number is the dividend?
3. Which number is the quotient?
4. Which number is the remainder?

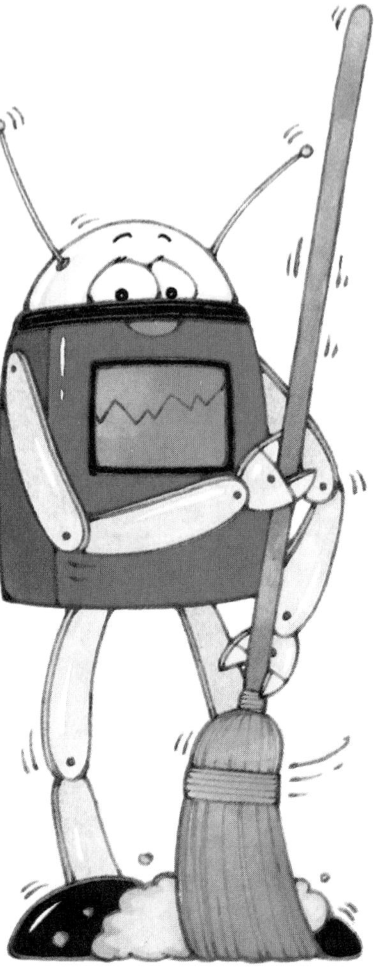

Sometimes, Always, Never

Which word should go in the blank, sometimes, always, or never? Explain your choices.

5. If a whole number ends in 0, you can __?__ divide it by 2 and get no remainder.
6. You __?__ check a division problem by multiplying the dividend by the divisor.
7. If the remainder is greater than the divisor, it is __?__ true that the quotient is too small.
8. The average of 4 numbers __?__ equals one of the four numbers.

Project

How tall is Robo-Land's average robot? Use the information given about each robot to find the average height of all 4 robots. Then compare each robot's height to the average. Which models are taller than average? Which are shorter than average? Is any robot exactly average?

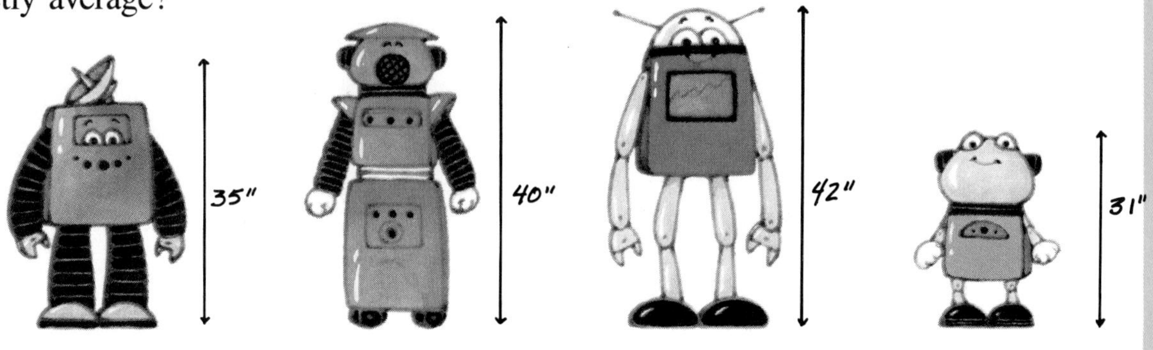

POWER PRACTICE/TEST

Part 1 Understanding

1. Explain how to find the quotient and remainder for 38 ÷ 5. Tell how to check the answer.

2. Since 36 ÷ 4 = ▥, then 360 ÷ 4 = ▥.

3. Tell why substituting a number can make estimation easier. Use 413 ÷ 6 as an example.

Estimate each quotient. Tell whether your estimate is over or under the exact quotient.

4. 217 ÷ 5

5. $7.75 ÷ 8

Part 2 Skills

Decide where to start dividing. Do not solve. Just write hundreds or tens.

6. $4\overline{)131}$

7. $6\overline{)849}$

8. $3\overline{)305}$

Divide and check.

9. 63 ÷ 5

10. $4\overline{)948}$

11. $8\overline{)825}$

12. $6\overline{)\$3.24}$

13. 80 ÷ 7

14. 552 ÷ 3

15. $9\overline{)987}$

16. $8\overline{)\$0.88}$

17. Divide 85 by 6

18. What is 670 divided by 4?

Use mental math to find the quotients.

19. $2\overline{)416}$

20. $7\overline{)\$7.49}$

21. $3\overline{)124}$

22. 160 ÷ 4

Part 3 Applications

23. A model truck is 4 times longer than its height. If it is 35 in. high, find its length. Tell the calculation method you used.

24. 114 cars used a parking garage near the auto show. They were parked in full rows of 8. How many cars were in the last row?

25. **Challenge** A bus driver drove 185 miles each day Monday through Thursday and 220 miles on Friday. What was her daily average?

ENRICHMENT
Discovering Prime Numbers

Here are the factor pair tables for the numbers up to 10. What patterns do you see?

Factors of 1
1 × 1

Factors of 2
1 × 2

Factors of 3
1 × 3

Factors of 4
1 × 4
2 × 2

Factors of 5
1 × 5

Factors of 6
1 × 6
2 × 3

Factors of 7
1 × 7

Factors of 8
1 × 8
2 × 4

Factors of 9
1 × 9
3 × 3

Factors of 10
1 × 10
2 × 5

1. Which number has just one factor?

2. Which numbers have three factors?

3. Study the factor tables above to discover how the numbers called **prime numbers** in the pattern below were chosen. Give the next 5 numbers in the pattern and their factor pair tables.
2, 3, 5, 7, ___, ___, ___, ___, ___.

4. Copy and complete this definition of prime numbers. A **prime number** is a number with exactly |||| factors.

5. Study the factor pair tables above to discover how the numbers called **composite numbers** in the pattern below were chosen. Give the next 5 numbers in the pattern and their factor pair tables.
4, 6, 8, 9, ___, ___, ___, ___, ___.

6. Copy and complete this definition of composite numbers. A **composite number** is a number, other than 1, that is not a |||| number.

7. Give all the prime numbers between 20 and 30.

8. Give all the composite numbers between 20 and 30.

CUMULATIVE REVIEW

1. Estimate the product of 83 and 683.

   A 48,000 B 5,600
   C 56,000 D 54,000

2. Find the product of $7.08 and 29.

   A $205.32 B $211.92
   C $203.32 D $204.32

3. A reasonable time to have a midmorning snack is ||||.

   A 6:15 p.m. B 6:15 a.m.
   C 10:45 p.m. D 10:45 a.m.

4. A nonstandard unit you might use to measure the length of a pen is a ||||.

   A span B thumb
   C step D cubit

5. Which distance is greater than a mile?

   A 5,280 ft B 2,000 yd
   C 1,760 yd D 60,000 in.

6. △ × ○ = □
   Which division equation is in the same fact family?

   A △ ÷ ○ = □
   B △ ÷ □ = ○
   C □ ÷ △ = ○

7. Which amount of rice weighs less than 3 pounds?

   A 45 oz B 48 oz
   C 60 oz D 72 oz

8. What is the quotient of 21 divided by 7?

   A 28 B 14
   C 3 D 147

9. 48 ÷ 6

   A 8 B 9
   C 7 D 10

10. $4\overline{)28}$

    A 4 B 9
    C 6 D 7

11. Vito rents a car for 10 days at a total cost of $248.80. About how much does the car cost per day?

    A $2.48 B $20
    C $48 D $25

12. After shopping, Ella had $4. She got a $7 belt, 3 books at $3 each, and a $14 skirt. How much did she start with?

    A $28 B $34
    C $31 D $30

11

GEOMETRY

THEME: MASKS

MATH AND FINE ARTS

DATA BANK

Use the Fine Arts Data Bank on page 480 to answer the questions.

1 What feature on the pattern for a sun mask is represented by a square shape?

2 How many triangles can you find on the sun mask pattern?

3 What feature on the pattern for a sun mask is represented by a rectangle shape?

4 **Use Critical Thinking** What two shapes on the pattern for a sun mask could you put together to make a rectangle?

These splendid masks from Africa show careful carving and interesting shapes in their design.

Space Figures and Plane Figures

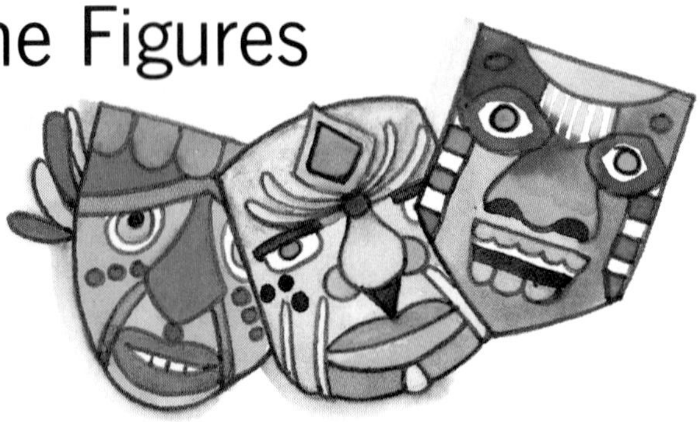

LEARN ABOUT IT

Many objects you see every day are shaped like these space figures.

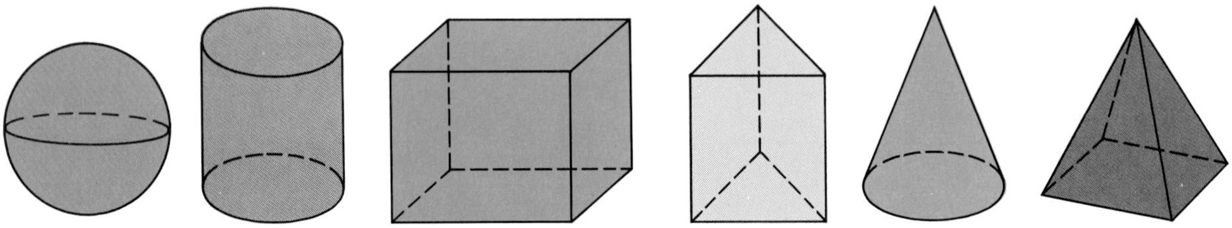

Sphere **Cylinder** **Rectangular Prism** **Triangular Prism** **Cone** **Pyramid**

EXPLORE Use Space Figure Models

Work in groups. Find the space figure for each riddle.

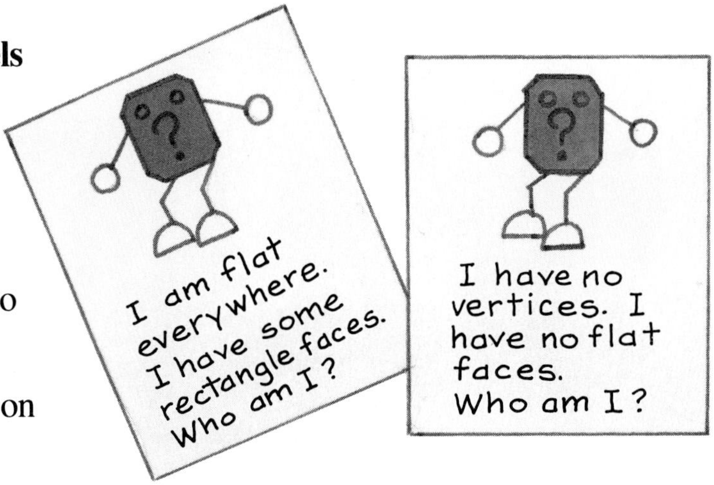

I am flat everywhere. I have some rectangle faces. Who am I?
I have no vertices. I have no flat faces. Who am I?

TALK ABOUT IT

1. Make up a riddle and give it to another group to solve.
2. Name the shapes of the faces on each space figure above.

The flat faces of a **space figure** are called **plane figures**. If all sides of a plane figure are straight and connected, it is a **polygon**.

A cube is a space figure with square faces. Each face is a plane figure and a polygon.

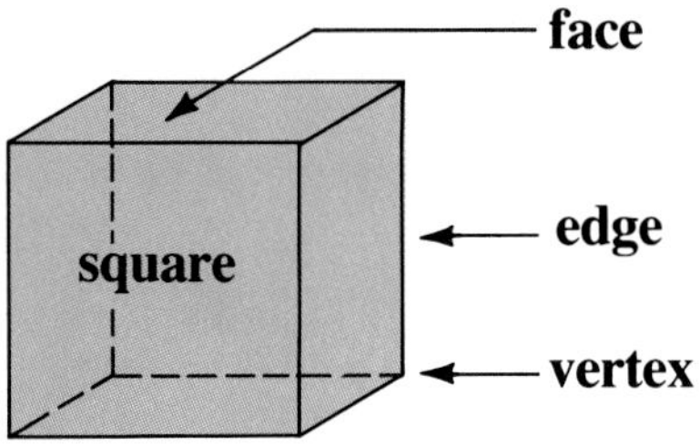

cube

TRY IT OUT

1. How many faces, edges, and vertices does a rectangular prism have? a triangular prism? a pyramid with a square base?

PRACTICE

Name the space figure for each riddle.

1. I have only two flat faces. I can roll.
2. I have just one flat face. I roll, but not straight.
3. I am flat all over. My faces are squares.
4. My faces are triangles. On top I have a point.
5. I have no flat faces, no corners and no edges.
6. My faces are two triangles and three rectangles.

APPLY

MATH REASONING Think about the object. What space figure is it like?

7. It holds ice cream.
8. It is a tomb in Egypt.
9. You bounce it or throw it.
10. It can hold crayons or cereal.

PROBLEM SOLVING

11. With her eyes closed Maria guessed what she held in her hands. It felt like a cylinder with one end open. It had a handle on the side. What was it?
12. Tomas used geometric shapes to decorate the mask he had made. He painted 17 triangles across the top and put 2 circles under each. Then he used circles for eyes, a rectangle for a nose, and another circle for a mouth. How many plane figures did he use?

USING CRITICAL THINKING Take a Look

Pretend you cut some clay space figure models down the middle. Each cut made two new identical faces. Imagine what each face looked like and draw a picture of it.

13. 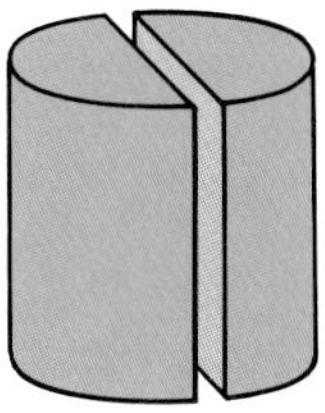

14. 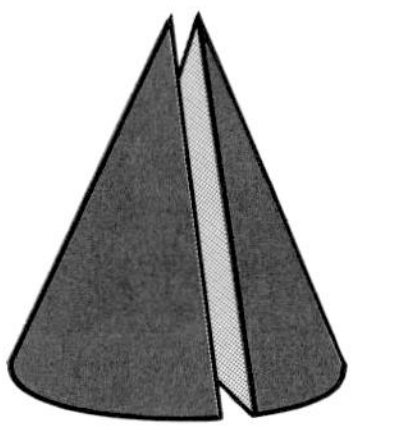

15. 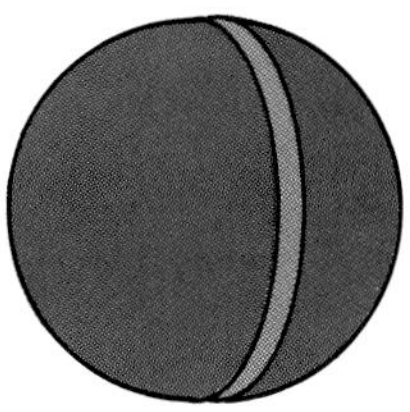

More Practice, page 521, set D

Polygons and Angles

LEARN ABOUT IT

Right Angle Protractor

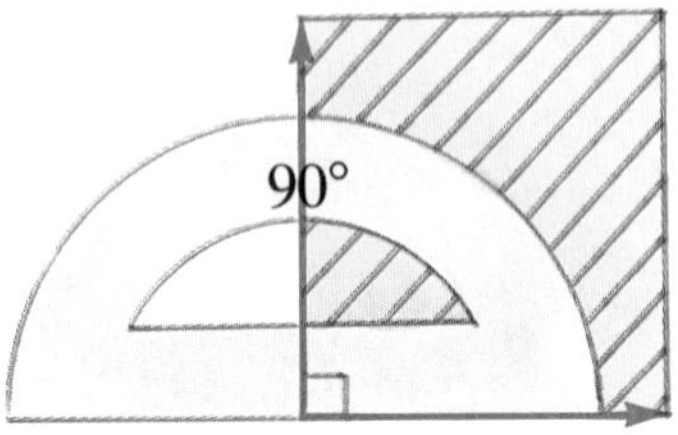

EXPLORE Use Real World Objects

Many objects around you suggest **angles.** In these pictures the red lines form angles. An angle has two **sides** that meet at the **vertex.** The corner of a square is a **right angle.** It measures 90°.

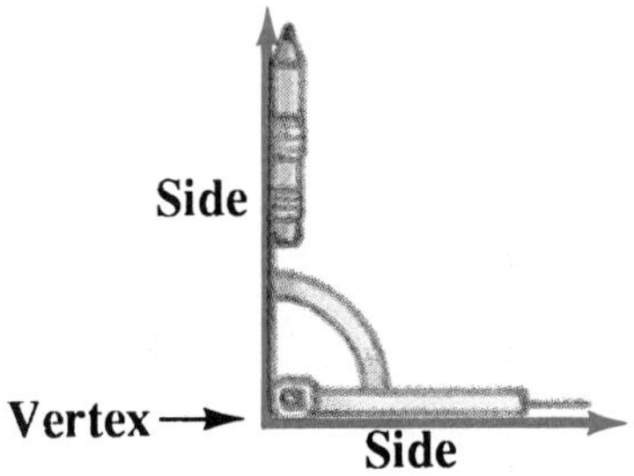

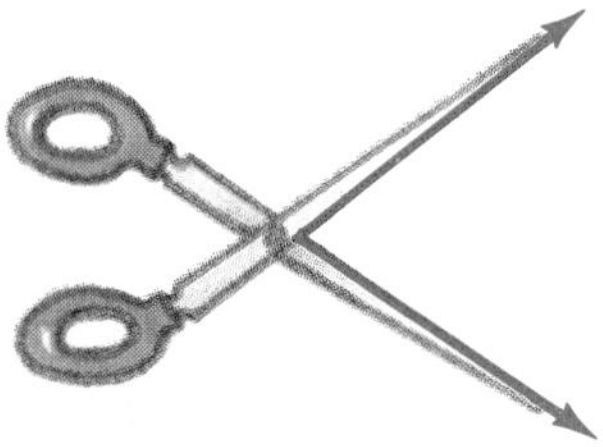

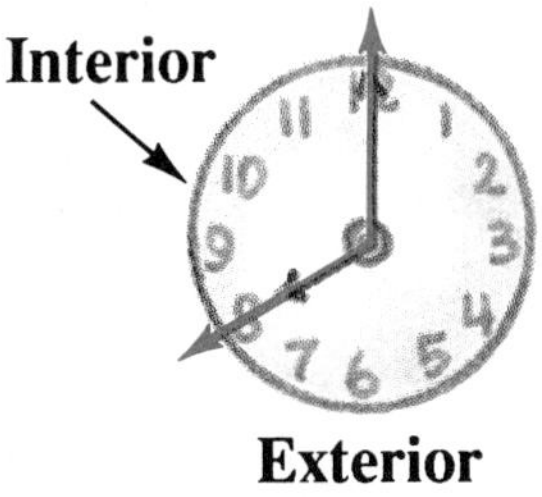

TALK ABOUT IT

1. Find angles in 5 other objects in your classroom.
2. How could you decide which of two angles is greater? Explain.

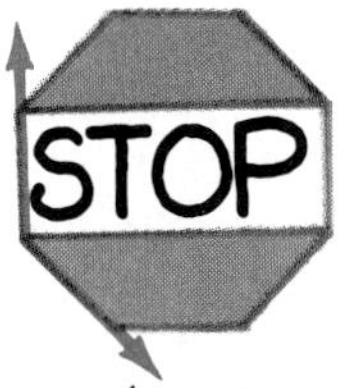

octagon
8 sides

An angle in each polygon is shown in red.

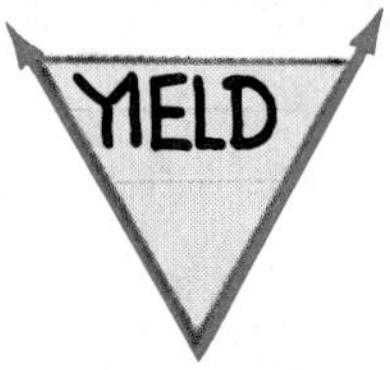

triangle
3 sides

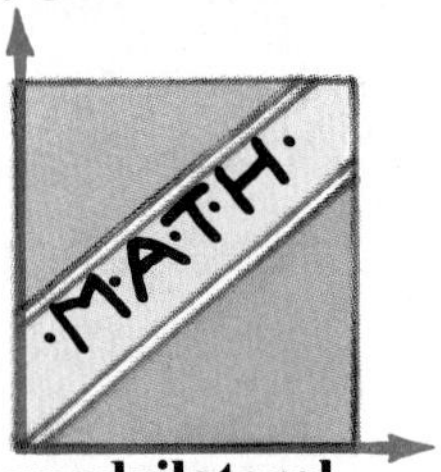

quadrilateral
4 sides

pentagon
5 sides

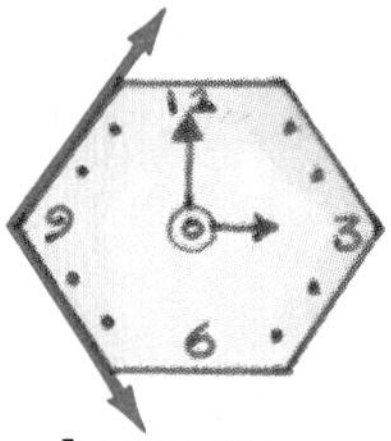

hexagon
6 sides

TRY IT OUT

1. Make a right angle model with folded paper. Use your model to draw a triangle with one angle less and the other angle greater than 90°.
2. Use your model to draw a polygon with all angles greater than 90°.

PRACTICE

Use your right angle model to decide if the red angle is less than 90°, more than 90°, or equal to 90°.

1. 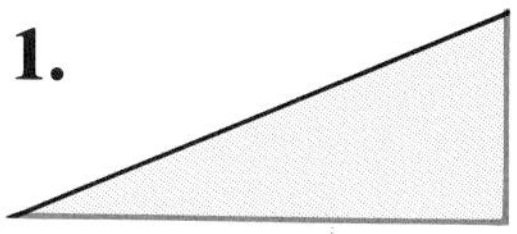

2. 

3. 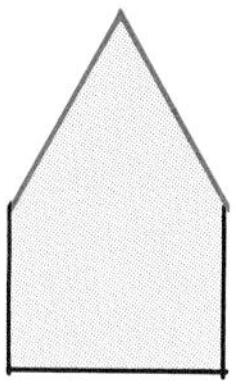

4. 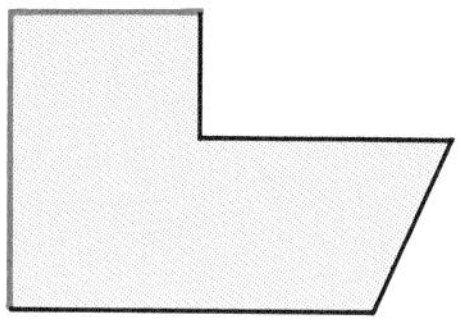

5. 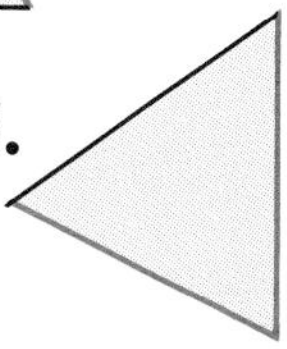

6. Name each polygon in exercises 1–5 and tell how many sides it has.

7. Tell how many right angles each polygon has in exercises 1–5.

APPLY

MATH REASONING

8. Draw a polygon that looks like this.

4 sides	1 angle more than a right angle
2 right angles	1 angle less than a right angle

PROBLEM SOLVING

9. Cathy made a square pen for her baby ducks. She used 24 feet of fence. How long was each side of the pen?

10. Tim took 120 steps to walk around a rectangular field. He took 20 steps to walk along the width of the field. How long is the field?

MIXED REVIEW

Divide.

11. $2\overline{)13}$ **12.** $6\overline{)45}$ **13.** $5\overline{)150}$ **14.** $8\overline{)\$8.00}$ **15.** $9\overline{)75}$

16. $6\overline{)360}$ **17.** $2\overline{)\$4.20}$ **18.** $8\overline{)240}$ **19.** $5\overline{)\$3.00}$ **20.** $4\overline{)\$8.64}$

More Practice, page 521, set E

Analyzing Polygons
Parallel and Perpendicular Lines

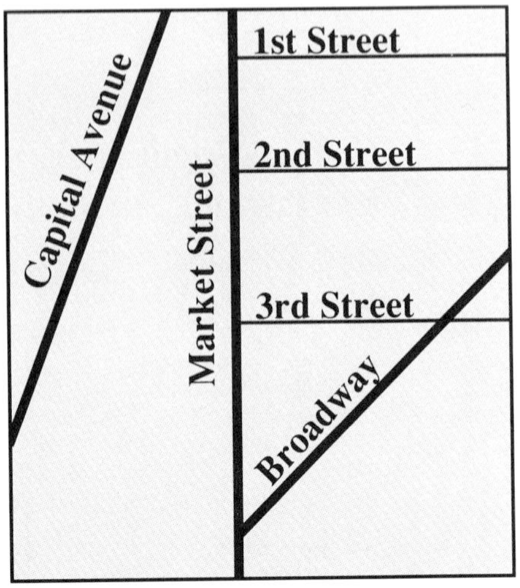

LEARN ABOUT IT

EXPLORE Use Tracing Paper

Use tracing paper to copy an example of each of the following from the map. Use street names to label your tracing.

1. A point on a corner of a triangle
2. A pair of lines that do not meet
3. A pair of lines that make a right angle
4. A pair of lines that meet and do not make a right angle

Intersecting lines meet in a point. **Parallel** lines lie on a flat surface and do not meet. **Perpendicular** lines meet to form a right angle.

Examples

intersection ⟶ **perpendicular lines**

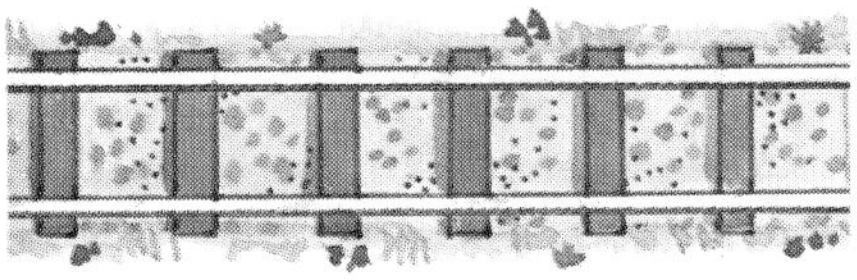

railroad tracks ⟶ **parallel lines**

TALK ABOUT IT

1. How would you use the words parallel and perpendicular to tell about the sides of a square?
2. Can a triangle have a pair of parallel sides? Explain.
3. Can a triangle have two pairs of perpendicular sides? Explain.

TRY IT OUT

1. Find some other objects around you that suggest parallel, perpendicular, or intersecting lines.
2. Fold paper to make models of intersecting, parallel, and perpendicular lines.

PRACTICE

Do you think the lines in these circles are parallel, perpendicular, or intersecting but not perpendicular?

1. 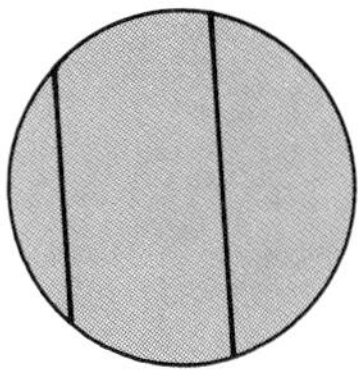

2. 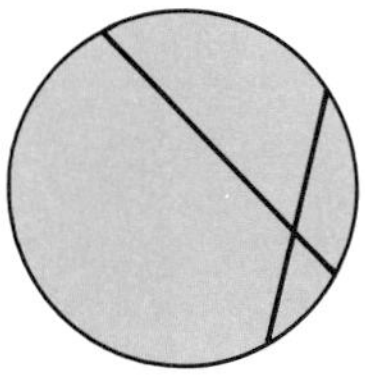

3. 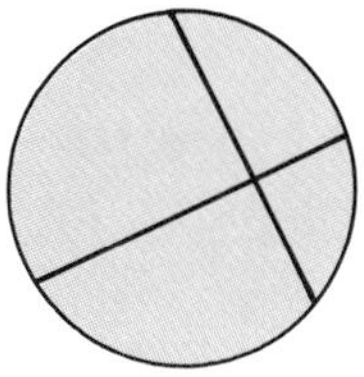

4. Make a pattern of squares like this. Then color pairs of lines that you think will be parallel, intersecting, or perpendicular when the pattern is folded to make a cube. Fold and tape to make the cube, then check your colored lines.

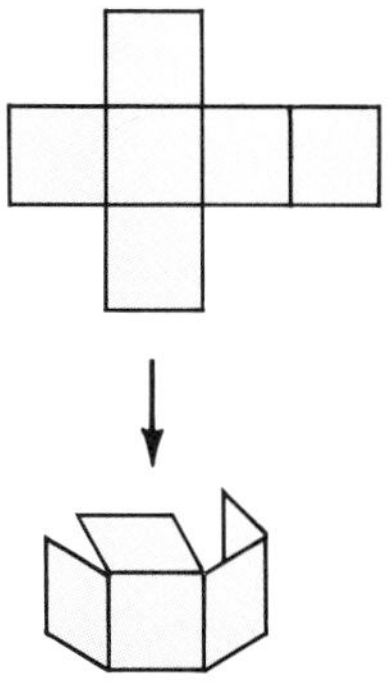

APPLY

MATH REASONING

5. At what times each day are the hands of a clock perpendicular with the minute hand pointing to 12?

6. At about what time would the clock hands be perpendicular when the hour hand is between 2 and 3?

PROBLEM SOLVING

7. Doli rode her bicycle up First Street to where it intersected Hill Street. Her plan was to make a perpendicular right turn and go one block, repeating this until she got back to First Street. If the blocks are rectangular, how many turns would she have to make?

8. Carl thought he would try and make a triangle with 2 parallel lines and 1 less than 90° angle. Is this possible? Explain.

COMMUNICATION Write to Learn

Copy and complete each sentence.

9. If bookshelves were not parallel to the floor, __?__.

10. If playground slides were perpendicular to the ground, __?__.

More Practice, page 522, set A

Symmetric Figures

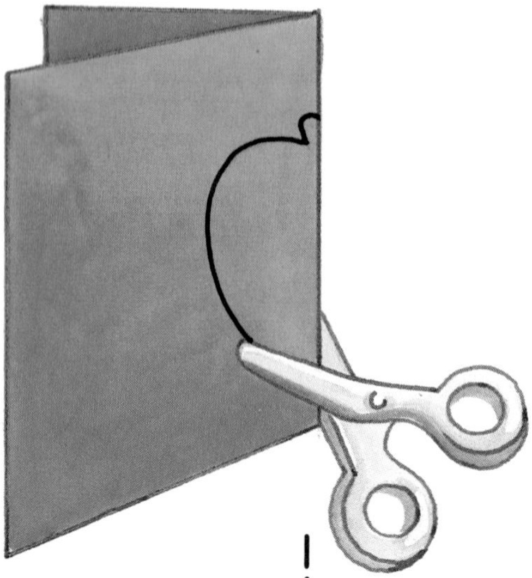

LEARN ABOUT IT

EXPLORE **Fold and Cut Paper**

You can fold a piece of paper and cut out a figure that has **symmetry**.

When folded along its **line of symmetry**, the two parts of the figure fit exactly upon each other.

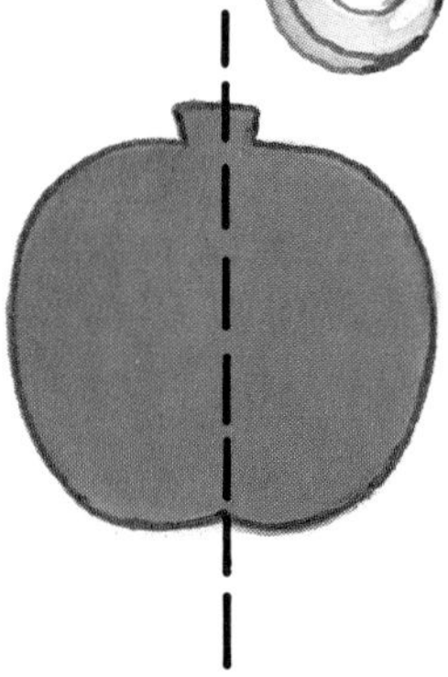

TALK ABOUT IT

1. How would you describe the line of symmetry of a figure?
2. Could a figure have more than one line of symmetry? Give an example.

■ What symmetric figure would you make with cuts like these? First predict and draw the figure. Then test your prediction.

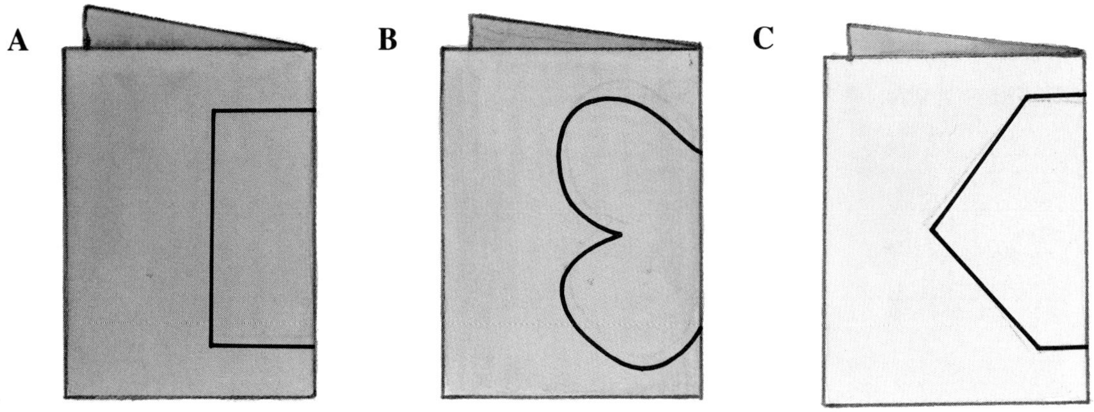

TRY IT OUT

Fold pieces of paper and cut out pieces that will make these symmetric figures when unfolded.

1. rectangle **2.** tall thin pumpkin **3.** triangle **4.** ball

PRACTICE

Draw what you think these figures will look like when cut and unfolded. Check by folding and cutting.

1. 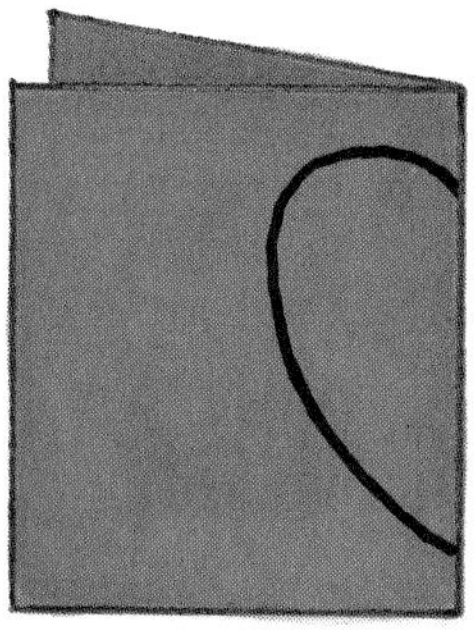

2. 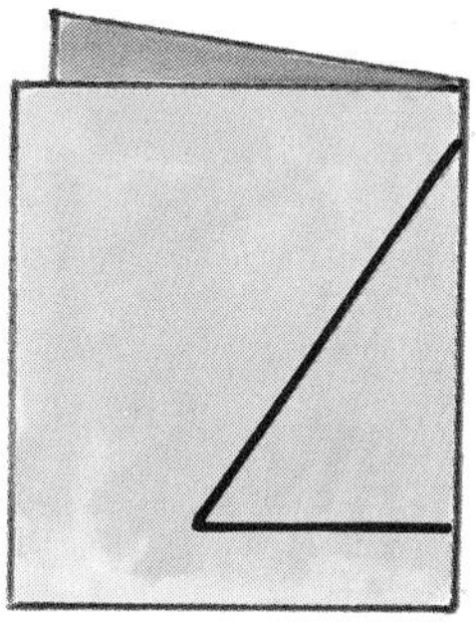

3. 

4. 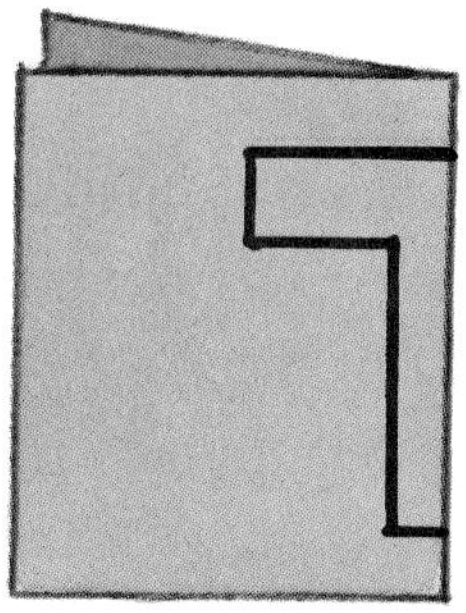

APPLY

MATH REASONING Does the dashed line appear to be a line of symmetry? Find a way to check to be sure.

5. 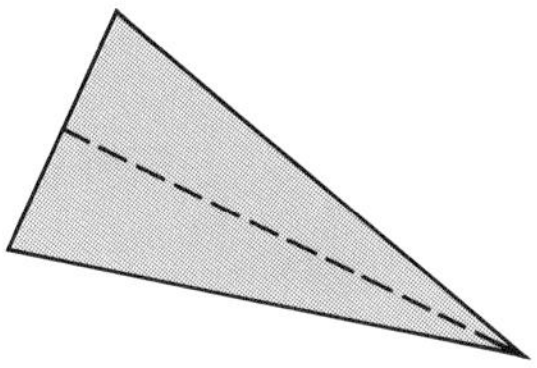

6. 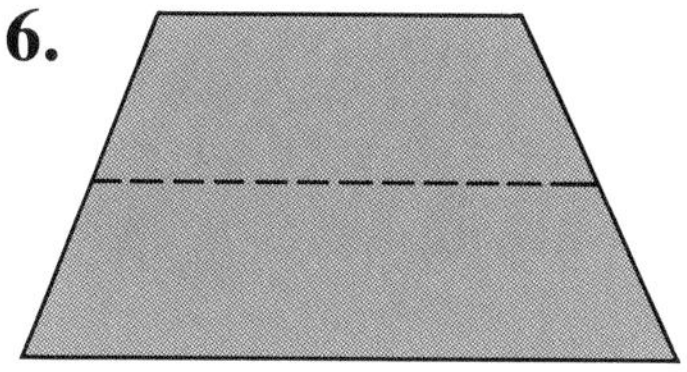

7. 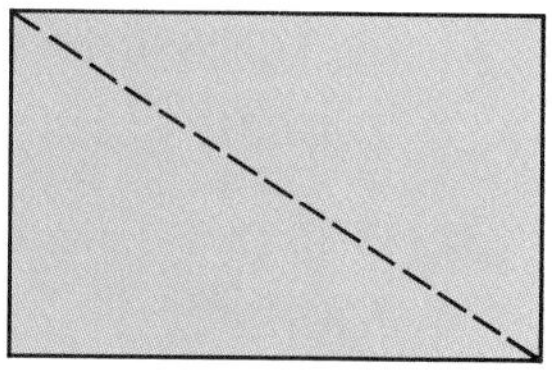

PROBLEM SOLVING

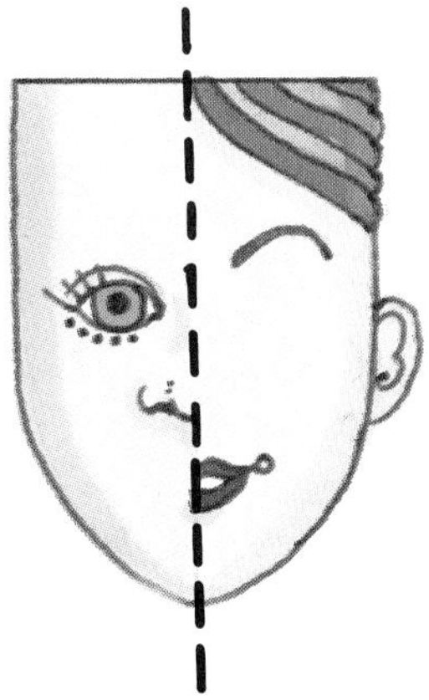

8. Tonya wanted the mask she was making to be symmetrical. It is pictured here, with some parts missing. Can you draw the mask and show the missing parts?
9. Nicolo wanted to draw a line of symmetry on the red cross sign on his first aid kit. Can you show 2 different ways he could do this? Draw pictures to show your answer.

COMMUNICATION Find Some Words

10. The word HIDE is a "symmetric word." How many other symmetric words can you find?

    Hint: Which capital letters in the alphabet are symmetric?

Classifying Angles and Triangles

LEARN ABOUT IT

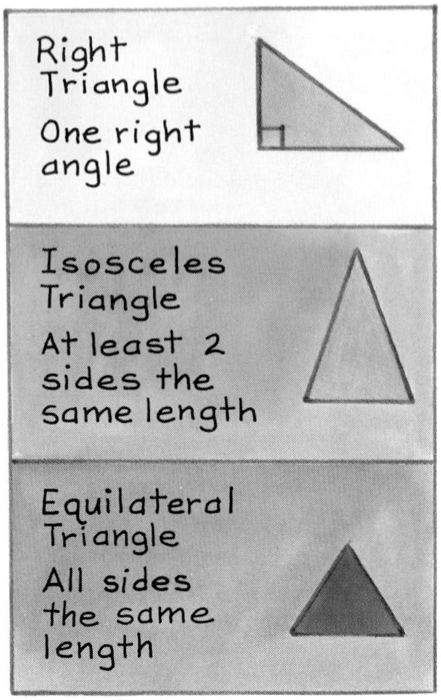

EXPLORE **Discover a Relationship**

Jimmy made these triangle cards to show three types of triangles. Trace and cut out two copies of the right triangle. Can you put the copies together to form an equilateral triangle? an isosceles triangle that is not equilateral? a figure that is not a triangle?

TALK ABOUT IT

1. Which of the triangles Jimmy made have an angle that measures less than 90°? more than 90°?
2. Is it possible to draw a right triangle that is also isosceles? Explain.
3. Is it possible to draw a right triangle that is also equilateral? Explain.

The angles in these triangles all have names.

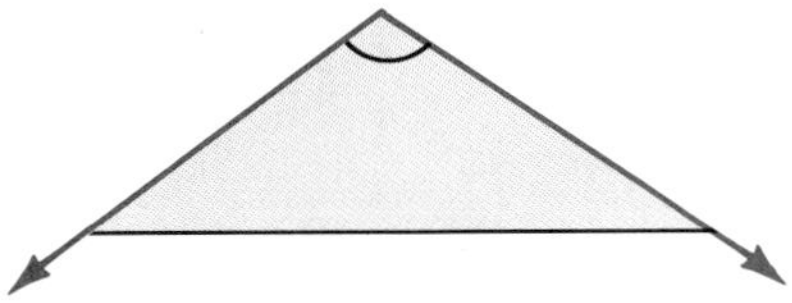

Obtuse Angle
Greater than 90°

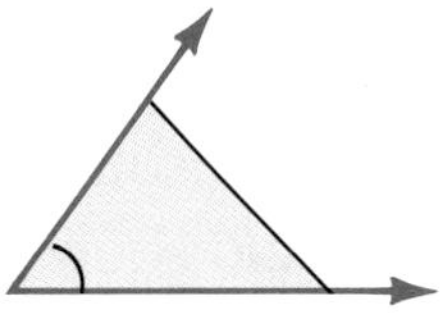

Acute Angle
Less than 90°

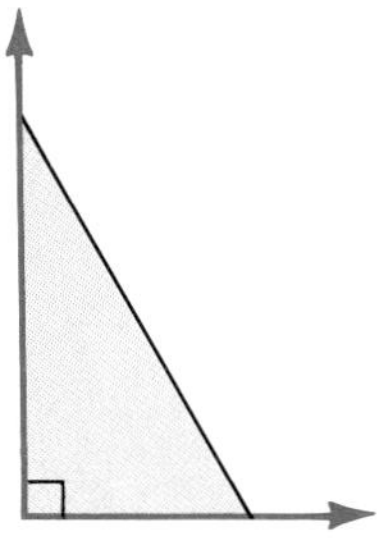

Right Angle
90°

TRY IT OUT

What kind of triangles are these? What kind of angle is the red angle?

1.

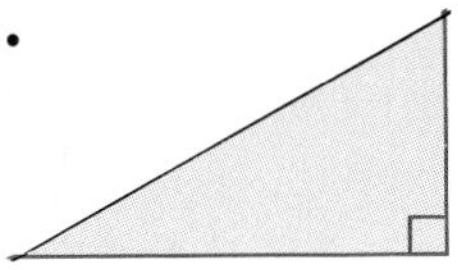

2.

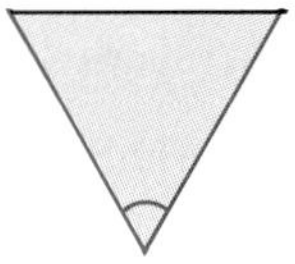

3.

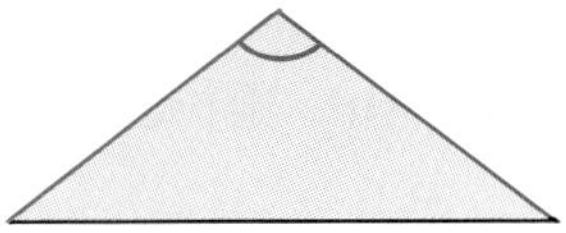

PRACTICE

Read the sentences. Tell which triangle each describes and give its name.

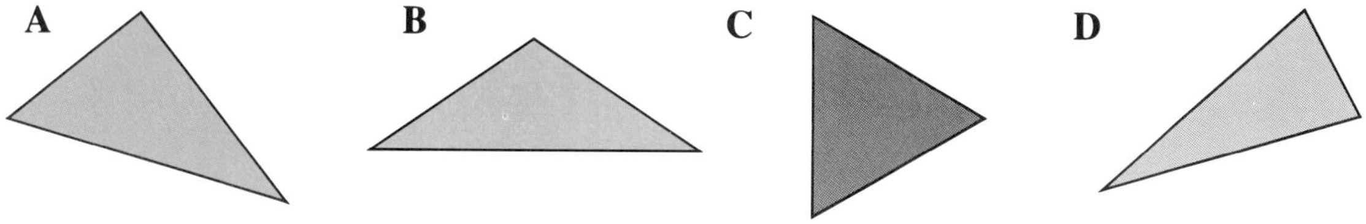

1. It has an obtuse angle and 2 sides the same length.
2. It has 3 acute angles and 3 sides the same length.
3. It has 3 acute angles and two sides the same length.
4. It has a right angle and all sides different lengths.

APPLY

MATH REASONING

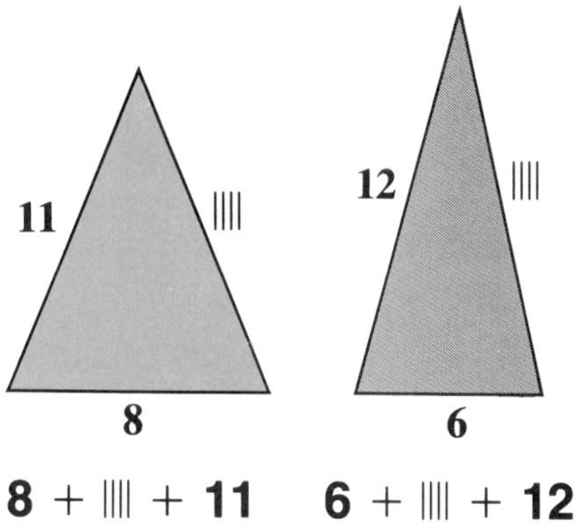

5. Two isosceles triangles have the same perimeter. Find the missing numbers. What is the perimeter of each triangle?

   8 + |||| + 11 = 12 + |||| + 6

PROBLEM SOLVING

6. Linnea had 22 ft of fencing to make a pen for her rabbits. She wanted the pen to be in the shape of a triangle and to have equal sides. She needed an extra foot to fasten the gate. How long should she make each side?

ESTIMATION

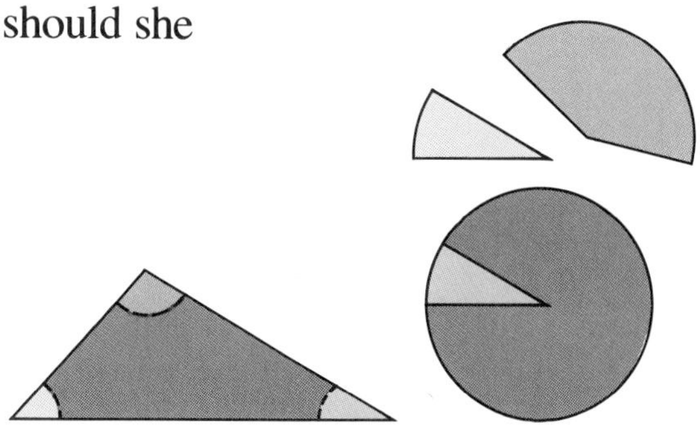

7. If you cut off the corners of a triangle will they fill half a circle? more than half a circle? less than half a circle? Cut out a triangle and check your estimate.

More Practice, page 522, set B

Classifying Quadrilaterals

LEARN ABOUT IT

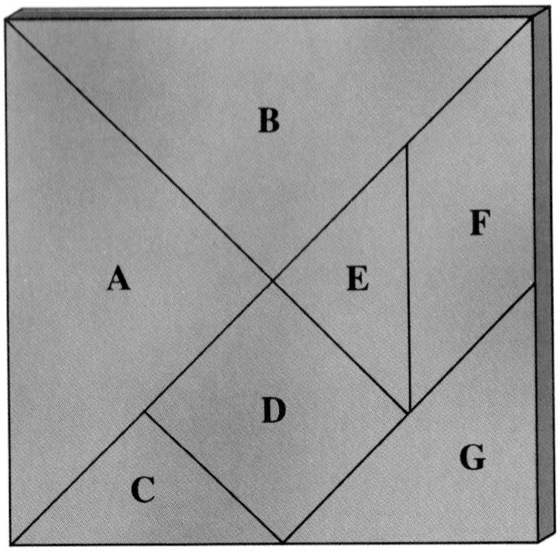

Tangram Puzzle

EXPLORE Use a Tangram Puzzle

- How many quadrilaterals of different shapes can you make using any combination of pieces A and B? Draw each one.
- How many different quadrilaterals can you make with pieces C, D, and E? Draw each one.

TALK ABOUT IT

1. Which of your quadrilaterals have at least one right angle?
2. Which have one pair of parallel sides?
3. Which have two pairs of sides that are the same length?
4. Which have all sides the same length?

Here are some types of quadrilaterals.

Square

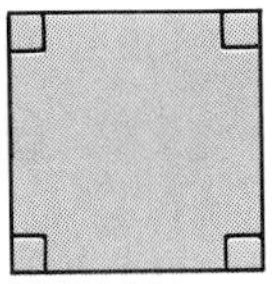

All sides the same length
All angles right angles

Rectangle

Two pairs of same-length sides
All angles right angles

Trapezoid

Exactly one pair of parallel sides

Parallelogram

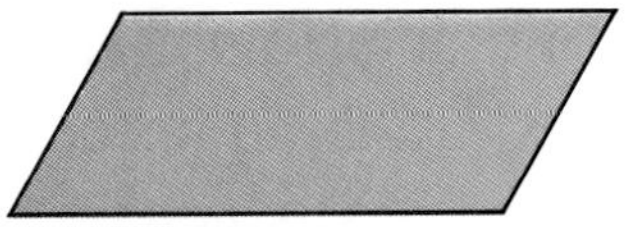

Two pairs of same-length sides
Two pairs of parallel sides

TRY IT OUT

1. Draw a picture of each type of quadrilateral turned to a different position than in the picture above. Write the names under your drawings.

PRACTICE

Draw and name the quadrilateral.

1. All of its sides are the same length. All of its angles are right angles.

2. It has two pairs of parallel sides. It has no right angles.

3. It has four right angles. Not all of its sides are the same length.

4. It has just one pair of parallel sides.

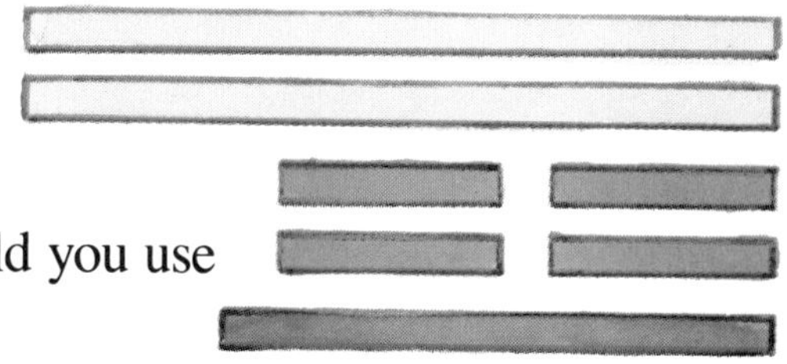

APPLY

MATH REASONING Which color of strips would you use to make the quadrilateral?

5. square **6.** rectangle **7.** trapezoid **8.** parallelogram

PROBLEM SOLVING

9. The Rivera's tool shed is shaped like a cube. Mrs. Rivera used half a can of paint to paint one inside wall. How many cans will she use to paint all the inside surfaces except the floor?

MIXED REVIEW

Check these quotients. Correct the answer if it is wrong.

10. $\begin{array}{r}8\\2\overline{)16}\end{array}$ **11.** $\begin{array}{r}8\text{ R}3\\4\overline{)35}\end{array}$ **12.** $\begin{array}{r}15\\5\overline{)75}\end{array}$ **13.** $\begin{array}{r}8\\3\overline{)25}\end{array}$ **14.** $\begin{array}{r}8\text{ R}8\\9\overline{)80}\end{array}$

Write the unit of measure you would use to find each amount.

15. the weight of one mushroom
ounces or pounds

16. the amount in a large container of milk
pints or gallons

More Practice, page 522, set C

Congruent Figures

LEARN ABOUT IT

EXPLORE **Use Tracing Paper**

When you make a mask you may need to make two figures exactly alike. Figures that have the same size and shape are **congruent**.

- Draw a triangle. Then use tracing paper to draw another triangle that is the same size and shape.
- Do the same for a quadrilateral.

TALK ABOUT IT

1. How do you know that the two shapes you drew are congruent?
2. How can you check to see if two cut-out shapes are congruent?

Here are some ways you can move triangle A to see if it will fit exactly on another triangle. If it will, the triangles are congruent.

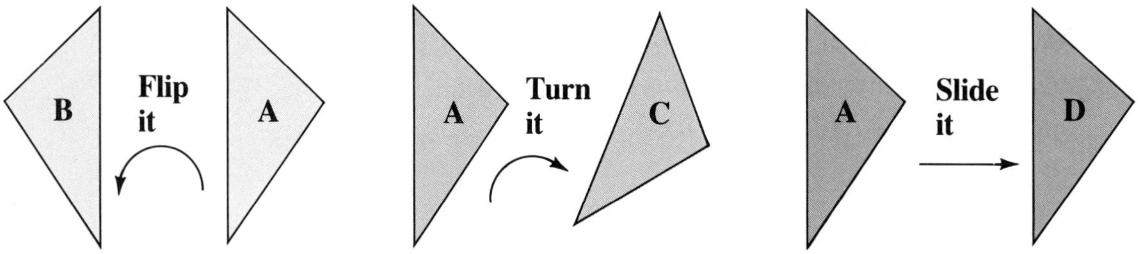

TRY IT OUT

Use tracing paper to decide which triangles are congruent to triangle A.

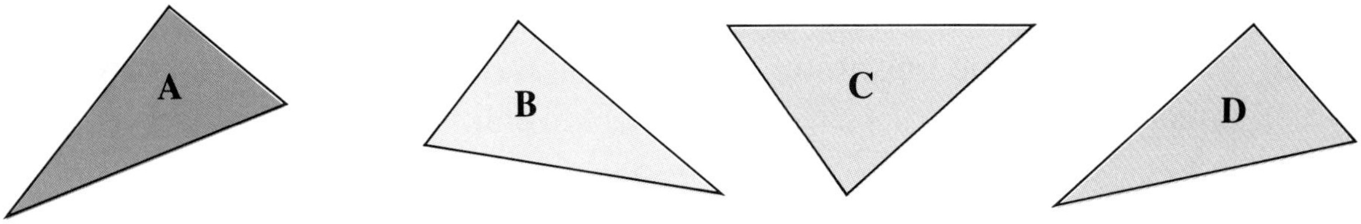

PRACTICE

Use tracing paper to decide which figures are congruent. You may need to slide, turn, or flip your tracing.

1.

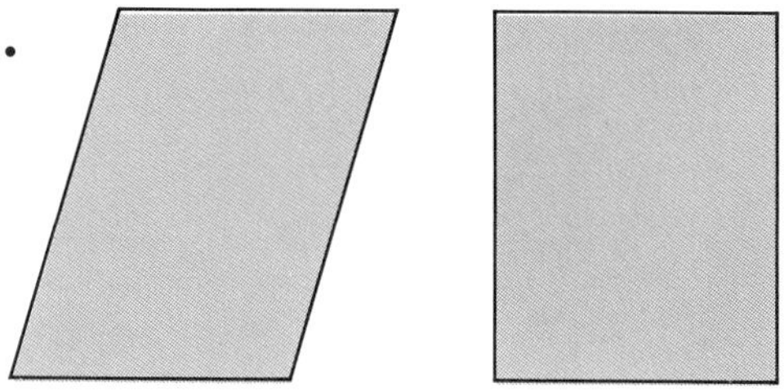

2.

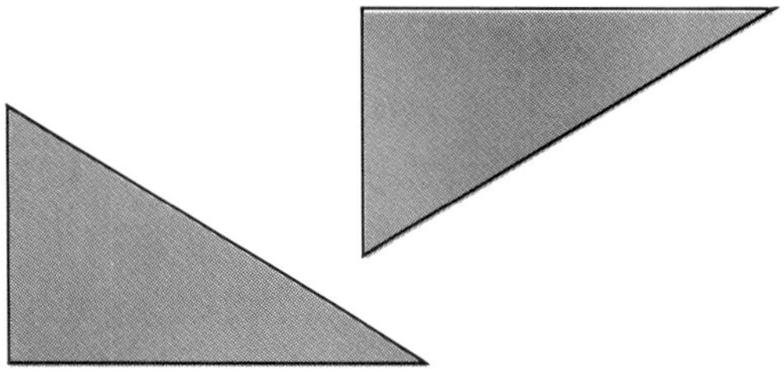

3. Draw 3 points. Then draw 3 segments to connect the points. What kind of polygon did you draw? Use tracing paper to make a congruent figure.

APPLY

MATH REASONING

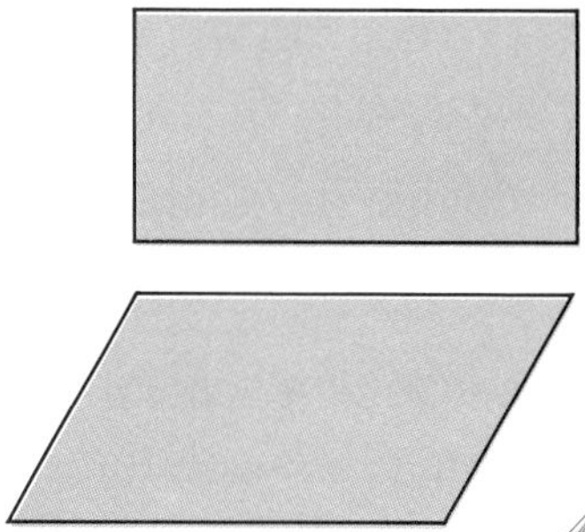

4. Name these two quadrilaterals. How are they alike? How are they different?

PROBLEM SOLVING

5. A new downtown office building has two identical wings. One wing is divided into 32 dental offices and 43 medical offices. How many offices are in the building?

6. **Fine Arts Data Bank** Name congruent polygons on the mask pattern in the Data Bank. See page 480.

DATA BANK

USING CRITICAL THINKING Comparing Polygons

7. Describe one of these figures to a partner. Have your partner try to draw a figure congruent to it, without looking at the book. Talk about the results.

A

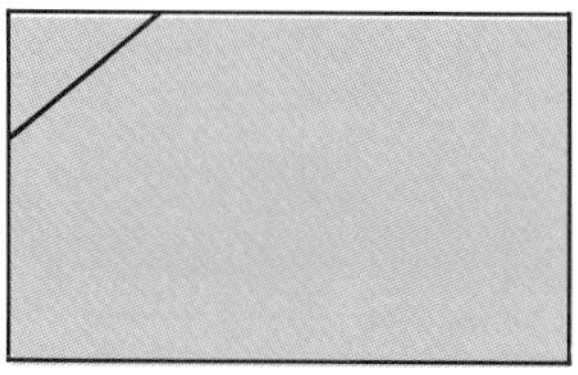

B

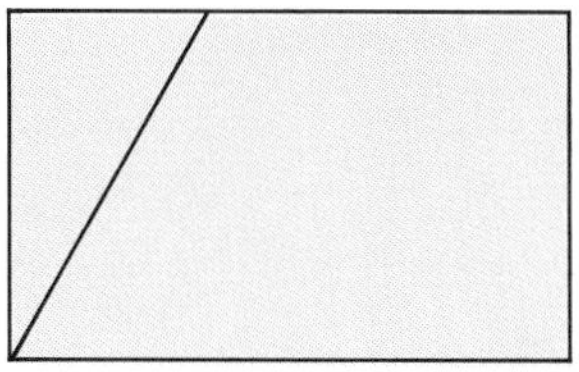

C

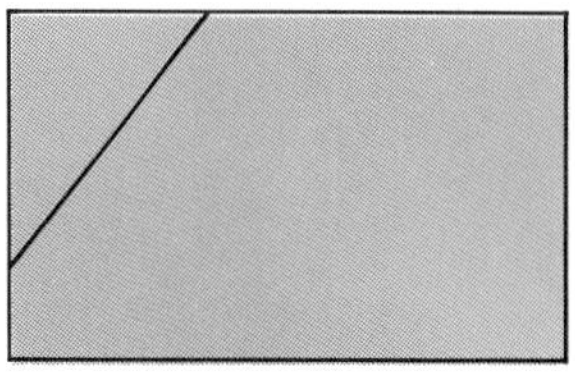

More Practice, page 522, set D

Curves and Circles

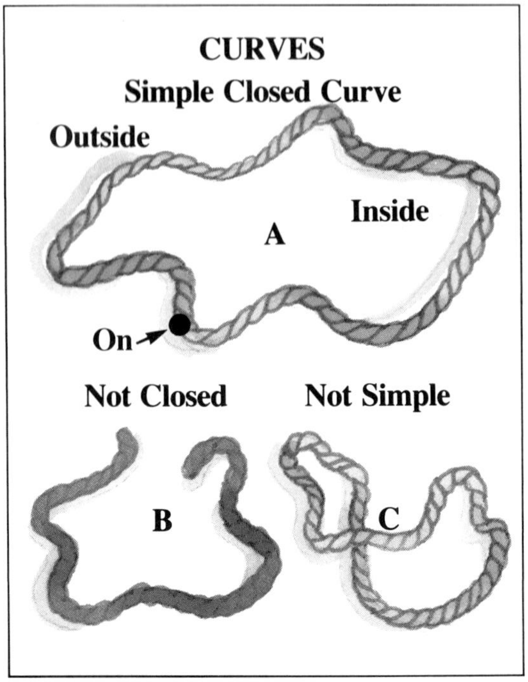

LEARN ABOUT IT

EXPLORE **Discover a Rule**

You have learned about geometric figures that have straight sides. Now you will learn about geometric figures that have **curves**.

Jenny glued yarn on a poster to show some things about curves.

TALK ABOUT IT

1. Why is curve B called "not closed"?
2. Which curve crosses itself?
3. You must cross a simple, closed curve to go from inside to outside. Is this true of curve B? Explain.

A **circle** is a special type of simple closed curve. The distance between the center of a circle and any point on the circle is always the same.

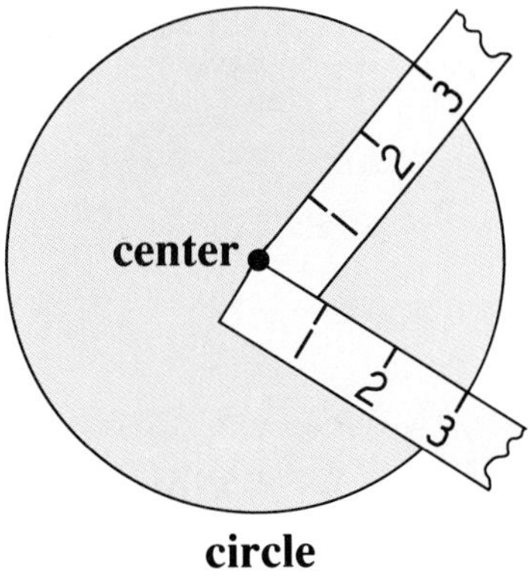

TRY IT OUT

Draw these. Where possible, mark and label points *inside*, *outside*, and *on* the curve.

1. a simple closed curve
2. a curve that is not closed
3. a curve that is not simple
4. Choose one of these methods to draw some different-sized circles.

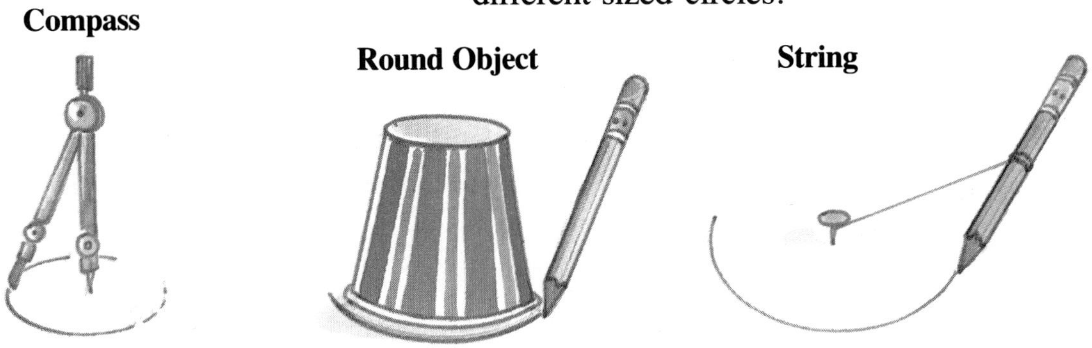

More Practice, page 523, set A

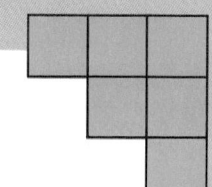

POWER PRACTICE/QUIZ

A **B** **C** **D** **E** **F**

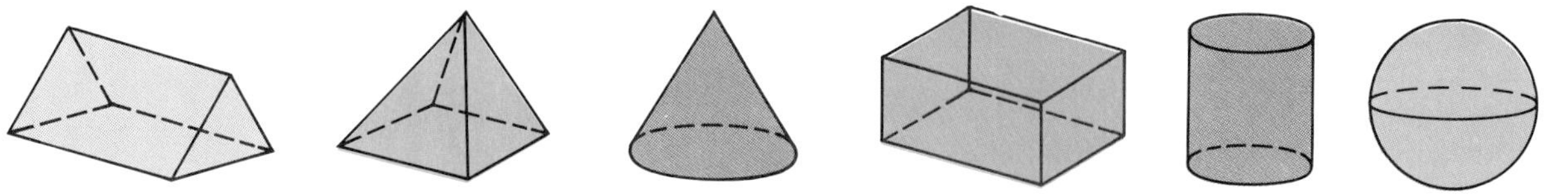

1. What is the name of each space figure?
2. Tell which of the figures' faces you could trace to make
   - a circle
   - a triangle
   - two different rectangles
   - a rectangle and a triangle
3. Which figures have curved edges? Which have straight edges?
4. Choose two figures. Tell how they are alike and different.

Use these polygons.

A **B** **C**

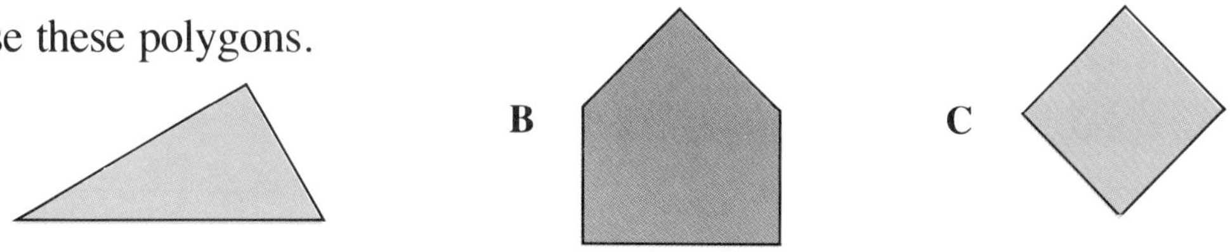

5. Name each polygon and tell how many sides it has.
6. Tell how many right angles each polygon has.
7. Which polygons have an angle that is less than 90°?

Draw the polygon that is described.

8. "I am a quadrilateral. Two of my sides are parallel. My other two sides are not parallel."
9. "I am a hexagon. Two of my sides are perpendicular and all have different lengths."

PROBLEM SOLVING

10. Ray tried to make a triangle with two perpendicular lines and one angle more than 90°. Is that possible? Tell how you know.

Liz has 5 sticks, one of each of these sizes: 2 in., 3 in., 3 in., 4 in., and 4 in.

11. How many different triangles can she make with a perimeter of 10 in. using just 3 sticks for the triangle?
12. Name the polygon, other than a triangle, Liz could make with a perimeter of 12 in. Which sticks would she use?

Coordinate Geometry

LEARN ABOUT IT

EXPLORE **Use Graph Paper**

You can use a pair of numbers to describe the location of a point. The numbers in the pair are called **coordinates**.

Here is how to graph the point for (3, 2).

1. Start at 0. Go **right** as many units as the first number. Go **up** as many units as the second number.
2. Mark the point.

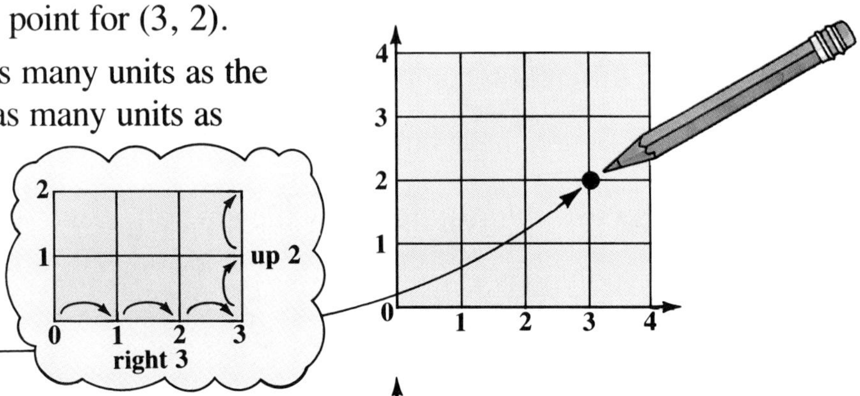

Choose some number pairs. Graph the points.

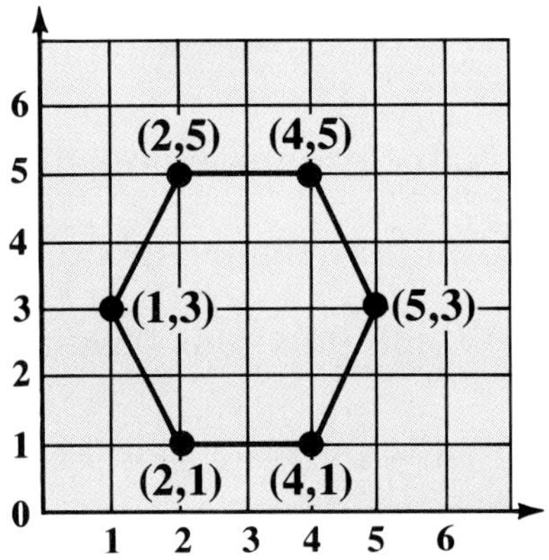

TALK ABOUT IT

1. Are (2, 1) and (1, 2) pairs for different points? Explain.
2. Tell how to find the number pair for a point on the grid.

You can graph a figure by graphing points and connecting them in order. The graph of these points is a hexagon.

(2, 5) → (1, 3) → (2, 1) → (4, 1) → (5, 3) → (4, 5) → (2, 5)

TRY IT OUT

Draw a pentagon shaped like a house by connecting points on graph paper. Give number pairs for the points and ask a classmate to draw the house.

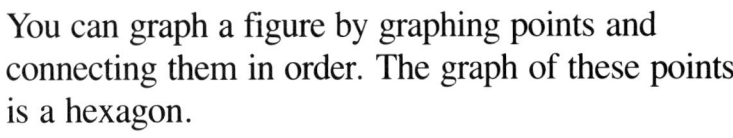

PRACTICE

Give the coordinates for the point that locates each object.

1. drum **2.** car

3. whistle **4.** key

Give the letter that is at the location given by these coordinates.

5. (1, 4) **6.** (3, 2)

7. 2, 1 **8.** (4, 4)

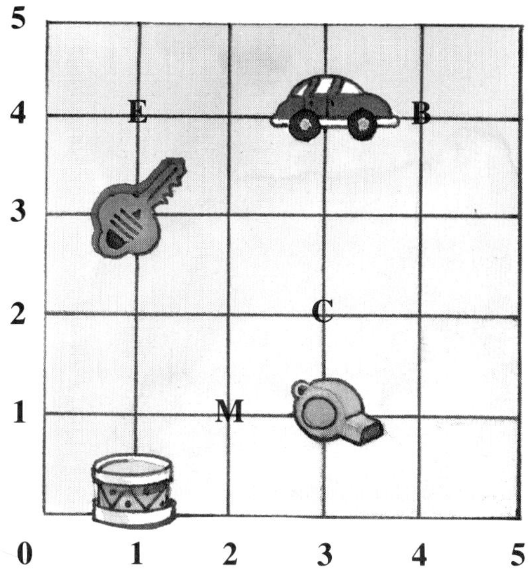

APPLY

MATH REASONING

9. Give the coordinates that could be graphed and connected to form these polygons.

a rectangle a square a triangle

PROBLEM SOLVING

10. An airport was at a location given on a map by the coordinates (0,0). A plane flying from the airport radioed back when it was at the location (1,2). It later radioed back at the locations (2,4), (3,6), and (4,8). Show all the plane's locations on a graph, find a pattern, and decide at what locations the plane will be when it radios back the next two times.

ALGEBRA

- Pick a number less than 10, say 4. Make it the first number of a pair.
- Subtract 1 from the first number. Make the answer the second number of the pair.

11. How many different number pairs can you make like this? List them.

12. Graph the pairs you found. What do you discover?

Similar Figures

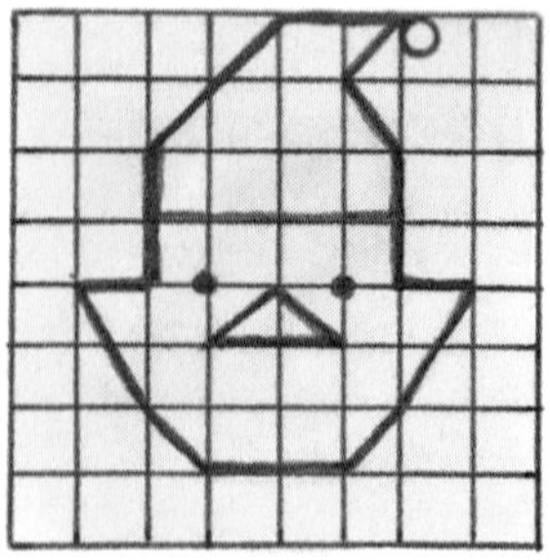

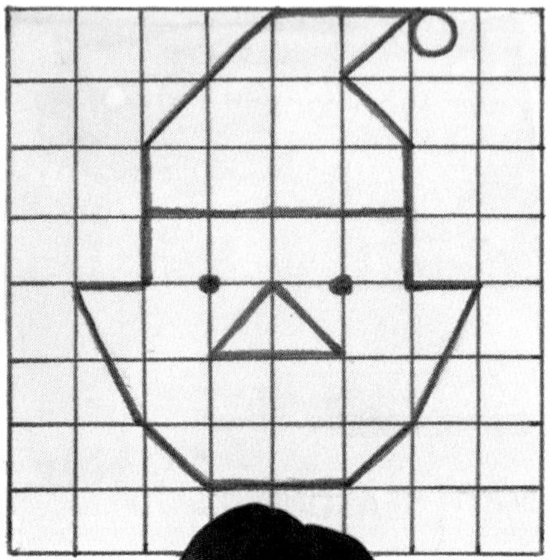

LEARN ABOUT IT

EXPLORE Use Graph Paper

You can use graphing to change the size of a figure. A mask pattern in a book was on a small grid. Chen wanted to make it larger, so he graphed the pattern on a larger grid.

Use graph paper with a different-sized grid to make a larger cat mask.

Cat Mask Pattern

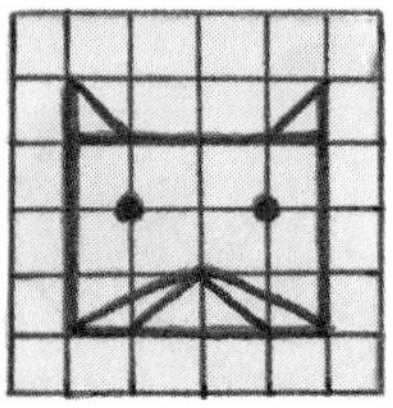

TALK ABOUT IT

1. What would you do to make the cat mask larger? to make it smaller?
2. Suppose you want a cat mask that is twice as large as the one in the picture. How would you choose the graph paper?

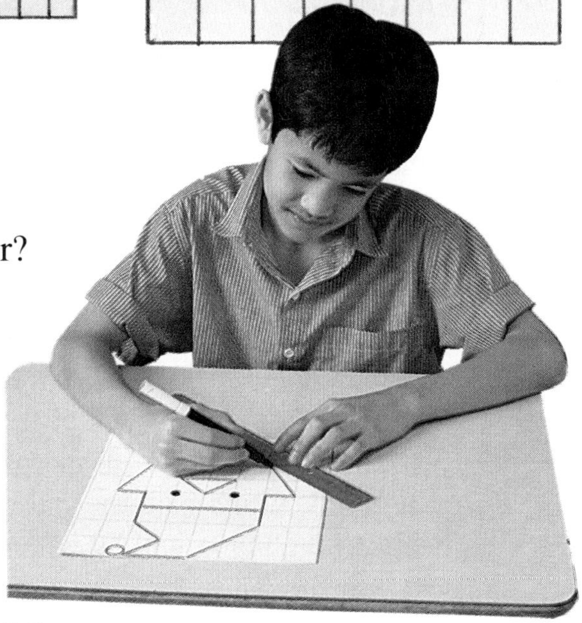

Two figures that have the same shape, but not necessarily the same size, are similar to each other.

TRY IT OUT

Write similar or not similar for each pair of figures.

1.

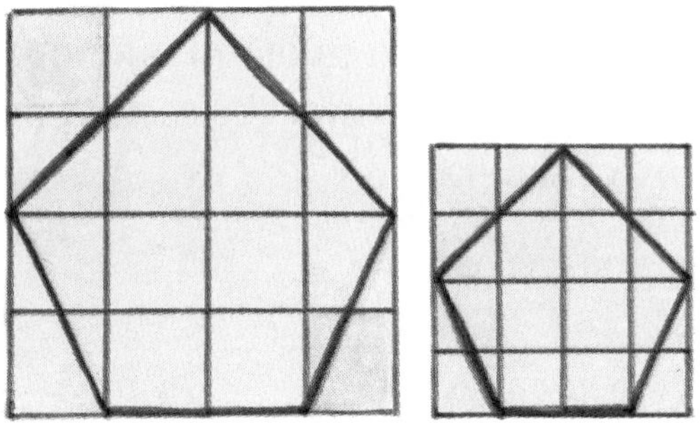

2.

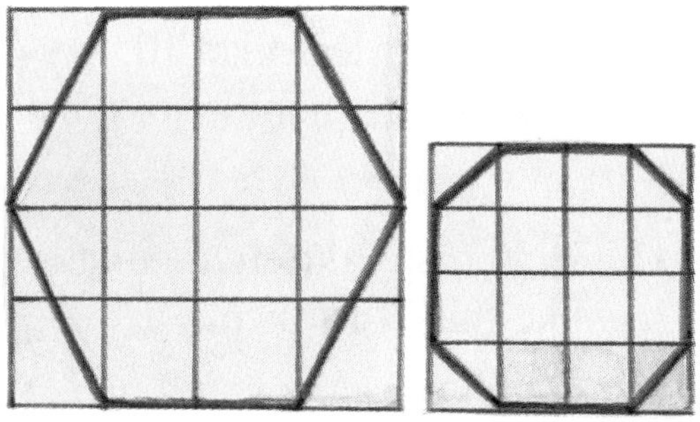

PRACTICE

Which figure in the row is similar to the first?

1.

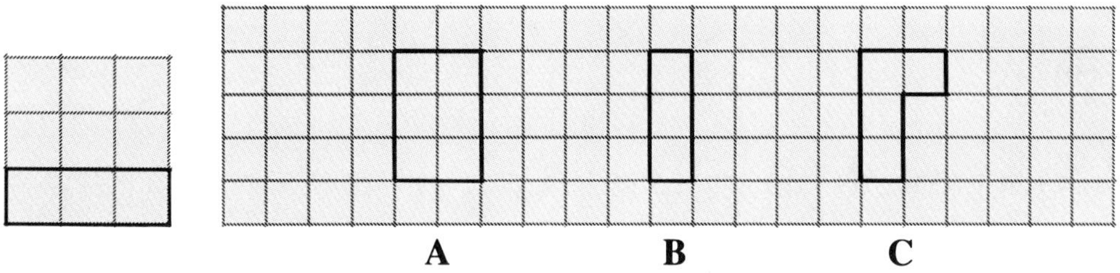

2.

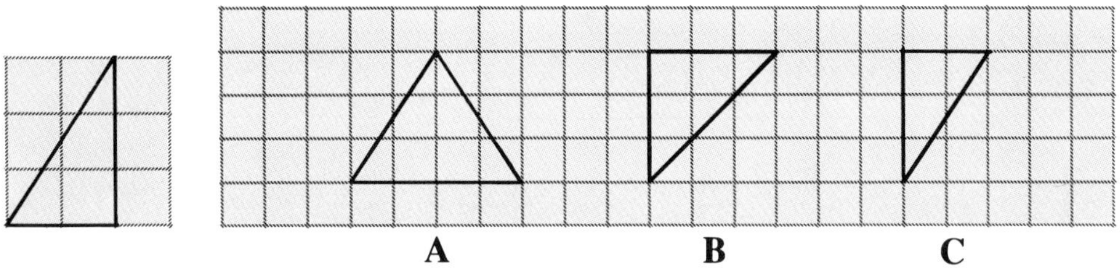

APPLY

MATH REASONING

3. Complete this sentence in 2 different ways. Use a single word each time. Any two __?__ that I draw will be similar to each other.

PROBLEM SOLVING

4. Fine Arts Data Bank Use different-sized graph paper to draw a sun mask similar to the one on page 480.

DATA BANK

5. Look for a pattern to solve this problem. Here are the first, second, third, and fourth "similar dot triangles." How many dots does the sixth one have?

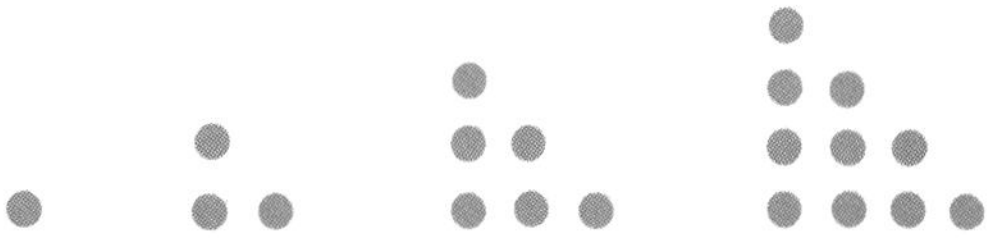

CALCULATOR

6. Figure B is similar to A. The sides of B are twice as long as the sides of A. Use a calculator to find the perimeters of both figures.

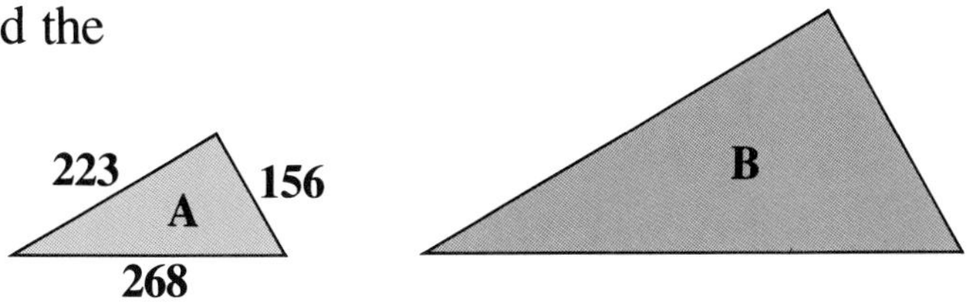

Problem Solving
Data from a Diagram

UNDERSTAND
FIND DATA
PLAN
ESTIMATE
SOLVE
CHECK

LEARN ABOUT IT

To solve some problems you must first locate the needed data in a diagram.

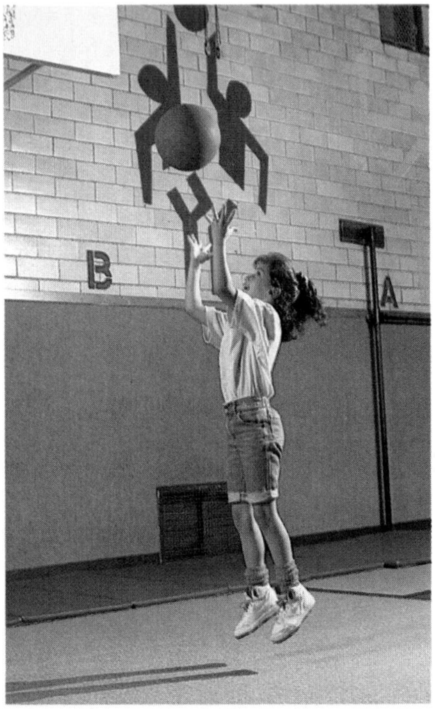

Rosita made a basket from the center line. How far did the ball travel?

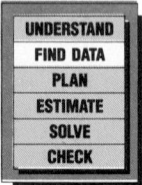

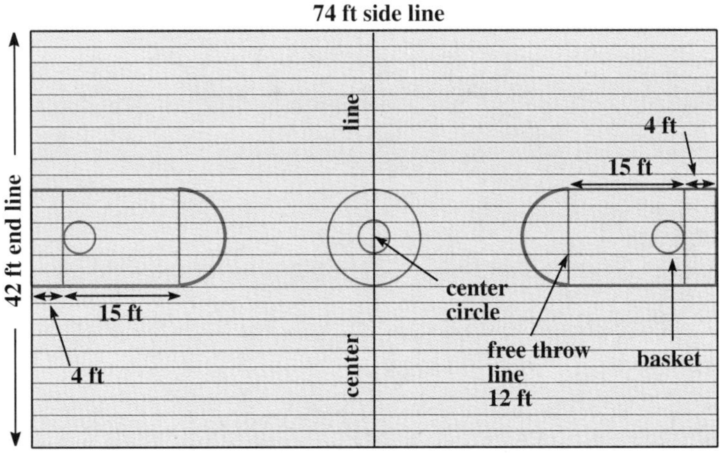

The sideline is 74 feet long. I'll divide that distance by 2 to find the center line.

$$2\overline{)74} = 37$$

The basket is 4 feet from the end line. I'll subtract to find the difference.

$$\begin{array}{r} 37 \\ -\ 4 \\ \hline 33 \end{array}$$

Rosita's ball traveled 33 feet.

TRY IT OUT

Solve.

1. Pablo's coach had the team jog around the perimeter of the court 12 times. How far did they jog?

2. Two parallel lines on the court have the same length. The sum of their lengths is 148 feet. Which lines are they?

3. What is the length of the court from basket to basket?

MIXED PRACTICE

Solve. Use any problem solving strategy.

1. Manny dribbled the ball the length of the court 15 times. How far did he go?

2. Each quarter in Ben's game lasts 8 minutes. How many seconds is this?

3. There are several pairs of congruent rectangles in the basketball court diagram. What is the perimeter of each of the largest rectangles?

4. The Heroines played 4 games. Use the graph and find their average score.

5. 47 fourth graders signed up for basketball. There are 5 more girls than boys. How many boys signed up?

6. After school Jayal practiced his hook shot. He threw the ball 47 times and sunk all but 16. How many baskets did he make?

7. **Talk About Your Solution**
   Solve. Georgia passed the ball from the middle of the center circle to the middle of the free throw line. How far was her pass? Explain your solution to a classmate. Compare your solutions.

Some Strategies

Act It Out
Use Objects
Choose an Operation
Draw a Picture
Make an Organized List
Guess and Check
Make a Table
Look for a Pattern
Use Logical Reasoning
Work Backward

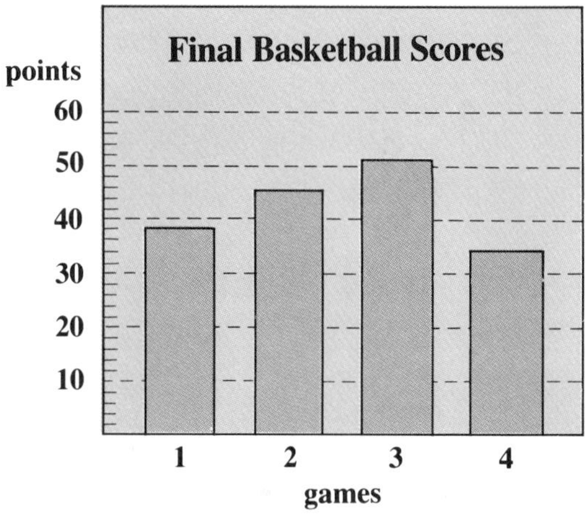

More Practice, page 523, set C

Applied Problem Solving
Group Decision Making

UNDERSTAND
FIND DATA
PLAN
ESTIMATE
SOLVE
CHECK

Group Skill:
Disagree in an Agreeable Way

Marty's mother has opened Round-the-World Diner near your school. She plans to serve foods from a different country each day of the week.

She has asked you to draw up a plan for arranging the tables, counter, and stools so that the largest number of customers can be seated at one time. Use graph paper to figure out a plan that you can show the owner.

Facts to Consider

1. 6 people can sit at a round table.
2. 4 people can sit at a square table.
3. You need to leave at least 3 squares between tables.

4. Customers can sit on stools on 1 side of the counter.
5. You need at least 1 square between each stool.
6. You need to leave some space at the door for the cash register.

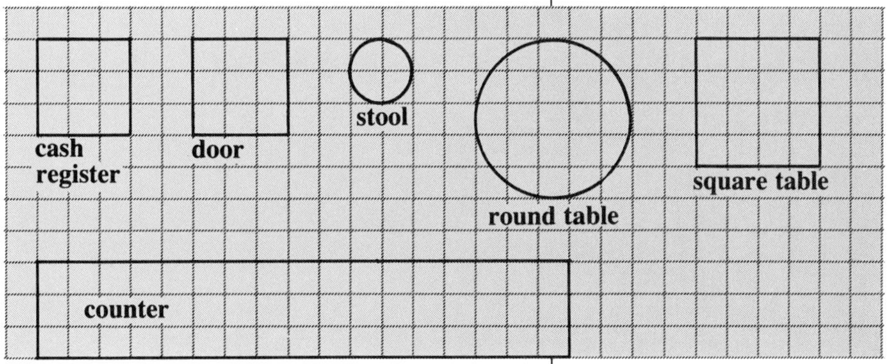

7. The diner is 24 squares wide and 31 squares long.
8. Here are the sizes of the furniture. Cut out copies of the patterns and trace around them on the graph paper to show your plan.

Some Questions to Answer

1. How many round tables can you fit in a row?
2. How many square tables can you fit in a row?
3. How many stools can you fit at the counter?
4. If a square table is against a wall, how many people can sit at it?
5. Did you leave enough room for the customers to get to their tables and to the cash register?

What Is Your Decision?

Use the furniture patterns and graph paper to show a plan that allows the most people to eat at the diner at the same time. Label the diagram so the owner understands your ideas.

WRAP UP

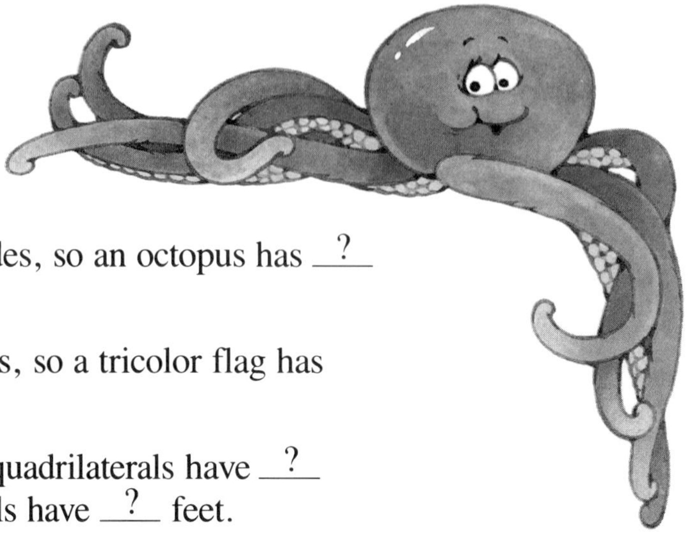

Number Prefixes

Complete each sentence.

1. An octagon has __?__ sides, so an octopus has __?__ tentacles.
2. A triangle has __?__ sides, so a tricolor flag has __?__ colors.
3. Ped means foot. Since quadrilaterals have __?__ sides, quadruped animals have __?__ feet.
4. A pentagon has __?__ sides. At the Olympics, the pentathlon involves __?__ events.
5. Pod also means foot. Insects are hexapods because they have __?__ feet.

Sometimes, Always, Never

Which word should go in the blank, sometimes, always, or never? Explain your choices.

6. Parallel lines __?__ intersect.
7. A trapezoid is __?__ a symmetric figure.
8. Congruent figures are __?__ similar as well.
9. Similar figures are __?__ congruent as well.
10. To plot the coordinates (5,7) on a graph, you __?__ go up 5 and over 7.

Project

Make a code with number pairs. First make a key by plotting alphabet letters at different points on a coordinate grid. Then think of a secret message. "Spell" the words in your message by giving the number pairs for each letter. Trade keys and codes with a friend. Read each other's messages.

POWER PRACTICE/TEST

Part 1 Understanding

1. Name an intersection in your town that suggests perpendicular lines.
2. What would happen if railroad tracks were not parallel?
3. Compare a square and a rectangle.
4. Compare a parallelogram and a trapezoid.
5. Draw these curves.
   a. simple b. not simple c. closed d. not closed

Part 2 Skills

Name an object shaped like each space figure.

6. sphere
7. cone
8. cylinder
9. pyramid
10. cube
11. rectangular prism

Name the polygon that has these features.

12. 5 sides
13. 8 sides
14. 6 sides
15. Trace this figure. Draw its line of symmetry.

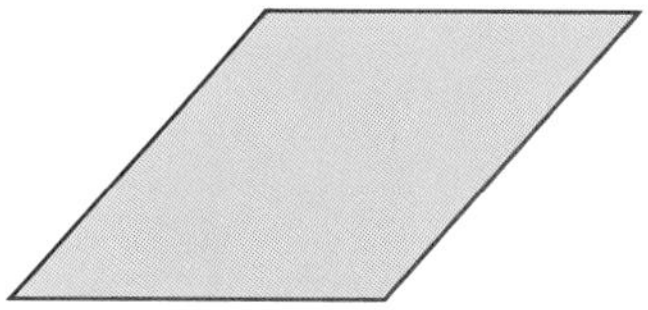

16. Which figure is congruent to this triangle?

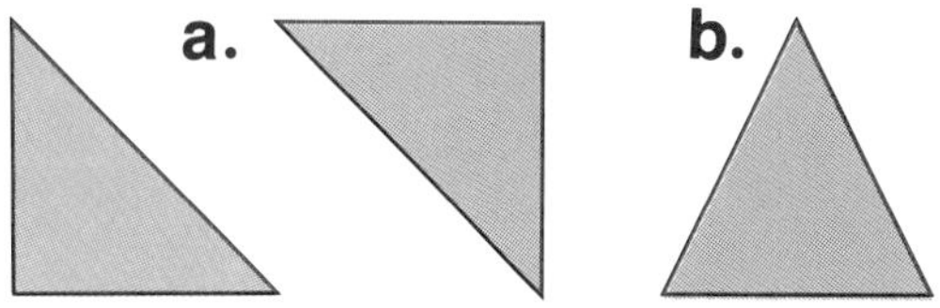

Part 3 Applications

17. A swim club built a pool shaped like a regular hexagon. One side is 43 ft long. What is the perimeter of the pool?
18. Randy is designing a patio in the shape of an isosceles triangle. Its perimeter must be 30 ft. Draw and label two possible patio diagrams.
19. **Challenge** A square fits along the two numbered edges of a grid. The coordinates (4,0) name its lower right-hand corner. Give the other coordinates.

ENRICHMENT
Modeling Changes in Geometric Figures

How can you flip, turn, or slide the pieces to change the tangram puzzle square into the figures shown? Use tangram pieces to show your solutions.

Start with a tangram puzzle square. Move only pieces A and B to make each figure below.

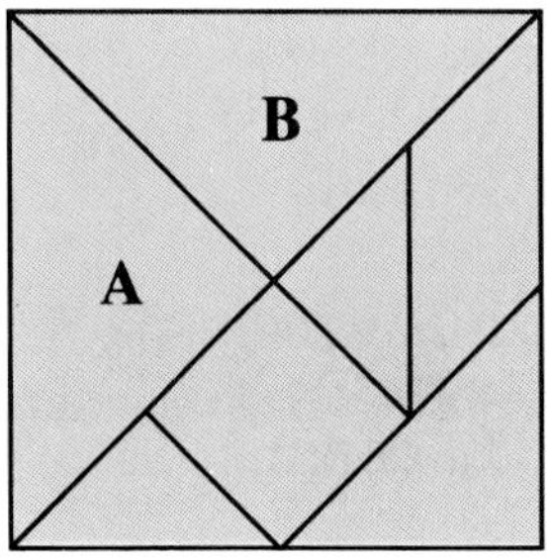

1 Rectangle

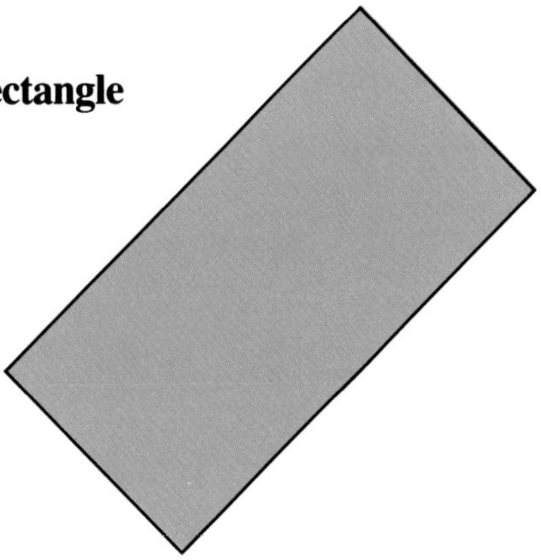

2 Parallelogram

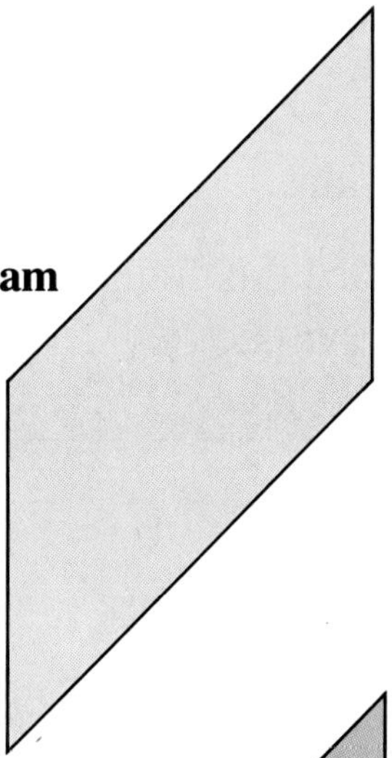

3 Triangle

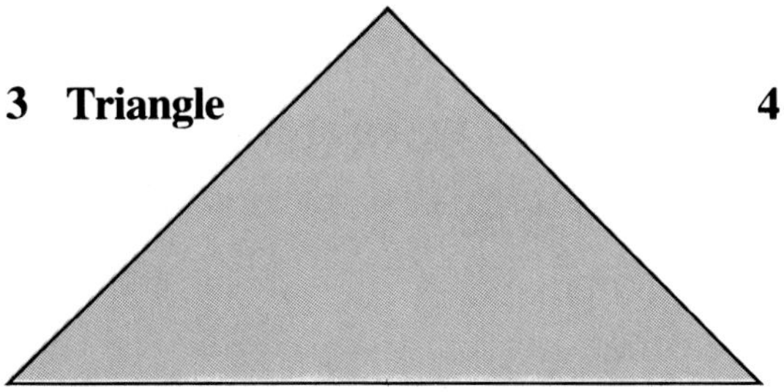

4 Trapezoid

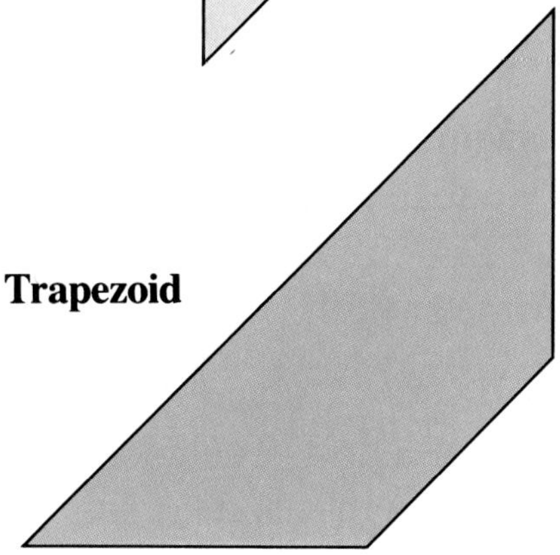

Cumulative Review

1. A passenger elevator can carry 900 pounds safely. How many adults weighing an average of 150 pounds each can safely ride in the elevator at the same time?

   A 6 B 8
   C 7 D 10

2. 11 yards = |||| feet

   A 22 B 44
   C 33 D 396

3. A good outdoor activity when it is 30°F is ||||.

   A raking leaves B sledding
   C swimming D gardening

4. $5\overline{)0}$

   A 5 B 1
   C 50 D 0

5. 64 ÷ 8

   A 6 B 8
   C 7 D 9

6. |||| × 9 = 45

   A 6 B 4
   C 5 D 3

7. If a function rule is <u>divide by 9</u>, what number should go in so that 8 comes out?

   A 72 B 81
   C 7 D 64

8. $6\overline{)23}$

   A 3 R3 B 4 R1
   C 4 D 3 R5

9. 240 ÷ 8

   A 3,000 B 30
   C 300 D 3

10. If you estimate these quotients using compatible numbers, which estimate will be an <u>under</u>estimate?

    A 396 ÷ 5 B 216 ÷ 3
    C 415 ÷ 7 D 114 ÷ 6

11. Find the average of 135, 153, 140, and 136.

    A 4 B 139
    C 141 D 564

12. $5\overline{)529}$

    A 105 R4 B 150 R4
    C 106 R1 D 104 R9

12

FRACTION CONCEPTS

THEME: LITERATURE

MATH AND LANGUAGE ARTS

DATA BANK

Use the Language Arts Data Bank on page 477 to answer the questions.

1 How many books did Laura Ingalls Wilder write? How many became Newberry Honor Books? How many did not?

2 How many servings of Johnny Cake would you get if you were to double the recipe?

3 In *Little House in the Big Woods,* Laura Ingalls Wilder writes that the story she is telling took place 60 years earlier. What year would that be?

4 **Use Critical Thinking** Laura and Mary get two cookies. Each nibbles half her cookie and saves the other half for Baby Carrie. Is this fair?

Children today like to read how Laura Ingalls lived long ago in the Big Woods and on the prairie.

Understanding Fractions
Regions

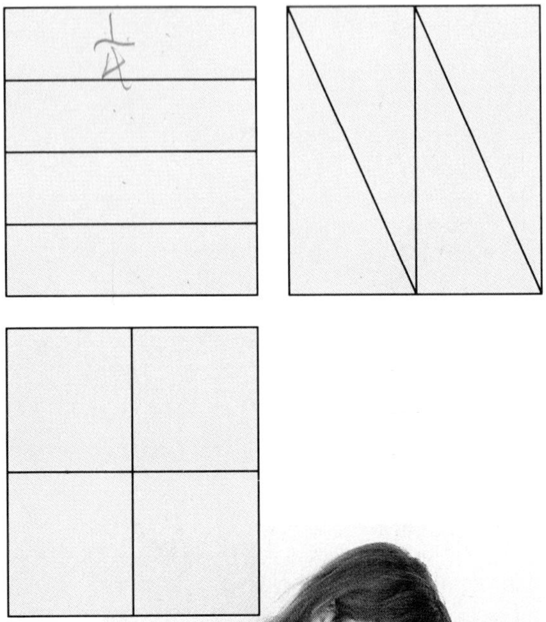

LEARN ABOUT IT

EXPLORE **Use Ruler and Scissors**

Work in groups. The teacher gave some fourth graders each a sheet of typing paper and asked them to divide it into fourths or four equal parts. These drawings show some of the ways they found.

Use paper, scissors, and a ruler to decide whether or not each of these methods shows fourths. Find other ways to show fourths.

TALK ABOUT IT

1. How do you know you have divided the paper into fourths?
2. Do the fourths have equal area even though they have different shapes? Explain.

You can write fractions to describe a part or parts of something.

one-fourth shaded	two-fourths shaded	three-fourths shaded	four-fourths shaded

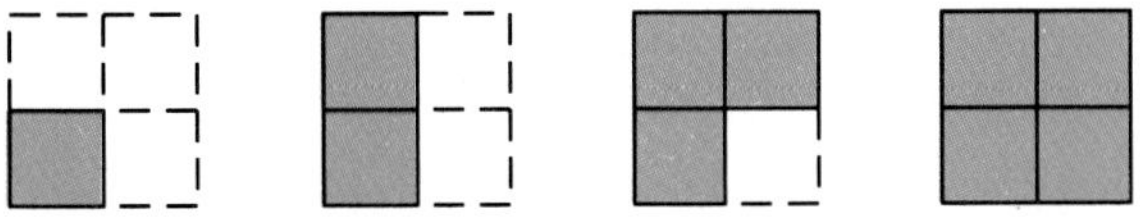

$\frac{1}{4}$	$\frac{2}{4}$	$\frac{3}{4}$	$\frac{4}{4}$

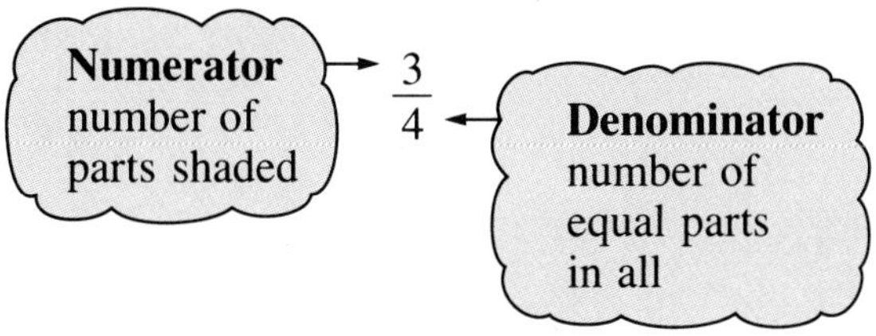

Numerator
number of parts shaded
$\frac{3}{4}$
Denominator
number of equal parts in all

TRY IT OUT

Draw 4 circles and divide each into 8 parts. Do this by hand and make the parts as equal as you can.

Color $\frac{1}{8}$, $\frac{3}{8}$, $\frac{5}{8}$, and $\frac{7}{8}$.

PRACTICE

Write the fraction.

1. What part of the fruit pie is eaten?

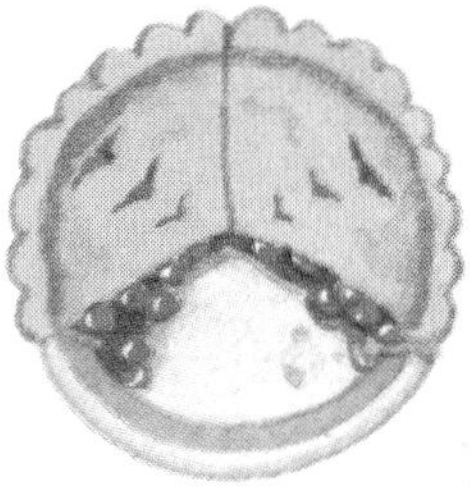

2. What part of the window is broken?

3. What part of the garden is planted?

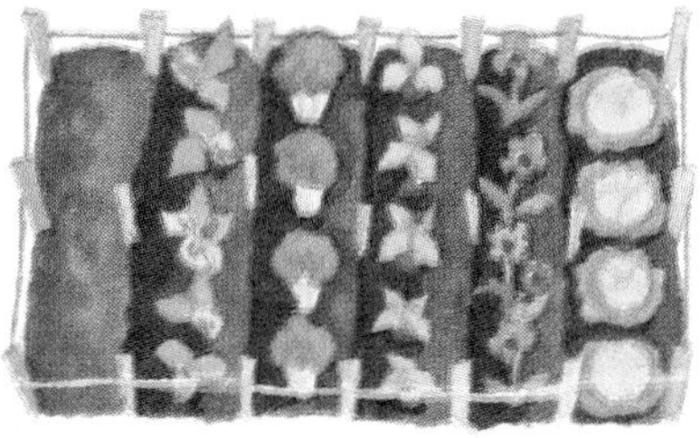

Write fractions to tell what part is shaded and what part is not shaded.

4. 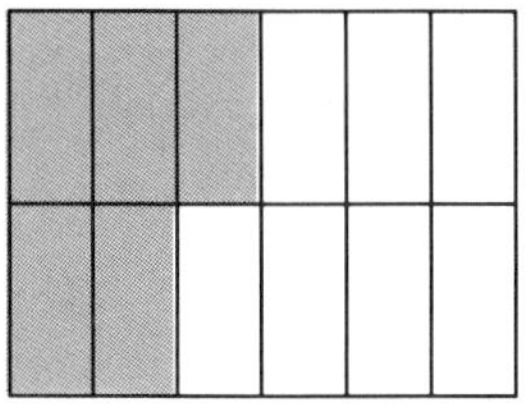

5. 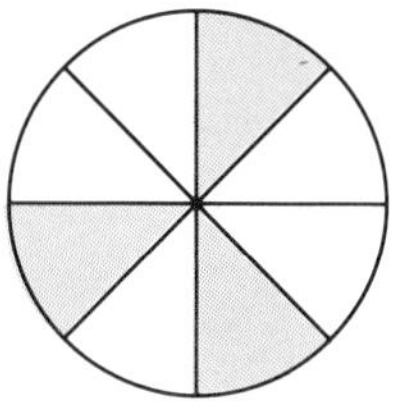

6. 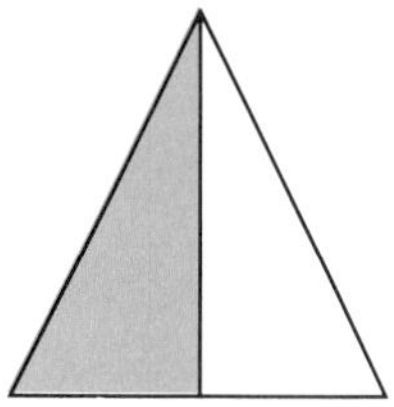

7. 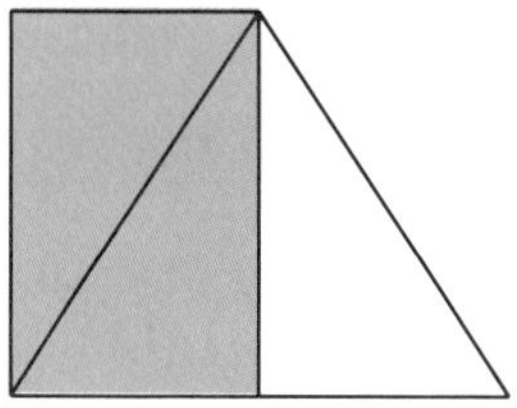

APPLY

MATH REASONING

8. Is the shaded part more or less than $\frac{1}{2}$?

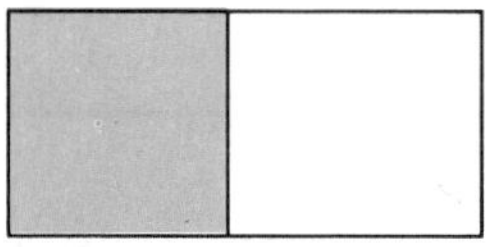

9. Is the shaded part more or less than $\frac{1}{4}$?

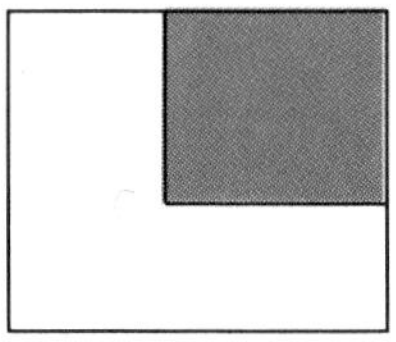

10. Is the shaded part more or less than $\frac{1}{3}$?

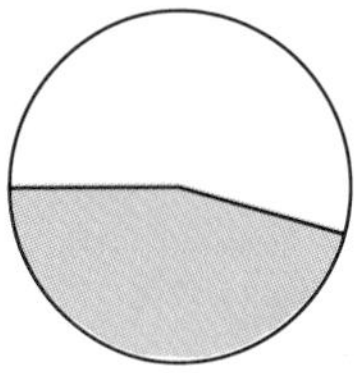

PROBLEM SOLVING

11. Miguel washed the living room window. It had 8 panes of glass. After he had washed 7 of them, what fractional part did he have left to wash?

USING CRITICAL THINKING Evaluate the Assumptions

12. "You got the bigger half of the granola bar!" Linette said to her sister. How would you answer this protest?

More Practice, page 523, set D

Understanding Fractions
Sets

LEARN ABOUT IT

EXPLORE **Think About the Situation**

In *Little House in the Big Woods,* Ma braided pieces of straw to make 6 hats. The 4 big hats were for Ma and Pa. The 2 small hats were for Laura and Mary.

TALK ABOUT IT

1. How many hats did Ma make?
2. How many of the hats were small?
3. How many of the hats were big?

You can use a fraction to tell what part of the hats were small.

number of small hats	2
total number of hats	6

We say **two-sixths** of the hats are small or $\frac{2}{6}$ of the hats are small.

Other Examples $\frac{3}{4}$ of the bonnets are red.

$\frac{2}{3}$ of the top hats are green.

TRY IT OUT

1. What fraction of the lockets are on ribbons?

2. What fraction of the parasols are yellow?

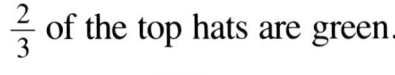

PRACTICE

Write the fraction for each ||||.

1. |||| of the toys are cornhusk dolls.

2. |||| of the fiddles have bows.

APPLY

MATH REASONING Give the fraction for each ||||.

3. |||| of the aprons have **some** red.
4. |||| of the aprons have **no** red.
5. |||| of the aprons have **all** red.

PROBLEM SOLVING

Draw a picture to help you solve the problem.

6. One Spring the Ingalls had 9 baby animals. $\frac{2}{9}$ of the animals were calves. The rest were piglets. How many were piglets?

7. **Language Arts Data Bank** DATA BANK What fraction of the books Laura Ingalls Wilder wrote became Newberry Honor Books? See page 477.

MIXED REVIEW

Divide. Show dollars and cents

8. \$3.45 ÷ 5
9. \$2.04 ÷ 4
10. \$0.70 ÷ 7
11. \$6.36 ÷ 6

Tell what the geometric shape is.

12. I have 4 sides. Each pair of sides is parallel. All my sides are equal.
13. I have three sides. No two sides are the same size.

Estimating Fractional Parts

LEARN ABOUT IT

EXPLORE Make a Decision

Laura told Ma at lunch that she had weeded about $\frac{3}{4}$ of the garden that morning. When Mary went to help finish the job she did not agree with Laura's estimate. What do you think?

Weeded Part

TALK ABOUT IT

1. Do you agree with Laura or Mary? Use an inch ruler to help you decide.
2. Which of these estimates do you think is best? Why?

$\frac{1}{4}$ $\frac{7}{8}$ $\frac{6}{10}$

Think about these fractions to help you estimate fractional parts.

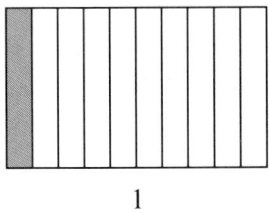

$\frac{1}{10}$ $\frac{1}{4}$ $\frac{1}{3}$ $\frac{1}{2}$

TRY IT OUT

Choose the best fractional estimate for the shaded part of each figure.

1. 

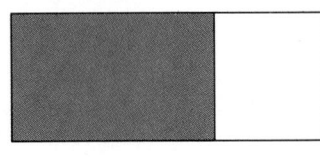

$\frac{1}{2}$ $\frac{2}{3}$ $\frac{9}{10}$

2. 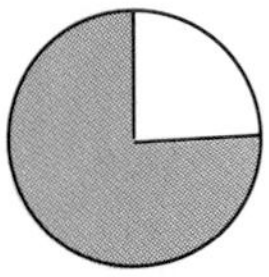

$\frac{2}{3}$ $\frac{3}{4}$ $\frac{9}{10}$

3. 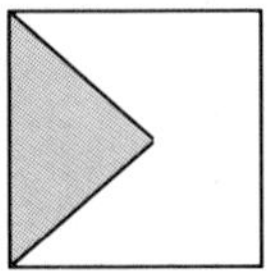

$\frac{1}{4}$ $\frac{1}{3}$ $\frac{1}{2}$

More Practice, page 524, set B

Problem Solving

MIXED PRACTICE

Solve. Use any problem solving strategy.

1. Guide dog schools train dogs for the blind. A school has been training 3 different kinds of dogs for 38 years. About 95 dogs are trained each year. How many dogs have been trained all together at the school?

2. The guide dog school had the same number of golden retrievers, Labrador retrievers, and German shepherds. There were 105 dogs in all. How many of each type of dog were there?

3. 5 out of every 10 dogs at the school pass the guide dog test. How many would pass out of 50 dogs?

4. For a 4-H project, Mary kept one of the dogs at her home until he was ready for guide dog training. She got him when he was 3 months old and kept him until he was 15 months old. How many days did she have the dog in all? Use 30 days for 1 month.

5. Carl is blind. He jogs 36 miles a week by holding onto his friend Kirk's shoulder. How many miles does he jog in a year?

6. Walter is 1 of 25 volunteers who records books on tape for the blind. 13 volunteers record science books. 17 record math books. Some record both kinds. How many record both kinds of books?

7. At the recording center, Jane reads books onto tape. She recorded these books.

Book	**Number of Pages**
Law	1,636
Math	356
Science	427
History	275

How many pages did she record in all?

8. A special machine can read a printed page out loud for visually handicapped people. It reads 900 words in 5 minutes. How many words does it read each minute?

More Practice, page 524, set C

Equivalent Fractions

LEARN ABOUT IT

EXPLORE **Use a Geoboard**

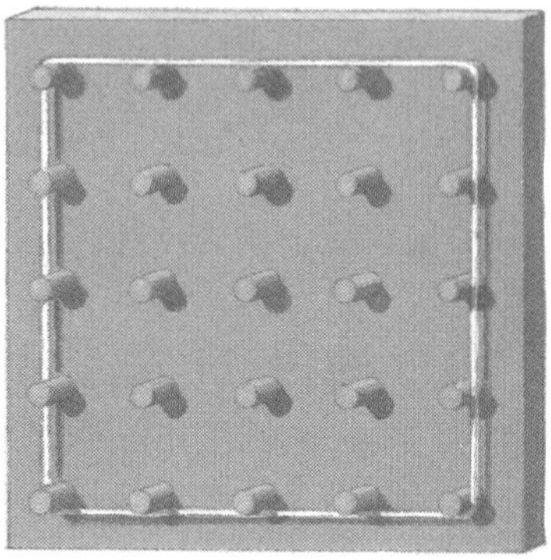

- Make this square on a geoboard. Divide it down the middle to show halves.
- Divide each of the halves into a number of equal parts in exactly the same way.
- Record the different ways to do this on dot paper. Think about how to use your dot paper pictures to write different fractions to describe half of the square.

TALK ABOUT IT

1. Pick out one of your squares. What fraction shows $\frac{1}{2}$ of the square?
2. Use your dot paper drawings to make a list of different fractions that show $\frac{1}{2}$ of the square.

Fractions that name the same amount are called equivalent fractions.

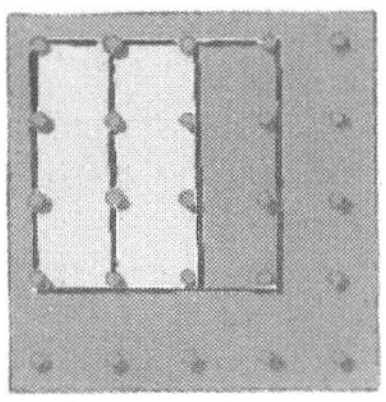

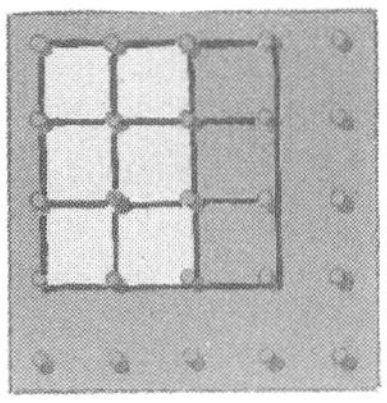

2 out of 3 parts are yellow → $\frac{2}{3} = \frac{6}{9}$ ← 6 out of 9 parts are yellow

$\frac{2}{3}$ is equivalent to $\frac{6}{9}$

TRY IT OUT

Copy and complete the equations.

1.

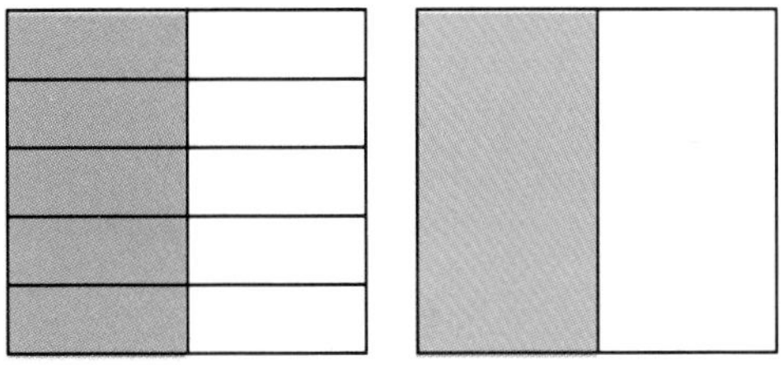

$\frac{5}{10} = \frac{|||}{|||}$

2.

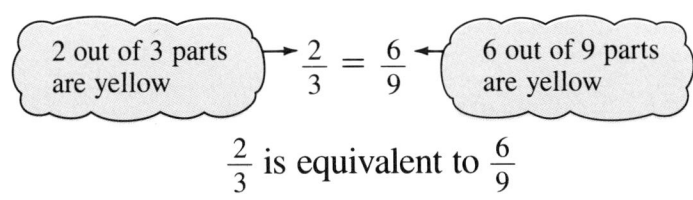

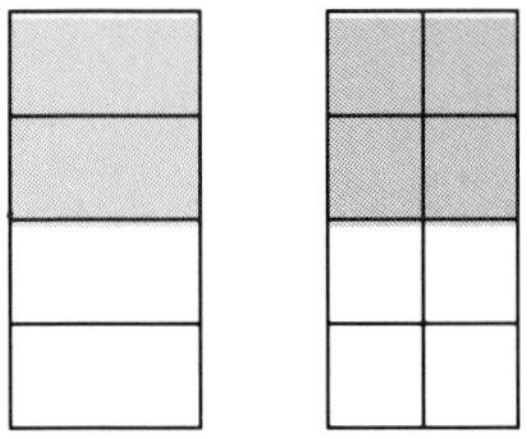

$\frac{2}{4} = \frac{|||}{|||}$

PRACTICE

Copy and complete the equations.

1. 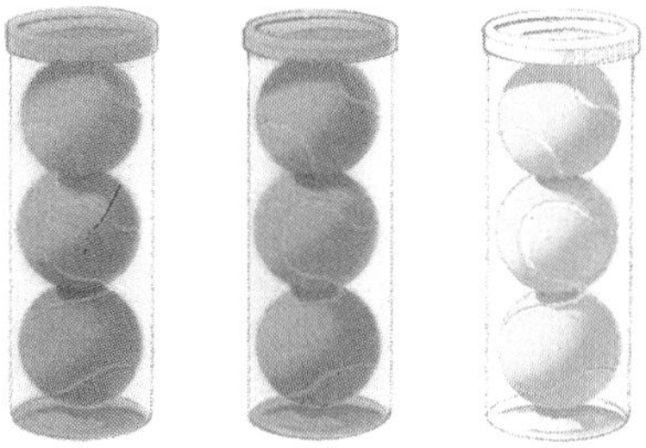 $\frac{2}{3} = \frac{|||}{9}$

2.  $\frac{1}{4} = \frac{2}{|||}$

3.  $\frac{2}{6} = \frac{|||}{|||}$

4. 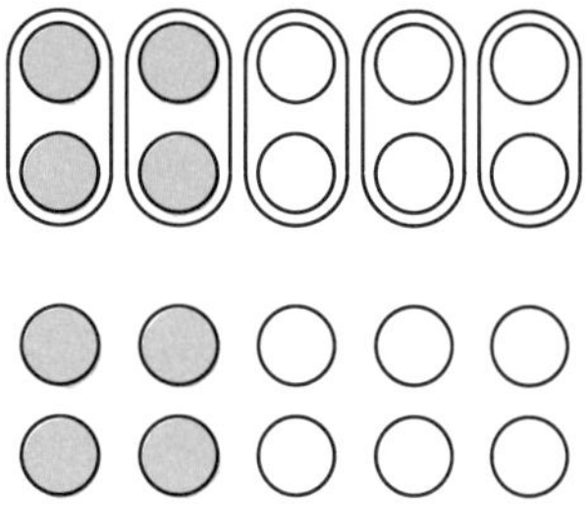 $\frac{4}{10} = \frac{|||}{|||}$

APPLY

MATH REASONING Write the fraction that does not belong. Use the pictures to help you.

5. $\frac{1}{2}$ $\frac{3}{4}$ $\frac{4}{8}$

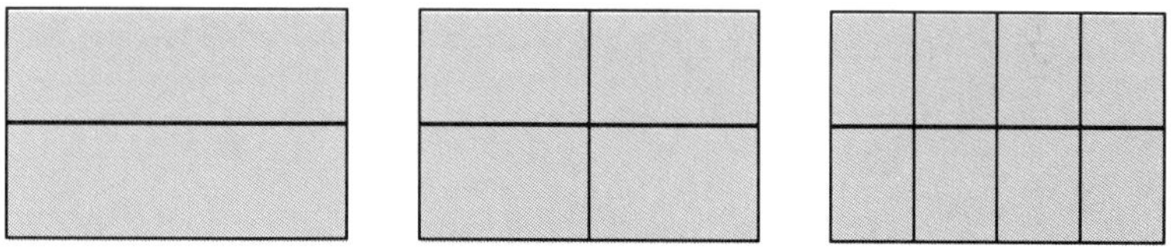

PROBLEM SOLVING

6. One of every 3 members of Jo's club had a computer. How many of the 12 members had a computer?

USING CRITICAL THINKING Give a Counterexample

Find an exception to the rule, if possible.

7. For any 2 equivalent fractions, the denominators are both even or both odd.

8. All fractions equivalent to $\frac{1}{3}$ have odd denominators.

More About Equivalent Fractions

LEARN ABOUT IT

EXPLORE **Think About the Situation**

At harvest time in *The Little House in the Big Woods,* teams, or pairs, of horses were hitched to a horsepower machine to run a machine called a separator.

TALK ABOUT IT

1. How many of the 4 teams are black? What fraction tells the part of the teams that are black?
2. Multiply the number of teams by 2. Multiply the number of black teams by 2. With these new numbers how can you write a fraction equivalent to the one in question 1?

To find equivalent fractions, multiply the numerator and the denominator by the same number.

Two-thirds and four-sixths are equivalent fractions.

×2

$\frac{2}{3} = \frac{4}{6}$

×2

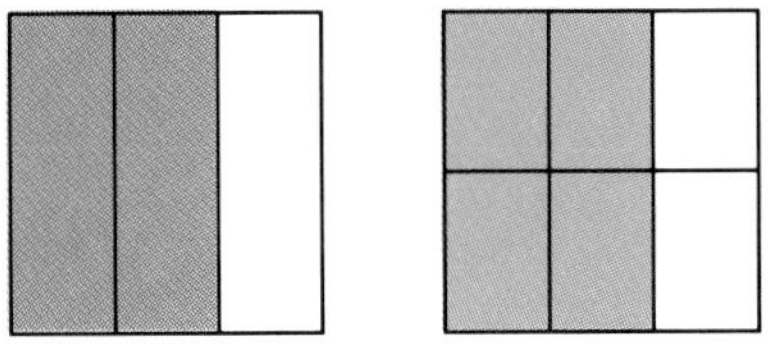

Other fractions equivalent to two-thirds.

×5

$\frac{2}{3} = \frac{10}{15}$

×5

×3

$\frac{2}{3} = \frac{6}{9}$

×3

TRY IT OUT

Multiply to find equivalent fractions.

1. ×2 $\frac{1}{4} = \frac{\square}{\square}$ ×2
2. ×3 $\frac{1}{4} = \frac{\square}{\square}$ ×3
3. ×2 $\frac{3}{5} = \frac{\square}{\square}$ ×2
4. ×3 $\frac{3}{5} = \frac{\square}{\square}$ ×3

PRACTICE

Multiply to find these equivalent fractions. Check with fraction pieces.

1. $\frac{1}{2} = \frac{|||}{|||}$ (×2 numerator, ×2 denominator)
2. $\frac{1}{2} = \frac{|||}{|||}$ (×3 numerator, ×3 denominator)
3. $\frac{5}{6} = \frac{|||}{|||}$ (×2 numerator, ×2 denominator)
4. $\frac{5}{6} = \frac{|||}{|||}$ (×4 numerator, ×4 denominator)

Multiply the numerator and denominator by 2, 3, and 4 to find the equivalent fractions.

5. $\frac{3}{4} = \frac{|||}{|||} = \frac{|||}{|||} = \frac{|||}{|||}$
6. $\frac{2}{5} = \frac{|||}{|||} = \frac{|||}{|||} = \frac{|||}{|||}$
7. $\frac{1}{8} = \frac{|||}{|||} = \frac{|||}{|||} = \frac{|||}{|||}$

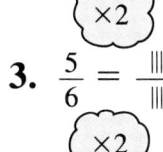

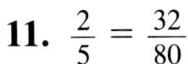

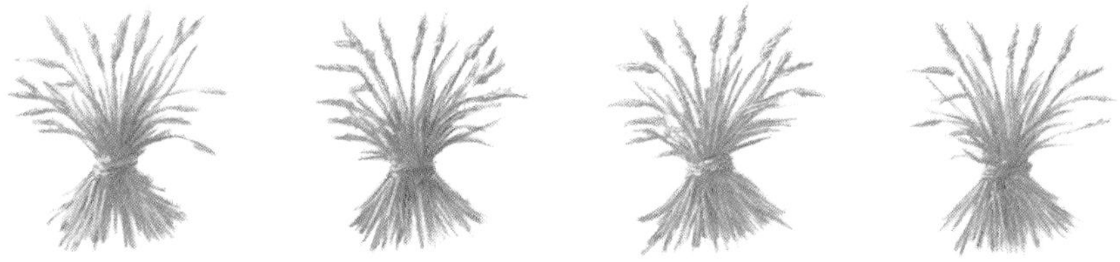

APPLY

MATH REASONING

8. If $\square = 15$, what is $\triangle$?
   $\frac{5}{8} = \frac{\square}{\triangle}$

9. If $\square = 10$, what is $\triangle$?
   $\frac{5}{8} = \frac{\square}{\triangle}$

PROBLEM SOLVING

DATA BANK

10. **Language Arts Data Bank** How can you measure the cornmeal to make Johnny Cake if you have only a tablespoon measure? Hint: 4 tablespoons equal $\frac{1}{4}$ cup. See page 477.

CALCULATOR

You can use a calculator to tell if 2 fractions are equivalent. Divide the numerator by the denominator. Are the calculator displays the same?

To see if $\frac{3}{5} = \frac{75}{125}$ is an equivalent fraction, do this.

[ON/AC] 3 [÷] 5 [=] 0.6

[ON/AC] 75 [÷] 125 [=] 0.6

11. $\frac{2}{5} = \frac{32}{80}$
12. $\frac{3}{4} = \frac{164}{224}$
13. $\frac{3}{8} = \frac{126}{336}$
14. $\frac{5}{6} = \frac{240}{288}$

More Practice, page 508, set F

Lowest-Terms Fractions

LEARN ABOUT IT

EXPLORE Think About the Situation

Tom says that $\frac{1}{2}$ of the fish in the aquarium are striped. Mary says that $\frac{6}{12}$ are striped.

TALK ABOUT IT

1. How many fish are there? How many are striped?
2. Who do you think is correct and why?
3. Which do you think is a simpler fraction, $\frac{1}{2}$ or $\frac{6}{12}$? Why?

A fraction is in lowest terms when no number except 1 will divide evenly into its numerator and denominator.

Find a number that will divide evenly into the numerator and denominator.

$$\frac{6 \div 2}{12 \div 2} = \frac{3}{6}$$

2 divides evenly. You could also have started dividing by 3 or 6.

Keep dividing until you cannot divide by any number except 1. The fraction is in lowest terms.

$$\frac{3 \div 3}{6 \div 3} = \frac{1}{2}$$

One-half is the lowest-terms fraction for six-twelfths.

TRY IT OUT

Reduce each fraction to lowest terms.

1. $\frac{6 \div 2}{8 \div 2} = \frac{|||}{|||}$ 2. $\frac{12 \div 4}{20 \div 4} = \frac{|||}{|||}$ 3. $\frac{6 \div 3}{15 \div 3} = \frac{|||}{|||}$ 4. $\frac{3}{9}$ 5. $\frac{9}{12}$

PRACTICE

Is the fraction in lowest terms? Answer yes or no.

1. $\frac{2}{4}$ **2.** $\frac{1}{8}$ **3.** $\frac{3}{15}$ **4.** $\frac{4}{5}$ **5.** $\frac{3}{9}$

If possible, reduce to lowest terms.

6. $\frac{10}{12}$ **7.** $\frac{6}{9}$ **8.** $\frac{2}{16}$ **9.** $\frac{4}{8}$ **10.** $\frac{1}{6}$ **11.** $\frac{18}{24}$

APPLY

MATH REASONING

For each pair, use mental math to reduce each fraction to lowest terms. Are they equivalent fractions?

12. $\frac{3}{6}, \frac{4}{8}$ **13.** $\frac{9}{12}, \frac{4}{6}$ **14.** $\frac{10}{15}, \frac{4}{6}$

PROBLEM SOLVING

15. Developing a Plan Tell which steps you could follow to solve this problem. Find all the correct choices. Jan has 12 tropical fish. Three are half-beaks, 2 are neons, and the rest are algae eaters. What fraction of the fish are algae eaters?

ALGEBRA

When a fraction in the IN row is put into a machine, the fraction in the OUT row comes out. Tell what rule the machine is using. Give the missing fraction.

16. Math Machine A

IN $\frac{1}{3}$ $\frac{4}{5}$ $\frac{2}{3}$ OUT $\frac{2}{6}$ $\frac{8}{10}$

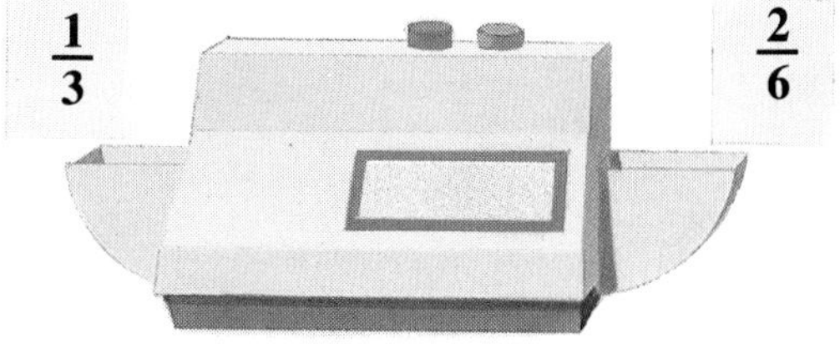

17. Math Machine B

IN $\frac{2}{5}$ $\frac{1}{2}$ $\frac{3}{4}$ OUT $\frac{8}{20}$ $\frac{4}{8}$

Comparing Fractions

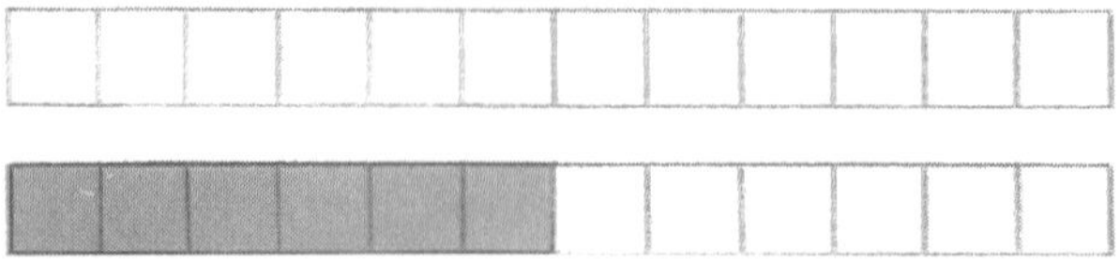

$\frac{1}{2}$

LEARN ABOUT IT

EXPLORE **Use Graph Paper**

- Cut some 12-unit strips from graph paper.
- Color a strip for each of these fractions.

  $\frac{1}{2}, \frac{1}{3}, \frac{1}{4}, \frac{1}{6}, \frac{1}{12}, \frac{2}{3}, \frac{3}{4}, \frac{5}{6}, \frac{5}{12}, \frac{7}{12}, \frac{11}{12}$
- Use your strips to help you complete some statements like these. $\frac{1}{2} < \frac{3}{4}$ $\quad \frac{1}{2} > \frac{1}{3}$

TALK ABOUT IT

1. How can you use the strips to show that $\frac{2}{3} < \frac{3}{4}$?
2. How can you look at your strips and easily write fractions with denominator 12 that are equivalent to $\frac{2}{3}$ and $\frac{3}{4}$? How can you use these fractions to show that $\frac{3}{4} > \frac{2}{3}$?

Fractions with the same denominator are easily compared on the number line.

Three-sixths is less than five-sixths.

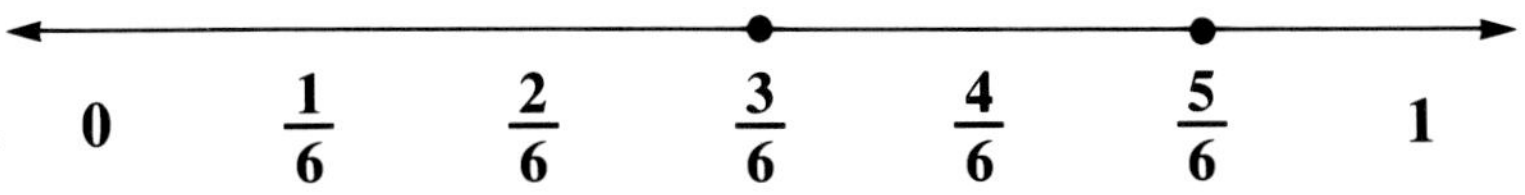

Fractions with unlike denominators can be compared by changing them to equivalent fractions with like denominators.

$\frac{1}{2} = \frac{3}{6} \qquad \frac{1}{3} = \frac{2}{6}$

Since $\frac{3}{6} > \frac{2}{6}$, we know that $\frac{1}{2} > \frac{1}{3}$

TRY IT OUT

Write $<$, $>$, or $=$ for each ||||. Use graph paper strips or write equivalent fractions to help you.

1. $\frac{1}{4}$ |||| $\frac{1}{3}$ **2.** $\frac{2}{3}$ |||| $\frac{1}{4}$ **3.** $\frac{5}{6}$ |||| $\frac{7}{8}$

PRACTICE

Write <, >, or = for each ||||.

1. $\frac{1}{3}$ |||| $\frac{1}{2}$ **2.** $\frac{2}{5}$ |||| $\frac{1}{2}$ **3.** $\frac{2}{6}$ |||| $\frac{3}{9}$ **4.** $\frac{1}{4}$ |||| $\frac{1}{5}$

5. $\frac{7}{8}$ |||| $\frac{3}{4}$ **6.** $\frac{2}{8}$ |||| $\frac{2}{3}$ **7.** $\frac{4}{20}$ |||| $\frac{1}{4}$ **8.** $\frac{5}{8}$ |||| $\frac{5}{6}$

APPLY

MATH REASONING

9. Which of these fractions are more than $\frac{1}{4}$ but less than $\frac{1}{2}$? $\frac{1}{6}, \frac{1}{5}, \frac{1}{3}, \frac{2}{3}, \frac{3}{8}$

PROBLEM SOLVING

10. Determining Reasonable Answers
Tell which of the answers seems reasonable. Sarah ate more than $\frac{1}{3}$ of a pizza and less than $\frac{2}{3}$ of it. The pizza was cut into sixths. How much could she have eaten?

a. $\frac{1}{4}$ pizza b. $\frac{5}{6}$ pizza c. $\frac{1}{2}$ pizza

d. none, there is no fraction between $\frac{1}{3}$ and $\frac{2}{3}$

MENTAL MATH

Think about pictures to help you discover a way to compare special fractions.

Which is bigger, $\frac{7}{8}$ or $\frac{5}{6}$?

$\frac{7}{8}$

$\frac{1}{8}$ is missing.

$\frac{5}{6}$

$\frac{1}{6}$ is missing.

Which is greater?

11. $\frac{3}{4}$ or $\frac{2}{3}$ **12.** $\frac{5}{6}$ or $\frac{8}{9}$

13. $\frac{9}{10}$ or $\frac{7}{8}$ **14.** $\frac{2}{3}$ or $\frac{5}{6}$

15. $\frac{4}{5}$ or $\frac{7}{8}$ **16.** $\frac{5}{7}$ or $\frac{3}{4}$

Exploring Algebra

LEARN ABOUT IT

Suppose you write the numerators and denominators of a set of equivalent fractions as number pairs. Then you graph them. What do you notice about the points?

1. Copy the table below. Write numbers for △ and □.

$$\frac{2}{3} = \frac{\triangle}{\square}$$

△	2	4	6				
□	3	6	9				

2. Graph the number pairs (△ , □) from the table above on a graph like this.

3. Connect the points on the graph. What do you notice?

4. Repeat using the fraction $\frac{2}{5}$. What do you notice about this graph?

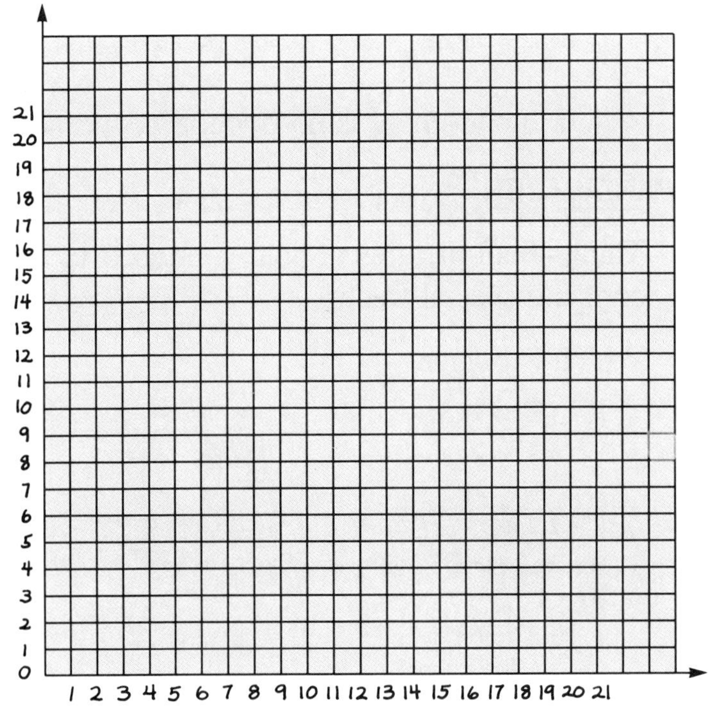

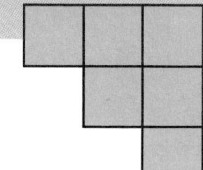

POWER PRACTICE/QUIZ

Write fractions to tell what part is red and what part is blue.

1. 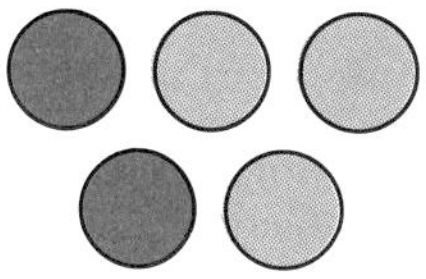

2. 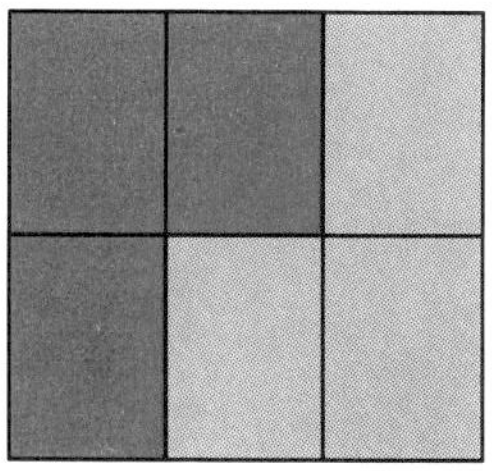

3. 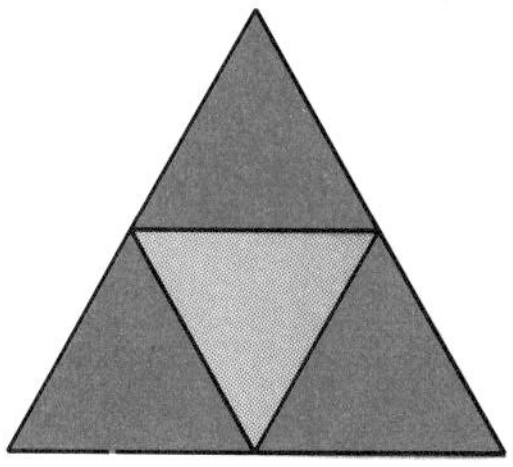

Copy and complete the equations.

4. 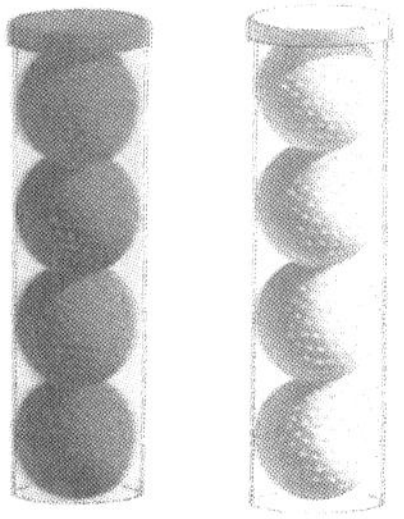

$\frac{1}{2} = \frac{\square}{8}$

5. 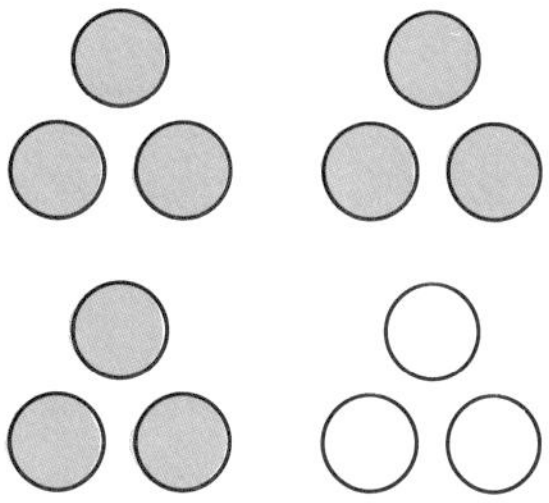

$\frac{3}{4} = \frac{\square}{12}$

Find equivalent fractions.

6. $\frac{3}{8} = \frac{\square}{\square}$ (×2 / ×2)

7. $\frac{1}{6} = \frac{\square}{\square}$ (×3 / ×3)

8. $\frac{1}{2} = \frac{\square}{\square}$ (×5 / ×5)

9. $\frac{3}{10} = \frac{\square}{\square}$ (×4 / ×4)

Reduce each fraction to lowest terms.

10. $\frac{6}{20}$ **11.** $\frac{12}{32}$ **12.** $\frac{5}{30}$ **13.** $\frac{15}{18}$ **14.** $\frac{16}{24}$

Write < or > for each ||||.

15. $\frac{1}{3}$ |||| $\frac{1}{4}$ **16.** $\frac{2}{3}$ |||| $\frac{3}{4}$ **17.** $\frac{2}{5}$ |||| $\frac{2}{3}$ **18.** $\frac{3}{5}$ |||| $\frac{2}{3}$

PROBLEM SOLVING

19. Nicholas ate $\frac{1}{3}$ of the pizza, Sebastian ate $\frac{3}{8}$, and Christine ate $\frac{7}{24}$. Did Sebastian eat the most? Tell how you know.

Mental Math
Finding a Fraction of a Number

LEARN ABOUT IT

EXPLORE **Think About the Situation**

Annie decided to give her friend Samantha $\frac{1}{4}$ of her walnut shell animals. She placed them in these four groups.

TALK ABOUT IT

1. Into how many equal parts did Annie divide her walnut shell animals?
2. How many animals will Annie give Samantha? Explain how you decided.

You can find $\frac{1}{2}$ of a number by dividing the number by 2.

To find $\frac{1}{3}$ of the number, divide it by 3.

To find $\frac{1}{4}$, divide by 4.

Here is how to find $\frac{3}{4}$ of a number.

- First find $\frac{1}{4}$ of the number

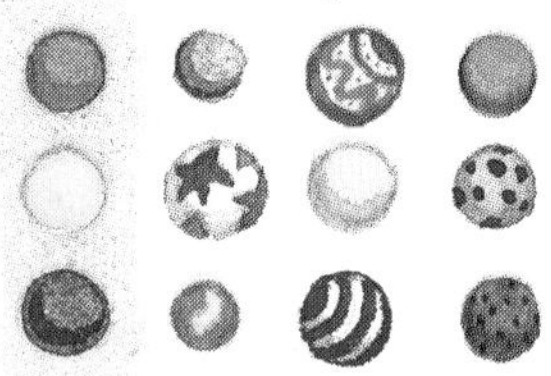

$12 \div 4 = 3$

$\frac{1}{4}$ of $12 = 3$

- Then multiply by 3.

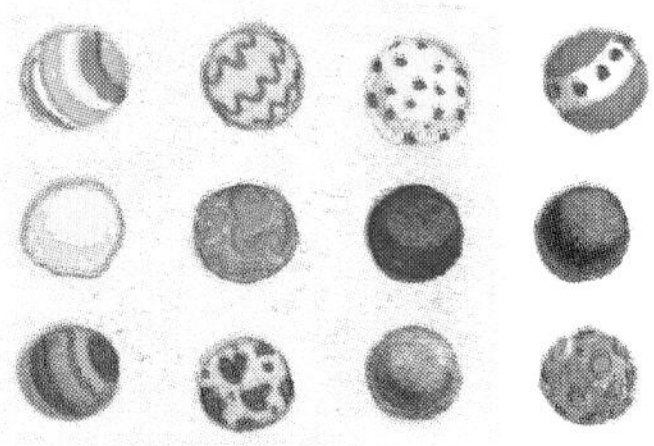

$3 \times 3 = 9$

$\frac{3}{4}$ of $12 = 9$

TRY IT OUT

Find the missing number. If you need help, draw or use objects.

1. $\frac{1}{3}$ of 9 = |||| $\frac{2}{3}$ of 9 = |||| **2.** $\frac{1}{4}$ of 12 = |||| $\frac{3}{4}$ of 12 = ||||

PRACTICE

Give the number for each ||||. Use the drawings or objects to help you.

1. $\frac{1}{4}$ of 8 = |||| $\frac{3}{4}$ of 8 = ||||

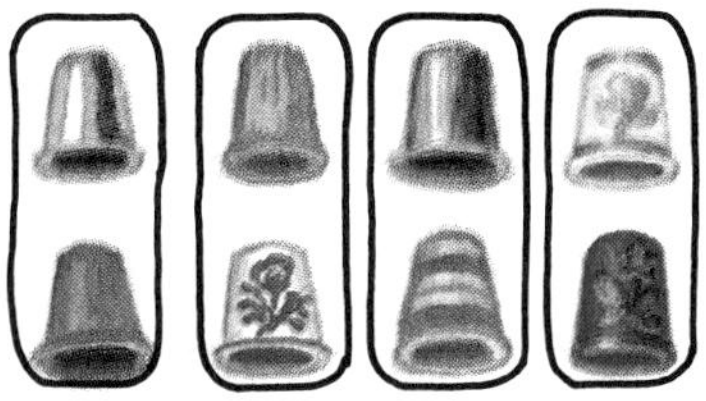

2. $\frac{1}{5}$ of 10 = |||| $\frac{3}{5}$ of 10 = ||||

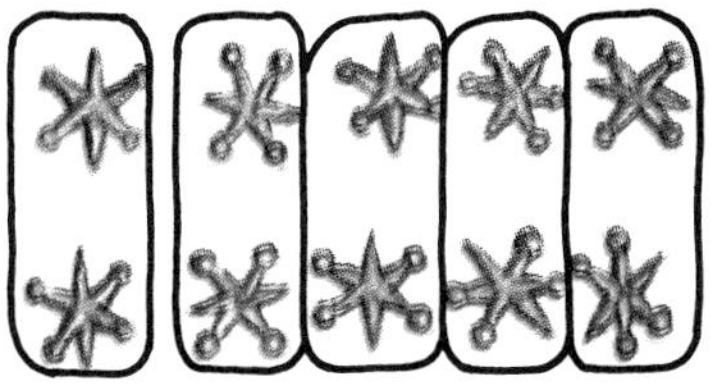

Give the number for each exercise.

3. $\frac{1}{2}$ of 14 **4.** $\frac{1}{8}$ of 32 **5.** $\frac{2}{5}$ of 20 **6.** $\frac{5}{6}$ of 36

APPLY

MATH REASONING

7. If this is $\frac{1}{3}$ of Carla's elf doll collection, how many elf dolls does she have in all?

PROBLEM SOLVING

8. Missing Data Tell what information you need to be able to solve this problem. Troy has 4 stamps with presidents on them, 8 space stamps, and the rest are stamps of inventors. What fraction of the stamps are space stamps?

CALCULATOR

You can use your calculator to find a fraction of a number.

To find $\frac{2}{3}$ of 126

Divide by the denominator. Enter: [ON/AC] 126 [÷] 3 [=] 42

Multiply by the numerator. Enter: [ON/AC] 42 [×] 2 [=] 84

9. $\frac{3}{4}$ of 312 **10.** $\frac{7}{8}$ of 3,648 **11.** $\frac{2}{5}$ of 755

More Practice, page 509, set B

Mixed Numbers

LEARN ABOUT IT

EXPLORE **Analyze the Situation**

Jake planned a quilt using quilt pieces that were each one fourth of a whole block. Look at these quilt blocks and pieces. Describe what you see in two different ways.

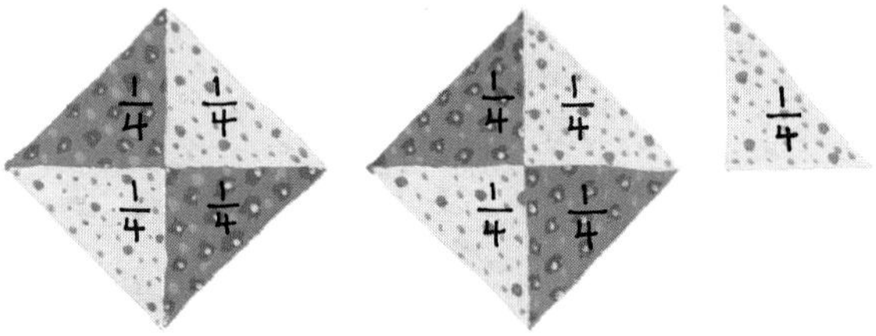

TALK ABOUT IT

1. How many fourths did Jake use?
2. How many whole quilt blocks did he make? How many fourths were left over?
3. Suppose Jake started with 15 fourths. How would you answer question 2?

Improper Fraction

$$\frac{9}{4} = 2\frac{1}{4}$$ **Mixed Number**

An improper fraction such as $\frac{9}{4}$ has a numerator greater than or equal to the denominator. You can write an improper fraction and a mixed number to describe Jake's quilt pieces.

$$\begin{array}{r} 2 \\ 4\overline{)9} \\ \underline{8} \\ 1 \end{array}$$

2 —**Number of wholes** → $2\frac{1}{4}$

1 —**Number of fourths** → $2\frac{1}{4}$

TRY IT OUT

Use fraction pieces to show the improper fraction. Write a mixed number for each fraction.

1. $\frac{5}{2}$ **2.** $\frac{6}{4}$ **3.** $\frac{7}{3}$ **4.** $\frac{8}{5}$ **5.** $\frac{12}{9}$

Write an improper fraction and a mixed number for each picture.

1. **2.** **3.**Write as a whole or mixed number. Draw pictures or use objects to help you.

4. $\frac{7}{3}$ **5.** $\frac{12}{2}$ **6.** $\frac{9}{4}$ **7.** $\frac{11}{5}$ **8.** $\frac{8}{6}$ **9.** $\frac{20}{5}$

MATH REASONING Match each statement with a reasonable number from the box.

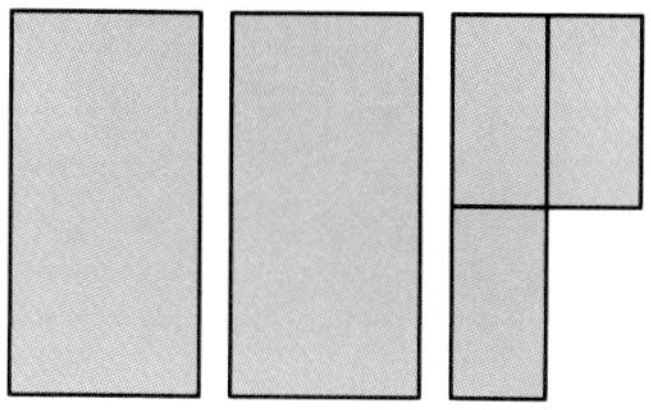

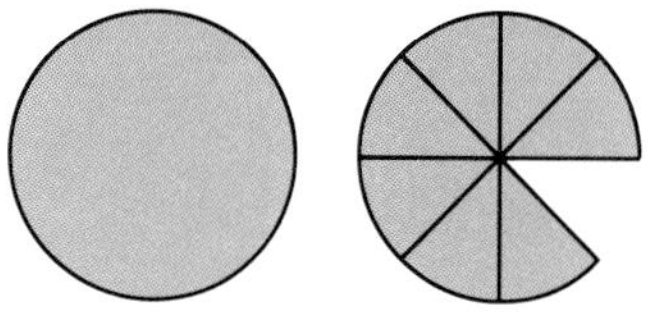

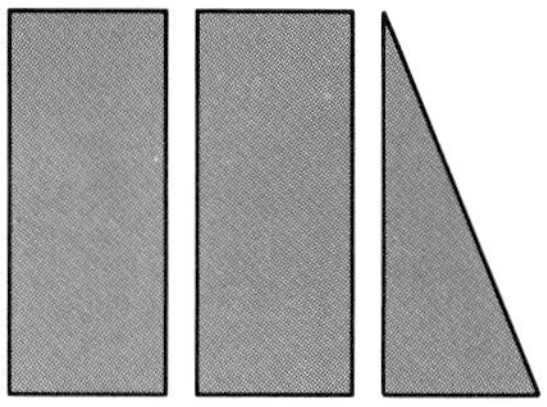

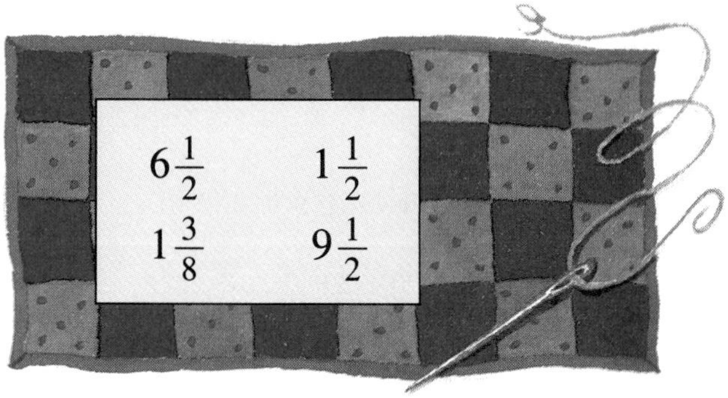

10. hours of school in a day

11. number of orange halves for a baseball team

12. age of a 4th grader

$$6\frac{1}{2} \qquad 1\frac{1}{2}$$
$$1\frac{3}{8} \qquad 9\frac{1}{2}$$

PROBLEM SOLVING

13. Tina used $3\frac{3}{8}$ yards of string to tie her quilt. Joe used $3\frac{1}{2}$ yards of string. Who used more string?

14. Each quilt tie takes $\frac{1}{8}$ yard of string. How many yards of string will Sue use if her quilt needs 36 ties?

MIXED REVIEW

Are these words symmetric? Write <u>yes</u> or <u>no</u>.

15. ALGEBRA **16.** HIDE **17.** BOOK **18.** CIDER

Draw a picture of each of these types of quadrilateral.

19. square **20.** parallelogram **21.** trapezoid **22.** rectangle

Problem Solving
Measuring to a Fractional Part of an Inch

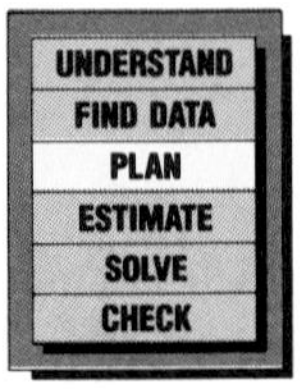

LEARN ABOUT IT

Sometimes you need to record a measurement to the nearest fractional part of an inch to get the data you need to solve a problem.

Reiko and Anita are making string bracelets. How long are their bracelets so far?

The length of Anita's bracelet to the nearest half inch is $2\frac{1}{2}$ inches.

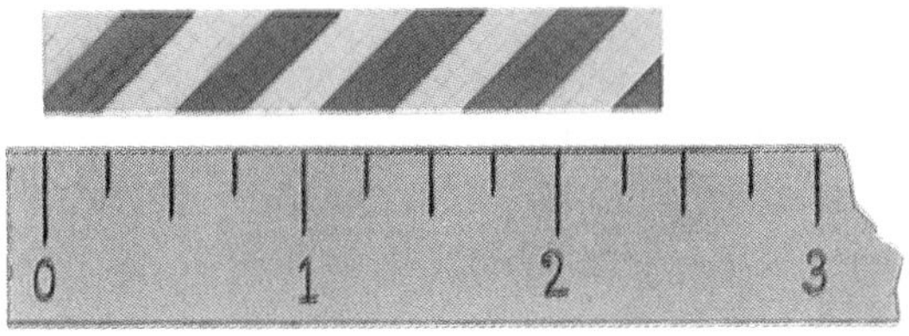

The length of Reiko's bracelet is $2\frac{1}{2}$ inches.

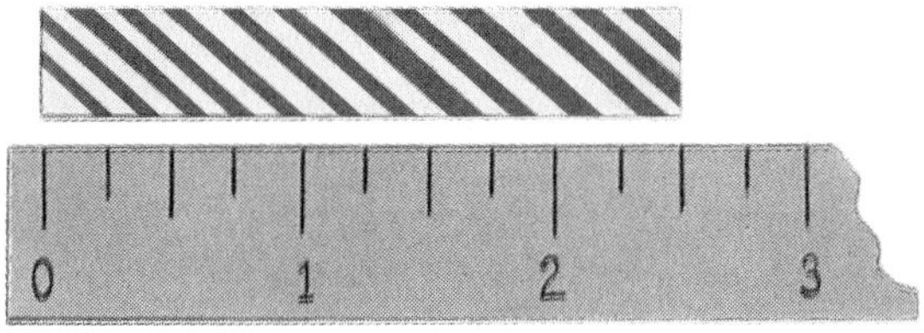

TRY IT OUT

Solve. Measure to the nearest $\frac{1}{2}$ inch to find the data needed.

1. Jane's finished lanyard is 8 inches long. Is Scott's lanyard so far more or less than $\frac{1}{4}$ the length of Jane's lanyard?

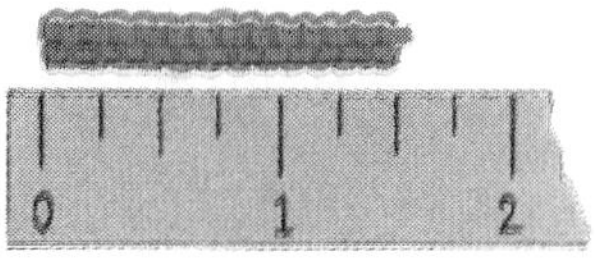

MIXED PRACTICE

Solve these problems. Use any problem solving strategy.

1. Sheryl wants to make a 6-inch long bracelet. Is she more or less than $\frac{1}{3}$ finished?

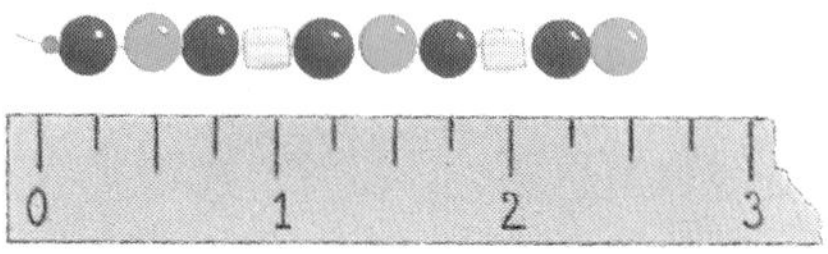

2. How many yellow beads will there be before the seventh red bead?

3. Sam made 24 bookmarks to sell. He's already sold $\frac{1}{3}$ of them. $\frac{3}{4}$ of them are made out of leather. How many did he sell?

4. Jana had some glass beads from the Bead Shop. She gave 13 to her sister Bella. Then she divided the rest into piles of 4 to make earrings. There were 5 piles. How many beads did Jana have in the beginning?

5. At Bob's Craft Supply, there are 23 different colors of yarn. Each ball costs $3.21 with tax. How much would it cost to get 2 balls of each color?

6. Roberto is making lanyard keychains as gifts. He needs 4 pieces of gimp for each keychain. He has cut 66 pieces of gimp. How many keychains can he make?

The fourth graders were planning what to make for their booth at the school holiday fair. They made a graph to show the results from the year before. Use their graph to answer these questions.

7. How much did the fourth graders earn the year before?

8. What fraction of their profits came from key chains?

9. How much money did they make selling both kinds of bracelets? What fraction of the profits was that?

Profits from School Fair

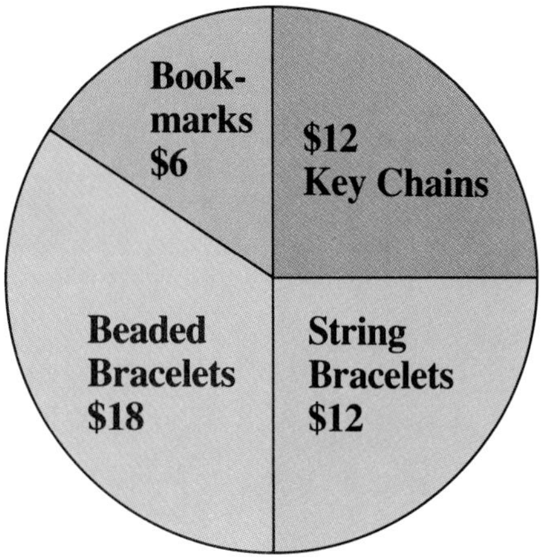

More Practice, page 524, set D

Data Collection and Analysis
Group Decision Making

UNDERSTAND
FIND DATA
PLAN
ESTIMATE
SOLVE
CHECK

Doing an Investigation

Group Skill:
Listen to Others

There are several different kinds of bike locks. Some open with keys and some have combinations. Some are chains and others are not. Predict what kind of bike lock is the most popular at your school. Conduct an investigation to find out.

Collecting Data

1. Discuss the kinds of bike locks students in your group have. Which is the most popular kind for your group?

2. Go to the bike rack at your school to find out what kinds of locks are on the bikes. Make a table to keep track of how many of each kind you find.

	combination lock	key lock
chain type	卌 III	I
not a chain type	卌 I	卌 卌 III

Organizing Data

3. Count how many locks you found in each category. Make a bar graph using this information.

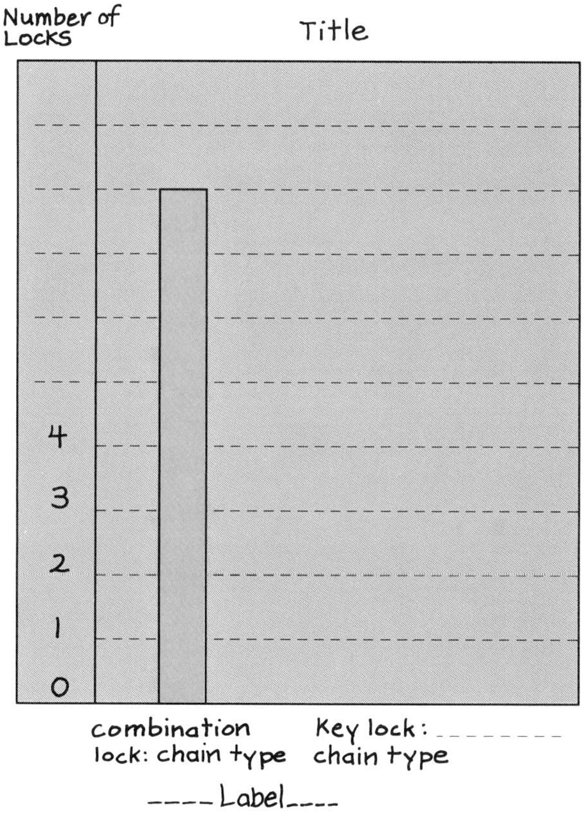

Presenting Your Analysis

4. Write a paragraph to tell what you found out. Were your predictions correct?

5. Give some reasons why you think one bike lock might be more popular than another.

Wrap Up

Fraction Match

Find a match.

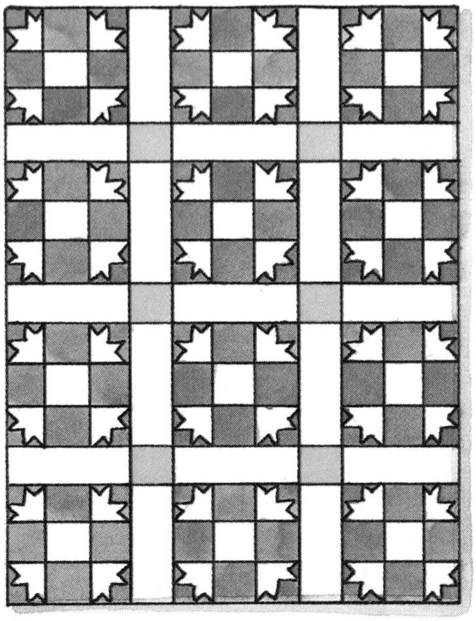

1. two tenths
2. a numerator of eight
3. a denominator of eight
4. a whole number
5. a mixed number
6. an improper fraction
7. a fraction equivalent to $\frac{1}{2}$
8. a fraction in lowest terms

a. $\frac{5}{4}$
b. 12
c. $\frac{7}{14}$
d. $\frac{2}{10}$
e. $\frac{6}{8}$
f. $3\frac{4}{6}$
g. $\frac{9}{13}$
h. $\frac{8}{14}$

Sometimes, Always, Never

Which word should go in the blank, sometimes, always, or never? Explain your choices.

9. Two equivalent fractions __?__ have the same nonzero numerator.
10. If the numerator and denominator are odd, the fraction is __?__ in lowest terms.
11. If the numerator and denominator are even, the fraction is __?__ in lowest terms.

Project

Don't let your eyes fool you! Each shape pictured is exactly $\frac{1}{4}$ of a square. Make 4 copies of each shape. Can you fit the pieces together to form a square?

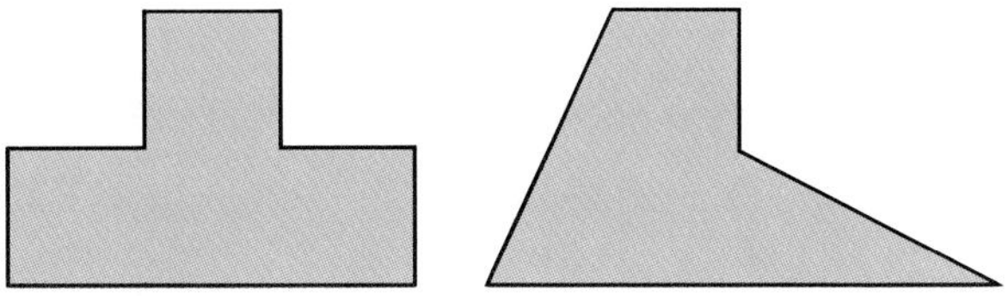

POWER PRACTICE/TEST

Part 1 Understanding

1. How much of this strip is red? blue? green? How much is not colored?

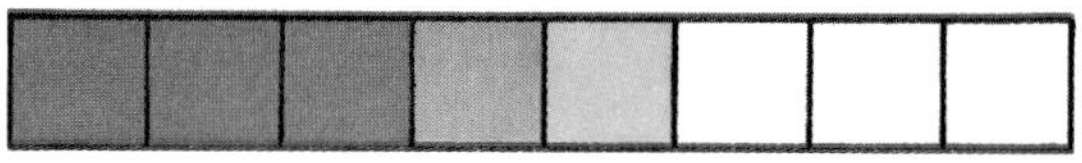

2. Write a fraction to tell what part of the group of triangles is red.

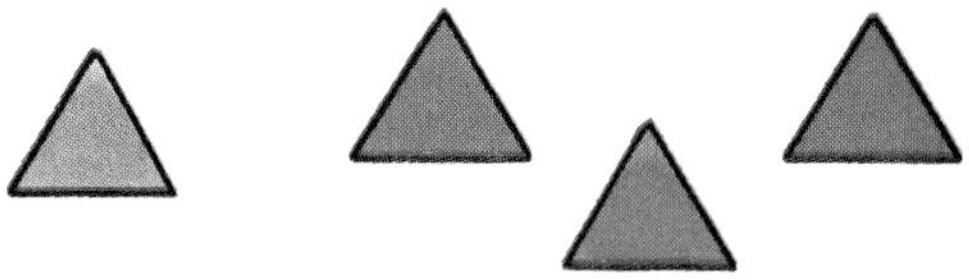

Part 2 Skills

Find the missing numbers for the equivalent fractions.

3. $\frac{1}{5} = \frac{3}{\square}$ **4.** $\frac{1}{4} = \frac{\square}{8}$ **5.** $\frac{4}{6} = \frac{\square}{24}$ **6.** $\frac{1}{2} = \frac{10}{\square}$

If possible, reduce to lowest terms.

7. $\frac{6}{18}$ **8.** $\frac{21}{24}$ **9.** $\frac{5}{25}$ **10.** $\frac{8}{10}$

Write $<$, $>$ or $=$.

11. $\frac{1}{3}$ |||| $\frac{1}{4}$ **12.** $\frac{3}{8}$ |||| $\frac{1}{2}$ **13.** $\frac{9}{16}$ |||| $\frac{18}{32}$ **14.** $\frac{5}{6}$ |||| $\frac{2}{3}$

Give the number.

15. $\frac{3}{4}$ of 20 **16.** $\frac{1}{6}$ of 30 **17.** $\frac{3}{8}$ of 24 **18.** $\frac{1}{2}$ of 40

Part 3 Applications

19. Sonya served melon quarters to 9 people. Give a mixed number for the amount of melon Sonya served.

20. Paul cut a honeydew into 6 pieces. He ate half the melon and his sister ate a third. How much is left?

21. Ray is 9 years and 10 months old. Express his age in years as a mixed number reduced to lowest terms.

22. **Challenge** Doug has 8 coins. $\frac{1}{2}$ are quarters, $\frac{1}{4}$ are dimes, $\frac{1}{8}$ are pennies, and the rest are nickels. How much money is this?

ENRICHMENT
Patterns of Equivalent Fractions

Use your centimeter ruler to make 6 cardboard strips, each 12 cm long.

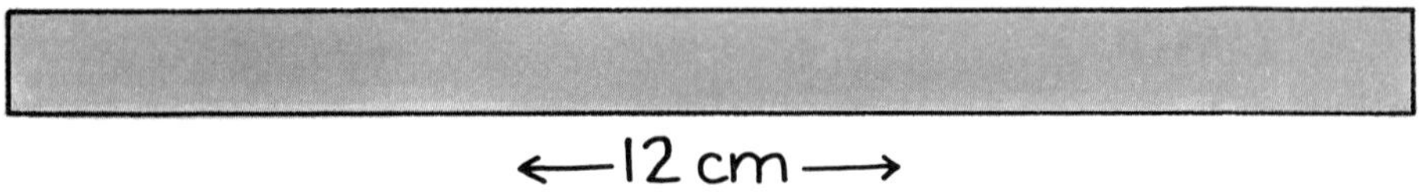

Here is how to use your ruler to make a fraction strip showing halves.

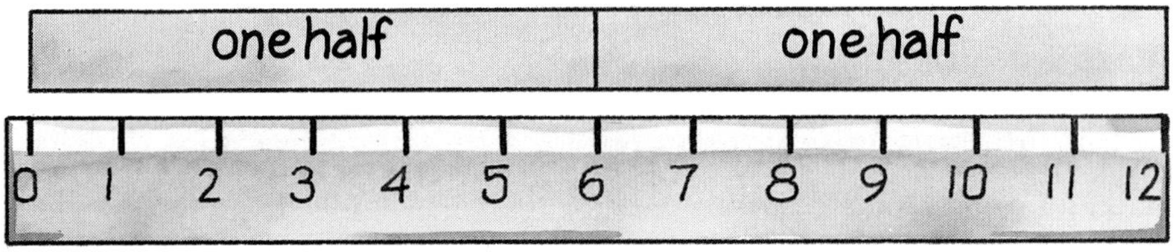

Make fraction strips showing halves, thirds, fourths, sixths, and twelfths.

Now lay strips together and cover part of them with a sheet of paper as shown.

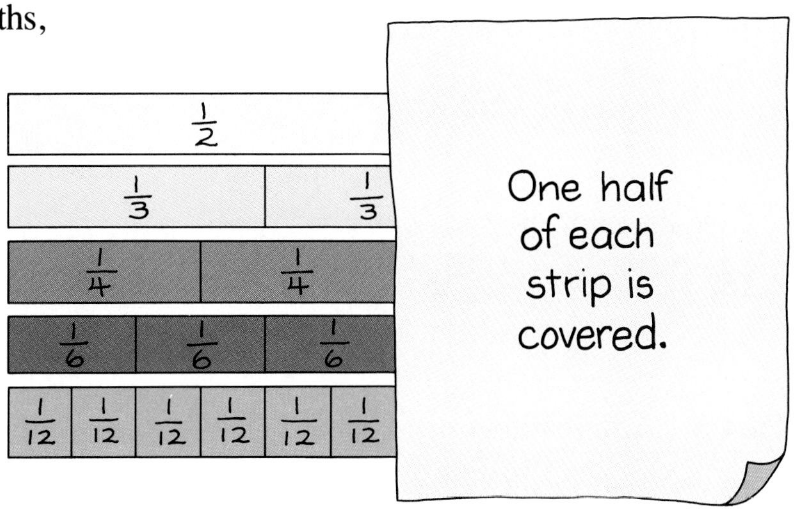

1. What pattern of equivalent fractions do you see in the part of the strips uncovered? Make a list of these fractions.

2. Move the paper so that the following parts of the strips are covered. List the patterns of equivalent fractions that are shown.

   a. $\frac{2}{3}$ b. $\frac{1}{4}$ c. $\frac{2}{6}$

Cumulative Review

1. $4\overline{)20}$

   A 6 B 4

   C 5 D 3

2. $7\overline{)56}$

   A 6 B 8

   C 7 D 9

3. $3\overline{)21}$

   A 5 B 6

   C 7 D 8

4. $4\overline{)93}$

   A 20 R3 B 24 R3

   C 23 D 23 R1

5. What is 860 divided by 3?

   A 293 R1 B 286 R2

   C 287 R1 D 353 R1

6. $5\overline{)\$7.85}$

   A \$1.55 B \$157

   C \$1.59 D \$1.57

7. Which of these things suggests a triangular prism?

   A ball B flag

   C roof D TV set

8. A space figure with no vertices is the ____.

   A pyramid B sphere

   C cone D rectangular prism

9. What kind of triangle is this?

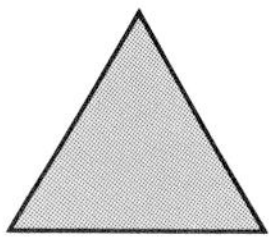

   A right B equilateral

   C scalene D obtuse

10. These two lines are ____.

   A intersecting B equilateral

   C perpendicular D parallel

11. How many different lines of symmetry can you draw for one square?

   A 0 B 2

   C 8 D 4

12. A quadrilateral that has exactly one pair of parallel sides is a ____.

   A trapezoid B rectangle

   C tangram D right angle

13

DECIMAL CONCEPTS

THEME: WINTER OLYMPICS

MATH AND HEALTH AND FITNESS

DATA BANK

Use the Health and Fitness Data Bank on page 482 to answer the questions.

1 A decade is 10 years. How many decades have passed since the first Winter Olympic Games were held?

2 What fraction of the winners of the Men's Slalom medals in 1984 and 1988 were from the United States?

3 What fraction of the winners of the Women's 500-Meter Speed Skating in the last 5 Olympics were from the United States?

4 **Use Critical Thinking** Do you think a course with 58 gates could be used for both a men's and a women's race? Support your conclusion.

Speed skaters from many different countries compete for gold, silver, and bronze medals in the Olympic Games.

Reading and Writing Decimals
Tenths

LEARN ABOUT IT

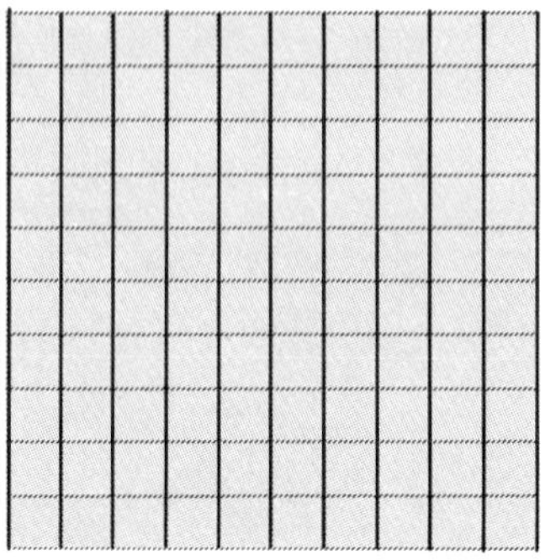

EXPLORE **Discover a Relationship**
Use graph paper and mark off three 10 by 10 squares. Divide your squares into 10 parts, like the square shown. In each square, color some of the 10 parts.

TALK ABOUT IT

1. What fraction of each square is colored?
2. What fraction of each square is not colored?
3. If you colored 10 tenths, how would you write it as a fraction? as a whole number?

A fraction or a mixed number that uses tenths can easily be written as a decimal.

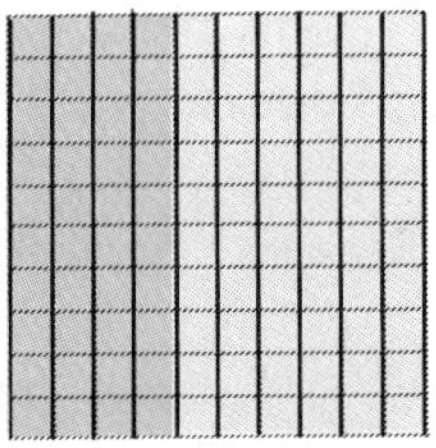

	Say	Write fraction	decimal
blue part	"four tenths"	$\frac{4}{10}$	0.4
yellow part	"six tenths"	$\frac{6}{10}$	0.6

decimal point

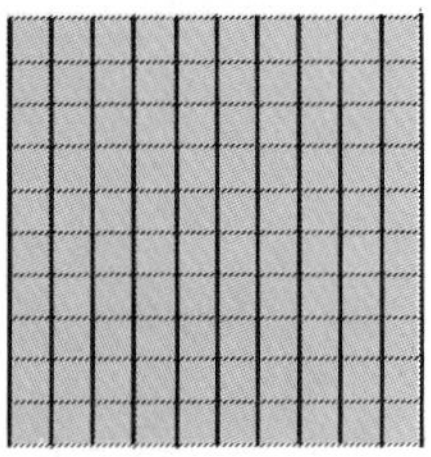

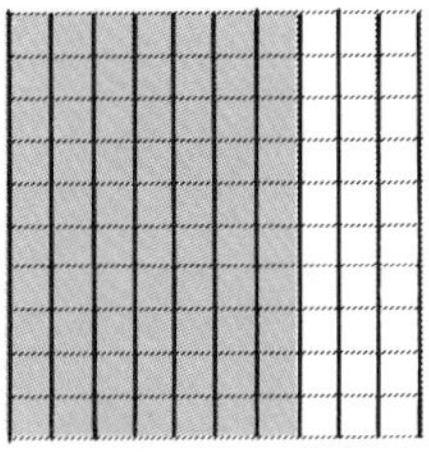

mixed number	decimal
$1\frac{7}{10}$	1.7

TRY IT OUT

Write the fraction for the colored part. Then write the decimal.

1. 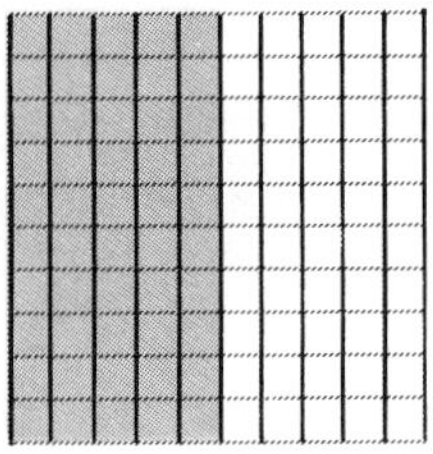

2. 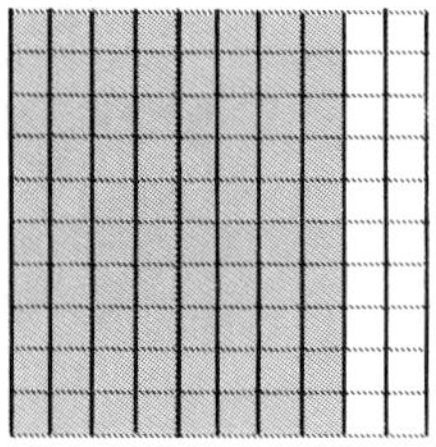

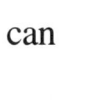

PRACTICE

Write the fraction and the decimal for the colored part.

1. green
2. yellow

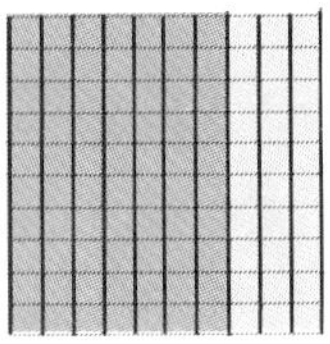

3. orange
4. white

Write a decimal for the amount.

5. one and nine tenths

6. twenty-one and three tenths

APPLY

MATH REASONING Give the numbers from the list in which the digit 3 has these values.

28.3	3.4	39.5
83.1	34.2	46.3

7. 30 **8.** 3 **9.** 0.3

PROBLEM SOLVING

10. Louann colored these 3 squares. If she had colored 2 more tenths what decimal would she have shown? if she had colored 2 less tenths?

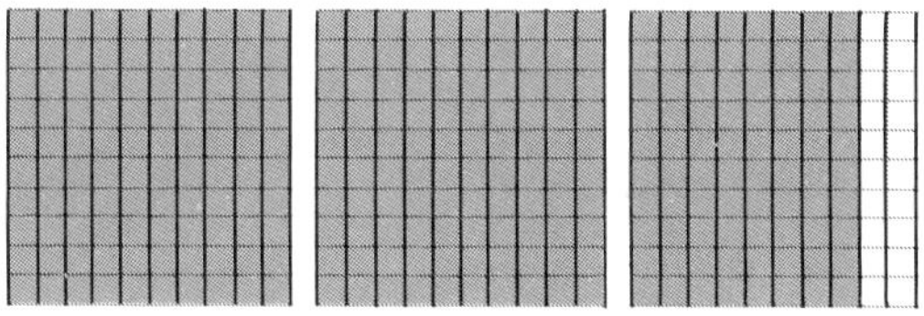

USING CRITICAL THINKING Analyze the Data

Which of the following statements is true about the distance walked by each student?

11. Some students might have walked more than 1.5 miles.
12. Some students might have walked 1.5 miles.
13. Some students might have walked less than 1.5 miles.

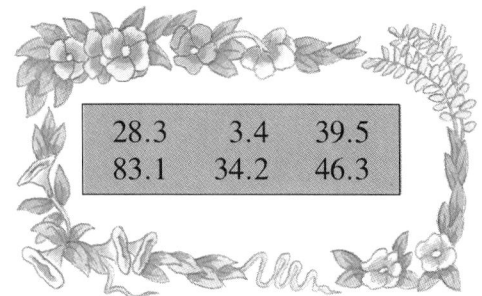

MARSHALL SCHOOL WALKATHON A SUCCESS
ALL STUDENTS WALKED AT LEAST 1.5 MILES

Reading and Writing Decimals
Hundredths

LEARN ABOUT IT

EXPLORE **Use Graph Paper**

To measure small amounts, you sometimes need to use a unit smaller than one tenth. Draw five 10 by 10 squares on graph paper. In each 10 by 10 square color in a different number of ones units.

TALK ABOUT IT

1. How many ones units are in each 10 by 10 square?
2. For each of your five squares, how many parts out of 100 are colored? How many are not colored?

Show	**Say**	**Write**	
		fraction	decimal
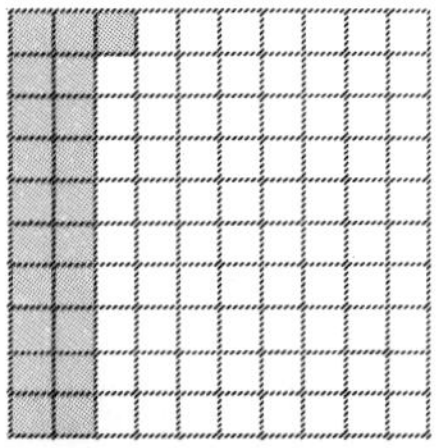	"twenty-one hundredths"	$\frac{21}{100}$	0.21
		mixed number	decimal
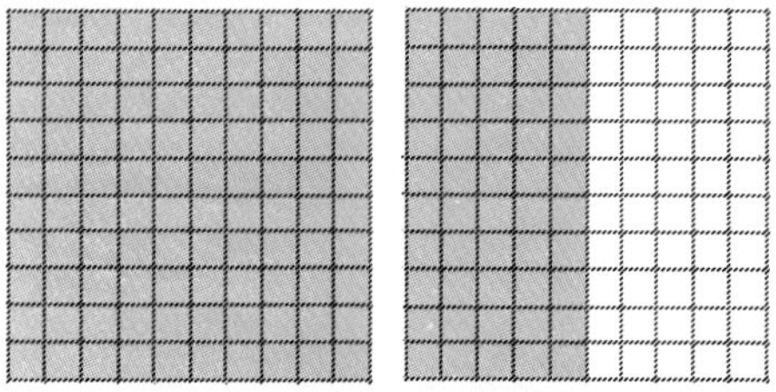	"one and five tenths" or "one and fifty hundredths"	$1\frac{5}{10}$ $1\frac{50}{100}$	1.5 or 1.50

Tens	Ones	Tenths	Hundredths
3	1 .	2	8

To find the value of a digit in a decimal number, think about its place. A decimal point always separates the ones place from the tenths place.

TRY IT OUT

Write a fraction or mixed number and a decimal to tell how much is colored.

1. 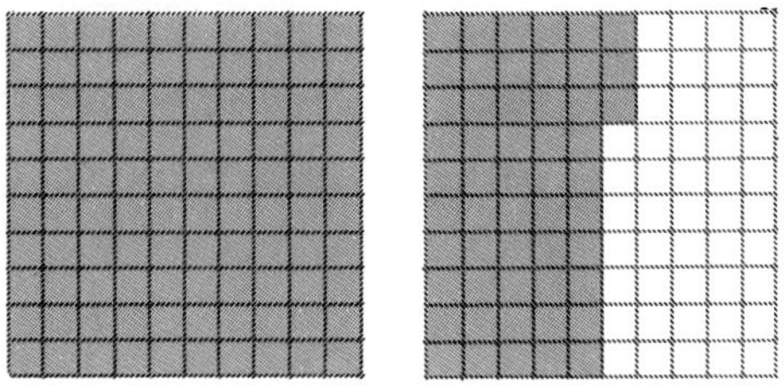

PRACTICE

Write a fraction or mixed number and a decimal to tell how much is colored.

1. 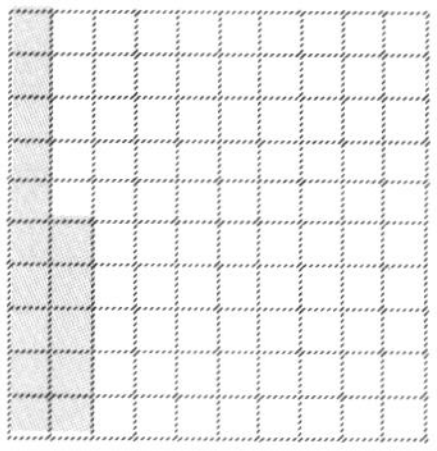

2. 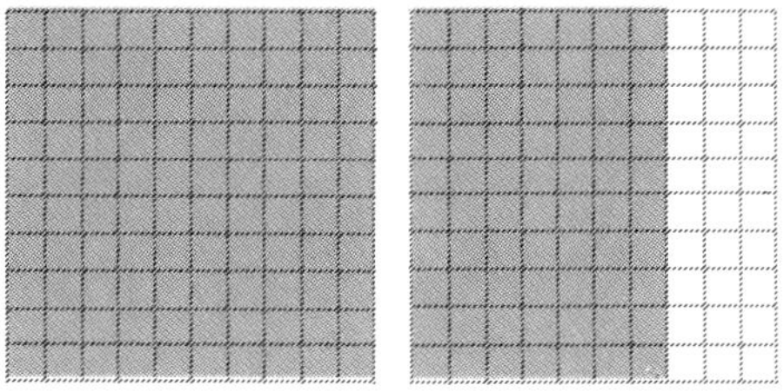

3. 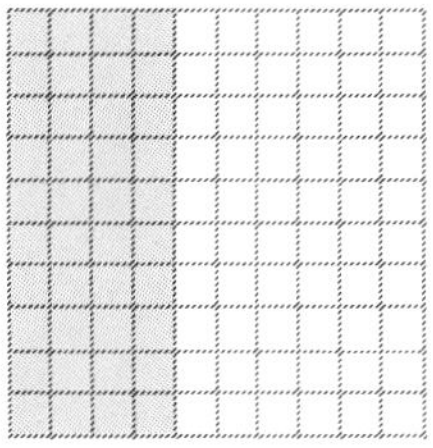

Write a decimal for each.

4. two and three hundredths

5. sixty-two hundredths

Write a word for each.

6. 1.18

7. 4.50

APPLY

MATH REASONING Give the numbers from the list in which the digit 7 has these values.

7.32	0.47	1.74
5.7	2.07	3.87

8. 7 **9.** 0.7 **10.** 0.07

PROBLEM SOLVING

DATA BANK

11. **Health and Fitness Data Bank** In which Olympic times for the 1980 and 1984 Men's Slalom does the digit 6 have a value of 0.6? In which times does the digit 6 have a value of 0.06? See page 482.

CALCULATOR

Change the number by adding or subtracting just once. Only one digit changes. Tell what you did to make each change.

12. Change 2.43 to 2.03.

13. Change 10.35 to 10.4.

14. Change 4.65 to 4.6

15. Change 7.10 to 8.

16. Change 34.68 to 4.68.

17. Change 1.65 to 1.6.

More Practice, page 525, set A

Decimals
Counting and Order

LEARN ABOUT IT

EXPLORE Use a Calculator

Use a calculator to count by tenths and then by hundredths. Try to guess the next decimal on the display before you press [=] each time.

[ON/AC] 0 [+] 0.1 [=] [=] [=]

Keep pressing the [=] key.

[ON/AC] 0 [+] 0.01 [=] [=] [=]

Keep pressing the [=] key.

TALK ABOUT IT

1. When you count by tenths, what decimal comes after 0.9? 1.9? 2.9? What decimal comes before 3.7? 4.2? 5?
2. When you count by hundredths, what decimal comes after 0.09? 0.19? 0.29? 0.99? What pattern do you see?

PRACTICE

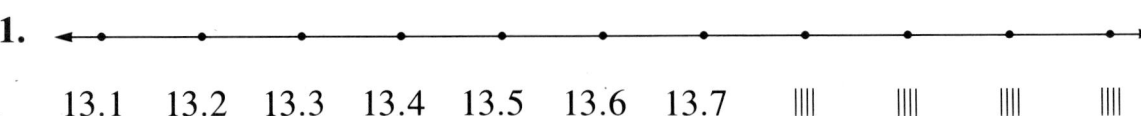

Give the next four decimals in the counting pattern.

1. 13.1 13.2 13.3 13.4 13.5 13.6 13.7 ____ ____ ____ ____

Write the decimal that comes after each number when you count by hundredths.

2. 8.34 **3.** 9.9 **4.** 7.43 **5.** 8.89 **6.** 8.99

Write the decimal that comes before each number when you count by hundredths.

7. 0.77 **8.** 1.5 **9.** 17.11 **10.** 35.4 **11.** 99.91

Write the decimal that comes between each pair of numbers when you count by hundredths.

12. 1.47 and 1.49 **13.** 3.4 and 3.42 **14.** 5.05 and 5.07

More Practice, page 525, set B

Power Practice/Quiz

Write a fraction and a decimal for the colored part.

1. red
2. blue

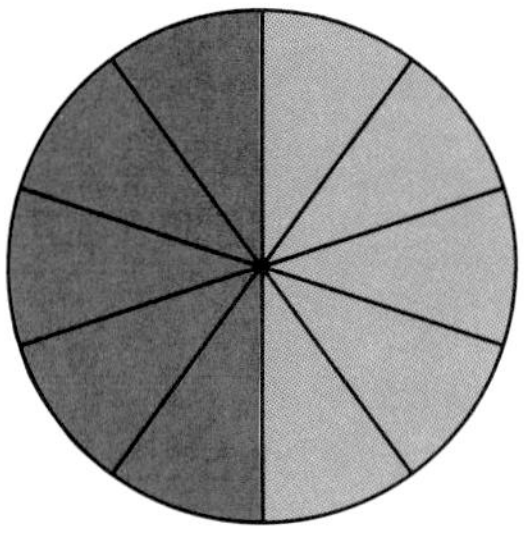

3. green
4. yellow

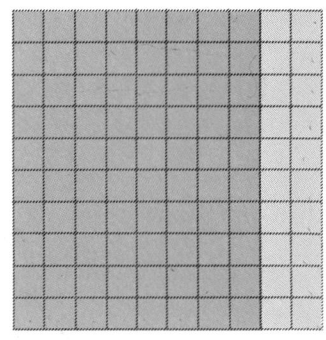

Write a fraction or mixed number and a decimal for the colored part.

5.

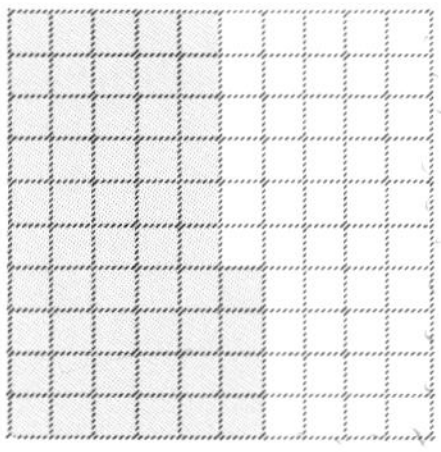

6.

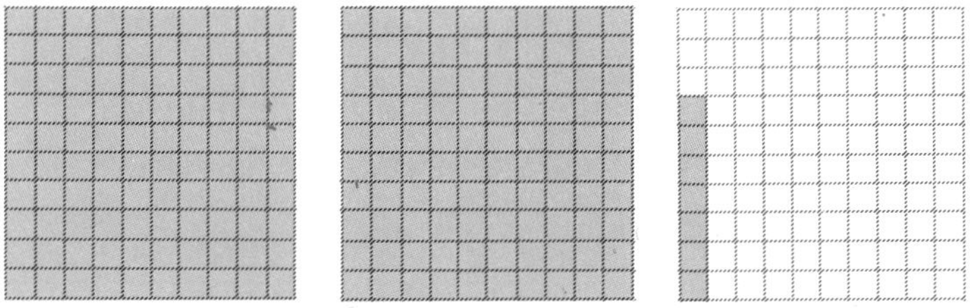

Write a decimal for the amount.

7. fifteen and seven tenths

8. ten and one tenth

Find the numbers in the list for which 5 has the value given.

9. 0.5

10. 50

11. 5

12. 0.05

6.35	53.41	125	74.5
65.8	0.95	9.57	256.9

PROBLEM SOLVING

13. Holly made up this puzzle problem. Can you solve it?
    The tenths digit of a 2-digit decimal number is 3 more than twice the ones digit. The ones digit is 2. What is the decimal number?

14. Rick painted 0.3 of this wall. Later he painted another 0.4. What decimal shows the amount of the wall Rick painted?

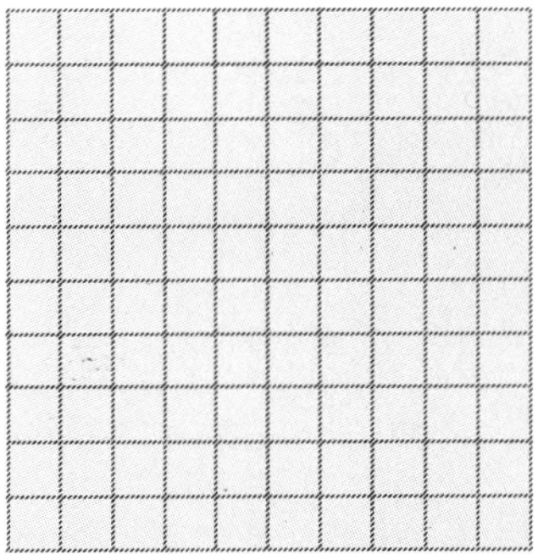

Comparing and Ordering Decimals

LEARN ABOUT IT

EXPLORE **Use Ones Blocks**

Larry measured how far he rode his bicycle each day. You can compare the distances by showing them with ones blocks. Each block counts for one tenth of a mile. These blocks show Monday's distance. Use blocks to show the other distances.

Larry's Riding Distances	
Monday	2.8 miles
Tuesday	2.1 miles
Wednesday	2.5 miles
Thursday	3 miles

Monday 2.8 miles

TALK ABOUT IT

1. Did Larry ride farther on Monday or Tuesday?
2. How can you list the distances in order from longest to shortest?

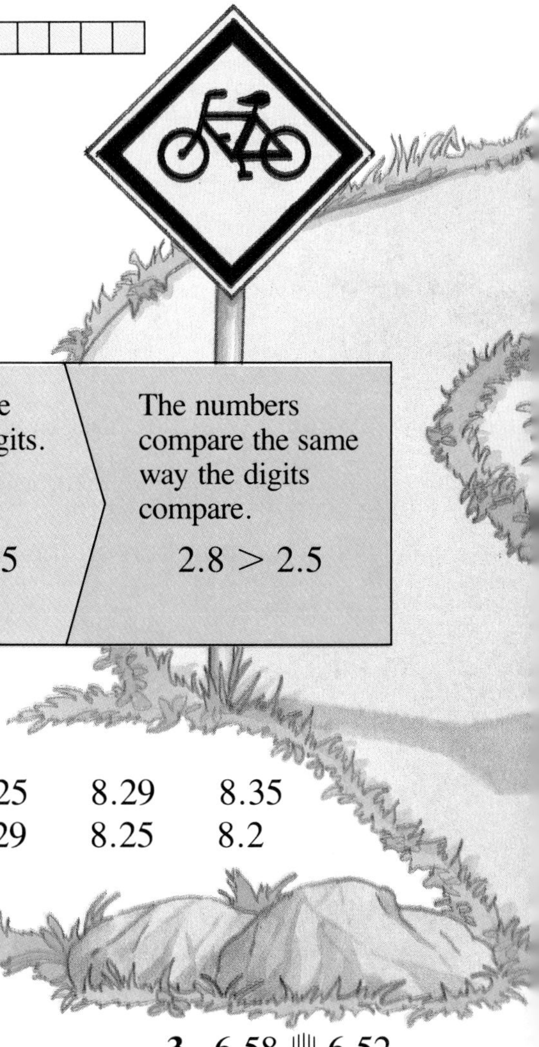

Here is another way to compare decimals.

Line up the decimal points.	Start at the left. Find the first place where the digits are different.	Compare these digits.	The numbers compare the same way the digits compare.
2.8 2.5	2.**8** 2.**5**	8 > 5	2.8 > 2.5

To order decimals such as 8.25, 8.2, 8.35, 8.29, compare the numbers two at a time.

List the numbers from least to greatest	8.2	8.25	8.29	8.35
or greatest to least.	8.35	8.29	8.25	8.2

TRY IT OUT

Write >, <, or = for each ▯.

1. 4.6 ▯ 5.3 **2.** 18.7 ▯ 18.3 **3.** 6.58 ▯ 6.52

4. Order these decimals from least to greatest. 3.45 3.54 3.49 3.52

PRACTICE

Decide whether each statement is true or false. If it is false, change the <, >, or = sign to make it true.

1. 4.38 < 4.42 **2.** 9.6 > 9.58 **3.** 8.3 = 8.03

4. 7.46 > 7.54 **5.** 0.5 > 0.51 **6.** 1.8 > 1.73

7. Order these numbers from greatest to least. 0.37, 0.41, 0.39

Use the number list to complete these exercises.

8. List the numbers greater than 8.5.

9. List the numbers less than 4.91.

10. List the numbers between 4.83 and 7.01.

11. Order the numbers between 4 and 8 from least to greatest.

8.73	3.2
8.49	7
4.9	4.38
7.1	8.05

APPLY

MATH REASONING

12. Use these digits to fit in the empty boxes. How many different decimals can you make greater than 25? What are they?

1 5 0 3

□□.□□

PROBLEM SOLVING

13. Larry's sister, Rhonda, also kept a record of her riding distances for the same days. On which days did Rhonda ride a shorter distance than Larry? Use the table on page 364.

Rhonda's Riding Distances	
Monday	2.6 miles
Tuesday	2.5 miles
Wednesday	2.8 miles
Thursday	2.9 miles

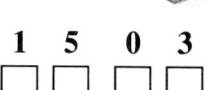

▶ MENTAL MATH Counting On

Use mental math and count on by tenths to find these sums.

14. 1.3 + 0.1 **15.** 3.4 + 0.2

16. 5.2 + 0.3 **17.** 2.7 + 0.3

More Practice, page 509, Set D

Rounding Decimals

LEARN ABOUT IT

EXPLORE **Study the Data**

Bill said that Dana and Seth each finished the race in 53 seconds.

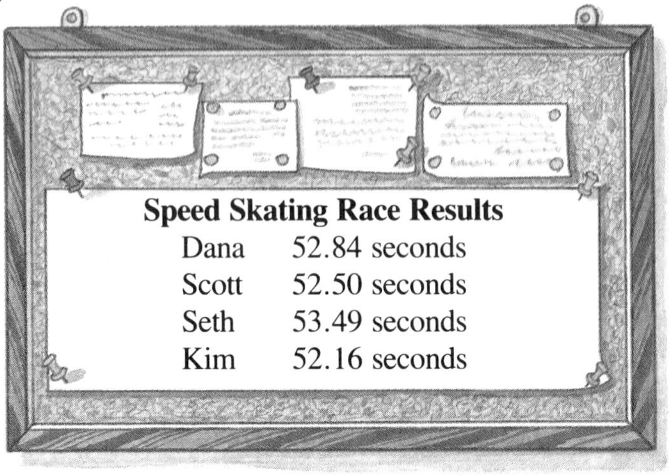

Speed Skating Race Results

Dana	52.84 seconds
Scott	52.50 seconds
Seth	53.49 seconds
Kim	52.16 seconds

TALK ABOUT IT

1. Were Dana's and Seth's race times the same? Explain.
2. Why do you think Bill used 53 seconds to describe their race times?
3. What whole numbers might Bill use to describe Kim's and Scott's finishing times? Explain why.

- Look at the digit in the tenths place. — 52.16
- Round up to the next whole number if the digit is 5 or more. Round down to the next whole number if the digit is less than 5. — 1 is less than 5, so 52.16 rounds to 52.

You can use a number line to be sure you have rounded correctly.

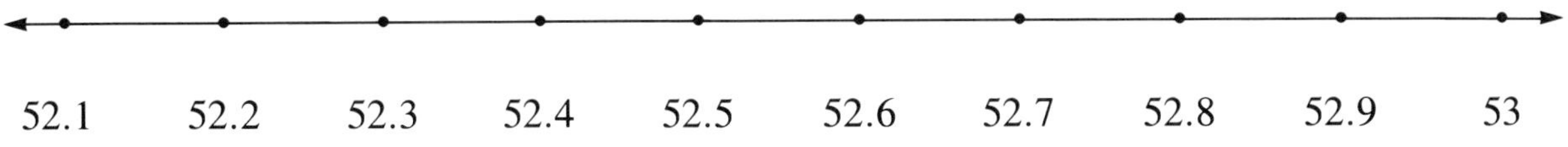

52.16 rounds to 52 52.50 rounds to 53 52.84 rounds to 53

TRY IT OUT

Round each number to the nearest whole number.

1. 3.8 **2.** 9.2 **3.** 75.8 **4.** 14.1 **5.** 92.5 **6.** 0.6

7. 25.11 **8.** 2.55 **9.** 46.35 **10.** 39.10 **11.** 99.99 **12.** 9.49

PRACTICE

Round each decimal to the nearest whole number.

1. 2.9	**2.** 4.8	**3.** 7.2	**4.** 3.7	**5.** 0.5
6. 18.3	**7.** 11.4	**8.** 46.5	**9.** 39.6	**10.** 49.8
11. 3.72	**12.** 4.88	**13.** 9.14	**14.** 5.63	**15.** 6.97
16. 17.83	**17.** 26.26	**18.** 81.17	**19.** 49.65	**20.** 99.50

21. Which numbers in the box round to 24 when rounded to the nearest whole number?

24.8	23.75	25.25
23.26	24.50	24.05
25.6	23.49	23.99

APPLY

MATH REASONING

22. Write 3 decimals that round to 5.

23. Write 3 decimals that round to 10.

24. Write 3 decimals that round to 50.

PROBLEM SOLVING

25. The men's World Speed Skating record for 500 meters is 38.00 seconds. The women's record is 41.80 seconds. Round to the nearest whole number to estimate the difference in the records.

26. **Health and Fitness Data Bank** Round to the nearest whole number to estimate the difference between Karen Enke's and Bonnie Blair's winning times. See page 482.

MIXED REVIEW

Use the list at the right to identify each figure.

cube
cone
sphere
cylinder
pyramid
rectangular prism

27. fish tank **28.** globe **29.** roll of paper

30. a volcano **31.** an orange

Decimals and Fractions

LEARN ABOUT IT

EXPLORE **Use Graph Paper**

You can find a decimal for a fraction. Cut four large 10 by 10 squares from graph paper. Fold and color a square to show each of these fractions.

$\frac{1}{4}$ $\frac{2}{4}$ $\frac{3}{4}$ $\frac{1}{2}$

Think about how a decimal could describe each colored part.

TALK ABOUT IT

1. How many small squares did you color for each fourth?

2. What decimal would you write for

$\frac{1}{4}$? $\frac{2}{4}$? $\frac{3}{4}$? $\frac{1}{2}$?

Each small square is a hundredth.

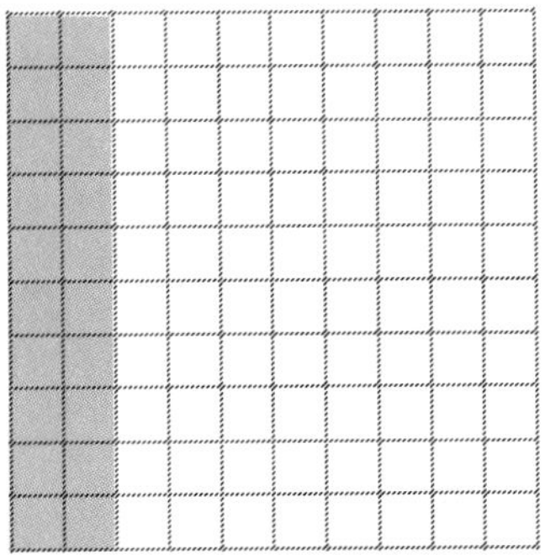

$\frac{1}{5}$ **0.20**

To use a 10×10 square to find a decimal for a fraction, first color the square to show the fraction. To find the decimal, count how many hundredth squares have been colored.

You can also use a calculator to find a decimal for a fraction. Since one meaning for $\frac{1}{4}$ is $1 \div 4$, use this keycode.

[ON/AC] 1 [÷] 4 [=]

TRY IT OUT

Count small squares and write a decimal for each fraction. Check with your calculator.

1.

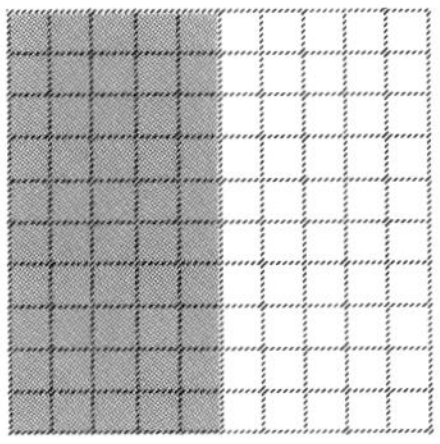

$\frac{1}{2}$

2.

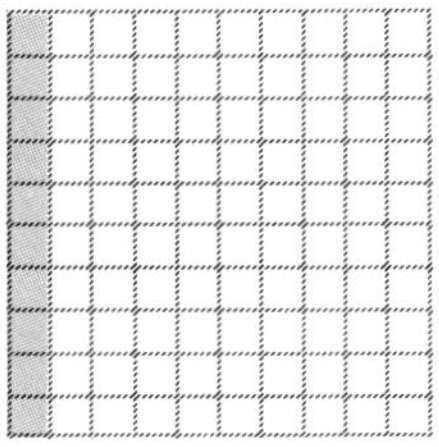

$\frac{1}{10}$

3. Use your calculator to find a decimal for $\frac{2}{8}$.

PRACTICE

Count small squares and write a decimal for each fraction. Check with your calculator.

1. $\frac{1}{4}$

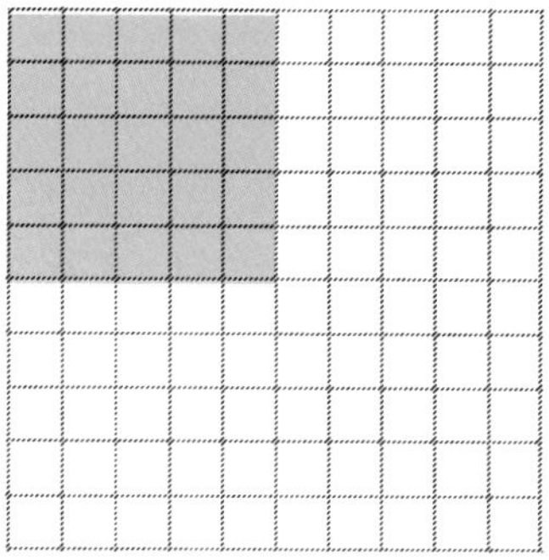

2. $\frac{3}{10}$

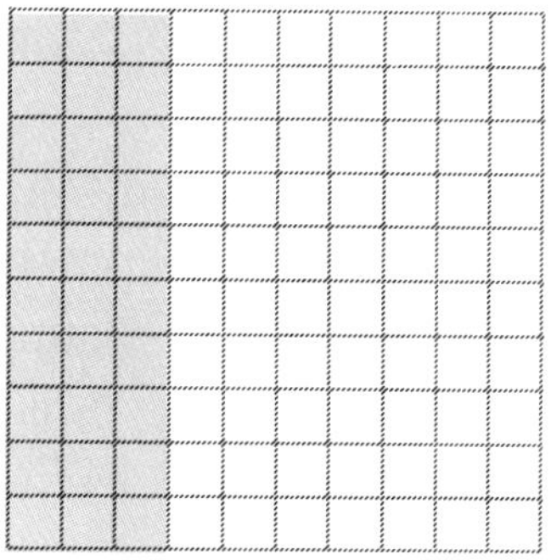

3. $\frac{4}{5}$

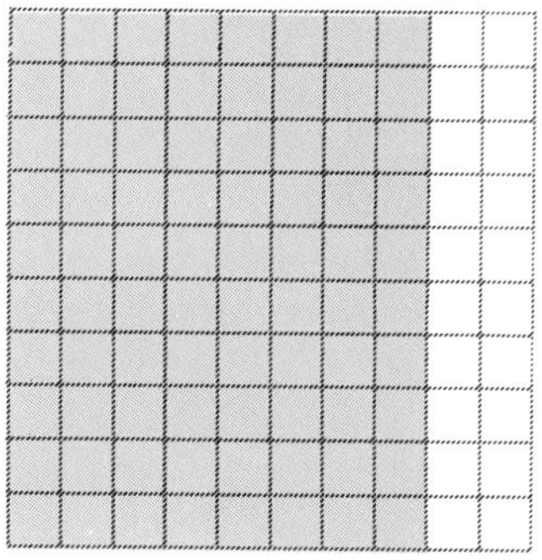

Use your calculator to find a decimal for these fractions.

4. $\frac{3}{5}$ **5.** $\frac{3}{4}$ **6.** $\frac{4}{8}$ **7.** $\frac{9}{10}$

APPLY

MATH REASONING Give the missing decimals.

8. If $\frac{2}{5} = 0.40$, then $\frac{4}{5} =$ ||||.

9. If $\frac{1}{4} = 0.25$, then $\frac{2}{4} =$ ||||.

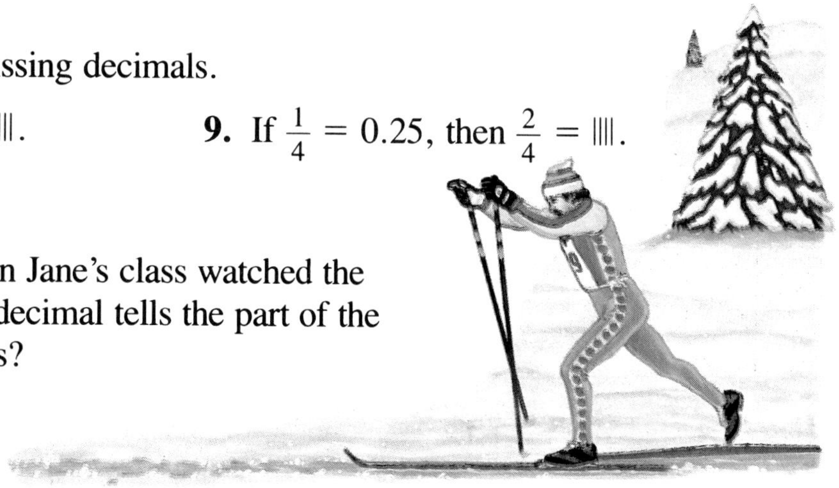

PROBLEM SOLVING

10. Ten out of 20 students in Jane's class watched the Olympic games. What decimal tells the part of the class that saw the games?

MIXED REVIEW

Tell if the angle is obtuse, acute, or right.

11. more than 90° **12.** 20° **13.** 134° **14.** 100° **15.** 90°

Write <u>yes</u> if the fractions are equivalent. Write <u>no</u> if they are not.

16. $\frac{2}{3}$ and $\frac{3}{6}$ **17.** $\frac{4}{5}$ and $\frac{16}{20}$ **18.** $\frac{4}{8}$ and $\frac{1}{2}$

19. $\frac{3}{10}$ and $\frac{2}{5}$ **20.** $\frac{3}{4}$ and $\frac{9}{12}$ **21.** $\frac{5}{6}$ and $\frac{4}{5}$

More Practice Bank, page 509, set F

Problem Solving
Determining Reasonable Answers

LEARN ABOUT IT

When you solve a problem, the last step is to check your work. You can ask yourself some questions.

- Is my arithmetic correct?
- Did I use the strategy correctly?
- Is my answer reasonable?

Malia needed 11 gallons of paint to paint her room bright pink. The paint cost $3.99 a gallon. How much did she pay for the paint?
Malia's answer: 78.29

To see if the answer is reasonable, I can use estimation.

I can round numbers and multiply.

$3.99 is about $4.
11 gallons is close to 10 gallons.

$\$4 \times 10 = \$40$

$78.29 is too high.

Malia's answer doesn't seem reasonable.

PRACTICE

Do not solve the problems. Decide if the answers are reasonable. If an answer is not reasonable, explain why.

1. Jesse paid $25.50 for 6 posters of cars. How much did each poster cost?

Jesse's answer:

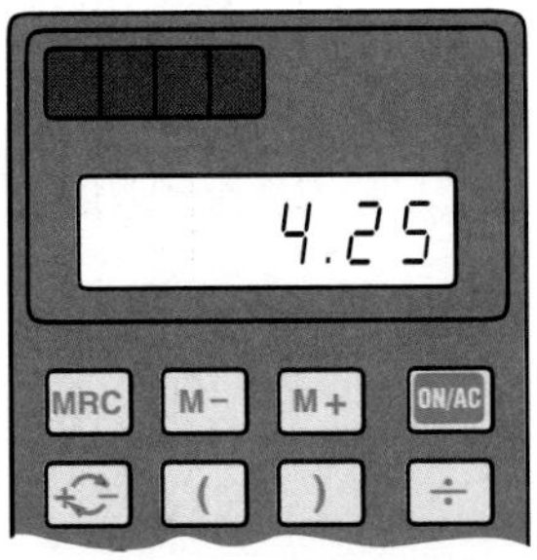

2. Willie is thinking of putting tiles in his room. He will need 125 tiles. Tiles cost a quarter each. How much would it cost to tile his room?

Willie's answer:

MIXED PRACTICE

Choose a strategy from the strategies list to solve these problems.

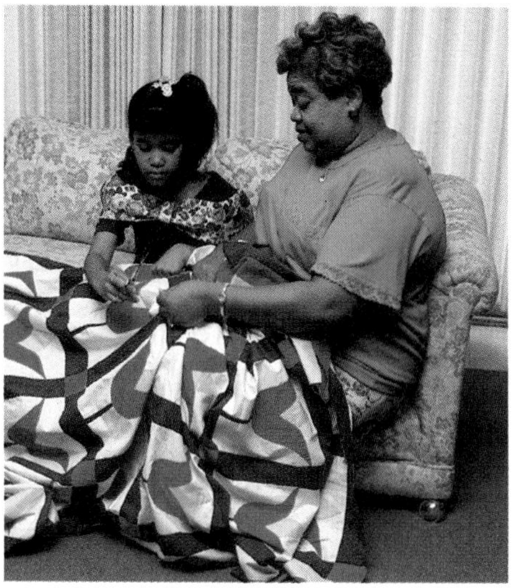

1. Rachel's mom bought Rachel a used TV for her room. It cost $126, and she paid it off in 9 months. How much did she pay each month?

2. It cost Sang-Ho $31 to mount 2 movie posters on cardboard. Mounting the large adventure poster cost $7 more than the comedy poster. How much did the comedy poster cost to mount?

3. Juan's aunt bought him a new study set:

desk	$49.49
chair	$69.95
computer table	$115.98
lamp	$46.58

She paid the bill off in 6 months. How much did she pay per month?

Some Strategies
Act It Out
Use Objects
Choose an Operation
Draw a Picture
Make an Organized List
Guess and Check
Make a Table
Look for a Pattern
Use Logical Reasoning
Work Backward

4. Mrs. Chung bought 12 rolls of wallpaper at $11.95 each. How much did the wallpaper cost?

5. Marla's grandmother made a quilt for her room. How many of this type of square were in the quilt?

6. The temperature in Bob's room in the garage was 50.6°F one night. His dad agreed to use $59.95 of the month's house budget to buy a space heater. Now there is $110.57 left in the budget. How much is the monthly house budget?

7. Masato had saved $25. She bought a wall hanging for her room with half of her money. How much did the wall hanging cost?

Applied Problem Solving
Group Decision Making

UNDERSTAND
FIND DATA
PLAN
ESTIMATE
SOLVE
CHECK

Group Skill:
Disagree in an Agreeable Way

You are a reporter for Children's Choice magazine. You need to look over some information on the four top children's cameras. Your job is to choose the best camera for kids to buy.

Facts to Consider

1. The photos taken with the cameras are of the same quality.
2. Some facts about the cameras are more important than others.
3. The camera you recommend should be the best in the important categories.
4. This is what you found out about the cameras.

Some Questions to Answer

1. Which is the best buy when you consider only the price? List the cameras from least expensive to most expensive.
2. Which cameras have the best film price?
3. Which cameras use the cheapest batteries?
4. Do you think a lighter or heavier camera would be better? How important is this fact?
5. Can you think of a way to organize your data to make a decision? Hint: you could start by assigning the numbers 1, 2, 3, and 4 in each category to show best to worst.

Name of Camera	Price	Film Price	Battery Price	Weight	Built-in Flash?	Automatic Rewind?
Kidcam	$56	$3.89	$5.00	12 oz	yes	yes
Wonder	$78	$4.39	$4.25	11 oz	yes	yes
Wizard	$58	$4.39	$4.25	9 oz	yes	no
Topper	$50	$3.89	$5.00	10 oz	no	yes

What Is Your Decision?

Which camera did you decide was the best? Explain your decision.

Wrap Up

Decimal Points

Choose the word or words that complete each sentence correctly.

decimal point
right
left
tenths
fraction
less
comma
mixed number

1. Fractions in __?__ can be written easily as decimals.
2. In a decimal, a __?__ separates the ones and tenths places.
3. The decimal 2.7 is equivalent to the __?__ $2\frac{7}{10}$.
4. In a place value chart, the hundredths place is to the __?__ of the tenths place.
5. The decimal 3.98 is a little __?__ than 4.

Sometimes, Always, Never

Which word should go in the blank, <u>sometimes</u>, <u>always</u>, or <u>never</u>? Explain your choices.

6. There are __?__ 2 digits written after a decimal point.
7. Two hundredths is __?__ equivalent to two hundred.
8. A number with two decimal places is __?__ greater than a number with only one decimal place.

Project

Use a digital stopwatch that shows tenths or hundredths of a second. Time how long it takes you to do a specific task. It might be to count to 100, climb a flight of stairs, or sharpen your pencil. Do the task 3 times. Record your time after each try. Then order the results from the slowest to the fastest time. Why do you think the times were different?

Power Practice/Test

Part 1 Understanding

1. Use graph paper to draw the following pictures. Label each with a fraction or mixed number and a decimal.

   a. three tenths **b.** 33 hundredths **c.** one and 2 tenths

2. Give a decimal in tenths and another in hundredths that can round to each number.

   a. 1 **b.** 5 **c.** 22 **d.** 40

Part 2 Skills

Write the decimal that comes before and after each number when you count by hundredths.

3. 0.43 **4.** 1.89 **5.** 11.06

Write <, >, or = for each ▥.

6. 5.20 ▥ 5.2 **7.** 3.7 ▥ 3.8 **8.** 5.9 ▥ 5.85

9. Order these decimals from least to greatest.

0.85, 0.91, 0.84, 0.93, 0.89

Write a decimal for the fraction.

10. $\frac{1}{2}$ **11.** $\frac{7}{10}$ **12.** $\frac{23}{100}$ **13.** $\frac{1}{4}$

Part 3 Applications

14. 13 team members each gave $5.50 for an end-of-season party. Estimate if this is a reasonable amount for a party that cost $60.

15. **Challenge** When rounded to the nearest one, I am 1. When rounded to the nearest tenth, I am 0.9. When rounded to the nearest hundredth, I am 0.86. Which am I?

a. 0.862 **b.** 0.868 **c.** 0.854

ENRICHMENT
Fraction and Decimal Patterns

You know that decimals and fractions are related.

$\frac{1}{2} = 0.5$ $\frac{4}{5} = 0.8$ $\frac{3}{4} = 0.75$

1. How can you use a calculator to convert a fraction to a decimal? Think: A meaning for $\frac{4}{5}$ is 4 divided by 5.

2. Find the decimal that equals $\frac{1}{5}$ on your calculator. Then use mental math to find the decimal for $\frac{3}{5}$. Check with your calculator. Explain your thinking.

Here's how to use your calculator to explore other relationships between fractions and decimals. You may find some interesting patterns!

3. Find the decimals that equal $\frac{1}{9}$, $\frac{2}{9}$, and $\frac{3}{9}$. What do you notice?

4. Predict the decimal equivalents for $\frac{4}{9}$, $\frac{7}{9}$, and $\frac{8}{9}$. Check with your calculator.

5. Imagine that your calculator had a wider display and more digits would fit across the display. How would this affect the decimals you found in problems 3 and 4?

6. Find the decimals that equal $\frac{4}{99}$ and $\frac{6}{99}$. Then predict the decimal for $\frac{8}{99}$. Explain what will happen in the decimals for $\frac{13}{99}$ or $\frac{46}{99}$. Check with your calculator.

7. Find a decimal pattern for fractions with a denominator of 999. Make a table to record at least 7 examples. Then describe your findings.

CUMULATIVE REVIEW

1. Look at the coordinate grid. Which coordinates name a point inside triangle P?

   A (1,2) B (2,2)
   C (2,3) D (4,5)

2. Which triangles on the coordinate grid are congruent?

   A P and R B Q and R
   C P and Q D P, Q, and R

3. Which of the triangles on the grid is similar to triangle R?

   A P B T
   C S D Q

4. Find the average of these test scores: 85, 92, 100, 90, and 88.

   A 89 B 92
   C 91 D 455

5. Choose the best fractional estimate for the shaded part.

   A $\frac{1}{6}$ B $\frac{1}{4}$
   C $\frac{1}{5}$ D $\frac{1}{3}$

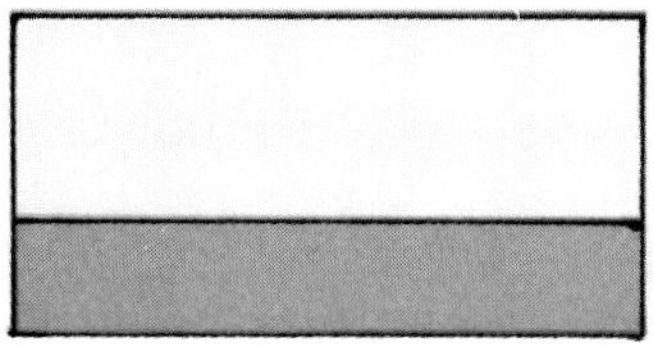

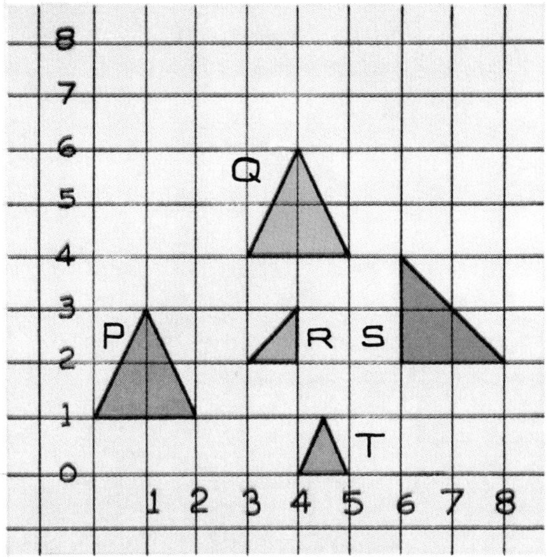

6. What fractional part of the letters in BANANAS are A's?

   A $\frac{1}{2}$ B $\frac{3}{7}$
   C $\frac{3}{4}$ D $\frac{4}{7}$

7. Which fraction is equivalent to $\frac{1}{4}$?

   A $\frac{4}{8}$ B $\frac{4}{16}$
   C $\frac{4}{12}$ D $\frac{4}{20}$

8. What is 58,620 rounded to the nearest thousand?

   A 59,000 B 58,600
   C 58,000 D 60,000

9. $2\overline{)817}$

   A 418 R1 B 408 R1
   C 409 R1 D 403 R1

14

METRIC MEASUREMENT

THEME: RAIN FORESTS

MATH AND SCIENCE

DATA BANK

Use the Science Data Bank on page 471 to answer the questions.

1 One type of tropical forest is the rain forest. Do the Florida Everglades receive enough rainfall to be considered a rain forest?

2 Would a forest that received 200.9 mm of rainfall per year be a rain forest?

3 What type of rain forest would you find 1,000 m high on a tropical mountain?

4 **Use Critical Thinking** If a tree in the emergent layer of a rain forest is 35 m high, can a tree in the canopy layer be 48 m high? Why?

This South American Indian finds food and shelter for his family in the Amazon rain forest of Brazil.

Centimeters, Decimeters, Meters, and Kilometers

LEARN ABOUT IT

1 dm = 10 cm
1 m = 10 dm = 100 cm

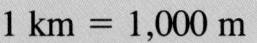

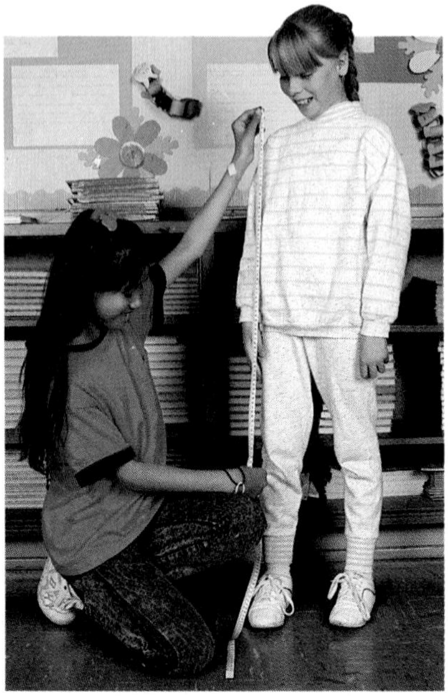

EXPLORE **Use a Metric Tape Measure**

The **centimeter** (cm), **decimeter** (dm), and **meter** (m) are metric units of length. Use a metric tape measure to measure your height and the lengths of some objects to the nearest centimeter. Record your measurements.

TALK ABOUT IT

1. How can you decide whether your height in centimeters is closer to 1, 2, or 3 meters?
2. About how many decimeters tall are you? Tell how you know.
3. Is decimeters a good unit of measure for your height? Explain.

The **kilometer** (km) is another metric unit of length. 1 km is about the same length as 5 city blocks. It takes about 10 minutes to walk a kilometer.

1 km = 1,000 m

TRY IT OUT

Measure the lengths of these objects in centimeters and decimeters. Then measure them to the nearest meter if you can.

1. your math book **2.** a piece of chalk **3.** your teacher's desk

Tell which measurement is longer or if they are the same length.

4. 4 dm 40 cm	**5.** 7 dm 2 m	**6.** 250 cm 3 m	**7.** 8,000 m 8 km

PRACTICE

Tell which object is wider or if they are the same width.

1. Table
Chalkboard

2. Window
Door

3. Chalkboard
Window

4. Door
Table

85 cm

2m

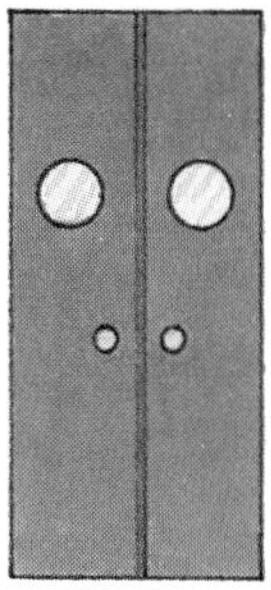

17 dm

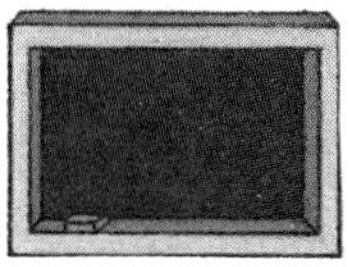

30 dm

Tell if the distance is greater than or less than 1 km.

5. 200 m

6. 1,500 m

7. 400 m

8. 1,000 cm

APPLY

MATH REASONING

9. Would a door 2 m tall fit into an opening 190 cm high?

10. Would a bookcase 250 cm tall fit into a classroom with a ceiling 3 m high?

PROBLEM SOLVING

11. A strip of rain forest is 600 dm long and 90 dm wide. Is the perimeter of the strip more or less than 100 m?

DATA BANK

12. **Science Data Bank** Which type of rain forest is found 2 km high on a tropical mountain? See page 471.

ESTIMATION

Estimate the height of these trees.

13. Tree A

14. Tree B

Tree A **6 m** **Tree B**

Estimating Length
Unitizing

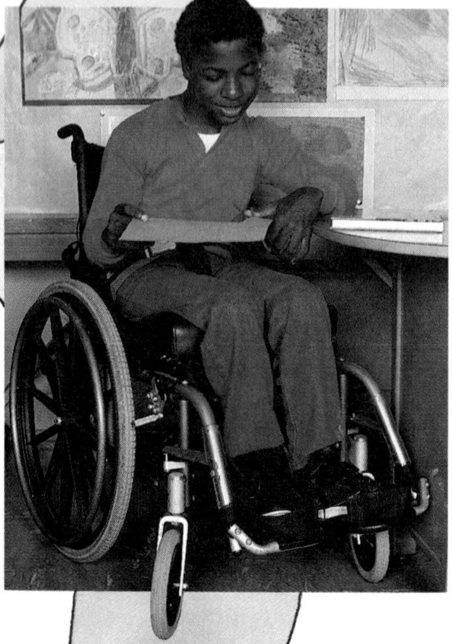

LEARN ABOUT IT

EXPLORE **Use Paper Strips**
Cut a strip of paper to match the width of one of your textbooks. Fold it into four parts. Estimate the length of one part in centimeters. Use that length to estimate the total width of your book.

TALK ABOUT IT

1. What is your estimated length for one part of the strip?
2. How can multiplication help you estimate the total width of your book?

You can use **unitizing** to estimate lengths.

- Visually or physically divide an object into equal parts.
- Estimate the length of one part.
- Multiply that estimate by the number of parts.

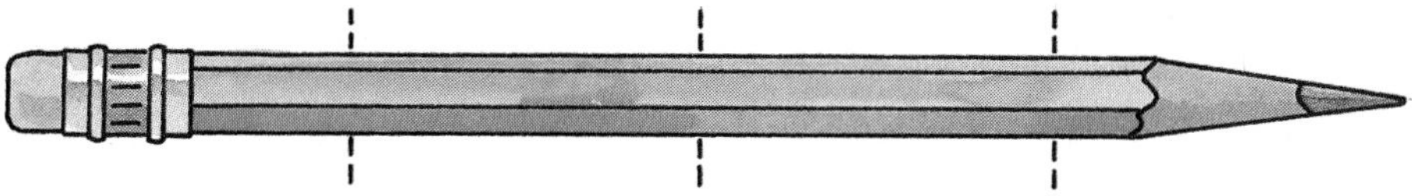

One part is about 3 cm long.
There are 4 parts.

4×3 cm $= 12$ cm
The total length is about 12 cm.

TRY IT OUT

Use unitizing to estimate the lengths of these objects in centimeters.

1. 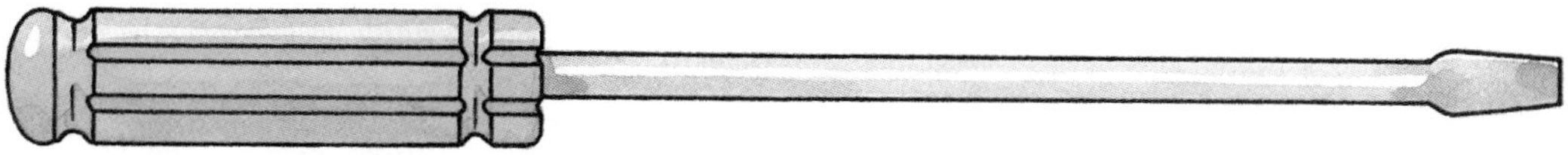

2. 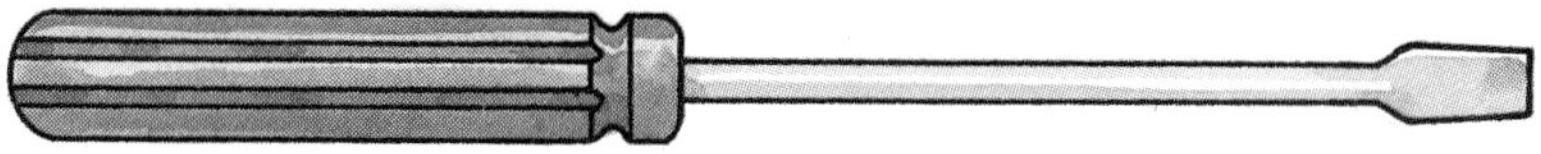

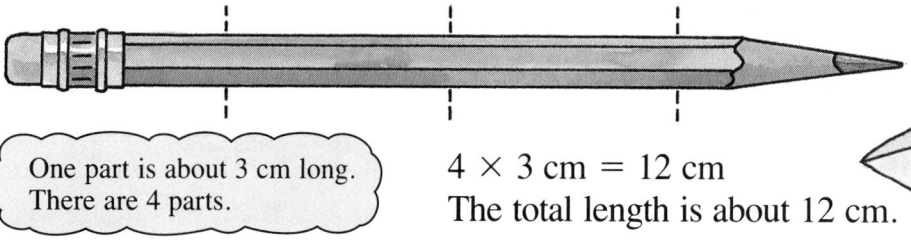

PRACTICE

Use unitizing to estimate each length. Then measure the length. Find and record the difference between the estimated and actual measures.

Record your data in a table like the one below.

Object	Estimate (cm)	Measure (cm)	Difference (cm)
1. Spelling book			

1. Spelling book
2. Desktop
3. Chalkboard
4. Chalkboard eraser
5. Table
6. Scissors

APPLY

MATH REASONING

7. Imagine that you estimated half of your classroom's width. How could you find an estimate for the whole classroom width?

PROBLEM SOLVING

8. Joe divided his bedroom length into 3 equal parts. He estimated that one of these parts is 2 m long. About how long is his bedroom?

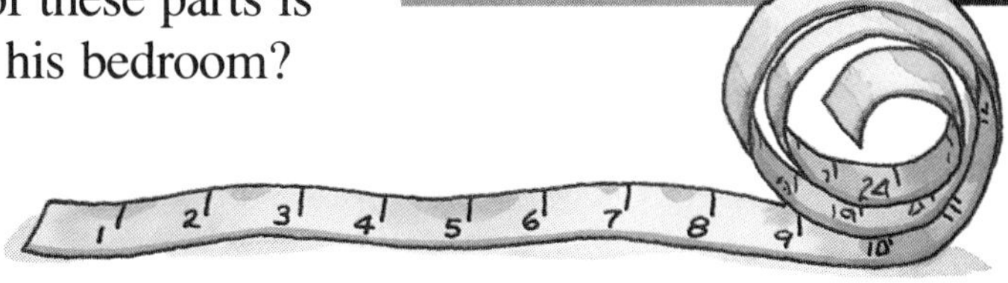

MIXED REVIEW

Write >, <, or = in each ▯.

9. $\frac{1}{5}$ ▯ $\frac{2}{15}$ **10.** $\frac{2}{3}$ ▯ $\frac{2}{4}$ **11.** $\frac{1}{5}$ ▯ $\frac{1}{4}$

Write each fraction as a whole or mixed number.

12. $\frac{8}{4}$ **13.** $\frac{11}{3}$ **14.** $\frac{7}{2}$ **15.** $\frac{15}{5}$ **16.** $\frac{10}{3}$

Write the decimals in order from least to greatest.

17. 7.34 7.23 7.38 7.29 **18.** 2.10 2.04 2.11 2.01

More Practice, page 525, set E

Millimeters

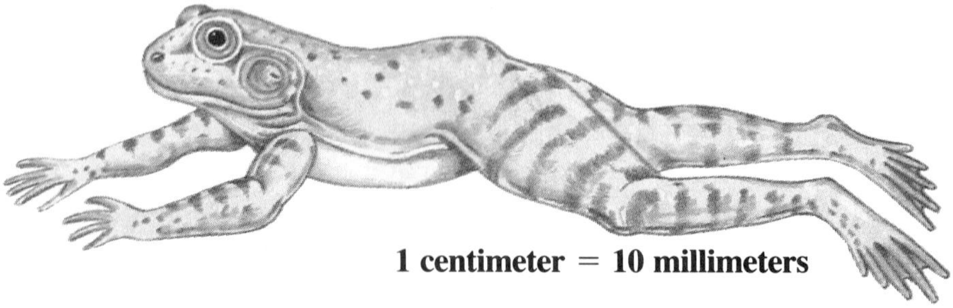

1 centimeter = 10 millimeters

LEARN ABOUT IT

The **millimeter** (mm) is a metric unit used for measuring length.

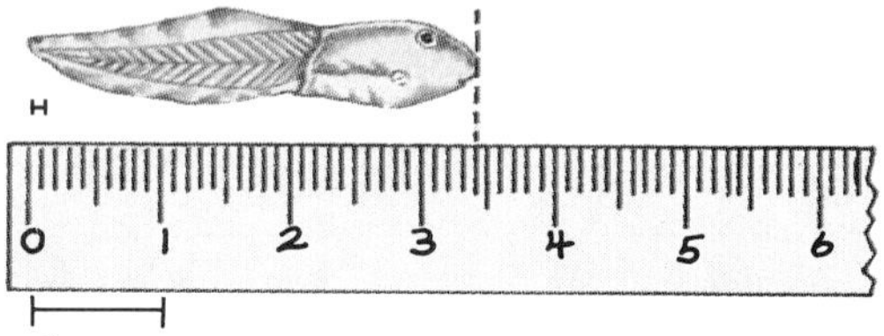

EXPLORE Solve to Understand

Dana had a Florida tree frog that was in the tadpole stage. She measured the tadpole every week and recorded its growth in a table. Read the ruler pictured to get the length of the tadpole the second week. Look for a pattern in the table.

TALK ABOUT IT

Week	1	2	3	4	5
Length mm	30	34	38	42	?

1. Is the tadpole's length the fourth week closer to 3 cm or 4 cm? The tadpole is __?__ cm __?__ mm long.
2. Using any table patterns you have found, how long would you expect the tadpole to be the fifth week?

You can use mental math to give a length in millimeters. Think of the object's length in centimeters and extra millimeters. Change the centimeters to millimeters and add the extra.

4×10 mm + 8 mm

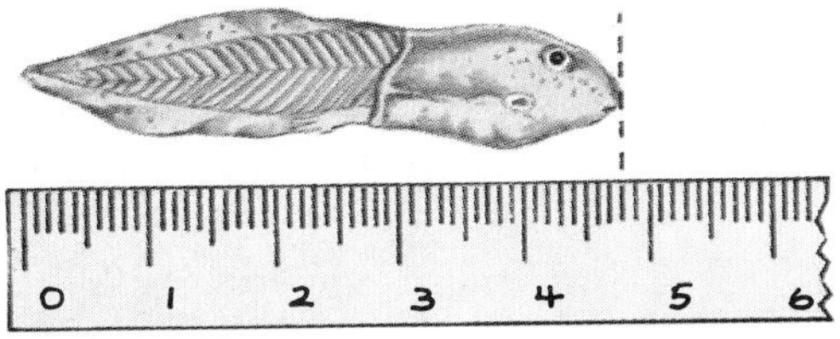

4 cm 8 mm = 48 mm

The tadpole is 48 mm long.

TRY IT OUT

Give the length of each tadpole in millimeters.

1. 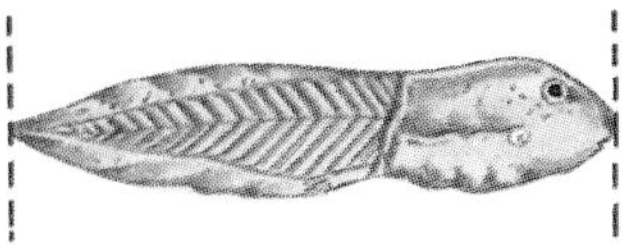

2. 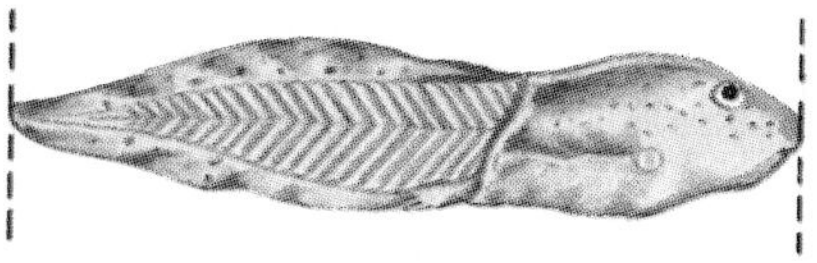

PRACTICE

Give the length of the tree frog in millimeters for each stage.

1. Egg **2.** Tadpole **3.** Adult frog

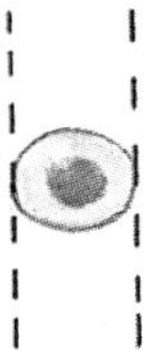

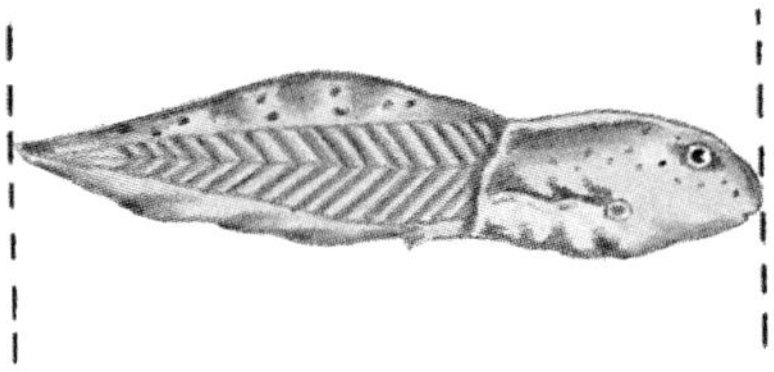

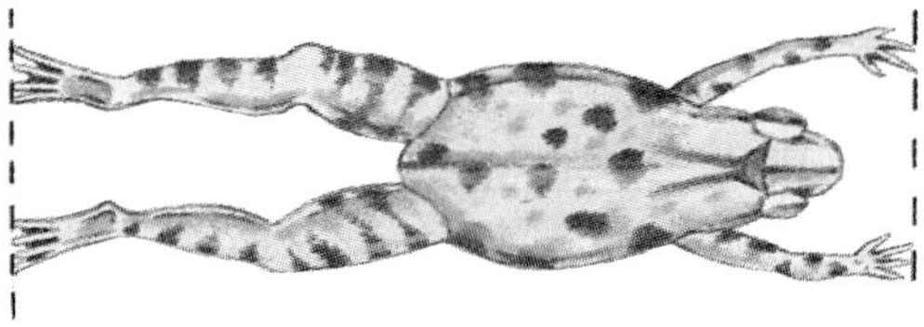

APPLY

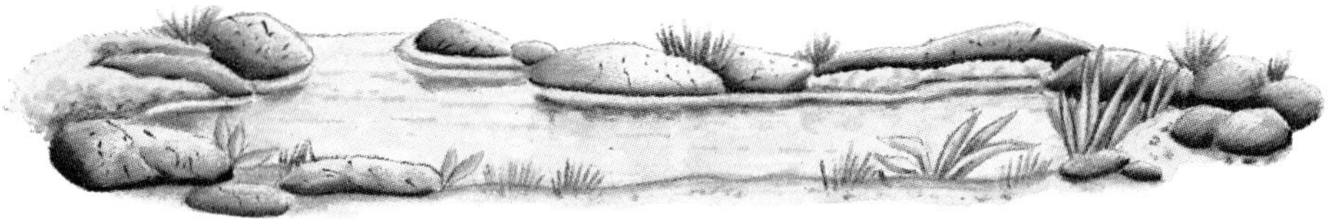

MATH REASONING

4. The red numbers show how much the frog's length increased each week. Find the pattern and complete the table.

Frog Length

Week	1	2	3	4	5	6	7	8
Length (mm)	2	4	8	14	22			

PROBLEM SOLVING

5. Miami, Florida, receives about 1,280 mm of rain per year. How much rain is that in centimeters?

6. Science Data Bank The Florida Everglades receive an average of 1,250 mm of rain each year. How much less is this than the wettest rain forest? See page 471.

CALCULATOR

Measure your height in centimeters. Use these keystrokes to enter 10 into the calculator's memory: [ON/AC] 10 [M+]. Then try each of the keystroke sequences below. Use the final number displayed and a metric unit (millimeter, centimeter, decimeter, meter, kilometer) to give your height.

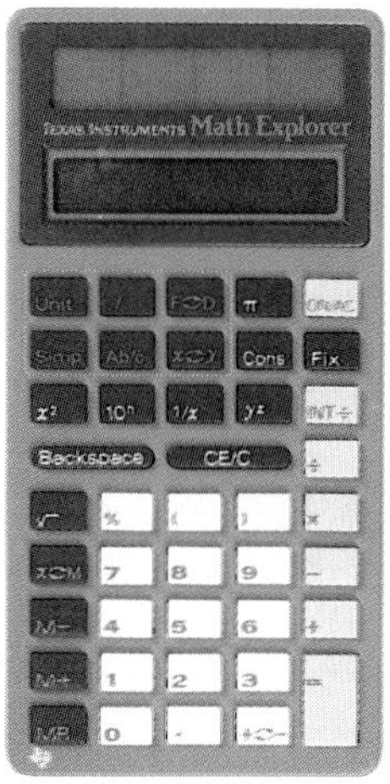

7. [CE/C] your height in cm [×] [MR] [=]

8. [CE/C] your height in cm [÷] [MR] [=]

9. [CE/C] your height in cm [÷] [MR] [=] [=] [=]

Problem Solving
Deciding When to Estimate

LEARN ABOUT IT

When you need only to use "about what is the measure," or to compare with a reference point, you can estimate. In other situations, you may want to actually measure. How the answer will be used often helps you decide.

Vicky is on boat patrol in the Florida Everglades. It is 10:53. She wants to go by boat to a wildlife area. At what time shall she tell her friends she will be back?

Vicky does not need to be back at an exact time.

She can estimate the time needed.

Jeff is practicing for an Everglades speedboat race. He wants to know how much greater his trial time is than the course record time of 9 minutes, 56 seconds.

Jeff needs to know exactly how many seconds faster he must go to beat the record.

Jeff should measure his trial time.

TRY IT OUT

Decide whether an estimate or an actual measure is needed. Tell why.

1. A carpenter is going to replace a door. The opening is twice as tall as it is wide. How tall should he cut the door?

2. You need to buy garden hoses and connect them together to reach from the faucet to a flower garden. Each hose is 20 m long. How many hoses will you need?

Power Practice/Quiz

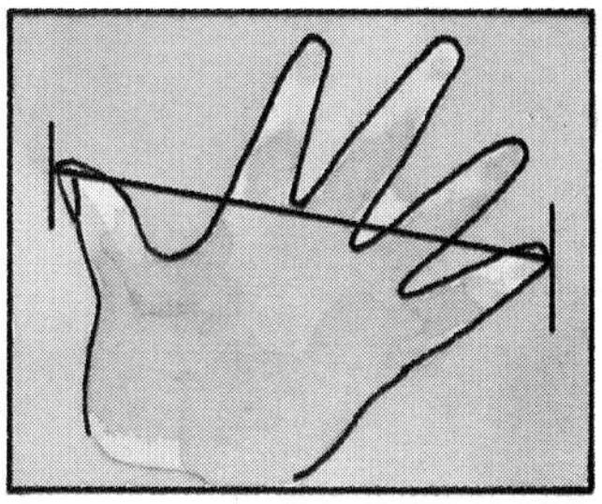

Measure your hand span to the nearest decimeter and the nearest centimeter.

1. Is your hand span closer to 1 dm, 2 dm, or 3 dm wide?
2. Is your hand span wider than a 15-cm hand span?
3. Which is wider, a 15-cm hand span or a 2-dm hand span?

Use unitizing to estimate these measurements. Then measure in centimeters to check.

4. length of your hand
5. height of a friend

Measure the height of the water in the rain gauge to the nearest millimeter.

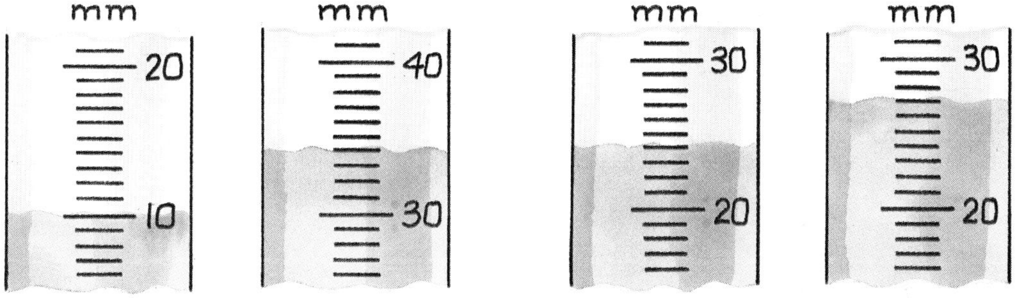

Tuesday **Wednesday** **Thursday** **Friday**

6. How much rain was there each day?
7. Which days had about 3 cm of rain?
8. Which days had about the same amount of rain?

PROBLEM SOLVING

9. Is the perimeter of this rug more or less than 5 m?
10. Reneé lives 2 km from Janice. Tia lives 850 m from Reneé. Who lives closer to Renee? How much closer?
11. What can you say about the heights of Tom, Dick, and Harry if Tom is 2 m tall, Dick is 20 dm tall, and Harry is 200 cm tall?

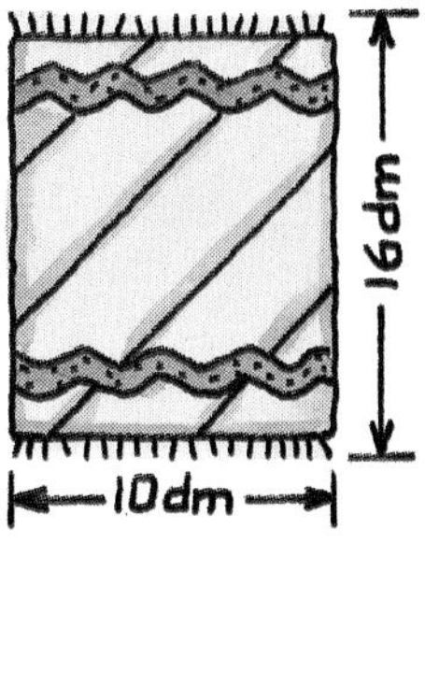

Area

The area of this table top is 12 square units.

LEARN ABOUT IT

EXPLORE **Use Graph Paper**

Draw as many different rectangles as you can that have 12 squares. Use only whole squares.

TALK ABOUT IT

1. How many different rectangles did you find?
2. Can regions with different numbers of rows have the same area? If so, give an example.

The **square centimeter** is a metric unit for measuring **area**.

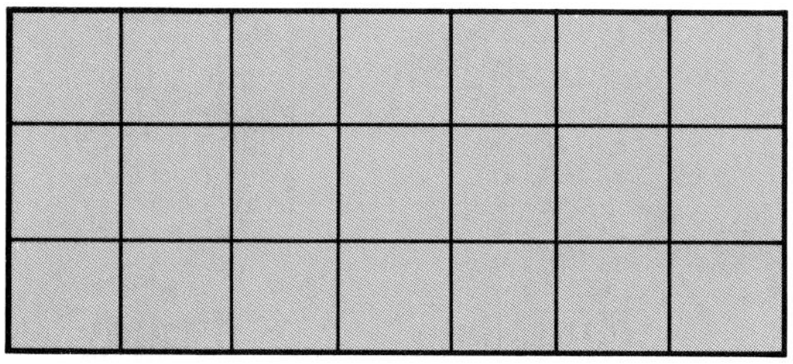

You can use multiplication to find the area of a rectangle.

3 rows × 7 in each row

$3 \times 7 = 21$ square centimeters

The area of the rectangle is 21 square centimeters.

TRY IT OUT

Give the area of each region in square centimeters. Use multiplication for the rectangular regions.

1.

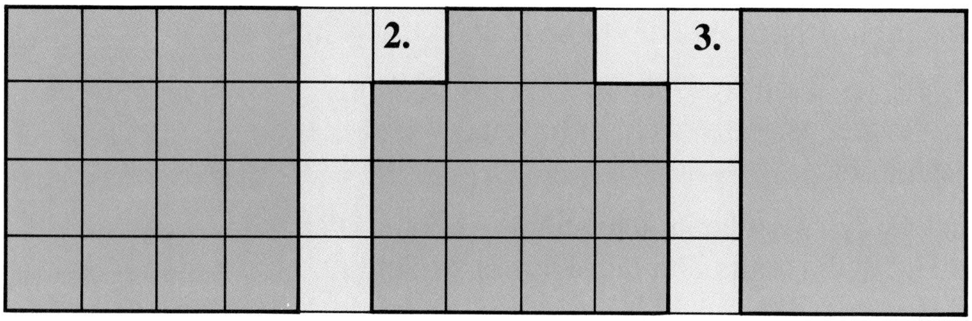

PRACTICE

Find the area of each region in square centimeters.
Use multiplication when you can.

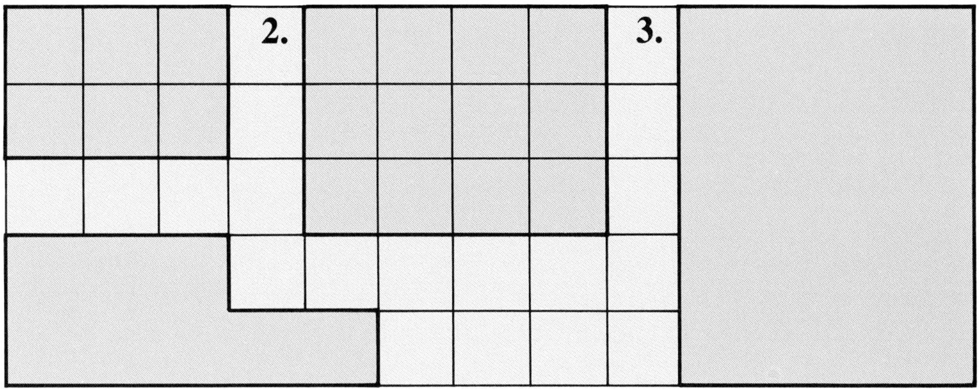

APPLY

MATH REASONING Use the figures below to answer these questions.

5. Which figures have the same areas, but different perimeters?

6. Which figures have the same perimeters, but different areas?

A B C

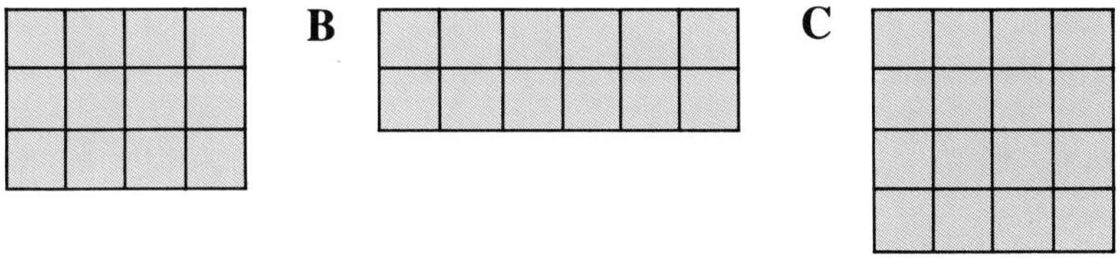

PROBLEM SOLVING

7. **Draw a Picture** Draw a rectangular region on graph paper. It should have an area of 12 square centimeters and a perimeter of 14 cm.

MIXED REVIEW

Round each number to the nearest whole number.

8. 45.1 **9.** 7.9 **10.** 21.6 **11.** 37.5 **12.** 61.3 **13.** 8.6

Tell which measurement is longer.

14. 20 cm
3 dm

15. 6 cm
2 m

16. 8 dm
8 m

17. 44,000 m
4 km

More Practice, page 526, set A

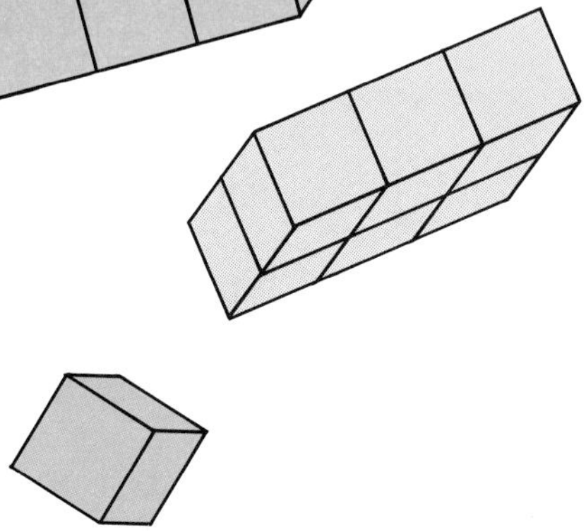

Volume

LEARN ABOUT IT

EXPLORE Use Cubes

Use cubes to make as many different rectangular prisms as you can. Each prism should be made with 12 cubes.

TALK ABOUT IT

1. How many different rectangular prisms were you able to make?
2. Suppose you have a rectangular prism with 3 rows of cubes and 4 in each row. How many cubes would there be in 1 layer? in 2 layers? in 3 layers?

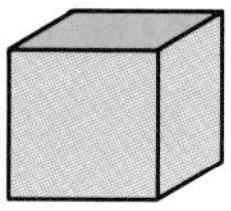

The **cubic centimeter** is a metric unit for **volume**.

You can use multiplication to find the volume of a rectangular prism.

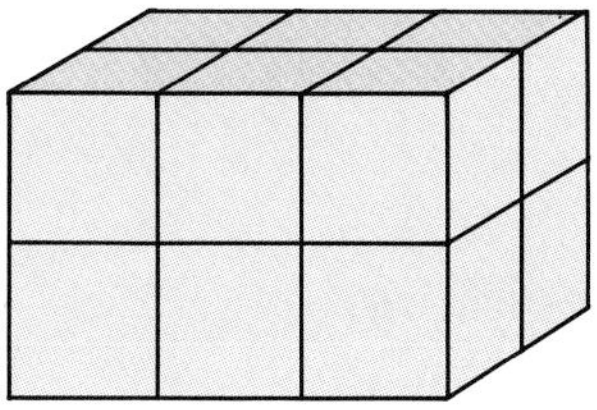

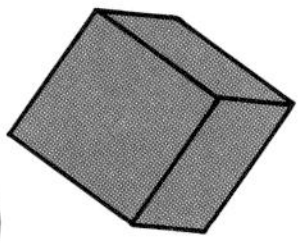

2 rows × 3 in each row × 2 layers

$2 \times 3 \times 2 = 12$ cubic centimeters

The volume is 12 cubic centimeters.

TRY IT OUT

Find the volume of each figure in cubic centimeters.

1. 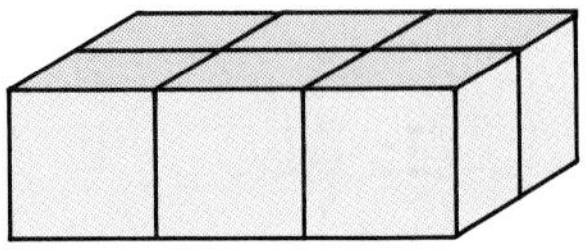

2. 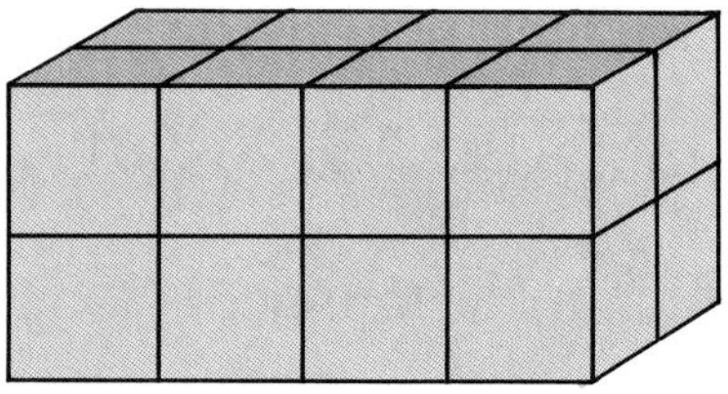

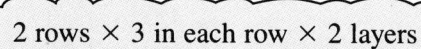

PRACTICE

Give the volume of each figure in cubic centimeters.

1. 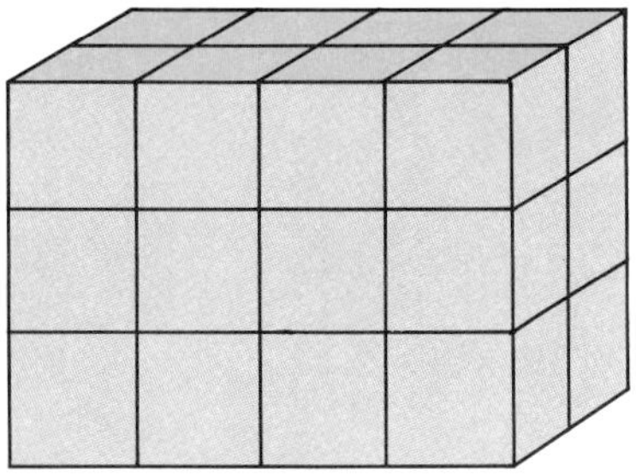

2. 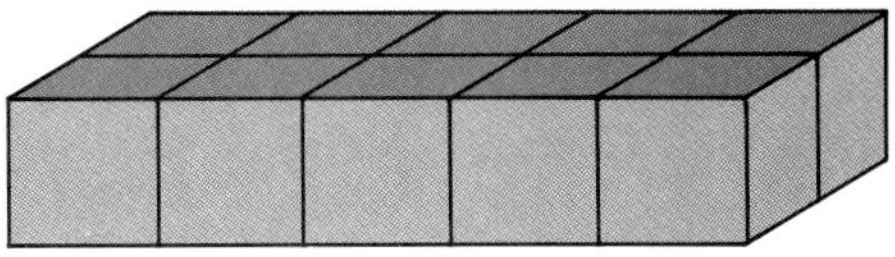

APPLY

MATH REASONING Find the volume of each figure in cubic units.

3. 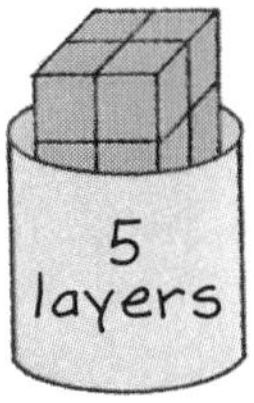

4. 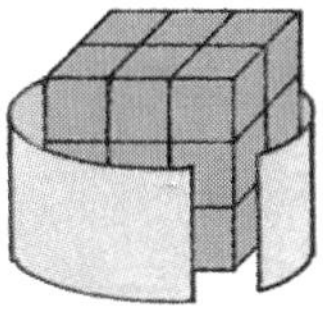

5. 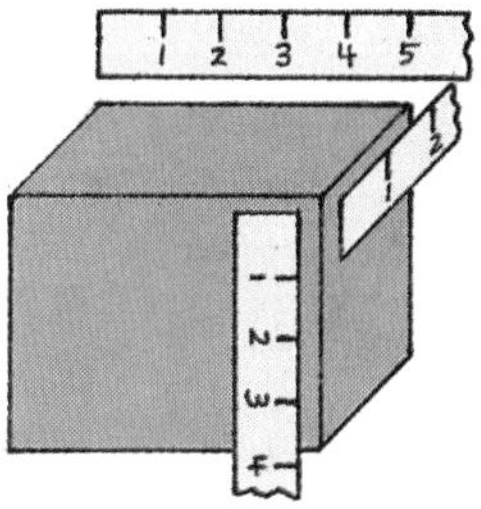

PROBLEM SOLVING

6. Dan filled a box with 6 layers of centimeter cubes. Each layer had 4 rows with 5 cubes in each row. How many cubes were in the box?

7. **Missing Data** Make up missing data and solve the problem. A box of blocks is 3 blocks long and 4 blocks wide. How many blocks are in the box?

USING CRITICAL THINKING Take a Look

Find the volume in cubic centimeters.

8. 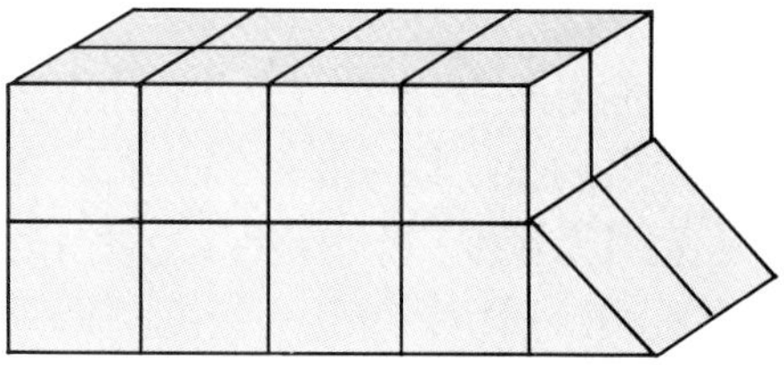

More Practice, page 526, set B

Problem Solving
Finding Related Problems

LEARN ABOUT IT

Many problems are related. That means they can be solved using the same strategy. When you are solving a problem, sometimes it helps if you think about a related problem.

Here are two related problems. They have both been solved by drawing a picture.

Ming, Becky, Tish, and Ken are in line for a tour of the Kennedy Space Center. Ming is ahead of Tish. Tish is between Ken and Ming. Ming is behind Becky. Who is last in line?

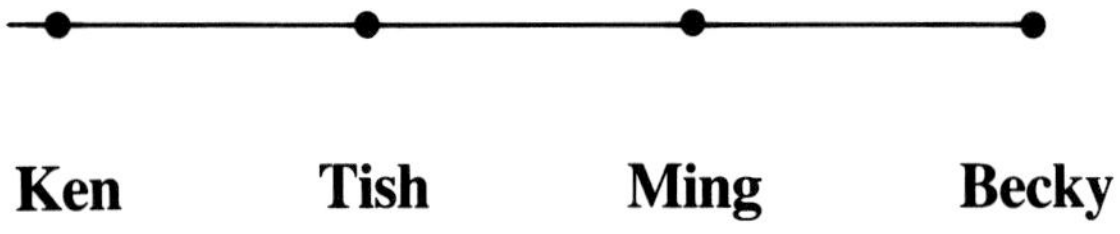

Ken is last in line.

Pedro went to 4 beaches in Florida. He went to Cocoa Beach before Jensen Beach. He went to Miami Beach after Palm Beach. He went to Palm Beach after Jensen Beach. What was the last beach he visited?

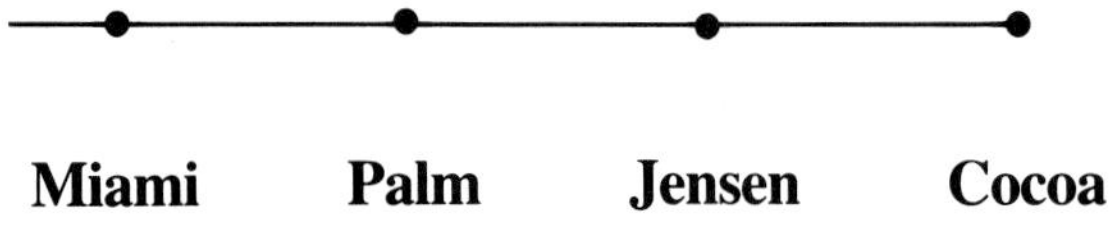

Pedro went to Miami Beach last.

TRY IT OUT

Solve. Explain why these two problems are related.

1. 22 of the fourth graders have been to Florida. 17 have been to Miami and 13 have been to Daytona Beach. How many have been to both Miami and Daytona Beach?

2. 34 students went on a field trip to Everglades National Park. 15 bought food for lunch at the park. 21 brought their own lunch. How many both brought their own lunch and bought food?

MIXED PRACTICE

Choose a strategy from the list or use other strategies you know to solve these problems.

Some Strategies
Act It Out
Use Objects
Choose an Operation
Draw a Picture
Make an Organized List
Guess and Check
Make a Table
Look for a Pattern
Use Logical Reasoning
Work Backward

Spanish Explorers in Florida

1513	Juan Ponce de León lands on the Florida coast looking for the legendary fountain of youth.
1539	Hernando de Soto leads an expedition through Florida.
1565	Pedro Menéndez de Avilés founds St. Augustine, the first permanent European settlement in the United States.

1. How many years passed between Juan Ponce de León's landing in Florida and the start of St. Augustine? Use the chart.

2. Georgia and her family drove 160 km to see the Florida Keys. They crossed 42 bridges. It took them 4 hours, and they drove the same distance each hour. How many kilometers did they drive each hour?

3. 16 years after Maine became one of the United States, Arkansas became a state. 9 years later, in 1845, Florida became a state. What year did Maine become a state?

4. The Florida peninsula is about 640 km long. Its widest part is about $\frac{1}{3}$ of its length. How wide is its widest part?

5. Postcards at Everglades National Park are 6 for \$3. How much would 36 postcards cost?

6. Daytona Beach, famous for car racing, is 37 km long. The width of the beach is 4 km longer than 4 times its length. How wide is Daytona Beach?

7. **Find a Related Problem**
Tell which of the problems on this page is related to this one. Then solve. Abe is 124 cm tall. At National Key Deer Refuge, he photographed a tiny deer that was half as tall as he is. How tall was the deer?

More Practice, page 526, set C

Capacity

LEARN ABOUT IT

EXPLORE **Use Containers**

You will need a 1-liter container plus several containers of different shapes and sizes. Estimate to put all the containers in order from the one that holds the least to the one that holds the most. Find a way to check your estimates.

TALK ABOUT IT

1. How did you decide on the order of the containers?

2. Does the tallest container always hold the most? Explain.

3. What method did you use to check your estimates?

You can use what you know about estimating with a benchmark to help you estimate capacity using the metric units **liter** (L) and **milliliter** (mL).

A teaspoon holds about 5 mL.
A tablespoon holds about 3 times as much as a teaspoon, so it holds about 15 mL.

A juice container holds about 1 L.
1 L = 1,000 mL.
A milk carton holds about the same as a juice container, so it holds about 1 L.

TRY IT OUT

Which unit, *liter* or *milliliter*, would make most sense to use when measuring the capacity of the object?

1. a medicine dropper **2.** a large pail **3.** a tea cup

Choose the better estimate of capacity.

4. a pitcher
a 3 L **b** 3 mL

5. a kitchen sink
a 20 L **b** 20 mL

6. a juice glass
a 150 L **b** 150 mL

PRACTICE

Which unit, *liter* or *milliliter*, would you use for measuring the capacity?

1.

2.

Choose the better estimate of capacity.

3.

a more than 1 L
b less than or equal to 1 L

4.

a more than 100 mL
b less than or equal to 100 mL

APPLY

MATH REASONING Write the missing numbers.

5. If 5 drops of water make 1 mL, then |||| drops make 1 L.
6. If a teaspoon of water is 5 mL, then |||| teaspoons make 1 L.

PROBLEM SOLVING

7. A bucket holds 6 L of water. After a rain it was one third full. How many L of water were in the bucket? How many mL?
8. A cup holds 250 mL. How many cupfuls would it take to make 1 L?

MENTAL MATH

Use mental math to answer the questions.

9. One large glass holds 300 mL. Do 3 glasses hold more or less than 1 L?
10. A small juice can holds 150 mL. Do 5 juice cans hold more or less than 1 L?

More Practice, page 526, set D

Grams and Kilograms

LEARN ABOUT IT

The **gram** (g) and the **kilogram** (kg) are metric units of **mass**.

EXPLORE **Use a Scale**
Work in groups. Put 5 objects in order from heaviest to lightest. Check your estimates by measuring each object's mass in grams.

TALK ABOUT IT

1. How did you compare the objects when you first put them in order?
2. If someone said that the largest object always has the greatest mass, would you agree or disagree? Explain.

Benchmarks like these can help you estimate the mass of objects.

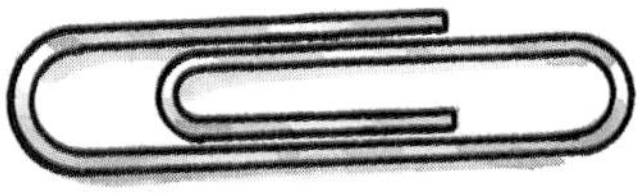

The mass of a large paper clip is about 1 g.

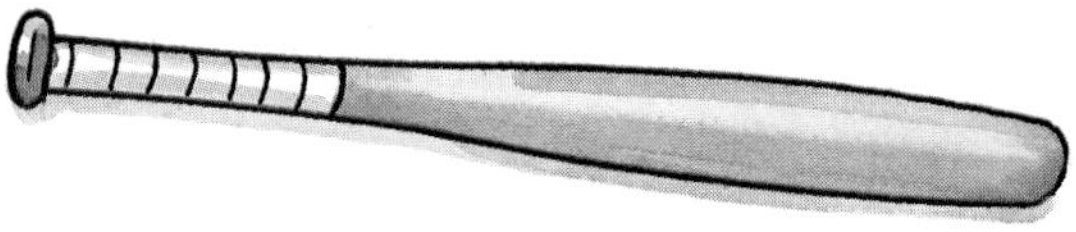

The mass of a baseball bat is about 1 kg. 1 kg = 1,000 g

PRACTICE

Use benchmarks. Estimate whether the mass of each object is 10 g or 1 kg.

1. 

2. 

3. 

More Practice, page 526, set E

Temperature
Degrees Celsius

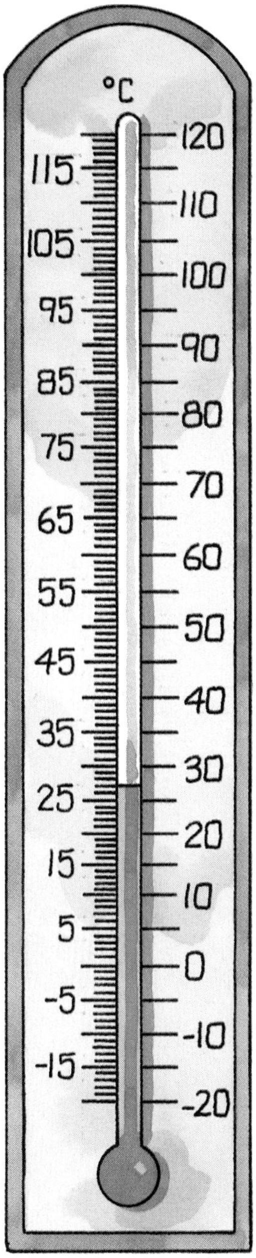

LEARN ABOUT IT

The metric unit for temperature is the **degree Celsius** (°C). On the thermometer at the right, the temperature is 27°C to the nearest degree.

EXPLORE **Try an Experiment**

Does the location of a thermometer make a difference in the temperature reading? To find out, place two thermometers outside in the sunshine, one with a glass over it.

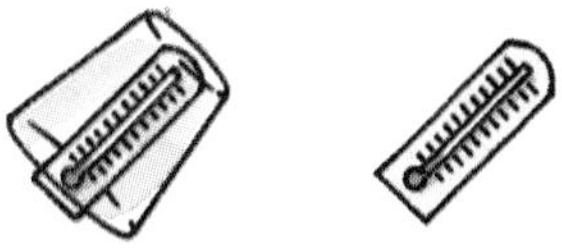

Record each temperature to the nearest degree every 30 minutes for 2 hours. Make a table to show the results.

TALK ABOUT IT

1. What did you find out in your experiment?
2. What was the greatest temperature? the least?
3. What was the greatest difference in the two temperatures?

PRACTICE

1. Make bar graphs to show the results of your experiment.

Record each temperature shown.

2. 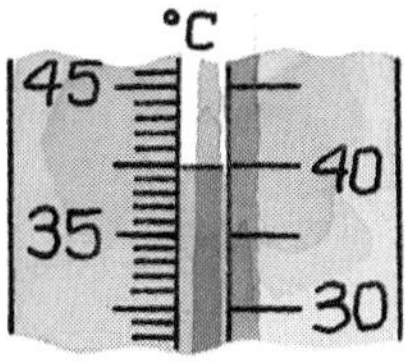

3. 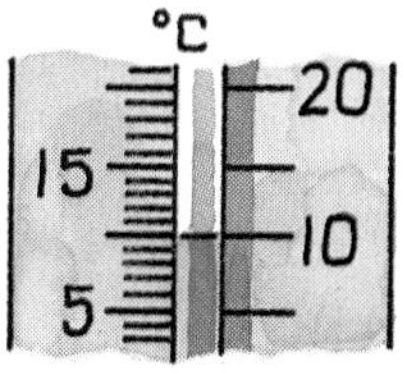

4. 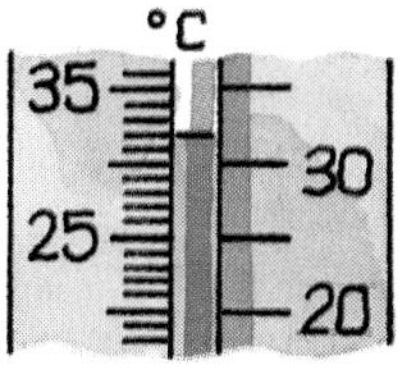

More Practice, page 527, set A

Data Collection and Analysis
Group Decision Making

UNDERSTAND
FIND DATA
PLAN
ESTIMATE
SOLVE
CHECK

Doing a Survey:
Group Skill:
Explain and Summarize

What animal do people think makes the best pet? Predict what animal you think most people will choose. Then conduct a survey to find out.

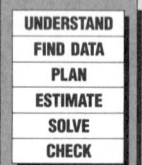

Collecting Data

1. Your group will ask a total of 30 people the survey questions. Decide how many people each student in your group will survey.
2. Write down the questions that you will ask. Make a table to record the answers.

What animal is the best to have as a pet? Why?

Animal	Why
dog	loyal
rabbit	gentle
bird	easy to care for
------	-------------
------	-------------
------	-------------

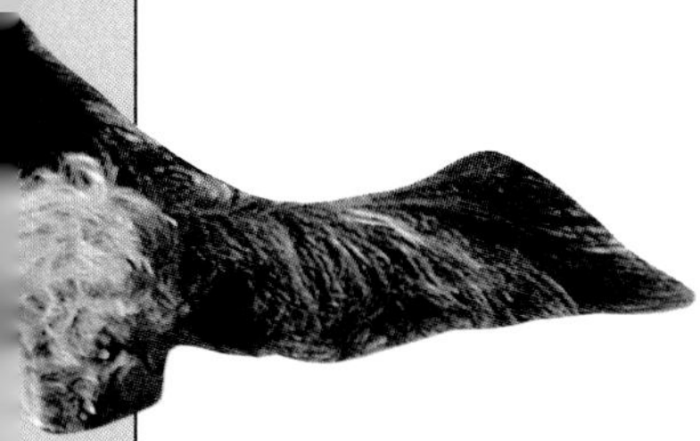

Organizing Data

3. Count how many times each animal was named. Make a bar graph to show how many people in your survey chose each animal. Adjust the scale to fit your data.

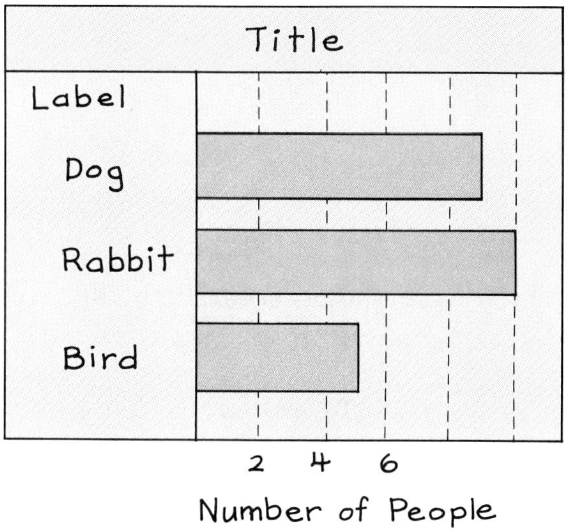

Presenting Your Analysis

4. Which animal was chosen by the most people? How many people named that animal?

5. Explain some of the reasons people chose a certain animal as the best pet.

6. Write at least three true sentences about the information in your graph.

Wrap Up

Measurement Mix-Up

Put these measurement cards in the correct categories.

a 4 sq cm | b 8 g | c 7 mm | d 4 L | e 10 cm

f 50 mL | g 3 dm | h 10 kg | i 5 m | j 40° C

k 12 cubic cm | l -7° C | m 4 km

1. length **2.** area **3.** volume

4. capacity **5.** mass **6.** temperature

Sometimes, Always, Never

Which word should go in the blank, sometimes, always, or never? Explain your choices.

7. A tall container will ___?___ have greater capacity than a short container.

8. The kilometer is ___?___ the most useful unit for measuring distance.

9. You ___?___ measure in milligrams to find the perimeter of a very small region.

Project

Find 2 containers with an estimated capacity of about 1 liter each. Find 2 containers that have the capacity of about 1 milliliter. Then use a liter measure and a milliliter measure to check the capacities of the containers you found.

Now look for a container larger than a liter. Estimate how many liters it will hold. Then do an actual measurement to check.

POWER PRACTICE/TEST

Part 1 Understanding

1. Use liter or milliliter to answer these problems.
A large spoon might hold 15 __?__.

A laundry sink might hold 25 __?__.

2. Use grams or kilograms to answer these problems.
The mass of a cement block may be 4 __?__.

The mass of a pencil may be 4 __?__.

3. Explain how to unitize to estimate the length of the toy car in centimeters.

4. David is making a window screen and a sand sifter with wire mesh. Explain for which object David needs an actual measure and for which he can use an estimate.

Part 2 Skills

5. Find the area in square centimeters.

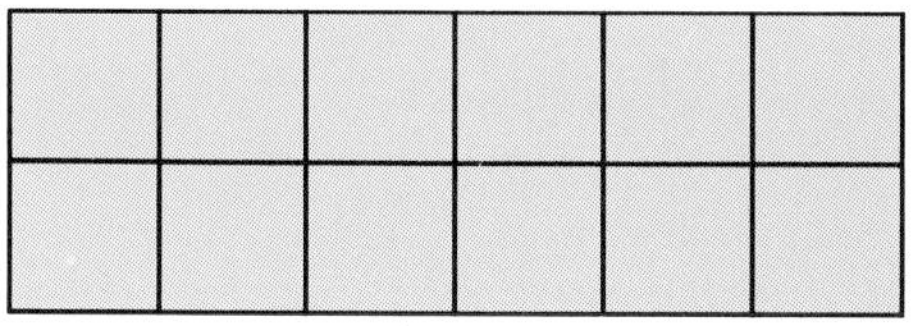

6. Find the volume in cubic centimeters.

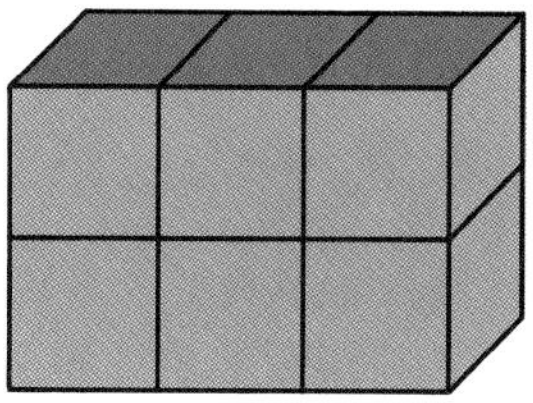

Measure to the nearest centimeter and millimeter.

7.

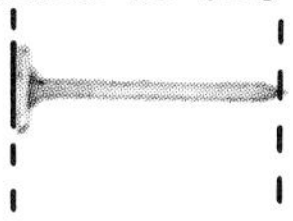

8.

Part 3 Applications

9. Sam's castle wall had 5 layers of cm cubes. Each layer had 8 rows of 7 cubes. What is the volume of Sam's castle wall?

10. **Challenge** Draw a figure whose area is an odd square number but whose perimeter is an even number.

Enrichment
Estimating Area

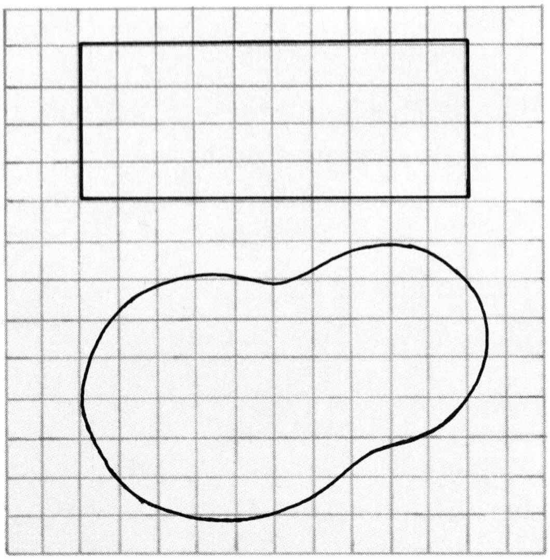

You can find the area of a rectangle by counting square units. But how can you find the area of other figures?

Look at the simple closed curve on this page. Then draw your own simple closed curve on centimeter grid paper.

1. What difficulty do you have when you try and find the area of the closed curves by counting square units?
2. Make a plan for counting units and partial units. Make a reasonable estimate of the area of your figure.

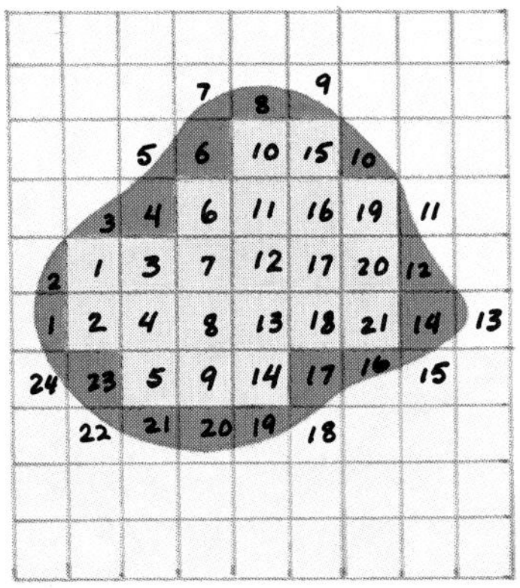

The count-and-average method gives a close estimate of the area of curved shapes. Here is what you do.

- Count the squares <u>totally</u> inside the figure.
- Count all the squares totally inside <u>or</u> partly inside the figure.
- Find the average of the two numbers.

3. How do you find an average?
4. Find the area of your closed curve with the count-and-average method. Compare this area with your earlier estimate.
5. Trace your foot on centimeter grid paper. First, estimate, then use the count-and-average method to find its area.

Cumulative Review

1. This is a(n) |||| triangle.

   A right B equilateral

   C obtuse D isosceles

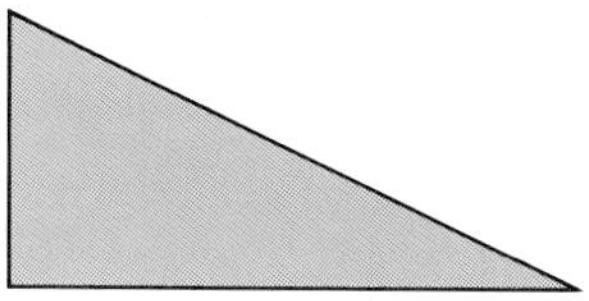

2. A rectangle is a special ||||.

   A parallelogram B square

   C trapezoid D curve

3. Which space figure is like this road marker?

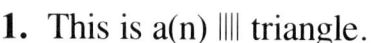

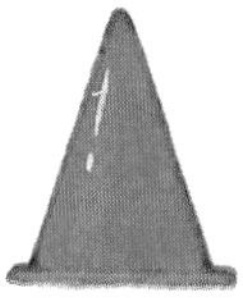

   A cube B cylinder

   C sphere D cone

4. Which fraction is reduced to lowest terms?

   A $\frac{6}{9}$ B $\frac{6}{7}$

   C $\frac{6}{18}$ D $\frac{6}{21}$

5. Choose the fraction that is greater than $\frac{2}{3}$.

   A $\frac{1}{2}$ B $\frac{3}{4}$

   C $\frac{2}{5}$ D $\frac{4}{6}$

6. Find $\frac{3}{7}$ of 28.

   A 12 B 9

   C 7 D 21

7. Which decimal is two and seven hundredths?

   A 2.07 B 2.70

   C 207.07 D 0.27

8. Choose the decimal in which the 3 equals 3 hundredths.

   A 302.64 B 1.37

   C 48.53 D 0.32

9. Which is between 5.7 and 5.78?

   A 5.8 B 5.74

   C 5.79 D 5.70

10. Dean won a vocal music prize for holding a note for 44.42 seconds. Find the time to the nearest second.

    A 40 B 50

    C 44 D 45

11. A ribbon is 0.25 yd long. Which fraction describes the same part of a yard?

    A $\frac{1}{4}$ B $\frac{2}{5}$

    C $\frac{2}{10}$ D $\frac{1}{3}$

15

ADDITION AND SUBTRACTION FRACTIONS AND DECIMALS

THEME: SPORTS

MATH AND HEALTH AND FITNESS

DATA BANK

Use the Health and Fitness Data Bank on page 483 to answer the questions.

1 Write a fraction for the maximum weight of a lawn tennis ball. Give an equivalent fraction for the fraction you wrote.

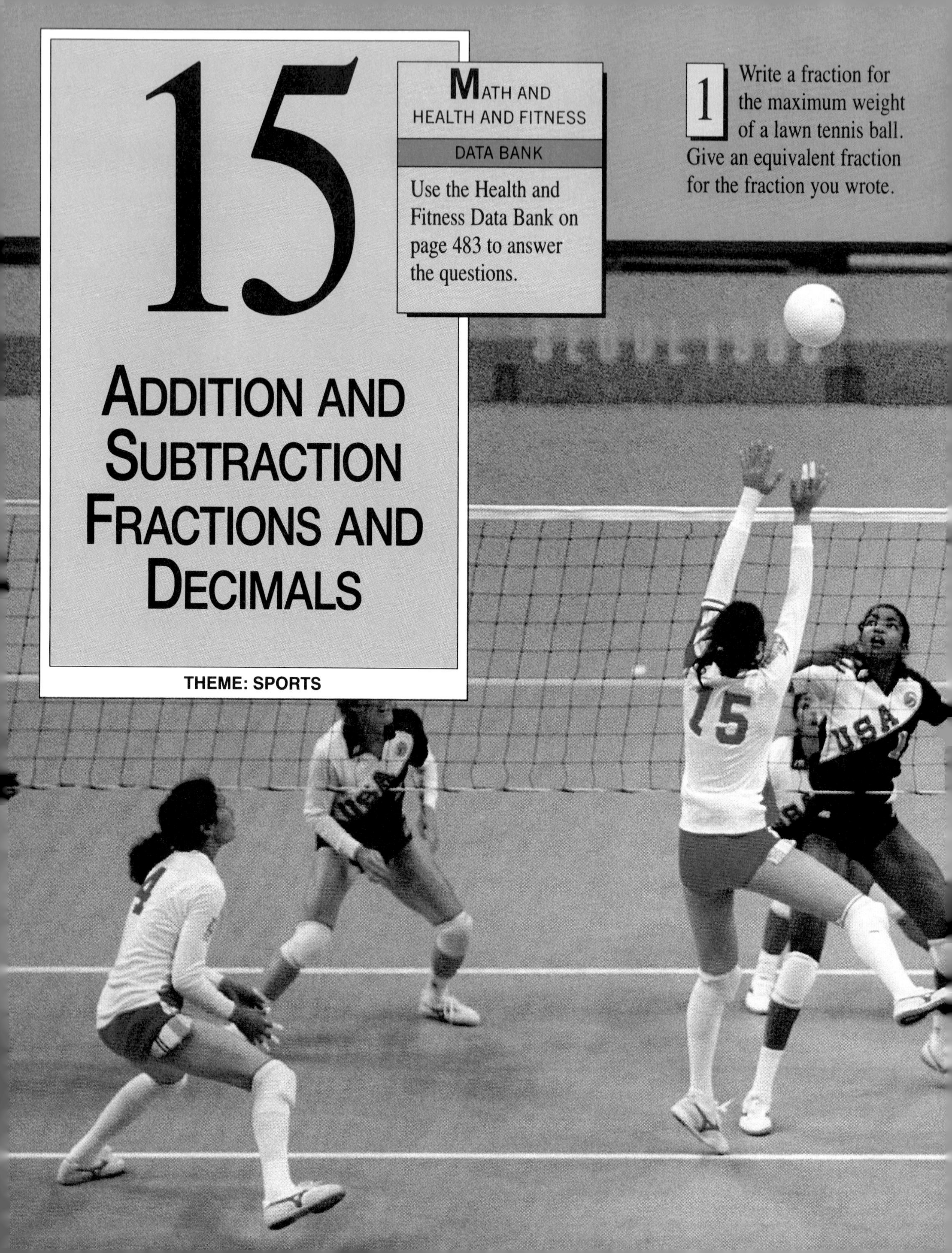

2 Would a table tennis ball weighing 2.49 grams meet the official weight standard?

3 Which ball bounces higher when dropped from a height of 6 feet, a lawn tennis ball or a soccer ball?

4 **Use Critical Thinking** If a volleyball and a basketball bounced the same height, which was bounced with more force? Explain.

Teams from the USA and China play an exciting volleyball game in the Olympic Games at Seoul, Korea.

Adding and Subtracting Fractions with Like Denominators
Making the Connection

LEARN ABOUT IT

EXPLORE Use Fraction Pieces

Work in groups. Use fraction pieces for eighths.

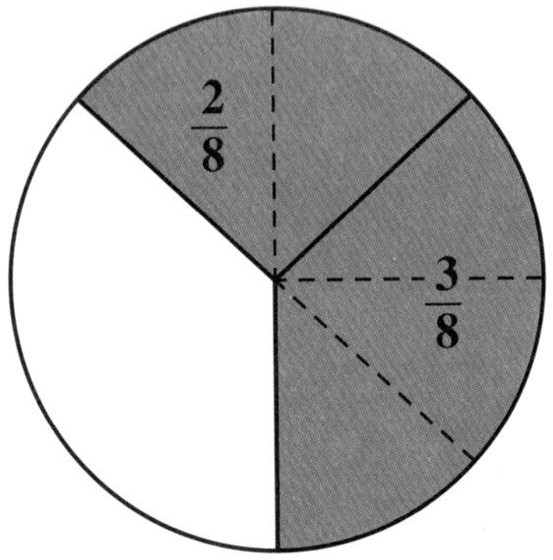

- Cover a part of the whole with some eighth pieces. Make a table to record the number of eighths you use. Next cover more of the whole with eighth pieces and record. Then tell how much of the whole you have covered all together.

1st part covered	2nd part covered	Total covered by the two parts
$\frac{2}{8}$	$\frac{3}{8}$	$\frac{5}{8}$

- Try this process again using different numbers of pieces. Then try it using sixth fraction pieces.

- Start with several eighth pieces covering part of the whole. Now pick up one of those pieces. Can you write a subtraction equation to record this?

TALK ABOUT IT

1. Look at one row of your table. Can you give an addition equation for that row?
2. In the subtraction activity, suppose you picked up all the pieces except one. Can you write another subtraction equation to record that action?

You have put fraction pieces together and taken them away to understand how to add or subtract fractions. Now you will see a way to record what you have done. This process can help you find sums and differences in problems such as $\frac{2}{8} + \frac{4}{8}$ and $\frac{5}{8} - \frac{3}{8}$.

	What You Do	What You Record
Addition		
1. What number in the fraction tells how many eighth pieces you are adding to $\frac{2}{8}$?	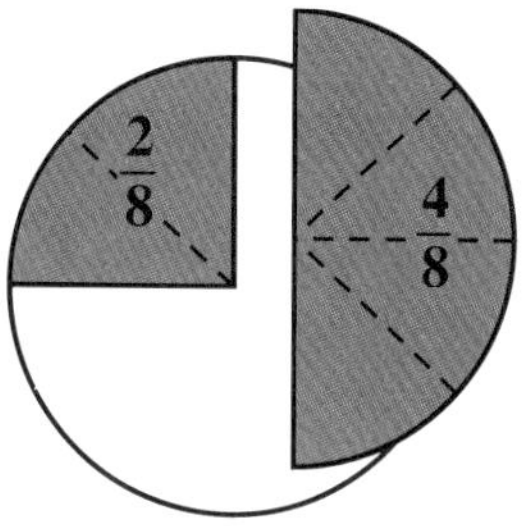	$\frac{2}{8} + \frac{4}{8}$
2. How many eighth pieces did you use in all? What is the sum of $\frac{2}{8}$ and $\frac{4}{8}$?	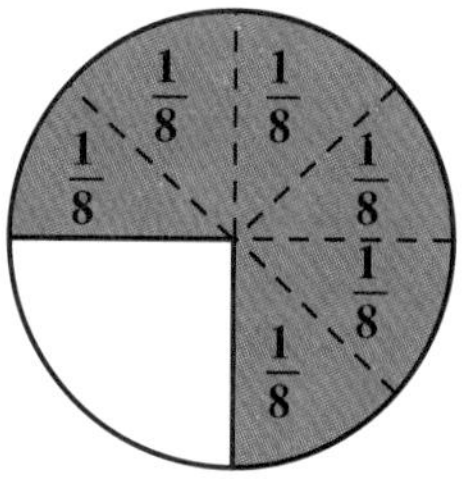	$\frac{2}{8} + \frac{4}{8} = \frac{6}{8}$
Subtraction		
3. How much of the whole is covered to start? **4.** How many pieces will you take away?	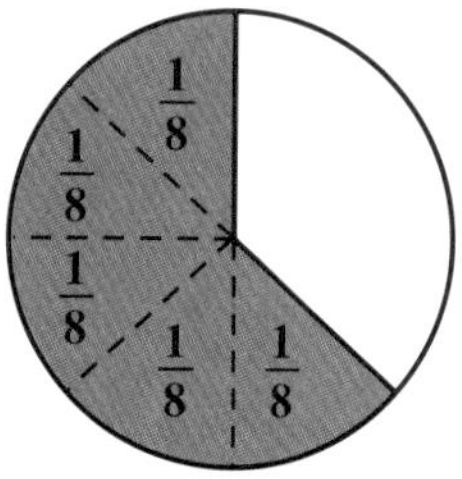	$\frac{5}{8} - \frac{3}{8}$
5. How many pieces are left? What is $\frac{5}{8}$ minus $\frac{3}{8}$?	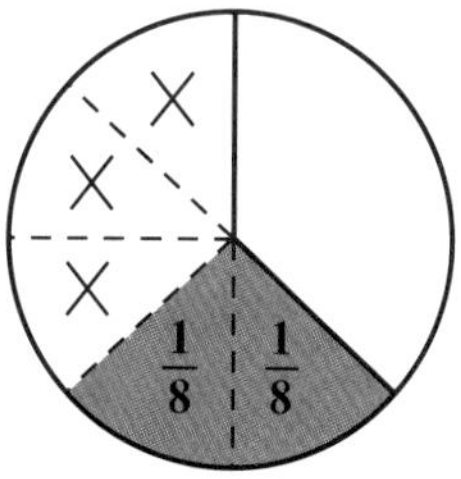	$\frac{5}{8} - \frac{3}{8} = \frac{2}{8}$

TRY IT OUT

Use fraction pieces to find the sums and differences. Reduce the answers to lowest terms.

1. $\frac{5}{8} + \frac{2}{8}$ **2.** $\frac{5}{6} - \frac{3}{6}$ **3.** $\frac{3}{4} - \frac{1}{4}$ **4.** $\frac{1}{5} + \frac{3}{5}$ **5.** $\frac{1}{3} + \frac{2}{3}$

Adding and Subtracting Fractions
Like Denominators

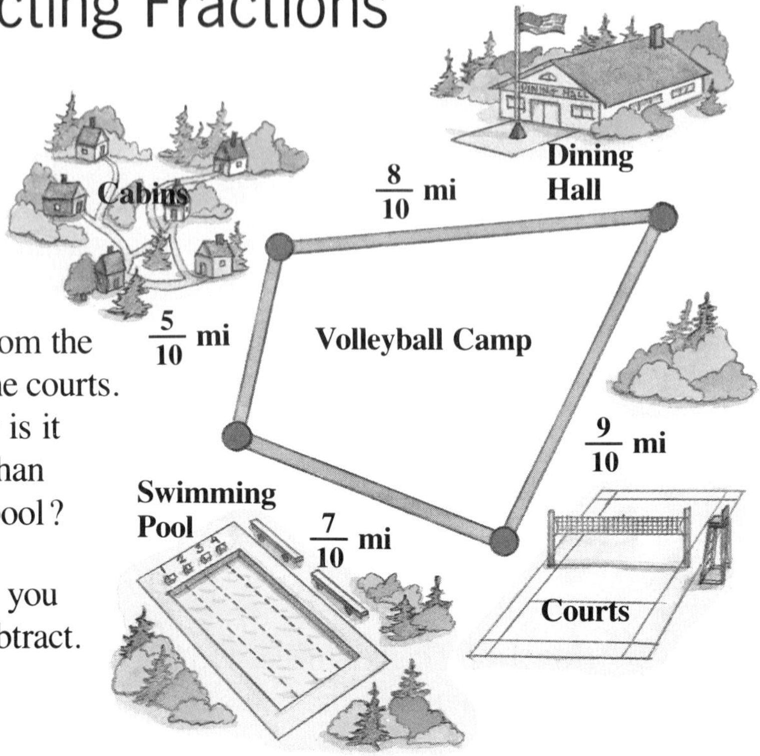

LEARN ABOUT IT

EXPLORE Think About the Process

At volleyball camp, Jorie jogged from the cabins past the swimming pool to the courts. How far is this? How much farther is it from the cabins to the dining hall than from the cabins to the swimming pool?

When two distances are combined, you add. To compare distances, you subtract.

Look at the denominators.	Add or subtract the numerators.	Write the sum or difference over the denominator. Simplify.
A $\frac{7}{10} + \frac{8}{10}$	$\frac{7}{10} + \frac{8}{10} = 15$	$\frac{7}{10} + \frac{8}{10} = \frac{15}{10} = 1\frac{5}{10} = 1\frac{1}{2}$
B $\frac{7}{10} - \frac{5}{10}$	$\frac{7}{10} - \frac{5}{10} = 2$	$\frac{7}{10} - \frac{5}{10} = \frac{2}{10} = \frac{1}{5}$

TALK ABOUT IT

1. How could you estimate to decide if the sum in A is more than 1?
2. Use complete sentences to give reasonable answers to the story problem.

TRY IT OUT

Add or subtract. Reduce to lowest terms.

1. $\frac{2}{6} + \frac{3}{6}$ **2.** $\frac{5}{10} + \frac{6}{10}$ **3.** $\frac{8}{9} - \frac{3}{9}$ **4.** $\frac{10}{12} - \frac{4}{12}$

PRACTICE

Find these sums and differences. Simplify.

1. $\begin{array}{r} \frac{2}{4} \\ -\ \frac{1}{4} \\ \hline \end{array}$ **2.** $\begin{array}{r} \frac{3}{8} \\ +\ \frac{4}{8} \\ \hline \end{array}$ **3.** $\begin{array}{r} \frac{4}{7} \\ -\ \frac{2}{7} \\ \hline \end{array}$ **4.** $\begin{array}{r} 5\frac{4}{10} \\ -\ 2 \\ \hline \end{array}$

5. $\frac{5}{8} + \frac{4}{8}$ **6.** $\frac{2}{6} + \frac{5}{6} + \frac{3}{6}$ **7.** $1\frac{3}{4} + 2$ **8.** $\frac{7}{8} - \frac{3}{8}$

9. Add $\frac{3}{5}$ and $\frac{4}{5}$.

10. Find the difference of $\frac{7}{9}$ and $\frac{2}{9}$.

APPLY

MATH REASONING Which sum is greater? Use mental math.

11. a $\frac{3}{4} + \frac{1}{4}$ **b** $\frac{3}{10} + \frac{6}{10}$ **12. a** $\frac{1}{8} + \frac{3}{8}$ **b** $\frac{4}{12} + \frac{3}{12}$

Which difference is smaller? Use mental math.

13. a $\frac{5}{8} - \frac{1}{8}$ **b** $\frac{8}{10} - \frac{7}{10}$ **14. a** $\frac{7}{8} - \frac{3}{8}$ **b** $\frac{3}{4} - \frac{2}{4}$

PROBLEM SOLVING

15. Jeanette played volleyball for $2\frac{3}{4}$ hours before lunch. She played for $1\frac{3}{4}$ hour after lunch. How much longer did she play before lunch than after lunch?

16. Health and Fitness Data Bank How much higher does a basketball bounce than a volley ball when dropped from a height of 6 ft? See page 483.

MIXED REVIEW

Write the fraction that does not belong.

17. $\frac{1}{2}$ $\frac{2}{4}$ $\frac{1}{3}$ **18.** $\frac{4}{6}$ $\frac{6}{12}$ $\frac{2}{3}$ **19.** $\frac{4}{16}$ $\frac{4}{8}$ $\frac{1}{4}$

20. $\frac{5}{6}$ $\frac{3}{9}$ $\frac{1}{3}$ **21.** $\frac{4}{12}$ $\frac{8}{16}$ $\frac{2}{6}$ **22.** $\frac{1}{10}$ $\frac{2}{5}$ $\frac{8}{20}$

Write a decimal for the amount.

23. one and forty-four hundredths

24. thirty-five and two tenths

25. twenty and one hundredth

26. six and eight tenths

More Practice, page 510, set A

Problem Solving
Data from a Recipe

LEARN ABOUT IT

The fourth graders at Tubman School are having an Italian dinner. They are making lasagna and spaghetti. How many cups of drained tomatoes will they need?

Lasagna
$\frac{1}{2}$ pound ground beef
2 cups mozzarella cheese
$\frac{1}{2}$ cup grated parmesan cheese
$\frac{1}{2}$ cup chopped onion
$2\frac{1}{2}$ cups drained tomatoes
$\frac{3}{8}$ ounce tomato paste
$\frac{1}{2}$ pound package lasagna noodles
$\frac{1}{4}$ cup mushrooms

Spaghetti
$2\frac{1}{2}$ pounds ground beef
$\frac{1}{3}$ cup grated parmesan cheese
$\frac{1}{4}$ cup chopped parsley
$1\frac{1}{4}$ cups mushrooms
$1\frac{1}{2}$ cups chopped onion
$1\frac{1}{2}$ cups drained tomatoes
$1\frac{1}{8}$ ounces tomato paste
$1\frac{1}{2}$ lb. spaghetti noodles

I'll find the data I need in the recipes.

Lasagna: $2\frac{1}{2}$ cups drained tomatoes

Spaghetti: $1\frac{1}{2}$ cups drained tomatoes

Now I can add to solve the problem.

$$\begin{array}{r} 2\frac{1}{2} \\ +\ 1\frac{1}{2} \\ \hline 3\frac{2}{2} = 4 \end{array}$$

The fourth graders will need 4 cups of drained tomatoes.

TRY IT OUT

Use the data in the recipes to solve these problems.

1. How many ounces of tomato paste do they need?

2. How many more cups of mushrooms are in the spaghetti than the lasagna?

MIXED PRACTICE

Solve. Use any problem solving strategy. Find the data you need in the recipes on page 410.

1. Ground beef costs $2.18 a pound. How much will the ground beef for both recipes cost?
2. How much ground beef would the students need if they doubled the recipes?
3. How much grated parmesan cheese do the students need for two recipes of lasagna?
4. There were 24 people at the dinner. 12 ate lasagna. 17 ate spaghetti. How many had both?
5. Each of the 24 guests who came paid $8.50. How much was collected in all?

Some Strategies
Act It Out
Use Objects
Choose an Operation
Draw a Picture
Make an Organized List
Guess and Check
Make a Table
Look for a Pattern
Use Logical Reasoning
Work Backward

6. At the cafeteria table, Mr. Pan, Mrs. Berns, and Mrs. Li sat in a row. Mr. Pan sat between Mrs. Berns and Mrs. Li. Mrs. Berns sat between Mr. Mantoya and Mr. Pan. In what order did the people sit?
7. A package of frozen lasagna that serves 2 people costs $3.38. How much would frozen lasagna for 1 person cost?
8. **Thinking About Your Solution**
   If the fourth graders doubled each recipe, how much tomato paste would they need in all?
   Write your answer as a complete sentence. Then write a description of how you solved the problem and name the strategy or strategies you used.

More Practice, page 527, set B

Adding Fractions with Models
Unlike Denominators

LEARN ABOUT IT

EXPLORE **Use Fraction Pieces**
Work in groups. Use halves, fourths, and eighths fraction pieces. Follow these steps several times, using different pieces each time.

- Cover a section of the whole with a piece or pieces that have one denominator. Then cover another section with a piece or pieces that have a different denominator.
- Trade pieces to cover the same sections so that all pieces have the same denominator.
- Find how many pieces in all.

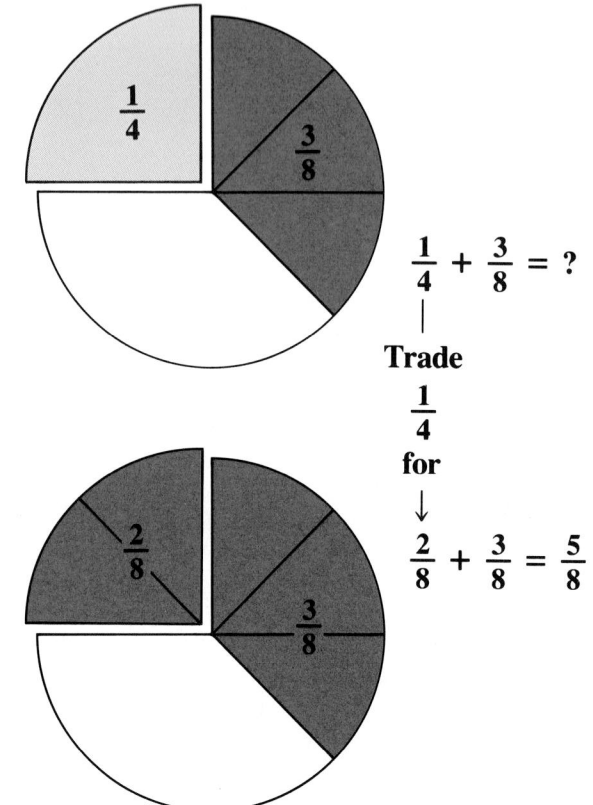

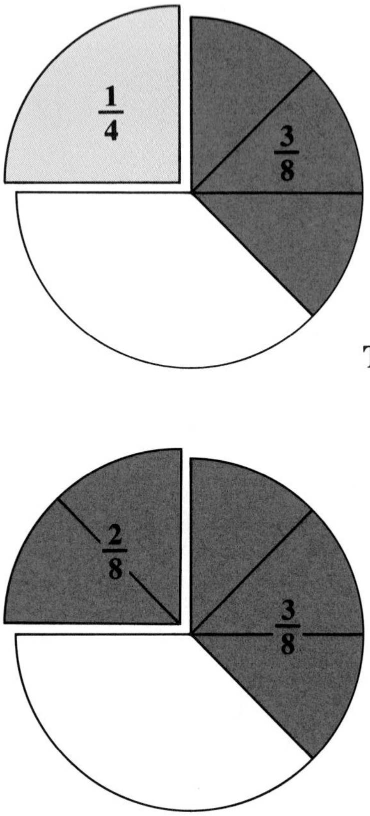

$\frac{1}{4} + \frac{3}{8} = ?$

Trade $\frac{1}{4}$ **for**

$\frac{2}{8} + \frac{3}{8} = \frac{5}{8}$

TALK ABOUT IT

1. Which pieces would you trade for $\frac{1}{2}$ when finding $\frac{3}{4} + \frac{1}{2}$? Explain.
2. Why does trading so that all pieces have the same denominator make it easy to add the fractions?

You can add fractions by changing them so that the denominators are alike. Fraction pieces can help you do this.

TRY IT OUT

Use fraction pieces to help you find each sum.

1. $\frac{5}{8} + \frac{1}{4}$ **2.** $\frac{1}{2} + \frac{3}{8}$ **3.** $\frac{1}{8} + \frac{1}{4}$ **4.** $\frac{1}{3} + \frac{1}{6}$

PRACTICE

Use fraction pieces to help you find each sum. Copy and complete the equation.

1. $\frac{1}{2} + \frac{1}{6}$

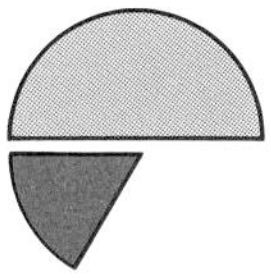

2. $\frac{2}{4} + \frac{3}{8}$

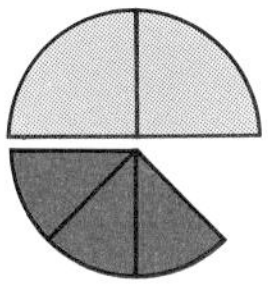

3. $\frac{1}{8} + \frac{1}{2}$

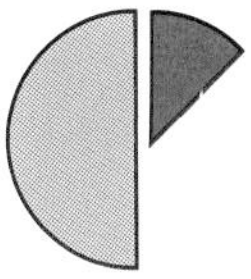

4. $\frac{2}{6} + \frac{1}{3}$

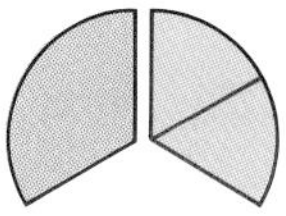

5. $\frac{1}{4} + \frac{2}{8}$ **6.** $\frac{4}{6} + \frac{1}{3}$ **7.** $\frac{2}{4} + \frac{1}{2}$ **8.** $\frac{2}{3} + \frac{1}{6}$

APPLY

MATH REASONING For each pair, use number sense to decide which will have the greater sum. Do not find the sums.

9. $\frac{5}{6} + \frac{1}{3}$ or $\frac{5}{6} + \frac{2}{3}$ **10.** $\frac{3}{8} + \frac{1}{4}$ or $\frac{3}{8} + \frac{3}{4}$

PROBLEM SOLVING

11. Jill practiced pitching for $\frac{1}{2}$ of an hour. She practiced hitting for $\frac{1}{4}$ of an hour. What part of an hour did she spend practicing?

12. **Missing Data** Tell what data is needed to solve the problem. Tim played basketball for $\frac{3}{4}$ hour and then rode his bike to the store and back. How many hours did he exercise?

▶ MENTAL MATH

Sometimes you can use mental math and compatible numbers to find fraction sums like $\frac{1}{3} + \frac{1}{5} + \frac{2}{3}$. $\frac{1}{3}$ and $\frac{2}{3}$ are compatible since they combine to make a whole number. Try these.

13. $\frac{4}{5} + \frac{3}{8} + \frac{1}{5}$ **14.** $\frac{7}{8} + \frac{5}{6} + \frac{1}{8}$

15. $\frac{9}{10} + \frac{1}{2} + \frac{1}{2}$ **16.** $\frac{3}{4} + \frac{1}{4} + \frac{3}{10}$

More Practice, page 510, set B

Subtracting Fractions with Models
Unlike Denominators

Thirds | Sixths

$$\frac{1}{3} \quad \frac{2}{3} \qquad \frac{1}{6} \quad \frac{2}{6} \quad \frac{3}{6} \quad \frac{4}{6} \quad \frac{5}{6}$$

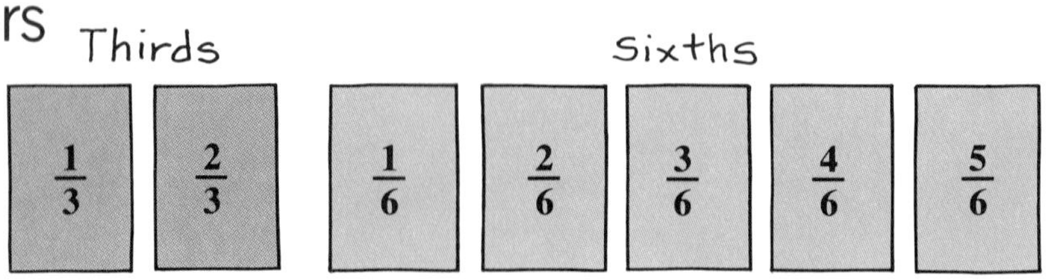

LEARN ABOUT IT

EXPLORE Use Fraction Pieces

Use the thirds and sixths fraction pieces and these fraction cards. Follow the steps several times and record your results.

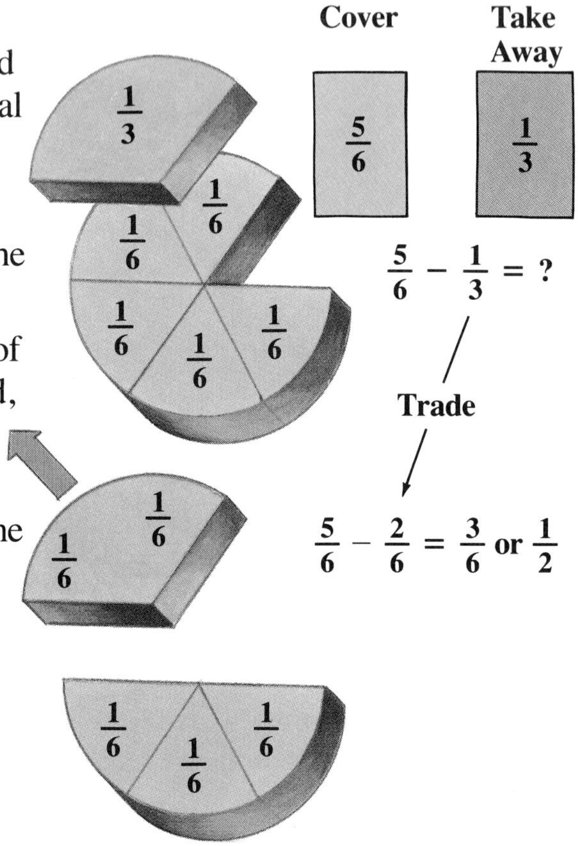

■ Choose a thirds and a sixths fraction card. The larger fraction is the *cover* fraction. The smaller is the *take away* fraction.

■ With fraction pieces, cover up the section of the whole shown on the *cover* fraction card, in this case, 5 sixths.

■ Trade the *take away* card for another card with an equivalent fraction that has the same denominator as the *cover* fraction.

■ Take away the part of the covered section shown on the new *take away* card.

■ Decide what part of the section is left. Complete an equation.

Cover $\frac{5}{6}$ Take Away $\frac{1}{3}$

$$\frac{5}{6} - \frac{1}{3} = ?$$

Trade

$$\frac{5}{6} - \frac{2}{6} = \frac{3}{6} \text{ or } \frac{1}{2}$$

TALK ABOUT IT

1. If you choose the $\frac{2}{6}$ piece and the $\frac{2}{3}$ piece, which is the *take away* piece? Explain.

2. When finding $\frac{2}{3} - \frac{1}{6}$, what piece will you trade to make the denominators the same?

You can subtract fractions by changing them so that the denominators are alike.

TRY IT OUT

Use fraction pieces to find each difference.

1. $\frac{5}{8} - \frac{1}{4}$ 2. $\frac{1}{2} - \frac{3}{8}$ 3. $\frac{3}{4} - \frac{1}{8}$ 4. $\frac{1}{3} - \frac{1}{6}$

PRACTICE

Use fraction pieces to find each difference.

1. $\frac{5}{8} - \frac{1}{2}$ **2.** $\frac{5}{6} - \frac{2}{3}$ **3.** $\frac{2}{3} - \frac{1}{6}$ **4.** $\frac{3}{8} - \frac{1}{4}$

5. $\frac{4}{6} - \frac{1}{2}$ **6.** $\frac{7}{8} - \frac{3}{4}$ **7.** $\frac{2}{3} - \frac{1}{2}$ **8.** $\frac{3}{4} - \frac{1}{2}$

APPLY

MATH REASONING For each pair, use number sense to decide which will have the greater difference. Do not subtract.

9. $\frac{5}{8} - \frac{1}{4}$ or $\frac{5}{8} - \frac{2}{4}$ **10.** $\frac{3}{10} - \frac{1}{5}$ or $\frac{7}{10} - \frac{1}{5}$

PROBLEM SOLVING

11. Bill did $\frac{1}{2}$ of his homework at school. He did $\frac{1}{4}$ of it before supper. What part of his homework did Bill have left to do after supper?

12. **Extra Data** Solve. Then tell what data is not needed. Tina played $\frac{3}{4}$ of the basketball game, Ann played $\frac{1}{2}$ of the game, and Jackie played $\frac{1}{8}$ of the game. How much more did Tina play than Jackie?

ESTIMATION

13. Write a fraction for the colored part of each strip. Tell if each fraction is closest to 0, closest to $\frac{1}{2}$, or closest to 1 whole.

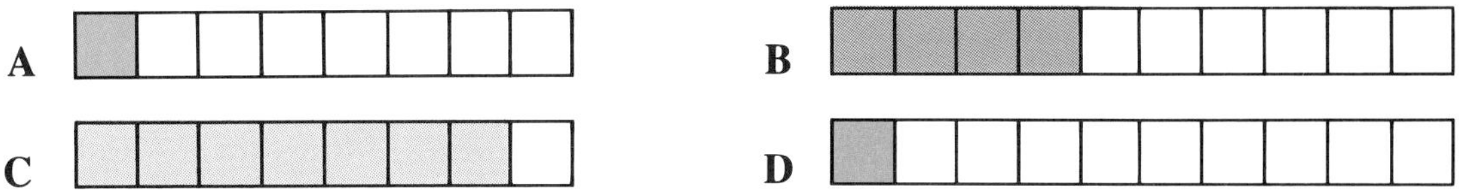

Replace each fraction below with 0, $\frac{1}{2}$, or 1 to estimate the sum or difference.

14. $\frac{9}{10} - \frac{1}{8}$ **15.** $\frac{4}{10} + \frac{7}{8}$ **16.** $\frac{3}{8} + \frac{4}{10}$ **17.** $\frac{9}{10} - \frac{7}{8}$

More Practice, page 510, set C

Exploring Algebra

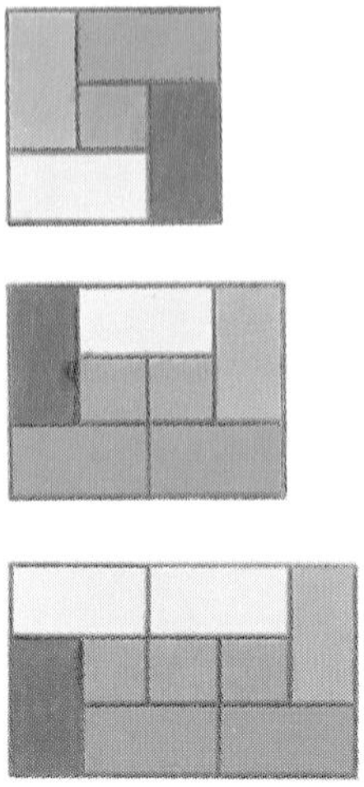

LEARN ABOUT IT

Notice how these patterns of geometric shapes grow. Continue the pattern by using objects or drawing pictures. Copy and complete the table.

S stands for the number of squares.

R stands for the number of rectangles.

<table>
<tr><td>S</td><td>1</td><td>2</td><td>3</td><td>4</td><td>5</td><td>6</td><td>7</td></tr>
<tr><td>R</td><td>4</td><td>5</td><td>6</td><td>||||</td><td>||||</td><td>||||</td><td>||||</td></tr>
</table>

TALK ABOUT IT

1. How do the numbers of squares in the table change?
2. How do the numbers of rectangles in the table change?
3. How do the numbers of rectangles relate to the numbers of squares?

TRY IT OUT

Look for a pattern. Use objects or draw a picture to help you show the next *T* design.

1. Copy and complete the table.
2. What would P be when N is 10?

1st

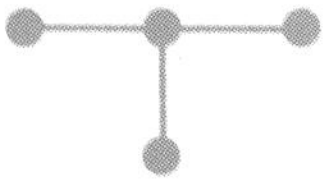

2nd

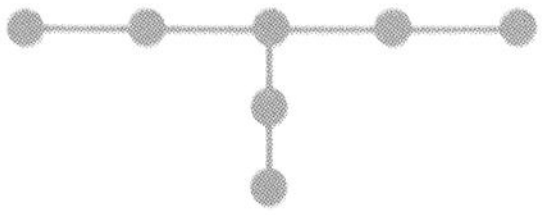

3rd

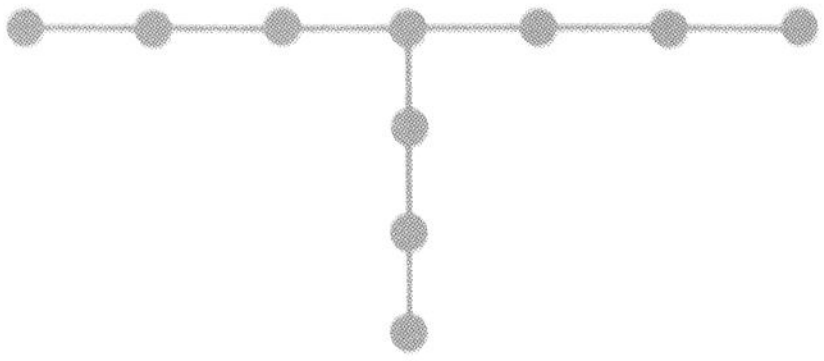

N stands for the number of the *T*.

P stands for the number of pegs needed to make it.

<table>
<tr><td>N</td><td>1</td><td>2</td><td>3</td><td>4</td><td>5</td><td>6</td><td>7</td></tr>
<tr><td>P</td><td>4</td><td>7</td><td>10</td><td>||||</td><td>||||</td><td>||||</td><td>||||</td></tr>
</table>

Power Practice/Quiz

Use fraction pieces if needed to find the lowest-terms sums and differences.

1. $\frac{3}{8} + \frac{2}{8}$

2. $\frac{2}{3} + \frac{1}{3}$

3. $\frac{7}{10} - \frac{3}{10}$

4. $\frac{4}{5} - \frac{1}{5}$

5. $\frac{4}{9} + \frac{7}{9}$

6. $\frac{7}{9} - \frac{4}{9}$

7. $\frac{5}{8} - \frac{3}{8}$

8. $\frac{2}{4} + \frac{3}{4} + \frac{1}{4}$

9. $\frac{2}{5} + \frac{3}{10}$

10. $\frac{1}{9} + \frac{2}{3}$

11. $\frac{3}{8} + \frac{3}{4}$

12. $\frac{11}{12} + \frac{5}{6}$

13. $\frac{8}{10} - \frac{3}{10}$

14. $\frac{4}{7} + \frac{3}{7}$

15. $\frac{7}{8} + \frac{4}{8}$

16. $\frac{3}{4} - \frac{1}{4}$

17. $\frac{3}{5} + \frac{2}{5}$

18. $1\frac{4}{9} + \frac{2}{9}$

19. $\frac{11}{12} - \frac{5}{12}$

20. $7\frac{2}{3} - 3\frac{2}{3}$

PROBLEM SOLVING

21. A cheese fondue recipe requires $1\frac{1}{4}$ pounds sharp Cheddar and $2\frac{3}{4}$ pounds Monterey Jack cheese. How many pounds of cheese is that all together? How much more Jack cheese than Cheddar cheese is needed?

22. A bread recipe calls for $2\frac{5}{8}$ cups wheat flour and $1\frac{1}{8}$ cups rice flour. How much flour is that all together? How much more wheat flour than rice flour is needed?

23. When Kathryn went from her house to the store and back, she jogged a total of $3\frac{7}{10}$ miles and walked a total of $2\frac{3}{10}$ miles. How much farther did she jog than walk? How far is it between her house and the store?

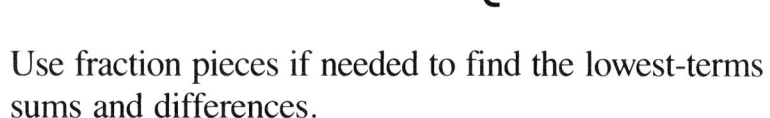

Adding and Subtracting Decimals
Making the Connection

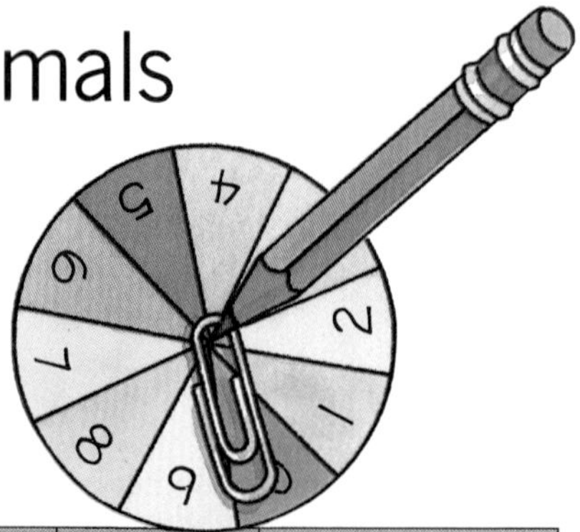

LEARN ABOUT IT

EXPLORE **Use a Place Value Model**

Work in groups. Use a spinner with the digits 0–9 and make piles of blocks.

Ones	Tenths	Hundredths

Trades

10 hundredths = 1 tenth

10 tenths = 1

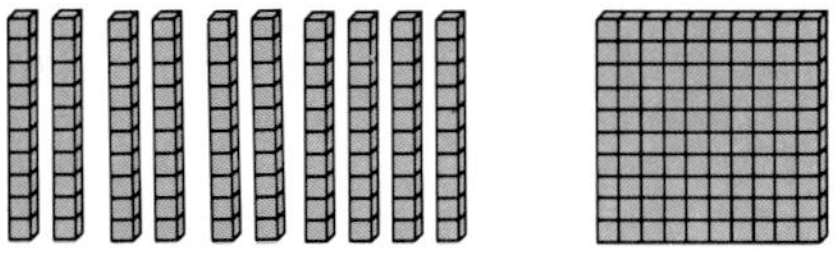

Activity 1

- Spin three times to give the number of ones, tenths, and hundredths blocks for a pile. Do this twice. Write the number for each pile in a table like the one shown.
- Push the two piles together and make all possible trades. Write the number for the combined pile in the table.

Activity 2

- Spin 3 times to give the number of hundredths, tenths, and ones blocks for a pile. Write the total number of blocks in the table.
- Spin to get the number of hundredths, tenths, and ones to take away from the pile. Re-spin as needed until the take-away number is less than the first number. Write the take-away number in the table.
- Take that number of blocks from the pile. Trade if needed. In a third row of the table, write how many are left.
- Do each of the activities several times. Make a separate table each time.

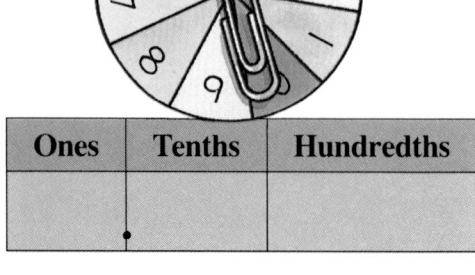

TALK ABOUT IT

1. Why is the ones column placed before the tenths and hundredths columns in the table?
2. Suppose you put 9 tenths with 7 tenths. What blocks would you have after you made a trade?

You have used blocks to show how many in all or how many are left. The addition example below will help you see that adding and subtracting decimals is just like adding and subtracting whole numbers except for lining up the decimal points.

What You Do	**What You Record**
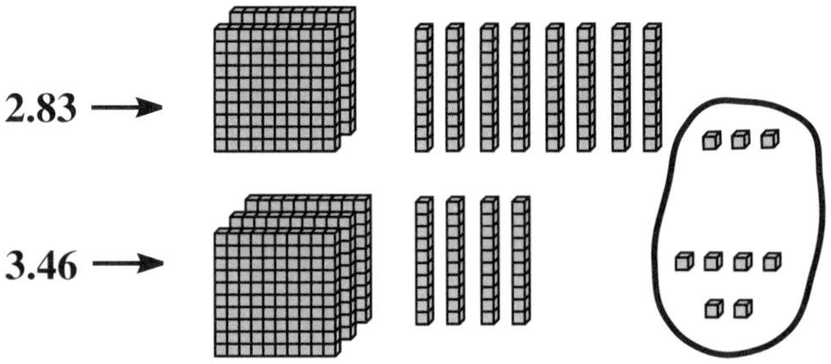	$\begin{array}{r} 2.83 \\ +\ 3.46 \\ \hline 9 \end{array}$

1. Are there enough hundredths to make a trade?

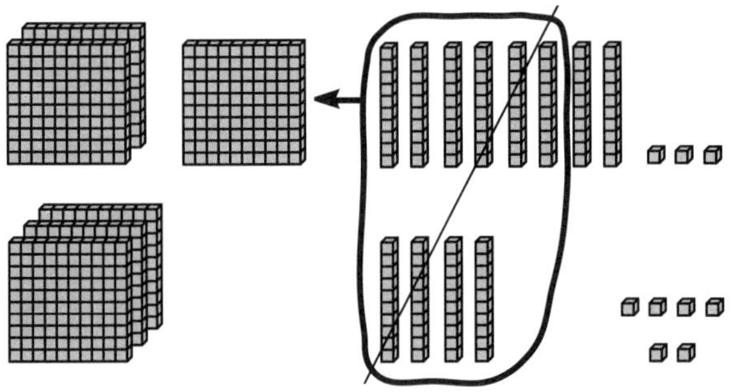

$\begin{array}{r} {}^{1} \\ 2.83 \\ +\ 3.46 \\ \hline 29 \end{array}$

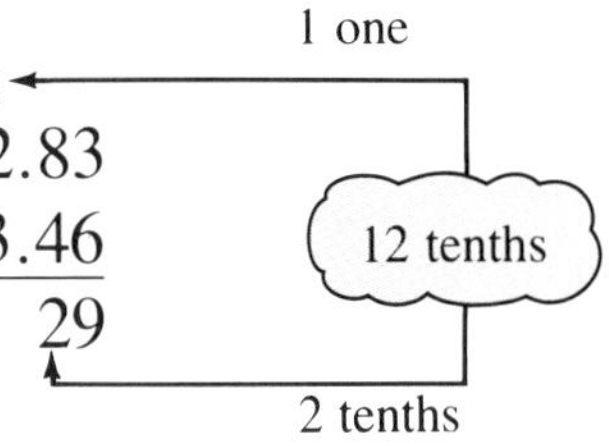

2. Are there enough tenths to make a trade?

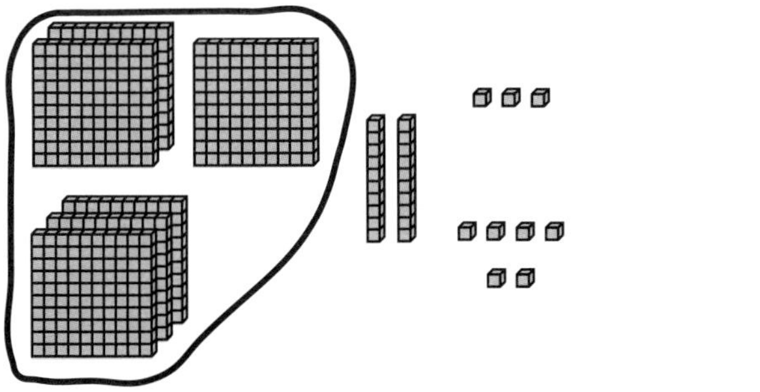

$\begin{array}{r} {}^{1} \\ 2.83 \\ +\ 3.46 \\ \hline 6.29 \end{array}$

3. How many ones are there after the trade?
4. What is the sum of 2.83 and 3.46?

TRY IT OUT

Use blocks to find these sums or differences. Record what you did.

1. 6.2 + 3.8 **2.** 1.64 + 5.37 **3.** 6.73 − 2.46 **4.** 4.37 − 1.75

Adding and Subtracting Decimals

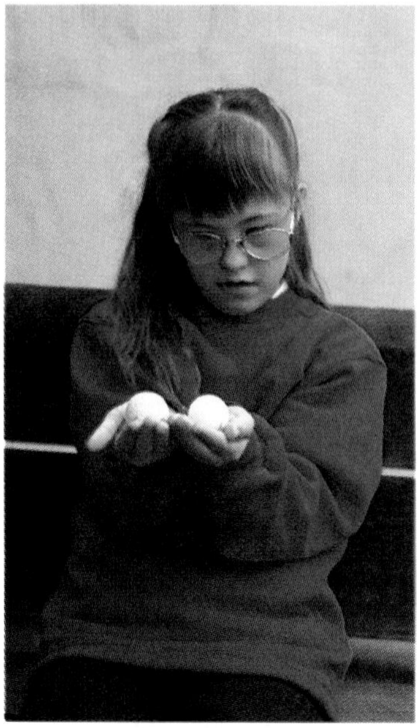

LEARN ABOUT IT

EXPLORE **Think About the Process**

A table tennis ball and a golf ball are nearly the same size. But a golf ball can weigh 45.90 grams and a table tennis ball weighs only 2.53 grams. How much do the two balls weigh together? How much more does the golf ball weigh than the table tennis ball?

When you add and subtract decimals, you must keep the decimal points in the proper place.

Line up the decimal points.	Add or subtract the hundredths. Trade if necessary.	Add or subtract the tenths. Trade if necessary.	Add or subtract the whole numbers. Place the decimal point.
45.90 + 2.53	45.90 + 2.53 3	1 45.90 + 2.53 43	1 45.90 + 2.53 48.43
45.90 − 2.53	8 10 45.~~90~~ − 2.53 7	8 10 45.~~90~~ − 2.53 37	8 10 45.~~90~~ − 2.53 43.37

TALK ABOUT IT

1. What trades did you make?
2. How would you have estimated the sum?
3. Use complete sentences to give reasonable answers to the story problems.

TRY IT OUT

1. 36.4
+ 27.8

2. 15.45
+ 6.19

3. 76.20
− 4.34

4. \$7.02
− 2.65

PRACTICE

1. 64.2 + 28.7 **2.** 33.8 + 17.6 **3.** 40.5 + 39.5 **4.** $57.20 − 4.84 **5.** 0.72 − 0.59

6. 0.89 + 0.53 **7.** $6.02 − $0.69 **8.** 24.61 + 16.18 **9.** 35.09 − 2.73

10. 42.30 − 18.80 **11.** $72.14 + 28.35 **12.** 36.05 − 9.18 **13.** 60.47 + 35.64 **14.** 56.58 − 29.74

15. 5.31 − 0.82 **16.** 43.00 + 17.06 **17.** 0.65 − 0.37 **18.** 30.54 − 8.38

APPLY

MATH REASONING Use mental math to find these sums. It may help to think of money or fractions.

19. 3.50 + 2.50 **20.** 0.25 + 0.75 **21.** 6.35 + 2.05 **22.** 3.04 + 5.01

PROBLEM SOLVING

23. Kevin's bowling ball weighed 5.44 kilograms. His sister Anne's weighed 4.08 kilograms. When Kevin carried both balls, how many kilograms did he carry?

24. Health and Fitness Data Bank How much greater is the maximum weight of a baseball than the maximum weight of a tennis ball? See page 483.

CALCULATOR

What numbers could you put between these calculator key codes to make the number sentences true?

25. [ON/AC] 4.0 [+] |||| [=] 5.5

26. [ON/AC] 3 [−] |||| [=] 2.99

27. [ON/AC] 3.5 [−] |||| [=] 3

28. [ON/AC] 2.9 [+] |||| [=] 3.2

29. [ON/AC] 4.99 [+] |||| [=] 5

30. [ON/AC] 6 [−] |||| [=] 5.9

More Practice, page 510, set D

More Adding and Subtracting Decimals

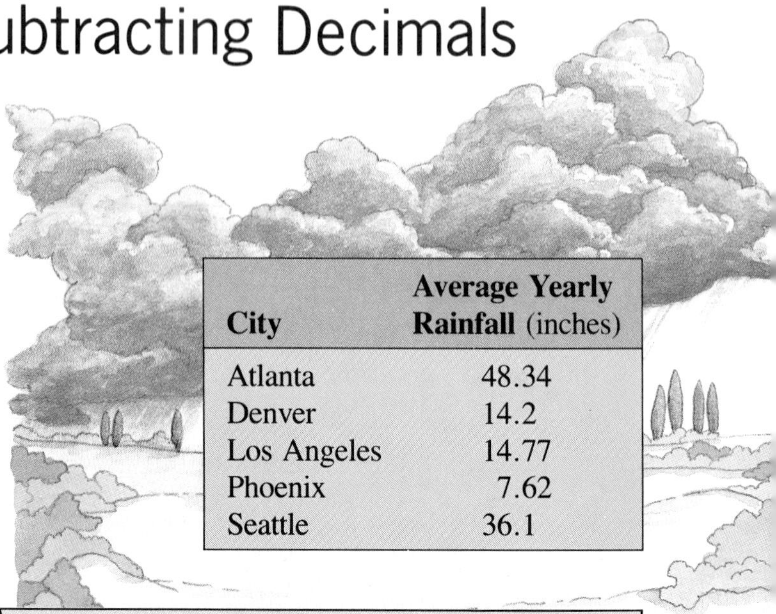

LEARN ABOUT IT

EXPLORE **Think About the Process**

The chart shows the average yearly rainfall for some cities. How much greater is the average rainfall for Denver than for Phoenix?

Since you are comparing two amounts, you subtract.

City	**Average Yearly Rainfall** (inches)
Atlanta	48.34
Denver	14.2
Los Angeles	14.77
Phoenix	7.62
Seattle	36.1

Write the problem. Line up the decimal points.

$$\begin{array}{r} 14.2 \\ -\ 7.62 \\ \hline \end{array}$$

14.2 is the same as 14.20.

Annex a zero to show both decimal parts as hundredths. Subtract.

$$\begin{array}{r} 14.20 \\ -\ 7.62 \\ \hline 6.58 \end{array}$$

TALK ABOUT IT

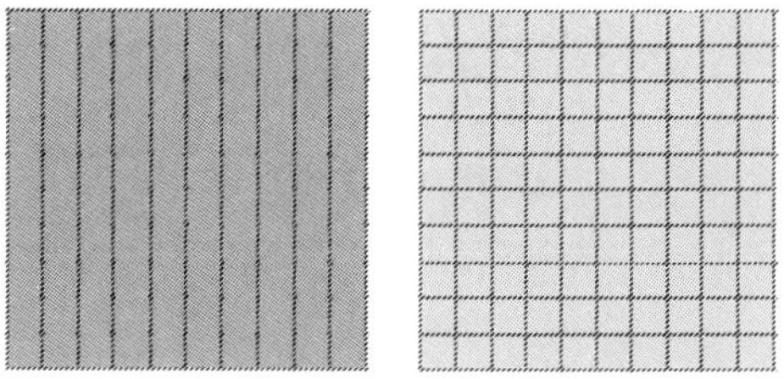

1. How could this picture help you explain why you can annex a zero and not change the value of the decimal number?
2. How would you have estimated the answer?
3. Use a complete sentence to give a reasonable answer to the story problem.

TRY IT OUT

Find the sums and differences. Annex zeros when you need them.

1. $\begin{array}{r} 42.7 \\ +\ 8.69 \\ \hline \end{array}$ **2.** $\begin{array}{r} 64.8 \\ -\ 21.34 \\ \hline \end{array}$ **3.** $\begin{array}{r} 2.69 \\ +\ 8 \\ \hline \end{array}$ **4.** $\begin{array}{r} 64 \\ -\ 18.3 \\ \hline \end{array}$ **5.** $\begin{array}{r} 93 \\ -\ 75.46 \\ \hline \end{array}$

PRACTICE

Find the sums and differences.

1. $\begin{array}{r} 14.2 \\ +\ 8.19 \\ \hline \end{array}$ **2.** $\begin{array}{r} 32.7 \\ -\ 12.43 \\ \hline \end{array}$ **3.** $\begin{array}{r} 8.96 \\ +\ 4 \\ \hline \end{array}$ **4.** $\begin{array}{r} 26.1 \\ +\ 4.27 \\ \hline \end{array}$ **5.** $\begin{array}{r} 48.72 \\ -\ 2.3 \\ \hline \end{array}$

6. 56.6 − 21.63 **7.** 40.07 + 9.9 **8.** 65.2 − 46

9. 29.1 + 4.52 **10.** 60.07 + 0.5 **11.** 47 − 28.34

APPLY

MATH REASONING Use mental math to find these sums and differences.

12. 2 − 1.5 **13.** 5 − 3.5 **14.** 14.5 − 8 **15.** 25 + 15.5

PROBLEM SOLVING

16. Use the table on page 422. Atlanta received 5.7 inches of rain in April and 6.4 inches in May. How much rain needs to fall during the rest of the year for Atlanta's rainfall to equal the yearly average?

17. **Data Hunt** What is the average yearly rainfall in your state? How much more or less rainfall does your state get than the wettest state? the driest state?

MIXED REVIEW

Tell which weighs the most.

18. nuts 326 grams
detergent 1,200 g
rice 1 kg

19. applesauce 725 g
pot roast 3 kg
potatoes 3,642 kg

20. tapioca 600 g
peaches 4 kg
vanilla 16 g

21. filet of sole 520 g
onion 435 g
butter 1 kg

Write L or mL for the unit you would use to measure each thing.

22. a raindrop **23.** a pitcher of milk **24.** a spoonful of honey

More Practice, page 511, set A

Estimating Decimal Sums and Differences

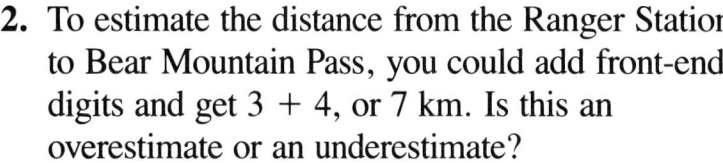

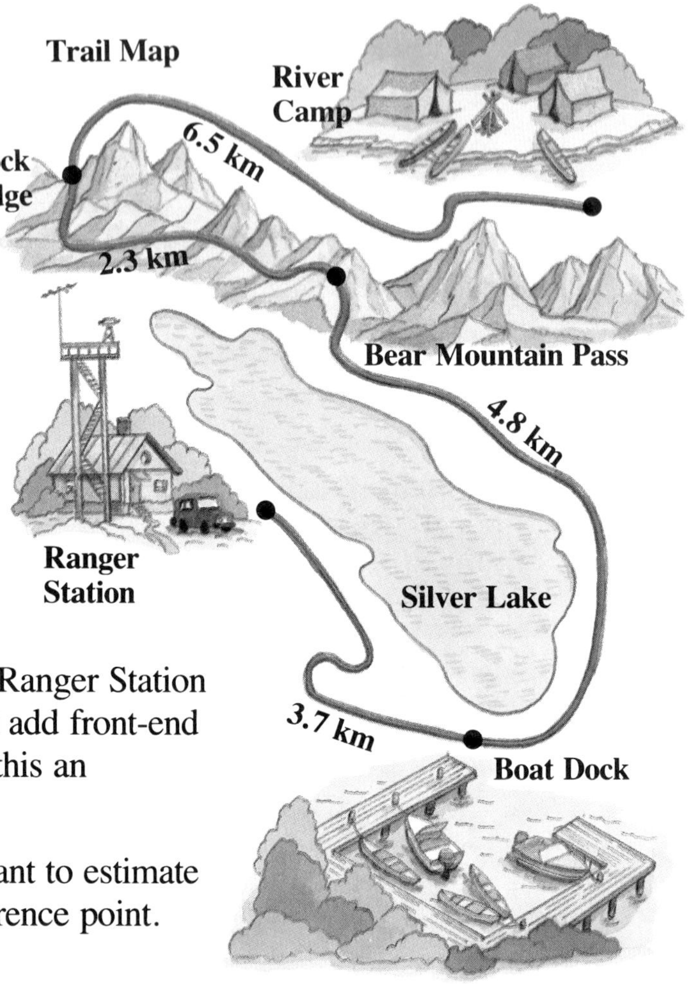

LEARN ABOUT IT

EXPLORE **Study the Map**

Megan is planning a backpacking trip. She does not want to hike more than 15 km a day. Can she hike from the Ranger Station to Eagle Rock Ridge in one day?

TALK ABOUT IT

1. Is the distance from the Ranger Station to the Boat Dock closer to 3 or 4 kilometers? Explain.
2. To estimate the distance from the Ranger Station to Bear Mountain Pass, you could add front-end digits and get 3 + 4, or 7 km. Is this an overestimate or an underestimate?

You can round decimals when you want to estimate a sum to decide if it is close to a reference point.

3.7 km + 4.8 km + 2.3 km = ||||

- round down, using front-end digits — 3 + 4 + 2 = 9
- round up — 4 + 5 + 3 = 12
- round to a chosen place — 4 + 5 + 2 = 11

rounded to the nearest whole number

The estimates are under 15 km.

TRY IT OUT

Estimate these sums or differences by rounding as indicated. Tell whether the answer is an *overestimate* or an *underestimate*.

1. 5.8 + 6.7 (up) **2.** 17.4 − 6.5 (down) **3.** 9.56 + 8.78 (up)

PRACTICE

Round down. Then estimate the sum.

1. $6.4 + 3.3$ **2.** $12.25 + 9.36$ **3.** $15.45 + 5.28$ **4.** $7.53 + 6.41$ **5.** $23.21 + 10.19$

Round up. Then estimate the difference.

6. $7.8 - 3.7$ **7.** $99.99 - 59.36$ **8.** $27.5 - 17.3$ **9.** $5.45 - 2.63$ **10.** $14.9 - 12.8$

Use rounding to estimate each sum or difference. Then decide whether the actual sum or difference is over or under the reference point 30.

11. $16.45 + 14.01$ **12.** $12.3 + 19.7$ **13.** $35.6 - 5.9$

APPLY

MATH REASONING

14. Megan bought a backpack for $29.58 and some wool socks for $5.25. She gave the clerk $40. Without counting, tell how much change she got.

a $4.17 **b** $5.17 **c** $3.17

PROBLEM SOLVING

15. Use the map on page 424 to solve this problem. Megan planned to hike from the Ranger Station to River Camp in two days. Is that distance more or less than 20 km?

16. The backpackers took five tents on the trip. Two tents could hold 4 people each, and 3 tents could hold 2 people each. How many people all together could the tents hold?

COMMUNICATION Write Your Own Problem

17. Write your own story problem. The problem should involve estimating and adding or subtracting decimals. It should have people in it and should have a reasonable answer.

More Practice, page 511, set B

Using Critical Thinking

LEARN ABOUT IT

Ellie showed this **flow chart** to Rosa. "Let's try to figure it out," said Rosa. "It might be fun, so I'll try the word *fun*!"

"What does *Is the word whole?* mean?" asked Ellie.

"I don't know," said Rosa, "but let's try the word *stop* before we stop!"

"Oh, now I see what it means!" said Ellie.

FUN

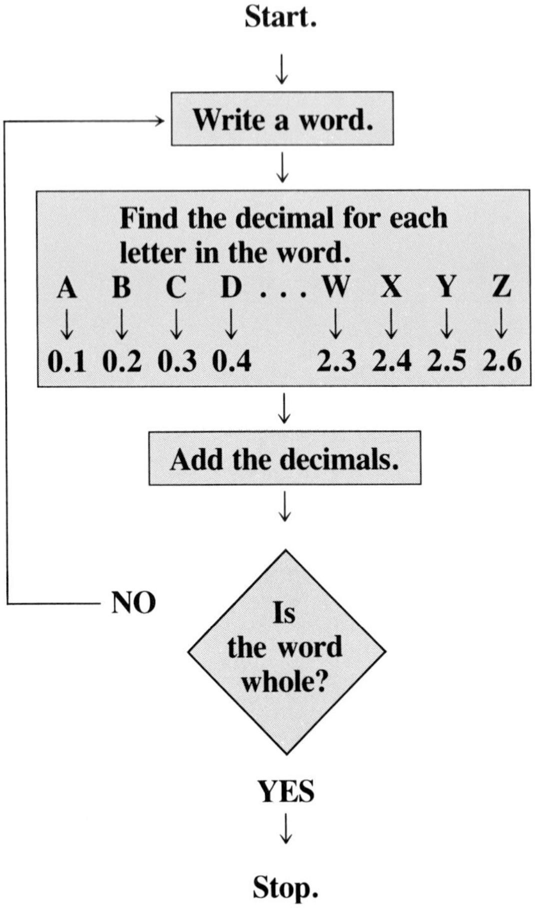
Start.
Write a word.
Find the decimal for each letter in the word.
A B C D . . . W X Y Z
0.1 0.2 0.3 0.4 2.3 2.4 2.5 2.6
Add the decimals.
Is the word whole?
NO
YES
Stop.

TALK ABOUT IT

1. A flow chart gives directions for doing something. What does this flow chart tell you how to do?
2. It is important to do the steps in order. What is the first step in this flow chart? What is the second step?
3. What is the decimal value for the word *fun*?
4. How did trying the word *stop* help Jill see what *Is the word whole?* means?

TRY IT OUT

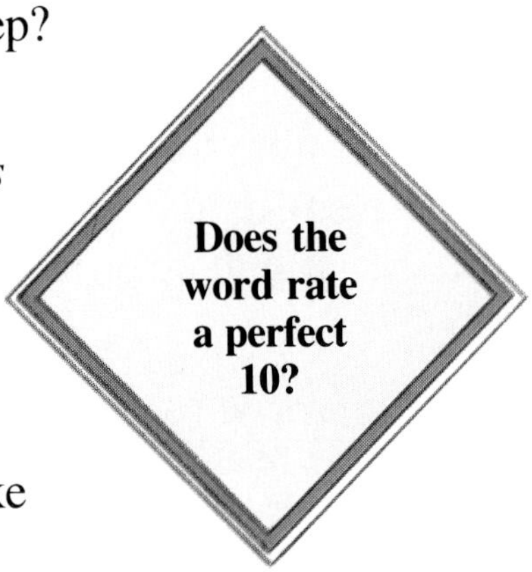
Does the word rate a perfect 10?

Suppose the diamond box in the flow chart looked like this. Which of these words would rate a perfect 10?

1. wizards **2.** fourth **3.** squares **4.** problems

Problem Solving

UNDERSTAND
FIND DATA
PLAN
ESTIMATE
SOLVE
CHECK

MIXED PRACTICE

Solve. Use any problem solving strategy.

Sizes of Penguins		
Penguin	Height	Weight
Fairy	35 cm	0.9 kg
Emperor	100 cm	45 kg at the most
extinct	?	135 kg

1. How much heavier than a fairy penguin is an emperor penguin?

2. One type of large penguin is now extinct. It was 10 cm shorter than 4 times the height of a fairy penguin. How tall was the penguin that is now extinct?

3. Emperors usually dive about 21 meters under water. They have been known to dive 13 times that deep to find large squid. How deep have they dived?

4. When a penguin pops 2 meters out of the water into the air, it is jumping 3 times its own height. For a tall man to jump 3 times his height, he would have to jump $5\frac{1}{2}$ meters out of the water. How much higher than the penguin does the human need to jump to jump 3 times his height?

5. Roberto can do a report on adelie, emperor, or little blue penguins. He can write it alone or with a partner. How many different choices does he have?

6. When a penguin toboggans, it can go as fast as 3.2 kilometers in 15 minutes. Estimate how far it could get in an hour.

7. The zookeeper divided the fish for the penguins into 6 buckets. Each bucket had 9 fish. She also put 15 fish into a bag. When the fish in the buckets and the bag had been fed to the penguins, the zookeeper still had 8 fish left in her pocket. How many fish did she start out with?

8. Penguin parents sometimes feed their young as much as 907 grams of food an hour. At that rate, how much food would a baby get in 12 hours?

More Practice, page 527, set C

Applied Problem Solving
Group Decision Making

UNDERSTAND
FIND DATA
PLAN
ESTIMATE
SOLVE
CHECK

Group Skill:
Disagree in an Agreeable Way

Your group wants to enter the school's kite-flying contest. You need to figure out how many kites the group will make, what materials you will need, and how much your kites will cost.

Facts to Consider

You will need to follow these directions to make one kite.

1. Cut a balsa wood stick 24 inches long and another one 30 inches long.
2. Cut notches in the ends of the sticks.

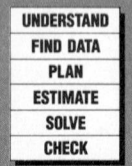

Cost of Materials

wrapping paper rolls small large extra large	 \$1.78 \$2.40 \$3.50	 4 feet long and $2\frac{1}{2}$ feet wide 6 feet long and $2\frac{1}{2}$ feet wide 6 feet long and 3 feet wide
balsa wood sticks	\$0.40 each \$0.45 each \$0.52 each	3 feet long 4 feet long 5 feet long
kite string, 1 ball	\$1.46	

3. Tie the sticks together so they make a small letter *t*.
4. Run 1 piece of string through all the notches and tie it. Now you have a frame.
5. Cut a piece of wrapping paper to cover your frame. Make it $\frac{1}{2}$ inch taller and $\frac{1}{2}$ inch wider than the frame so you can fold it over.
6. Glue the wrapping paper to the frame.
7. Punch 2 holes in the paper and attach the flying string.
8. Make a tail.

Some Questions to Answer

1. How many kite sticks can you cut from a 3-foot balsa wood stick? a four-foot stick? a five-foot stick?
2. How many kites can you cut from one small roll of wrapping paper? from a large roll? from an extra-large roll?
3. How many kites will your group make?
4. Do you need more than one ball of kite string?
5. Can you think of a way to save money when you buy your materials? Hint: It might help to draw a picture or diagram to plan the least wasteful use of materials.

What Is Your Decision?

Make a list of the materials you will need. Tell how much it will cost to make the kites.

WRAP UP

What Comes First?

Choose the phrase that correctly completes the sentence.

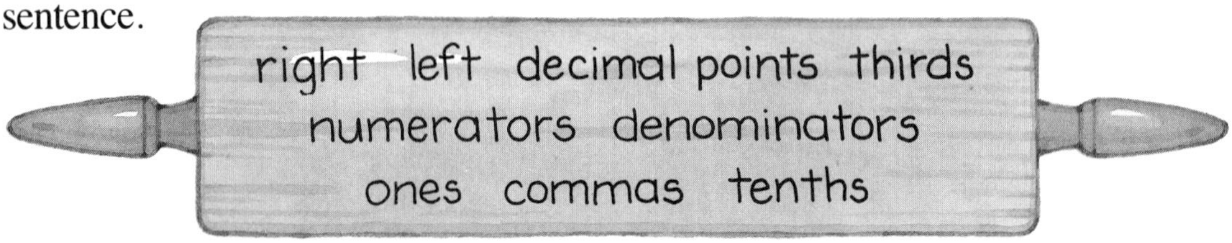

1. When you add or subtract fractions, first look at the __?__.
2. When you add or subtract decimals, first line up the __?__.
3. When you add fractions with like denominators, first add the __?__ and write the sum over the denominator.

Sometimes, Always, Never

Which word should go in the blank, sometimes, always, or never? Explain your choices.

4. To add or subtract fractions, you __?__ add or subtract denominators.
5. The sum of two mixed numbers is __?__ a mixed number.
6. If you annex extra zeros to the right of the last decimal point, the value of the decimal __?__ stays the same.

Project

Find a recipe for making something special you like to eat. Rewrite the recipe so it will make twice as much as the original recipe.

POWER PRACTICE/TEST

Part 1 Understanding

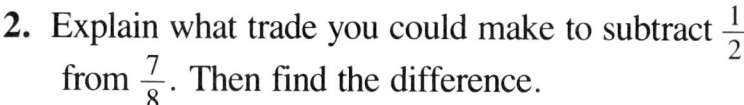

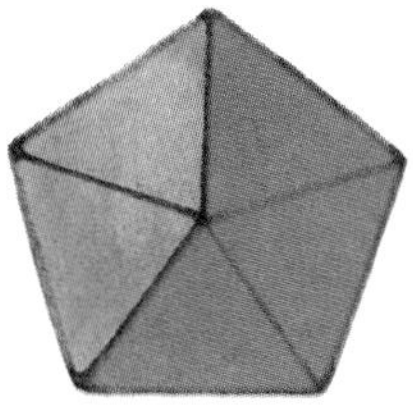

1. Use fractions to tell how much of the pentagon is red and how much is blue.
2. Explain what trade you could make to subtract $\frac{1}{2}$ from $\frac{7}{8}$. Then find the difference.
3. Find a pattern. Give the next 3 numbers in each row. P stands for perimeter and A stands for area.

P (in cm)	4	8	12	16	?	?	?
A (in sq cm)	1	4	9	16	?	?	?

Part 2 Skills

Add or subtract. Reduce answers to lowest terms.

4. $\frac{7}{10} - \frac{2}{10}$ **5.** $\frac{5}{6} + \frac{5}{6}$ **6.** $\frac{6}{7} + \frac{4}{7}$

7. $\frac{1}{4} + \frac{1}{2}$ **8.** $\frac{1}{8} + \frac{3}{4}$ **9.** $\frac{2}{3} - \frac{2}{9}$

Add or subtract.

10. $0.63 - 0.28$ **11.** $3.74 + 8.26$ **12.** $42.22 + 30.89$ **13.** \$23.50 − \$ 9.62

14. $4.52 + 7.7$ **15.** $44 - 35.01$ **16.** $13.7 + 0.68$

Part 3 Applications

17. At breakfast time, Dan was 20 km from his goal of hiking 500 km per month. If he hiked 12.9 km before lunch and 7.4 km after lunch, did he reach his goal?

18. **Challenge** A campfire stew recipe calls for $2\frac{1}{2}$ cups of water. Dan doubles the recipe. His canteen holds $1\frac{1}{4}$ cups. How many times must he fill it to make the stew?

ENRICHMENT
Puzzling Fractions

Think of this hexagon as one unit.

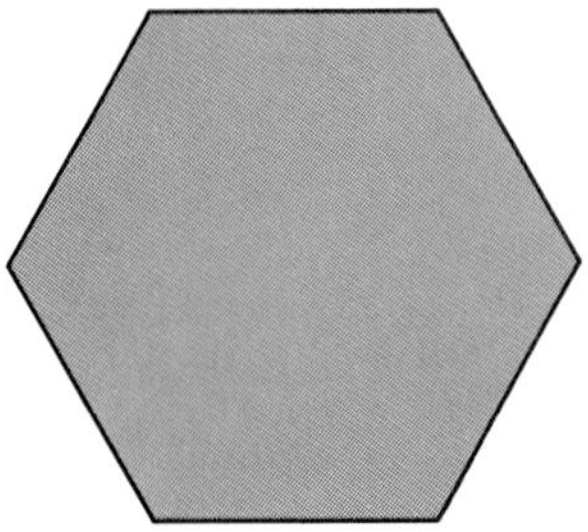

These shapes are fractional parts of the hexagon.

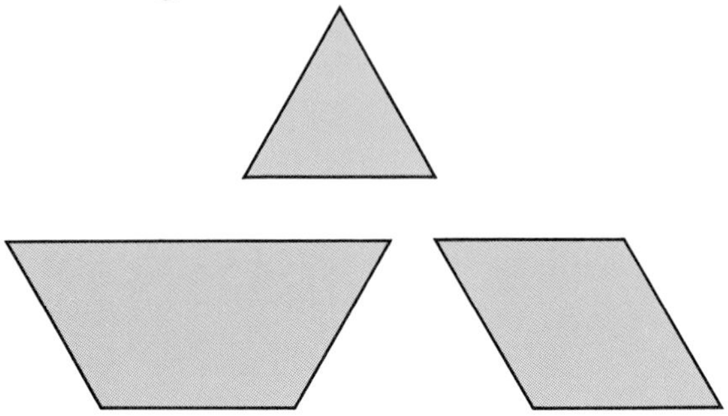

1. Tell what fractional part of the hexagon each piece is. Use pattern blocks or tracing paper if you need help.

Write what fractional part of the original hexagon each of these pieces is. Then add the fractions in each problem. Write the sum as a fraction in lowest terms, a whole number, or a mixed number.

2.

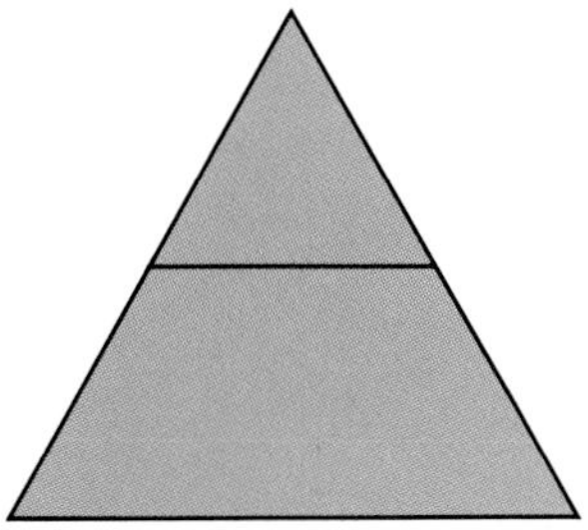

3.

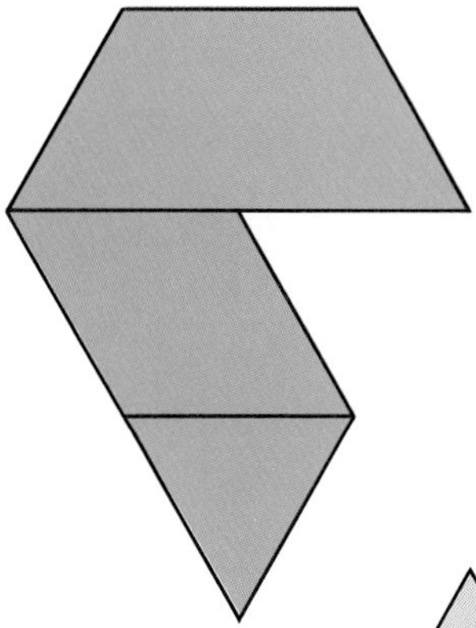

4.

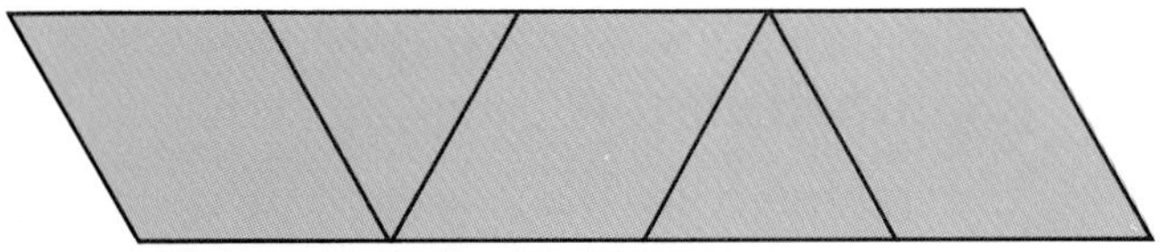

5.

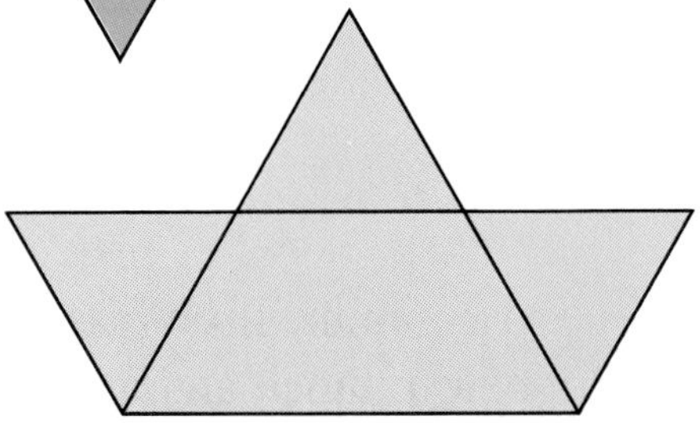

6. Make a 3-piece quadrilateral, the sum of whose pieces is $\frac{5}{6}$.

Cumulative Review

1. Which fraction is equivalent to $\frac{5}{8}$?

   A $\frac{8}{5}$ B $\frac{40}{64}$
   C $\frac{10}{24}$ D $\frac{25}{32}$

2. Which fraction is reduced to lowest terms?

   A $\frac{9}{14}$ B $\frac{9}{12}$
   C $\frac{9}{15}$ D $\frac{9}{27}$

3. Find $\frac{4}{5}$ of 40.

   A 24 B 10
   C 8 D 32

4. Which is a reasonable estimate of 12 × \$3.09?

   A \$27 B \$15
   C \$30 D \$36

5. Which number has 5 in the tenths place?

   A 54.2 B 2.64
   C 2.54 D 50.03

6. Which decimal is less than 3.1?

   A 3.10 B 3.08
   C 3.21 D 4.0

7. Find a decimal equal to $\frac{4}{5}$.

   A 0.8 B 0.5
   C 0.4 D 0.1

8. Which is a reasonable length for a watermelon?

   A 48 km B 48 m
   C 48 dm D 48 cm

9. About what air temperature is reasonable for a swim in an outdoor pool?

   A 10°C B 100°C
   C 43°C D −5°C

10. Which weighs about 3 kg?

    A a balloon B a stove
    C a crayon D a cat

11. A juice bottle holds 200 mL. How many bottles are needed to hold 1 L of juice?

    A 10 B 4
    C 5 D 50

12. A string bean is just under 4 cm. Which could be its length in mm?

    A 45 mm B 4 mm
    C 38 mm D 387 mm

16

DIVISION 2-DIGIT DIVISORS

THEME: LITERATURE

MATH AND LANGUAGE ARTS

DATA BANK

Use the Language Arts Data Bank on page 478 to answer the questions.

1 How many families are living on Krakatoa? How many Krakatoans are children?

Before airplanes were invented, people used hot-air balloons to fly high above the earth.

2 Krakatoan inventions include a balloon merry-go-round. How many children can ride the balloon merry-go-round at a time?

3 The book *Twenty-One Balloons* was first published in 1947. How many years after the actual explosion of Krakatoa was this?

4 **Use Critical Thinking** Everyone escapes the volcano on a balloon platform. How many of each size balloon are on each side of the platform?

Mental Math
Special Quotients

LEARN ABOUT IT

EXPLORE Think About the Situation

You can use basic division facts and mental math to help you find special quotients. At an amusement park 20 people can ride the Log Water Slide at once. Jane wondered how many rides it would take for the 180 people waiting in line.

TALK ABOUT IT

1. How can you use multiplication and the guess and check strategy to answer Jane's question?
2. How many groups of ten people are waiting in line? How could thinking of tens help you find the quotient?

Here is a quick way to find quotients like 180 ÷ 20 using mental math.

To find **180** ÷ **20**, find **18** ÷ **2**

18 tens ÷ 2 tens = 9

$$\begin{array}{r} 9 \\ 2 \text{ tens} \overline{)18 \text{ tens}} \end{array}$$

180 ÷ 20 = 9

$$\begin{array}{r} 9 \\ 20\overline{)180} \end{array}$$

TRY IT OUT

Divide, using mental math. Check by multiplying.

1. 90 ÷ 30	**2.** 320 ÷ 40	**3.** 280 ÷ 70	**4.** 560 ÷ 80
5. 400 ÷ 50	**6.** 420 ÷ 60	**7.** 450 ÷ 90	**8.** 810 ÷ 90

PRACTICE

Divide, using mental math. Check by multiplying.

1. 40 ÷ 20 **2.** 600 ÷ 6 **3.** 400 ÷ 80 **4.** 810 ÷ 9

5. 180 ÷ 6 **6.** 280 ÷ 40 **7.** 630 ÷ 70 **8.** 250 ÷ 50

9. 160 ÷ 20 **10.** 540 ÷ 90 **11.** 720 ÷ 80 **12.** 120 ÷ 30

13. $50\overline{)300}$ **14.** $90\overline{)90}$ **15.** $60\overline{)180}$ **16.** $70\overline{)490}$

17. How many 40s are in 160?

18. How many 80s are in 320?

19. What is 480 divided by 60?

APPLY

MATH REASONING Use mental math to decide if the quotients are equal or unequal.

20. 200 ÷ 2 and 2,000 ÷ 20

21. 600 ÷ 60 and 6,000 ÷ 60

22. 400 ÷ 5 and 4,000 ÷ 50

23. 210 ÷ 7 and 2,100 ÷ 70

PROBLEM SOLVING

24. There are 30 seats on the ferris wheel. 240 people are waiting in line. If the ferris wheel is full for each ride, how many rides will it take for everyone to have a turn?

25. Toby's father bought 4 five-day passes to Fun Park. The total cost was $160. How much did each pass cost?

ESTIMATION

Estimate the quotients using front-end digits. Substitute a compatible basic fact when helpful.

26. $22\overline{)183}$ **27.** $67\overline{)487}$ **28.** $81\overline{)324}$ **29.** $82\overline{)641}$

30. $42\overline{)359}$ **31.** $78\overline{)236}$ **32.** $53\overline{)324}$ **33.** $34\overline{)122}$

34. 456 ÷ 94 **35.** 284 ÷ 31 **36.** 133 ÷ 62

More Practice, page 511, set C

Dividing by Tens
1-Digit Quotients

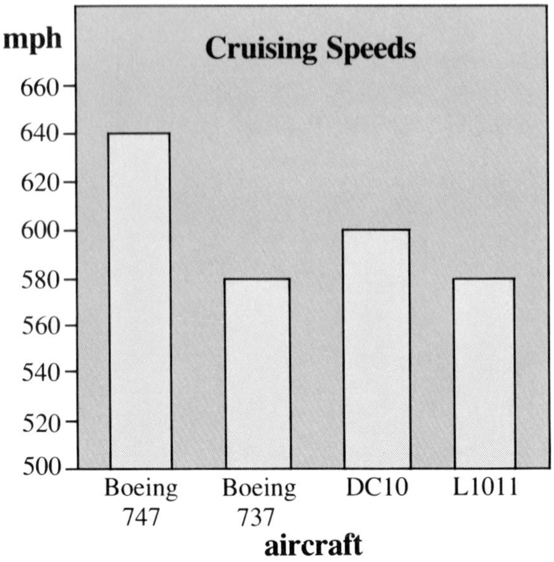

LEARN ABOUT IT

EXPLORE Think About the Process. The table shows the cruising speed of some modern jet aircraft. How far does the Boeing 737 fly in 1 minute?

This is how to find the correct quotient.

Use front-end digits and basic facts to estimate the quotient.	Divide using your estimate.
6 tens)58 tens 60)580	■ Divide ■ Multiply ■ Subtract ■ Compare 9 R40 60)580 540 40

TALK ABOUT IT

1. How can you use multiplication to see if your answer is reasonable?
2. Answer the question in a complete sentence.

Other Examples

A
6 R18
40)258
240
18

B
2 R12
30)72
60
12

C
8 R40
70)600
560
40

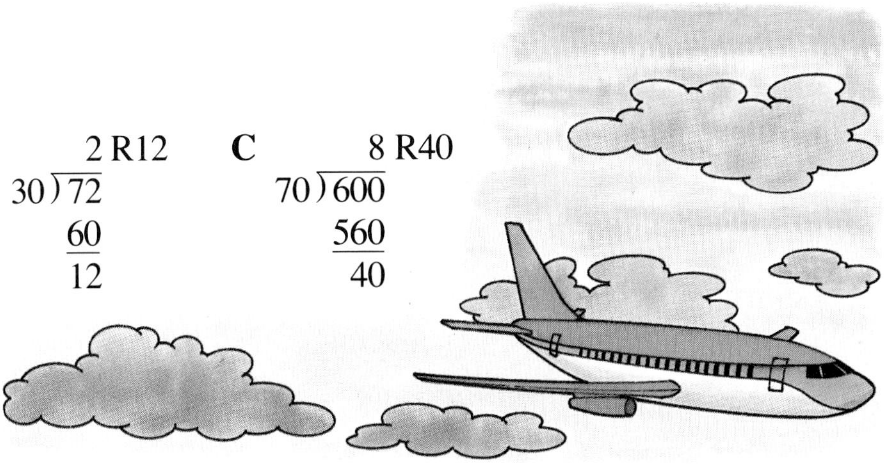

TRY IT OUT

Divide and check.

1. 30)68   **2.** 20)94   **3.** 50)325   **4.** 60)400   **5.** 90)618

PRACTICE

Divide and check.

1. $10\overline{)93}$ **2.** $20\overline{)67}$ **3.** $40\overline{)83}$ **4.** $20\overline{)54}$ **5.** $60\overline{)248}$

6. $30\overline{)159}$ **7.** $50\overline{)313}$ **8.** $80\overline{)500}$ **9.** $90\overline{)193}$ **10.** $30\overline{)251}$

11. $70\overline{)400}$ **12.** $60\overline{)195}$ **13.** $30\overline{)285}$ **14.** $50\overline{)491}$ **15.** $10\overline{)79}$

APPLY

MATH REASONING Estimate these quotients.

16. $60\overline{)372}$ **17.** $20\overline{)126}$ **18.** $30\overline{)189}$ **19.** $50\overline{)449}$

20. Find at least three numbers that when divided by 30 do not have a remainder.

PROBLEM SOLVING

21. Determining Reasonable Answers
There were 16 people in one row of an airplane. The row had 6 more adults than children. How many children were there? Decide which answer is reasonable.

a 2 children **b** 4 children **c** 5 children **d** 6 children

22. How far does the DC 10 airplane fly in one minute? Use the data from the graph on page 438.

MIXED REVIEW

Use mental math to divide.

23. 40 ÷ 20 **24.** 26 ÷ 13 **25.** 36 ÷ 12 **26.** 63 ÷ 21 **27.** 90 ÷ 30

28. Write 4 decimals with a number in the tenths place that rounds to 5.

29. Write 4 decimals with numbers in the tenths and hundredths places that round to 10.

More Practice, page 511, set D

Dividing
1-Digit Quotients

LEARN ABOUT IT

EXPLORE **Think About the Process**

In the book *Twenty-One Balloons*, a hydrogen balloon such as the *Globe* must carry bags of sand. These bags, called ballast, weigh 33 pounds each. How many bags of ballast could the professor make from 265 pounds of sand?

Use rounding to help you find the quotient.

Round the divisor. Use front-end digits and basic facts to estimate the quotient.

Think 3)26

30
↖
33)265

- Divide
- Multiply
- Subtract
- Compare

$$\begin{array}{r} 8\ \text{R1} \\ 33\overline{)265} \\ -\ 264 \\ \hline 1 \end{array}$$

TALK ABOUT IT

1. Why is 8 a better estimate than 80?
2. Use a complete sentence to give a reasonable answer to the story problem.

TRY IT OUT

Divide and check.

1. 18)37 **2.** 23)86 **3.** 13)34 **4.** 57)\$2.28 **5.** 90)369

6. 96 ÷ 45 **7.** 48 ÷ 36 **8.** 425 ÷ 85

PRACTICE

To what number would you round the divisor when estimating the quotient?

1. $28\overline{)68}$ **2.** $64\overline{)93}$ **3.** $23\overline{)76}$ **4.** $85\overline{)\$8.76}$

Divide and check.

5. $29\overline{)92}$ **6.** $18\overline{)42}$ **7.** $32\overline{)53}$ **8.** $54\overline{)83}$

9. $72\overline{)377}$ **10.** $21\overline{)85}$ **11.** $19\overline{)143}$ **12.** $64\overline{)\$5.76}$

13. $63\overline{)260}$ **14.** $25\overline{)\$2.00}$ **15.** $47\overline{)255}$ **16.** $32\overline{)\$2.24}$

APPLY

MATH REASONING Use mental math to solve these problems.

17. $12\overline{)24}$ **18.** $25\overline{)50}$ **19.** $15\overline{)30}$ **20.** $25\overline{)75}$

Guess and check to solve these equations.

21. $9 \times n = 108$ **22.** $96 = 4 \times n$ **23.** $7 \times n = 98$

PROBLEM SOLVING

24. For stopping, a hydrogen balloon needs 2 mooring ropes each 33 feet long. How many mooring ropes could be cut from a rope 325 feet long?

25. Language Arts Data Bank DATA BANK The valve for letting out the hydrogen should require a pull of between 33 and 44 pounds. About how many times more than the greatest recommended pull was the pull of each balloon's valve on the flying platform? See page 478.

USING CRITICAL THINKING Support Your Conclusion

26. Decide if this statement is sometimes true, always true, or never true. Show some examples to support your conclusion. Start with a 1-digit divisor. Then try a 2-digit divisor.

> If you double the divisor in a problem, the quotient will also double.

Changing Estimates

LEARN ABOUT IT

EXPLORE **Solve to Understand**

Over the weekend, 495 people bought tickets for a double-decker bus tour. 325 people bought tickets for the single-decker bus tour. A double-decker bus holds 72 passengers and a single-decker bus holds 46 passengers. How many full buses will the company need for each tour and how many people will be on a partly filled bus?

TALK ABOUT IT

1. How do you know that you should divide in this problem?
2. Which pairs of numbers will you need to divide?

When you divide you will sometimes discover that you need to change your estimate.

A

$$\begin{array}{r} \scriptstyle 70 \nwarrow \quad 7 \\ 72\overline{)495} \\ -\ 504 \end{array} \leftarrow \text{Too large} \qquad \begin{array}{r} \scriptstyle 70 \nwarrow \quad 6\text{ R}63 \\ 72\overline{)495} \\ -\ 432 \\ \hline 63 \end{array}$$

B

$$\begin{array}{r} \scriptstyle 50 \nwarrow \quad 6 \\ 46\overline{)325} \\ -\ 276 \\ \hline 49 \end{array} \begin{array}{l} \\ \\ \leftarrow \text{Too small} \\ \leftarrow \text{more than 46} \end{array} \qquad \begin{array}{r} \scriptstyle 50 \nwarrow \quad 7\text{ R}3 \\ 46\overline{)325} \\ -\ 322 \\ \hline 3 \end{array}$$

6 full double-decker buses and an extra bus with 63 people are needed. 7 full single-decker buses and an extra bus with 3 people are needed.

TRY IT OUT

Decide which estimates must be changed. Then finish the division.

1. $17\overline{)88}$, estimate 4
2. $28\overline{)86}$, estimate 2
3. $16\overline{)97}$, estimate 4
4. $42\overline{)82}$, estimate 2

PRACTICE

Divide. Change your estimate if necessary.

1. $38\overline{)46}$ **2.** $22\overline{)85}$ **3.** $53\overline{)125}$ **4.** $44\overline{)243}$ **5.** $64\overline{)312}$

6. $32\overline{)248}$ **7.** $35\overline{)142}$ **8.** $19\overline{)184}$ **9.** $77\overline{)543}$ **10.** $93\overline{)651}$

11. $42\overline{)289}$ **12.** $85\overline{)686}$ **13.** $65\overline{)391}$ **14.** $29\overline{)133}$ **15.** $74\overline{)636}$

16. $182 \div 27$ **17.** $167 \div 54$ **18.** $364 \div 39$ **19.** $332 \div 82$

20. $428 \div 56$ **21.** $895 \div 93$ **22.** $85 \div 26$ **23.** $646 \div 91$

24. Find 543 divided by 61. **25.** Find 699 divided by 86.

APPLY

MATH REASONING Decide which quotient is larger without solving the problem.

26. $2{,}383 \div 42$ or $2{,}383 \div 52$

27. $423 \div 17$ or $323 \div 17$

PROBLEM SOLVING

28. 138 students from Elm School will take single-decker buses on a field trip. Each bus holds 46 passengers. How many buses do they need?

29. The wax museum is very popular. In one day it averages 424 visitors. About how many visitors does it average every 2 weeks?

ALGEBRA

Find at least 5 pairs of numbers for the $\square$ and $\triangle$ in each problem.

30. $\square \div \triangle = 40$

31. $\square \div \triangle = 20$

More Practice, page 511, set F

Problem Solving
Mixed Practice

Choose a strategy from the strategies list to solve these problems.

Some Strategies
Act It Out
Use Objects
Choose an Operation
Draw a Picture
Make an Organized List
Guess and Check
Make a Table
Look for a Pattern
Use Logical Reasoning
Work Backward

1. Teresa's school took a field trip to see the Monarch Butterfly Refuge. 108 students went on the trip. 12 students went in each van. How many vans made the trip?

2. The drive to the monarch refuge was 45.75 miles. The students hiked 1.2 miles to get to the grove. Then they hiked back to the vans and drove home. How far did they go in all?

3. To get to the preserve for the winter, one monarch flew 216 miles. Another flew 13 times as far. How far did the second monarch fly?

4. When a caterpillar hatches from its egg, its length is $\frac{3}{16}$ of an inch. The guide said one caterpillar grew to be $1\frac{1}{16}$ inches long. How much did it grow?

5. At the nature store, the students bought a total of 12 souvenir keychains. They paid $24 in all. How much did each keychain cost?

6. Jose bought peanuts at the nature store. He gave 5 peanuts to each of the 6 people in his group. He ate 7. Then he had 9 peanuts left. How many peanuts did he buy?

7. The largest known butterfly has an 11.02 inch wingspan and weighs 0.88 ounces. The smallest known butterfly has a wingspan of 0.26 inches. What is the difference in their wingspans?

More Practice, page 527, set D

POWER PRACTICE/QUIZ

Find each quotient.

1. $30\overline{)150}$	**2.** $80\overline{)560}$	**3.** $60\overline{)360}$	**4.** $50\overline{)200}$
5. $20\overline{)80}$	**6.** $40\overline{)160}$	**7.** $70\overline{)420}$	**8.** $90\overline{)810}$

Divide and check.

9. $10\overline{)27}$	**10.** $30\overline{)275}$	**11.** $80\overline{)410}$	**12.** $70\overline{)608}$
13. $14\overline{)98}$	**14.** $39\overline{)245}$	**15.** $82\overline{)600}$	**16.** $54\overline{)387}$
17. $45\overline{)337}$	**18.** $68\overline{)540}$	**19.** $27\overline{)190}$	**20.** $74\overline{)435}$
21. $24\overline{)\$1.44}$	**22.** $51\overline{)32}$	**23.** $64\overline{)435}$	**24.** $35\overline{)99}$
25. $30\overline{)260}$	**26.** $90\overline{)580}$	**27.** $20\overline{)149}$	**28.** $47\overline{)\$2.35}$

PROBLEM SOLVING

A nickel wrapper holds 20 nickels and a penny wrapper holds 50 pennies.

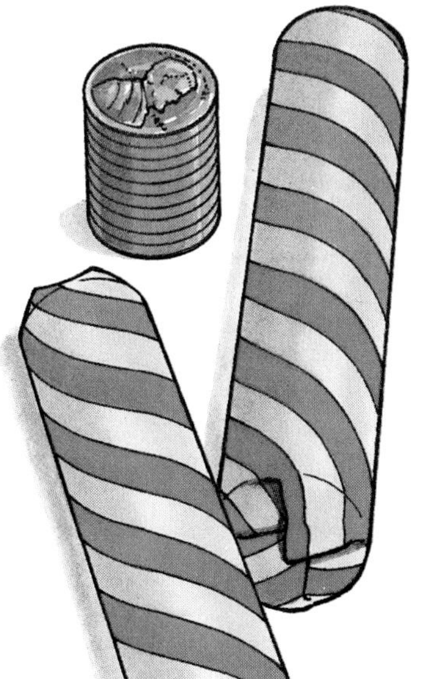

29. If J. J. has 100 nickels, how many nickel wrappers will he fill?

30. How many penny wrappers will Rita fill with 487 pennies? How many pennies will be left over?

31. Gina has 320 pennies and 144 nickels. How many coin wrappers will she need? How much money will be left over?

32. How many nickel wrappers will Tony fill if he has $1.00 in nickels?

Dividing by Tens
2-Digit Quotients

LEARN ABOUT IT

EXPLORE **Think About the Process**

Our year has 365 days. In the book *Twenty-One Balloons* the Krakatoan calendar has 20 months in a year and only 360 days. If the months all have the same number of days, how many days are in each Krakatoan month?

Here is how to divide by a multiple of 10.

Divide the tens.		Divide the ones.	
■ Estimate ■ Divide ■ Multiply ■ Subtract ■ Compare	$\begin{array}{r} 1 \\ 20\overline{)360} \\ \underline{20} \\ 16 \end{array}$	■ Bring down ■ Divide ■ Multiply ■ Subtract ■ Compare	$\begin{array}{r} 18 \\ 20\overline{)360} \\ \underline{20} \\ 160 \\ \underline{160} \\ 0 \end{array}$

TALK ABOUT IT

1. How do you decide where to write the first quotient digit?
2. How would you have estimated the answer?
3. Use a complete sentence to give a reasonable answer to the story problem.

TRY IT OUT

Divide and check.

1. $10\overline{)673}$ **2.** $50\overline{)617}$ **3.** $60\overline{)875}$ **4.** $40\overline{)\$4.80}$

5. $40\overline{)932}$ **6.** $50\overline{)835}$ **7.** $20\overline{)\$6.00}$ **8.** $70\overline{)864}$

PRACTICE

Divide and check.

1. $60\overline{)255}$ **2.** $30\overline{)742}$ **3.** $20\overline{)285}$ **4.** $50\overline{)750}$

5. $10\overline{)678}$ **6.** $20\overline{)400}$ **7.** $30\overline{)386}$ **8.** $40\overline{)495}$

9. $675 \div 50$ **10.** $\$9.60 \div 80$ **11.** $526 \div 40$ **12.** $921 \div 30$

13. How many 40s are in 810? **14.** How many 20s are in 665?

APPLY

MATH REASONING Estimate each quotient.

15. $790 \div 10$ **16.** $420 \div 30$ **17.** $800 \div 40$ **18.** $900 \div 50$

Write each example using both kinds of division symbols. Do not solve.

19. 38 divided into 423 **20.** 174 divided by 83

PROBLEM SOLVING

21. It takes about 700 cubic feet of free hydrogen to lift 50 pounds. How many cubic feet of hydrogen does it take to lift one pound?

22. **Language Arts Data Bank** DATA BANK The size of Professor Sherman's balloon, the *Globe*, was 10 times the size of the standard balloon in 1883. What was the size of the *Globe*? See page 478.

MIXED REVIEW

Find the sums. Then write the answers as mixed numbers and reduce them to lowest terms.

23. $\frac{2}{3} + \frac{4}{3}$ **24.** $\frac{4}{10} + \frac{8}{10}$ **25.** $\frac{3}{6} + \frac{5}{6}$ **26.** $\frac{8}{9} + \frac{1}{9}$

27. $7\frac{5}{10} + 3\frac{3}{10}$ **28.** $2\frac{5}{11} + 5\frac{6}{11}$ **29.** $4\frac{2}{8} + 1\frac{4}{8}$ **30.** $2\frac{6}{7} + 3\frac{5}{7}$ **31.** $1\frac{4}{15} + 7\frac{14}{15}$

Dividing
2-Digit Quotients

LEARN ABOUT IT

EXPLORE Think About the Process

A Jersey cow needs about 300 gallons of water and 3,750 pounds of grass per month. She gives about 900 gallons of milk a year. How much milk does she give in a month?

Decide where to start.	Divide the tens if possible.	Divide the ones.
12)900 12 > 9 There are not enough hundreds. 12 < 90 Start by dividing 10s.	7 12)900 − 84 6	75 12)900 − 84 60 − 60 0

TALK ABOUT IT

1. Explain how you used the "bring down" step.
2. How would you have estimated the final quotient?
3. Give a reasonable answer using a complete sentence.

TRY IT OUT

Divide. Decide if you start with the hundreds or the tens.

1. 30)674	**2.** 60)275	**3.** 40)384	**4.** 80)945
5. 38)745	**6.** 43)875	**7.** 67)540	**8.** 16)$9.28

PRACTICE

Find the quotients. Check your answers.

1. $28\overline{)793}$ **2.** $52\overline{)523}$ **3.** $36\overline{)582}$ **4.** $70\overline{)856}$ **5.** $42\overline{)652}$

6. $23\overline{)477}$ **7.** $57\overline{)704}$ **8.** $35\overline{)986}$ **9.** $88\overline{)935}$ **10.** $13\overline{)\$8.32}$

11. $3.57 ÷ 17 **12.** 894 ÷ 43 **13.** $8.36 ÷ 44 **14.** 483 ÷ 24

15. What is 500 divided by 28? **16.** How many 12s are in 908?

APPLY

MATH REASONING Use estimation to decide which of these cannot be correct.

17. $\begin{array}{r} 38\text{ R}6 \\ 21\overline{)804} \end{array}$ **18.** $\begin{array}{r} 38\text{ R}2 \\ 19\overline{)572} \end{array}$ **19.** $\begin{array}{r} 17\text{ R}4 \\ 48\overline{)820} \end{array}$ **20.** $\begin{array}{r} 10\text{ R}4 \\ 32\overline{)645} \end{array}$

PROBLEM SOLVING

21. If you bought 5 quarts of milk for $4.80, how much did you pay per quart?

22. Ted poured the milk from his two cows, Bossie and Daisy, together to make a gallon of milk. Bossie always gives twice as much milk as Daisy. What fraction of the gallon of milk did each cow give?

CALCULATOR

A number is divisible by another number if their quotient is a whole number and the remainder is 0. Use your calculator to answer these questions.

23. Which of these numbers is divisible by 4?
252 187 72 356 234

24. 224 is divisible by which of these numbers?
2 4 24 46 56

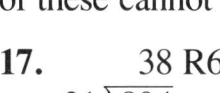

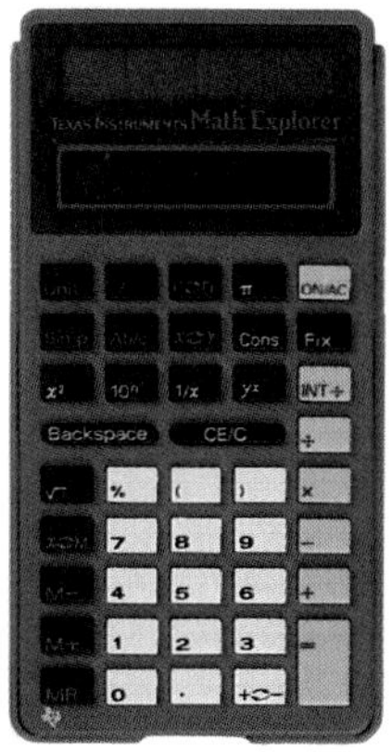

More Practice, page 512, set B

Problem Solving Using a Calculator

UNDERSTAND
FIND DATA
PLAN
ESTIMATE
SOLVE
CHECK

LEARN ABOUT IT

For some division problems, a calculator shows the quotient as a decimal number. It is helpful to know how to use these quotients.

The fourth grade class is making totem poles 30 in. high to sell at a school fair. How many can they cut from a board 144 in. long?

144 ÷ 30

4.8

They can make 4 totem poles. There is not enough wood to make a fifth.

Everyone who plays a game at the fair will receive a prize. The organizing committee wants to buy 750 prizes, which come in bags of 1 dozen each. How many bags of prizes should they buy?

750 ÷ 12

62.5

62 bags will not be enough. The committee should buy 63 bags.

TRY IT OUT

Use a calculator to help solve these problems. Remember to interpret the decimal quotient and write the answer in a complete sentence.

1. Some students are making ribbons for awards. Each award uses 15 in. of ribbon. How many awards can they make from a roll of ribbon 110 in. long?
2. The third graders need 450 cups for the refreshment booth. If 1 bag of cups contains 36 cups, how many bags should they buy?
3. One class is going to sell strawberries in baskets. They plan to pick 12 dozen and put them into 20 baskets. How many strawberries will be in each basket?
4. Aiko cut a 365 ft string into 15 ft pieces for the Amazing Maze booth. How many 15 ft pieces did she cut?

MIXED PRACTICE

Use any problem solving strategy to solve these problems.

1. 38 fourth graders worked at the fair. 17 worked at the refreshment booths and 25 at the game booths. How many students worked at both types of booth?

2. Everyone tried the Obstacle Course booth. Danielle was 3.5 seconds slower than Diego going around the course. Use the table to find out what her time was.

Obstacle Course

Name	Time
Diego	54.8 seconds
Mary	54.9 seconds
Barney	57.2 seconds

3. The second time around the obstacle course Mary went 2.3 seconds faster than the first time. How fast did she go the second time around?

4. Michael worked at the ticket booth. He sold 127 tickets at $0.25 each. How much money did he collect?

5. The school made $1,062 by selling 581 raffle tickets for a handmade quilt. The quilt cost $178 to make. How much did the school profit by selling the quilt?

6. Students formed teams of 12 for the tug-of-war. 136 students wanted to play. How many complete teams could they form?

7. Large balloons cost $0.75 and small balloons cost $0.50. Chapa sold 32 large and 17 small balloons. How much money did she earn for the school?

8. The students at the Make-Your-Own Button booth needed 248 stickers. Each package has 16 stickers. How many packages did they need to buy?

9. The police department registered 57 bicycles at the fair. There were 11 more racing bikes than mountain bikes. How many racing bikes did they register?

More Practice, page 527, set E

Data Collection and Analysis
Group Decision Making

UNDERSTAND
FIND DATA
PLAN
ESTIMATE
SOLVE
CHECK

Doing a Survey
Group Skill:
Explain and Summarize

People of all ages and cultures like to play games. Do games change? Have you ever wondered about the kinds of games played by adults when they were your age? Make a questionnaire to find out.

Collecting Data

1. Brainstorm with your group to think of some things you could ask people about games they played as children.
2. Write at least two multiple choice questions using your ideas. A multiple choice question gives a choice of more than one answer. Here are some examples.

When you were about 9 years old, what kind of game did you play?
a. ___ outdoor game
b. ___ indoor game
c. ___ singing game
How did you play your game?
a. ___ alone
b. ___ with one other person
c. ___ with a group

3. Give your questionnaire to one or two people. If they find any question that is unclear, rewrite it.
4. Make enough copies of your questionnaire to give to families of your classmates to complete.

Organizing Data

5. Make a table to record the information from your questionnaire. You can use tally marks to count the answers.

Sample Table

	a.	b.	c.
	in-door	out-door	sing-ing game
1. What kind of game did you play?	𝍸 III	𝍸 𝍸 II	𝍸 II
	alone	with 1 person	with a group
2. How did you play your game?	𝍸 I	𝍸 𝍸 I	𝍸 𝍸

6. Make a pictograph for one of the questions to show the results.

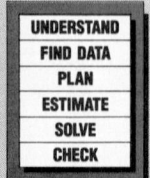

Organizing Data

1. What kind of game did you play?	
a. indoor	○○○○○○○○
b. outdoor	○○○○○○○○○○○○
c. singing	○○○○○○○

Each ○ means ___ people

How many answers will you have each symbol show?

These Inupiat Indian children from Kotzebue, Alaska, kick high playing Stick Kick.

Presenting Your Analysis

7. Which choice had the most tally marks for your first question? For the second question?

8. Prepare to tell the class three or four things you learned from your questionnaire.

9. How does the pictograph help you understand the data? Would another kind be better? Why?

10. Compare the results to the answers you would expect to get from students your age today.

WRAP UP

Answers in Division

To answer a division word problem you must understand which of the following is needed.

A quotient and remainder **B** quotient only

C remainder only **D** quotient, increased by 1

In these exercises, tell whether you need to use A, B, C, or D. Then give the answer. Use this division exercise to help you.

$$\begin{array}{r} 29\text{ R}11 \\ 25\overline{)736} \\ -\underline{50} \\ 236 \\ -\underline{225} \\ 11 \end{array}$$

Colin's class collected 736 cans in the clean-up drive. They put 25 cans in each bag.

1. How many bags does the class need in all?

2. How many bags can the class fill completely?

3. How many cans are left over when 29 bags are filled?

Sometimes, Always, Never

Which word should go in the blank, sometimes, always, or never? Explain your choices.

4. Dividing by a 2-digit divisor __?__ gives a 2-digit quotient.

5. If a remainder has 2 digits, the divisor will __?__ be a 1-digit number.

Project

Make cards for the digits 1–5. Place them in the pattern shown to create division examples like these. You may use a calculator to help.

□□)□□□

A a 1-digit quotient **B** a 2-digit quotient

C an even remainder **D** an odd remainder

Power Practice/Test

Part 1 Understanding

1. Explain how to use basic division facts and mental math to divide 360 by 40.
2. Why is rounding an important first step when you are finding a quotient?
3. Give two general rules for when you should change an estimated quotient in division.
4. Determine the number of digits in the quotients of $40\overline{)295}$ and $31\overline{)726}$ without dividing

Part 2 Skills

Divide and check.

5. $480 \div 60$	**6.** $97 \div 20$	**7.** $318 \div 60$	**8.** $175 \div 23$
9. $48\overline{)303}$	**10.** $56\overline{)\$3.92}$	**11.** $33\overline{)128}$	**12.** $46\overline{)419}$
13. $60\overline{)791}$	**14.** $73\overline{)952}$	**15.** $38\overline{)270}$	**16.** $51\overline{)\$3.57}$

Part 3 Applications

17. When Tina divided 138 by 8, her calculator showed 17.25 as the quotient. What does this tell about her answer?
18. When Randy used mental math to divide 525 by 52, he got 100 R3 as the quotient. How can you tell that his answer is not reasonable?
19. Gary used up 2 boxes of toothpicks to build 5 identical houses. If a box had 475 toothpicks, how many toothpicks were in each house?
20. **Challenge** 12 women shared a $750 prize, then each gave $5 of her winnings to charity. What did each person win? How much did the group give to charity?

ENRICHMENT
Division Tools

What is going on in this division puzzle? Hint: Each tool stands for a different digit from 1 to 9.

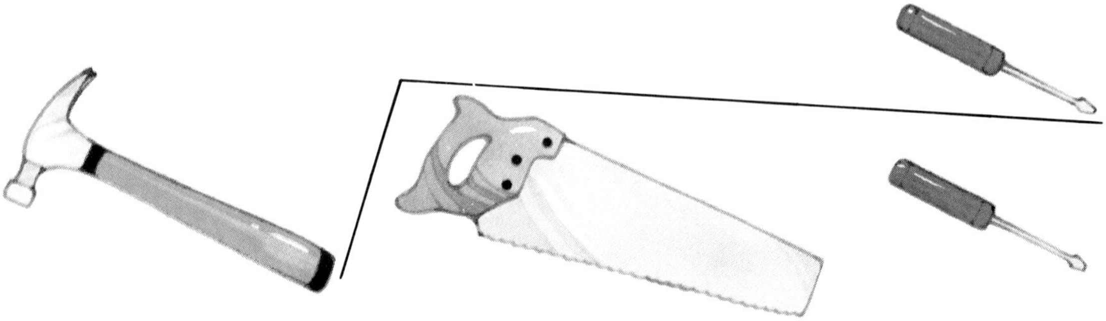

1. Solve the division puzzle by replacing each tool with a digit. Be sure your solution works.
2. Compare your solution with a classmate's. Explain why your solutions might be different. Then work with your classmate to show another way the puzzle could be solved.
3. Try this division puzzle. Remember, each tool stands for a different digit from 1 to 9. Hint: Find a relationship between the screwdriver and the hammer.

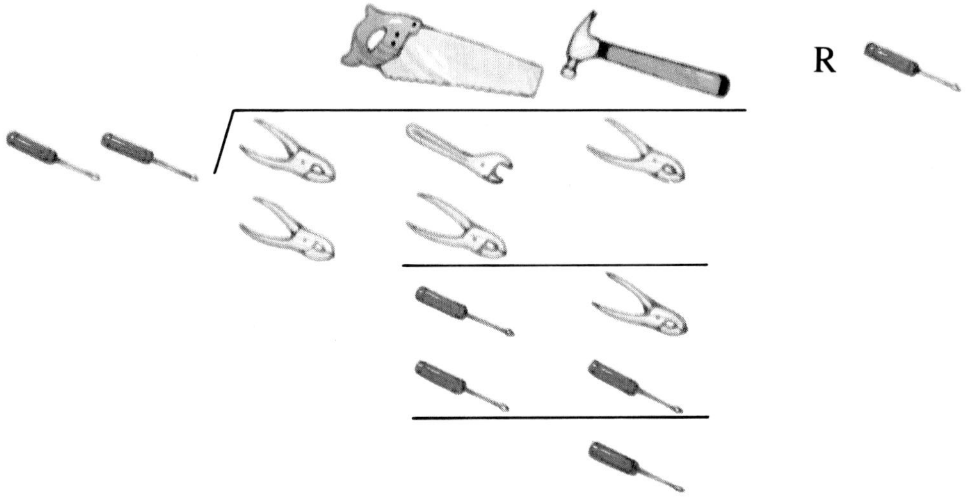

Cumulative Review

1. Which decimal rounds to 25?

A 26.35 B 25.61

C 25.09 D 20.7

2. Which decimal belongs between 0.7 and 0.72?

A 0.8 B 0.69

C 0.70 D 0.71

3. Theo estimated 9 cm for the length of part of a stick. About how long is the stick?

A 18 cm B 27 cm

C 36 cm D 3 cm

4. Choose a reasonable measure for the height of a table.

A 75 cm B 75 dm

C 75 m D 75 km

5. The shading shows how many sixths remain. What fraction tells how much is not shaded?

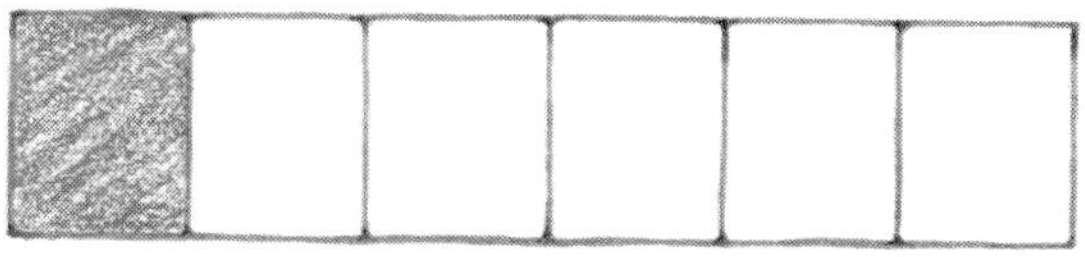

A $\frac{4}{5}$ B $\frac{1}{6}$

C $\frac{5}{6}$ D $\frac{1}{2}$

6. $\frac{9}{12} + \frac{5}{12}$

A $\frac{1}{3}$ B $1\frac{1}{6}$

C $1\frac{1}{2}$ D $\frac{12}{14}$

7. A recipe asks for $\frac{5}{8}$ cup orange juice and $\frac{1}{8}$ cup lemon juice. How much more orange juice is needed?

A $\frac{3}{4}$ cup B $\frac{5}{8}$ cup

C $\frac{1}{2}$ cup D $\frac{1}{4}$ cup

8. $0.62 + 0.89$

A 0.51 B 1.41

C 0.151 D 1.51

9. $53 - 4.26$

A 57.26 B 48.74

C 49.26 D 49.64

10. A bus holds 60 people. How many buses are needed to take 288 people on a field trip?

A 5 B 6

C 4 D 5 R12

11. Gino paid \$8.64 for a dozen cans of oil. What was the cost per can?

A \$0.86 B \$7.20

C \$0.72 D \$0.70

Resource Bank and Appendix

Resource Bank

APPENDIX

Place Value: Hundreds, Tens, and Ones

These models help you understand numbers.

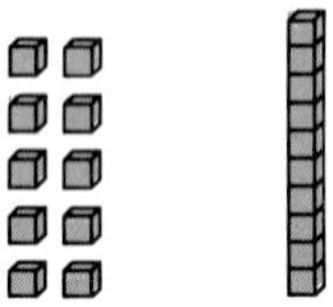

ten ones = one ten (10)

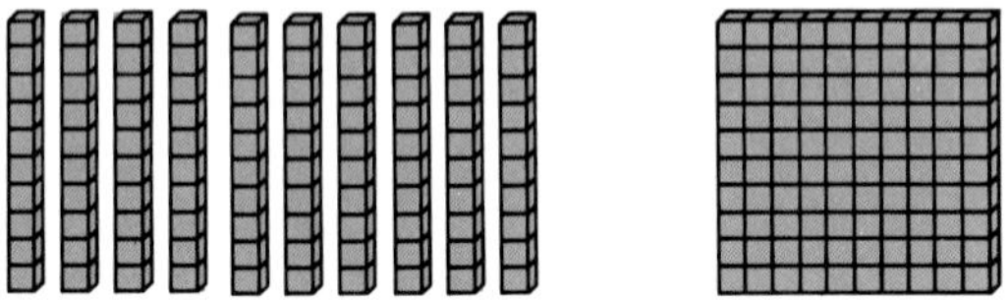

ten tens = one hundred (100)

This model shows the meaning of 232.

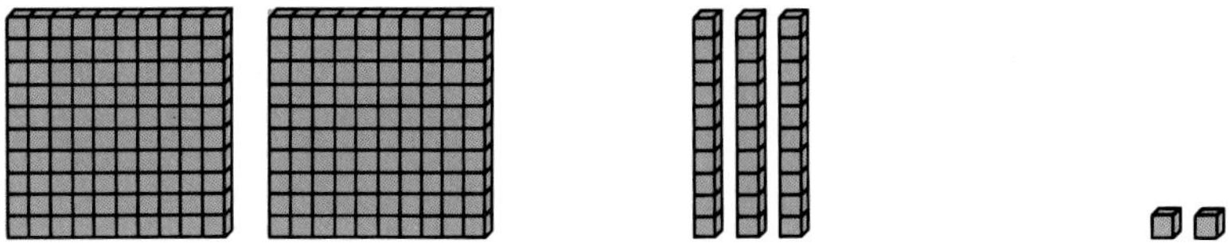

2 hundreds , 3 tens , 2 ones = 232

TRY IT OUT Read each number. Tell the meaning of the red digit.

Example: 426 The 2 means 2 tens.

1. 342	**2.** 639	**3.** 19	**4.** 401	**5.** 823
6. 436	**7.** 808	**8.** 42	**9.** 791	**10.** 92

Practice the Facts: Addition

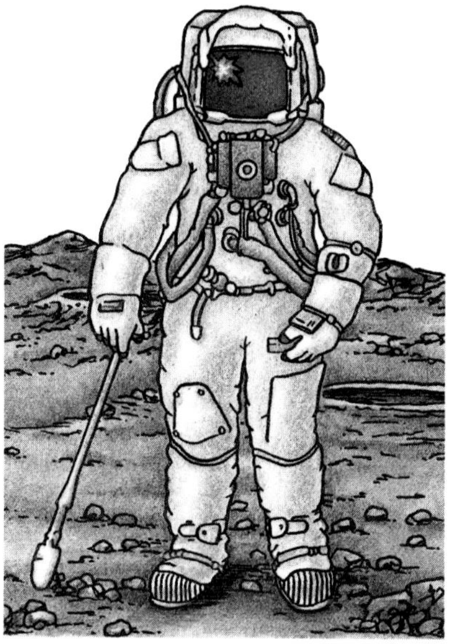

During the Apollo 12 moon mission Charles Conrad walked for 8 hours on the moon. Alan Bean walked for 7 hours. What is the total number of hours they walked on the moon?

Since we want the total number of hours, we add.

7	+	8	=	15
Addend		Addend		Sum

7	Addend
+ 8	Addend
15	Sum

They walked for a total of 15 hours on the moon.

Practice. Add.

1. 4 + 9 = **2.** 6 + 5 = **3.** 3 + 2 =

4. 6 + 3 = **5.** 1 + 9 = **6.** 5 + 7 =

7. 8 + 5 = **8.** 4 + 3 = **9.** 7 + 6 =

Practice. Add.

10.	**11.**	**12.**	**13.**	**14.**
5	9	8	4	3
+ 6	+ 1	+ 5	+ 4	+ 7

15.	**16.**	**17.**	**18.**	**19.**
0	8	6	7	1
+ 8	+ 2	+ 4	+ 8	+ 6

Adding: One Trade

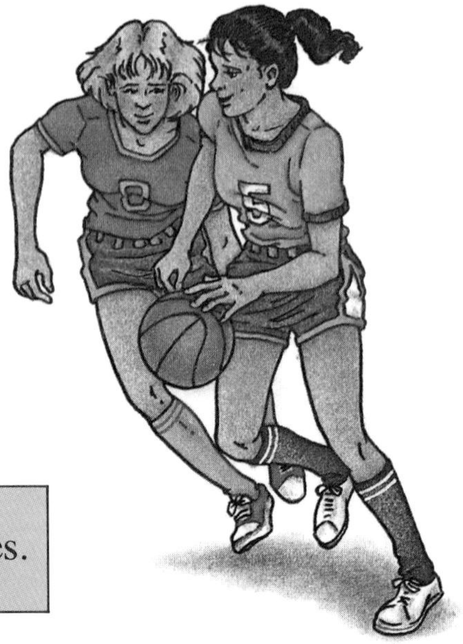

Emma plays on a women's basketball team. In the championship game she scores 38 points in the first half and 26 points in the second half. How many points does she score in all?

Since we want the total, we add.

$$\begin{array}{r} 38 \\ +\ 26 \\ \hline \end{array}$$

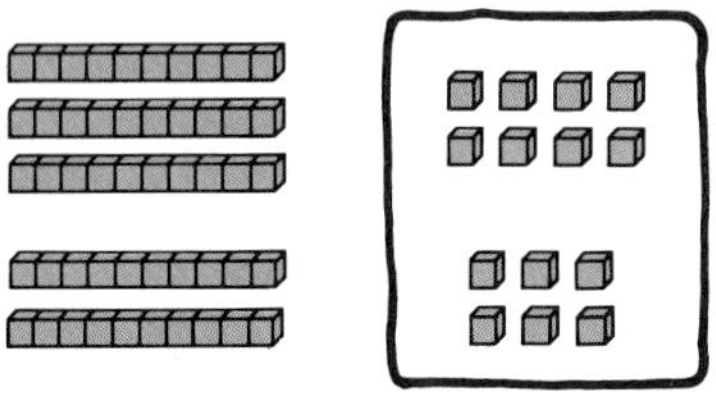

Add the ones.

$$\begin{array}{r} {}^{1} \\ 38 \\ +\ 26 \\ \hline 4 \end{array}$$

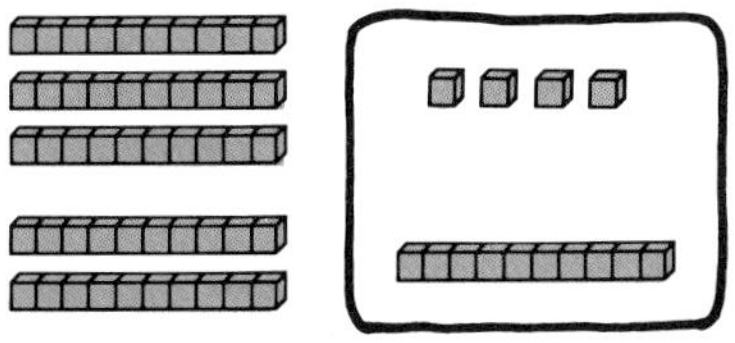

Trade if necessary.

14 ones = 1 ten and 4 ones.

$$\begin{array}{r} {}^{1} \\ 38 \\ +\ 26 \\ \hline 64 \end{array}$$

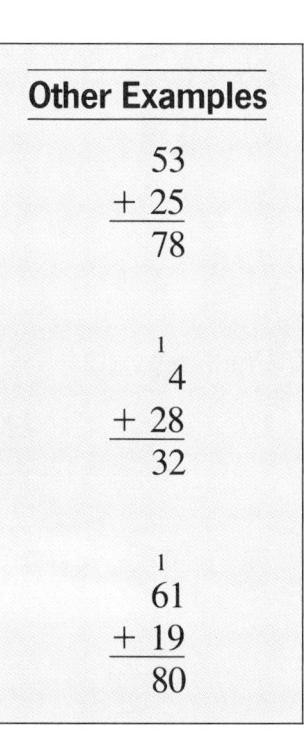

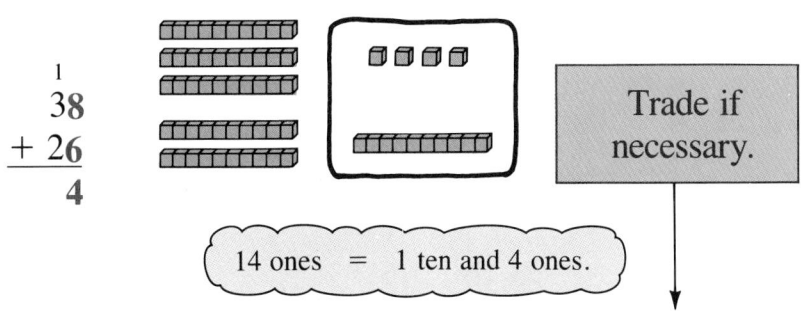

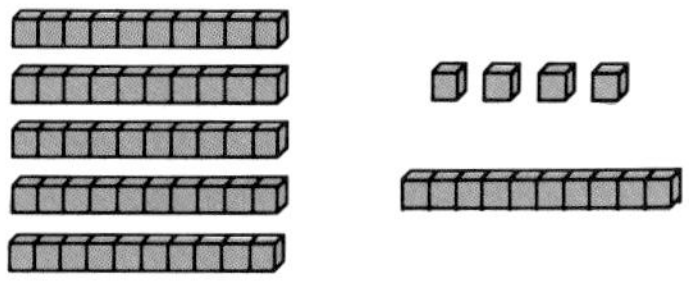

Add the tens.

Other Examples

$$\begin{array}{r} 53 \\ +\ 25 \\ \hline 78 \end{array} \qquad \begin{array}{r} {}^{1} \\ 4 \\ +\ 28 \\ \hline 32 \end{array} \qquad \begin{array}{r} {}^{1} \\ 61 \\ +\ 19 \\ \hline 80 \end{array}$$

Emma scores 64 points in the championship game.

Try it out. Add.

1. $\begin{array}{r} 24 \\ +\ 18 \\ \hline \end{array}$ **2.** $\begin{array}{r} 91 \\ +\ 41 \\ \hline \end{array}$ **3.** $\begin{array}{r} 26 \\ +\ 36 \\ \hline \end{array}$ **4.** $\begin{array}{r} 9 \\ +\ 79 \\ \hline \end{array}$ **5.** $\begin{array}{r} 38 \\ +\ 38 \\ \hline \end{array}$

Practice the Facts: Subtraction

Jane Goodall studied chimpanzees in Africa. One group of chimps had 13 members. Another group had 7 members. How many more chimps were in the larger group?

Since we want to find how many more, we subtract.

$13 - 7 = 6$ difference

$$\begin{array}{r} 13 \\ -\ 7 \\ \hline 6 \end{array}$$ difference

Practice. Subtract.

1. $15 - 6 =$ **2.** $17 - 8 =$ **3.** $10 - 5 =$

4. $11 - 4 =$ **5.** $13 - 2 =$ **6.** $7 - 0 =$

7. $9 - 7 =$ **8.** $16 - 8 =$ **9.** $6 - 6 =$

Practice. Subtract.

10. $\begin{array}{r} 12 \\ -\ 8 \\ \hline \end{array}$ **11.** $\begin{array}{r} 10 \\ -\ 3 \\ \hline \end{array}$ **12.** $\begin{array}{r} 7 \\ -\ 5 \\ \hline \end{array}$ **13.** $\begin{array}{r} 13 \\ -\ 6 \\ \hline \end{array}$ **14.** $\begin{array}{r} 17 \\ -\ 9 \\ \hline \end{array}$

15. $\begin{array}{r} 9 \\ -\ 4 \\ \hline \end{array}$ **16.** $\begin{array}{r} 11 \\ -\ 2 \\ \hline \end{array}$ **17.** $\begin{array}{r} 5 \\ -\ 5 \\ \hline \end{array}$ **18.** $\begin{array}{r} 8 \\ -\ 3 \\ \hline \end{array}$ **19.** $\begin{array}{r} 6 \\ -\ 4 \\ \hline \end{array}$

Subtracting: One Trade

Elizabeth bought 36 stamps of famous American women. She traded 18 of them with her friends. How many American women stamps did she have left?

Since we want to find how many she had left, we subtract.

$$\begin{array}{r} {\scriptstyle 2\ 16} \\ 3\!\!\!/6 \\ -\ 18 \\ \hline \end{array}$$

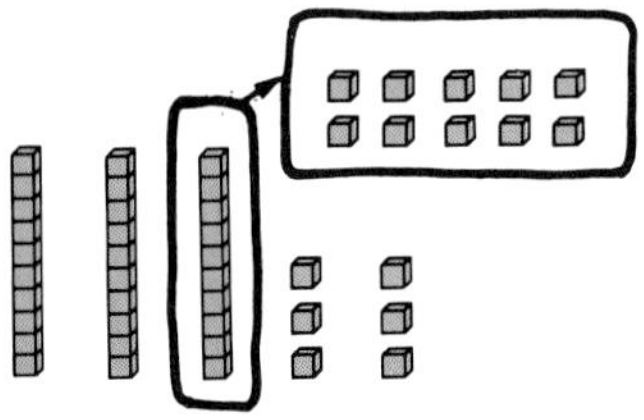

Trade 1 ten for 10 ones.

$$\begin{array}{r} {\scriptstyle 2\ 16} \\ 3\!\!\!/6 \\ -\ 18 \\ \hline 8 \end{array}$$

Subtract the ones.

$$\begin{array}{r} {\scriptstyle 2} \\ 3\!\!\!/6 \\ -\ 18 \\ \hline 18 \end{array}$$

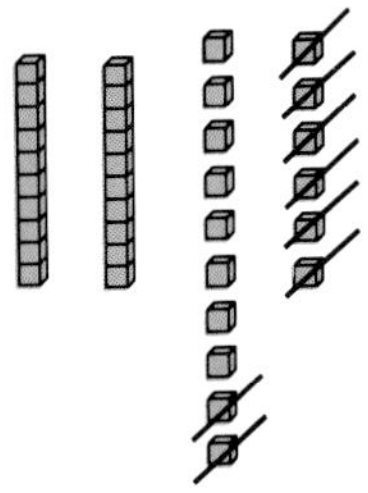

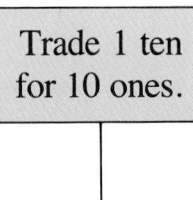

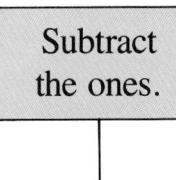

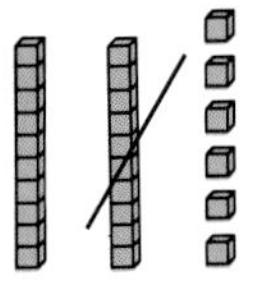

Subtract the tens.

Other Examples

$$\begin{array}{r} {\scriptstyle 5\ 12} \\ 6\!\!\!/2 \\ -\ 36 \\ \hline 26 \end{array}$$

Check
$$\begin{array}{r} {\scriptstyle 1} \\ 26 \\ +\ 36 \\ \hline 62 \end{array}$$

$$\begin{array}{r} {\scriptstyle 3\ 14} \\ 4\!\!\!/4 \\ -\ 19 \\ \hline 25 \end{array}$$

$$\begin{array}{r} {\scriptstyle 1\ 15} \\ 2\!\!\!/5 \\ -\ 17 \\ \hline 8 \end{array}$$

She had 18 stamps of American women left.

Try it out. Subtract. Check by adding.

	1.	2.	3.	4.	5.
	74	58	66	21	85
	− 29	− 18	− 48	− 8	− 56

Multiplying: Trading Ones

Antoine throws 25 clay bowls each day on his pottery wheel. How many bowls will he make in 3 days?

Since we want the total for equal amounts, we multiply.

$$\begin{array}{r} 25 \\ \times\ 3 \\ \hline \end{array}$$

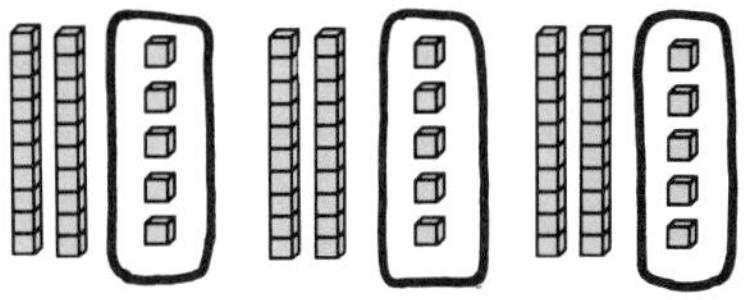

15 ones

Multiply the ones.

$$\begin{array}{r} ^{1} \\ 25 \\ \times\ 3 \\ \hline 5 \end{array}$$

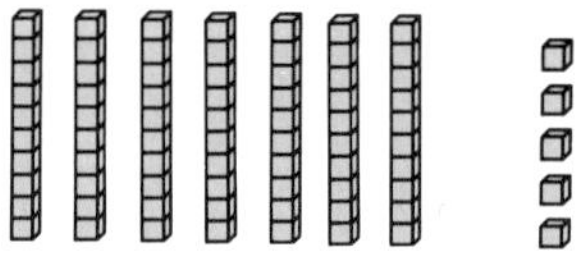

15 ones = 1 ten and 5 ones

Trade if necessary.

$$\begin{array}{r} ^{1} \\ 25 \\ \times\ 3 \\ \hline 75 \end{array}$$

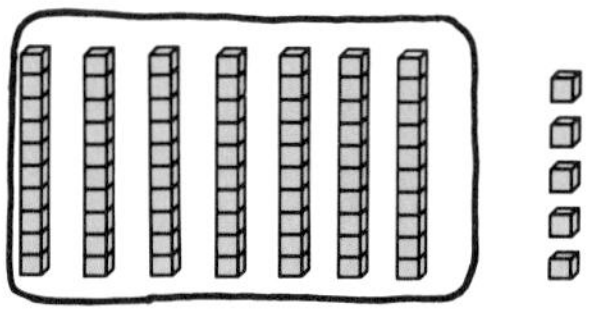

7 tens

Multiply the tens. Add any extra tens.

Other Examples

$$\begin{array}{r} 23 \\ \times\ 2 \\ \hline 46 \end{array}$$

No trade necessary.

$$\begin{array}{r} ^{2} \\ 17 \\ \times\ 3 \\ \hline 51 \end{array}$$

$$\begin{array}{r} ^{3} \\ 15 \\ \times\ 6 \\ \hline 90 \end{array}$$

Antoine makes 75 bowls in 3 days.

Try it out. Multiply.

1. $\begin{array}{r} 22 \\ \times\ 3 \\ \hline \end{array}$ **2.** $\begin{array}{r} 36 \\ \times\ 2 \\ \hline \end{array}$ **3.** $\begin{array}{r} 17 \\ \times\ 3 \\ \hline \end{array}$ **4.** $\begin{array}{r} 14 \\ \times\ 6 \\ \hline \end{array}$ **5.** $\begin{array}{r} 19 \\ \times\ 2 \\ \hline \end{array}$

Adding Fractions: Like Denominators

You can write fractions to describe a part of something.

cheese pizza

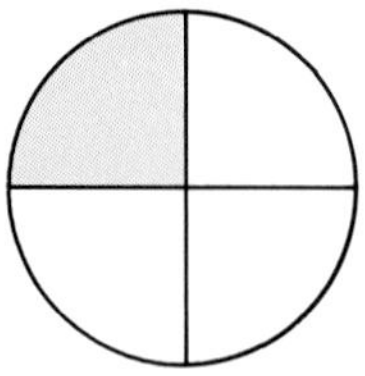

$\frac{1}{4}$ of the pizza is shaded.

sausage pizza

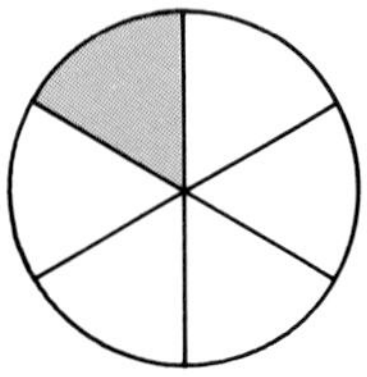

$\frac{1}{6}$ of the pizza is shaded.

pineapple pizza

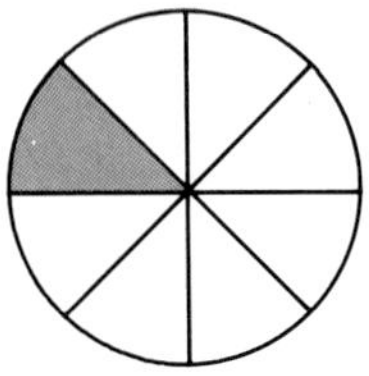

$\frac{1}{8}$ of the pizza is shaded.

1. Which piece of pizza is the largest?

2. Which piece of pizza is the smallest?

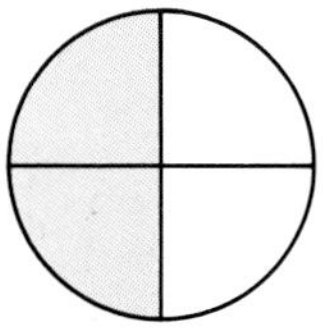

Christa ate 2 pieces of cheese pizza.
She ate $\frac{1}{4} + \frac{1}{4}$ or $\frac{2}{4}$ of the cheese pizza.

$\frac{1}{4} + \frac{1}{4} = \frac{2}{4}$

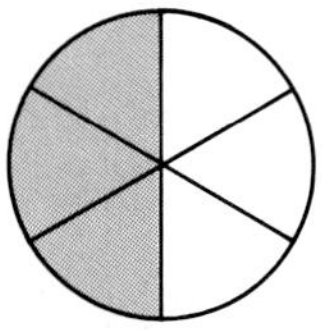

Jim ate 3 pieces of sausage pizza.
He ate $\frac{1}{6} + \frac{1}{6} + \frac{1}{6}$ or $\frac{3}{6}$ of the sausage pizza.

$\frac{1}{6} + \frac{1}{6} + \frac{1}{6} = \frac{3}{6}$

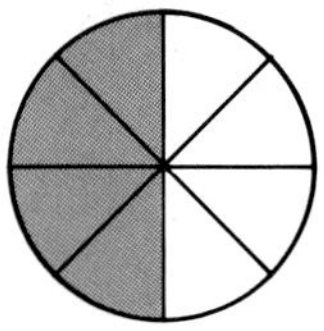

Quan ate 4 pieces of pineapple pizza.
She ate $\frac{1}{8} + \frac{1}{8} + \frac{1}{8} + \frac{1}{8}$ or $\frac{4}{8}$ of the pineapple pizza.

$\frac{1}{8} + \frac{1}{8} + \frac{1}{8} + \frac{1}{8} = \frac{4}{8}$

Find the sums. Add.

1. $\frac{5}{10} + \frac{4}{10} =$

2. $\frac{2}{9} + \frac{6}{9} =$

3. $\frac{1}{6} + \frac{2}{6} =$

4. $\frac{1}{3} + \frac{1}{3} =$

5. $\frac{2}{5} + \frac{2}{5} =$

6. $\frac{3}{7} + \frac{2}{7} =$

Subtracting Fractions: Like Denominators

The fourth grade class sold pieces of pizza at the school fair. Jose cut the cheese pizza into 4 equal pieces. He sold 2 pieces. How many pieces did he have left?

Since we want to find how many are left, we subtract.

cheese pizza

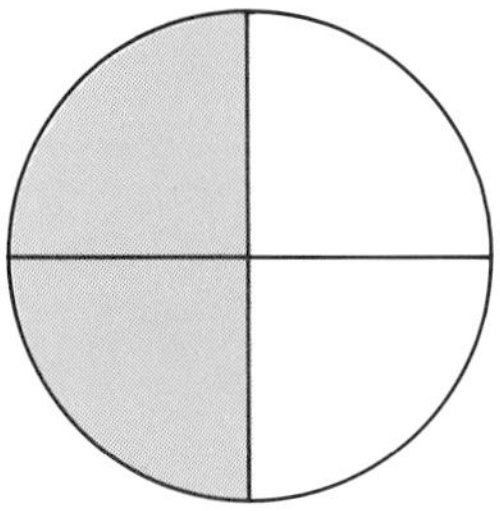

$\frac{4}{4} - \frac{2}{4} = \frac{2}{4}$

sausage pizza

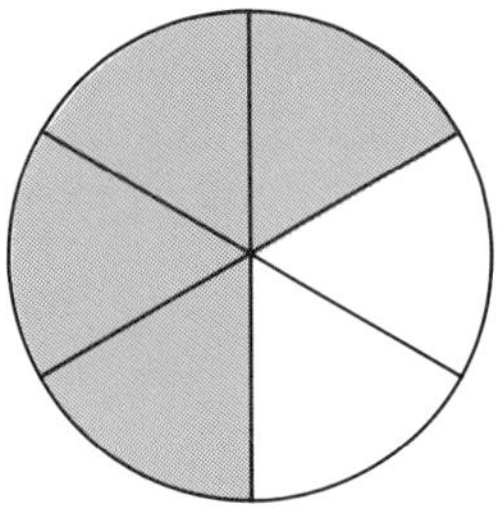

$\frac{6}{6} - \frac{2}{6} = \frac{4}{6}$

pineapple pizza

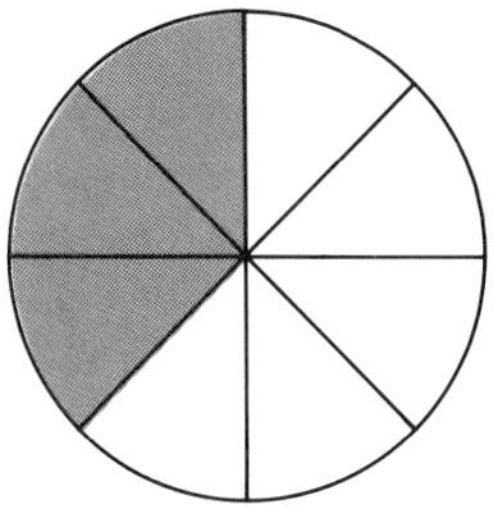

$\frac{8}{8} - \frac{5}{8} = \frac{3}{8}$

He had 2 pieces or $\frac{2}{4}$ of the cheese pizza left.

1. Michelle sold 2 pieces of sausage pizza. How many pieces did she have left?

2. James sold 5 pieces of pineapple pizza. How many pieces did he have left?

Find the differences. Subtract.

1. $\frac{7}{10} - \frac{2}{10} =$

2. $\frac{3}{5} - \frac{2}{5} =$

3. $\frac{3}{8} - \frac{1}{8} =$

$\frac{4}{9} =$

5. $\frac{5}{6} - \frac{4}{6} =$

6. $\frac{2}{3} - \frac{1}{3} =$

Math and Science Data Bank

Life Spans of Small Wild Animals

Because of predators, hunters, and automobiles, in the wild most of these animals live an average of one year. But they can live longer.

	In the Wild	In Captivity
	Years Possible	Years Possible
Cottontail Rabbit	3	5
Raccoon	6	14
Squirrel	12	20
Box Turtle	80	123
White-footed Mouse	2	8

Daytime Activity of Red-Backed Salamander

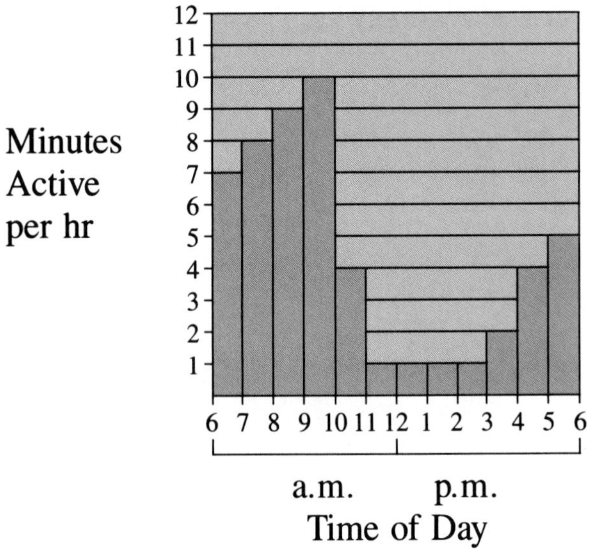

Math and Science Data Bank

Heartbeat Rates of Birds

Bird	Heartbeats per minute
Sparrow	500
Starling	390
Crow	379
Ostrich	65
Peregrine Falcon	347

Wingbeats Per Second

Hummingbird weighing 2 g	50
Hummingbird weighing 4 g	32
Hummingbird weighing 6 g	24

Birds lay a group, or clutch, of eggs that hatch together. Some birds lay more than one clutch each year.

Number of Eggs Laid

Bird	Usual Number of Eggs in a Clutch	Usual Number of Clutches Laid in a Year
Barn Owl	5	2
Coot	8	2
Peregrine Falcon	3	1
Hummingbird	2	2
Lark	4	3
King Penguin	1	1
Ostrich	14	1
Starling	6	2

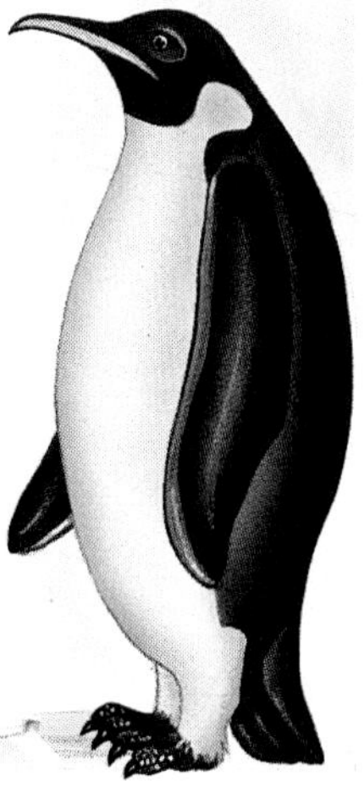

Math and Science Data Bank

Planets in Our Solar System

Planet	Number of Earth days to go around the sun	Number of Satellites	Diameter in km
Mercury	88	0	5,000
Venus	225	0	12,000
Earth	365	1	13,000
Mars	687	2	7,000
Jupiter	4,333	16	143,000
Saturn	10,759	23	121,000
Uranus	30,685	15	51,000
Neptune	60,188	2	45,000
Pluto	90,700	1	3,000

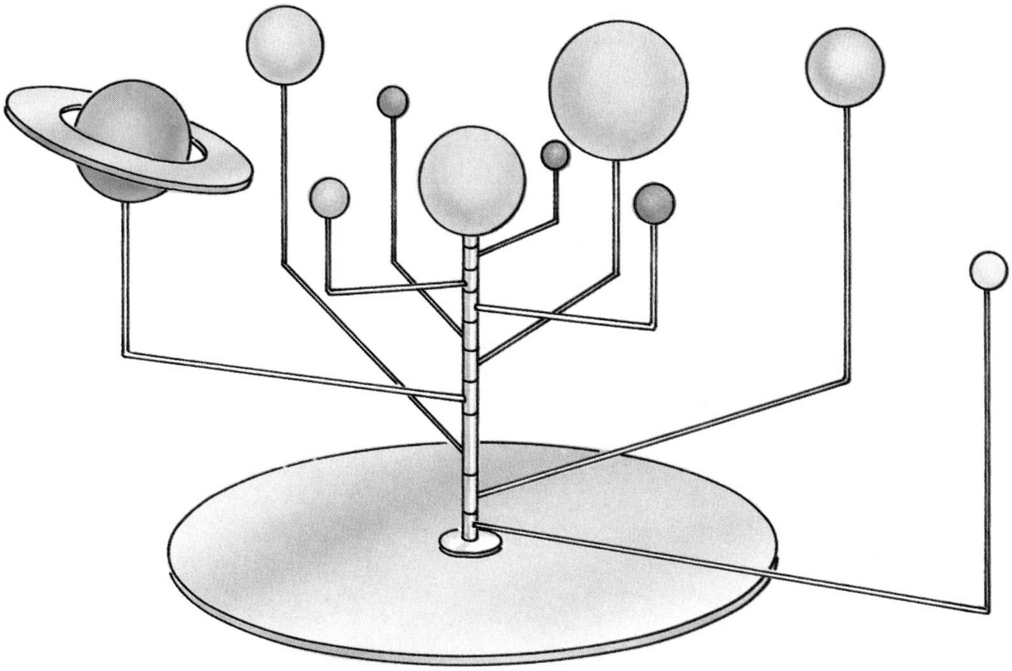

Math and Science Data Bank

Average Rainfall Per year

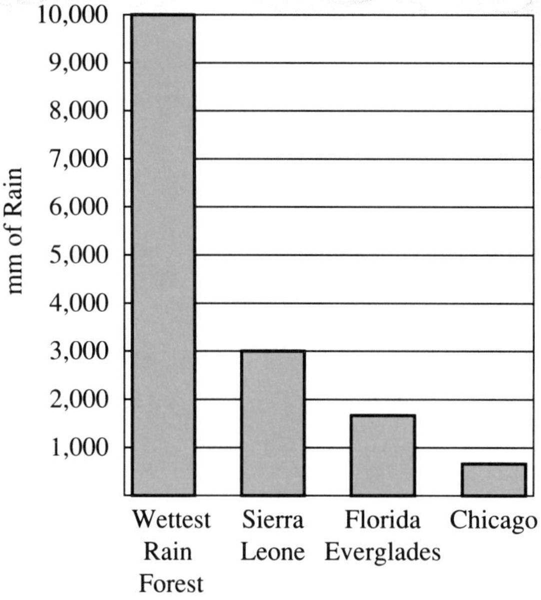

Note: Minimum rainfall for a rain forest is 2,000 mm per year.

Types of Rain Forest on a Typical Tropical Mountain

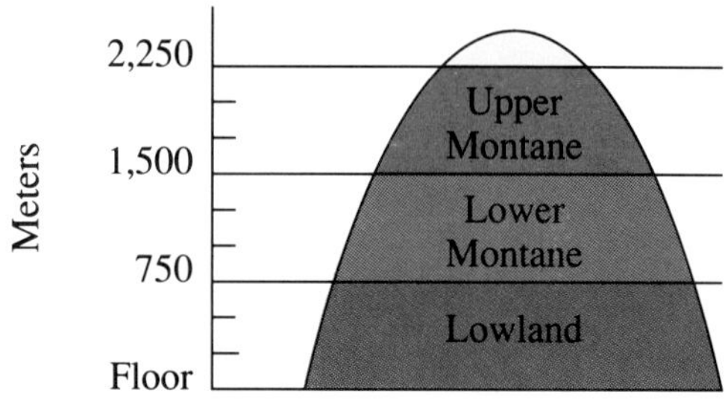

Layers of Vegetation in a Tropical Rain Forest

Math and Social Studies Data Bank

Old Indian Dwellings in the Southwest

	Number of Rooms
Canyon de Chelly, Arizona	
White House	80
Antelope House	50
Mummy Cave	55
Chaco Canyon, New Mexico	
Pueblo Bonito	800
Mesa Verde, Colorado	
Cliff Palace	225
Long House	150
Spruce Tree House	114

Math and Social Studies Data Bank

U.S. Peaks More Than 14,000 Feet Above Sea Level

State	Number of Peaks
Alaska	18
California	12
Colorado	53
Washington	1

Some Rivers Formed in the Rocky Mountains

River	Length in Miles	Direction of Flow	Mouth
Colorado	1,400	west	Gulf of California
Missouri	2,714	east	Mississippi
Rio Grande	1,800	east	Gulf of Mexico
Arkansas	1,400	east	Mississippi River
Snake	1,038	west	Columbia River

Math and Social Studies Data Bank

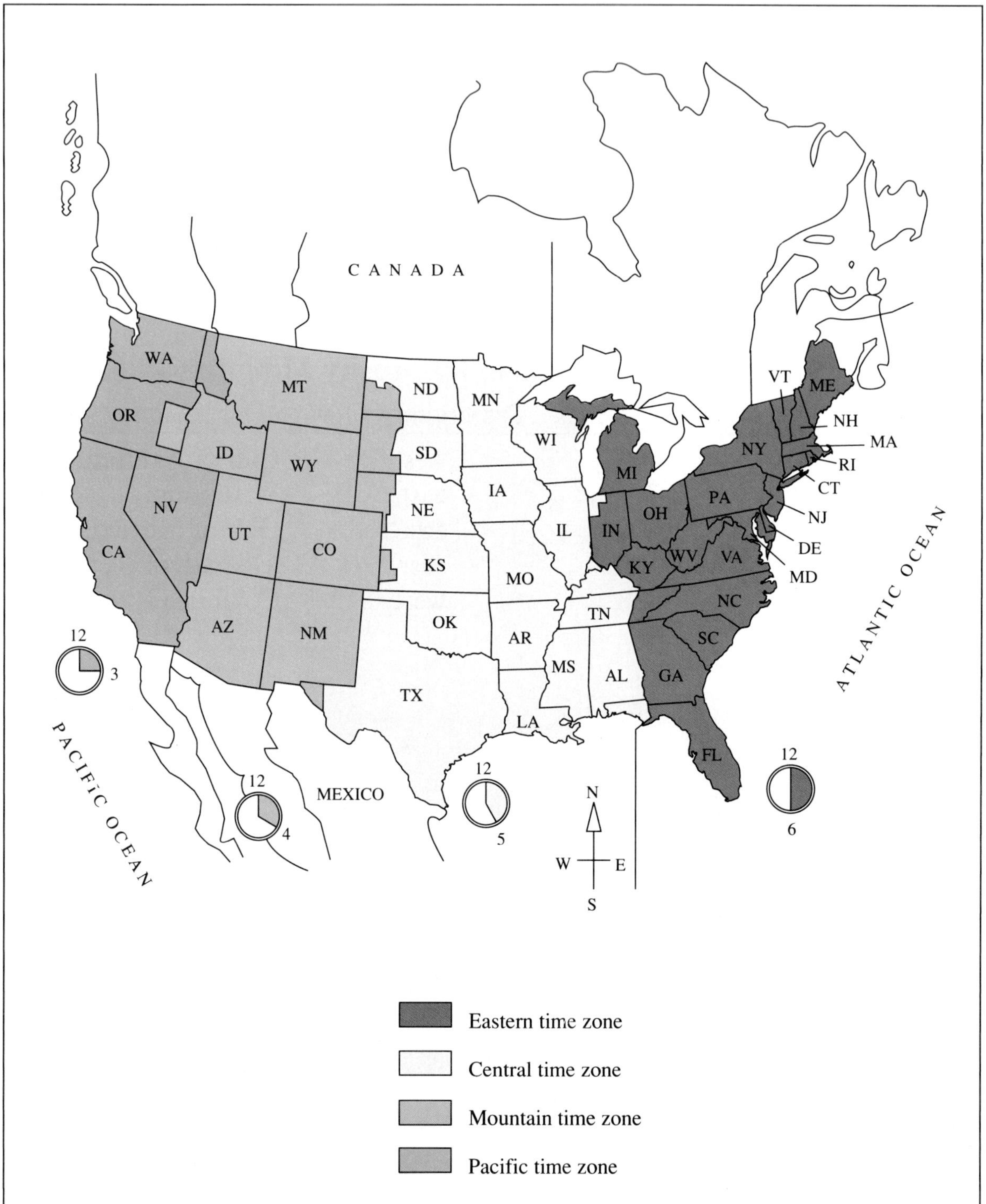

Math and Social Studies Data Bank

Lengths of Historical Ships

Kind of ship	Length
Viking longship	150 ft
Viking cargo ship	54 ft
Man-of-war carrack	120 ft
Merchant carrack	100 ft
Columbus' *Santa María*	90 ft
Columbus' *Pinta*	75 ft
Pacific Islander war canoe	100 ft
Pacific Islander vaamotu	60 ft

Crew Sizes of Historical Ships

Kind of ship	Size of crew
Small Viking ship	6 sailors
Viking longship	70 sailors
Viking cargo ship	30 sailors
Columbus' *Santa María*	50 sailors
Columbus' *Pinta*	30 sailors
Pacific Islander war canoe	90 warriors

Math and Language Arts Data Bank

Tall Facts from American Tall Tales

Pecos Bill

Pecos Bill was the make-believe hero of the cowboys of the Southwest.

- During a drought, Pecos Bill had to lasso 9 miles of the Rio Grande River each morning to feed his cattle.
- Bill could rope a herd of cattle at one throw.

Paul Bunyan

Loggers made up stories about a giant, Paul Bunyan, and Babe, his blue ox.

- To grease Paul's hotcake griddle, 5 men skated on it with a slab of bacon tied to each foot.
- The Gumbaroo Paul captured in the woods had 16 pairs of rubber legs.

Joe Magarac, the Steel Man

Joe was a folk hero of men who worked in steel mills.

- Joe made 4 steel rails at a time with one hand by squeezing them out between his fingers.

Alfred Bulltop Stormalong

Alfred was a hero in stories told by deep-water sailors.

- He was 4 fathoms tall. He fought a sea monster 10 fathoms long. A fathom is a sailor's measure equal to 6 feet.
- Once Alfred tied an octopus's arms in knots that took a month of Sundays to untie.

Math and Language Arts Data Bank

Books by Laura Ingalls Wilder

	Year of Publication
Little House in the Big Woods	1932
Farmer Boy	1933
Little House on the Prairie	1935
On the Banks of Plum Creek *(Newberry Honor Book)*	1937
By the Shores of Silver Lake *(Newberry Honor Book)*	1939
The Long Winter *(Newberry Honor Book)*	1940
Little Town on the Prairie	1941
These Happy Golden Years	1943
The First Four Years	1971

Recipe for Johnny Cake

Served at threshing time in *Little House in the Big Woods*

1 egg	½ teaspoon salt
¾ cup corn meal	1½ cups buttermilk
½ teaspoon baking soda	1 tablespoon melted butter

Beat the egg. Stir in the corn meal, baking soda, salt, and buttermilk. Pour the mixture into a 1-quart baking dish greased with the melted butter. Bake at 400° for 20 to 25 minutes. *Amount: 6 servings.*

Math and Language Arts Data Bank

Fact and Fiction
from the book *Twenty-One Balloons*
by William Pene du Bois

Fact

- The standard size of a hydrogen balloon in 1883 was 600 cubic yards.
- The volcanic island of Krakatoa in the Pacific Ocean blew up in 1883 in the greatest explosion ever. The sound was heard 3,000 miles away.

Fiction

- 80 people live on Krakatoa in families of 4 with 2 children in each family.
- A balloon merry-go-round made of 8 boats connected in a circle could land on the ocean. Each boat held 2 children and was attached to a balloon.
- The rectangular balloon platform on which the Krakatoans and the professor escaped was lifted by 10 large balloons alternating with 10 smaller balloons. A large balloon was at each corner. Each shorter side had 3 large balloons.
- To land the platform, Professor Sherman had to pull apart the valves that let the hydrogen out of the balloons. Each valve required a 150-pound pull.

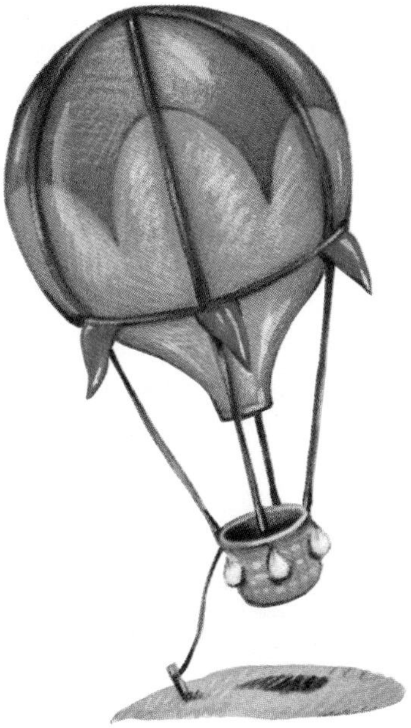

Math and Fine Arts Data Bank

"Double Airplane" Controller for 9-String Marionette

To make the 2 T bars you need 2 wood strips that are 10 inches long and 2 wood strips that are 7 inches long. Each of the 9 strings in the diagram is labeled by the part of the puppet to which it is to be attached. To string the puppet you need 2 pieces of string that are 60 inches long and 5 pieces of string that are 30 inches long.

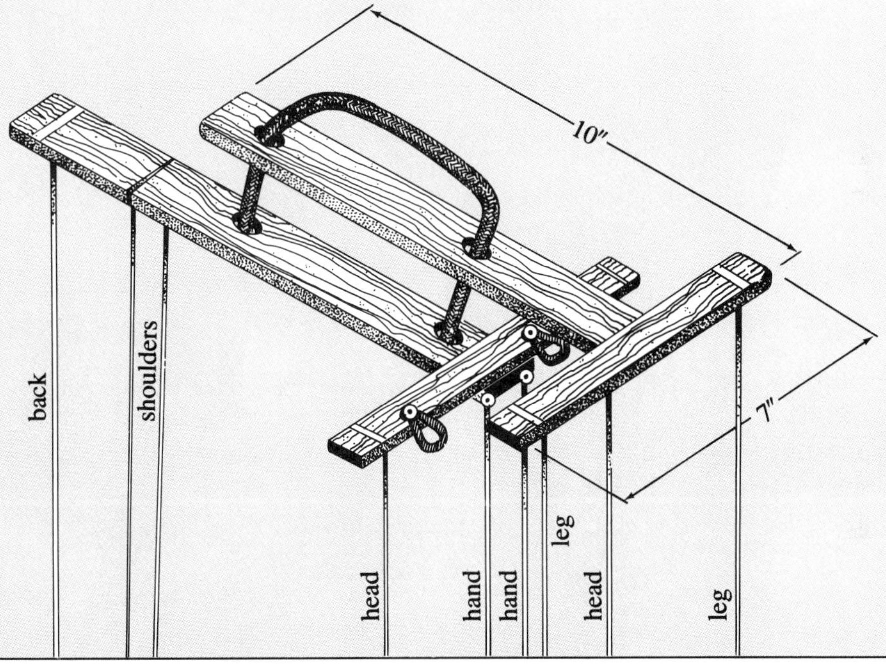

Japanese Bunraku Puppet Theater

The puppets weigh about 70 pounds each and are between 3 and 4 feet tall.
The female puppets are each worked by 3 people.
The male puppets are each worked by 4 people.
The people working the puppets are dressed in black and can be seen on the stage as they work the puppets.
Singers and readers present the story.

Math and Fine Arts Data Bank

Pattern for a Sun Mask

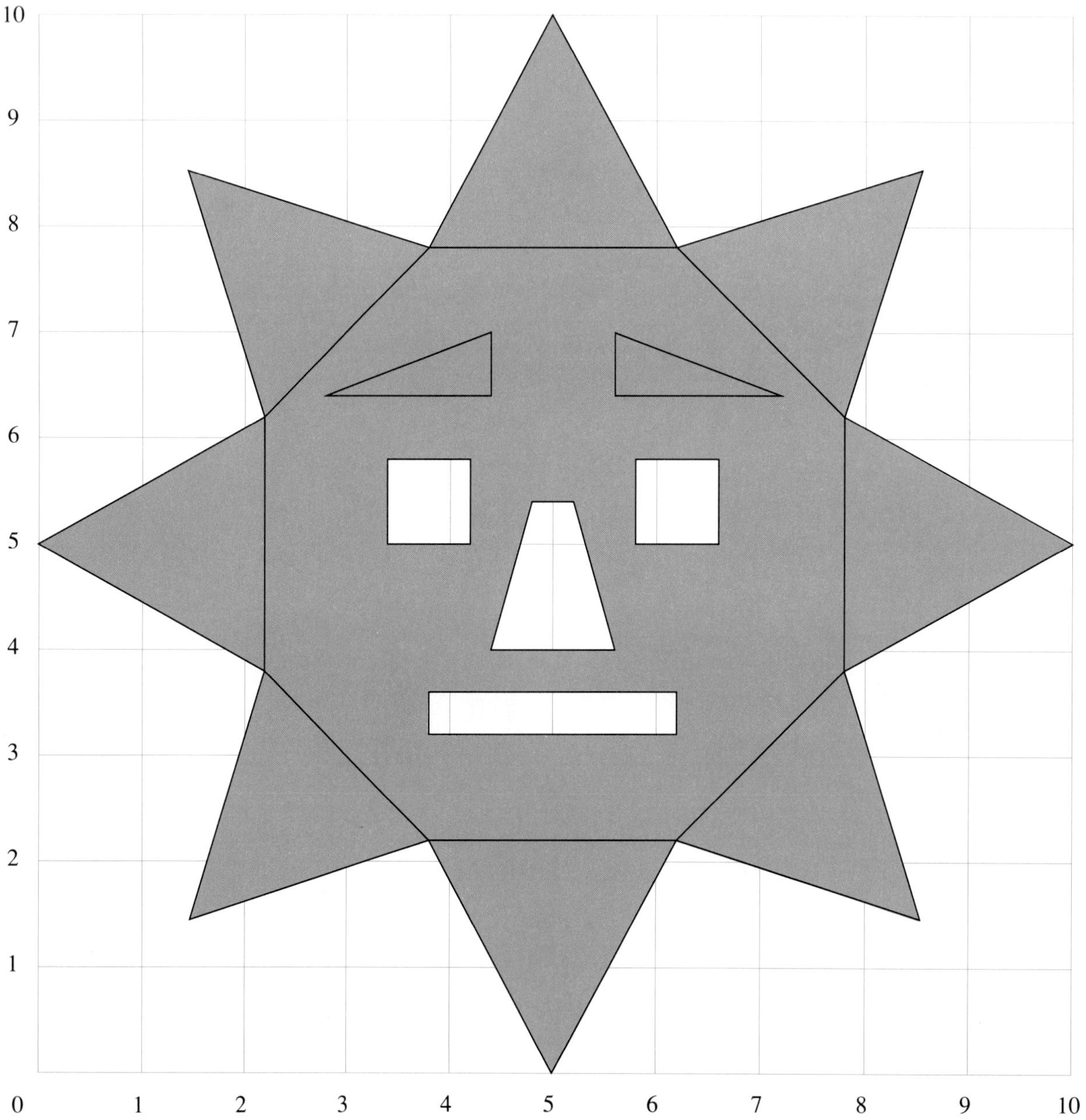

Math and Health and Fitness Data Bank

World Records for Fourth Graders Single Rope Skills Events

Event	Number of jumps
Single Speed	272
Double Speed	292
Double Unders	296
Double Unders/Crosses	53
Triple Unders	39
Pogo Jumping	5,064
Hoppity Hop Jumping	390

NOTE: Single Speed has a time limit of 1 minute. Double Speed allows 30 seconds for each partner. The other events have no time limit.

Aerobic Points for Energy Used in Exercise

Activity	Aerobic Points for 1 hour of activity
Jumping Rope	24
Running	30
Walking	3
Swimming	15
Baseball	2

Average Resting Heartbeat Levels Heartbeats Per Minute

Math and Health and Fitness Data Bank

Facts about Winter Olympic Games

- The first Winter Olympic Games were held in 1924.
- The race course for the Men's Slalom skiing event must have between 55 and 75 gates. The course for the Women's Slalom must have between 40 and 60 gates.

Speed Skating: Women's 500-Meter Race

Year	Winner of Gold Medal	Time
1960	Helga Haase	45.9 seconds
1964	Lydia Skoblikova, USSR	45.0 seconds
1968	Ludmila Titova, USSR	46.1 seconds
1972	Anne Henning, United States	43.33 seconds
1976	Sheila Young, United States	42.76 seconds
1980	Karin Enke, East Germany	41.78 seconds
1984	Crista Rothenburger, East Germany	41.02 seconds
1988	Bonnie Blair, United States	39.10 seconds

Alpine Skiing: Men's Slalom

Year and Medal	Winner	Minutes	Seconds
1980			
Gold Medal	Ingemar Stenmark, Sweden	1	44.26
Silver Medal	Phil Mahre, United States	1	44.76
Bronze Medal	Jacques Luethy, Switzerland	1	45.06
1984			
Gold Medal	Phil Mahre, United States	1	39.41
Silver Medal	Steve Mahre, United States	1	39.62
Bronze Medal	Didier Bouvet, France	1	40.20
1988			
Gold Medal	Alberto Tomba, Italy	1	39.47
Silver Medal	Frank Woerndl, East Germany	1	39.53
Bronze Medal	Poul Frommelt, Liechtenstein	1	39.84

Math and Health and Fitness Data Bank

Official Weights of Sport Balls

	Minimum	Maximum
Lawn Tennis	56.7 grams	58.5 grams
Baseball	141.7 grams	155.9 grams
Softball	177.2 grams	198.4 grams
Croquet	461.0 grams	477.0 grams
Table Tennis	2.4 grams	2.53 grams

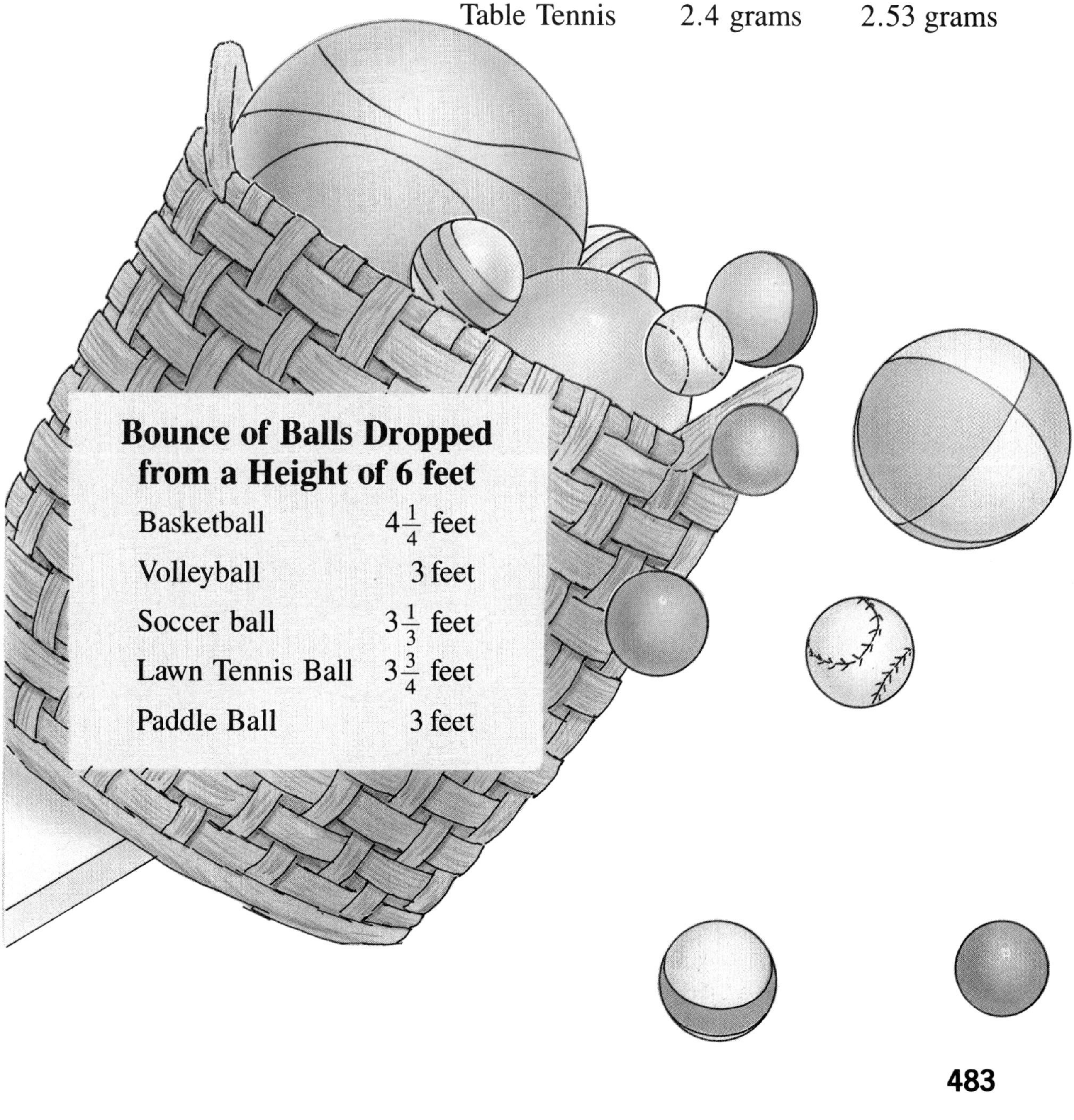

Bounce of Balls Dropped from a Height of 6 feet

Basketball	$4\frac{1}{4}$ feet
Volleyball	3 feet
Soccer ball	$3\frac{1}{3}$ feet
Lawn Tennis Ball	$3\frac{3}{4}$ feet
Paddle Ball	3 feet

Counting and Counting Patterns

Try these key codes to make your calculator count on by twos.

[ON/AC] [+] 2 [=] [=] [=] [=] . . .

[ON/AC] [+] 2 [Cons] [Cons] [Cons] [Cons] . . .

Entering [+] 2 or [+] 2 [Cons] sets up a **constant**, a number that stays the same. Each time you press [=] or [Cons] the calculator will add 2 to the number in the display.

Now try counting backward by 4s. Start at 70.

Enter [ON/AC] 70 [−] 4 [=] [=] [=] [=] . . .

or [ON/AC] [−] 4 [Cons] 70 [Cons] [Cons] [Cons] [Cons] . . .

The display should show 66, 62, 58, 54, and so on.

What is the largest number your calculator can display? Enter as many 9s as you can on your calculator. Most calculators can display eight 9s, or 99,999,999. What happens when you add 1? The number is too large for many calculators. The display shows an **overflow error**.

Activity

Is the target number in the counting pattern? Write yes or no.

	Start at	Count	Target Number
1.	20	on by 8	68
2.	14,000	on by 96,000	700,000
3.	700,000	on by 7,000,000	Error
4.	5,000	back by 64	4,680
5.	17,000	back by 810	560,000

Whole Number Addition and Subtraction

To do an addition or subtraction problem, enter the key code just the way you say the problem. Try these.

Say	Enter	Display
four plus eight equals	[ON/AC] 4 [+] 8 [=]	12
twenty minus five equals	[ON/AC] 20 [−] 5 [=]	15
eighty-nine minus fourteen equals	[ON/AC] 89 [−] 14 [=]	75
sixty-nine plus thirty equals	[ON/AC] 69 [+] 30 [=]	99
six hundred six minus fifty equals	[ON/AC] 606 [−] 50 [=]	556
four thousand seven plus fifty equals	[ON/AC] 4007 [+] 50 [=]	4057

Addition and subtraction problems with more than two numbers work the same way. Try these.

Problem	Enter	Display
23 + 45 + 91 =	[ON/AC] 23 [+] 45 [+] 91 [=]	159
97 + 11 + 67 − 22 =	[ON/AC] 97 [+] 11 [+] 67 [−] 22 [=]	153
93 − 21 − 16 − 30 =	[ON/AC] 93 [−] 21 [−] 16 [−] 30 [=]	26
345 − 45 + 16 − 6 =	[ON/AC] 345 [−] 45 [+] 16 [−] 6 [=]	310

Activity

Complete the web. The outside ring is the sum of the three inside rings.

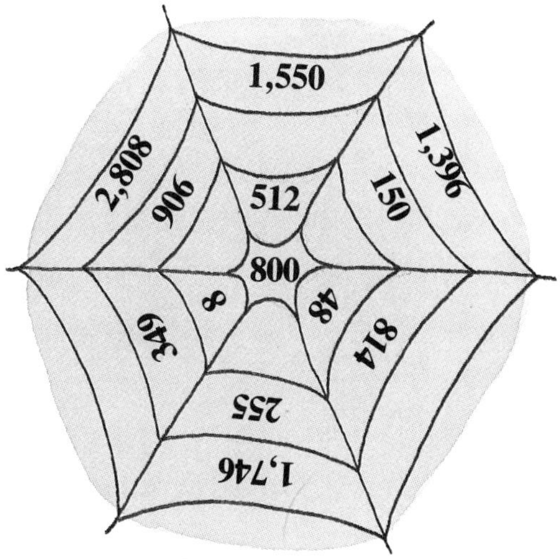

Whole Number Multiplication

Here are some ways you can find the total of 5 sevens.

[ON/AC] 0 [+] 7 [=] [=] [=] [=] [=]

[ON/AC] 7 [+] 7 [+] 7 [+] 7 [+] 7 [=]

[ON/AC] 5 [×] 7 [=]

Use your calculator to find 9 eights, 32 twelves, and 215 nineteens.

Suppose you want to multiply 22, 45, 113, and 2,045 each by 15. If your calculator has a **multiplication constant**, you can enter the constant, [×] 15, and then multiply each number by the constant.

[ON/AC] 22 [×] 15 [=] 45 [=] 113 [=] 2045 [=]

[ON/AC] [×] 15 [Cons] 22 [Cons] 45 [Cons] 113 [Cons] 2045 [Cons]

Your display should show 330, 675, 1,695, and 30,675.

Multiply 12, 33, 432, 2,341, and 44,153 by 1. Is your display the same as the number multiplied? That is because 1 is the **identity** number for multiplication.

Multiply 14, 65, 315, 3,516, and 47,936 by 0. Does your display show 0 after each operation? The product of any number and 0 is 0.

Activity

Can you solve all of these problems in less than two minutes?

1. 16×16 **2.** 41×1 **3.** 0×55 **4.** $1{,}600 \times 16$ **5.** 1×213

6. 14×16 **7.** 88×0 **8.** 16×14 **9.** $8{,}564 \times 1$ **10.** 765×0

Whole Number Division

How many 9s are there in 45? You can count the number of times you can subtract 9 from 45.

Enter [ON/AC] 45 [−] 9 [=] [=] [=] [=] [=]

or [ON/AC] 45 [−] 9 [=] [−] 9 [=] [−] 9 [=] [−] 9 [=] [−] 9 [=]

Or divide 45 by 9. Enter [ON/AC] 45 [÷] 9 [=].

To divide 96, 88, 80, 48, and 16 each by 8, you can enter the **division constant**, [÷] 8, and then divide each number by that constant.

Enter [ON/AC] 96 [÷] 8 [=] 88 [=] 80 [=] 48 [=] 16 [=]

or [ON/AC] [÷] 8 [Cons] 96 [Cons] 88 [Cons] 80 [Cons] 48 [Cons] 16 [Cons]

Your display should show 12, 11, 10, 6, and 2.

Divide 174 by 5. Your display should show 34.8. With the Math Explorer calculator, you can use the [INT ÷] key to do division with remainders.

Enter	Display
[ON/AC] 174 [INT ÷] 5 [=]	34 Q 4 R

The quotient is 34. The remainder is 4.

Divide 9, 56, 179, and 6,543 by 0. Dividing by zero is not logical. The calculator will display a **logic error**.

Activity

Find the number in each row that cannot be divided evenly by the divisor. What is the remainder?

Divisor							
7	14	105	147	91	318	574	182
13	52	325	533	107	858	533	221
41	82	205	574	902	2,091	1,025	297
23	92	391	322	690	1,079	598	1,863

Order of Operations: Memory Keys

To do a problem involving more than one operation, first multiply and divide, then add and subtract. For example, to do 6 × 7 + 4 × 13 you first find 6 × 17. Next find 4 × 13. Then add the two products.

Enter	Display
[ON/AC] 6 [×] 17 [=]	102
[ON/AC] 4 [×] 13 [=]	52
[ON/AC] 102 [+] 52 [=]	154

Sometimes you will want to remember the result of one calculation while you do another one. This can be done with **memory keys**.

[M+]	adds the display to the calculator's memory
[M−]	subtracts the display from the calculator's memory
[MR]	recalls the total in memory

Find 6 × 17 + 4 × 13.

Enter	Display
[ON/AC] 6 [×] 17 [=] [M+]	102
4 [×] 13 [=] [M+]	52
[MR]	154

Unlike some calculators, the Math Explorer does operations in the correct order. You can enter the problem just as it is written.

[ON/AC] 6 [×] 17 [+] 4 [×] 13 [=] 154

Activity

Match each expression in Column A with the expression in Column B which equals it. Remember to use the correct order of operations.

A	B
152 ÷ 4 + 16 × 4	88 + 166 − 16 × 5
12 × 12 − 32 ÷ 8	8 × 5 + 5 × 20
180 − 77 ÷ 7 + 5	19 × 3 + 180 ÷ 4

Decimals

Enter decimals on your calculator in the same way you enter whole numbers. Remember to press the decimal key. Enter these decimals.

Decimal Number	Key Code	Display
three tenths	[ON/AC] [.] 3	0.3
three hundredths	[ON/AC] [.] 03	0.03
four and one tenth	[ON/AC] 4 [.] 1	4.1

Notice that the calculator places a zero in front of the decimal point if no whole number is entered.

Add and subtract decimals just like you add and subtract whole numbers. Enter money amounts as decimals. Try these.

Problem	Key Code	Display
6 − 0.43 =	[ON/AC] 6 [−] .43 =	5.57
\$7.05 + \$23.62 =	[ON/AC] 7.05 [+] 23.62 =	30.67
\$6.58 − \$3.18 =	[ON/AC] 6.58 [−] 3.18 =	3.4

The display for the last problem shows 3.4, which in dollars is \$3.40.

Activity

Find the mistake Carlos made in his checkbook. His ending balance should be \$646.64. Make any necessary corrections in his balances.

Check No.	Date	To	Checks	Deposits	Balance
					546.12
324	4/1	AP Auto	450.00		96.12
	4/7	(Pay Check)		757.18	853.30
325	4/9	Al Barr	276.89		585.41
326	4/9	Sam's Food	81.12		504.29
327	4/11	Cable TV	29.90		474.39
	4/13	(Interest)		217.40	691.79
328	4/15	Sal's Toys	36.15		655.64

Fractions and Decimals

To find the decimal equivalent of a fraction, you can use your calculator to divide the numerator by the denominator.

Find the decimal for $\frac{1}{2}$, $\frac{3}{8}$, and $\frac{12}{5}$. Your calculator should show 0.5, 0.375, and 2.4.

The [F⇄D] key on the Math Explorer calculator is a fraction/decimal key. To change $\frac{1}{4}$ to a decimal, enter [ON/AC] 1 [/] 4 [F⇄D].

Find the decimals for $\frac{1}{2}$, $\frac{3}{8}$, and $\frac{12}{5}$ using the [F⇄D] and [/] keys.

Now find the decimal for $\frac{3}{4}$.

Enter	Display
[ON/AC] 3 [/] 4 [F⇄D]	0.75
Press [F⇄D] again.	$\frac{75}{100}$

Pressing [F⇄D] the second time changes the decimal 0.75 back to a fraction. The N/D → n/d in the display means that the fraction is not in simplest form. To simplify the fraction, enter [Simp] [=] until N/D → n/d disappears from the display.

Activity

Find the one fraction that does not have an equivalent decimal, and the one decimal that does not have an equivalent fraction.

Fractions

$\frac{21}{24}$ $\frac{36}{16}$ $\frac{5}{2}$

$\frac{35}{50}$ $\frac{33}{20}$

$\frac{20}{24}$ $\frac{24}{32}$ $\frac{20}{25}$

Decimals

2.5 .7 1.65

.75 1.7 2.25

.8 .875

Adding and Subtracting Fractions

To add or subtract fractions on a calculator, change them to decimals.

Add $\frac{1}{2} + \frac{7}{8}$.	Enter	Display
	[ON/AC] 1 [÷] 2 [=]	0.5
	[ON/AC] 7 [÷] 8 [=]	0.875
	[ON/AC] .5 [+] .875 [=]	1.375

To add or subtract mixed numbers, first change the mixed number to an improper fraction. For example, $2\frac{1}{2} + 1\frac{4}{5} = \frac{5}{2} + \frac{9}{5}$.

[ON/AC] 5 [÷] 2 [=] [M+]	2.5
9 [÷] 5 [=] [M+]	1.8
[MR]	4.3

To add or subtract fractions on the Math Explorer, enter the key code just the way you write the problem. Here are some examples to try.

Problem	Key Code	Display
$\frac{5}{6} - \frac{1}{3}$	5 [/] 6 [−] 1 [/] 3 [=]	$\frac{3}{6}$
	[Simp] [=]	$\frac{1}{2}$
$2\frac{7}{8} + \frac{6}{16}$	2 [Unit] 7 [/] 8 [+] 6 [/] 16 [=]	2 u $\frac{20}{16}$
	[Ab/c]	3 u $\frac{4}{16}$
	[Simp] 4 [=]	3 u $\frac{1}{4}$

Note that the [Ab/c] key changes improper fractions to mixed numbers.

Activity

Use the digits 1, 2, 3, 4, 5, 6, 7, 8, and 9. Make a true equation.
(Hint: The sum and differences are equal to $2\frac{1}{4}$ or 2.25.)

$$\frac{\square}{\square} + \frac{\square}{\square} = \frac{\square}{\square} - \frac{\square}{\square}$$

Computer Technology: Finding Total Amounts

Daryl was in the checkout counter at the supermarket. He had 5 items in his cart. He had only $10. He decided to estimate the total cost of the 5 items to see if he had enough money.

Bread	$1.39
Ground Beef	2.96
Apples	1.39
Cereal	2.49
Milk	1.15

Estimate the total cost. Do you think Daryl had enough money?

You can use the computer program below to practice your addition estimation skills.

```
10  PRINT "ESTIMATING TOTAL AMOUNTS": PRINT "SELECT HOW MANY
    NUMBERS TO ADD. THE": PRINT "COMPUTER WILL DISPLAY THE
    NUMBERS.": PRINT "ESTIMATE THE TOTAL. DO NOT USE": PRINT "PAPER
    AND PENCIL."
20  T = 0
30  PRINT : INPUT "HOW MANY NUMBERS TO ADD? ";N
40  PRINT : FOR I = 1 TO N
50  P = INT (995 * RND (1))/100: PRINT "$";P
60  T = T + P
70  NEXT I
80  PRINT : INPUT "ESTIMATE THE TOTAL. ";T1
90  PRINT : PRINT "THE EXACT TOTAL IS ";T
100 PRINT : PRINT "YOU MISSED THE TOTAL BY ";INT (100 * ABS (T-T1))/100
110 END
```

Estimating Length

Choose something in your classroom to measure. It can be a chalkboard, your desk or table, or even a book. Estimate the length in centimeters. Now measure to find the actual length. How close was your estimate?

The computer program below will give you more practice in estimating length. You will be given a unit segment and an unmarked segment. You must estimate the length of the unmarked segment. The computer will tell you how close your estimate was to the actual length.

```
 10  PRINT : PRINT : PRINT "ESTIMATING PRODUCTS"
 20  F1 = INT (90 * RND (1) + 1):F2 = INT (90 * RND (1) + 1)
 30  P = F1 * F2
 40  PRINT "ESTIMATING THIS PRODUCT."
 50  PRINT : PRINT TAB(15 - LEN (STR$ (F1)))F1: PRINT
 60  PRINT TAB(12)"x"; TAB(15 - LEN (STR$ (F2)))F2
 70  PRINT TAB(12)"___"
 80  PRINT : INPUT "ESTIMATE = ";P1
 90  PRINT : PRINT "THE EXACT PRODUCT IS ";P"."
100  D = ABS (P - P1): IF D < 10 THEN GOTO 120
110  PRINT "YOUR ESTIMATE IS OFF BY ";D: GOTO 130
120  PRINT P1;" IS A VERY GOOD ESTIMATE."
130  PRINT : INPUT "DO YOU WANT TO TRY ANOTHER PROBLEM? ";Y$
140  IF LEFT$ (Y$,1) = "Y" THEN GOTO 10
150  END
```

Estimating Capacity

Kristy made a graph to show the number of gallons of water in a tank. Each  shows one gallon of water. Count the stars to find how many gallons are in the tank. How many gallons are there?

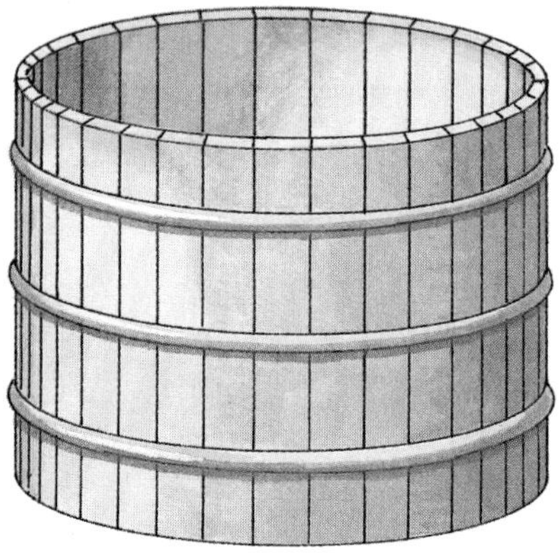

Now estimate how many gallons the empty tank will hold.

You can use the computer program below to try other estimation problems.

```
 10  PRINT : PRINT : PRINT “ESTIMATING PRODUCTS“
 20  F1 = INT (90 * RND (1) + 1):F2 = INT (90 * RND (1) + 1)
 30  P = F1 * F2
 40  PRINT “ESTIMATE THIS PRODUCT.“
 50  PRINT : PRINT TAB(15 – LEN (STR$ (F1)))F1: PRINT
 60  PRINT TAB(12)“x“; TAB(15 – LEN (STR$ (F2)))F2
 70  PRINT TAB(12)“___“
 80  PRINT : INPUT “ESTIMATE = “;P1
 90  PRINT : PRINT “THE EXACT PRODUCT IS “;P“.“
100  D = ABS (P – P1): IF D < 10 THEN GOTO 120
110  PRINT “YOUR ESTIMATE IS OFF BY “;D: GOTO 130
120  PRINT P1;“ IS A VERY GOOD ESTIMATE.“
130  PRINT : INPUT “DO YOU WANT TO TRY ANOTHER PROBLEM? “;Y$
140  IF LEFT$ (Y$,1) = “Y“ THEN GOTO 10
150  END
```

Function Tables

Can you see a pattern between the input and output numbers in the function table?

What are the two missing output numbers for the table? What is the rule that is used to get the output numbers?

The computer program below will give you more practice in finding rules and numbers for function tables.

Function Table

Input	Output
12	36
3	9
11	33
8	?
10	?

```
10  FOR I = 1 TO 5:X(I) = INT (20 * RND (1) + 1)
20  IF X(I) = X(I − 1) THEN 10
30  NEXT I
40  A = INT (10 * RND (1) + 1)
50  PRINT : PRINT : PRINT "INPUT | OUTPUT": PRINT "______|______": PRINT " |"
60  GOSUB 190
70  IF X(5) < 10 THEN PRINT " "X(5)" | ?": GOTO 90
80  PRINT " "X(5)" | ?"
90  PRINT : PRINT : PRINT "FUNCTION TABLES": PRINT "THERE IS A
    PATTERN BETWEEN THE INPUT": PRINT "AND OUTPUT NUMBERS IN THE
    FUNCTION": PRINT "TABLE. STUDY THE TABLE AND SEE IF YOU": PRINT
    "CAN FIND THE PATTERN. WHAT IS THE"
100 INPUT "MISSING NUMBER IN THE TABLE? ";M: PRINT : IF (J = 1) AND
    (M = X(5) + A) THEN PRINT "CORRECT.": GOTO 140
110 IF (J = 2) AND (M = X(5) * A) THEN PRINT "CORRECT.": GOTO 150
120 IF J = 1 THEN PRINT "NOT CORRECT.": GOTO 140
130 IF J = 2 THEN PRINT "NOT CORRECT.": GOTO 150
140 PRINT "THE RULE IS: INPUT + ";A:" = OUTPUT": GOTO 160
150 PRINT "THE RULE IS: INPUT X";A;" = OUTPUT"
160 INPUT "DO YOU WANT ANOTHER FUNCTION TABLE? ";Y$
170 IF LEFT$ (Y$,1) = "Y" THEN GOTO 10
180 END
190 J = INT (2 * RND (1) + 1)
200 ON J GOTO 210,230
210 FOR N = 1 TO 4: IF X(N) < 10 THEN PRINT " "X(N)" |"X(N) + A: NEXT N:
    RETURN
220 PRINT " "X(N)" | "X(N) + A: NEXT N: RETURN
230 FOR N = 1 TO 4: IF X(N) < 10 THEN PRINT " "X(N)" | "X(N) * A: NEXT N:
    RETURN
240 PRINT " "X(N)" | "X(N) * A: NEXT N: RETURN
```

Smallest Difference

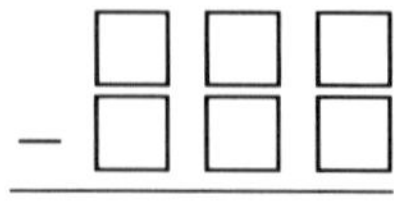

Joan and Nikko wre playing the game of Smallest Difference. Joan had the 6 digits, 3, 5, 3, 2, 0, 7 to put in the boxes in the subtraction problem. She wanted the answer to be as small as possible. Nikko had the digits 4, 3, 9, 9, 7, 0. She wanted to get a smaller difference than Joan.

What problem would you make with Joan's digits? What would you make with Nikko's digits? Who would win?

You can play the game of Smallest Difference on the computer. Think about some strategies that may help you win some games.

```
10  PRINT “SMALLEST DIFFERENCE GAME“
20  PRINT “EACH PLAYER RECEIVES 6 DIGITS. USE THE“: PRINT “6 DIGITS
    TO CREATE A SUBTRACTION“
30  PRINT “PROBLEM WITH THE SMALLEST POSSIBLE“: PRINT
    “DIFFERENCE. THE PLAYER WITH THE“: PRINT “SMALLEST DIFFERENCE
    WINS THE GAME.“
40  FOR P = 1 TO 2
50  PRINT : PRINT “PLAYER “;P;“, YOUR NUMBERS ARE:“: PRINT
60  FOR C = 1 TO 6:B = INT (10 * RND (1))
70  PRINT B“ “;: NEXT C: PRINT : PRINT
80  INPUT “TYPE THE TOP NUMBER. “;T(P)
90  INPUT “TYPE THE BOTTOM NUMBER. “;B(P)
100 IF B(P) > T(P) THEN GOTO 80
110 D(P) = T(P) – B(P): NEXT P
120 PRINT : PRINT “PLAYER 1“,“PLAYER 2“: PRINT
130 PRINT TAB(6 – LEN (STR$ (T(1))))T(1); TAB(22 – LEN (STR$ (T(2))))T(2):
    PRINT: PRINT TAB(2)“–“; TAB(6 – LEN (STR$(B(1))))B(1); TAB(18)“–“;
    TAB(22 – LEN(STR$ (B(2))))B(2)
140 PRINT TAB(2)“___“; TAB(18)“___“: PRINT : PRINT TAB(6 – LEN (STR$
    (D(1))))D(1); TAB(22 – LEN (STR$ (D(2))))D(2)
150 PRINT : IF D(1) = D(2) THEN PRINT “TIE SCORE OF “;D(1): GOTO 180
160 IF D(1) < D(2) THEN PRINT “PLAYER 1 WINS.“: GOTO 180
170 PRINT “PLAYER 2 WINS.“
180 PRINT : INPUT “WANT TO PLAY ANOTHER GAME?(Y/N) “;Y$
190 IF LEFT$ (Y$,1) = “Y“ THEN 40
200 END
```

Fractions of a Number

There are 24 students in Melissa's music class. $\frac{3}{8}$ of the students can play a musical instrument. How many students can play a musical instrument?

You can use the set of 24 stars to help you think about the problem. There are 8 stars in each row. There are 3 rows of stars. What is $\frac{3}{8}$ of 24?

Computers can help you learn about fractions. The computer program below will give you more problems like the one above to solve.

```
 10  N = INT (10 * RND (1) + 1)
 20  D = INT (10 * RND (1) + 1): IF D <= N THEN 10
 30  M = INT (9 * RND (1) + 1) * D
 40  PRINT : PRINT : FOR R = 1 TO M/D
 50  FOR C = 1 TO D
 60  PRINT "*";: NEXT C: PRINT : NEXT R
 70  PRINT : PRINT : PRINT "FINDING FRACTIONS OF A WHOLE NUMBER":
     PRINT "THERE ARE ";M;" TOTAL STARS. THERE ARE ";D
 80  PRINT "STARS IN EACH ROW. THERE ARE ";M/D;" ROWS OF": PRINT
     "STARS. WHAT IS ";N;"/";D;" OF ";M;
90   INPUT "STARS? ";A:A1 = (N/D) * M: PRINT
100  IF A = A1 THEN PRINT "CORRECT."
110  IF A <> A1 THEN PRINT "SORRY."
120  PRINT N:"/";D;" OF ";M;" = ";A1: PRINT
130  FOR R = 1 TO M/D
140  FOR C = 1 TO N
150  PRINT "*";: NEXT C: PRINT : NEXT R
160  PRINT : INPUT "DO YOU WANT ANOTHER PROBLEM? ";Y$
170  IF LEFT$ (Y$,1) = "Y" THEN 10
180  END
```

Probability Spinner

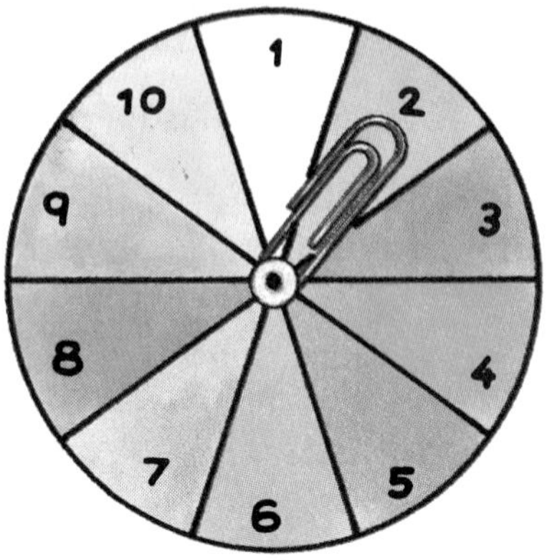

Raymond used a spinner divided into 10 sectors of equal size for a probability experiment. He decided to spin the spinner 100 times and record the number for each spin. He thought that each of the numbers 1 to 10 would come up 10 times. Do you think this will happen? What would happen in 1,000 spins?

Computers can be programmed to simulate some probability problems. The program below can be used to simulate a spinner with any number of equal sectors. It can simulate the number cube by choosing a spinner with 6 sectors. To simulate a coin toss, choose a spinner with 2 sectors. You can choose any number of trials.

```
 10  PRINT "PROBABILITY SPINNER": PRINT "THIS IS AN EXPERIMENT IN
     PROBABILITY.": PRINT "CHOOSE A SPINNER WITH ANY NUMBER OF":
     PRINT "EQUAL PARTS. CHOOSE ANY NUMBER OF": PRINT "SPINS. THE
     COMPUTER WILL QUICKLY GIVE": PRINT "THE OUTCOME."
 20  PRINT : INPUT "HOW MANY SECTORS OF EQUAL SIZE? ";X
 30  DIM D(X)
 40  FOR N = 1 TO X:D(N) = 0: NEXT N
 50  INPUT "HOW MANY SPINS DO YOU WANT? ";Y
 60  FOR I = 1 TO Y:R = INT (X * RND (1)) + 1
 70  LET D(R) = D(R) + 1: NEXT I
 80  PRINT "NUMBER","FREQUENCY"
 90  FOR N = 1 TO X: PRINT N,D(N): NEXT N
100  END
```

Computer Graphs

Joyce wanted to make a graph of the data in a table of record animal ages. She decided to show a star, *, for every 2 years of age for each of the animals.

Make a graph of the data in the table. Use Joyce's plan.

Record Ages of Animals	
Elephant	62
Hippopotamus	54
Rhinoceros	40
Bear	34
Monkey	26

Computers can be used to quickly and accurately show data in graph form. The program below is a simple example. You must make some choices when using the program.

```
10  PRINT : PRINT : PRINT "COMPUTER GRAPHING": PRINT "ENTER THE
    FOLLOWING INFORMATION AND THE": PRINT "COMPUTER WILL CREATE
    A GRAPH."
20  PRINT : INPUT "HOW MANY NUMBERS FOR THE GRAPH? ";N
30  DIM N$(N): DIM X(N)
40  PRINT "FOR EACH ITEM, TYPE THE NAME AND THE": PRINT "NUMBER
    SEPARATED BY A COMMA."
50  FOR I = 1 TO N: INPUT N$(I),X(I): NEXT I
60  S = 1: FOR Q = 1 TO N:S1 = INT (X(Q)/23 + 1): IF S1 > S THEN S = S1
70  NEXT Q: INPUT "TYPE THE NAME OF THE GRAPH. ";G$
80  PRINT : PRINT TAB(20)G$
90  PRINT "________________________________________"
100 FOR I = 1 TO N: PRINT N$(I),
110 FOR J = 1 TO INT (X(I)/S + .5): PRINT "*";: NEXT J
120 PRINT : NEXT I
130 PRINT "________________________________________": PRINT
140 PRINT "EACH * = ";S
150 END
```

More Practice Bank

Set A For use following page 7.

Find these sums.

1.	2.	3.	4.	5.	6.
6	7	8	9	0	4
+ 5	+ 7	+ 3	+ 7	+ 8	+ 6

7. (3 + 9) + 4 **8.** 3 + (9 + 4)

Set B For use following page 15.

Add. Break apart an addend if needed.

1.	2.	3.	4.	5.	6.	7.
14	15	10	12	7	16	11
+ 7	+ 7	+ 3	+ 4	+ 0	+ 9	+ 2

Set C For use following page 17.

Add. Use compensation if needed.

1.	2.	3.	4.	5.	6.	7.
13	10	17	18	6	12	15
+ 6	+ 4	+ 8	+ 9	+ 2	+ 7	+ 6

Set D For use following page 31.

Write > or < for each ||||.

1. 73,112 |||| 73,211 **2.** 468,101 |||| 468,011

3. 676 |||| 667 **4.** 538 |||| 358

Set E For use following page 37.

Round to the nearest ten or hundred.

1. 28 |||| **2.** 83 |||| **3.** 65 |||| **4.** 34 |||| **5.** 295 |||| **6.** 703 ||||

Set F For use following page 39.

Round to the nearest thousand or dollar.

1. 4,499 **2.** 8,207 **3.** 2,600 **4.** 5,653 **5.** \$1.79 **6.** \$68.16

Set A For use following page 55.

Find these sums and differences.

1. 300 + 600
2. 80 − 40
3. 700 + 500
4. 16,000 − 8,000
5. 1,200 + 1,500
6. 800 + 600

Set B For use following page 57.

Estimate the sums and differences by rounding.

1. 75 + 34
2. 42 − 33
3. 242 + 757
4. 318 − 186
5. 683 − 321
6. 1,684 + 7,450

Set C For use following page 61.

Find the sums.

1. 715 + 916
2. 685 + 77
3. 263 + 98
4. 702 + 859
5. 457 + 382
6. 375 + 829

Set D For use following page 63.

Add.

1. 64, 47, 28, + 35
2. $3.83, 5.35, 7.68, + 0.54
3. 746, 75, 434, + 8
4. 563, 87, 412, + 29
5. $1.95, 6.28, 1.39, + .97
6. 52, 43, 18, + 77

Set E For use following page 66.

Estimate the sums. Use front-end estimation.

1. 24, 33, + 14
2. 46, 38, + 17
3. 342 + 461
4. 602 + 813
5. 630, 742, + 253
6. 312, 403, + 614

Set A For use following page 71.

Subtract.

1. $\begin{array}{r} 529 \\ -\ 179 \\ \hline \end{array}$ 2. $\begin{array}{r} 615 \\ -\ 340 \\ \hline \end{array}$ 3. $\begin{array}{r} 7{,}136 \\ -\ 472 \\ \hline \end{array}$ 4. $\begin{array}{r} 148 \\ -\ 95 \\ \hline \end{array}$ 5. $\begin{array}{r} 390 \\ -\ 36 \\ \hline \end{array}$ 6. $\begin{array}{r} 370 \\ -\ 114 \\ \hline \end{array}$

Set B For use following page 73.

Subtract.

1. $\begin{array}{r} 508 \\ -\ 179 \\ \hline \end{array}$ 2. $\begin{array}{r} 605 \\ -\ 346 \\ \hline \end{array}$ 3. $\begin{array}{r} 1{,}006 \\ -\ 788 \\ \hline \end{array}$ 4. $\begin{array}{r} 505 \\ -\ 149 \\ \hline \end{array}$ 5. $\begin{array}{r} 2{,}001 \\ -\ 135 \\ \hline \end{array}$ 6. $\begin{array}{r} 402 \\ -\ 58 \\ \hline \end{array}$

Set C For use following page 75.

Use compensation to find these sums and differences.

1. $\begin{array}{r} 763 \\ +\ 97 \\ \hline \end{array}$ 2. $\begin{array}{r} 596 \\ +\ 35 \\ \hline \end{array}$ 3. $\begin{array}{r} 841 \\ -\ 499 \\ \hline \end{array}$ 4. $\begin{array}{r} 589 \\ -\ 405 \\ \hline \end{array}$ 5. $\begin{array}{r} 687 \\ +\ 163 \\ \hline \end{array}$ 6. $\begin{array}{r} 386 \\ -\ 79 \\ \hline \end{array}$

Set D For use following page 79.

Find the sums and differences. Use a calculator if necessary.

1. $\begin{array}{r} 2{,}964 \\ +\ 5{,}682 \\ \hline \end{array}$ 2. $\begin{array}{r} 6{,}587 \\ +\ 2{,}744 \\ \hline \end{array}$ 3. $\begin{array}{r} 4{,}532 \\ +\ 1{,}607 \\ \hline \end{array}$ 4. $\begin{array}{r} 4{,}430 \\ -\ 726 \\ \hline \end{array}$ 5. $\begin{array}{r} 6{,}429 \\ -\ 5{,}161 \\ \hline \end{array}$ 6. $\begin{array}{r} 7{,}000 \\ -\ 2{,}674 \\ \hline \end{array}$

Set E For use following page 119.

Find the products.

1. $\begin{array}{r} 4 \\ \times\ 1 \\ \hline \end{array}$ 2. $\begin{array}{r} 1 \\ \times\ 3 \\ \hline \end{array}$ 3. $\begin{array}{r} 2 \\ \times\ 0 \\ \hline \end{array}$ 4. $\begin{array}{r} 0 \\ \times\ 3 \\ \hline \end{array}$ 5. $\begin{array}{r} 2 \\ \times\ 1 \\ \hline \end{array}$ 6. $5 \times 4 = 20$
 $4 \times 5 = n$

Set F For use following page 121.

Find the products.

1. $\begin{array}{r} 2 \\ \times\ 2 \\ \hline \end{array}$ 2. $\begin{array}{r} 2 \\ \times\ 7 \\ \hline \end{array}$ 3. $\begin{array}{r} 2 \\ \times\ 8 \\ \hline \end{array}$ 4. $\begin{array}{r} 4 \\ \times\ 2 \\ \hline \end{array}$ 5. $\begin{array}{r} 5 \\ \times\ 2 \\ \hline \end{array}$ 6. $\begin{array}{r} 5 \\ \times\ 3 \\ \hline \end{array}$ 7. $\begin{array}{r} 5 \\ \times\ 8 \\ \hline \end{array}$

More Practice Bank

Set A For use following page 123.

Multiply.

1. 6×9 2. 7×9 3. 9×0 4. 9×9 5. 2×9 6. 1×9 7. 9×5

Set B For use following page 125.

Multiply.

1. 6×3 2. 3×4 3. 5×4 4. 3×9 5. 4×3 6. 3×3 7. 7×4

Set C For use following page 131.

Find the products. Break apart one of the factors if needed.

1. 7×6 2. 8×5 3. 6×8 4. 7×7 5. 7×8 6. 9×9 7. 5×6

Set D For use following page 133.

Find the products.

1. 6×9 2. 8×8 3. 6×7 4. 6×6 5. 8×6 6. 6×7

Set E For use following page 135.

Copy and complete each set of multiples.

1.

×	0	1	2	3	4	5
5	0	5	10	▯	▯	▯

2.

×	0	1	2	3	4	5
2	0	2	4	▯	▯	▯

Set F For use following page 147.

Find the products. Write answers only.

1. 5×30 2. 2×700 3. 3×200 4. $6 \times 1{,}000$ 5. $2 \times 8{,}000$

Set A For use following page 151.

Multiply and then add 4. Write answers only.

1. 2×5 2. 6×7 3. 3×2 4. 7×4 5. 8×7

Set B For use following page 155.

Find the products.

1. 53×4 2. 72×5 3. 24×4 4. 45×6 5. 86×5 6. 12×8

Set C For use following page 157.

Find the products.

1. 130×4 2. 161×7 3. 128×3 4. 116×5 5. 411×8 6. 247×2

Set D For use following page 159.

Find the products.

1. 605×3 2. 250×7 3. 708×2 4. 435×8 5. 582×5 6. 641×5

Set E For use following page 162.

Find the products.

1. $(2 \times 3) \times 3$ 2. $(4 \times 1) \times 10$ 3. $5 \times (4 \times 2)$

4. $4 \times (2 \times 100)$ 5. $5 \times (2 \times 3)$ 6. $(3 \times 3) \times 10$

Set F For use following page 163.

Find the missing numbers using your calculator.

1. $382 + 526 + 55 = 261 + 118 + \square$ 2. $407 + 89 + 281 = 292 + 43 + \square$

Set A For use following page 165.

Find the products.

1. 4,512 × 7	**2.** 1,475 × 6	**3.** 7,004 × 5	**4.** 2,359 × 3	**5.** 5,267 × 8

Set B For use following page 167.

Multiply.

1. $0.45 × 7	**2.** $5.26 × 8	**3.** $3.02 × 4	**4.** $8.59 × 9	**5.** $12.78 × 5

Set C For use following page 179.

Find the products. Write answers only.

1. 90 × 50 **2.** 50 × 60 **3.** 60 × 40 **4.** 80 × 30 **5.** 20 × 60

Set D For use following page 181.

Estimate the products. Round numbers to the nearest ten.

1. 12 × 29 **2.** 38 × 21 **3.** 61 × 49 **4.** 352 × 19 **5.** 18 × 19

Set E For use following page 183.

Multiply.

1. 63 × 80	**2.** 48 × 30	**3.** 75 × 40	**4.** 43 × 10	**5.** 27 × 60	**6.** 38 × 20

Set F For use following page 185.

Find the products.

1. 12 × 23	**2.** 31 × 42	**3.** 43 × 11	**4.** 30 × 24	**5.** 14 × 12	**6.** 44 × 34

Set A For use following page 193.

Find the amounts.

1. $\begin{array}{r} \$4.73 \\ \times\ \ 36 \\ \hline \end{array}$ **2.** $\begin{array}{r} \$9.06 \\ \times\ \ 53 \\ \hline \end{array}$ **3.** $\begin{array}{r} \$5.61 \\ \times\ \ 42 \\ \hline \end{array}$ **4.** $\begin{array}{r} \$8.34 \\ \times\ \ 16 \\ \hline \end{array}$ **5.** $\begin{array}{r} \$3.10 \\ \times\ \ 45 \\ \hline \end{array}$

Set B For use following page 239.

Use counters to find the quotients.

1. $8 \div 2 =$ **2.** $24 \div 3 =$ **3.** $14 \div 2 =$

4. $2\overline{)16}$ **5.** $3\overline{)21}$ **6.** $2\overline{)12}$

Set C For use following page 243.

Divide.

1. $3\overline{)21}$ **2.** $2\overline{)18}$ **3.** $3\overline{)27}$ **4.** $2\overline{)8}$ **5.** $3\overline{)12}$

6. $2\overline{)16}$ **7.** $3\overline{)24}$ **8.** $2\overline{)14}$ **9.** $3\overline{)9}$ **10.** $2\overline{)12}$

Set D For use following page 245.

Divide.

1. $20 \div 5 =$ **2.** $16 \div 4 =$ **3.** $10 \div 5 =$

4. $40 \div 5 =$ **5.** $25 \div 5 =$ **6.** $36 \div 4 =$

Set E For use following page 248.

Find the quotients.

1. $0 \div 8$ **2.** $9 \div 1$ **3.** $0 \div 2$ **4.** $4 \div 1$ **5.** $87 \div 87$ **6.** $0 \div 6$

Set F For use following page 251.

Find the quotients.

1. $35 \div 7 =$ **2.** $54 \div 6 =$ **3.** $12 \div 6 =$ **4.** $21 \div 7 =$

5. $30 \div 6 =$ **6.** $42 \div 7 =$ **7.** $28 \div 7 =$ **8.** $18 \div 6 =$

Set A For use following page 253.

Divide.

1. $8 \div 8 =$	**2.** $27 \div 9 =$	**3.** $56 \div 8 =$
4. $81 \div 9 =$	**5.** $32 \div 8 =$	**6.** $63 \div 9 =$

Set B For use following page 267.

Find the quotients and remainders. Check your answers.

1. $2\overline{)13}$ **2.** $4\overline{)22}$ **3.** $7\overline{)16}$ **4.** $6\overline{)15}$ **5.** $8\overline{)65}$ **6.** $9\overline{)39}$ **7.** $5\overline{)47}$

Set C For use following page 269.

Find the quotients. Write answers only.

1. $80 \div 4$ **2.** $80 \div 8$ **3.** $60 \div 2$ **4.** $40 \div 2$ **5.** $360 \div 4$ **6.** $560 \div 8$

Set D For use following page 271.

Estimate by rounding to the nearest ten. Write estimated answers only.

1. $91 \div 3$	**2.** $75 \div 4$	**3.** $58 \div 2$	**4.** $49 \div 5$
5. $252 \div 5$	**6.** $423 \div 7$	**6.** $357 \div 9$	**8.** $182 \div 3$

Set E For use following page 275.

Find the quotients and remainders.

1. $5\overline{)68}$	**2.** $8\overline{)94}$	**3.** $2\overline{)91}$	**4.** $6\overline{)53}$	**5.** $4\overline{)79}$
6. $3\overline{)55}$	**7.** $7\overline{)81}$	**8.** $9\overline{)86}$	**9.** $3\overline{)92}$	**10.** $8\overline{)82}$

More Practice Bank

Set A For use following page 279.

Find the quotients and remainders.

1. $7\overline{)884}$ **2.** $6\overline{)893}$ **3.** $4\overline{)450}$ **4.** $2\overline{)335}$ **5.** $8\overline{)889}$ **6.** $6\overline{)696}$ **7.** $4\overline{)510}$

Set B For use following page 283.

Divide and check.

1. $3\overline{)124}$ **2.** $7\overline{)810}$ **3.** $6\overline{)200}$ **4.** $2\overline{)137}$ **5.** $4\overline{)543}$ **6.** $9\overline{)425}$ **7.** $5\overline{)663}$

Set C For use following page 285.

Divide.

1. $7\overline{)636}$ **2.** $6\overline{)604}$ **3.** $9\overline{)98}$ **4.** $2\overline{)801}$ **5.** $5\overline{)750}$ **6.** $3\overline{)91}$ **7.** $4\overline{)431}$

Set D For use following page 289.

Divide.

1. $4\overline{)\$5.92}$ **2.** $7\overline{)\$4.41}$ **3.** $8\overline{)\$8.00}$ **4.** $3\overline{)\$0.78}$ **5.** $6\overline{)\$2.70}$

Set E For use following page 335.

Fill in the $\square$ to create an equivalent fraction.

1. $\frac{2}{3} = \frac{\square}{6}$ **2.** $\frac{3}{6} = \frac{\square}{12}$ **3.** $\frac{1}{4} = \frac{\square}{8}$ **4.** $\frac{1}{2} = \frac{2}{\square}$ **5.** $\frac{3}{5} = \frac{\square}{10}$

Set F For use following page 337.

Multiply the numerator and denominator by 2, 3, and 4
to find a set of equivalent fractions.

1. $\frac{3}{8} = \frac{\square}{\square} = \frac{\square}{\square} = \frac{\square}{\square}$ **2.** $\frac{3}{4} = \frac{\square}{\square} = \frac{\square}{\square} = \frac{\square}{\square}$ **3.** $\frac{5}{9} = \frac{\square}{\square} = \frac{\square}{\square} = \frac{\square}{\square}$

Set G For use following page 339.

Reduce each fraction to lowest terms.

1. $\frac{6}{8}$ **2.** $\frac{3}{9}$ **3.** $\frac{4}{16}$ **4.** $\frac{18}{24}$ **5.** $\frac{8}{12}$ **6.** $\frac{15}{25}$

More Practice Bank

Set A For use following page 341.

Write $>$, $<$, or $=$ for each ||||.

1. $\frac{1}{5}$ |||| $\frac{1}{3}$ 2. $\frac{1}{2}$ |||| $\frac{1}{3}$ 3. $\frac{1}{10}$ |||| $\frac{1}{5}$ 4. $\frac{1}{4}$ |||| $\frac{1}{5}$ 5. $\frac{2}{4}$ |||| $\frac{5}{10}$

Set B For use following page 345.

Solve.

1. $\frac{2}{5}$ of 5 2. $\frac{3}{4}$ of 24 3. $\frac{4}{5}$ of 15 4. $\frac{2}{4}$ of 16 5. $\frac{3}{8}$ of 24 6. $\frac{3}{4}$ of 16

Set C For use following page 347.

Write each fraction as a whole number or a mixed number.
Reduce all fractions to lowest terms.

1. $\frac{40}{6}$ 2. $\frac{12}{2}$ 3. $\frac{11}{4}$ 4. $\frac{15}{2}$ 5. $\frac{9}{3}$ 6. $\frac{39}{9}$

Set D For use following page 365.

Give $>$ or $<$ for each ||||.

1. 2.27 |||| 2.35 2. 7.6 |||| 7.54 3. 9.4 |||| 9.36

4. 4.8 |||| 3.9 5. 6.27 |||| 6.29 6. 2.5 |||| 2.6

Set E For use following page 367.

Round each decimal number to the nearest whole number.

1. 64.53 2. 11.4 3. 29.5 4. 6.8 5. 5.25 6. 93.1 7. 9.2

Set F For use following page 369.

Write the decimal for each fraction.

1. $\frac{1}{4} =$ 2. $\frac{2}{10} =$ 3. $\frac{3}{5} =$ 4. $\frac{4}{10} =$ 5. $\frac{1}{2} =$ 6. $\frac{2}{5} =$

MORE PRACTICE BANK

Set A For use following page 409.

Add or subtract. Reduce to lowest terms.

1. $\frac{3}{5} + \frac{1}{5}$

2. $\frac{11}{10} - \frac{6}{10}$

3. $\begin{array}{r} 4\frac{5}{8} \\ +\ 4\frac{2}{8} \\ \hline \end{array}$

4. $\begin{array}{r} 8\frac{6}{10} \\ -\ 7\frac{3}{10} \\ \hline \end{array}$

5. $\begin{array}{r} 3\frac{1}{2} \\ +\ 2\frac{1}{2} \\ \hline \end{array}$

Set B For use following page 413.

Add. Use models if necessary.

1. $\begin{array}{r} \frac{1}{6} \\ +\ \frac{2}{3} \\ \hline \end{array}$

2. $\begin{array}{r} \frac{6}{10} \\ +\ \frac{3}{5} \\ \hline \end{array}$

3. $\begin{array}{r} \frac{2}{8} \\ +\ \frac{2}{4} \\ \hline \end{array}$

4. $\begin{array}{r} \frac{1}{3} \\ +\ \frac{5}{6} \\ \hline \end{array}$

5. $\begin{array}{r} \frac{3}{10} \\ +\ \frac{3}{5} \\ \hline \end{array}$

6. $\begin{array}{r} \frac{4}{10} \\ +\ \frac{1}{2} \\ \hline \end{array}$

Set C For use following page 415.

Subtract.

1. $\begin{array}{r} \frac{5}{8} \\ -\ \frac{1}{2} \\ \hline \end{array}$

2. $\begin{array}{r} \frac{1}{2} \\ -\ \frac{1}{8} \\ \hline \end{array}$

3. $\begin{array}{r} \frac{2}{3} \\ -\ \frac{2}{6} \\ \hline \end{array}$

4. $\begin{array}{r} \frac{6}{8} \\ -\ \frac{1}{2} \\ \hline \end{array}$

5. $\begin{array}{r} \frac{7}{8} \\ -\ \frac{3}{4} \\ \hline \end{array}$

6. $\begin{array}{r} \frac{7}{10} \\ -\ \frac{1}{5} \\ \hline \end{array}$

Set D For use following page 421.

Add or subtract.

1. $\begin{array}{r} 53.68 \\ +\ 4.19 \\ \hline \end{array}$

2. $\begin{array}{r} 42.7 \\ +\ 69.1 \\ \hline \end{array}$

3. $\begin{array}{r} 4.83 \\ +\ 1.47 \\ \hline \end{array}$

4. $\begin{array}{r} 58.26 \\ +\ 17.35 \\ \hline \end{array}$

5. $\begin{array}{r} 8.3 \\ +\ 7.2 \\ \hline \end{array}$

6. $\begin{array}{r} 7.64 \\ -\ 3.16 \\ \hline \end{array}$

7. $\begin{array}{r} \$47.20 \\ -\ 19.80 \\ \hline \end{array}$

8. $\begin{array}{r} 47.52 \\ -\ 8.73 \\ \hline \end{array}$

9. $\begin{array}{r} 47.60 \\ -\ 17.82 \\ \hline \end{array}$

10. $\begin{array}{r} 32.75 \\ -\ 12.08 \\ \hline \end{array}$

MORE PRACTICE BANK

Set A For use following page 423.

Add or subtract.

1.	2.	3.	4.	5.
$42.7 + 8.69$	$64.8 - 21.34$	$2.69 + 8$	$64 - 18.3$	$93 - 75.46$

Set B For use following page 425.

Round to the nearest whole number, then add or subtract.

1.	2.	3.	4.	5.
$32.46 - 17.83$	$26.41 - 14.82$	$13.40 + 6.17$	$28.65 + 19.82$	$67.62 - 53.46$

Set C For use following page 437.

Divide.

1. $20\overline{)80}$ **2.** $60\overline{)180}$ **3.** $10\overline{)90}$ **4.** $40\overline{)240}$ **5.** $90\overline{)360}$ **6.** $70\overline{)420}$

Set D For use following page 439.

Divide.

1. $50\overline{)285}$ **2.** $30\overline{)95}$ **3.** $90\overline{)508}$ **4.** $60\overline{)185}$ **5.** $20\overline{)99}$ **6.** $70\overline{)383}$

Set E For use following page 441.

Divide and check.

1. $15\overline{)48}$ **2.** $47\overline{)96}$ **3.** $33\overline{)47}$ **4.** $25\overline{)56}$ **5.** $39\overline{)34}$ **6.** $14\overline{)30}$

Set F For use following page 443.

Divide. Change your estimates if necessary.

1. $13\overline{)35}$ **2.** $12\overline{)49}$ **3.** $19\overline{)427}$ **4.** $18\overline{)72}$ **5.** $23\overline{)45}$

6. $31\overline{)91}$ **7.** $27\overline{)588}$ **8.** $14\overline{)83}$ **9.** $35\overline{)80}$ **10.** $42\overline{)813}$

Set A For use following page 447.

Divide and check.

1. $20\overline{)\$7.00}$ **2.** $70\overline{)955}$ **3.** $30\overline{)812}$ **4.** $40\overline{)579}$ **5.** $50\overline{)805}$

Set B For use following page 449.

Divide and check.

1. $14\overline{)279}$ **2.** $22\overline{)354}$ **3.** $41\overline{)892}$ **4.** $35\overline{)961}$ **5.** $46\overline{)703}$

Set C For use following page 5.

Use counters to help you solve these problems.

1. Steve has saved \$11. He bought a record for \$5. Then he earned \$7 more. How much money does he have now?

2. Jack has \$12. Jin has \$15. Jin spends \$7. Jack does not spend any money. Now how much more money does Jack have than Jin?

Set D For use following page 9.

Write the fact family for each pair of addends.

1. 5, 9 **2.** 3, 4

Set E For use following page 11.

Solve.

1. Mike wanted to spot a dozen blue jays on his hike. By noon he had seen 5 blue jays. How many more blue jays does he have to spot?

2. Holly found 11 acorns in the forest. Her brother Ted found 16 acorns. How many fewer acorns did Holly find than Ted?

Set F For use following page 27.

Write the place value of each red number.

1. 3,620 **2.** 739 **3.** 19 **4.** 402 **5.** 924 **6.** 589

More Practice Bank

Set A For use following page 29.

Write the standard number. Use a comma to separate thousands.

1. thirty-six thousand

2. five hundred seventy-nine thousand

Set B For use following page 35.

Solve.

1. Riku is shorter than Betty. Fran is taller than Betty. Donna is shorter than Riku. Who is the tallest girl?

2. Nadine is younger than Garrett. Joan is older than Garrett. Ed's age is between Garrett's and Joan's. Who is the youngest?

Set C For use following page 41.

Write the standard number.

1. eight million, seven hundred twelve thousand

2. forty-nine million

Set D For use following page 43.

Pretend you gave the clerk $10.00 to buy some items. The prices are below. Tell what coins and bills the clerk would give you for change.

1. $7.78 **2.** $8.82 **3.** $5.65 **4.** $9.22 **5.** $4.38 **6.** $2.15

Set E For use following page 45.

Decide without counting if each amount can buy a $2.00 kite.

1.

2.

Set A For use following page 77.

1. At the store, Rebecca selected a bag of apples that cost $1.05, a bunch of bananas that cost $1.50, and several pears that cost $2.30. At the checkout counter, Rebecca found she only had $4.00. What is the difference between the money she had and the total cost of the apples, bananas, and pears?

2. There are 10 boys and 12 girls in Domingo's class. The classroom had 20 desks. How many people in Domingo's class had to sit at a table?

Set B For use following page 81.

Tell if you need an exact answer or an estimate. Explain why.

1. You are a checkout clerk at a grocery store. The customer pays for his $8.95 purchase with a $10.00 bill. How much change do you give the customer?

Set C For use following page 91.

Use the graphs on page 90 to answer these questions.

1. One autumn the snow could be found as low as 11,000 ft. Which mountains on the bar graph were capped with snow?

2. If 200 of the campers from the pictograph stayed in trailers that year, how many campers stayed in tents?

Set D For use following page 93.

1. Make a bar graph like the one on page 90 with the data from this table.

	Blue Spins in 300 tries
Spinner 1	90
Spinner 2	140
Spinner 3	50

Set A For use following page 97.

1. Copy the line graph on page 96. Then draw these points and connect them to the line. Add to the graph if necessary.

More Mountain Temperatures (°F)

6,000 ft up	39°	7,000 ft up	35°

2. How many points on the graph are above 50°F?

Set B For use following page 101.

1. At the annual spelling bee, only 3 of the 62 students on Team A misspelled a word. There were 35 boys and 27 girls on Team A. How many students on Team A spelled every word correctly?

2. Team B won the contest with 185 points. Team A scored 140 points and Team C scored 176 points. By how many points did Team B beat Team C?

Set C For use following page 103.

1. At the count of three, Debbie and Ian each hold up 1 to 5 fingers. If the number of fingers they each hold up matches, Debbie gets a point. If the number of fingers does not match, Ian gets a point. Is this a fair or unfair game? Why?

2. Ian and Debbie change the rules. They decide to hold up 1 or 2 fingers each time. If the number of fingers matches, Debbie gets a point. If the number of fingers does not match, Ian gets a point. Is this game fair or unfair. Why?

Set D For use following page 105.

1. Clarinda wrote the letters of the alphabet on a piece of paper so that the entire page was covered. Then she shut her eyes and put her finger on the paper. Do you think it was more likely that she picked out a consonant or a vowel? Why?

Set A For use following page 117.

Tell whether addition or multiplication is best and why.

1. José has 6 dollars. Each dollar is worth 4 quarters. How many quarters can José get for his dollars?
2. James has 1 quarter, 2 dimes, and 3 nickels. What is the total amount of money he has?

Set B For use following page 129.

Write each question in a different way. Then solve.

1. Abdul's softball team won 9 games each year for 3 years in a row. What is the total number of games that Abdul's team won over the 3-year period?
2. In July Abdul hit 15 home runs. In August he hit 3 home runs. What is the difference in the number of home runs?

Set C For use following page 137.

Fill in the data needed to complete the table. Then solve.

1. Muffins cost $1.50 for a "baker's dozen" at the bakery. There are 13 muffins, or one extra muffin in a "baker's dozen." How many muffins can you buy for $6.00?

cost	$1.50	$3.00		
muffins	13	26		

Set D For use following page 169.

Make a table to help solve the problems.

1. Dan decided to do 5 more push-ups each week to get ready for the swim meet. How many push-ups was he doing after 8 weeks?
2. Carol added 2 more laps to her workout each week. How many laps was she running after 6 weeks?

MORE PRACTICE BANK

Set A For use following page 195.

Tell which calculation method you would choose. Then solve.

1. The fourth grade class held a car wash. They charged $3.75 to wash each car. On Saturday, they washed 52 cars. How much money did they collect on Saturday?

2. An additional $5.75 was charged to wax a car after it was washed. What was the total charge to wash and wax a car?

Set B For use following page 197.

1. Movie companies use cameras that shoot 24 pictures each second. If a camera has shot 1,348 pictures, how many more pictures does it need to have shot a full minute? (60 second = 1 minute)

2. A slow-motion camera takes 54 pictures each second. If a director puts one minute of slow-motion pictures with 720 regular-speed pictures, how many pictures does he have? (60 seconds = 1 minute)

Set C For use following page 207.

Write each time.

1. 

|||| : |||| ||||

|||| minutes to ||||

2. 

|||| |||| : |||| ||||

|||| minutes to ||||

3. 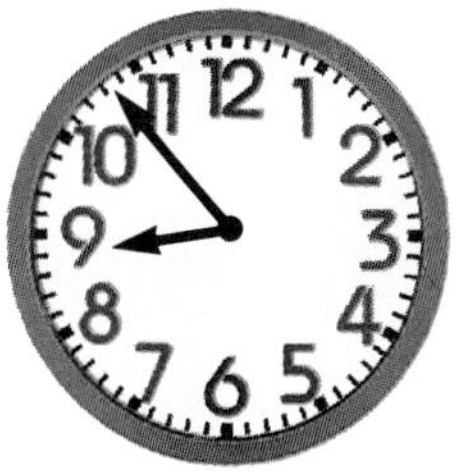

|||| : |||| ||||

|||| minutes to ||||

Set D For use following page 208.

Write whether each time is a.m. or p.m.

1. Lois got up early and ate breakfast at 7:00 ||||.

2. Guy was out of school and roller-skating by 3:15 ||||.

Set A For use following page 209.

Use the August calendar on page 209 to name these dates.

1. On August 16 the parade committee decided to meet again in a week. When will they next meet?
2. The parade and street fair will be held the last Saturday in August. What date should everyone circle on their calendars?

Set B For use following page 211.

Give the times.

1. What time was it 5 hours before 2:00 p.m.?
2. What time will it be 25 minutes after 8:50 a.m.?

Set C For use following page 213.

Solve. Find as many answers as you can.

1. Which coins make $0.25?
2. Pilar has 24 pennies. Into how many rows can she arrange the coins and still have an equal number of coins in each row?

Set D For use following page 215.

Solve.

1. Mr. Blacksmith's draft horse is 4 cubits tall. When he compares a hand span and a cubit, he finds there are about 4 hand spans in 1 cubit. How many hand spans tall is his horse?
2. Mr. Blacksmith paced around the horse corral to find its size. He found it was 20 steps wide and 22 steps long. What was the perimeter of the corral?

Set E For use following page 217.

Write inches, feet, or yards to make the statement reasonable.

1. The basketball player is 6 __?__ tall.
2. The classroom is 5 __?__ wide.

Set A For use following page 220.

1. On a map of South Carolina, 1 thumb width stands for 75 miles. There are 13 thumb widths between Middleton and Seaside City. How many miles apart are the two towns?

Set B For use following page 222.

Find the perimeter of each figure.

1.

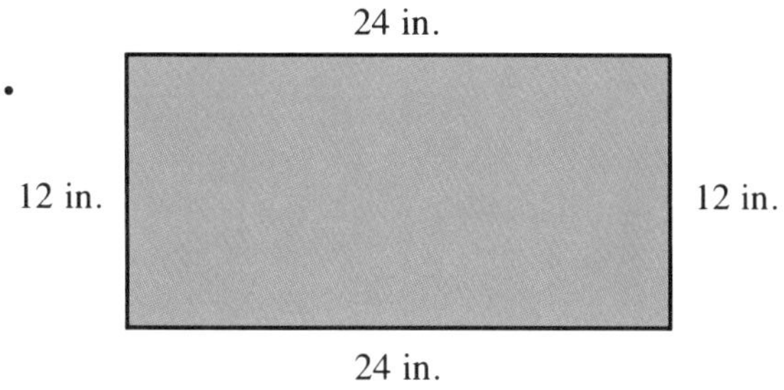

2.

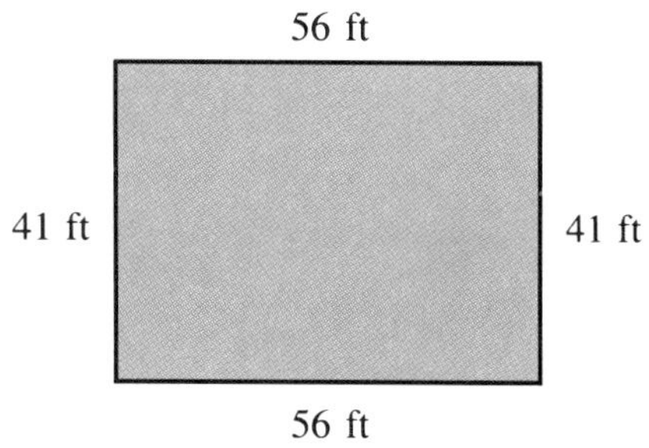

Set C For use following page 223.

Choose the better estimate.

1. How wide is the desk?

   A 1 foot   B 1 yard

2. How long is the street?

   A 4 yards   B 4 miles

Set D For use following page 225.

Solve using data from the chart on page 224.

1. What is the total population of the two cities that get the most rainfall in Texas?
2. Which city has about 3 times as many people as Austin?

Set E For use following page 227.

Use the relationships shown on page 226 to solve.

1. The cook made 5 gallons of vegetable soup. How many quarts is this?
2. The cook made 8 quarts of fruit punch for a party. How many pints is this?

Set A For use following page 228.

Choose pounds or ounces to estimate these weights.

1. Portable TV

   20 ___?___

2. Orange

   8 ___?___

Set B For use following page 229.

Choose the best estimate.

1. Hot water faucet
   - A 60°F
   - B 90°F
   - C 150°F
2. Cool fall day
   - A 90°F
   - B 40°F
   - C 10°F
3. Inside a freezer
   - A 10°F
   - B 40°F
   - C 60°F

Set C For use following page 241.

Find the products and quotients.

1. $4 \times 3 = n$
$3 \times 4 = n$
$12 \div 3 = n$
$12 \div 4 = n$
2. $5 \times 2 = n$
$2 \times 5 = n$
$10 \div 2 = n$
$10 \div 5 = n$
3. $3 \times 5 = n$
$5 \times 3 = n$
$15 \div 5 = n$
$15 \div 3 = n$
4. $2 \times 4 = n$
$4 \times 2 = n$
$8 \div 4 = n$
$8 \div 2 = n$

Set D For use following page 247.

Estimate the answer. Then solve.

1. 4 friends earned \$36 for unloading firewood from a truck. How much money did each get?
2. A cord of firewood costs \$127. If Mountain Ski Lodge burns 5 cords of firewood each winter, how much do they spend on firewood?

Set E For use following page 257.

1. A bus left the downtown station and traveled 2 hours before stopping. The rest stop lasted 20 minutes. The bus then traveled an hour and a half before arriving in Middletown at 4:30 p.m. What time did the bus leave for Middletown?

More Practice Bank

Set A For use following page 277.

Solve.

1. Noriko wants to take 250 photographs of the wedding. On her portrait camera she can take 7 photographs for each roll of film. How many rolls of film does she need?

Set B For use following page 280.

Find the average of these numbers.

1. 233, 205, 248, 258
2. 91, 85, 119, 103, 142, 132

Set C For use following page 287.

Tell which calculation method you will use. Then solve.

1. A hot-air balloon traveled 86 mi in 3 hours. If on the average the balloon traveled the same distance each hour, about how many miles did it travel each hour?
2. It costs $6.85 for each person to ride in a hot-air balloon. About how much would it cost altogether for 8 people to ride in a hot-air balloon?

Set D For use following page 299.

Name each space figure or plane figure.

1. 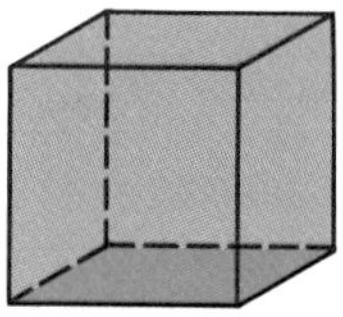
2. 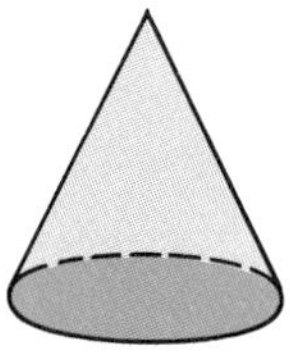
3. 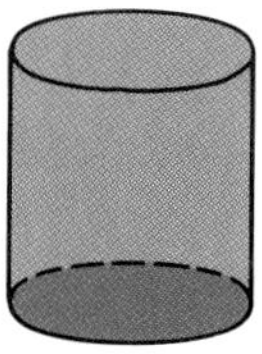
4. 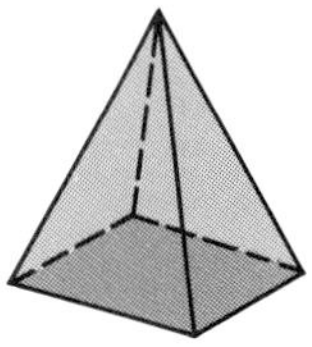
5. 
6. 

Set E For use following page 301.

Name each polygon.

1. 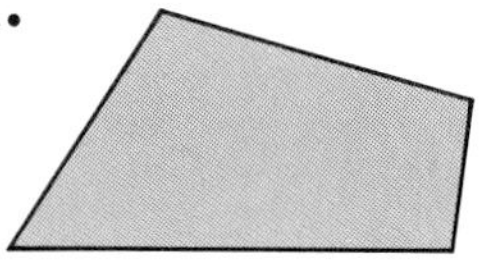
2. 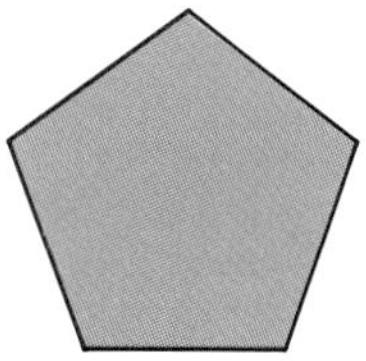
3. 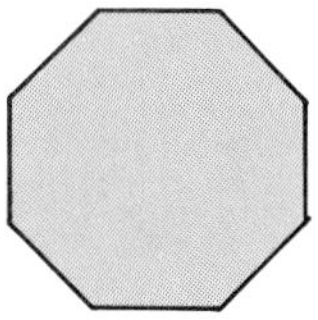
4. 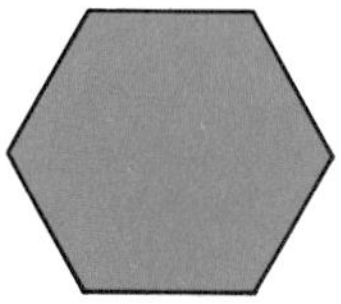

Set A For use following page 303.

Tell which of the following lines are parallel, intersecting and perpendicular, or intersecting but not perpendicular.

1.
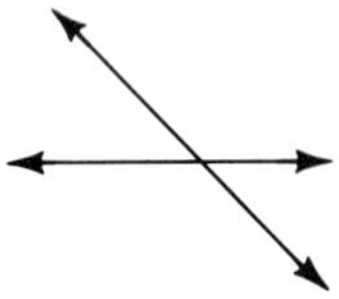

2.
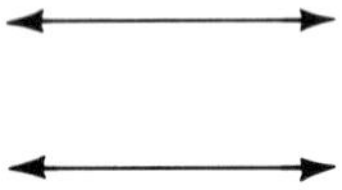

3.
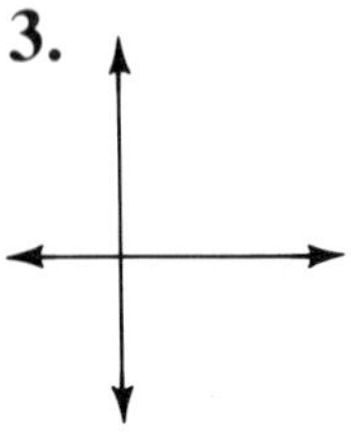

4.
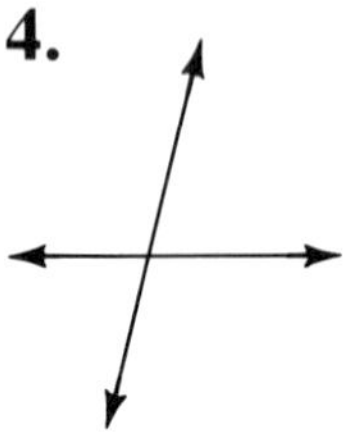

5.
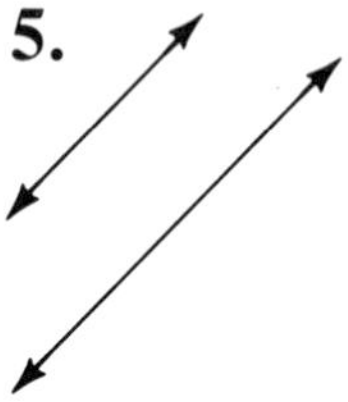

6.
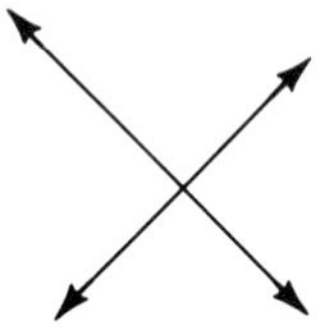

Set B For use following page 307.

Name the triangles and angles.

1.
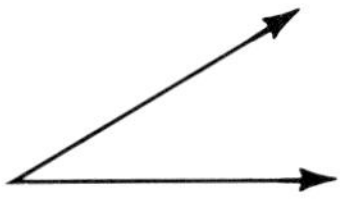

2.
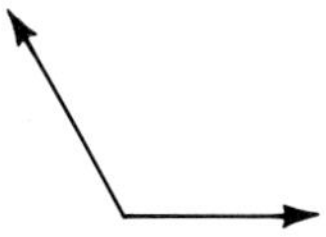

3.
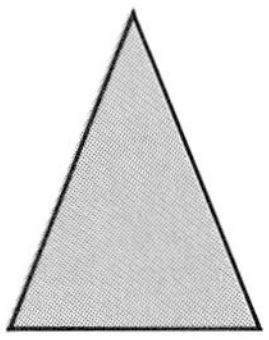

4.
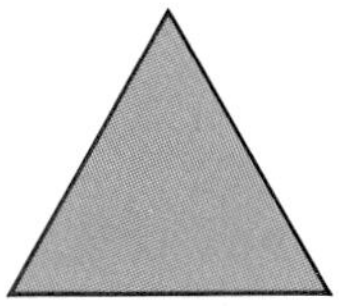

5.
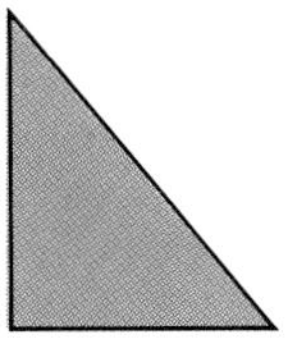

Set C For use following page 309.

Name the quadrilateral.

1.

2.
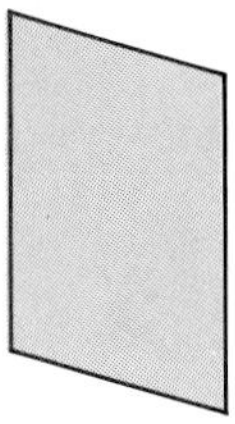

3.

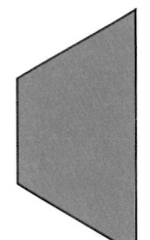

4.

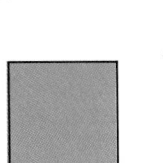

5.
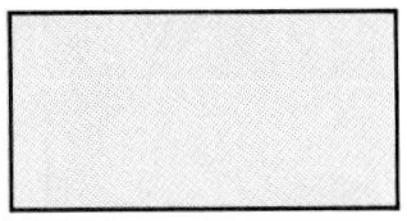

Set D For use following page 311.

Which figures are congruent and which are not congruent?

1.
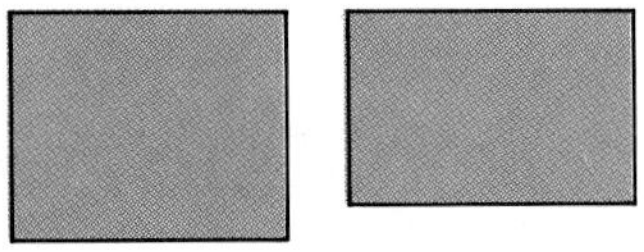

2.
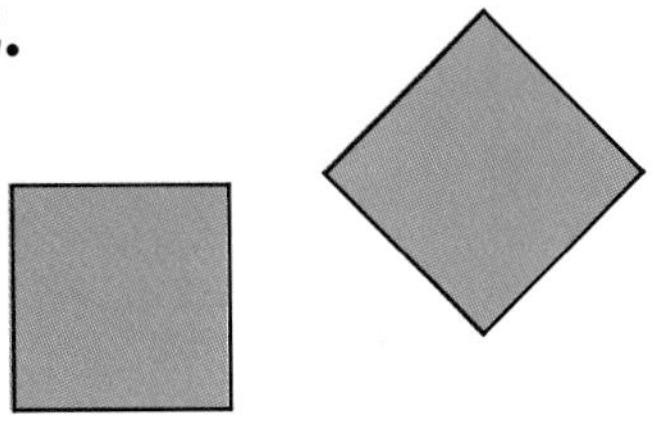

3.
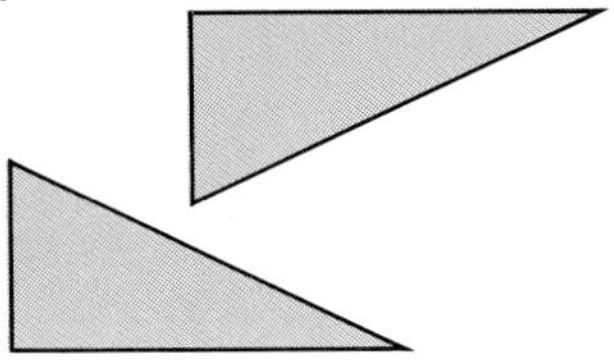

More Practice Bank

Set A For use following page 312.

Name the curves.

1. 
2. 
3. 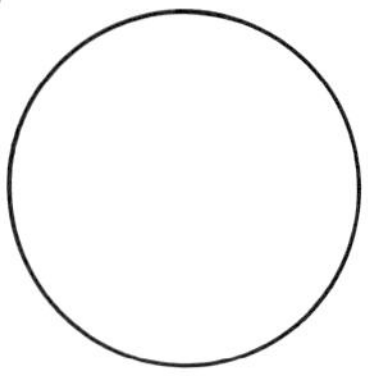
4. 
5. 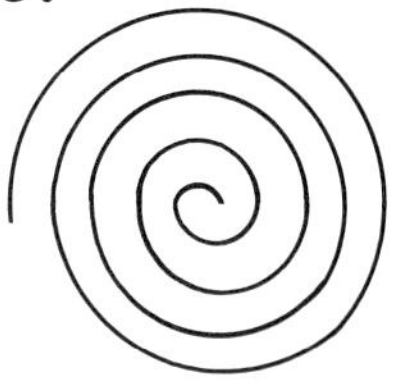

Set B For use following page 317.

Which figure is similar to the first?

1. 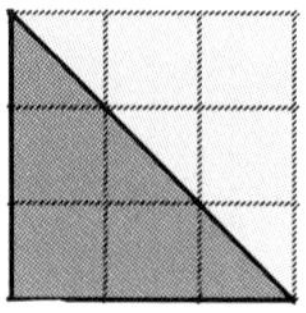

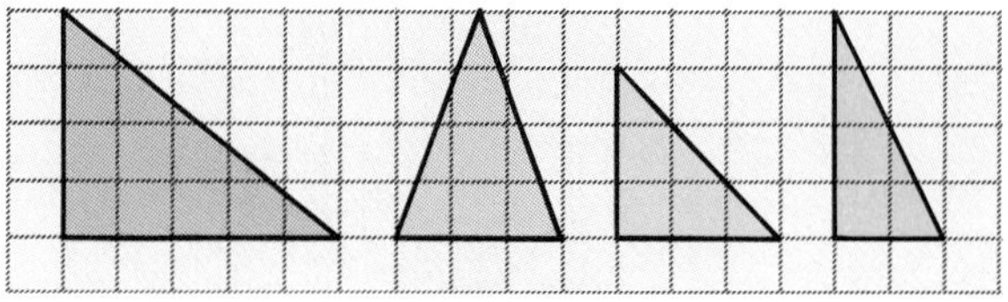

A B C D

Set C For use following page 319.

Use the diagram on page 318 to solve these problems.

1. When Paul was blocked on the left side of the net, he dribbled around the perimeter of the rectangular lane in front of the net to the right side. How far did he dribble?
2. How much longer would the side line be if it was twice as long as the end line?

Set D For use following page 329.

Write a fraction to tell what part is shaded.

1. 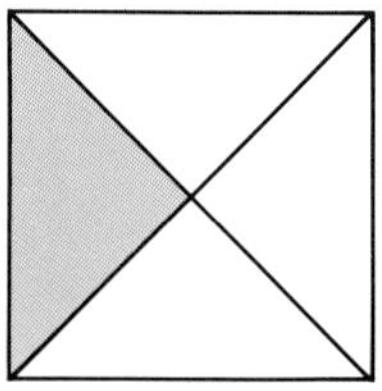
2. 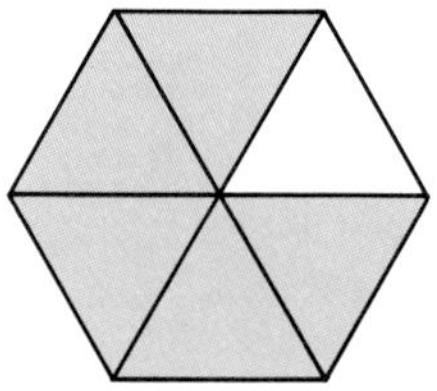
3. 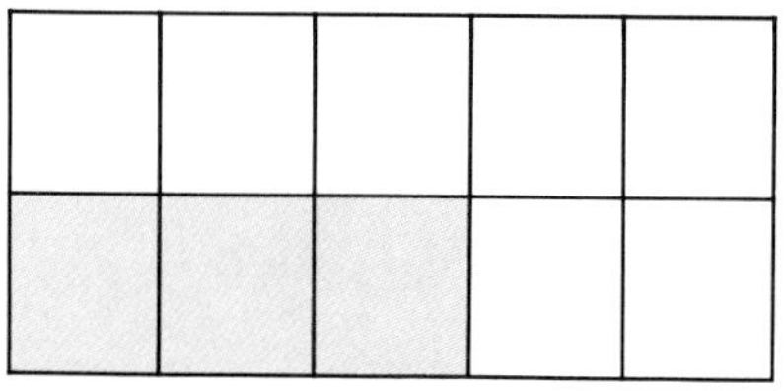

MORE PRACTICE BANK

Set A For use following page 331.

Write a fraction for each ||||.

1. 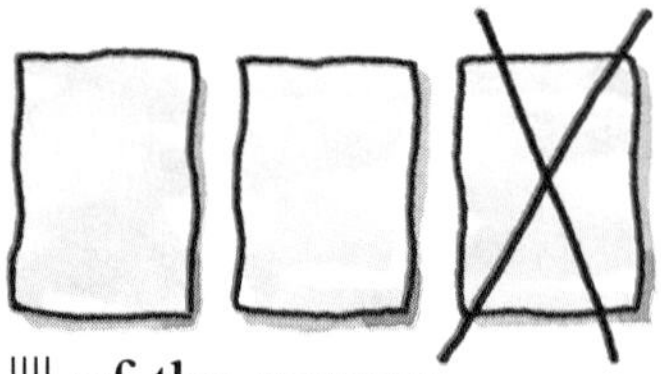

|||| of the papers have an X.

2. 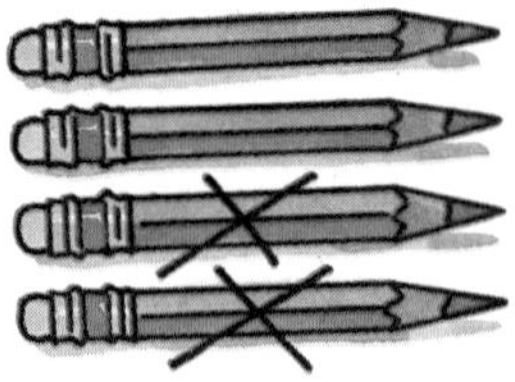

|||| of the pencils have Xs.

3. 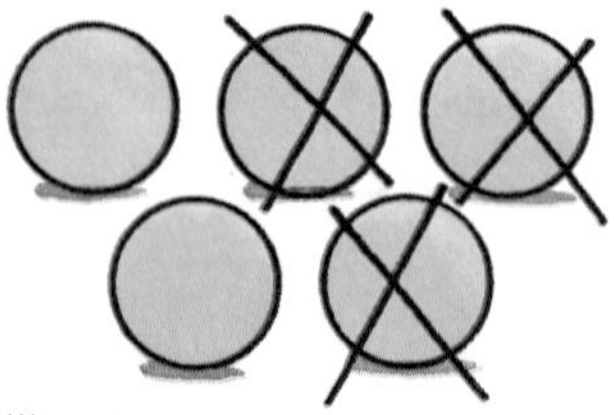

|||| of the balls have Xs.

Set B For use following page 332.

Estimate what part of each figure is shaded.

1. 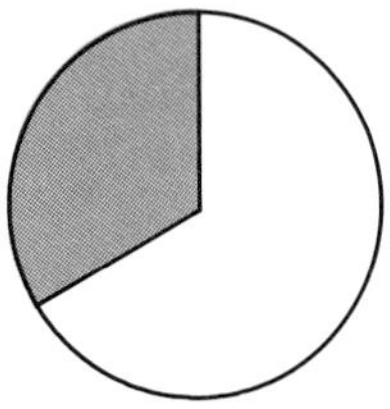

2. 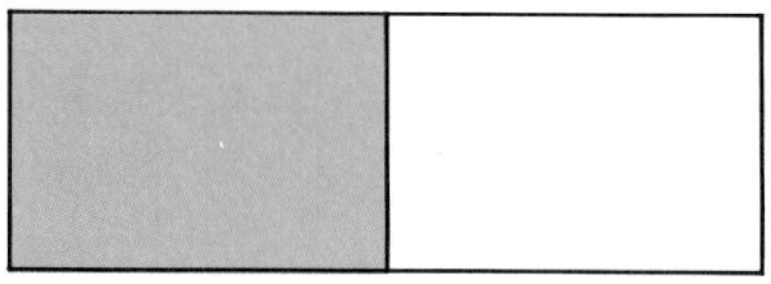

3. 

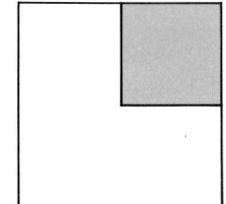

Set C For use following page 333.

1. Don had 10 checkers. He made two stacks. One stack had 2 more checkers than the other. How many checkers were in each stack?

2. At the end of the checker contest, Bernie had won more games than Emily. Emily won more games than Dale. Kate won more games than Emily but was not in second place. In what order did they finish?

Set D For use following page 349.

1. 

Lila knitted a row this long in 2 minutes. She wants to try again and keep up this speed for 10 minutes. If she succeeds, how long will her knitted row be? Measure to the nearest $\frac{1}{4}$ inch.

2. 

Jonathan was gluing a path made of beans onto his picture. To stretch from the house to the pond the path needed to be about 9 inches long. How many more beans will he need? Measure to the nearest $\frac{1}{2}$ inch.

More Practice Bank

Set A For use following page 361.

Write a decimal for each.

1. three and six hundredths

2. two and thirty-six hundredths

Set B For use following page 362.

Write the decimal that comes after each number when you count by hundredths.

1. 9.25 **2.** 10.1 **3.** 6.36 **4.** 7.79 **5.** 5.98 **6.** 8.99

Set C For use following page 371.

Do not solve the problems. Tell why the answers are reasonable or not reasonable.

1. $\frac{7}{8}$ of Lincoln Public School voted for class president. 1,992 students go to the school. How many students voted in the election?

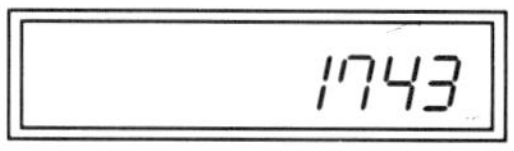

2. One candidate sold campaign buttons for $0.89 each and donated the money to the school orchestra. The donation was $426.31. How many buttons did the candidate sell?

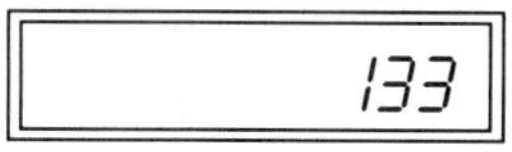

Set D For use following page 383.

Fill in each blank with cm, dm, m, or km.

1. The distance across town is 20 __?__.

2. My piano is 2 __?__ high.

3. Her necklace is 3 __?__ long.

4. The caterpillar is 6 __?__ long.

Set E For use following page 383.

Use unitizing to estimate these lengths in centimeters.

1.

2.

MORE PRACTICE BANK

Set A For use following page 389.

Use cm graph paper to draw these figures.

1. a rectangle of 28 square centimeters.
2. an area of 14 square centimeters.

Set B For use following page 391.

Give the volume of the following.

1. A stack of blocks with 4 rows, 4 boxes in each row, and 2 layers = |||| cubic centimeters.
2. A stack of blocks with 6 rows, 3 boxes in each row, and 3 layers = |||| cubic centimeters.

Set C For use following page 393.

Solve these problems. Then tell how they are related.

1. Ana built a rectangular yard fence. Two sides were 98 m and two sides 105 m. How much fence was this?
2. Ian has a square bulletin board. Each side is 96 cm. What is the perimeter of the bulletin board?

Set D For use following page 395.

Choose the better estimate of capacity.

1.

A 4 L **B** 4 mL

2.

A 1 L **B** 1 mL

3.

A 200 L **B** 200 mL

Set E For use following page 396.

Estimate the weight of each object.

1.

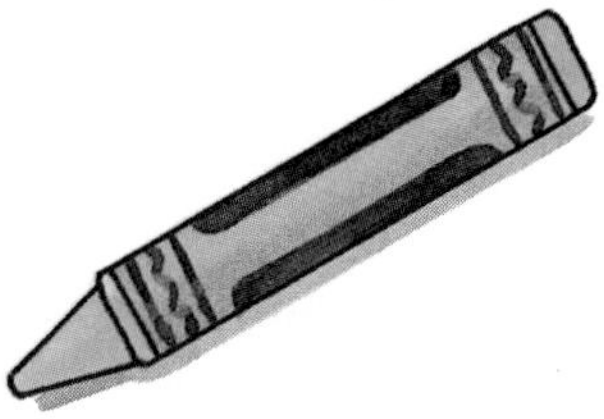

A 6 g **B** 6 kg

2.

A 2 g **B** 2 kg

3.

A 8 g **B** 8 kg

MORE PRACTICE BANK

Set A For use following page 397.

Record each temperature.

1. 

2. 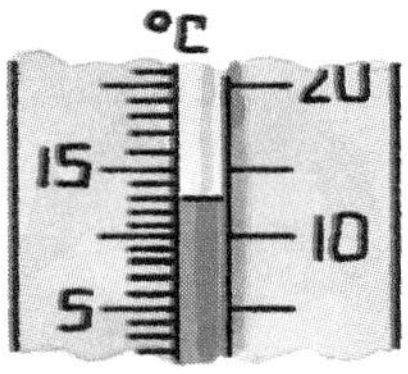

3. 

Set B Use following page 411.

Use the recipes on page 410 to answer these questions.

1. How much ground beef do you need to make both spaghetti and lasagne?
2. The spaghetti recipe calls for how many more ounces of tomato paste than the lasagne recipe?

Set C For use following page 427.

1. A bus going to the city had 3 empty seats—1 in front, 1 in back, and 1 in the middle. It stopped at Island Shopping Mall to pick up a man and a woman. How many ways could they sit down?
2. There were 20 passengers left on the bus when it got to the city. There were 2 more men than women. How many men were on the bus?

Set D For use following page 444.

1. Hawaii has an average of 177.6 cm of rain per year. Nevada has an average of 18.8 cm. What is the difference in average rainfall between Hawaii and Nevada?
2. Chicago had 85.1 cm of rain one year. The following year 96.62 cm of rain fell. How much rain did Chicago have in the two years?

Set E For use following page 451.

Use a calculator to help solve these problems.

1. Louise divided 81 old comic books among 5 friends. How many comic books did each friend get?
2. Mr. Lopez read a book to his grandchildren. He read 11 pages per day. The book had 75 pages. How many days did it take Mr. Lopez to finish the book?

TABLE OF MEASURES

Metric System		Customary System	
Length			
1 centimeter (cm)	10 millimeters (mm)	1 foot (ft)	12 inches (in.)
1 decimeter (dm)	100 millimeters (mm) 10 centimeters (cm)	1 yard (yd)	36 inches (in.) 3 feet (ft)
1 meter (m)	1,000 millimeters (mm) 100 centimeters (cm) 10 decimeters (dm)	1 mile (m)	5,280 feet (ft) 1,760 yards (yd)
1 kilometer (km)	1,000 meters (m)		
Area			
1 square meter (m^2)	100 square decimeters (dm^2) 10,000 square centimeters (cm^2)	1 square foot (ft^2)	144 square inches ($in.^2$)
Volume			
1 cubic decimeter (dm^3)	1,000 cubic centimeters (cm^3) 1 liter (L)	1 cubic foot (ft^3)	1,728 cubic inches ($in.^3$)
Capacity			
1 teaspoon	5 milliliters (mL)	1 cup (c)	8 fluid ounces (fl oz)
1 tablespoon	12.5 milliliters (mL)	1 pint (pt)	16 fluid ounces (fl oz) 2 cups (c)
1 liter (L)	1,000 milliliters (mL) 1,000 cubic centimeters (cm^3) 1 cubic decimeter (dm^3) 4 metric cups	1 quart (qt)	32 fluid ounces (fl oz) 4 cups (c) 2 pints (pt)
		1 gallon (gal)	128 fluid ounces (fl oz) 16 cups (c) 8 pints (pt) 4 quarts (qt)
Weight			
1 gram (g)	1,000 milligrams (mg)	1 pound (lb)	16 ounces (oz)
1 kilogram (kg)	1,000 grams (g)		
Time			
1 minute	60 seconds (s)	1 year (yr)	365 days 52 weeks 12 months
1 hour (h)	60 minutes (min)		
1 day (d)	24 hours (h)		
1 week (w)	7 days (d)	1 decade	10 years
1 month	about 4 weeks	1 century	100 years

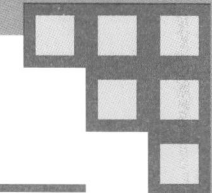

PERFORMANCE ASSESSMENT

Chapter 1 Addition and Subtraction: Concepts and Basic Facts

Suppose you and three friends buy some tropical fish. Each of you gets three bags, but when you arrive home, you discover that the bags have different numbers of fish in them.

Can you find a way for each of you to give exactly one bag to someone else, so that all of you end up with the same number of fish? (What is that number?) Explain in writing how you worked to get an answer to the problem.

Chapter 2 Place Value and Money

Imagine that you are hired by the Ding Dong Ping Pong Ball Company. Every month the company manufactures a boxcar load of Ping-Pong table tennis balls, but they are not counted or put into packages. They are just dumped into a big boxcar.

The Ding Dong president wants to know how many balls are made each month. She also wants the balls put into packages so they can be shipped and sold easily.

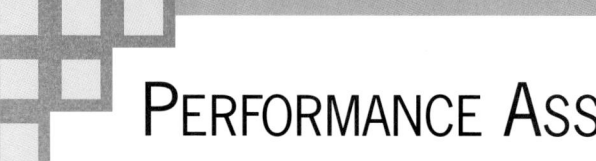

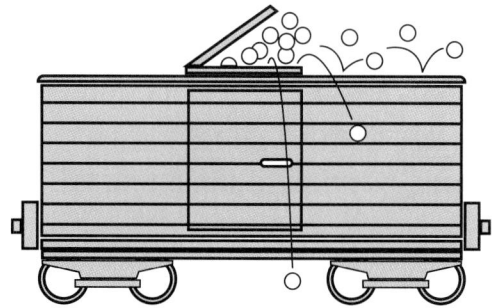

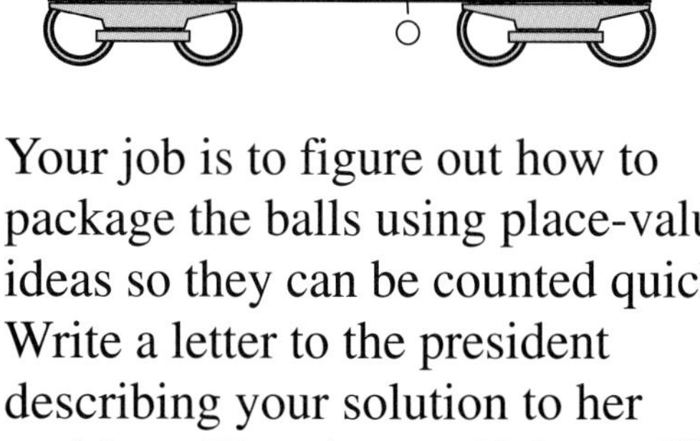

Your job is to figure out how to package the balls using place-value ideas so they can be counted quickly. Write a letter to the president describing your solution to her problem. Use pictures if they will help you do your job.

PERFORMANCE ASSESSMENT

Chapter 3 Addition and Subtraction of Whole Numbers

Here are the number of balls made by Ding Dong's main competitor, Slam Bang Table Tennis Company. The smudges are where the ball-counting clerk accidentally spilled chocolate syrup on the record sheet.

Can you estimate how many balls Slam Bang made in the first six months of the year?

January	12,03●91
February	9,090,90●
March	10,333,●4
April	11,223,344
May	15,000,739
June	14,025,●

What are the greatest and least numbers that could have been made? Tell how you solved the problem.

Chapter 4 Data, Graphs, and Probability

In the first month of school last year, a teacher noticed that out of 31 students in his class, 19 were less than 5 feet tall. The next month 17 students were less than 5 feet tall. The month after that 16 students were less than 5 feet tall. In the fourth month only 13 students were less than 5 feet tall.

What do you think happened during the rest of the year?

A new student entered the class in the eighth month of the year. Would you guess that the student was over or under 5 feet tall? Why?

Chapter 5 Multiplication Concepts and Basic Facts

You are to try to reach a goal number. First choose four different numbers from 0 through 9. Then multiply any two of those numbers, add another number to that product, and finally subtract the last number from that sum. You can use the four numbers in any order to get to your goal.

Example: Goal 19

Numbers Chosen: 3, 4, 5, and 6

$$3 \times 6 = 18$$
$$18 + 5 = 23$$
$$23 - 4 = 19$$

Repeat this for the goal numbers of 9, 12, 29, and 50. Explain your thinking for the last problem.

Chapter 6 Multiplying by 1-Digit Factors

Find out how many times your heart beats in a minute. (Your teacher will help you.) If you are not sure, use 70 beats per minute. Estimate how many times your heart will beat in—

- 3 minutes
- 7 minutes
- 9 minutes

Do you think your heart will beat exactly that many times? Why or why not?

Explain how you came up with your estimates.

Chapter 7 Multiplying by 2-Digit Numbers

Did you know that the letter “e” is used more often in books written in English than any other letter?

Select a page in your reading book and a page in your social studies book. Count the number of times “e” is used on each page.

Make an estimate as to how many times the letter “e” appears in the first seventy-five pages of your reading book and in your social studies book. Are your two estimates close together or far apart? Why do you think this is? Explain how you made each estimate.

Chapter 8 Time and Customary Measurement

This measurement chapter covered a lot of information! You studied time: minutes, a.m. and p.m. hours, and calendars. You studied distance measurement: length in inches, feet, yards, and miles. You studied capacity: cup, pint, quart, and gallon; weight: pounds and ounces; and temperature: Fahrenheit degrees.

Make up a story about preparing, serving, and eating dinner with several friends or your family. Use as many of the time and measurement ideas as you can in your story. You can draw pictures if you like!

Chapter 9 Division Concepts and Basic Facts

A teacher wants to make cooperative work groups with not more than 9 students in each group and not more than 9 groups in the room. Also there has to be the same number of students in each group. There are 36 students in the room. What choices for group size and numbers of groups does the teacher have?

What number of students from 1 through 50 will allow this teacher the most choices for group size? Explain how you found your answer.

Chapter 10 Division: 1-Digit Divisors

Sandy has just shown you the work below and has asked you if it is correct. It is not. Figure out what the answer should be and explain how you could help Sandy understand a better way to do long division.

Sandy's Work

```
    403 R 6
 7)307
   28
   27
   21
    6
```

Chapter 11 Geometry

On a piece of graph paper, draw a quadrilateral that is not a rectangle, not a trapezoid, not a parallelogram and not a square. Label the coordinates in each of the four corners of the figure. On another piece of graph paper, draw a quadrilateral that is double the area of the first quadrilateral, and label the coordinate points.

Are the two figures that you drew congruent? Why or why not? Are they similar? Why or why not?

Does either figure have a line of symmetry? How do you know?

Chapter 12 Fraction Concepts

Make a list of the approximate number of hours you spend each day doing different activities. Here are some examples of how people spend their time: sleeping, eating, attending school, traveling to and from school, doing chores, playing, reading, and watching television.

When you have made your list, tell what fraction of the day you spend doing each activity. Then list them in order, from the activity you spend the most time doing, to the one you spend the least time doing. Did any of the results surprise you? Why or why not?

Performance Assessment

Chapter 13 Decimal Concepts

Is the United States money system based on decimals? Tell why you think it is or is not, giving reasons to support your belief. Include examples.

Chapter 14 Metric Measurement

Use centimeter graph paper and tape to construct a cube. Explain how to find the volume of your cube.

Suppose you want to cover your cube with colored paper. How many square centimeters of paper will you need to cover your cube? Explain how you can find out.

Suppose you made each side of your cube twice as long as it presently is. What would be the volume of your cube then? How would you know?

Performance Assessment

Chapter 15 Addition and Subtraction: Fractions and Decimals

Teresa asked her friends what part of a whole pizza they each wanted. Here is what they said:

Juan	$\frac{1}{3}$	Tanya	$\frac{1}{4}$
Lin	$\frac{1}{2}$	Rafael	$\frac{1}{4}$
Harry	$\frac{1}{4}$	Teresa	$\frac{1}{4}$

How many pizzas should Teresa order? If each pizza costs $8.95, is $20 enough? If so, how much change will she get back?

Chapter 16 Division: 2-Digit Divisors

```
       ■■ R ■■
■■)■■■
```

Make up seven different division problems that have 2-digit divisors and 3-digit dividends. They must also satisfy the following conditions:

The first problem must have a remainder of 0.
The second problem must have a 1-digit quotient.
The third problem must have a 2-digit quotient.
The fourth problem must have a remainder greater than 24.
The fifth problem must have a remainder between 0 and 10.
The sixth problem must have an even-numbered quotient.
The seventh problem must have an odd-numbered quotient.

Pick two of your examples and explain how you came up with them.

GLOSSARY

a.m. A way to indicate the times from 12:00 midnight to 12:00 noon.

acute angle An angle that is smaller than a right angle and measures less than 90°.

addends Numbers that are added together to form a sum.

Example:
$$\begin{array}{r} 3 \\ +\ 5 \\ \hline 8 \end{array} \quad \leftarrow \text{addends (3 and 5)}$$

angle Two rays from a single point.

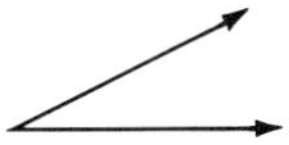

area The measure of a region, expressed in square units.

associative property See grouping property.

average The quotient obtained when the sum of the numbers in a set is divided by the number of addends.

bar graph A graph that shows information by using bars.

benchmark A point of reference from which measures can be estimated.

capacity The volume of a space figure given in terms of liquid measurement.

centimeter (cm) A unit of length in the metric system. 100 centimeters equal 1 meter.

|———| ← 1 centimeter

circle A closed curve in which all the points are the same distance from a point called the center.

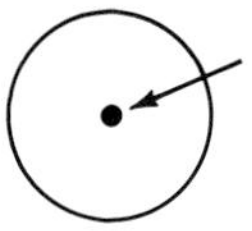

circle

clustering Using numbers that are close to, or cluster around, a rounded number, making it easy to estimate.

commutative property See order property.

compatible numbers Pairs of numbers that "go together" to make mental math easier.

compensation A mental math technique in which a sum or difference is changed into an easier sum or difference with the same answer. In addition, one addend is increased and the other decreased. In subtraction, each number is increased or decreased the same amount.

cone A solid figure that has a circular bottom.

congruent figures Figures that have the same size and shape.

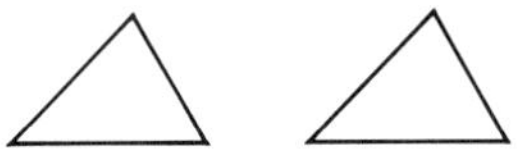

congruent triangles

constant A number entered on a calculator which allows you to do operations using that number without re-entering it.

coordinates The two numbers in a number pair.

cube A space figure that has squares for all of its faces.

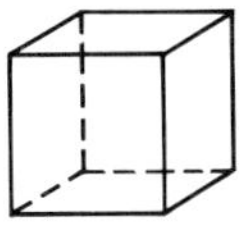

cup (c) A unit for measuring capacity. 4 cups equal 1 quart.

cylinder A space figure that has a circle for a face.

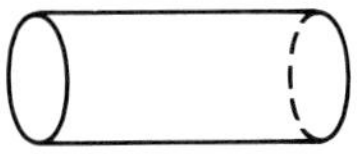

cylinder

decimal A number that uses a decimal point to show tenths, hundredths, and so on.

3.2 ← decimal
↑
decimal point

GLOSSARY

decimeter (dm) A unit of length in the metric system. 1 decimeter equals 10 centimeters.

degree Celsius (°C) A unit for measuring temperature in the metric system.

degree Fahrenheit (°F) A unit for measuring temperature in the customary system of measurement.

denominator The number below the line in a fraction.

$\frac{3}{4}$ ← denominator

difference The number obtained by subtracting one number from another.

digits The symbols used to write numerals: 0, 1, 2, 3, 4, 5, 6, 7, 8, and 9.

display The window on a calculator that shows the numbers as they are entered and the results of the calculations.

dividend A number to be divided.

$7\overline{)28}$ with quotient 4 ← dividend

divisor The number by which a dividend is divided.

divisor → $7\overline{)28}$ with quotient 4

edge One of the segments making up any of the faces of a space figure.

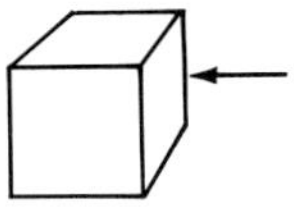

END An instruction in a computer program that tells the computer to stop.

equation A number sentence that uses the equal sign.

Examples: $9 + 2 = 11$
$8 - 4 = 4$

equilateral triangle A triangle with all sides the same length.

equivalent fractions Fractions that name the same amount.

Example: $\frac{1}{2}$ and $\frac{2}{4}$

estimate To find an answer that is close to the exact answer.

even number A whole number that has 0, 2, 4, 6, or 8 in the ones place.

face One of the plane figures (regions) making up a space figure.

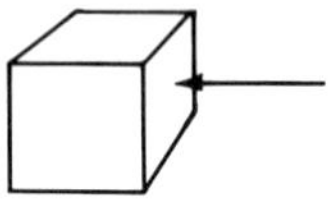

fact family A group of related facts using the same set of digits.

factors Numbers that are multiplied together to form a product.

factors → $6 \times 7 = 42$

flowchart A chart that shows a step-by-step way of doing something.

foot (ft) A unit for measuring length. 1 foot equals 12 inches.

fraction A number that expresses parts of a whole or a set.

Example: $\frac{3}{4}$

front-end estimation The estimation technique of adding the leading digits of addends, then using the other places to adjust the estimate.

gallon (gal) A unit for measuring capacity. 1 gallon equals 4 quarts.

GOTO An instruction in a computer program that tells the computer to jump to a specified line.

gram (g) The basic unit for measuring mass in the metric system. The mass of a paper clip is about 1 gram.

graph A picture that shows information in an organized way.

grouping property When the grouping of addends or factors is changed, the sum or product is the same.

greater than The relationship of one number being larger than another number.

Example: $6 > 5$, read "6 is greater than 5."

GLOSSARY

half gallon A unit for measuring capacity. 1 half gallon equals 2 quarts.

hexagon A polygon with six sides.

improper fraction A fraction in which the numerator is greater than or equal to the denominator.

inch (in.) A unit for measuring length. 12 inches equal 1 foot.

intersecting lines Lines that meet in a point.

isosceles triangle A triangle that has at least 2 sides the same length.

key codes An arrangement of letters and numbers that tell what order to press the keys on a calculator to find an answer.

kilogram (kg) A unit of mass in the metric system. 1 kilogram is 1,000 grams.

kilometer A unit of length in the metric system. 1 kilometer is 1,000 meters.

length The measure of distance from one end to the other end of an object.

less than The relationship of being smaller than another number.
Example: $5 < 6$, read "5 is less than 6."

line A straight path that is endless in both directions.

line graph A graph that shows information by using lines.

line of symmetry A line on which a figure can be folded so that the two parts fit exactly.

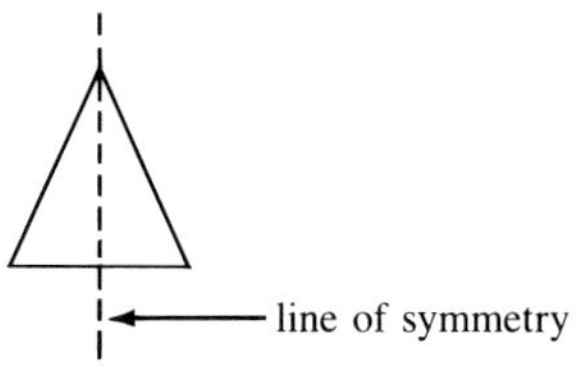

liter (L) A metric unit used to measure capacity. 1 liter equals 1,000 milliliters.

logic error The message on a calculator display that shows an operation is not logical.

Logo A special computer language that is used for computer graphics.

lowest terms A fraction is in lowest terms if the numerator and denominator have no common factor greater than 1.

memory keys The keys marked with M that instruct the calculator to remember the result of one calculation while you do another one.

meter (m) A unit of length in the metric system. 1 meter is 100 centimeters.

mile (mi) A unit for measuring length. 1 mile equals 5,280 feet.

milliliter (mL) A metric unit for measuring capacity. 1,000 milliliters equal 1 liter.

millimeter (mm) A unit of length in the metric system. 10 millimeters equal 1 centimeter.

mixed number A number that has a whole number part and a fractional part, such as $2\frac{3}{4}$.

multiple A number that is the product of a given number and a whole number.

multiple-choice question A written question that gives more than one choice for an answer.

negative number A number that is less than zero.

number pair Two numbers that are used to give the location of a point on a graph.
Example: (3,2)

numeral A symbol for a number.

numerator The number above the line in a fraction.

$\frac{3}{4}$ ← numerator

obtuse angle An angle that is greater than a right triangle and measures more than 90°.

octagon A polygon with eight sides.

odd number A whole number that has 1, 3, 5, 7, or 9 in the ones place.

one property In multiplication, when either factor is 1, the product is the other factor. In division, when 1 is the divisor, the quotient is the same as the dividend.

order property When the order of addends or factors is changed, the sum or product is the same.

ordinal number A number that is used to tell order.
Example: first, fifth

ounce (oz) A customary unit for measuring weight. 16 ounces equal 1 pound.

overflow error The message on a calculator display showing that a number is too large for the display window.

p.m. A way to indicate the times from 12:00 noon to 12:00 midnight.

parallel lines Lines that do not intersect.

parallelogram A quadrilateral with 2 pairs of same-length sides and two pairs of parallel sides.

pentagon A polygon with five sides.

perimeter The distance around a figure.

period A group of three digits set off by a comma in larger numbers.

perpendicular lines Lines that intersect to form a right angle.

pictograph A graph that uses pictures to show quantities.

pint (pt) A unit for measuring capacity. 2 pints equal 1 quart.

place value The value given to the place a digit occupies in a number.

Example: 3 5 6

hundreds' place (3)
tens' place (5)
ones' place (6)

plane figures Figures that lie on a flat surface.

Examples:

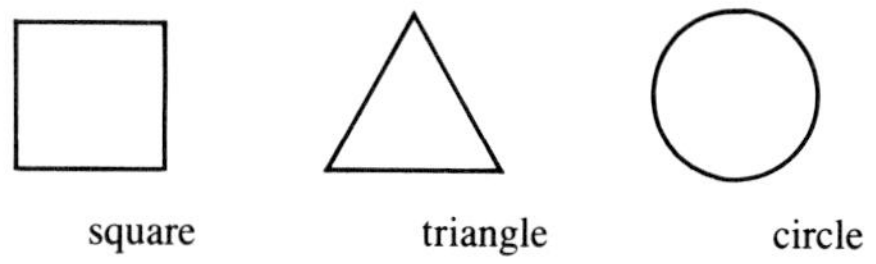

point A single, exact location, often represented by a dot.

polygon A closed figure formed by line segments.

pound (lb) A customary unit for measuring weight. 1 pound equals 16 ounces.

prime number A whole number greater than 1, whose only factors are itself and 1.

PRINT An instruction in a computer program that tells the computer to print something.

probability The chance that something will or will not happen.

product The result of the multiplication operation.

$$6 \times 7 = 42 \longleftarrow \text{product}$$

program The set of instructions that tells a computer what to do.

quadrilateral A polygon with four sides.

quart (qt) A unit for measuring capacity. 1 quart equals 4 cups.

questionnaire A written list of questions used to gather information.

quotient The number (other than the remainder) that is the result of the division operation.

$45 \div 9 = 5.$ (5 ← quotient)

$$\begin{array}{r} 6 \\ 7\overline{)45} \\ -\,42 \\ \hline 3 \end{array} \quad 6 \longleftarrow \text{quotient}$$

rectangle A plane figure with two pairs of same-length sides and four right angles.

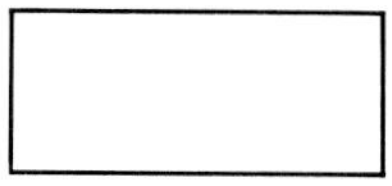

rectangular prism A space figure with six faces. It has the shape of a box.

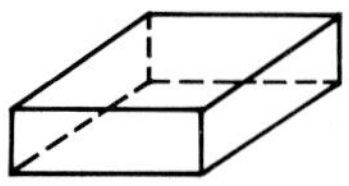

reference point A point from which something is measured or to which something is compared.

remainder The number less than the divisor that remains after the division process is completed.

Example:
```
   6
7)47
 -42
   5  <- remainder
```

right angle An angle that has the same shape as the corner of a square.

right angle protractor A tool used to measure right angles.

rounding Replacing a number with a number that tells about how many.

Example: 23 rounded to the nearest 10 is 20.

RUN What appears on the video screen when a computer program is used.

similar figures Two or more figures having the same shape but not necessarily the same size.

space figure A figure that is not flat but that has volume.

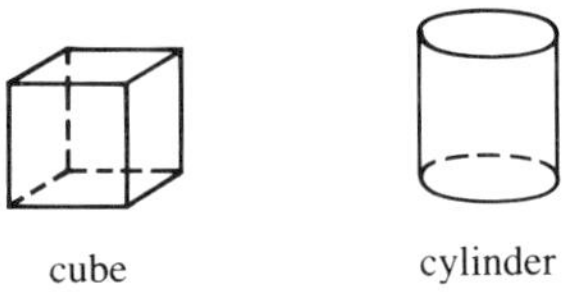

sphere A space figure that has the shape of a round ball.

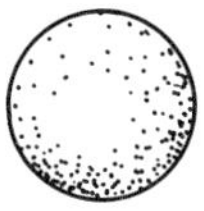

square A plane figure that has four equal sides and four equal corners.

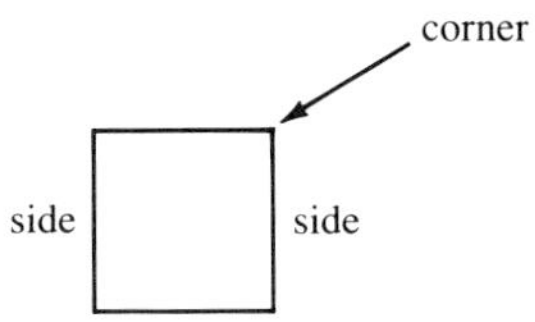

sum The number obtained by adding numbers.

Example:
```
  3
+ 2
  5  <- sum
```

symmetric figure A plane figure that can be folded in half so that the two halves match.

ton A unit for measuring weight. 1 ton equals 2,000 pounds.

trading To make a group of ten from one of the next highest place value, or one from ten of the next lowest place value.

Examples: 1 hundred can be traded for 10 tens; 10 ones can be traded for 1 ten.

trapezoid A quadrilateral with exactly one pair of parallel sides.

triangle A plane figure with three segments as sides.

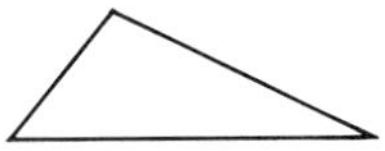

unit An amount or quantity used as a standard of measurement.

unitizing Visually or physically dividing an object into equal parts to estimate length.

vertex (vertices) The common point of any two sides of a polygon.

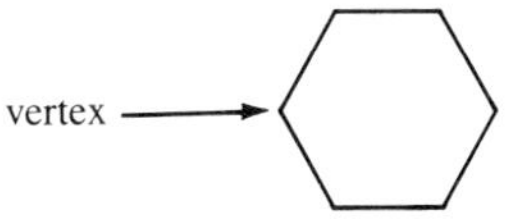

volume The number of units of space that a space figure holds.

yard (yd) A unit for measuring length. 1 yard equals 3 feet.

zero property In addition, when one addend is 0, the sum is the other addend. In multiplication, when either factor is 0, the product is 0.

INDEX

INDEX

INDEX

ACKNOWLEDGMENTS

Illustration Acknowledgments

Anthony Accardo p. 461, 462, 463, 465, 493, 497

Angela Adams p. 91, 92, 93, 94, 95

Randy Chewning p. 43, 44, 54, 55, 58, 63, 65, 68, 70, 71, 72, 73, 74, 75, 84, 152, 228, 229, 272, 352, 353, 354, 382, 383, 387, 396, 397, 418, 522, 524, 525, 526, 527

Suzanne Clee p. 147, 149, 151, 155, 158, 159, 164, 165

Daniel Del Valle p. 381, 383, 383, 391, 394, 395

Len Ebert p. 28, 29, 30, 34, 35, 36, 37, 39, 40, 41, 110, 112, 160, 200, 202, 374, 376, 377

Andrea Fong p. 472, 481

Simon Galkin p. 359, 360, 362, 364, 363, 366, 369, 370, 371, 408, 413, 414, 416, 422, 424, 426, 427, 464, 485, 494, 497, 498

Jeff Hukill p. 470, 483

Arlan Jewel p. 334, 335, 336, 337, 338, 339, 340, 343, 348, 349

Heather King p. 4, 5, 6, 7, 8, 9, 10, 15, 16, 17, 21, 298, 299, 300, 301, 302, 304, 305, 306, 309, 312, 314, 315, 316, 318

Barbara Lanza p. 260, 276, 277, 402, 430

Morissa Lipstein p. 50, 90, 102, 209, 232, 233, 234, 386, 392, 393, 396

Laura Lydecker p. 329, 330, 331, 332, 344, 345, 346, 347

Laurie Marks p. 146, 152, 157, 162, 167, 168, 178, 179, 184, 186, 194, 195, 196

Jane McCreary p. 119, 122, 130, 132, 135, 136, 137, 140, 142, 143, 156, 166, 172, 187, 192, 214, 215, 216, 217, 282, 283, 300

Susan Nelson p. 438, 439, 440 441, 442, 443, 444, 445, 446, 448, 449, 450, 451

Rik Olson p. 96, 98, 99, 100, 101, 104, 105, 109, 266, 267, 270, 271, 278, 284, 285, 286

Rick Sams p. 475, 479

Margaret Sanfilippo p. 168, 169

Ed Sauk p. 20, 181, 316, 328, 333, 361, 367, 369, 371, 418, 420, 425

Nancy Schill p. 12, 15, 61, 64, 68, 77, 80, 81

Seventeenth Street Studios
Valerie Winemiller p. 254

Blanche Sims p. 6, 14

Rosalind Solomon p. 468, 469, 471

Rhonda Voo p. 473, 476, 477, 482

Ann Wilson p. 207, 220, 221, 223, 226, 227, 238, 239, 240, 241, 242, 243, 245, 249, 252, 253, 257, 262, 292, 294, 322, 400, 401, 402, 403, 430, 431, 454, 456, 457

Jeannie Winston p. 116, 117, 118, 120, 121, 123, 131, 133

Photo Acknowledgments

Table of Contents: iii Ken Karp*; iv Nick Pavloff*; v Nick Pavloff*; vi Nick Pavloff*; vii Nick Pavloff*; viii Ken Karp*; ix Lawrence Migdale*; x Ken Karp*; xi Ken Karp*; xii Stephen Frisch*; xiii Elliott Smith*; xiv Nick Pavloff*.

Chapter 1: 2-3 Stephen Frisch*; 5 John Gerlach/Animals, Animals; 9 Wayland Lee*/Addison-Wesley Publishing Company; 11 Jeff Foott/Tom Stack & Associates; 16 Janice Sheldon*; 18-19 Janice Sheldon*

Chapter 2: 24-25 Craig Aurness/Woodfin Camp & Associates; 32 Janice Sheldon*; 38B Janice Sheldon*; 38T John Running; 42 Janice Sheldon*; 47 Stephen Frisch*; 48 Janice Sheldon*.

Chapter 3: 52-53 Stephen Frisch*; 56 Janice Sheldon*; 58 Ken Karp*; 60 Ken Karp*; 62 Janice Sheldon*; 68 Nick Pavloff*; 76 Ken Karp*; 78 NASA; 79 Jet Propulsion Lab; 80 Nick Pavloff*; 82-83 Janice Sheldon*.

Chapter 4: 88-89 Spencer Swanger/Tom Stack & Associates; 98 Janice Sheldon*; 100 Wayland Lee*/Addison-Wesley Publishing Company; 102 Ken Karp*; 103 Ken Karp*; 104 Janice Sheldon*; 105 Janice Sheldon*; 106 Wayland Lee*/Addison-Wesley Publishing Company; 107 Wayland Lee*/Addison-Wesley Publishing Company; 108 Wayland Lee*/Addison-Wesley Publishing Company.

Chapter 5: 114-115 Lawrence Migdale; 120 Wayland Lee*/Addison-Wesley Publishing Company; 122 Nick Pavloff*; 124-125 Wayland Lee*/Addison-Wesley Publishing Company; 126 Ken Karp*; 128B Janice Sheldon*; 128T Wayland Lee*/Addison-Wesley Publishing Company; 129 Janice Sheldon*; 136 Janice Sheldon*; 138 Lawrence Migdale*.

Chapter 6: 144-145 Charles & Elizabeth Schwartz/Animals, Animals; 148 Janice Sheldon*; 150 Ken Karp*; 152 Nick Pavloff*; 162 Nick Pavloff*; 170-171 Janice Sheldon*.

Chapter 7: 176-177 Owen Franken/Stock, Boston; 180 Janice Sheldon*; 182 Janice Sheldon*; 183 Janice Sheldon*; 187 Janice Sheldon*; 188 Janice Sheldon*; 190 Ken Karp*; 192 Ken Karp*; 198-199 Nick Pavloff*; 202 Stephen Frisch*.

Chapter 8: 204-205 Bill Gallery/Stock, Boston; 210 Stephen Frisch*; 211 Wayland Lee*/Addison-Wesley Publishing Company; 212 Stephen Frisch*; 213 Stephen Frisch*; 218 Janice Sheldon*; 219 Janice Sheldon*; 223B Wayland Lee*/Addison-Wesley Publishing Company; 223T Janice Sheldon*; 224 WesThompson/The Stock Market; 225 Matt Bradley/Tom Stack & Associates; 230-231 Janice Sheldon*.

Chapter 9: 236-237 Martine Franck/Magnum Photos, Inc.; 238 Janice Sheldon*; 239 Janice Sheldon*; 244 Janice Sheldon*; 246 Ken Karp*; 247 Ken Karp*; 248 Janice Sheldon*; 250B Ben Simmons/The Stock Market; 250T Martine Franck/Magnum Photos; 251 Ben Simmons/The Stock Market; 255 Ken Karp*; 256 Janice Sheldon*; 258-259 Janice Sheldon*.

Chapter 10: 264-265 D. Puleston/Photo Researchers, Inc.; 268B Wayland Lee*/Addison-Wesley Publishing Company; 268T Janice Sheldon*; 269 Wayland Lee*/Addison-Wesley Publishing Company; 274 Ken Karp*; 280 Janice Sheldon*; 287 Bob McKeever/Tom Stack & Associates; 288 Janice Sheldon*; 289B Wayland Lee*/Addison-Wesley Publishing Company; 289C Janice Sheldon*; 290 Ken Karp*.

ACKNOWLEDGMENTS

Chapter 11: 296-297 Aldo Tutino/Art Resource, New York; 310 Janice Sheldon*; 316 Ken Karp*; 318 Ken Karp*; 319 Elliott Smith*; 320 Stephen Frisch*.

Chapter 12: 326-327 Ken Karp*; 328 Ken Karp*; 340 Janice Sheldon*; 341 Janice Sheldon*; 342 Janice Sheldon*; 346 Ken Karp*; 350 Janice Sheldon*.

Chapter 13: 356-357 Mike Powell/Allsport; 368 Ken Karp*; 371 Nick Pavloff*; 372 Wayland Lee*/Addison-Wesley Publishing Company; 373 Janice Sheldon*.

Chapter 14: 378-379 Lionel Delevingne/Stock, Boston; 380 Janice Sheldon*; 382 Janice Sheldon*; 383 Janice Sheldon*; 385 Wayland Lee*/Addison-Wesley Publishing Company; 388 Ken Karp*; 396 Janice Sheldon*; 398 Janice Sheldon*.

Chapter 15: 404-405 Focus On Sports; 406 Ken Karp*; 410 Janice Sheldon*; 411 Janice Sheldon*; 420 Nick Pavloff*; 428 Janice Sheldon*.

Chapter 16: 434-435 Phillip Wallick/The Stock Market; 436 Michele Burgess/The Stock Market; 437 Wendell Metzen/Bruce Coleman Inc.; 442 Wayland Lee*/Addison-Wesley Publishing Company; 444 W. Perry Conway/Tom Stack & Associates; 449 Wayland Lee*/Addison-Wesley Publishing Company; 453 Lawrence Migdale*.

*Photographed expressly for Addison-Wesley Publishing Company, Inc.

Special thanks to The Nature Company, Corte Madera, California; Bubba's Diner, San Anselmo, California; Easy Street Cafe, San Anselmo, California.